WORLD LEADERSHIP

WORLD LEADERSHIP

How Societies Become Leaders and
What Future Leading Societies Will Look Like

Neil Hamblin

Living Tree

Living Tree Publishing
Stafford, Virginia

Published in the United States by Living Tree Publishing Company.

Living Tree Publishing
PO Box 671
Stafford VA 22555-0671
livingtreepublishing.co

Cover design by Robin Locke Monda
Formatting by Polgarus Studio

Published in 2017.

1.0.2

ISBN: 978-0-9992388-0-6 (epub)
ISBN: 978-0-9992388-1-3 (paperback)
ISBN: 978-0-9992388-2-0 (hardcover)

Manufactured in the United States of America.

To Christine

History is not everything, but it is a starting point. History is a clock that people use to tell their political and cultural time of day. It is a compass they use to find themselves on the map of human geography. It tells them where they are but, more importantly, what they must be.

    – John Henrik Clarke

Contents

Figures

Tables

Prologue

Russia invades Crimea, immediately raising cries that it is trying to resurrect the Soviet Union. China flexes its muscles in the South China Sea, claiming sovereignty over disputed islands. North Korea launches a missile, deliberately antagonizing its neighbors. Iran seeks nuclear energy, despite having the fourth-largest oil reserves on the planet. ISIS springs up to launch attacks on two neighboring countries and Europe, vowing to restore the caliphate. Meanwhile, the United States has to contend with doubters from abroad and within by saying: "Rumors of my demise are greatly exaggerated." Each of these societies is vying for power in a different way. Every one of them wants to put its stamp on global affairs.

The appeal of leadership is strong. Some nations are permanent members of the United Nations Security Council, while others rotate through. Some nations are members of the G-20 industrial council, but most are not. Some nations are considered viable to host the Olympic Games, while most are not in contention. How is it that some countries are heard whenever they talk, while others feel they have to commit acts of terrorism to be heard? How do some societies get to be the leaders?

While it is easy to trace the present situation back to the wars of the twentieth century, it is more instructive to look at a longer-term perspective to ask: How has anyone gotten to be a leader? How does a society, in general, become a leader?

I stumbled my way onto this subject several years ago. In 2005 I saw a PBS program called *Guns, Germs and Steel*. It was a film version of the Pulitzer Prize–winning book of the same name, which delved into the issue of why some societies were *haves* while others were *have-nots*. I was fascinated by it. It described how being a *have* was primarily the result of geography, which drove differences in how societies had evolved over time. While I found this insight compelling, the film also reminded me of a book I had read years earlier called *The Rise and Fall of the Great Powers*, another monumental work. That book dealt with a similar subject, though it had a modern focus. It explained how societies needed to keep military strength and economic strength in balance to become a power. Somehow, it seemed to me, that if the books could be combined, they would tell the whole story. I decided to make it my hobby for next two or three weekends. My intent was to create some high-level understanding of the issue and put it to rest. Five years later, I put it to rest.

My analysis showed that leadership is driven by innovation (no surprise there), but not just any innovation. Only a handful of innovations have ever made a difference when it comes to leadership: the vast majority make our lives better, but few have made a society into a leader. (Guns and steel are among them, but there are others.) Furthermore, to be a leader, is it important that a society not only acquire the right innovation but also respond appropriately to it and even be transformed by it. That will grow its leadership power. Perhaps more interesting is finding that some of these innovations triggered civilization's advancement, moving humankind in discreet steps from cave dwellers to the modern world. Perhaps even more interesting is finding that we are on the verge of another such advance (in historical timing, that is—it still may be generations away), one that has not happened since the birth of the nation-state in the 1600s.

Toward the end of the analysis, I became increasingly aware that someone besides me should know all of this. So after a two-year break, I began writing this three-part book. In Part I, I explain leadership from a historical perspective, trace its root causes, and create a framework for understanding how leading societies rise to power. In Part II, I use this framework to project into our future, to show how things will likely unfold in the generations to come. In Part III, I address the *so what* question by describing how a society can prepare for our future. In addition, I provide an example of how the framework can be useful for analyzing today's affairs. (Twenty years of consulting experience has shown me that only analysts and engineers really care about frameworks; everyone else wants answers.)

This book, understandably, will by its nature generate some controversy. Some will even have objections to it. I may as well address some of those objections up front.

One objection I expect to hear is that it is too general—too high level. To this I would say that such is the nature of strategic analysis. The answers I was looking for did not lie within any one discipline—not history, technology, sociology, or psychology; rather, the issue of societal leadership cuts across all of these and more. The challenge was getting these to blend together to tell a seamless and accurate story; and that story has to provide direction rather than explain any single point in glorious detail. Scientific analysis, where something needs to be statistically proven to be acceptable, requires less breadth and more depth (though I do use statistical regression at one point in the book). As it is, I went into just enough detail to understand how an issue contributes to *world leadership*.

Another objection will be that it is reductionistic—an oversimplification. Again, I would say that such is the nature of this kind of analysis. Exploring unimportant details is the quickest way either to lose the message (the forest through the trees) or to waste time on things that do not matter. Instead, the key is to separate the signal from the noise—the critical issue from the myriad of details that one could examine—stopping once you've proven it (although I may have indulged my weakness for mechanical technology in the firearms section; please forgive me).

Some will think it audacious that I tried to predict the future.[1] Many will think it would have been wiser to simply look into the past and leave it at that (which was my original intent). However, doing so would not have benefitted anyone—interesting I would hope, but not beneficial. Far better that I attempt to use this understanding to inform us about our world to come, so

---

[1] I have an entire chapter on this later in the book.

we can plan for it, rather than leave it to loose speculation, or worse, lose the opportunity altogether.

Some might be concerned that it gives too much information to the world, especially with all the bad actors out there. I see, however, a greater risk in not doing so. The world is going to transform, and history shows that people generally do not handle it well (they tend to start wars). Much better that people know what is coming and plan for it so that no one is surprised or forced into knee-jerk reactions that get people killed (does World War I come to mind?). If we all know what is coming, it is more likely we will be able to craft an acceptable outcome for everyone.[2]

I could see some complain that this book does not give specific advice, or at least not country-specific advice. It is not meant to. This is a book for the world, not for any one country. Many examples come from the United States simply because I live there, but to be accurate (let alone credible), the analysis has to apply everywhere. As such, the advice tends to be of a global nature. Countries need to determine their own long-term goals and strategy using this information (or not), along with whatever other information they deem relevant.

Some might object to my use of a social evolution model in the analysis. These models show how humankind has progressed over time. (Even using the term "progressed" may be offensive to some.) In times past, the models have been used to justify all sorts of abuses, but the one I crafted is essential for understanding how societies became leaders. Moreover, it was not meant to convey any kind of superiority of one people over another. Differences in rates of social progress were eloquently explained by Jared Diamond in his 1996 Pulitzer Prize–winning book. If that was not enough, a few years later, the Human Genome Project removed any lingering doubt about human equality by proving that we all came from the same small gene pool and we have not been around long enough for anything but surface differences to have evolved in us genetically. This means that social progress cannot be linked genetically to any group of humans; rather, it is the result of environmental differences such as climate, geography, and the availability of

---

[2] More will be said about this at the end of the book.

key natural resources. I would hope that by now we are beyond any confusion about one group of people being superior to another.

Finally, I can imagine someone challenging my use of online sources, especially tertiary sources—online encyclopedias such as Wikipedia and Britannica online. Truth be told, I could not have done the analysis without them. Online sources—along with search engines, home office products, computers, printers, scanners, and software—were essential for doing this analysis. Using electronic media and office software, I could find data in one hour that would have taken a team of research assistants a month to do not even ten years earlier. When I started this analysis in 2005, the world was on the cusp of this new wave of data availability. Without these tools, that data would have remained inaccessible. Of course that does not mean that all online data is correct. (What? The Internet lies?) I developed some guiding principles called *The 5 Cons of Online Data Sourcing* to help discern what to keep and what to pass over.[3] I believe the tools and guiding principles enabled me to capture a pretty accurate picture of our world. In any event, if despite my best effort something fell through the cracks, I apologize. Nonetheless, I would continue to use online sources, since throwing out the baby with the bathwater does not seem wise. Is it better to forego the insights available to us for fear that a minor detail may not be accurate or precise enough? I do not think so.

When all has been said and done, this book looks into our past and into our future through the lens of societal leadership to help people make better decisions today. Those in policymaking positions would be especially wise to pay close attention. I am not promoting any particular political agenda; rather, I am providing context and background for decision making. (Any specific policy issue would require the examination of issues not covered in this book.) I hope this backdrop helps us avoid some of the mistakes made by past generations, and by our own generation in the recent past. In the end, I hope to get ideas on the table for discussion—ideas that will impact our lives, and even more so, the lives of our children's children. This book is not meant to be the final word; rather, it is meant to *start the discussion.*[1]

---

[3] *Con* doesn't mean "against" in this context. I explain these principles in the appendix.

Chapter 1
Overview

My grandmother used to make quilts. She made each one of us grandchildren at least one quilt. Because I lived with her for a year during my childhood, I got to see her in action. While I watched her make entire quilts, I could never tell what the eventual pattern was going to look like from the material she had scattered on her bed. Often she would hold a piece of cloth against a half-formed quilt, and then set it aside to find another one that fit better. I was never sure whether she started with a pattern or whether she just made it up as she went along. Whichever the case, the results were always beautiful when she was done.

World leadership is an eclectic and potentially confusing subject. It does not fit into any single school of thought or discipline; rather, it cuts across many. Because of this, it is probably best to begin with an overview before delving deeper into any piece of it. This chapter provides a *Reader's Digest* version of the rest of the book. (Spoiler alert: skip this chapter if you do not want to know the answer up front.)

Societal Levels

Since the dawn of civilization, humankind has been moving forward, developing new technology, raising its standard of living, and making life easier for itself. This conclusion is inescapable: few of us have ever lived in roaming bands, had to follow herds for sustenance, or had to grow food to survive. Most of us live relatively settled lives, in comfortable homes, with available education, with our lives more or less predicated on what our parents did.

Our ancestors came from less developed societies, but they are ones that incrementally led to our current status. They built machines, cured diseases, and gave us comforts we now take for granted. This path humankind has taken gives us insight into how human development has progressed and how it will likely continue. It also gives us insight into what makes some societies into leaders and which societies are more likely to become future leaders.

A look back through history has shown humankind's progression through five societal levels:

- Bands,
- Tribes,
- Chiefdoms,
- Fiefdoms, and
- Nation-states.

Bands are characterized by groups of a half-dozen to a few dozen people, generally all of one family. They nomadically follow their food source, usually a herd of reindeer, buffalo, or some other animal. They also gather berries, nuts, and other foodstuffs from the local environment to supplement their diet.

Tribes are groups of a few dozen to a few hundred people who live together, most often in a single extended family. They grow their food and raise their own herds. Because of this, they live relatively settled lives around stationary food sources, such as a stream or farms with crops and domesticated herds.

Chiefdoms are groups ranging from a few hundred to thousands. They generally include groups of unrelated people who recognize the authority of the same chieftain or big man. They live stationary lives and have even developed cities and performed other public works projects designed to further their existence.

Fiefdoms are groups ranging from a few thousand to hundreds of thousands. They are governed by a single royal family, and membership cuts across family, ethnic, and linguistic lines. And while members recognize the authority of a single royal family, they have scribes and other civil servants who further support the realm, which often includes large cities, standing armies, and expanded territories. They have developed roads, commerce law, and other forms of infrastructure designed to increase wealth and self-identification.

Nation-states are societies of hundreds of thousands to hundreds of millions who are governed by a central authority who acts more or less based on a written code, a constitution. Often multilingual and multiethnic, these peoples are joined together by a set of common values. Government leaders are chosen by process (whether by elections or by military coup) not by heredity. They enjoy a higher standard of living than any of the levels before them.

These are the five basic ways human societies have organized themselves for mutual sustainment and support. With each level, populations have grown larger and territory has expanded. With each level, the standard of living has gone up for its citizens. This effectiveness is caused by each subsequent level's greater ability to manage resources. Each level's ability to provide a higher standard of living and greater influence than the previous level has meant that once a society has moved to a higher level, it has never intentionally chosen to go back to a prior level.

The leadership insight in all of this is that though there are a few ways a society has become a leader, the most powerful has been to advance to a "higher" level first. This pattern has repeated itself throughout history. From tribes that amalgamated neighboring bands to European colonialism in Africa, a society on a higher level was able to dominate those on lower levels, usually with considerable bloodshed. Higher-level societies inherently possess more leadership power than the lower-level ones. This means the society that first transitions to a higher level will have more power than rivals who remain at the lower level. Historically, higher-level societies have used that power to overrun or bully neighbors into submission.

Innovation

Innovation has been the primary driver behind societal-level change, though not every innovation has impacted leadership the same way. The vast majority of innovations brought greater convenience and comfort to mankind, but only a handful drove societal-level change.

Elevating innovations were the primary drivers of societal-level change. For each societal-level change, there was one elevating innovation.

- Language elevated bands to a new level,
- Property rights led to the formation of tribes,
- Criminal justice led to the formation of chiefdoms,
- Writing led to the formation of fiefdoms, and
- Printing led to the formation of nation-states.

Some of these innovations would be considered technology (printing), but others were not (property rights). Nevertheless, they were all innovations: *the application of an insight to solve a problem.* Elevating innovations changed the way societies managed their resources, which in turn resulted in societal-level change.

But elevating innovations could not do the job alone—societies needed another innovation to make them useful. Another innovation had to prepare a society to receive the elevating innovation; otherwise, it would have no effect. Therefore, for each societal-level change, there was also one *preconditioning innovation* that prepared a society for the elevating innovation.

- Food production established the need for property rights,
- Labor specialization enabled the existence of criminal justice,
- Mathematics enabled the existence of writing, and
- Christianity enabled the effectiveness of printing.

Some of these innovations seem intuitive (food production), while others do not (Christianity). Some of them were invented almost everywhere (labor specialization), while others were invented only in a few places (mathematics). Yet each one of them played a role in developing society, and none were obvious before they were invented. While we take them for granted, there was a time when the world did not know them—someone had to invent them; somewhere had to take a risk to create them, usually to solve a problem. So working in tandem, the preconditioning innovation and the elevating innovation brought about a change in resource management that resulted in societal-level change.

However, this was not the only way a society could become a leader. The second way a society became a leader was by acquiring a dominating innovation first. Dominating innovations were innovations that gave a society more leadership power than its rivals, without changing societal levels. These innovations were

- Metallurgy,
- Horse warfare,
- Gunpowder,
- Petroleum propulsion, and
- Nuclear weapons.

Unlike the other transformative innovations, multiple dominating innovations could exist at the same societal level, though not at the same time. Each dominating innovation gave the society that acquired it first the power to dominate its rivals. Ancient Sumer, in present-day Iraq, increased its power when it invented bronze production.[1] The Hittites rose to power with iron working. Islamic societies obtained gunpowder from eastern Asia to create empires. Great Britain invented petroleum propulsion (i.e., the steam engine) and secured its lead in the world. And America, as well as the Soviet Union, dominated world affairs in the latter half of the twentieth century through its nuclear arsenals.

The limitation of the dominating innovation was that its power only lasted while the first society to acquire it had a monopoly on its use. Once other societies acquired it, leadership power dissipated until parity was ultimately

---

[1] Sumer had already invented writing, which made it into a regional power. Bronze working further enhanced the society's status.

reestablished. Therefore, unlike power generated from societal-level change, which was permanent, dominating innovation power was temporary (though "temporary" in historical timing could last for centuries). Simply put, as long as societies were competing at the same societal level, the one with a dominating innovation monopoly was the leader.

A third (and final) way a society became the leader was through better management of its leadership power sources. There are four leadership power sources:

- Population,
- Wealth,
- Military strength, and
- Foreign reach.

Within the same societal level, while no one had a dominating innovation monopoly, the society that best cultivated and balanced these four power sources became the leader. Hence America could begin its rise with post–Civil War industrialism, and Japan would rise during its Meiji period.

During the Middle Ages and Early Modern period, many societies invested in military strength, though often at the expense of their economies—their wealth. While a large population may have helped Russia to raise a large army in the nineteenth century, when it came at the expense of economy, it led to instability and weakness. Despite whatever military potential one might have, isolationism (the absence of foreign reach) would ensure one's leadership remained impotent. Hence it was growing all four leadership power sources in balance that enabled societies to advance in times when no one had a clear innovation advantage.

So, those are the three ways societies historically have risen to positions of leadership:

- Jump to a new societal level first,
- Acquire a dominating innovation first, or
- Better manage the four leadership power sources.

The Future

This understanding begs the question of where the future lies. If these trends continue, what will the future look like, and who will be the leader?

If the trend continues, the next societal level will be the *nation-union*—a grouping of nations linked together for mutual support. This doesn't necessarily mean that nations will disappear, only that nations will be more tightly integrated for mutual support—to the point where they form their own identity.

It may be no surprise that the next elevating innovation has already arrived: *computing*. Of all the innovations in existence today, only computing has the potential to change the way societies manage their resources. Strong parallels already exist between computing today and printing before the birth of the nation-state. However, more time is needed for computing to develop to the point where it can change resource management.

The next preconditioning innovation will most likely be *nuclear fusion*. The next preconditioning innovation will likely come from the energy field. A cheap and abundant energy source has the potential to change our world, setting the stage for nation-unions. The best candidate for this is nuclear fusion, though it will be a couple of generations before scientists can determine whether it will really work. Other candidates may come along in the meantime, but fusion is in play right now.

What this all means is that for future world leadership, it is still within anyone's reach. While some societies already have an advantage, there is still time for regions to position themselves for the impending transition. It is far from clear when this transition will take place, but it could be just generations (not millennia) away. And just as Europe benefitted from the transition to nation-states, whoever makes the next transition first will become the world's next leader. The region that is best positioned for this transition before it happens will most likely become the leader. However, because decades of preparation are required for such positioning, societies that want to be a leader tomorrow would be wise to begin preparing for it today.

Figure 1 is a diagram of everything we have discussed. Like a quilt pattern formed from disparate pieces of information, it presents history from a perspective of societal progression and shows how innovation has led to societal-level change at different points in our history. The figure shows how within a societal level, dominating innovations drove leadership. It also speaks to how leader power has continually increased over time. Finally, it projects a future world that is not so far away that it should be ignored.

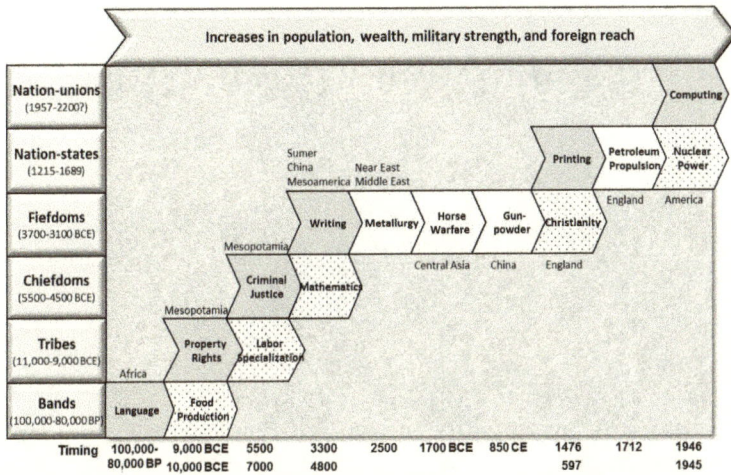

Figure 1. Human societal levels and transformative innovations.

In the end, a look at human societal progression tells us another story as well. It speaks of the never-ending cycle of competition between societies to be first, to obtain advantage over another, and to seek security or prosperity at someone else's expense. This competition has both fueled mankind's progress and led to bloodshed and tragedy. While this motivation has been profitable for some, it is one thing that we will likely have to change in our future. Before any societal-level change occurs, societies will have to resolve not to compete against each other in the ways they have in the past: there is too much potential for wrongdoing on a grander scale for such behavior. A world more focused on problem solving instead of rivalry will be required for the future. However, we need to begin planting those seeds today.

The next few decades or centuries could be a time of radical upheaval; alternatively, it could be a time of relatively smooth transition. Which path we take depends upon the decisions made by societies in the coming decades. It is hoped that knowing this transition is coming may be enough to take some of the fear, sting, and insecurity out of it. Planning and cooperation may be able to overcome knee-jerk reactions, allowing the next transition to be quite a bit smoother and more peaceful than the last one. Equity, fairness, and nonconfrontation are a possibility. The choice is ours.

Part I

OUR PAST

Chapter 2
Societal Level Progression

When my kids were young, I ordered an illustrated picture book of world history. My intent was to ensure that my four-year-old daughter gained the confidence she needed from understanding her world. While she would not read the words anytime soon, I was sure she would flip through the pages and absorb an entire education in world history. I began leafing through the pages to see what I had bought.

The first chapter or two were about the Stone Age. By the third chapter, I came to civilization. I read through a few pages about an early kingdom that had risen to power, reigned for a while, and was then conquered by another kingdom. I flipped a few pages forward. Another kingdom rose to power, survived awhile, and then was conquered. I flipped a few more pages forward. I read how another kingdom rose up, ruled awhile, and then fell. Next chapter. More kingdoms rose, ruled awhile, and then fell. I jumped forward in time. More rose, ruled, and then fell. It seems this pattern repeated itself throughout our entire history. By the end of the book, I was depressed. Has our entire human existence been the story of one kingdom rising up then falling, one kingdom chasing after another? Is that all we have done? Have we not made any more progress than that?

Then I thought: Wait a minute. We have made more progress than that. We do not roam the woods searching for food anymore. We do not miss a meal if we miss the shot. Most of us do not live in mud huts anymore. We may choose to do some of these things if we want that experience, but we do not have to rely on them anymore. I grabbed a pen and started jotting down some notes. We started out as families. Then we became tribes. Then we became city-states or kingdoms. Then we became nation-states. There! We have made progress.

I put the book on the shelf, and my depression was blunted. The funny thing is that I do not recall ever seeing my kids causally pick up that book or any other book on world history. It seems they preferred, well, kid things. Go figure.

Societal Levels

A study of leadership first requires an understanding of *societal levels*. Societal levels are the ways humans have organized themselves for mutual support and sustainment. Societal levels are the prism through which we can view our long and often chaotic history. Humankind has progressed through five societal levels. Those five levels are

- Bands,
- Tribes,
- Chiefdoms,
- Fiefdoms, and
- Nation-states.

Generally speaking, bands are families that roam the land following herds or finding edible plants for food. They usually have a half-dozen to a few dozen members. Tribes are extended families that grow crops and raise animals for food. They range in size from a few dozen to a couple of hundred members. Chiefdoms are multifamily groups who align themselves under the authority of a single chieftain. They range in size from a few hundred to a few thousand members, with some of the larger ones even reaching into the ten thousands. Fiefdoms are groups whose members align themselves under the authority of a single royal family. These range in size from a few thousand to hundreds of thousands of members. Nation-states are groups aligned under a common legal code or constitution. These can range from a few hundred thousand to hundreds of millions of members. In general, humankind progressed from bands, to tribes, to chiefdoms, to fiefdoms, and finally to nation-states. While there are lots of perturbations to this straightforward path, this by-and-large has been the case.

So how do these five societal levels help our understanding of leadership? It is simple. Whichever society reached the next level first became the leader. In a region composed of bands, whichever band became the first tribe dominated. In an area composed of tribes, whichever tribe became the first chiefdom dominated. In an area full of chiefdoms, whichever chiefdom became the first fiefdom dominated. Among fiefdoms, the first nation-state dominated.

This has been the pattern throughout the ages. Across the world, tribes have always been stronger than bands because they are larger and can better coordinate activities, such as hunting and fighting. In Mesopotamia and Egypt, early chiefdoms rose to power from among local tribes. In Sumer and Maya, early fiefdoms rose to power in their respective regions, dominating local chiefdoms. England, the first nation-state, eventually became the British empire, dominating other fiefdoms, as well as lower-level societies, in the process. The transition and subsequent rise to power was not instant: it may have taken decades or even centuries. However, once on top, the leading society dominated others for generations.

Model Caveats

There is a danger in using such characterizations of human progress. Such characterizations are not new. In fact, they were popular back in the nineteenth century for all the wrong reasons. Such models usually put Europeans at the leading edge of the progression and were used to justify colonizing other parts of the world. Later, such progressions became discredited as being biased and self-serving. Still later, they reemerged, albeit in a new form, having usefulness in explaining human development.[II]

The danger of such models is abuse. Models can be used to further one's self-interest at the expense of others. Such models usually blunder because their underlying question is wrong. If a model was invented to answer the question "Why shouldn't Europeans colonize the world?" then it will naturally align to that question (though a good model may still not support the proposition).

This model was framed by asking: "How are world leaders made?" Stated as such, the question is not biased, and so the model is country neutral. The answer should apply equally to any society that meets the characteristics of a world leader. Many studies have shown that there is no inherent difference in humans. I support the idea that any people on earth could have progressed through these levels under the right conditions—conditions that include geography and climate, as well as natural plants and animals.[III]

The other way models are abused is when they are stretched beyond their intended purpose. Some general models try to answer many questions within a subject. These become popular if they answer enough questions to be useful. However, danger arises when a model is stretched beyond what it is intended to do.

The five-step model presented in this book is based on resource management. Other societal-progress models have used different numbers of steps, but this one has five since there have been five basic ways in which humankind has managed its resources. Resource management turns out to be the primary driver behind leadership power. In all likelihood, the world's next leader will come from a society that uses technology to manage resources in a new way. Hence, a model based on resource management is on the right track.

...

With this tool we can better understand our history. These levels give us a way to break up our history into comprehensible chunks. No longer is history just one endless continuum of one kingdom conquering another—it now has discreet breakpoints that enable us to focus in on a particular time and region to understand how leadership came about. It is a tool.

Chapter 3
Societal Levels through History

In April 2002, a group of hunter-gatherers from Botswana took the government of Botswana to court. They were seeking to reverse the practice of resettlement away from their ancestral homeland located in the Central Kalahari Game Reserve. The resettlement began in 1997 when the government first encouraged them, then forced them to relocate to a city built for them several hours away. "People have been encouraged to move out to give themselves and their children the benefits of development," declared one public official. However, some nongovernmental organizations (NGOs) believed the real reason behind the move was government support of cattle ranching and diamond mining interests that wanted the land.

The San people have lived in southern Africa for 30,000 years. San is the name given to a broad collection of up to 100,000 hunter-gatherers who inhabit parts of six southern African countries. They live as their ancestors did millennia ago, and are one of the few remaining hunter-gatherer groups in the world.

Seeking to preserve their way of life, they fought back. With the help of NGOs, they filed a lawsuit against the government. The case took more than two years to work its way up to the Supreme Court of Botswana, but in the end the high court sided with the San. It declared that indigenous people had an inherent right to their ancestral homeland.

Such a collision between cultures in our world today is the result of a complex social evolution that has occurred over several thousand years. That a group of hunter-gatherers would file suit in a national court to protect their land rights against diamond mining interests shows just how complex humans' modern-day affairs have become. But it did not start out this way. So how did such a situation come to be? [IV]

Five Societal Levels

The San in Botswana are an example of a *band*. Bands are groups of hunter-gatherers who typically live in groups of 5 to 80 people. Bands are nomadic. They roam from place to place, foraging for food or following herds of wild animals for their sustenance. Typically the men will hunt and the women will gather wild fruits and vegetables. Bands may stay in one general area, but there is no concept of land ownership—it is simply there for everyone to use.

The members of the band are all related in some way, either biologically or by marriage. As such, bands are the original form of human society—basically a family or an extended family.

Finding food is the occupation of everyone in the band, and everyone works for his or her food. Even the head of the band has to work to provide food for himself and his family. Correspondingly, bands are egalitarian and decisions are made by consensus. Every adult has a say in decisions that affect the entire band. The head of the band facilitates discussion that helps build the consensus.

Bands were eventually replaced by *tribes* as the most common form of human society. The first tribes appeared in the Fertile Crescent (Figure 2) around 11,000 BCE. Tribes ranged in size from a few dozen to a few hundred people. They first emerged around naturally abundant, yet stationary food sources that eliminated the need for roaming and foraging.

In some ways, tribes were essentially bands joined through intermarriage. Multiple bands could coexist around an especially productive growing area, usually around a nearby river. This close proximity made it easy to give sons and daughters in marriage to other bands, increasing the size of the society. As the tribe grew, it developed its own identity, though the original familial lines, now termed clans, were still recognized. However, the tribe never grew beyond the point where not everyone knew each other.

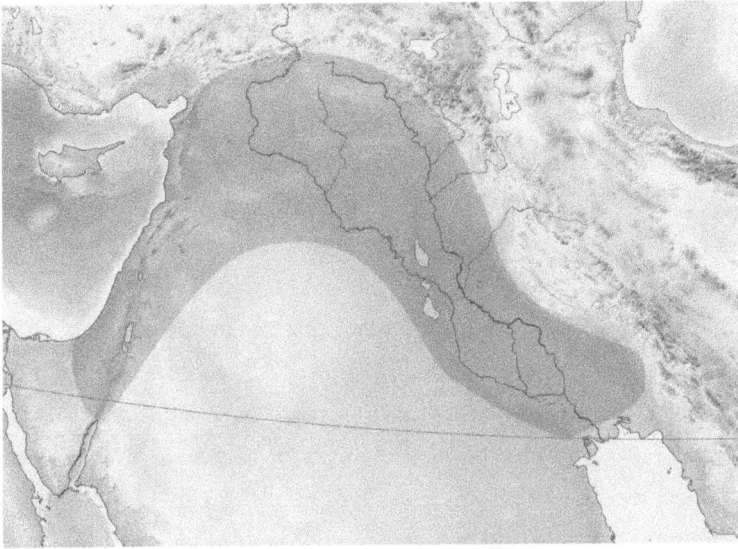

Figure 2. The Fertile Crescent.
Source: By Sémhur derivative work: Rafy (Middle East topographic map-blank.svg) [CC-BY-SA-3.0 (http://creativecommons.org/licenses/by-sa/3.0/)], via Wikimedia Commons.

In tribes, everyone still has the basic job of producing food, whether by raising animals or by growing their own fruits and vegetables. Any kind of specialty craft is done as a side hobby and does not displace anyone from producing his or her own food.

Tribes retain the egalitarianism of the band. Tribes are run by tribal councils. Sometimes the most influential member of the council will assume a quasi-head of the tribe status, but this is not a formal position. It is an informal one based on influence and respect within the tribe. Decision making is still by-and-large made as a group with every council member having equal say in the decision.

Eventually tribes gave way to *chiefdoms* as the leading form of human society. Chiefdoms also emerged in the Fertile Crescent, but much later than tribes—

around 5500 BCE. As with tribes, they also began to appear in every other part of the world as the centuries passed. Chiefdoms ranged in size from a few thousand to tens of thousands of people. Chiefdoms were composed of several villages, often with the most powerful village becoming the capital or seat of power.

While not all people within a chiefdom were related to each other, or even knew each other, they all generally belonged to the same ethnic and linguistic group. And while most people were still involved in food production, non-food-production-related jobs, such as craftsmen, emerged to fills the needs of an increasingly complex society.

In chiefdoms, social stratification began to emerge. Ruling classes began to make decisions, and commoners followed them. The egalitarianism of earlier societal levels dissolved. This centralized decision-making authority enabled the development of public works project such as dams, canals, storehouses, or other projects for "the public good." It also led to a redistributive economy, where food was collected by officials during harvest time, stored, and meted out to people in the months following the harvest. Some of it also went to pay taxes to the ruling class. Each chiefdom also had a chieftain—a public official with preeminent authority over the realm. He used his relatives to help him oversee the chiefdom and enforce his decrees, establishing the basis for royalty. In the chiefdom, allegiance to, or at least the recognition of, the chieftain became a part of a member's identify.

In time, chiefdoms were replaced by *fiefdoms* as the leading and predominant form of human society. Fiefdoms typically had populations from the tens of thousands to the hundreds of thousands and covered hundreds or even thousands of square miles. The first fiefdoms appeared around 3700 BCE. As with previous societal levels, fiefdoms first arose in the Fertile Crescent and later appeared in other places around the globe, including the Americas and Africa.

Fiefdoms were large enough that they had to cut across linguistic and ethnic lines. Their identity and cohesion was based primarily on allegiance to a common ruler—a king, a duke, an emperor—as well as a defined border and a paramount capital city. The city-states of the ancient world were fiefdoms: Babylon, Athens, Rome, Tenochtitlan—were all fiefdoms. Some may have begun as villages, but they were all fiefdoms by the time of their preeminence. Over time, fiefdoms broaden beyond the city-state model, taking the form of kingdoms, duchies, tsardoms, and emirates.

In a fiefdom, the ruler retains the authority to make key decisions such as when to go to war or when to form an alliance with a neighboring fiefdom. The ruler uses relatives to help him run the realm, but more extensively than in chiefdoms. Relationship to the ruler is well defined, and even a royal pecking order emerges based on proximity. The royal family is an extension of the ruler, having authority over specific aspects or parts of the realm. However, civil servants handle much of the day-to-day operations of the fiefdom, leaving the royal family to perform an oversight role. Leadership is passed down from one member of the royal family to the next, across generations, to ensure power continuity within the family.

The current societal level, the *nation-state*, began in 1689 when England passed its Bill of Rights, effectively establishing rule-of-law for governance. The nation-state then spread around Europe and the world to become the predominant societal level, displacing fiefdoms. The United States, Russia, England, Namibia, Australia, and China are all nation-states. Nation-states typically have millions to hundreds of millions of citizens, and can range in size from a small island to the greater part of a continent.

Nation-states typically have multiple ethnic and linguistic groups within well-defined borders. Identity and cohesion are based on a common allegiance to a constitution or other written code, as well as the shared history or struggle required to create it.

Nation-states operate based on constitutions and the legal code derived from them. In these complex societies, the written code allows decision making to be vested in the hands of multiple people (i.e., representative democracy) or remain with a single individual (i.e., a dictator). Leadership is acquired through election or another process. Force is illegitimately used in a nation-state with a weak constitution or a weak loyalty to it. Oversight and enforcement come from a sophisticated network of delegated authority and expansive civil service.

These five societal levels reflect the basic ways humankind has organized itself for mutual sustainment and support throughout its history. Table 1 summarizes the key attributes of those societal levels.[v]

Table 1: Growth in Societies

	Population	Territory	Membership	Center of Authority	Public Works
Bands	Dozens	None (roaming)	Single family/clan	None (roaming)	None
Tribes	Hundreds	One village	Extended family/clan	Village	None
Chiefdoms	Thousands	Region containing several villages	Groups of clans within a single ethnic/linguistic group	Paramount Village	Small-scale of projects
Fiefdoms	Hundreds-of-thousands	Large geographic area (e.g., isthmus, mountain range)	Non-related people, but within a common ethnic/linguistic group	City-state	Large scale public architectural programs
Nation-states	Hundreds of Millions	Fractions of a continent	Multi-ethnic, multi-linguistic	Capital	Continuous investment in infrastructure development

An Erratic Path

These five levels simply explain humankind's progress. So why does our history not look more like this idealized model? History has been a lot more erratic than this, and this erraticism has obscured the levels. In fact, there are five basic ways in which reality has deviated from an idealized step-by-step progression.

The first deviation is that different parts of the world started their progressions at different times. Largely due to geography, this complicating deviation alone is enough to create confusion when trying to understand how societies have progressed.

The second deviation is that societies progressed at different rates; in fact, not all societies have made it through all five levels. There are still bands in Africa, tribes in the Amazon, chiefdoms in northern Pakistan, and fiefdoms in the Middle East (e.g., the United Arab Emirates). In addition, nowadays it is sometimes easy to confuse a fiefdom with a nation-state. When a modern society is run by a family, and leadership is passed along relational lines, the society is still a fiefdom even though it may have cell phones and nuclear weapons (e.g., North Korea). Even dictators who come to power through a coup d'état may eventually pass leadership to a family member, reverting that society to a fiefdom. This leads to the next deviation.

A third deviation is the fallback. A fallback occurs when a society reverts to a previous level after spending time at a higher level. Though not common, fallbacks have been some of most dramatic events in human history. Europe experienced a fallback with the end of the Roman Empire. Rome had been a fiefdom led by an emperor. After it fell, provinces such as Gaul, which had been under Roman rule for centuries, established themselves as independent chiefdoms. These chieftains then fought each other for dominance. Eventually, these societies returned to the more advanced level of fiefdom, under new leadership. In Gaul, the local chiefdoms were reunited under Clovis, who became the first ruler of the Franks.

A fourth deviation is the false start—the reverse of the fallback. A false start occurs when a society reaches a new level, holds it for a time, and then reverts back to the lower level. Both ancient Greece and Rome became democracies (i.e., nation-states) for a time, and then ultimately reverted to fiefdoms run by kings and emperors. Chiefdoms emerged from tribes sporadically—popping up and reverting for centuries until the chiefdom was finally able to sustain itself as a way of life.

The fifth deviation is overlap. One can see all five levels still at work in the world today. While the majority of societies have moved to the nation-state, you still have fiefdoms such as Saudi Arabia, Jordan, Morocco, Indonesia, and North Korea. These societies all have reigning monarchs with real political power. You can still see chiefdoms today—modern chieftains take the form of warlords and militia leaders. They are still common in places like Somalia, Iraq, Afghanistan, or tribal regions of Pakistan. Even tribes still exist in Amazonia and New Guinea, and bands, such as the Khoisan and the Clo-e, still exist in Africa and South America.

Furthermore, when a new societal level appears, the old levels do not disappear entirely; rather, they take on new forms. The family is still the basic unit of human development, just like it was during the band era. The extended family remains intrinsically important to most people, just as it did during the tribal era. As mentioned, militias still operate around the world much as chiefdoms did. And constitutional monarchies preserve a role for the royal family, even if it is more symbolic than political these days. Lower levels change when they fit underneath a higher level because they are part of who we are. Having been part of our experience for thousands of years has made them so.

With these deviances understood, humankind's progress becomes clearer. That progress has followed a path that is uneven and erratic, with fits and starts. Yet it also becomes clear how important each of these societal levels remains to us today.

A Case Study: Britain

Perhaps the clearest way to see the progression of societal levels is to follow one society through all five levels. Britain is a good candidate for this because it is an island. It has well-defined borders—the sea—which means it is easy to tell what evolved naturally and what was brought by a foreign invader. (It is harder to see changes in areas that have been crisscrossed by centuries of invasions.)

Modern humans in Britain date back to around 30,000 years ago. A land bridge was exposed between Britain and continental Europe during the ice ages as glaciers expanded and sea levels lowered. This land bridge would appear and disappear repeatedly over time. At this time, much of northern Europe was populated by bands of roaming hunter-gatherers who followed animal herds. At one point when the land bridge was exposed, hunter-gatherers followed animal herds onto what was then a peninsula. The final ice age in Britain waned around 10,000 years ago: the glaciers retracted, the sea level rose, an island was created, and forests grew. By 8,500 years ago, the hunter-gathering bands trapped on the island became its first permanent residents.

Tribes first began to appear in Britain around 4500 BCE when the hunter-gatherer bands started adopting a sedentary agricultural lifestyle. Earnest transition occurred primarily between 4300 and 3300 BCE, as is evidenced by the widespread clearing of forests across Britain for farming.

By the end of this transition time, some settlements had grown quite large in the fertile areas around Boyne, Orkney, eastern Scotland, Anglesey, the upper Thames, Wessex, Essex, Yorkshire, and the river valleys of the Wash. These settlements were centers of both farming and animals herding. Initially native cattle and pigs were raised, but later sheep, goats, wheat, and barley were introduced from the mainland.

Chiefdoms emerged in Britain in the Middle Bronze Age, 2500–1500 BCE. The transition may have been instigated by migrations from the continent, especially from the Beaker culture. Around 2700 BCE the Beaker culture brought new ideas and people to the island. The cultural change was significant. They brought pottery making, bronze making, and other craftsmanship, along with new rituals such as individual burial of the dead. After a couple of centuries, the influence of the Beakers began to change the way the rest of the island lived.

By around 1600 BCE, Britain had become a major exporter of bronze goods to the continent. By around 1500 BCE, hillforts and other large public works began to rise. As the population grew, chiefdoms grew larger in size and number. Consequently, they began fighting each other more, which in turn created the need for more defensible cities. Hillfort building reached its peak in the late Iron Age, around 100 BCE.

Between 500 and 100 BCE, Celts migrated from mainland Europe. These chiefdoms were primarily warriors, fighting each other as much as anyone else. They were also craftsmen, bringing an enhanced knowledge of metal working to the island. By 100 BCE, iron bars were used as currency, and both internal trade and trade with continental Europe flourished, largely due to Britain's extensive mineral reserves. Roman records show Britain exporting hunting dogs, animal skins, and slaves to the continent, in addition to possessing large farmsteads that produced food in industrial quantities.

Fiefdoms were brought to Britain by the Roman invasion in 43 CE. Late Iron Age Britain was composed of dozens of small chiefdoms. Most of the ones in the south were aligned with Rome and paying tribute. In the 40s CE, the anti-Roman Catuvellauni displaced the pro-Roman Trinovantes as the most powerful chiefdom in southeastern Britain. This change put at risk their status as a client-state. Emperor Claudius responded by invading Britain. In the early campaigns, Roman forces defeated eleven southern chiefdoms, whose resistance had been led by Caratacus, chief of the Catuvellauni. The overall conquest of Britain took four decades, however. It finally ended when Roman legions subdued what is now the northeast coast of Scotland in 84 CE.

The conquest of present-day Scotland would be temporary though, for the Roman legions were eventually pulled back south to a line that would be demarcated by Hadrian's Wall, built in 122 CE. This effectively separated the Roman Empire from the non-Roman "barbarians" of the northern chiefdoms. Three centuries later, Rome left Britain in 410 CE.

The final years of Roman rule saw new migrations to England from mainland Europe. The Angles, the Saxons, and the Jutes, arrived and set up fiefdoms that pushed the Celtic chiefdoms into the corners of the isle. The kingdoms of Northumbria, Mercia, East Anglia, and Wessex became the strongest, while the kingdoms of Kent, Sussex, and Essex, as well as several smaller territories, also became a political presence (Figure 3).

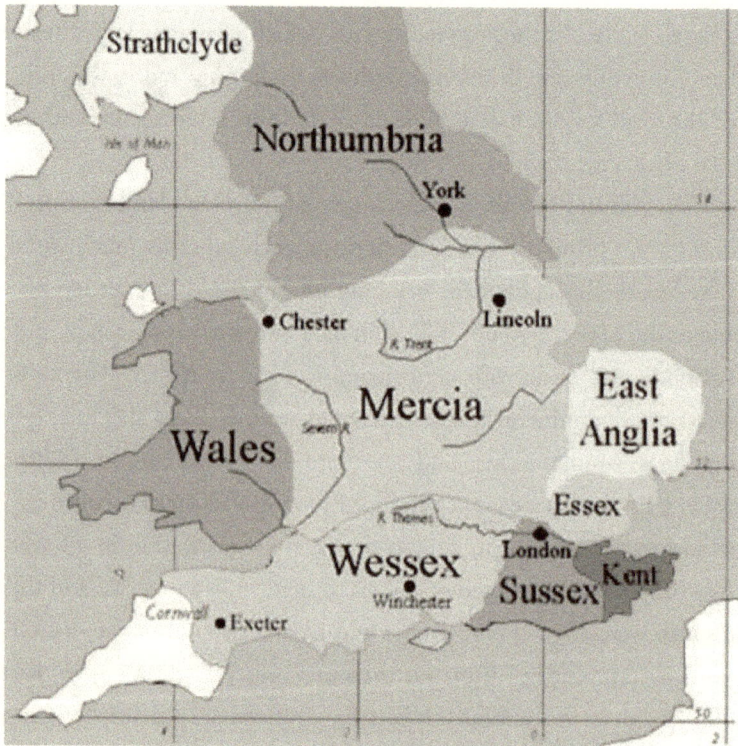

Figure 3. Anglo-saxon Kingdoms

In the ninth century, Danish vikings invaded and remained a threat for almost a century. After the Vikings had largely been expelled, kingdoms began to consolidate under the conquests of Wessex. By the end of the century, Britain was more or less unified, though conflicts with the Danes would continue for decades to come.

When William I took control of Britain after winning the Battle of Hastings in 1066 CE, one fiefdom was simply replacing another. From a societal-levels perspective, this major event was the continuation of something started by the Romans a thousand years earlier. Eventually this would soon change, however.

The seeds of the nation-state were planted in England with the signing of the Magna Carta in 1215 CE. Before this, the law was considered an extension of the king's word. With the Magna Carta, the two diverged—the king's word, his wishes, and his desires even became subordinated to the law. However, it would take centuries for this fully to take hold.

In time, England would build structures to support this concept. By the thirteenth century, King's Councils were held, where barons and the archbishop were invited to discuss matters of taxation and judgments. This would eventually become the House of Lords. Eventually, representatives from towns and counties were allowed to attend the meetings, and later would form their own council. By the fourteenth century, this had become the House of Commons. The two Houses became British Parliament.

In the sixteenth century, power began to shift from the king to Parliament. By 1689, a Bill of Rights was passed, giving Parliament sole authority for passing and repealing all laws; this eliminated the king's legislative authority and established the modern world's first nation-state.

So from Britain we can easily discern all five societal levels. Except for the temporary fallback to chiefdoms after the fall of Rome, the isle steadily progressed in sequence through all five levels. Most of the world went through something similar, though the timing differed from region to region and the steps are not quite as clear. This brings up another question: How do we know that this progression is not more like walking up a ramp than stairs?[VI]

Discrete Levels

One could ask: Why call them *levels*? Why not say progress was a long continuum? As mentioned earlier, all five discrete levels still exist somewhere in the world today. They still provide a useful way of life for some people around the world, despite being millennia old. This means that each level is, by itself, a stable, steady-state form of governance. Furthermore, when looking at how the levels formed in the first place, one can see that more time was spent at a level than in the transition to a level. As a result, progress looks more like a staircase than a ramp.

Bands had the longest transition. While it is difficult to say how long, we can use as a rough estimate the time it took for language to develop. Before 100,000 years ago, humankind did not have the voice box or facial control to produce the speech we know today. By the time humankind left Africa roughly 80,000 years ago, it had developed not only speech but also hunting, gathering, and organizing skills that would enable it to populate the globe. As such, a broad transition estimate would be 20,000 years. Humankind then stayed at this band level until replaced by tribes. Tribes became a sustainable way of life in roughly 9,000 BCE, so bands were the leading (only) societal level for 70,000 years (give or take a few thousand).

The transition from band to tribe took around 2,000 years. Tribes first appeared in the Fertile Crescent around naturally abundant food sources around 11,000 BCE. By about 10,000 BCE, agrarian tribes were forming villages in the eastern Fertile Crescent, near the Euphrates River. By 9000 BCE, agrarian tribes were forming in the western Fertile Crescent, near the Jordan River. After this, tribal living became a sustainable way of life as villages began to proliferate across the Fertile Crescent. Tribes would be the leading societal level until replaced by chiefdoms around 4500 BCE, meaning that tribes were the leading form of society for about 4,500 years.

Chiefdoms took about a thousand years to develop. They first appeared in the Samarra culture of northern Mesopotamia around 5500 BCE. Over the next thousand years, in first northern then southern Mesopotamia, a hereditary chieftain elite emerged, signaling the shift away from tribal methods of governance. The first social stratification appeared as a two-tier society was formed—royalty and commoners. Centralized administration began, and conflict mediation methods were introduced. The first cities appeared: Eridu was founded in 5400 BCE. Public works projects began. Projects included large-scale irrigation with canal networks. By 5000 BCE, large-scale crop irrigation was fully developed. Public works also included temple and shrine building.

By 4500 BCE, the chiefdom level of society had stabilized and began proliferating throughout the region and into surrounding regions. Eridu had become the major city in the region, and Uruk was on the rise. Trade networks sprang up between these early cities and began to stretch from the Mediterranean coast to present-day Oman. Chiefdoms would be the leading form of society from 4500 BCE until they were replaced by fiefdoms around 3100 BCE. As such, their duration was about 1,400 years.

The transition to fiefdoms took about 600 years. In southern Mesopotamia, particularly in Sumer, cities starting growing beyond chiefdom size around 3700 BCE. Whereas a chiefdom settlement might have a central city of about 10 hectares (27 acres) and surrounding villages of about 1 hectare each (2.7 acres), by 3700 BCE, Uruk covered 70–100 hectares (175–250 acres). Trade networks between these emerging city-states began to flourish, expanding as far north as the Caucasus region. By 3500 BCE, urban settlements had developed complex configurations, and population swelled as large cities began to proliferate.

By 3400 BCE, city-states such as Uruk were expanding their authority into surrounding regions and even colonizing territory. The region between northern and southern Mesopotamia filled in as new city-states popped up. They began developing a more sophisticated administrative support structure, and by 3200 BCE, a full civil service structure was in place. Responsibility for governance shifted from the priest-chieftains to kings. In addition to their religious duties, the priests assumed more administrative functions such as food inventory management and redistribution. By 3100 BCE a large city might have 10,000 to 20,000 people, and the central city itself covering over 250 acres (a square kilometer). Multilevel social stratification was firmly in place.

Fiefdoms would reign as the leading form of society far longer than any other societal level—from about 3100 BCE until 1689 CE, when the first sustainable nation-state was created. This means it had a duration of 4,789 years.

As we have already discussed, the nation-state began when England passed its Bill of Rights in 1689, forever shifting political power away from the king and placing it in the hands of representatives. The transition began with the acceptance of the Magna Carta in 1215 and therefore took 474 years. Since the nation-state is still the leading form of governance in the world, it constitutes the most recent step—one that is still growing.

Table 2 summarizes the resulting staircase effect. Transitions were only a portion of previous levels' durations. The overlap between one level's transition and the previous level's duration ranged from 3% to 43%. If progress had been a ramp instead of a staircase, then the overlap would have been 100%. As it were, each societal level enjoyed a period of stability, without much changing, before another level started brewing underneath the surface.

Table 2: Societal Level Durations and Transitions

	Floor	Step 1	Step 2	Step 3	Step 4
Nation-states					474
Fiefdoms				600	4,789
Chiefdoms			1,000	1,400	
Tribes		2,000	4,500		
Bands	20,000	70,000			
Overlap	N/A	3%	22%	43%	10%

These long periods of stability also suggest that an equilibrium existed at each societal level. This means that the form of governance worked in concert with the surrounding environment. When something in the environment changed, disrupting the equilibrium, a new form of governance began coalescing, seeking to establish equilibrium in the new environment. When the new form of governance was mature (i.e., a new equilibrium was achieved), it could propagate and the world shifted to a new societal level.

So history shows us that societal progress was uneven, but it was uneven in a consistent way. There were times of stability and times of transition. Centuries could go by with not much happening; then boom (relatively speaking) humankind was facing something new. Understanding these levels, and what causes them, can give us insight into our world and into leadership.[VII]

Societal Levels and Leadership

So what do societal levels and leadership have in common? It is simple: the society that reached a new societal level first became the leader. In Sumer, cities such as Eridu became the first chiefdoms and rose to power. Later, city-states such as Uruk became the first fiefdoms and began to dominate the region, even colonizing much of it. In fact, Sumer became the most powerful region on earth at the time, advancing ahead of other areas and expanding its influence and authority. Later, the Maya would do the same thing when they became the Western Hemisphere's first fiefdom. England became the modern world's first nation-state, and laid the basis for the British empire; while other factors contributed, the foundation was established when it became a nation-state. Way back during the tribal era, this same phenomena apparently happened as well. Jericho, one of the first agrarian tribes, remained a regional power into biblical times. (Perhaps one band crossed from Africa into Asia ahead of others. Who knows?) At every societal level, the *first mover* became the leader.

The first mover became the leader because a higher-level society can coordinate more resources than a lower-level one can. Resources are the people, assets, and capital used to make a society work. Each societal level uses different methods to coordinate those resources, and resources, properly coordinated, generate power that translates into dominating force. So the society that reaches the higher level first has a power advantage over other societies still at a lower level. If the higher-level society chose to use that power to establish dominance (and they always did), then that society became the regional leader.

Because of this difference in resource coordination, whenever societies at different levels clashed, the higher-level society won. In North America, chiefdoms such as the Iroquois Confederacy and the Powhatans could dominate regional tribes. In the sixteenth century, Spain, a fiefdom, conquered Native American chiefdoms (though germs and disease contributed to this). In the early twentieth century, the United States, a nation-state, ended the Spanish empire, which was still a fiefdom. A lower-level society may harass the higher-level society, and a lower-level society may even stave off defeat long enough to cause a higher-level to decide to withdraw from a region. However, in an existential fight, the higher-level society wins.

Resource coordination is the key. Higher-level societies have methods that give them an ability to coordinate resources more effectively than lower levels. They can manage more resources, from a greater variety of places, from farther away, in more complex arrangements. With the ability to coordinate more resources, the first movers can dominate and amalgamate lower-level rivals, thereby expanding their territory, gaining more resources, and gaining even more power. Once beaten, lower-level societies are subsumed into higher-level ones. Sometimes the mere threat of force is enough to make this happen. Whether by force or threat, the higher level dominates. So throughout history reaching a higher societal level first has been the surest and strongest way to become a leader.[VIII]

...

So, humankind has progressed through five societal levels, from bands to nation-states, though the path was erratic and in some places incomplete. That is how a band of hunter-gatherers could challenge a national government in its own supreme courts. But what really is a societal level? Is it a solid platform or more like a cloud? We need to peel the back the onion and take a deeper look.

Chapter 4
Governance Bases

In the third grade, when I was learning about molecules, I saw them as mostly red and blue balls held together by Popsicle sticks. It was the next year when I learned real molecules were not red and blue balls; rather, they were mostly empty space, I was shocked. I learned that if a hydrogen atom were the size of a football field, the nucleus would be a marble on the 50-yard line and the electron would be a grain of sand on the goal line. In between it is all empty. How in the world does anything stand up?

In some ways societal levels are like molecules. I describe them as platforms, but they are really more ethereal than that. Societal levels are really *the different ways societies use authority to manage resources.* This involves deciding who has the authority, how much authority they have, and how that authority is to be used. Societal levels change when societies change how they use authority. Only the successful changes take hold—the ones that fail rarely make it into history. But let us take it one step at a time.

Resource Management

A society's resources can be lumped into three categories: labor, material, and capital. *Labor* is the people, the workforce, those who are performing societies activities. *Material* is the work-stuffs, the tools, the raw materials needed to perform that work. *Capital* is the money used to pay for the work. All societies use these three types of resources to make things happen, whether it is growing food, building pyramids, or launching rockets.

Resource management is the use of authority to make decisions on how resources are applied for society's benefit, and how those decisions are enforced. *Authority* refers to the individual or individuals assigned to make decisions on a society's behalf. In every society, someone makes decisions: decisions about other people, about material, and about where capital in invested. The right to make those decisions is authority. Authority varies in the scope and the power it receives from society to manage those resources. The expectation that goes along with that authority is that the authorized individuals will manage society's resources to craft a better way of life for the people of that society, making it better than would have been possible had such authority not been awarded. This expectation may be stated or implied, decided outright or inherited by tradition or default. *Enforcement* is the way each society ensures the authority's decisions are followed. Each societal level, therefore, represents a different way in which those three elements—authority, decision making, and enforcement—came together to create a better life for the people in a society.

Bands were essentially families, either one immediate family or an extended family composed of a few immediate families (brothers and cousins). Any decision involving one immediate family was simply made by the head of the family. When a decision involved a few families, the decision was made by consensus—the heads of each immediate family would meet to decide the course of action. Meetings were egalitarian: no one had any authority over anyone except his own family. Leadership took the form of individuals who could facilitate discussions and help the group reach consensus on an issue. All adult males, and in some bands females, had a say in the decision. The head of the family had no official role or title—he simply led his family. There was no enforcement structure, but everyone had given input so they usually went along with the group's decisions.

This decision-making process is still used by modern hunter-gatherer bands. The Cinta Larga were a modern band in the Amazon region of South America. The abundance of wild game, coupled with the difficulty of farming in their climate, caused the Cinta Larga to retain a hunter-gatherer lifestyle. That lifestyle still used a decision-making process ruled by consensus well into the twentieth century. As author Candace Millard described in *River of Doubt*, her account of Theodore Roosevelt's journey down the Amazon River tributary:

> The Cinta Larga would not allow their village chief to tell them how to live their lives. Instead, the chief's job was to oversee the tribal ceremonies—an important role, because the Cinta Larga did not have a written language.... Not only did the chief not command the village as a whole, he did not have power over any family within it but his own. Each man was the chief of his own family, which consisted of as many wives as he could convince to marry him and as many children as his wives could bear.

This requirement for consensus in decision-making had at least one modern-day impact. In 1912, after losing a comeback bid for the presidency, Theodore Roosevelt immersed himself into another one of his famous adventures. He was traveling down the River of Doubt in South America when the Cinta Larga spotted his party. The band had to decide what to do with the invaders. Millard continues:

> Because the Indians did not have a traditional chief, they were forced to make all of their decisions by consensus. If it was time to move the village, for instance, they had to agree on the time and location of the move. When it came to dealing with the expedition, the Cinta Larga were divided. Some of them believed that they should remain invisible to the outsider. Others, however, argued that they should attack. These men had invaded their territory, and there was no reason to believe they did not mean the Indians harm. By attacking first, the Cinta Larga would have the upper hand. They would also be able to loot the expedition, which was carrying valuable provisions and tools—especially those made of metal.

Because the Cinta Larga could not agree, Roosevelt and his party were able to pass out of their territory unmolested.

Tribes were intermarried families and clans. Everyone in a tribe was related to each other either by bloodline or by marriage. Large tribes could have multiple layers of distant cousins. In such a large group, total consensus was not feasible. Decision making therefore passed to a smaller group—a council of elders who would make decisions for the much larger group. The elder council had a representative from each clan, but it used consensus to make decisions.

Councils were egalitarian—no one had any more authority than anyone else. Leadership sometimes took the form of a particular council member who had more influence than his peers, however. His tools were respect and persuasion, but his position was not formal—even he still had to grow his own food and raise his own livestock.

Tribes had no formal enforcement body. Each council member made sure his clan obeyed council decisions. Because council members were typically the patriarchs of their respective clans, family relationships and respect ensured people abided by decisions made.

Tribes still function like this today. In northeast Ghana, the Frafra are a group of tribes that share a common history and language. They number about 30,000 and have lived as tribes for thousands of years. The Frafra are mainly farmers, though they supplement their subsistence through hunting. Frafra society is egalitarian, and tribal decisions, such as land allocation, are made by the elder council. They are known for their masks and other works of art (Figure 4).

Figure 4. Frafra mask.
Source: Photo by author.

In fact, a University of Iowa art exhibit aptly described their tribal lifestyle:

> Frafra societies are comprised mainly of farmers, without social or political stratification. They are not divided among occupational castes or groups since most of them simply till the land and engage in occasional hunting. They had no internal system of chiefs, and all important decisions were made by a council of elders consisting of the oldest members of each of the village lineages. Religious leaders do maintain some political authority, determining the agricultural cycle and parceling out land for cultivation.

A chiefdom was the first societal level where not everyone was related to each other. They did share a common language and ethnicity, however. In a chiefdom, authority was given to an individual rather than rely on group consensus. The chieftain could settle disputes, coordinate resource sharing, and oversee public works projects. A portion of the chiefdom's produce was sent to him as tribute, allowing him to take on this responsibility as a full-time role. Tribute also supported family members, who helped by enforcing the chieftain's decisions.

The chieftain position was a hereditary right, passed down from father to son (or on rare occasion through a matrilineal line). His relatives helped by enforcing his decisions. This was the beginning of social stratification, where those who were a relative of the chieftain became royalty, those who had a personal relationship with the chieftain formed the upper class, and those who were neither became commoners. Smaller chiefdoms may have only had two levels, while larger chiefdoms developed multiple levels.

Chiefdoms still exist today in many parts of the world, albeit in a different form. The contemporary warlord is a kind of chieftain. Warlords are typically men who have gained power in remote regions in the absence of any higher authority. A warlord's rise in power is rooted in his ability to fund a militia. Not everyone is related to each other, but everyone pledges loyalty to the warlord. Key positions go to family members. Today, a warlord may even run a business on the side, often operating in the gray area between legitimacy and organized crime. The militia and civilians under their control may number into the thousands, and they often subjugate other local leaders. They also form relations with other warlords, and may even become preeminent among them. Such has been the case in Afghanistan in recent years, where the reemergence of warlords has been both a problem and a support to the struggling federal government. As Foreign Policy magazine described in 2010:

> [Preeminent Afghan warlords] Dostum and Ismail Khan had much in common. Both devoted considerable energy to managing the unruly mass of small-time warlords and petty military leaders, using a mix of persuasion and coercion.... Even a regular, disciplined army trained by a foreign mission (like the Afghan National Army today) would find it difficult to crush the thousands of small armed groups loyal to petty military commanders spread around Afghanistan.

So chiefdoms are alive and well today, though they take a different form. Whether it be warlord, sheik, small-town boss, or even a midsize business, each reflects aspects of a societal level that once dominated human civilization for millennia.

In fiefdoms, the ruler's authority was farther reaching than it was under chiefdoms. While fiefdoms and chiefdoms were similar, fiefdoms were simply grander than chiefdoms. Leadership was still passed along hereditary lines, but in fiefdoms it had led to dynastic rule. Social stratification had gone from a couple of layers to multiple layers, and in some cases had developed into a full-fledged caste system. In addition, the ruler's decisions were enforced not only by relatives but also by a fully developed civil service.

The civil service was composed of people who were not related to the ruler. Civil servants could be chosen at least in part by their natural talent and how well they performed in training. Civil servants assumed the administrative duties of the realm, freeing up the ruler's relatives to perform an oversight role. Now the ruler was not limited to using relatives, so he could expand his power, using commoners to perform administration (e.g., scribes) or enforcement duties (e.g., tax collection). Guided by the ruler's policies, multilayer bureaucracies developed. Conflict resolution passed from a duty performed by the royal family to one performed by a state police and judiciary.

Fiefdoms are still common today. Saudi Arabia is perhaps the clearest example. Arabia has been run by the Saud royal family since 1932. There has never been a national election. In Saudi Arabia, the king's word is law, and the king is subject only to his own royal decree. There is no written constitution, other than the Quran and the Sunnah (the traditions of Muhammad). No political parties exist—the immense Saud family dominates the political system with royal family members occupying all key ministerial positions and the thirteen regional governorships. Enforcement comes from having family members in key posts to oversee the civil service and make sure it follows the king's dictates.

Some modern monarchies have full parliaments that run the day-to-day ministries and make some lower-level decisions. However, even in these, the royal family still makes nearly all of the key decisions.

Nation-states are societies run by people who act in accordance with a written constitution. In the nation-state, leaders are no longer accepted along hereditary lines; rather, they emerge through processes defined by law. Decisions can be made by elected officials, as is the case in a representative democracy, or a dictator, who comes to power through a military or civil service structure that was created by the laws of the land. Enforcement comes through an expanded civil service, which acts in accordance with policies and procedures derived from the constitution and its subordinate laws. Enforcement no longer comes through royal rule. In this environment, social stratification disappears. Today, most of the world is composed of nation-states—the nation-state is the current leading societal level.

The United States is a nation-state with a constitution and representative democracy (Figure 5). Its decision makers are chosen in periodic elections, as is its president. Its president is charged with enforcing the laws that representatives create. Authority is granted, on a time limited basis, to representatives and the president, with terms limited to two, four, or six years.[IX]

Figure 5. Constitution of the United States

So each societal level reflects a different approach for managing resources. While societies tailored the approach to suit their own tastes, all societies at the same level used the same basic approach. Because of this, each approach could be called a *governance basis*—and every society at the same level is built upon the same foundation. Table 3 summarizes these governance bases.

Table 3: Governance Basis of Each Societal Level

	Governance Basis	Authority	Decision-making	Enforcement
Bands	Consensus	Head of the family	Consensus	None
Tribes	Council consensus	Elder council	Consensus	Informal relationship
Chiefdoms	Non-familial authority	Chieftain	Sole discretion	Chieftain family
Fiefdoms	Remote authority	Ruling fief	Sole discretion	Royal family + Civil Service
Nation-states	Rule-of-law	Surrogates	By process	Civil Service

At each societal level, a governance basis identified how a society used authority to manage its resources. It identified who made the decisions, how those decisions were made, and how those decisions were enforced.

Bands operated on a consensus basis, with each head of a family either making the decision or having equal input into the decision. There were no formal enforcement mechanisms since compliance was strictly voluntary.

Tribes operated on a council consensus basis. A council of elders used consensus to make decisions affecting the entire tribe. Sometimes a "big man" would stand out among peers on the council, but consensus was still the order of the day. Enforcement came through personal relationships since everyone in the tribe knew each other.

Chiefdoms operated on a nonfamilial authority basis. This gave direct decision-making authority to the chieftain, who was not necessarily a relative, but someone well known in the local region. This was done, presumptively, because he would make life better for everyone. He used his own family members to enforce his decisions. Furthermore, chiefdoms developed coercive tools to help with enforcement such as rituals and affectations of importance (i.e., a big staff, a large house, a monopoly on violence, or an ability to hear the gods).

Fiefdoms operated on a remote authority basis. This gave direct decision-making authority to a person who may live far away—someone whom most people would never meet. A royal family oversaw enforcement within the fiefdom as governors, ministers, or in other titled positions. Day-to-day operations and enforcement was left in the hands of civil servants.

Nation-states operate on the basis of rule-of-law. Decisions are made by surrogates using a process established by law. Surrogates (representatives or other) are chosen by a process established in law. Decisions are enforced by civil servants organized into agencies structured by law or regulation.

Therefore, changing the governance basis resulted in resources being managed over more people and a wider area by concentrating authority and enforcement into the hands of proportionally fewer people. While every society had its own variations in how it did this—how it structured and operated its government—all societies on the same level use the same basic approach. Even dictatorships are based on rule-of-law, though their governments use rule-of-law differently from representative democracy. In short, a governance basis can be thought of as an operating principle, while the governments themselves are structures built to affect that principle. The intent of both principle and structure is to create a stable and ideally prosperous way of life for people in a society. This is as true today as it was in the band era, and whether the society is a nation of over a billion people or a single family.[X]

Governance Bases and Societal Levels

So each societal level had its own governance basis. In reality, it is more accurate to say that each governance basis created its own societal level. Changing the governance basis changed the societal level. The growth a society experienced was really just a manifestation of that change.

The most obvious difference between societal levels is the size of communities. Bands ranged from a half-dozen to a few dozen members. Tribes ranged from a few dozen to a couple hundred members. Chiefdoms ranged from a few hundred to thousands. Fiefdoms ranged from thousands to hundreds of thousands. And nation-states ranged from hundreds of thousands to hundreds of millions. At each step, changing the governance basis enabled societies to grow. However, that growth was not the societal-level change itself—rather, it was the result of it.

Actually, it is more precise to say that changing the governance basis did not cause growth; rather, it enabled growth to continue. Such was the case when bands found naturally abundant food sources in the Fertile Crescent. Bands settled around these food sources and grew in size. They reached a limit to that growth, however, that challenged them to do things differently. At some point, they changed the way they used authority to manage resources, and the tribal council was born. This was the point at which they became tribes. Under new management, they could continue to grow. As it was, changing the governance basis was both a response to growth and a facilitator of further growth.

...

So, if the best way to become a leader is to reach a new societal level first, and a new societal level is really a change in governance basis, and a change in governance basis is really a change in the way societies manage their resources, then a society can become a leader simply by changing the way it manages its resources. Right? Not so fast.

Changing one's governance basis does not happen by decision. *Change* in general is so difficult for people that a society has to be forced to do it—"voluntarily" forced that is—prodded by its own self-interest. So what causes a society to change its governance basis? In a word: innovation.

Chapter 5
An Overview of Innovation

For two years in the 1990s, I lived on the north side of Chicago, in a neighborhood composed of apartment buildings and single-family homes. Parking was always in short supply, and I often had to park two or three blocks from my apartment building. Walking home in the winter could get messy when streets were covered with snow and ice.

The first major snowfall of 1994 dropped several inches on the city. By morning most people had dug out their cars and gone to work. Sometimes a person left a chair where his car had been. It seemed as though, once it was free of snow, the space (which was already a scarce commodity) became more valuable. What is more, its "owner" expected to use it again when he got off work, justifying this by the investment he had made in clearing it. Now he was going to keep it, at least until the snow melted. I never saw anyone challenge this unofficial rule, though I am sure it happens from time to time. Even if one disagrees with making chair-claims, it seems we understand them. On some basic level, property rights are intuitive to us (ask any three-year-old). I never claimed my space with a chair, even when I had spent twenty minutes clearing it. And when I was gone, I am sure it did not take but a minute for someone to grab the cleared space, the fruit of my labor.

Innovation: What Is It?

Societal-level change is driven by innovation. Most people would find this intuitive. We have grown accustomed to technology being a driver of change in our society. Recently, social media has reinforced this point quite well: creating new ways to communicate that we could not have imaged a generation ago. For societal-level change, it is useful to see *how* innovation drives that change.

A typical definition for innovation is "something new or different introduced; or, the act of innovating; the introduction of new things or methods." The first definition captures the idea that innovation is something new—a new product or concept. The second definition identifies it as a process—the action of introducing something new, something also required for change to happen. For this study, we will combine these by saying innovation is *an idea or insight applied to solve a problem or exploit an opportunity.*

Fundamentally, innovation is about insight: seeing what others do not see, or seeing it before others see it. Insight comes from looking at a situation from a new perspective—whether by diving into the details or by stepping back to look at the big picture. It comes from having seen something similar in a slightly different form or from having already solved a similar problem in a different context. Sometimes it comes by combining things that had never been combined before. However insights are generated, they are first born in some person's mind.

Another aspect of innovation is *application.* Insights alone are not enough to drive change—someone has to *do* something with them. The insight has to yield a new approach, a device, a methodology, a tool, or something else that accomplishes a purpose. It has to make a difference somehow. That purpose is most meaningful when it solves a problem or seizes an opportunity relevant for society. In most cases, innovation starts with a problem. It could be a small one or a major one, but someone somewhere wants it resolved. In other cases, there is an opportunity to do something better or to satisfy a hidden need. Making cars in a variety of colors is not complex, but it is innovative when it satisfies people bored with "any color you want as long as it is black."

Also note that innovation is not necessarily restricted to technology. Technology relates specifically to the application of science to do things differently. While this is probably the most common form of innovation today, it is not the only form. Innovation is broader.

So with innovation defined, we can return to the question of how it drove societal-level change. In fact, we can even address the original, broader question of what drove societal leadership? The key insight here is that not all innovations were created equal—some had more impact than others.[XI]

Four Kinds of Innovation

When it comes to understanding how some societies became leaders over others, one needs to consider four types of innovation: elevating innovations, preconditioning innovations, dominating innovations, and comforting innovations.

Elevating innovations were the biggest driver of societal-level change. In fact, each of these created a new societal level. The elevating innovations were

- Language,
- Property rights,
- Criminal justice,
- Writing, and
- Printing.[1]

Each of these drove a change in the way authority was used to manage resources in a society. Once that change happened, societies could grow, prosper, and build leadership power that led to dominance over rivals. Each of these had a major impact on the societies of its day and is still an indispensable part of our world.

Preconditioning innovations worked in tandem with elevating innovations to drive societal-level change. The preconditioning innovations were

---

[1] Each of these will be discussed at length in later chapters.

- Food production,
- Labor specialization,
- Mathematics, and
- Christianity.

Preconditioning innovations created the conditions needed for change to happen. For each societal level, a preconditioning innovation changed the environment before the elevating innovation came along. This created the conditions needed for the elevating innovation to be effective. Either innovation alone would have had no effect. They were partners, one pair for each societal level change: food production and property rights for tribes; labor specialization and criminal justice for chiefdoms; mathematics and writing for fiefdoms; and Christianity and printing for nation-states. A one-two punch drove societal-level change.

Dominating innovations are a third type of innovation that impacted leadership. These did so without driving any change in societal levels. The dominating innovations were

- Metallurgy,
- Horse warfare,
- Gunpowder,
- Petroleum propulsion, and
- Nuclear weaponry.

These innovations gave societies power over rivals. They were, in fact, capital weapons—in a war, the side with them won. Only when both sides acquired them did power begin to equalize. As such, dominating innovations drove leadership change when everyone was on *the same societal level*. They generated less power than did the combination of elevating and preconditioning innovations because they did not change societal levels. However, they gave the societies that acquired them first the power to rise into a leadership position.

The last type of innovation is *comforting innovations*. These are by far the most common form of innovation. They are everything not included in the types above. They had no impact on leadership, but they did improve people's lives. The rake, the vacuum cleaner, and the toothbrush are comforting innovations that have made our lives better (especially that last one), but none of them have altered societal leadership. We acknowledge them to recognize that innovation goes way beyond simply determining who is going to have power in the world—innovation speaks to life itself.

Innovation Families

The innovations mentioned above are quite general. When we think of innovations today, we tend to think about something specific, perhaps an enhancement to an existing device, such as a Smartphone, or a new process, such as a new way to sequence DNA. These are indeed remarkable innovations. However, to understand how leadership works, we need to think in terms of broad, basic categories—*innovation families* even. An innovation family is a grouping of related innovations that perform the same general task or support the same objective. Metallurgy contains gold smelting, copper smelting, bronze smelting, iron smelting, and even steel working. These are causally related innovations. Gold smelting gave people the insight and experience to try copper smelting. Copper smelting led to bronze smelting as people added tin to the process. Bronze smelting led to iron smelting as people began working with higher temperatures. Iron smelting led to steel making, as people learned to control carbon content. This causality continues all the way to today, with more specific innovations along the way such as the Bessemer process for the mass production of steel. Innovation families capture all of these related innovations much like parents, children, and grandchildren form human families.

Knowing the *originating innovation* is critical when defining an innovation family. The originating innovation starts the chain of causality. An originating innovation is created when someone tries something new—a new approach, a new material, or perhaps applying an existing approach or material to a new problem. For petroleum propulsion, the originating innovation was a steam pump built in 1712 to remove water from mines.

While many originating innovations were developed before recorded history, it is not always necessary to go back that far. The causal chain begins when a new idea adds far more value than anything that preceded it—to the point where it can be considered the start of the chain. Metallurgy was preceded by pottery making, where humankind first learned to bake goods in a fire. However, the process of heating ore instead of clay was such value added that we can use that as the starting point for the family. More precisely, we could even use bronze smelting as the originating innovation since only with that did metal become strong enough to create durable weapons and tools.

All innovations within the family after the originating innovation are *spin-off innovations*. These descendants of the originating innovation continue to transform societal process by making incremental improvements on the original idea. They make it faster, cheaper, larger (or smaller), stronger, or more powerful. Sometimes they apply the originating innovation in a new way or to a new area. The internal combustion engine was a spin-off of the steam engine, moving the fire chamber inside the block. The typewriter was a spin-off of movable type printing, placing the type at one's fingertips. Paper was a spin-off of writing since it replaced animal skins, clay, or stone with a more plentiful medium. Muskets were a spin-off within gunpowder, being a tool that focused the blast to launch a projectile.

Often a spin-off innovation will belong to two or more families. The diesel tractor can belong with either food production or petroleum propulsion. This does not present a problem because it is primarily the originating innovation that is most critical in understanding history and leadership; spin-off innovations help to identify the originating innovation and provide scope to the innovation family.

So for every originating innovation, there was a multitude of spin-off innovations that continued to advance the idea. Once an originating innovation established a family, its spin-offs continued to update and adapt the idea for the changing times. While a spin-off innovation had an incremental impact on society, an originating innovation had a paradigm-shifting impact on society. By separating originating innovations from spin-offs, and by focusing on the originating innovations, it is easier to see how an idea changed the world, and leadership.

The Innovation–Leadership Connection

Each *transformative innovation*, whether elevating, preconditioning, or dominating, changed leadership in some way. Elevating and preconditioning innovations worked together to drive societal-level change. As a result, they had the greatest impact on leadership. Dominating innovations enabled a society to rise to power as long as all societies were at the same societal level and the society had a monopoly on its use. Because of these limitations, it had a substantial impact on leadership, but less than the first two transformative innovations. Comforting innovations had no impact on leadership. Spin-off innovations, when separated from their originating innovation, had little impact on leadership—they were not transformative like their originating ancestors were.

Viewing innovation and leadership in this way makes it clear that only a handful of innovations ever had a real impact on leadership: the originating transformative innovations. When a society invented and embraced these, it became the leader.[2] The society could use the innovation to amass leadership power. If it gained a head start over rivals, it could make itself into a power before anyone could catch it, leading to power that would last a dynasty. [XII]

Innovation or Intuition?

Some innovations may seem so obvious that one might question whether they are worthy to be called innovations. Is growing food innovative? Bear in mind that what seems obvious to twenty-first-century humankind was hardly obvious when these innovations were first created. Even something as intuitive as property rights had to be invented at some point in our past, even if it was invented in multiple places.

Most innovations spread across the world from a single or a few separate points of invention. Gunpowder was invented in one place: China. Everyone else got it from there. By contrast, specialized labor can be found all over the world. Does it matter whether that idea was conceived by one person or by

---

[2] There is another way a society could become a leader without depending so heavily on these innovations. This will be discussed in a later chapter.

many people? In terms of societal leaders, the answer is no; the impact on leadership is no different whether it came from one place or several. The impact the innovation had on leadership makes it important, not whether it had one inventor or a multitude. (Nonetheless, most innovations did have a single origin. Even the bow and arrow, found all over the world, likely had a single origin in Africa, prior to humankind's first emigration.) One could go even further to argue that any society with the same needs and materials could have created any of the innovations, given enough time.[XIII]

...

Innovations solve problems facing a society at a particular time. Some innovations are complex and may target weighty issues. Others are so simple that they may seem intuitive and target smaller problems. Some change the world, and others claim parking spaces you have just shoveled. Some you hope catch on, while others you hope do not. I hope chair-claims do not catch on: they always seemed rude to me.

Chapter 6
Elevating Innovations

In the late 1980s, I drove to Detroit one weekend to see an old friend, play some golf, and see a girl I had met a few weeks earlier. After a five-hour drive from Cincinnati, I arrived at John's apartment. We ate something, and then hit some balls at a local driving range. That evening I met Christine in the lobby of a downtown hotel, where she was attending her family reunion. We walked through the lobby, down the hall, toward what I assumed would be a medium-sized room with a couple of dozen people. Instead I walked into a gargantuan ballroom with over a thousand people in it. It was bright and noisy, people were mingling, kids were running, and the hive was buzzing. We eventually found one of her first cousins, and she began to catch up. We met some of her aunts and uncles when we sat down for dinner.

It was strange to me to overhear people talking with relatives they had just met. The typical conversation involved trying to find out how they were related. Do you know Great Aunt Aleen? Are you a Baskin or a Vaughn? How long have you lived in that part of the country, and where were you before then?

By the end of the evening, groups had formed. The Baskins were in one corner, the Vaughns in another, and the Peays in another. After being politely social, people wanted to relax with people they knew. Having a common ancestor made you kin, but it did not mean you were going to hang out with these people. Overall, it was a fun night. The following year, I was invited to the new, and smaller, Baskin reunion.

The Change Process

Of the many innovations throughout history, elevating innovations were most responsible for creating new leaders in the world. They did so by changing the way a society managed its resources.

For each societal-level shift, there was one elevating innovation. When an elevating innovation came along, it initiated a sequence of events that culminated in level change. The change did not happen overnight—sometimes it took generations or even centuries. However, once begun, the transformation continued steadily until complete. While other innovations would later support and reinforce the change, the elevating innovation initiated the change.

A society had to transform to embrace the elevating innovation. If a society did not change the way it used authority, it did not change societal level. However, once the society made the change, the door to new opportunities began to open—ones that had not existed before. As the opportunities were exploited, the society grew in power and stature. Some of these transformations are well documented. Ones further back in history are less well documented, but the pattern of transformation still holds true.

Language

Language is the first elevating innovation. It appeared sometime after 100,000 years ago in Africa. Before language, only protolanguage existed. Protolanguage was the grunts, hand signals, facial expressions, and body language that facilitated communication before speech. Protolanguage carried no specific content, so humans were limited in the types of training, collaboration, and development they could perform.

Two prominent theories exist for the appearance of language. The first notes that the FOXP2 "language gene," which is required for the facial and mouth control needed to pronounce modern words, did not reach its present form until between 100,000 and 200,000 years ago. The human voicebox did not reach its modern level of development until around 100,000 years ago. This would have been the first time that humans could have pronounced modern words. Once so enabled, language followed.

Another theory says that at roughly the same time, the human brain changed the way it organized information. A protein-rich diet, produced by the abundance of shellfish found along the eastern shore of southern Africa, promoted genetic improvements in the way the brain organized information, leading to language and other development.

These two theories may be somewhat intertwined. Since the early twentieth century, linguists have known that language plays a role in how the mind structures information.[1] This was proven in the 1970s, when a man who had no language suddenly appeared at a language class in southern California. He had grown up deaf in a rural Mexican village with parents who did not know sign language. As a result, he did not even know language existed. He survived by mimicking the motions people made with their mouths and hands. Amazingly, he found his way into a developmental program for the hearing impaired. There, a researcher named Susan Schaller discovered him and began working with him, introducing him first to the idea of language, and then to English itself. Years later, he stated how acquiring language had "rewired" his brain—he could not even recall *how* he thought before language: "I think differently. I can't remember how I thought."[2]

Language gave humankind a capability it did not have before. The Great Leap Forward started around 80,000 years ago. At that time, humankind began a rapid advance in development. We see remnants of this in the caves of eastern South Africa: the world's first jewelry, cultural artifacts, ritual objects such as ornamental shell beads, inscribed ostrich shell,; needles, and sophisticated bone-engraving awls. Local trade routes were established, and clearing land by fire began. Tool development took off: fishhooks were invented, sophisticated stone working began, and bows and arrows appeared. Along with these tools came better fishing techniques, and more sophisticated hunting techniques that targeted larger game. There were changes in the way bands organized themselves for hunting and gathering, and some researchers

[1] Sapir–Whorf is the accepted theorem on this issue, though several versions of it exist.
[2] Susan Schaller, *A Man Without Words* (Berkeley: University of California Press, 2012).

believe that the number of people who could coexist in a single group went from about a half dozen to sixty. All of this happened within a 20,000-year period. It is hard to imagine such development occurring without language—the generations of experience needed to build such skills could not have accrued without language.

The Great Leap Forward coincides with another ancient phenomenon: the Great Human Migration. That is when modern humans ventured from Africa to Asia around 80,000 years ago. By 74,000 years ago, humans were in India. (Tools dating to that time were found at a site in India; they are almost identically matched to tools found in Africa.) By 45,000 years ago, humankind had reached New Guinea and Australia (which were connected by a land bridge back then). By 40,000 years ago, modern humans had reached Europe. Such widespread migration would not have been possible without language and its resultant skills. While Neanderthal was limited to Europe, this new human could spread around the globe. It is clear that language changed the way humankind managed resources (i.e., hunting, fishing, food distribution, and organization), and is therefore the first elevating innovation, creating the bands that would inhabit the earth for millennia.[XIV]

Property Rights

Property rights are the second elevating innovation. Property rights emerged in prehistoric times. The first property rights were assigned to objects held in one's possession. While a person was using an objective—a rock, a piece of shellfish, or an animal carcass—it was his. However, once he set it down, and it was clear he was not using it anymore, his claim expired.

This changed somewhat when tool development began. Even back then, humans (like some animals) linked an object to a person who had worked on it. Therefore, if a person took the time to fashion an arrowhead from a piece of stone, others considered the arrowhead to belong to that person, even when he was not holding it in his hands. This was the case for all objects provided they looked distinctive from something anyone could pick up from the ground. As such, the earliest property rights were informally attached to tools, gathered food, weapons, and temporary habitations—things people had had to invest time and effort to acquire or develop.

In hunter-gatherer societies, land belongs to no one. In prehistoric times, bands roamed within a territory, setting up camp and staying in one place as long as food was available. When food became harder to find, the band would move to another area—a better hunting ground, a better fishing hole; for example, foraging in one place lasted until all of the berries were picked, and then they found another location. Multiple bands roamed within an area. In general, deference was shown to the band already occupying a particular spot. Once that party departed, however, it was again up for grabs.

Initially there were no property rights over animals. Animals were wild game; if an animal was found, a hunter was free to kill it. The first exception to this was dogs. Dogs were domesticated around 13,000 BCE, at the end of the last ice age. Dogs were bred down from wolves. As they became visibly distinctive from wolves, they would no longer be considered wild. Property rights became attached to dogs as members of a band began to see a relationship between a particular dog and a band member. It was easy to see a particular dog's affinity for one man by its behavior and to assign property rights to its apparent master. It was observed or presumed that this person fed and trained the dog. Hence, deference was shown to this relationship using the same invested labor principle that had existed for millennia between people and objects.

When agriculture developed around 9,000 BCE, it became necessary to attach property rights to land. For agriculture to work, a family had to make a considerable investment of time and effort up front in seeding and nurturing crops—long before a single grain could be harvested. If the family lost the land it had cultivated, it risked starvation, so this up-front investment had to be protected to make this way of life work.

Property rights became attached to land in the same way that they had been attached to objects or dogs—by deference to invested labor. As long as other band members could tell that a piece of property had been worked, they could show deference to someone for having done that work. Once a family started turning over soil, it became obvious that someone was working that plot. In this way, property rights could take on a permanency with land in the same way they had with tools and weapons—existing even if a person was not standing on the plot. This helped ensure that a family's up-front labor investment would not be lost through encroachment.

Land was nearly always held by individual families rather than by an entire band. It was simply too easy to shirk work or overconsume the harvest when property belonged to the band as a whole. Instead, property remained with individuals or their families, and they had full ownership of the resulting harvest. To make this work, however, everyone in the band had to know which plots of land belonged to which families—and that any attempt to encroach on someone else's property would be met with the scorn, discipline, and social norms of punishment within the band.

Likewise, when husbandry arrived a thousand years later, property rights were assigned to animals as well. Fortunately, assigning rights to livestock was made easier since bands already had been doing that with dogs for millennia. Just as with dogs, livestock was owned by the individual or the single family, not the band. As such, members of the band had to know which animals belonged to which families.

Over time, bands developed various ways to signal ownership. As animals became domesticated, they looked less like their wild cousins, reducing the likelihood they would be mistaken for wild game. In addition, branding was introduced. Ear notching was also used. Furthermore, simple comfort in the presence of humans would have given away the fact that the animal had been domesticated, let alone if it were found in a crude form of corral.

In time, most bands would stop roaming and settle into agrarian living. Because agrarian living supports a denser population than does nomadic foraging, the size of bands grew. In time, there would be competition for the most productive soil and the best grazing areas. Keeping herds separated became more difficult. Disputes between families became more common. In this environment, the consensus approach to governance did not work well. Until now, disputes were settled by consensus, and every adult male had a vote. If not everyone agreed, disputes were not settled. If two families claimed the same plot of land, there was no resolution mechanism. As bands grew larger, disputes grew worse.

Local economics compounded this problem. Land value increases in more densely populated areas (that was true back then as it is today). As a band grows, the value of its land grows, particularly the most fertile areas near water or the best grazing land. In this scenario, the old regime of deference to invested labor breaks down—an interloper has more incentive to challenge the owner for the property. Though everyone in the band was related, the larger the band, the more distantly related people were and the more conflict there would be unless something could be done to halt it.

By necessity, the tribal council was born. Instead of having the head of every family attend a dispute-resolution meeting—a practice no longer feasible given the size of the group—now only the head of each clan (group of families) would attend. This person, usually the patriarch of an extended family (cousins and so forth), would make the decision on behalf of his clan. While the council would still make decisions using consensus, the meetings were at least kept to a reasonable size—one more conducive to dialog. In addition, since patriarchs were one step removed from the emotions of the dispute, they could make more dispassionate—and on average fairer—decisions. Furthermore, having the revered family patriarch as part of the decision-making process meant that clans would comply out of respect.

With this new form of institutional authority assigning and enforcing property rights, the tribe was born. Archeological evidence suggests the earliest permanent settlements emerged in the Fertile Crescent around 11,000 BCE around natural supplies of wild grains and game. Active food production was commonplace by around 9000 BCE. At some time during this two-thousand-year transition (probably closer to the end), property rights over land and livestock became a common practice and tribal councils were a common form of governance.

Once formed, councils began making other decisions relating to the welfare of the tribe, such as where to plant and how to best use the land for overall productivity. (Even today, decisions over land allocation and use are a primary responsibility for tribal councils.) Land still belonged to families though, allocated through clans, not to the tribe as a whole. Council decisions were final. Societal-level shift had taken place.

This new tribal structure proliferated throughout Mesopotamia starting around 9000 BCE; eventually every region in the world would adopt it. It was the governance structure that could allow agriculture and husbandry to expand.[xv]

Criminal Justice

The third elevating innovation is criminal justice. Today's criminal justice system includes everything from the local police and district attorney to the Federal Bureau of Investigation, Drug Enforcement Administration, the prison systems, and all agencies charged with enforcing the law. However, it did not start out that way. Things were much simpler once—though every bit as essential.

Tribal life was violent. In nearly every tribe, some form of violence was a leading cause of death. One report estimates that violence accounted for up to 30 percent of all deaths within Amazonian tribes prior to European contact.[3] Even today, tribalism is behind much of the violence still seen in Africa.

This violence occurred not only between tribes but also within tribes. High murder rates were the norm. Violence grew out of disputes over territory, honor, revenge, women, and possessions—what causes arguments today often caused murder back then. While bands also had high murder rates, having more people living closer together only increased the opportunity for violence.

Disputes within tribes could be settled with the help of a common relative who acted as a mediator. This common relative was typically older and was respected by both parties. If he was found quickly enough, the dispute could be settled before it became violent. As tribes grew, however, it became harder to find a common relative—one who both parties knew. This is problematic in conflicts: when tempers flare, time is of the essence. In fights between clans, there may be no common relative at all—clans were only distantly related so common relatives may have all died. In addition, a tribal council was

[3] Timothy Wall, "Amazonian Tribal Warfare Sheds Light on Modern Violence, Says MU Anthropologist," *University of Missouri, News Bureau*, October 2, 2012, http://munews.missouri.edu/news-releases/2012/1002-amazonian-tribal-warfare-sheds-light-on-modern-violence-says-mu-anthropologist.

ineffective for resolving this type of conflict, since they could not meet quickly enough. As a result, violence was the norm for settling grievances.

Criminal justice was the solution. Instead of finding a common relative, tribes began having one person settle disputes for everyone—even across clans. This person would be readily available for settling disputes because it would be his full-time job. He could be found quickly because his hut was centrally located, and it may even be adorned so people would easily recognize it. Parties would no longer be allowed to fight each other or take revenge— only this selected person would have the right to exercise violence to settle the dispute or enforce justice. His relatives would be called upon to help him enforce his decisions and carry out his sentences. In this way, criminal justice was born.

Often, the Big Man—the most influential person on the tribal council— was chosen for this role of adjudicator. However, even that was not enough to make this new approach work—he needed authority. He needed authority so that all members of the tribe would obey the decisions he made. He needed a position of great honor, respect, and deference. Therefore, the position of chieftain was created. He would have an honored seat at the table of elders. He would wear special dress to set him apart. He would carry a staff as a symbol of his authority. He would be honored at tribal ceremonies. He would go a step further by making the decision-making process a court of honor, surrounded by pomp and ceremony. And all of this seemed to work.

The shift in authority from tribal council to chieftain, along with deputation of the chief's relatives, brought violence under control. Now a larger society could live together with less fighting. While tribes were limited to a couple of hundred members (the maximum number of people who can know each other personally), now society could grow into the thousands. Eventually, this centralized decision-making authority would be applied to other areas such as food redistribution and public works. As his role continued to expand, the chieftain acquired a monopoly on information (from multiple human sources or from the gods), and he used it to exercise more authority, such as dictating when to plant crops or when to raise a militia because enemies were threatening. Eventually, this position would become hereditary, passed down from father to son, further separating this position and royal lineage from the rest of the people, the commoners. The chiefdom was born.[XVI]

Writing

The fourth elevating innovation is writing. It is hard to imagine a world today without written language. In most societies, it is so important that children start learning to write by the age of five. In some parts of the world, however, oral traditions still satisfy the needs of a simpler lifestyle. There, written language is not required for daily living. There was a time when the entire world was like this.

By reducing violence, chiefdoms grew larger and more complex. They covered more people and a larger territory. The chieftain and his now royal family grew more powerful. Social stratification emerged as those close to him grew in power. Public works projects grew larger and more sophisticated, building irrigation canal networks, food storage facilities, temples, and roads.

As society grew, the chieftain's ability to manage his realm became strained. Even his relatives could only be in so many places at one time to watch over things, so it became increasingly difficult to enforce decisions over a greater population and area. In effect, a chieftain's meaningful authority was limited to a few thousand people and a few hundred square miles.

Around 3300 BCE, writing appeared in Sumer. It would later appear in China and Mesoamerica, and from these three places, it would spread around the world. In Sumer it began when someone discovered that making a different kind of stroke on the outside of clay jar (a bulla) could represent a different kind of object inside the jar. Until then, simple tally marks had been used to denote only the number of objects in the jar. Over time, writing grew more sophisticated as different symbols were added, until they were finally able to reflect spoken language. In addition, clay and stone materials were replaced by animal skins, papyrus, parchment, and other more transportable materials. Now a person could send a message without it being corrupted by the messenger's faulty memory or interpretation.

With writing, a ruler could record his decisions on papyrus or any of the new materials developed. He could have the papyrus carried to the far reaches of his realm and read without loss of meaning. With writing, he could expand his realm beyond its current limits. There was a limitation, however. Only a few people could read and write, and he still only had a few relatives to watch over his territory. To further enlarge his territory, something else had to change.

The solution was to enlist commoners in administering the realm. Now nonrelatives could perform minor roles, while kinsmen would be reserved for major posts. Scribes would be enlisted to capture his decisions on papyrus. Messengers would be used to traverse the territory delivering messages. A royal seal would verify that the message came from the king. Troops, led by an officer, would accompany the messengers to enforce decrees. All of these people would be selected, at least in part, based on their ability, and trained in their roles.

The civil service enabled a ruler to expand his territory. Now a larger group of people could see laws that had been written down. Remote posts could receive direct instructions from the ruler or another high-ranking official. Laws could be reread as often as necessary to ensure they were fully communicated and obeyed. With writing, rule could even cut across language barriers as interpreters were hired to translate laws into other dialects. The expanded realm could now include people of different linguistic and ethnic backgrounds. Suddenly there was an exponential jump in the size of a society that could be governed by a single ruler.

To help manage the larger territory, legal scrolls could be stored and revisited from time to time, helping to create a legal memory that lasted longer than any single ruler. Dynasties developed. With these, there was greater consistency across successive kings, which helped to stabilize the larger society.

This expansion of authority was the beginning of the fiefdom. The ruler's family shifted to an oversight role and backed out of the minor tasks involved in running the realm. With the addition of a civil service—scribes, temple administrators, and so forth—social stratification further increased. Whereas chiefdoms only had two or three levels of society, a fiefdom could have a half dozen. Below the royal family were priests and astrologers, and then high-ranking civil servants who would reign in social standing above commoners.

Within a hundred years of the advent of writing, the world's first city-state, Uruk, became a power in ancient Sumer (3200 BCE). Within a century of receiving writing, Egypt established its first dynasty (3100 BCE). Writing and the fiefdom appeared concurrently during the Xia dynasty in China (2070–1600 BCE). And in Mesoamerica, fiefdom empires emerged after the advent of writing, including the Zapotec (500 BCE) and the Maya (250 CE).[4] After these early pioneers, other societies adopted writing and began their transition. Eventually, the fiefdom would become the second-longest-running level in human history (after bands), dominating for over four thousand years.

Writing allowed the will of the ruler to be carried out far away from the person himself, and by a group of people not related to the ruler. This was possible by establishing a civil service, which could expand the ruler's ability to enforce his decrees. With the sovereign's will communicated in writing, and a civil service in place, early fiefdoms could dominate their chiefdom rivals, establishing some of the world's first empires—empires that would last for centuries.[XVII]

Printing

The fifth elevating innovation is printing. Today we take it for granted, but if you are reading this book in hardcopy, paperback, or even ebook, you are benefitting from printing at this very moment. There is also a good chance that you are reading this book in a country governed by rule-of-law. Again, you are benefitting from printing.

Before the 1500s, governance by rule-of-law had been tried but failed. Either it lacked the ability to make and execute decisions or it lacked a cohesion needed to hold society together. The Athenian democracy lasted about a century before its inability to coordinate warfare led to its defeat at the hands of rival Sparta. Internal bickering over the conduct of the war led to some disastrous decision making, which ultimately resulted in the democracy's downfall.

While the Roman Republic did not have this problem, it had another problem—cohesion. The Roman Republic began at the same time as the Athenian democracy. It lasted over four times longer, however, because Rome was better able to translate democracy into action than Athens was. After its founding, the Roman Republic grew in power and might. In time, however,

---

[4] Maya writing began as early as 250 BCE, but Maya civilization entered its Golden Age around 250 CE.

the republic unraveled. Rule-of-law was not taken seriously enough to override the personal agendas of powerful men. Eventually, some of its leaders would have their own militias running through the streets of Rome contending for power. This situation called for a strong leader, such as Julius Caesar, to reassert order and authority.

The first modern attempt at rule-of-law began when King John of England acceded to the Magna Charta in 1215. When he accepted the document (a decision in which he had no choice), King John accepted that he was bound by laws he did not create—he became subject to the law, not over it. Yet despite this, and the emergence of two houses of Parliament, power remained mostly with the king for a couple of centuries. Legislators simply did not have the means to rival kingly authority.

Then in the 1450s, Johannes Gutenberg of Mainz, Germany, a former goldsmith and cloth printer, determined that metal could be used to create durable, individual letter type for printing. At that time, woodblock printing was the practice—with its large hand-carved wooden blocks inked and pressed onto paper. While this was effective at preserving art and literature, it was labor intensive and costly. Individually movable type, on the other hand, could be rearranged and reused to create any printed page, for any publication, thereby greatly reducing the cost of books.

Gutenberg experimented with, and found, the right alloy for the type. He also found the right oils for the ink. He created a hand mold and a letter cavity—a matrix to rapidly cast the type. He created a *form* to assemble the lettering for a page. He created a movable undertable that cycled the paper through the press. He reinvented the screw press so it applied pressure evenly across the page. With these inventions, he made printing into an assembly line. The cost of books plummeted, making them affordable for readers and profitable for printers.

The movable type printing presses spread rapidly across Europe. Within two decades, they were all over the continent. In 1476, the printing press arrived in Britain, brought from the mainland by William Caxton, a merchant/diplomat, who had spent time in Cologne, Germany. His intent was to print his English language translation of a French book on ancient Troy.

Printing rapidly changed religion, commerce, industry, and academia throughout Europe. Sacred documents that had only been seen by the privileged few were now available to everyone. Laypeople could share information about their trade and develop written procedures to create the first industry standards. Units of measure standardized as scholars and craftsman began to work together as never before. Peer review of scholarly works emerged as documents were shared across the continent.

Moreover, for the first time in history, knowledge could accumulate. Instead of struggling to preserve their knowledge, societies could now accumulate it. While writing enabled some collective knowledge retention, printing enabled knowledge to accumulate faster than it ever did before. No longer would knowledge fade when a leading thinker died. With printing, each generation could add its own research to the collective body of knowledge. This was the case in nearly every field—academia, trade, commerce, business, or religion.

Perhaps nowhere was the change wrought by printing more impactful than in the legal field. Printing allowed the mass reproduction of legal works, from existing and new laws, to proceedings of court cases, to points of view on legal matters. Now that a wider audience gained greater access to this information, some things about the law began to change.

Law acquired greater permanency. Printed laws were shared and reviewed by more people, so they were less likely to be forgotten. With more people reading them regularly, including the growing number of law students and professors, the laws remained on people's minds and were less likely to be lost.

Laws also became more consistent. As more people gained access to printed laws, more people were available to identify the inconsistencies between them, and more people then began working to remove those inconsistencies. Also, when someone came up with a new law, there were more people to review it, alongside preceding laws. Legal precedent arose. Even laws across regions were harmonized.

Like knowledge in general, laws could accumulate. Subsequent laws would now build on earlier laws—refining them, enhancing them, and making them more specific to a particular situation. With all of these changes, the *corpus juris* was built up and solidified. The collective body of law within English society became more robust, more precise, more reliable, and more credible.

More precise laws afforded less room for loose interpretation by the courts.

A tighter legal code reduced the number of capricious rulings coming from the courts as lawmakers found themselves bound to the printed word. This led to a more consistent judiciary.

In time, people came to rely more on consistent laws, procedures, and metrics. They seemed to enable things that were not possible before—longer-distance trade, greater fairness in legal cases, larger commercial ventures, more tools to build the economy, and better preparation for warfare. Moreover, people came to know what to expect, thereby reducing some of life's uncertainty. As life improved, rule-of-law gained credibility as a form of governance.

As people's faith shifted to procedures and rules, it shifted away from rulers. Life under rule-of-law became preferable to life under lordship. Eventually, authority shifted from king to lawmakers. The growing importance of law shifted authority to those who could best make the laws. The king's role became increasingly ceremonial.

Printing expanded the civil service. Now agencies and institutions charged with running the government and enforcing laws could be set up by policy to address specific aspects of governmental affairs. Managing colonies, working with labor unions, collecting taxes, or overseeing military operations—all of these would be guided by policy, which now had a consistency and a permanency it never had before. Printed policy enabled centralized control of decentralized execution. Thousands of miles from the seat of power, officials could operate with semiautonomy, provided they adhered to the bounds of policy. Standardized procedures meant faster enforcement, and the pace of governance—and life in general—increased. And all of this further reduced the need for a royal family to oversee enforcement.

With society's belief in rule-of-law, governance gained a cohesion it had lacked before printing. Even powerful men were less likely to challenge a system embraced by the majority of the population. People had no intention of going back to the old days of arbitrary rulings and uncertainty. At that point it became a fait accompli that the king would be removed from power and governance by rule-of-law adopted.

In 1689, about two centuries after the arrival of the printing press on British soil, England became the world's first sustainable nation-state, with the passage of the Bill of Rights. Other nations would follow suit. A larger, more solid *corpus juris* provided the cohesion needed to hold both government and society together—a cohesion that was a product of printing.[XVIII]

Elevation

The elevating innovations led directly to societal-level change. Table 4 summarizes these changes. Each of these innovations was the result of someone trying to solve a problem faced by society. For each innovation, someone or some group had an insight that led to solving a problem. Today, many of these solutions may seem obvious, but they were not obvious at the time. Some of these innovations were developed in one place, while others were developed independently in multiple locations. Whichever the case, the innovation changed how authority was used in society—how it was assigned and the type of decisions that it could make. Ultimately, these were decisions about how society's resources would be used and how those decisions would be enforced. This shift in authority did not lead to societal-level change—it *was* societal-level change. It changed the governance basis. After the shift, the society accrued more power, expanded its borders, conquered its neighbors, exalted itself, and gained a sustainability it did not have before. These were the trappings of change.

Table 4: Elevating Innovations Triggering Societal-Level Change

	Initial Governance Basis	Elevating Innovation	Resulting Governance Basis	
Bands	Consensus	Property Rights	Council Consensus	**Tribes**
Tribes	Council Consensus	Criminal Justice	Non-familial Authority	**Chiefdoms**
Chiefdoms	Non-familial Authority	Writing	Remote Authority	**Fiefdoms**
Fiefdoms	Remote Authority	Printing	Rule-of-law	**Nation-states**

...

Such was the role of the elevating innovations—changing the governance basis. As societies grew larger and individuals became less familiar with each other personally (like large family reunions), societies had to change the way they managed their resources. Elevating innovations provided the ability to do this; however, they could not have done it alone. They needed assistance from another innovation—the preconditioning innovations—to be useful. Preconditioning innovations had to set the stage for the elevating innovations to work.

Chapter 7
Preconditioning Innovations, Part I

Sometimes an innovation is just ahead of its time. The concept is sound and the execution is good, but the world just is not ready for it. Sometimes it takes another innovation to come along to make the world ready for it.

Take the parachute, for example. The parachute was designed in the 1480s by Leonardo Da Vinci (Figure 6). It saw limited, sporadic development over the next few centuries, and was even embraced by adventurous balloonists in the eighteenth century. However, it was not until World War I, with the advent of aerial combat, that nations had a sustained need for parachutes. After the war, they set about parachute development, and by World War II, entire divisions of men were using them to fly into combat zones. Today, parachutes have slowed space shuttles returning from orbit, and parachute-based glide suits enable people to fly forward as much as they fall. Hence, the parachute, which sat mostly dormant for over four centuries, suddenly became an essential tool with a variety of uses, but not until the airplane came along to make it a necessity.

Figure 6. Da Vinci's parachute in sketch, c. 1480s, and its first test flight in 2000.

Or take the Sega Channel. The Sega Channel was released in 1993 as a way to download videogames over cable television. For $15 a month, families in North America could view a rotating list of fifty games on their household TV screen, and select one to download and play. At its peak, the Sega Channel had well over a hundred thousand subscribers. However, technical limitations hampered further growth. One problem was that you could not save games; they were erased upon exit, so you had to start over each time you played. A bigger problem was that cable TV providers had to upgrade their lines to carry the signal, generating cost for the local cable companies. Even with upgraded lines, interruptions while downloading were commonplace, forcing the consumer to re-download, often multiple times. In 1998, Sega decided to cancel the service rather than upgrade it for new, more advanced controllers.

Today on-demand downloading is commonplace with programs such as Xbox Live and Playstation. These products use the Internet to allow users to scroll through a menu of games for download. The games are a generation more sophisticated as well, allowing multiple players to interactively compete against one another, concurrently. So the innovation of downloadable games was a sound one, but it needed the Internet to make it work.

Elevating innovations were the primary drivers behind societal-level change. However, none of them would have had any effect had it not been for a preconditioning innovation. The preconditioning innovation changed the environment so that the elevating innovation could add value. Without the preconditioning innovation, the elevating innovation would not have existed, would not have been necessary, or would not have been useful.

There were four preconditioning innovations—one for each elevating innovation (except language): food production preconditioned the environment for property rights; labor specialization preconditioned for criminal justice; mathematics preconditioned for writing; and Christianity preconditioned for printing. In each case, societies were initially facing some barrier or hurdle in their existing environment. The preconditioning innovation removed, or at least reduced, the hurdle. After this, almost as a side effect, the change wrought by the preconditioning innovation made the elevating innovation useful or feasible. This in turn began societal-level change. This four-step pattern repeats itself every societal-level change. While some preconditioning innovations may seem so intuitive or obtuse that they hardly deserve to be called innovations, each one performed an indispensable function.[XIX]

Food Production

The first preconditioning innovation is food production. Food production made property rights essential.

As we discussed earlier, until about thirteen thousand years ago hunter-gatherer bands were the only form of society in the world. Bands roamed a local area, moving from one hunting-gathering spot to the next in search of food. In this environment, property rights were only applied to objects—tools, weapons, or shelters; game killed; or dogs, which were first domesticated about fifteen thousand years ago. In short, property rights were afforded to those things in which someone had invested their labor—then they would be considered to belong to someone. Property rights could never be applied to land or animals since these things could not be owned—they were openly available for anyone to use (like oceans today). Once someone moved off a good campsite, it was up for grabs. Only after someone had killed an animal did it become that person's property.

Now, ancient southwestern Asia was an area naturally rich with cereal grasses and game. In addition to natural abundance, the region's warm and wet climate promoted biodiversity and growth. In fact, the region was so abundant that bands could stop roaming and simply harvest what was continuously available in the same spot. There was enough food, year-round, that they did not have to search for it. (This still happens in some parts of the world today.) This abundance led to substantial population growth in the region.

Then around 10,900 BCE, the Younger Dryas began. This was a colder, drier period that lasted roughly twelve hundred years. During this time, temperatures across the northern hemisphere dropped on average 4°F–10°F (2°C–6°C); the glaciers even advanced a final time, covering much of the hemisphere. This sudden climate change caused much of the natural abundance in southwestern Asia to shrink or disappear altogether. This was problematic for a population that had ballooned in recent centuries. People were forced to live in the remaining pockets of food abundance—and they were shrinking. Some returned to hunting and gathering, but there was not enough game to support the larger population.

One solution was to produce more food from the remaining pockets of natural abundance. This was initially done using proto-agriculture. Proto-agriculture involves clearing away the brush, vegetation, and weeds surrounding naturally growing plants, trees, and bushes. Proto-agriculture may also include clearing the land through burning to encourage new growth, cutting down encroaching trees, loosening the soil near plants to aerate it, digging small channels near plants to help pool water, pruning the plants, and even replanting branches that had broken off. In short, proto-agriculture is everything except moving the saplings or seeds to a new location. The earliest evidence of proto-agriculture dates to about 23,000 BCE at a site in the western Fertile Crescent, on the shores of the present-day Sea of Galilee in Israel. It is likely this practice would have been known in the eastern Fertile Crescent as well by the Younger Dryas period. It certainly would have been applied with vigor in light of a shrinking food supply.

At some point, someone tested the idea of moving the saplings or seeds to a new area. The first move may have only been a few feet, but it worked. And it caught on. Now growth could expand beyond the natural pockets—in short, agriculture had begun. When the climate finally returned to normal, agriculture was poised to explode—which it did.

Husbandry came about a thousand years afterward. Sometime between 9000 and 8000 BCE, goats were bred from wild bezoars, and sheep were bred from wild mouflon. By 8000 BCE, goat herding and sheep herding were common throughout Mesopotamia. Within another fifteen hundred years, pigs would be bred from boars and cattle from aurochs, adding to livestock.

It would take over a thousand years for agrarianism to fully develop. Techniques had to be developed, new types of cereal grasses had to be planted, understanding of the soil had to develop, and ways to foster yield had to be learned. Developing the symbiosis between farming and husbandry—where grain was grown to feed animals and animals were grown to pull plows and help grow grain—would take centuries. Nevertheless, a steady progression had begun—one that continues even today.

The new agrarian life coexisted alongside hunting and gathering for much of this time. People would split their time between the two lifestyles, often on a seasonal basis, with part of the year spent planting and harvesting and the remainder spent hunting and gathering. (This still happens today.) Ultimately, however, agrarianism won out. Agrarianism could provide more food for the same amount of time and effort expended, with lower risk.[1] Fully developed agriculture could sustain ten to one hundred times the population density that hunting and gathering could. With this kind of productivity, food production spread and the population grew. By around 9,000 BCE, agrarian villages were starting to proliferate throughout the region.

Now, for agrarian living to take hold, the old approach of property rights by labor invested had to be applied to things that had always been held in common, namely, land and animals. People had to recognize that a plot of ground turned over and developed was separate and distinct from open country. People had to see that a domesticated animal behaved differently from a wild one, so it should not be killed for game. Furthermore, people had to have some idea of who had invested their labor into that land or that animal. As such, a paradigm shift was needed to protect the investment that

---

[1] In southwestern Asia, shortages of wild game also played a role in the shift—gazelle populations were being decimated during this time.

people were now making in growing food—people tilling a field whose harvest was not expected for months had to be assured they would receive the fruits of their labor. Nevertheless, a new mind-set took hold, giving ownership rights to people who had invested their labor to create the food.

Undoubtedly, these new property rights were informal at first, with people generally recognizing and respecting their neighbor's work. However, with increased population came increased conflict over land and animals. Some plots of land were simply better than others for farming. Some pastureland was better than others for grazing. If a person set aside farming to do seasonal hunting, was he still entitled to the same land when he returned? Was simply occupying a spot not being actively worked enough to claim it? It is sometimes hard to tell one goat from another, and with more people living close together, it was easy to get herds mixed up. Finally, with a growing population, the social norms of the band (i.e., close family ties) were fading and hence less reliable for dispute resolution. Violence increased.

The solution was to formalize the assignment of property rights over land and animals. This meant they had to be permanently assigned by a recognized formal body. Of course, such a body did not exist, so one had to be created. This new body had to cross bands and even clans (a group of bands) to represent their respective views. So the heads of clans would meet to decide who owns what, and would resolve any disputes that arose. The tribal council was born.

The concept took hold, and it was replicated throughout Mesopotamia. Under this new structure, agrarian villages could spread to new areas away from natural abundance as long as water was available. The tribe was born.[XX]

Labor Specialization

The second preconditioning innovation is labor specialization. Labor specialization made criminal justice feasible.

With a new tribal structure in place, a sedentary lifestyle, and food production fully developed, the population grew and tribes proliferated. In this sedentary life, women could have more children—one every year or two instead of every three or four years. (Children no longer had to be able to keep up with a mobile family.) As a result, tribes grew in both size and number.

Feeding this growing population was a full-time job, however, for everyone. Everyone worked in food production—every man, woman, and child who was old enough was planting, hoeing, irrigating, or raising an animal. The family's survival depended on it. There were no jobs outside of food production, so there were no craftsmen. If someone made baskets, it was a side job, after the day's work had been done. If someone made clay pots, it was in addition to that individual's food-producing duties, done in those rare moments of downtime. Sometimes the very old or the very young would do more of these jobs, but since each family had to raise its own food, it would have been a limited practice.

As mentioned before, a growing population had another effect. Larger tribes meant more people were living closer together than ever before. Ultimately, tribes reached an inherent size limit—the size at which not everyone can know each other personally—usually a couple of hundred. Beyond this point, when a dispute happened, the informal mechanism for resolving the dispute, a personal relationship, broke down. When that happened, disputes often turned violent. Life in a tribe was violent—the larger the tribe, the more violence there was. When there was a common relative nearby, he or she could become the mediator in a dispute. In larger tribes, however, finding a common relative took longer, so more arguments turned violent. Death from homicide was common in tribal life: an estimated 15%– 30% of all tribal deaths were caused by homicide.

Another aspect of agrarian life was food storage. Harvests only came in a couple of months out of the year, so grain had to be stored so people could eat year-round. Grain was stored in baskets, and in a village, water was brought up from a nearby stream and stored in watertight pots. Baskets and pots had been sporadically made for centuries, but an agrarian lifestyle required them in abundance.[2]

---

[2] Pottery shards dating to 18,000 BCE were found in China. In the Near East, a ceramic object was found in northern Mesopotamia dating to around 8000 BCE, though some scholars believe it was a piece of accidentally fired clay rather than of pottery. Basketry is thought to be an even older practice, though archaeologists find more evidence of durable pottery shards than basket fragments.

The need for such items would eventually become greater than that which could be met by a family member making them as a side job. Full-time basketry and pottery making was unheard of at this time—everyone had to produce food to survive. Fortunately, this paradigm began to shift as food production began to exceed consumption needs. At this point, a family member, and later people from outside of the family or clan, could make baskets and pottery on a full-time basis in exchange for food. Undoubtedly, this risky move began inside the family, where the new weaver or potter was sure to receive some portion of the family meal. Eventually, it became a profession outside the family, with full-time practitioners exchanging baskets and pots for grain. Now there would be enough baskets and pots to meet demand. Basketry and pottery making spread throughout the Fertile Crescent between 7000 and 6500 BCE. These were the first form of specialized labor, but that was only the beginning.[XXI]

In time, the number of people not directly involved in food production would grow. Craftsmen and artisans emerged, making weapons, jewelry, and even adorning pottery. Eventually priests would arise—in this new environment, people could do a host of activities besides growing food.

Labor specialization caused a fundamental shift in the economy of the period. Bands and tribes had a reciprocal economy (or gift economy), where one person would give another a gift and expect to receive something of roughly equal value in return at some future time. These gifts were exchanged without money, contract, or even immediacy. Informal credit was extended, and then repaid. This economy worked because trade was limited—there was little to exchange, and exchanges were usually made between members of the same tribe, where social customs and family ties helped govern the process.

With specialized labor, the economy gradually changed. Specialized labor increased the number of items available for exchange: baskets, pottery, ornaments, and weavings all became objects of trade. Long-distance trade between tribes emerged. Long-distance trade created a barter economy, where two-way exchange was immediate and no credit was extended since it was less likely to be repaid.

While intratribal trade still relied on reciprocal exchange, it would become more common to pay with grain. Grain payments offered more immediate exchange. By 6000 BCE grain and even cattle were a form of currency in the Fertile Crescent. This foreshadowed the market economy that would develop millennia later. Metal currency would not appear until after 3000 BCE.

So with labor specialization, reciprocal exchange was still used within a tribe, though barter exchange emerged between tribes. However, a more fundamental shift was afoot—a redistribution economy was emerging. When labor specialization began within the family, there was no doubt family members would share their food. As it spread from the family to the clan, there was still little risk to the craftsman because the family patriarch would ensure everyone was fed. Food and crafted items would be collected and redistributed so that overall everyone benefitted from the exchange. The patriarch would in effect govern the local economy. In exchange, the patriarch, who was probably too old to hunt or farm by this time, would keep a portion of the collection for his own needs.

After centuries of labor specialization and clan-level food redistribution, an opportunity arose. The tribal world was still violent. Fights were still commonplace. Disputes within a clan might be adjudicated, but disputes across clans often turned deadly. However, if clan patriarchs could receive a portion of the collection, could not someone on the tribal council receive a portion of the collection to resolve disputes? Could not the Big Man—the de facto chairman of the tribal council— adjudicate disputes in exchange for food? With life so violent, it was sure to be a full-time job, so clans would have to provide him with food so he did not have to grow his own. However, now someone would be available all the time to settle cross-clan disputes and make life a little more peaceful.

The Big Man—now the chieftain—was given authority to adjudicate disputes, pronounce restitution, and punish offenders. He needed help, so he enlisted his own family to support him. He received regular food payments from clans and families across the tribe—every family had to contribute.

It worked; violence declined. Now someone had the authority to make decisions to resolve disputes. Family members ensured decisions made were enforced. The inherent limit on the number of people who could live together increased, and the population of new societies grew into the thousands. The new societies could even include multiple tribes, as long as they recognized the authority of the chieftain.

In time, the chieftain would be asked to do more than resolve disputes. He presided over ceremonies, set the date of harvests, and held feasts. He retained craftsmen to perform more non-food-producing duties, such as making ritual objects for ceremonies. To feed them, he assumed responsibility for all food collection and reallocation within the chiefdom. A redistribution economy had emerged.

Redistribution started out simply at first—after a harvest, the chieftain threw a big feast, at the end of which tribes and clans were allowed to take home a share of the food stores—enough to last them until the next harvest. While a tribal council could never have coordinated such a thing, it became feasible under a chieftain. In time, it would grow more sophisticated. Of course, the chieftain, his family, and later his staff, would take their cuts off the top as tribute.

Labor specialization took hold around 7000 BCE, about the time basketry and pottery began to spread throughout southwestern Asia. Chiefdoms emerged in the Fertile Crescent around 5500 BCE, presumably about the time the chieftain received authority. During the period in between, labor specialization preconditioned the environment so that criminal justice could exist. Hence, labor specialization is the second preconditioning innovation.[XXII]

Mathematics

The third preconditioning innovation is mathematics. Mathematics made writing useful.

Hunter-gatherer bands had little need for mathematics. Most hunter-gatherer languages only had words *one, two,* and *many*: that was all they needed in their environment. Some hunter-gatherer bands knew the concept and the value of counting, however. The Lebombo bone is a baboon fibula discovered in Swaziland, South Africa. It dates to around 35,000 years ago. It has twenty-nine notches cut into it, suggesting it was used to count something. Similarly, the Wolfe bone from Czechoslovakia was dated to around 30,000 years ago and had fifty-five notches cut into it. The Ishango bone, discovered in Congo, dates back 20,000 years and has three columns of tally marks running its entire length. Hence, mathematics began as counting. Some prehistoric people saw value in making tally marks, where one scratch onto a bone stood for one item of something.

Writing emerged in three places around the world: Mesopotamia, China, and Mesoamerica. The rest of the world acquired it, either in substance, form, or concept, from one of these places.[3] Each one provides insight on how mathematics and writing were linked.

By the fifth millennium BCE in Mesopotamia, independent tribes had coalesced into chiefdoms, and a period of urbanization was under way. Smaller villages surrounded larger paramount villages. Public works projects began. An extensive canal network was built to link villages. Temples and cemeteries were built. Trade networks extended farther and conveyed a greater variety of wares. Society stratified into royalty and commoners, and the chieftain's kin performed administrative duties in the temple and its granaries. They also continued mediating conflicts and enforcing order. By the fourth millennium BCE, a tribute economy was in full force: harvests were collected under the supervision of the royal priests, and food was reallocated to feed the populations and collect tribute.

Figure 7. Protowriting on Kish Tablets, Sumer, c. 3500 BCE

All of this was accomplished without the benefit of writing. Only protowriting existed at the time. Protowriting was symbolic. Like today's Nike swoosh or a cattle brand, it meant something symbolic, but it did not convey spoken language. Protowriting had existed around the globe for centuries (Figure 7), and people who were familiar with the symbols knew to what the writing referred. However, there was nothing to read.

In a growing and vibrant economy like that of Mesopotamia,

---

[3] This is a hotly debated topic. Some researchers also consider Egypt and the Indus River Valley as having invented writing separately. I'll touch on one of these, Egypt, at the end of this section.

redistribution management became a crucial function. Knowing how much grain was collected and stored in the temple granaries was an economic necessity. The more accurate and precise the transactions, the more efficiently the economy operated and the less likely it was that people would starve. Even along trade routes, merchants needed to know how much and what type of items were being traded to ensure that they were not being lost or stolen. This need for transaction precision gave rise to the field of accountancy; however, a number system would have to evolve to make it work: counting had to move beyond simply making notches in a bone.

As agriculture developed in the Fertile Crescent, the idea of using tokens to track items took hold. A token was a clay object that represented an exchanged item—a cow, a sheep, or an amount of grain. People tracked how many animals were in the herd or how much grain had been stored in a granary by adding or removing tokens from a pile.

By the fourth millennium BCE, tokens were being placed in clay bullae—round, sealed jars (Figure 8). These bullae carried the number of tokens involved in a transaction. With these, someone on the receiving end could know how many items were supposed to be in the transaction, like a modern-day packing slip. If there was any doubt, the customer could simply break open the bulla and count the tokens. If the number of exchange items did not match the number of tokens, something had been lost or stolen along the way.

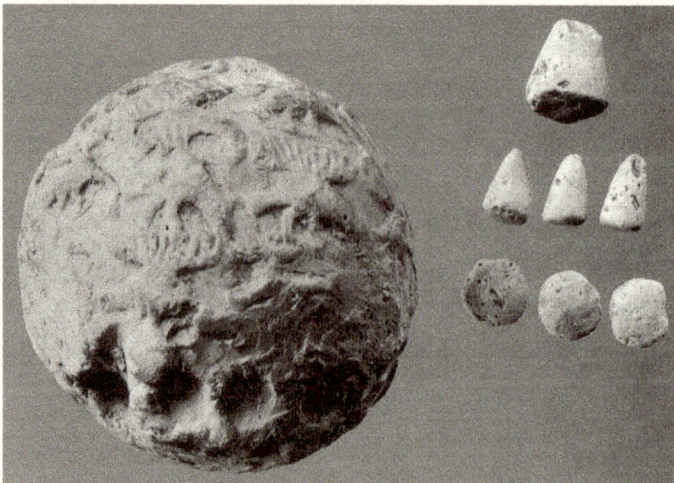

Figure 8. Clay bulla and tokens

After a while, the process of breaking open a bulla to verify a transaction became cumbersome. Eventually, someone had the insight to put a mark on the outside whenever a token was put inside. That way, anyone could read how many tokens were inside without breaking the bulla.

Around 3300 BCE, someone had another insight—skip the first step altogether. Simply mark the clay without putting tokens inside; if there happened to be a discrepancy between the clay marks and the number of exchange items, then something had been lost or stolen. In fact, you did not even need a round jar—a flat piece of clay worked just fine. With that, modern mathematics was born. This new accounting made transactions more precise and the economy more robust. By 3000 BCE, Sumer had a highly refined system of accounting and metrology (weights and measures).

However, mathematics had a side effect. When it became clear that a stroke could mean *one*, and a different stroke could mean *twelve*[4], it eventually became clear that another type of stroke could mean a *cow*, and another, a *pig*: strokes not only could be used to count but also could denote the type of object being exchanged. Eventually, different strokes would represent who received them and who submitted them—as well as *when* the transaction took place, *why* it took place, and even *where*.

Eventually strokes went beyond commerce and expanded into other walks of life. At this point, writing diverged from mathematics. A new form of expression replaced protowriting—no longer was writing to be only symbolic. Writing now had the power to convey spoken language: a person could read someone else's words, captured on clay or stone or papyrus, miles from where it had been inscribed. Historical dates and events were captured; ceremonies were planned; stories about the gods were written; fables were put forth; and ideas were conveyed. Cuneiform had emerged.

Now the ruling sovereign could convey his will through writing. A civil service was created. Now nonrelatives would be trained for a particular job to carry out the ruler's written intent. With this expanded capability, the city-state emerged: Eridu and Uruk being among the first two. The fiefdom had arrived.

---

[4] That part of the world developed a base-12 number system. The modern world uses a base-10 number system.

Chiefdoms began to appear in China around 4000 BC. By around 6000 BCE, several cultures had experienced elevated economies due to either rice cultivation in the east or millet cultivation in the northwest—signs of food surplus. Over the next thousand years, labor specialization, in the form of sophisticated pottery making, appeared and spread across China. By around 5000 BCE, cultures along the east coast were making jade objects and fine ceramics. Later, around 4000 BCE, the Painted Pottery Culture began, in which several cultures started making pottery and lacquerware objects as a form of fine art rather than just for utilitarian reasons.

By 5000 BCE, the population started to grow with villages appearing across central and eastern China. Village layouts became more formal, suggesting higher levels of coordination. By 4000 BCE several cultures were building stamped-earth walls around their towns for protection. This centrally coordinated public work was evidence that the chiefdom had arrived. Social stratification appeared during the fourth millennium BCE as well. The Liangzhu culture of the lower Yangtse River region developed magnificent tombs for their royalty during this time, furnished with jade objects, pottery, lacquerware, ivory, and even mural paintings. Tombs for commoners had none of these. By the end of the Neolithic era, thousands of villages with large populations overlooked terraced valleys across China; in addition, carpentry, weaving, and needlework were well-established professions.

Protowriting in China dates back to the seventh millennium BCE. The earliest protowriting—found in Jiahu, Henan Province—dates back to between 6600 and 6200 BCE. It was still being used as late as 2500 BCE in northeast China, and continued sporadically thereafter.

Chinese numbers date back to around 4000 BCE. Like Mesopotamians, the Chinese needed to keep account of their crops and animals. The first accounting records—notches cut into wood to track items exchanged and stored—date to around this time. They also needed to track the seasons for planting. Legend has it that the Chinese calendar was invented around 2600 BCE by the Yellow Emperor, Huangdi. The Chinese zodiac also dates back to around this time. Legend also has it that the Yellow Emperor invented Chinese characters and numbers above 10,000 during this time. Modern

Chinese numbers date back to the Shang dynasty (1600–1100 BCE), but the Shang number system was quite advanced—it included algebraic equations, negative numbers, geometry, and decimals. Such sophistication indicates a predecessor had existed centuries before the Shang.

Chinese writing emerged sometime before 2000 BCE.[5] The earliest clear evidence of language-bearing writing is characters written on a flask found at Taosi in north-central China. Dated to around 2000 BCE, the flask shows what appear to be the Chinese characters for *civilized, bright, fate,* and *walled-town.* Also by 2000 BCE, records of livestock and goods were being written on shells and bones, indicating that numbers had already begun to shift protowriting into language-bearing script by then. By the Shang dynasty, writing, as well as numbers, were complex, indicating they had both been in existence for centuries before their founding in 1600 BCE.[6]

The emergence of writing coincides with China's transition to fiefdom. Dynastic rule began in China in 2070 BCE with the Xia dynasty. Initially thought to be mythical, historical evidence suggests an alliance of a dozen chiefdoms located along the Yellow River in north-central China. Historical writings say that its first ruler, Yu the Great, rose to power after finding a way to control flooding along the river.

The Xia established multilevel social stratification that included graduated ranks of nobility based on how closely a person was related to the king; at the other end of this stratification was China's first slave class. The Xia had a penal code (the Penal Code of Yu) and a standing army. They had a calendar with twelve lunar months, and they tracked the movements of the sun, moon, and stars for seasonal planting and stockbreeding.

Taosi was an early Xia capital. Founded around 2400 BCE, archeology reveals a settlement in transition from chiefdom to fiefdom. It had a rich

---

[5] It is difficult to precisely identify when writing emerged since much of the information between 2200 and 1500 BCE was destroyed. Between 213 and 210 BCE, the Qin dynasty conducted a purge where many books were burned. Called the Burning of Books and Burying of Scholars, ancient works were destroyed, and 460 Confucian scholars were buried alive. It was Qin's attempt to eradicate divisive thinking and dissent. In 207 BCE, the Qin capital city was sacked by rebels from the Western Jin; the imperial library and official archives, which contained untold numbers of ancient documents, were burned.

[6] Modern Chinese writing is derived from Shang script.

cemetery, high defensives walls, and a complex city layout, common to other chiefdoms. In the latter part of its existence, it showed increasing signs of sociopolitical stratification and what appears to be the beginning of royal court administration. It was destroyed by invaders around 1900 BCE.

Yu the Great ruled for forty-five years, and then passed the throne to his son, Qi. There were seventeen kings in the Xia dynasty before they fell to the Shang around 1600 BCE.

A thousand years later, Mesoamerica would see the same process of mathematics infusing precision into protowriting to create language-bearing script. Like the Chinese and other societies, Mesoamericans tracked the seasons for agricultural reasons. However, they had a far more compelling reason to keep track of the stars and time—to precisely set the dates of their religious ceremonies. What is most unique about Mesoamerica, though, is that different societies developed different writing systems from the same number system. In addition, how well a society used its number system largely drove how sophisticated its writing became, which in turn drove how powerful the society would become.

In Mesoamerica, the Olmec were one of the early powers. They are known for their magnificent works of art, which include the famous Olmec heads. The Olmec reigned from roughly 1400 BCE to 400 BCE. They were located on the southern-most shores of the Gulf of Mexico, in the southeast corner of the present-day state of Veracruz. It appears the Olmec shifted from tribe to chiefdom around 1400 BCE, as is evidenced by an increased concentration of population, the rise of social stratification, the emergence of craft specialization, and the emergence of long-distance trade. At that time, small villages began to spring up around the paramount villages of San Lorenzo and La Venta, where temples likely existed.

The Olmec had protowriting by 900 BCE. The Humboldt Celt is a stone carving with protowriting on it. It was carved around this time. It appears to represent some form of greeting between the rulers of different villages. The Cascajal Block also has protowriting on it and dates to about this time, or perhaps even a couple hundred years earlier.

There is no evidence, however, that the Olmec developed a number system. Consequently, while there are multiple sources of protowriting, their writing does not go beyond this stage. (Centuries later, after they had ceased to be a major power, they did develop a writing system called epi-Olmec, however, after being influence by surrounding societies.)

The Olmec do not appear to have shifted beyond chiefdom either. While they developed a form of redistributive economy, they never had a civil service structure, a standing army, or a priestly caste. They remained a chiefdom throughout their reign, influencing the surrounding tribes though never controlling them outright.

The Zapotec were the first Mesoamerican people to create a number system and a writing system. They were also the first to shift to a fiefdom. They reigned between 600 BCE and 700 CE, in Mexico's southern state of Oaxaca. They were at least casual stargazers, having built what many researchers believe was an observatory in their capital city of Monte Alban. Apparently, stargazing was part of their religion. They were polytheistic, and their religion periodically required a tribute be paid to the gods, sometimes in the form of human sacrifice. The Zapotec were known to have conquered other tribes and sacrificed the prisoners they captured to their gods.

The Zapotec priests needed a way to plan their upcoming religion ceremonies. To do this, they created two calendars. One was a solar calendar, based on a 365-day year. It had eighteen 20-day months and a 5-day period at the end of the year. It was most useful for setting the date for crop plantings and other seasonal events. The second was a 260-day sacred calendar. This was used to plan religious ceremonies. The sacred calendar was so important to the Zapotec that parents would often name their children for the date they were born (e.g., 6 Monkey, 5 Deer). When the two calendars were combined, they formed a 52-year cycle called a Calendar Round. The Zapotec considered time to be cyclical rather than lineal.

To support these calendars, the Zapotec created a vigesimal, or base-20, number system.[7] In it, a dot represented a one, and a bar represented five.

---

[7] We have a decimal number system, or base-10, where each digit represents ten. Ancient Babylonia used a base-60 number system.

These, and a zero, were combined to create the system (Figure 9). This system worked well with their 20-day-per-month calendar system. This number system would be adopted by all other Mesoamerican societies.

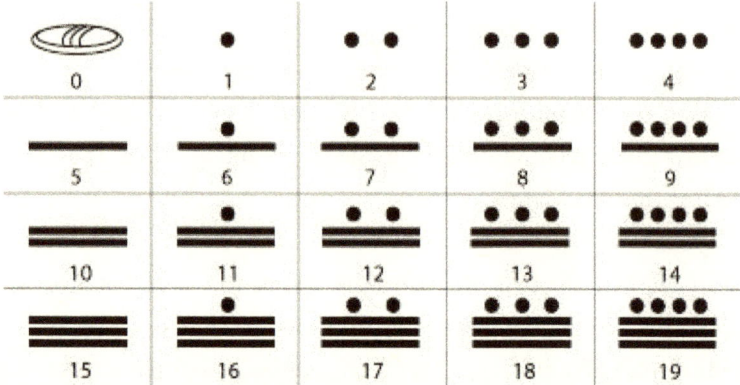

Figure 9. Mesoamerican Number System.
Source: Ryan Johnson and Cristen Conger, "How the Mayan Calendar Works," HowStuffWorks.com, December 27, 2007, http://people.howstuffworks.com/mayan-calendar.htm

By around 600 BCE, the Zapotec developed writing. They inherited protowriting from the Olmec, but they needed the ability to write out the date-names on calendars. Because so many people were named after their birthdate, historical records show many of these in reference to individuals. The date-names combined numerals with a glyph—a character that represented the month. Eventually verbs and other nouns were added, and the language expanded into a logographic (one glyph per spoken word) and logosyllabic (one glyph per spoken syllabic) writing system.

Major events were carved into stone towers, or stellae. By 200 BCE over three hundred stone stelae existed. Their stories tended to focus on military conquests, which showed scenes of captives taken and places conquered. Later carvings describe the political structure of society, denoted royalty, portrayed genealogical lines, and identified historic landmarks.

Soon after the advent of writing, the Zapotec became Mesoamerica's first fiefdom. The Zapotec political structure changed from a large village surrounded by small hamlets to a large confederacy centered at Monte Alban, their capital. Monte Alban was built around 500 BCE and became Mesoamerica's first city-state. At its peak, Monte Alban had a population between 10,000 and 15,000, with another 20,000 in the surrounding countryside. The Zapotec remained powerful until about 700 CE. By 750 CE the city was largely abandoned for unknown reasons.

The Maya had the most sophisticated use of numbers in ancient Mesoamerica; consequently, they had the most sophisticated writing system and the most sophisticated society. Their astronomy and time tracking surpassed any other empire in the world. During its Classic era, 250–900 CE, the Mayan empire dominated the Yucatan Peninsula, southern Mexico, part of central Mexico, and part of Central America.

The Maya shifted from tribes to chiefdoms around 1000 BCE. By that time, labor specialization had begun, and prestige goods, including obsidian mirrors and jade jewelry, were being traded along networks that radiated outward from the central lowlands of southern Mexico. Construction of complex irrigation canals and other public works began. Paramount villages with large central plazas and earthen mounds began to appear. Standing armies emerged, and chiefdoms near the Pacific Coast rose to power.

The Maya inherited the Zapotec calendars and number system. However, while the Zapotec only dabbled in stargazing, the Maya obsessed over it. Mayan religion required that the Maya please the gods with a ceremonial outpouring of human blood and sacrifice (another inheritance from the Zapotec). These ceremonies had prescribed times that had to be dutifully observed, or the entire cosmos would cease to run smoothly, devolving into chaos and mayhem. As a requirement, the priests had to precisely know when to hold these ceremonies, as well as when to undertake other projects such as planting, harvesting, or going to war. Priests even had to know which days were inherently lucky or unlucky.

These precise timing requirements demanded an extensive knowledge of the stars, so the Maya developed unparalleled celestial accounting. They built temples that doubled as observatories. They developed rigorous maps of the constellations and planetary movements. They mapped the phases of the Moon and Venus. They created precise tables of celestial calculations. They forecasted solar eclipses and conjunctions of Venus. In short, Maya priests became the most sophisticated astronomers of their day.

The Maya expanded the Zapotec two-calendar system, adding a third called the Long Count calendar. Day one of this calendar was August 11, 3114 BCE—the date they believed the world was created. (There were multiple creations and destructions in the Mayan religion.) They created larger time cycles than the 52-year Calendar Round, enabling them to ascribe dates millions of years into the past and future.[8] They measured the solar year with greater precision than any civilization would for centuries to come.

Undergirding this use of calendars was the vigesimal (base-20) number system they inherited from the Zapotec; however, their use of mathematics far surpassed that of their predecessor. Their religious and calendric needs required calculating huge sums: stone inscriptions show mathematical calculations running into the hundreds of millions, and dates so long it took several lines to represent them.

Mayan writing began around 300 BCE. That is when the earliest of identifiable Maya script can be found in painted inscriptions in caves. Mayan writing initially focused on the empire's religion and its elements—celestial astronomy, divination, horoscopes, almanacs, patron deities, and ceremonies. Over time Mayan writing broadened to include political structure, the social status of key people, key historical conquests, and the sacrifice of enemy leaders captured in battle. In time, Mayan writing would be the most complete and complex of any Mesoamerican writing systems, containing more than eight hundred identifiable glyphs.

Eventually, the Maya developed books. They emerged about the same time Europe was switching from scrolls to codices (leaf-books). The Maya created thousands of them—capturing their history, religion, and way of life far more comprehensively than stone carvings ever could (Figure 10). Years later, the Spanish would destroy all but four of them in massive burnings designed to expunge paganism from the people.

---

[8] Contrary to popular belief, in the Mayan calendar system, December 21, 2012, indicated the end of the 400-year Bak'tun cycle, not the end of the world.

Figure 10. A Mayan codex.
Source: Photo by author.

The Maya transitioned to a fiefdom around 300 BCE, at the beginning of what is considered the Maya's Late Preclassic era. Much of the developments for which the Maya are known—cities with large central plazas and imposing temple pyramids; ornamental architectures with vaulted ceilings, stone carvings, and painted murals; and further expansion of the trade network—all began during the Late Preclassic era. By the famed Classic era, these were already in place and fully functioning, representing the height of Mayan civilization.

Around 300 BCE, the Maya installed their first priest-kings called *ajaw*. Political power centralized around emerging city-states. The city-states of Kaminaljuyu and El Mirador grew especially powerful, though several emerged as well. Kaminaljuyu, located along southern Mexico's Pacific Coast, controlled mineral quarries and trade routes that enabled them to extend control over hundreds of square miles. Across the Mayan empire, societies grew more complex—population surged, social stratification deepened, public works projects assumed grander ambitions, and agricultural sophistication rose to feed the denser population. During this same time period, warfare escalated.

For reasons still unknown, the late Preclassic era ended rather abruptly, with most of the power of these early city-states rapidly collapsing. Rearchers have offered various hypotheses, including a volcanic eruption, dynastic crises, or ecological problems. In any case, the ruins of this period provided the foundation for an even greater period of Maya civilization in the Classic era.

The highpoint of Maya rule occurred during the Classic era, between 250 and 900 CE. During this time, all the previous developments matured: urban planning, architecture, astronomy, mathematics, writing, and artisty. Mayan civilization stretched across southern Mexico and into Guatemala and Honduras, with a population in the millions. Dozens of city-states dotted the region, each with elaborate temples, palaces, and observatories. Each had its own royal court, whose members resided near the central plaza of the city. Various castes of lesser officials inhibited the rest of the city. Commoners lived in modest homes outside the city. Farming, wars, religious ceremonies, ball courts, and games dominated their way of life. Trade reached into northern Mexico, the Caribbean Islands, and Panama.

This way of life continued for centuries, but it ultimately collapsed around 900 CE. Internal strife in the royal courts of city-states is considered to be a likely cause. This resulted in civil wars that brought down several city-states. Warfare between city-states also increased during this time. It is likely this internecine fighting ended the once great Mayan civilization.

The Mixtec rose soon after the Maya fell. The Mixtec were late starters in Mesoamerica. They transitioned to chiefdoms between 500 and 750 CE, and like others, they began to exhibit signs of urbanization, social stratification, and public works such as temples, terrace farming, and irrigation systems.

Like the Maya, the Mixtec practiced ceremonial blood sacrifice to maintain balance in the universe and used the same two-calendar system to plan their sacred ceremonies. However, unlike the Maya, they did not believe in the cycle of creation, destruction, and recreation, so they had less need to track time as vigorously. Consequently, they had less need for the sophisticated calculations the Maya performed. They did not even use the bar-and-dot notation the Maya used—they replaced the bar-notation for *five* with five dots—though the older, more ceremonial, notation was still used for monumental inscriptions.

As a consequence, Mixtec writing was simpler than Mayan writing, using more pictograms than language-bearing glyphs. Their words mainly conveyed the names of people and places; the rest of a story would be told through pictures. Nevertheless, the Mixtec produced books. These books focused on historical events, rather than astrological or calendric forecasts. Mixtec writings captured events back to around 950 CE—mostly royal births, marriages, and deaths; wartime alliances and battles; and religious pilgrimages.

The Mixtec transitioned to fiefdoms in the tenth century. They formed the first dynasties through political marriages and alliances. Society further stratified into royalty, lesser nobles, artisans, peasants, and slaves. They built "great houses" for the royal families. They began to expand beyond the hillsides, first into adjacent valleys, and then into the Valley of Oaxaca.

Mixtec city-states formed throughout southern Mexico. A tribute economy emerged, as the city-states began collecting both materials and services from subordinated villages. A corps of officers and administrators, overseen by a member of the royal family, managed the process. Artisanry reached a new level as stonecutters, potters, and goldsmiths fashioned magnificent works.

The Mixtec were never quite as cohesive as the Maya were, however. While Mayan city-states were relatively independent, Mixtec city-states were even more so—often foe as much as friend. They forged alliances among themselves as well as with other people. They fought among themselves as much as with other people.

By the eleventh century, Mixtec city-states were consolidating through warfare. By the end of the twelfth century, their society reached its height. By 1350 CE, they had taken the city of Monte Alban from the Zapotec, who still existed but were not as powerful. Yet despite these accomplishments, the Mixtec remained fragmented. They were conquered by the Aztec in the late fifteenth century.

The Aztec were late arrivals to an area dominated by city-states in the thirteenth century. A number of city-states inhabited the area surrounding

Lake Texcoco in central Mexico when the Mexica arrived around 1248 CE. The Mexica drained swampland and began farming maize, beans, squash, potatoes, avocados, and tomatoes. They also hunted and fished local game. In 1325, they founded the town of Tenochtitlan on a swampy island in Lake Texcoco[9] and became a tributary to the city-state of Azcapotzalco.

In 1428 CE Tenochtitlan formed an alliance with the city-state of Texcoco as well as smaller city-states to defeat Azcapotzalco. Another large city-state, Tlacopan, then joined to form the triple alliance that would become the Aztec. In 1440 Moctezuma I became leader of the Aztec. He led wars of conquest that expanded Aztec borders beyond Lake Texcoco. A campaign to the east acquired territory that reached the Gulf of Mexico. A campaign to the south conquered the Mixtec and reached the Pacific Ocean. Tenochtitlan came to dominate the alliance.

The Aztec established a tribute economy. Vassal states sent goods to the capital cities in accordance with established quotas. Tribute items included forms of currency (feathers, cacao, grain, cotton cloth, gold nuggets, and tin pieces); fashioned goods (beads, cloth, incense, adorned suits, warrior costumes, and shields); or staples (food, firewood, animals, syrup, and paper). Local authorities, called *calpixque*, collected tribute every three months, six months, or twelve months, depending upon the items and the distance of the vassal state.

Ordinary citizens paid taxes. Farmers paid taxes based on the crops they produced; artisans paid taxes based on the value of their services; and merchants paid taxes on goods sold. The central marketplace in Tenochtitlan was so large that an estimated 50,000–60,000 people visited on weekly shopping days. Tlatelco, Technochtitlan's sister city, had up to 60,000 visitors per day selling wares in its marketplace. Goods were assigned to different streets—animals to one, gold and silver to another; stones, clay, wood, herbs, coal, vegetables, fruit, honey, cotton, animal skins, china, and seeds all had their own sections. Twelve judges oversaw the marketplace, standing ready to enforce accurate measurements, resolve disputes on the spot, and punish offenders.

---

[9] This may have occurred in 1345.

The Aztec kept meticulous records. The calpixque kept a census of the local population down to a household level. They knew how much land each landholder possessed. They documented all tribute collected—1400 blankets, 650 blouses. They had it shipped to the capital cities, where warehouse stewards received the items and kept detailed accounts of warehouse inflow, inventory, and redistribution. Tribute overseers maintained records of incoming and outgoing goods from all of the central warehouses. Records were kept on paper—one steward reportedly had an entire house full of accounting codices (books). The Tribute Record of Tlapa recorded thirty-six years of tribute payments from Tlapa province. (It resembled a spreadsheet with 5 columns and 145 rows, recording tribute received between 1486 and 1522 in three-month increments.)

The Aztec became sophisticated mathematicians to meet their tribute accounting needs. The Aztec inherited the vigesimal number system and the two-calendar systems from earlier Mesoamerican societies. (They used the Mixtec version, which used only dots for numbers, though they retained the older bar-and-dot system for artistic inscriptions on monuments.) They adapted the number system by adding higher value units: a flag became 20; a feather became 400; a bag of incense became 8,000. The number 8,420 would be shown as one bag, one feather, and one flag. The number was connected by a line to a pictogram of the tribute item (a blanket). With this, they were able to track huge amounts of tribute coursing through the empire.

The Aztec exacted tribute from landholders based on land value. To assess land value, they calculated the area of the parcel, even irregularly shaped parcels. The calpixque had five formulas to calculate the total area of a plot, including the formula for a rectangle and a trapezoid. They created additional units of measurement to make it more precise. While their standard unit for length was the *rod* (about 2.5 meters), they introduced smaller units that included an arrow, a heart, a hand, and a bone.

Aztec writing evolved to support their precise accounting and commercial needs. The Aztec used Mixtec characters, but treated them differently—leveraging space and size to convey more precision in Aztec accounting statements. Aztec writing could also record historic events with the same precision that accounting used. Aztec books recorded an ongoing history of wars, conquests, great victories, and celebrations; feasts and ceremonies; dreams, illusions, omens, superstitions, and rites; royal marriages and royal succession; diseases; and even the weather for major events. They did not have the long texts that Mayan writing had, but they were able to capture history in pictorial presentations nonetheless. Language evolution would keep pace with the expanding and diversifying commercial activities. Within decades of its founding, the commercial traffic was so great that the Aztec language, Nahuatl, became the lingua franca for all of central Mexico.

The Aztec were able to dominate central Mexico within a century and a half of their founding. By the beginning of the sixteenth century, Tenochtitlan had an estimated 200,000 residents. The area surrounding Lake Texcoco may have had as many as 300,000–700,000 residents. At its peak, the Aztec empire exerted influence, through conquest or commerce, over an estimated 6,000,000 people.[10] Its clout reached as far south as Guatemala.

The Aztec empire flourished until 1521 when it was brought down by an alliance of Spaniards and indigenous Aztec enemies. Hernán Cortés and his soldiers arrived in November 1519 and put down the final Aztec resistance in August 1521—an estimated 240,000 people died in the campaign, and Tenochtitlan lay in ruins.[11] Cortés built present-day Mexico City on the ruins.

Mesoamerica presents the strong link between numbers and writing. In each case, numbers preceded writing. Where numbers did not exist, writing remained in the protowriting stage. A society's needs drove the sophistication of its number system. The number system in turn drove the sophistication of the writing system. The Maya had the most sophisticated writing, followed by the Aztec; the Zapotec and Mixtec had simpler systems; and the Olmec never developed a number system nor went beyond protowriting.

This scale was not a matter of natural progression. The Mixtec and Aztec had simpler systems than the Maya, though they came later. It was a matter of investment. The societies that developed and used numbers and writing most effectively became most powerful—they transitioned from chiefdom to

---

[10] Some researchers say upward of 11,000,000.
[11] Many are thought to have died because of smallpox brought by the Spaniards.

fiefdom, and went on to become dominant societies (like the Aztec).

A final place worth examining is Egypt. The Egyptians represent a society that acquired writing early, though it appears they borrowed the concept of writing from Sumer, their long-distance trading partner.

Egypt began transitioning to chiefdoms around 5000 BCE. Craft industries were well established in several places by that time. Specialties included utilitarian and ornamental pottery, stoneware, basket weaving, textile weaving, bead making, woodworking, crafted tools, and taxidermy. A redistributive economy was emerging, probably first at a tribal level, with food centrally managed to ensure stores were available for year-round consumption. Prestige goods were being created to support a higher economic class. Societies began socially stratifying with signs of chieftaincy appearing— scepters, royal accoutrements, royal sections added to cemeteries, and prestige items buried with royal or high-ranking officials. More centralized administration led to more organized village layouts. By 4300 BCE, the town of Merimda, northwest of Cairo, had reached a population of about 2,000— ten times the sustainable population for a tribe.

Far to the south, in what would become Nubia, another site had begun transitioning to a chiefdom even earlier—starting around 5500 BCE. Nabta Playa had socially stratified into royalty, elites, and commoners; conducted massive public works projects, which included building a megalithic structure used in regional religious ceremonies; and even studied astronomy—they built the Calendar Circle, a collection of small stones that aligned to sunrise on the summer solstice. The site was abandoned in 4200 BCE due to a return of arid conditions to the area.

Protowriting in Egypt began by around 4000 BCE. Symbols were painted on Gerzean pottery that dates to about that time. They resemble characters that would later appear as hieroglyphics. Gerzean culture in general (also known as Naqada II) flourished between 3500 and 3200 BCE and is known for its pottery and other ceramics.

In Egypt, unlike the other societies we have studied, the number and writing systems appear at the same time—both around 3300 BCE. A tomb in Abydos, Egypt (some 320 miles south of Cairo), was found in the early

1990s. It contained numerous artifacts, some of which had inventory tags on them. These tags, over 150 in total, recorded the delivery of the items and their sources. Forty-three tags had numbers on them as well to indicate either the quantity of items or the size of the item.

A century before that discovery, a macehead had been found at an archeological survey at Hierakonpolis (south of Luxor). Called the Narmer macehead, it captured the exploits of the first pharaoh, Narmer (also known as Menes), as he united Upper and Lower Egypt around 3100 BCE. It is thought to have been made for one of the jubilees held during his reign in the early thirty-first century BCE. It contains both numbers and writing as well—inscriptions on it record some of the bounty he collected during his invasion of Lower Egypt, including 400,000 cattle, 1,422,000 sheep, and 120,000 men. A cosmetics palette, the Narmer palette, found alongside the macehead, also contained writing detailing his conquests. (The ancient Egyptians used palettes to grind cosmetics; however, this palette is so large it is thought to be a ceremonial object.)

During this time, Egyptian writing was mostly pictographic. Over time, it became simpler and more useful, and even evolved into two scripts—one for priests and one for commoners. Full language-bearing script did not appear until around 2750 BCE, by which time about eight hundred hieroglyphs existed.

The issue with having both numbers and writing appearing simultaneously is that there would have been no time for *precision infusion*——the process of converting protowriting to writing by gradually including more content-bearing characters. As such, it is likely that both Egyptian numbers and writing were inspired by Sumerian numbers and writing. Egyptian traders, from the western end of the Fertile Crescent, would have been able to observe their Sumerian trading partners, from the eastern end of the Fertile Crescent, tracking exchange items and inventory using impressions in clay. Once they believed it was beneficial to do the same (perhaps after the Sumerians dispensed with bullae), they could have adopted the concept for themselves, creating their own number and writing systems.[12] While it is possible that both Sumerian and Egyptian number and writing systems developed independently and simultaneously in each location, it is the less likely scenario.

In any event, soon after writing was acquired, Egypt began dynastic rule. By 3100 BCE, King Narmer had united Upper Egypt and Lower Egypt into a single country that stretched from the Mediterranean to the first cataract (waterfall) at Aswan.[13] He moved his capital from Abydos in the south to Memphis in the north. He created a central administration where civil servants were overseen by royal governors. They met in newly constructed open-air temples built from sandstone and wood.

Around 3000 BCE the dynasty undertook expansion through military conquests, saw its economy expand, began massive building projects, and developed lavish works of art. Colonies appeared in southern Israel.

The next dynasty continued with advances in mathematics, writing, the sciences, religion, the arts, and agriculture. They created a calendar. Later dynasties continued military expansion into the Sinai, building projects, and artistic development. Brick making, metalworking, woodworking, and stone carving all advanced. In the fourth dynasty (2613 to 2494 BCE), the great pyramids in Giza were built. Egypt had become one of the world's early empires.

...

Mathematics is the preconditioning innovation for writing. Mathematics trained people to make their writing precise—it trained them to expect the same precision in writing as they had when using numbers to account for food, tribute, or stars. Over time, writing became precise enough to convey

---

[12] This process occurred again in 1821 when Sequoya, a Cherokee blacksmith living in Alabama, completed a written script for the Cherokee language after seeing how beneficial English writing was. It also occurred in the early 1960s when Shong Lue Yang invented a written script for a Hmong dialect in Laos.

[13] There are several variants of this story. Some scholars say the conquest was by a different king or even several kings over multiple reigns. Some believe it was a peaceful unification rather than a conquest. The date for unification even ranges between 3150 and 2950 BCE. In any case, it happened soon after Egypt acquired writing.

spoken language. When this occurred, new possibilities became available—
possibilities that early societies exploited to become leaders in their region.[XXIII]

Chapter 8
Preconditioning Innovations, Part II

In July 2004, I was working on a project in Wiesbaden, Germany, when one Saturday I took a boat cruise up the Rhine River. It was a beautiful sunny day, so I grabbed a seat on the top deck before the crowd arrived. We left the dock and began our slow cruise up the winding river. Provincial towns, green hills, and lush vineyards lined the hillsides above the river.

One of the novel features that also lined the hillsides was castles. Over forty of them lie along the banks of the Middle Rhine (Figure 11). I asked a crewmember why there were so many castles along this stretch of the river. The easygoing deckhand told me it is because that section of the river is narrow and winding. I ask him why that matters, and he said it was easier for the castles to bomb the ships, since they had to slow down so much to manage the river. Still missing the point, I asked why they wanted to bomb ships. He told me that in the Middle Ages, castles were built above the river to force the ship owners to pay a toll. If they did not pay, cannons fired on them. When I asked why they tolerated this, he told they had no choice—castles were built to withstand sieges. If the merchants led the townspeople in an attack on the castle, and the castle was strong enough to defend itself and withstand the siege, the toll remained. If the castle was overrun, the toll ended. The castle at St. Goar withstood a siege that lasted over a year.

Figure 11. A Castle on the Middle Rhine River, Germany.
Source: Photo by author.

I was awestruck. That would be called extortion today. Can you imagine someone firing on a barge going up the Ohio River? Back then it was a normal practice, however. It was a different world. Nevertheless, that era left a legacy of castles that could endure not only yearlong sieges but also centuries of history.

Christianity

Christianity is the last preconditioning innovation. It may seem odd to call a religion an innovation, but if you ignore the theological content and focus on the impact it had on society, it becomes clear that it had the same characteristics as the three previous innovations—namely, that there was a problem in society this innovation fixed; as a by-product, it enabled another innovation to work better or, in this case, to have greater impact; and that other innovation would go on to drive societal-level change. But what problem did Christianity solve?

Despite the development of criminal justice and civil service structures that included royal police forces, fiefdoms were still violent places—very violent by today's standards. In the early Middle Ages, Viking raids ravaged northern Europe. Starting with the Lindisfarne monastery in 793 CE, Vikings raided rich targets with such fury and violence that it struck terror into the hearts of people far and wide. The British Isles were a favorite target, but nowhere was safe—other parts of Europe and even parts of Asia fell victim. These were privateering ventures, often led by low-level nobles in search of easy plunder and riches not afforded by a farming lifestyle. Later, they would take on a more state-sponsored nature after Viking settlements had grown up in conquered territory.

This high level of violence persisted throughout the Middle Ages, embedded in the culture. As Harvard professor, Steven Pinker, pointed out in his essay, "A History of Violence,"

> In sixteenth-century Paris, a popular form of entertainment was cat-burning, in which a cat was hoisted in a sling on a stage and slowly lowered into a fire.... Today, such sadism would be unthinkable in most of the world.

Even French writer Alexandre Dumas (*The Three Musketeers*, *The Count of Monte Cristo*) glorified duels and sword fights that seemed to occur with regularity in sixteenth-century France.

And none of this begins to touch on state-sponsored warfare, which continued well into the twentieth century. European states found it an acceptable way for royals to achieve personal goals, such as acquiring a throne, by throwing armies at each other. However, the violence experienced by people in their daily lives—that which occurred when a person was walking down the street—perhaps is the most startling difference between the Middle Ages and the modern era.

Such violence was not only a European problem. Mesoamerican societies practiced ritual human sacrifice well into the sixteenth century. Sacrificing mainly to Huitzilopochtli, the Aztec took it to an unprecedented level. While starting at an estimated 10,000 victims a year, Aztec sacrifices rose to a staggering 50,000 per year just prior to the Spanish arrival. They even bragged about it. At the rededication of the Pyramid of the Sun at Tenochtitlan in

1487, Aztec records report 80,400 sacrifices over a four-day period. (Few scholars take this at face value, however; they expect the real number is somewhat lower.)

All of this violence had a side effect—it kept the local sovereign in a position of power. In a dangerous environment, a person will naturally turn to someone in a position of strength for protection—it is human nature: a prostitute will turn to a pimp for protection; a new prison inmate will cling to a veteran inmate for protection; in a corporate downsizing, a lower-level worker will buddy up to a senior-level director to avoid being laid off.

This happens to societies as well—whenever a threat looms, societies will find a strong leader to coordinate an effective response. In 1932, America turned to Franklin Roosevelt to tackle the Great Depression; in 1933, Germany turned to Adolf Hitler to end the chaos the Weimar Republic could not; and in 1940, Britain turned to Winston Churchill to defend it against the German war machine. This happens in all walks of life: the sheriff who saves the town in the old West; the corporate leader who saves the company and even the industry; or the presidential candidate who preaches getting tough is the answer to all of our problems.

Now when violence and chaos exist in perpetuity, the position of a strong leader remains permanent. The tribal chieftain in Waziristan does not negotiate with elders before taking action. The central African warlord does not get approval before acting decisively. A king (baron, lord) can direct his appointed sheriff to enforce his laws. He can call up his militia to respond to a threat. So in the violent world of the Middle Ages, fiefdoms—which are built around a sovereign ruler—were the only way to maintain order in society.

But society would change. In the first century, Christianity arrived in Europe. It started on the eastern coast of the Mediterranean Sea. Christians believe that a man named Jesus was crucified by Roman authorities and afterward rose from the dead. This convinced them he was the Son of God, come to restore a relationship between humans and a celestial Father. Christianity spread to Asia Minor, Greece, and Rome during the first century.

During the second and third centuries, Christianity spread around the Mediterranean Sea with help from evangelists, monks, and merchants. It spread along the southern coastline through Libya to Carthage, which were then Roman provinces. Along the northern coastline, it spread past Rome into France, which then was called Gaul.

By the fourth century, an estimated 10 percent of the roman population had been converted. Armenia, a Roman province just north of where Christianity began, made it the state religion in 301 CE. However, Christianity still had to compete with pagan gods. In Rome, the last and severest persecution took place under Diocletian from 303 to 311 CE. After that, Constantine came to power and issued the Edict of Milan, which granted Christianity equal footing with other religions in the empire. In 380 CE, Theodosius issued the Edict of Thessalonica, which made the Nicene version of Christianity the state religion of the Roman Empire.

By the end of the fourth century, Christianity had spread southward and became firmly rooted in Egypt, Nubia, and Arabia. (Evangelists had come to these places in the first century, but by the fourth century they had an established bishopric.)

Christianity also spread eastward, reaching Mesopotamia and Parthia in the second century. In the third century, the Persians replaced the Parthians, and they were less receptive to the new religion, though it remained in pockets. By the fourth century, there was a vibrant Christian community in India, having been started by the Apostle Thomas in the first century. Christianity spread deeper into Asia, first into Georgia and then beyond. Centuries later, Nestorian Christians would be found on Genghis Khan's court.

By the fifth century, Western Rome was collapsing. Chiefdoms began invading each other's territory, conquering their opponents, and settling on their land. People sought protection from the church when the state proved unable to provide it. (In 452 CE, Pope Leo went to Attila the Hun's camp and persuaded him not to sack Rome.) After Rome fell in 476, the Church was the only stable governance in Western Rome. It began sending out missionaries to convert pagan tribesmen and stabilize remote regions. Monasteries became centers of learning. Ireland was converted to Christianity in the middle fifth century largely due to the efforts of Patrick. The Franks converted to Christianity when their king, Clovis, converted at the end of the fifth century.

In the late sixth century, Britain was reintroduced to Christianity. It had been first introduced in the third century, but it was pushed into small pockets after the fall of Rome. Britain was fully converted in the seventh century. In the eighth century, Germany was converted by an English priest named Boniface, who later became the bishop of Mainz. He was martyred after he chose to leave his position and return to preaching to pagan tribes. In the ninth century Orthodox missionaries converted the Slavic countries of Eastern Europe, present-day Slovakia, Bulgaria, and Czechoslovakia. In the tenth century, Catholic missionaries converted central Europe—present-day Hungary and Poland. Orthodox missionaries converted Russia, with support from Queen Olga and her son, Prince Vladimir, who brought in priests from Byzantium.

Scandinavia was the last region to convert, doing so in the tenth through twelfth centuries. A Danish king, Harold Bluetooth, converted in the middle tenth century; a Norwegian king, Olaf I, converted at the end of the tenth century; Iceland converted in the early eleventh century; and Sweden finally converted in the middle twelfth century, when the first archdiocese was established at Uppsala.

Conversion was not without problems, however; there were numerous setbacks along the way. Islam replaced Christianity in North Africa in the seventh century, cutting off the Christian communities in the south from those in Europe. By the ninth century, Islamic forces were attacking Spain and southern Italy. Later, Islamic and Mongol conquests cut off Christian areas in Asia from those in Europe. Furthermore, the Christian church was marred with internal strife, most pointedly between the Orthodox Church based in Constantinople and the Catholic Church based in Rome. Nonetheless, by the end of the twelfth century, Europe was basically a Christian society.

Tracing the spread of Christianity reveals a few things. First, the spread mostly occurred after the fall of Rome. Second, it was not quick—it took centuries. Third, even after Christianity had been introduced into an area, it often took decades or even centuries to take hold. And fourth, there was continual resistance to it. Change of any kind is difficult, and this was no exception. As such, any impact Christianity had on a society would have been experienced gradually, over time.

As described before, Europe in the Middle Ages was a violent place; however, recent discoveries have shown that the violence declined over time. In fact, between the High Middle Ages and late Middle Ages, communal violence declined almost tenfold (Figure 12). This happened across Europe—in England, Germany, France, Italy, the Netherlands, and Belgium. However violent those societies were in the early Middle Ages, they became safer as centuries passed.[1]

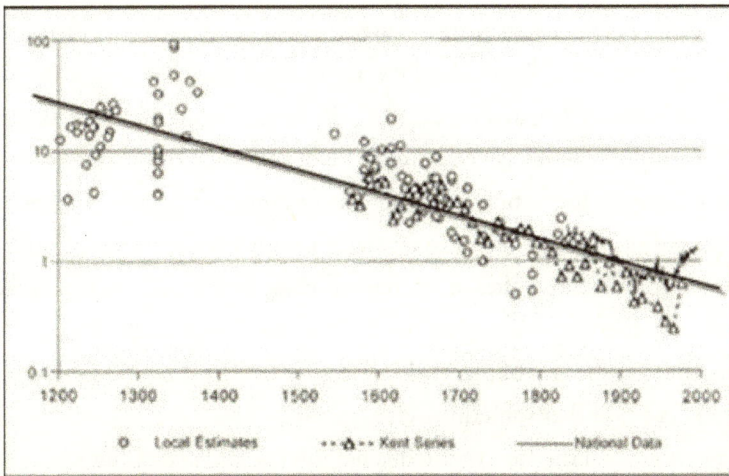

Figure 12. Gradual decline of homicide rates in England.

Source: Reprinted with permission from Manuel Eisner, "Modernization, Self-Control, and Lethal Violence: The Long-Term Dynamics of European Homicide Rates in Theoretical Perspective," *British Journal of Criminology* 41, no. 4 (2001): 622 (line added by author).

Scholars offer several ideas on why this occurred, most of which center on the development of political institutions and on sociological reasons. Some

---

[1] This does not say that all violence was eliminated; nor does it address state-sponsored wars between fiefdoms. This focus is on violence within a society, within a person's daily life.

scholars point to the gradual development of criminal justice institutions, which more effectively controlled violence. Some point to the growth of institutions of higher learning, which enculturated ideas about the value of human life that reduced the level of violence in society. Some point to greater commercial interaction, which gave people the incentive to cooperate rather than kill each other. Other scholars point to the enlargement of societies, which made more people feel they were a part of society and therefore less likely to commit violence against it. Still others reason that a longer life span increased the perceived value of human life, making people less likely to strike against their fellow man.

All of these factors likely helped to reduce the level of violence in societies across Europe. More specifically, they likely reinforced the downward trend in violence after it had started. However, another factor had to initiate the trend. More sophisticated justice systems would not appear until after the nation-state was fully birthed in the early modern era. (While the transition to the nation-state began in 1215 CE, it would be centuries before more effective criminal justice systems would be developed.) Institutions of higher learning likely helped, but most people (among whom the violence was occurring) did not have access to education until later centuries. Commerce did grow, particularly after a merchant class developed in the fifteenth century. Societies also grew, after the birth of the nation-state. And life spans did lengthen, at the end of the Middle Ages. It is likely that all of these factors reinforced a trend that something else started.

Knowing when the trend started is helpful for understanding what caused it. By the time the first records on local homicide rates were kept in the thirteenth century, the decline was already under way. A social system is like an inertial system, a fluid system, an electrical system, or any other type of system—it does not change direction instantaneously (it takes time for a ship to adjust course). So for violence to have been in steady decline by the thirteenth century, it had to have begun dropping before then. The data shown suggests that violence started to decline in England in the early Middle Ages, most likely in the seventh century. (See the endnotes for details.)[XXIV]

The beginning of the decline corresponds to the spread of Christianity across Britain. Christianity had been reintroduced by Augustine in 597 CE.

After several decades, most of the kingdoms on the isle were converted. This would suggest that Christianity had the primary impact since nothing else of so great a magnitude occurred during that time. Again, one must keep in mind, however, that the data shows the homicide rate in daily life—the life of normal people. It does not count combat deaths in wars between fiefdoms, nor does it suggest intrigue and murders among those competing for the thrones of societies declined. That kind of violence continued unabated.

What happened in Britain happened on a larger scale across Europe. The decline in violence happened in societies across Europe during this same period. The beginning of the decline in violence across Europe corresponds to the spread of Christianity. But how did the spread of Christianity lead to the decline in violence?

Back in the fourth century, Christianity had helped put an end to the gladiator fights. Christianity (along with other actions) began to introduce a principle that all human life had value to God and therefore was not to be wasted. Centuries later, after Christianity had spread to Scandinavia, this principle changed people's attitudes about violence, and helped to end the Viking raids. While other factors played a part—the decline of the slave trade (which had been their cash cow), better coastal defenses, and a rise in centralized authority—even some of these, to an extent, are the indirect result of Christianity. In time, the raids became both less tolerable and less profitable, and eventually came to an end.

The Church actively worked to reduce violence by eradicating practices that devalued human life. The Church helped end slavery in Europe by proclaiming that one Christian could not own another one. The Church helped end polygamy in Europe, thereby elevating the status of women. The Church took an aggressive stance against concubinage and divorce as well, declaring that the marital relationship was a sacred and permanent one. The Church helped remove the last vestiges of human sacrifice from Europe.[2] And finally, the Church helped end infanticide, no longer considering it an acceptable form of birth control.

---

[2] While most human sacrifice had been eradicated by the Roman Empire, it did still occur in remote places into the early Middle Ages.

The Church also ran programs aimed directly at reducing violence in daily life. The Peace of God and subsequent Truce of God movements actively sought to reduce violence by prohibiting it on certain days of the week. Local councils worked to convince people that violence did not have to be a normal part of life. These grassroots councils spread across Western Europe in the tenth and eleventh centuries and remained in effect for centuries until giving way to more formal criminal justice systems.

Perhaps the Church's greatest impact came by working with governments and forming institutions. It worked with French kings, who were some of the first monarchs to establish laws aimed at the civil treatment of people. Clovis I, first king of the Franks, though violent himself, late in life established a church council that established thirty-one laws directed at securing humane treatment of both friend and foe alike. Later, Charlemagne established centers of learning and a formal legal system. England saw the blossoming of a legal code in several kingdoms after Christianity was reintroduced. Christian monasteries became repositories of knowledge, technology, and education across Europe in the early and High Middle Ages. Later, the Church established the first universities in Europe. New laws and institutions helped stabilize a European society still reeling after the fall of Rome.

These principles, programs, laws, and institutions slowly convinced people that human life had value and needed to be treated with more respect. While wars between states continued unabated, and court intrigues continued, gradually people began treating each other with greater civility. While it took centuries to take hold, a greater respect for human life caused the reduction in European violence throughout the Middle Ages.[3]

The gradual reduction of violence in European had an interesting side effect: it reduced the need for a strong local sovereign to keep order. Just as high levels of violence require a strong authoritarian leader to maintain order, lower levels of violence result in less need for such a position. After World War II, the British people voted out Winston Churchill and his Conservative Party in July 1945, in favor of Clement Attlee and his Labour Party, believing they would be more effective at handling the postwar environment. In a

---

[3] See the endnotes for a modern example of this.

society with less violence, people acquire other priorities, such as economic development or social services. They will eventually start looking for a leader who can deliver such things.

The reduced need for a sovereign also creates possibilities for other forms of government. Perhaps without even being aware of it, the role of a king is not as important as it used to be. In fact, the entire militaristic feudal order—of king to barons to knights to commoners—is not quite as important. No one has to coordinate local defenses against Viking raids anymore. And while there still needs to be someone who can defend the country against foreign invaders, that defense can be coordinated in different ways, so other governance options become possible.

At the end of the late Middle Ages, the printing press arrived on England's shore. In a calmer, more tranquil society, printing could now help to introduce rule-of-law, which it did in a few principle ways.

First, printing created a more systematic society. The printing process forced the printing industry to become more standardized and systematic to maximize efficiency and profits. Because printing touches every other field of endeavor, this systematic approach was passed along to other industries as well. Standardization took place across society, as weights and measures were standardized, language was standardized, commercial practices were standardized, and agricultural practices were standardized. The idea of standard operating procedure emerged. The scientific method was developed. Every field of science, business, and academia became more process oriented. Following the rules suddenly became fashionable.

When this adherence to process touched the legal field, it gave traction to rule-of-law. Birthed back in 1215, rule-of-law never fully caught on. While there were two houses of Parliament, power still rested with kings. If the king was weak, then power rested with the barons. The idea of having commoners or their representatives make meaningful decisions was not taken seriously at senior levels. But now, society's leading legal minds and thinkers were beginning to ponder what it would be like to fully govern by process, by rule-of-law.

A second impact of printing was that it allowed for the accumulation of knowledge. Before printing, hand-copied old manuscripts, containing laws or even the wisdom of the ages, were in danger of being lost. Copying was done by hand and relegated to a few assiduous monks or scholars. One fire, one flood, or general aging over time could ruin a document, causing a work of knowledge to disappear forever. With printing, that changed. Now great works could be printed and disseminated, ensuring that the loss of a document in an unfortunate event would not spell the destruction of knowledge, since it could be found elsewhere. What is more, with more copies available, more scholars could build upon these works, correcting earlier mistakes, and adding new material to them. Knowledge could now accumulate, and the advent of practices such as peer review helped ensure the right new information was retained.

When this form of accumulation was applied to the legal field, the *corpus juris*—the body of law—began to grow. And as it grew, the law became more robust, more refined, and more credible. No longer would it reflect the whims of a sovereign or the capriciousness of the royal courts. It was becoming something new, something wholly credible unto itself. The principle of *stare decisis*—legal precedence—emerged, giving the law an internal consistency check it had not had before. And as more people saw the law for the first time, through printed books, the legal profession grew. Law schools began producing lawyers, barristers, and legal clerks all intent on refining the legal system and using it to make society better. People became vested in the law.

A third impact that printing had was that the printed word itself became more credible. Before printing, words on paper only meant something if they had a royal stamp or something else to give them authority. With printing, however, words could convey the experience of hundreds who had done something before—those who had experience in a particular industry, or studied a particular issue, or debated a legal case. As a result, the printed word itself gained credibility. While putting something in writing did not necessarily make it true, it at least deserved to be looked at. With increased literacy across society, this feeling spread. Commoners could believe that something in print probably meant something, or at least should not be dismissed outright. As such, the printed word gained more credibility. When this became widespread, it set the stage for rule-of-law.

With printing having transformed society, and the reduction in violence having made a sovereign ruler and his fealty less necessary, the only thing that stood between English society and a new way of governance was the old feudal structure. By the 1600s, it was obvious that a group of professional lawyers with the ability to craft legislation could guide the country better than a single king and his cronies.

Violent structural change began in 1642 when the English Civil War started. For nine years the forces of Parliament battled the forces of the king. No ruler gives up power willingly, and King Charles I was not inclined to do so either. After seven years of warfare, the king was defeated, and beheaded. It took another two years to close out hostilities. It then took another generation for England to learn *how* to govern by rule-of-law. (During this time, it even restored the monarchy under the king's son, Charles II.) In 1689, however, England passed reform laws that gave power to Parliament, but left the king in a ceremonial oversight role.

All of this happened within roughly two centuries of printing's arrival in England, but none of it would have happened had not Christianity already reduced the violence in society so rule-of-law could take hold. As such, Christianity was the fourth preconditioning innovation.[xxv]

Working Together

The preconditioning innovations worked in tandem with elevating innovations to drive societal-level change. However, exactly how they did that was different in each case (Figure 13).

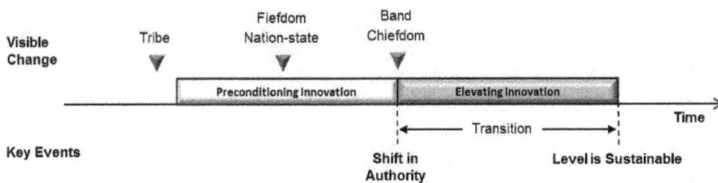

Figure 13. Societal-level change.

Technically, a new societal level began when a society made a shift in authority. Tribes were formed when authority shifted to the tribal council to enforce property rights. Chiefdoms were formed when authority shifted to a chieftain to execute criminal justice. Fiefdoms were formed when authority was delegated (in writing) to a civil servant. The nation-state was formed when authority shifted from king to Parliament. Except for this last shift, the dates for beginning new societal levels have been lost to history.

The shift in authority, however, just marked the beginning of a transition period. Transition was not complete until the new societal level was sustainable. A societal level became sustainable when governance structures were in place to sustain it. Tribes became sustainable after councils and all of their attendant protocols were established. Chiefdoms became sustainable after the royal family was established to support the chieftain's new role and all the affectations of leadership were in place. Fiefdoms became sustainable after the civil service structure was established, including institutions to hire and train personnel. Nation-states became sustainable after laws, institutions, and procedures were in place for running a government according to policy. The dates for sustainability are subjective, or lost to history altogether.

Sometimes a visible change to society began with the arrival of the elevating innovation, but not always (Table 5). Bands acquired new capabilities soon after language skills appeared. The earliest chiefdoms likely grew soon after chieftains received authority to adjudicate disputes. In contrast, societies sometimes began to change before the elevating innovation arrived. Mathematics enabled Mesopotamian societies to grow before writing was invented. Christianity began to mollify medieval Europe before printing arrived. In one case, societies began to change even before the preconditioning innovation arrived. Villages in Mesopotamia began to grow where food was naturally abundance; however, food production was needed for villages to proliferate.

Table 5. Relative Timing of Visible Change and Elevating Innovation

	Visible Change	Trigger	Elevating Innovation Start	Relative Timing
Band	100,000-80,000 B.P.	Start of Language	Language, c. 100,000-80,000 B.P.	Coincided
Tribe	11,000-9,000 B.C.	Natural food sources	Property Rights, c. 9,000 B.C.	Began Before
Chiefdom	5500-4500 B.C.	Start of criminal justice	Criminal Justice, c. 5500 B.C.	Coincided
Fiefdom	3700-3100 B.C.	Mathematics matured	Writing, c. 3300 B.C.	Began before
Nation-state	1215-1689 A.D.	Christianity calmed society	Printing, 1476 A.D.	Began before

In each case, however, the preconditioning innovation preceded the elevating innovations, changing the environment so the latter innovation could become elevating. Food production created the need for land and animal property rights. Labor specialization enabled criminal justice to be a full-time job. Mathematics changed writing so it could carry language. Christianity reduced violence so printed words could be obeyed.

Conversely, if these innovations had never existed, the latter innovations would not have existed or never would have been effective. If food production had not existed, property rights would not have been attached to land or animals. If labor specialization had not existed, everyone still would be producing his or her own food. If mathematics had not existed, writing would still be only symbolic. Had Christianity not existed, violence would still be too high for rule-of-law to catch on.[4] Together, the two types of innovation drove societal-level change—without one, the other would not have existed, or if it had existed, it would not have been elevating.

---

[4] Only the first societies that transitioned to nation-state had to be Christian; other societies transformed once they saw how well it worked (e.g., Soviet Union and Peoples Republic of China).

...

So, human societal progression is a story of innovation and resource management change. Only eight innovations drove societal-level change. Once a society acquired these, and made the structural changes to employ them, it reached the next societal level first and became the reigning leader for a long time. However, these were not the only innovations that drove leadership change. There were others, but they did it in a different way: they used a simpler, more direct approach.

Chapter 9
Dominating Innovations, Part I

I took my son to his first hockey game when he was seven years old. He was excited about seeing the Washington Capitals play. On the drive in, he made a comment about how funny it was to name a team after a building. I told him they are not the Washington *Capitols*; they are the Washington *Capitals*, with an *a*. He asked what that meant. I told him "capitol" was a building; "capital" had several meanings. Washington, DC, is the capital of the United States, so the team name is making a reference to us living here in the nation's capital. Another meaning of "capital" is that it is something that cannot be beaten. In the 1800s, battleships were called capital ships because nothing could beat them except other battleships. So if you had one, you won. If the other guy had one, he won. If you both had one, then the victory was up for grabs. To a seven-year-old, that sounded a lot cooler than a building.

In previous chapters we have discussed the elevating and preconditioning innovations. These innovations changed societal leadership at different points in our history. There is, however, another group of innovations to consider: the dominating innovations.

Dominating innovations created leadership power, typically in the form of increased wealth and military strength. They created so much power that if a society had one, it could dominate any society that did not have one. This provided a second way for a society to become a leader. The dominating innovations are

- Metallurgy,
- Horse warfare,
- Gunpowder,
- Petroleum propulsion, and
- Nuclear power.

These changed leadership without driving a change in societal levels. They did not change resource management, so they created less power than that created during a societal-level shift. In addition, the increased power was temporary: it lasted only until other societies acquired the same innovation. Once the monopoly was broken, the power differential dissipated, and dominance began to wane. Nonetheless, in those long spans between societal-level changes, dominating innovations often determined who would become the leader.

Metallurgy

Metallurgy was the first dominating innovation. It started around 4000 BCE in what is now modern-day Turkey. Metallurgy began as an outgrowth of pottery making: the fires used to bake clay pots eventually became ones used to melt metal ore. The first metal smelted was copper; however, metallurgy became dominating when bronze was invented about a thousand years later.

The Bronze Age began in Sumer around 3000 BCE: the same people who first gave the world agriculture also developed bronze metallurgy (Figure 14). Early bronze was made from copper and arsenic; however, arsenic was replaced by the less hazardous tin around 2500 BCE.

Bronze could be used to make stronger and sharper tools and weapons than either copper or stone, which were both still in use at the time. Axes, saws, and other farm tools, as well as arrowheads, armor, helmets, and swords, could all be fashioned from the new metal. It not only made agriculture easier but also generated military might. Industry grew as well, with bronze objects becoming popular manufacturing and trade items. Trade routes spread throughout the Near East as Sumer needed continued access to raw materials.

All of this increased the power of the southern Mesopotamian city-states

(Figure 14). Unfortunately, the city-states primarily invested this additional power in fighting each other. For almost two thousand years, Sumerian city-states warred against each other. First Lagash rose to power, and then Umma became a regional power.

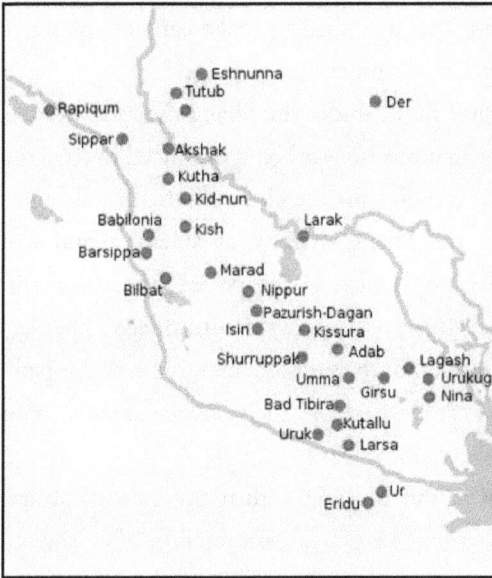

Figure 14. Sumer, third millennium BCE.
Source: By Ciudades_de_Sumeria.svg: Crates derivative work: Phirosiberia
(Ciudades_de_Sumeria.svg) [CC BY 3.0
(http://creativecommons.org/licenses/by/3.0)], via Wikimedia Commons.

Ultimately, the Sumerian monopoly on metallurgy slipped when Akkad of northern Mesopotamia acquired it. Akkad's proximity to Sumer and its location along the metals trade routes ensured the Akkadians would eventually be able to develop it. In 2270 BCE, the Akkadians overthrew Lagash, who had returned to power. Eventually Akkad, under its leader, Sargon, would become an empire stretching from the Persian Gulf to northern Syria.

Later Sumer would return to power with various city-states waxing and waning in control. All the while, bronze metallurgy spread across western Asia. Sumer, further weakened by population loss due to agricultural shifts, finally and permanently fell as a power in 1940 BCE, toppled by the Amorites of Syria and Canaan.

While bronze metallurgy helped strengthen Sumer and Akkad as regional leaders, this cannot be said everywhere because leadership also depended on political conditions. In China, there was only one power when bronze metallurgy was developed around 2100 BCE, the Xia dynasty. Bronze spears, arrowheads, and axes unearthed from that time period reflect a more consistent process than that used to make earlier artifacts. However, it was still early in bronze development.

By around 1500 BCE, under the Shang dynasty, bronze metallurgy had come of age. Excellent bronze was being produced in large quantities to make ornamental status symbols for the elite or agricultural tools. Weaponry also advanced during the Shang dynasty as smelting and casting techniques matured. New weapons, such as the poleax, the lance, the spear, and the dagger axe, and bronze helmets were introduced. Quality standards were established, techniques for their employment were developed, and even tactics for using them were devised. As such, advancements in bronze weaponry advanced war fighting in general.

Of course, all of this brought with it the industry to mine, smelt, craft, and trade bronze items. Large-scale production of ornamentation, weapons, tools, and vessels expanded, employing large labor forces, requiring a multitude of transportation assets, and bringing with it government oversight of operations. Bronze metallurgy had reached into the fabric of society.

However, none of this changed the leadership situation. The Shang dynasty had come to power early in the development of bronze metallurgy, so the innovation did not play a role in the Shang's rise. Nor did it play a role in the Shang's fall, since its rival and successor, the Zhou, also had it. Ultimately, bronze metallurgy continued to develop in China and reached its high point centuries later during the Warring States period, when innovations such as adding chromium oxide in order to make swords more rust resistant were introduced.

So while bronze metallurgy could make a society into a power, it only did so if the society had a monopoly on its use. Alternatively, it could strengthen an established power, as long as the power retained such a monopoly. This same pattern can be seen in iron metallurgy.

Iron metallurgy uses iron instead of bronze to form objects. It was invented by the Hittites around 2000 BCE in what is modern-day Turkey. While iron objects had existed before in different parts of the world, they were fashioned from meteoric iron fragments. The Hittites invented the first process for smelting iron from iron ore.

The process was slow to evolve, however. Early iron objects did not resemble those produced today. Ancient iron making required building a large fire and blowing air over it to make it hot enough to remove the oxygen from iron ore. The facility was called a bloomery and produced a spongelike mass called a bloom. The bloom was then hammered repetitively to force out impurities, resulting in an early form of wrought iron.

Initially, iron objects were used primarily for ornamentation—iron was still too soft to have military value. Nonetheless, these objects helped the Hittite empire grow wealthy. Iron objects were highly valued and sought after by foreign rulers. By the fourteenth century, the Hittites had a thriving iron trade.

Hatti's weapons, by contrast, were still made from bronze. Iron swords did not appear until the twelfth century BCE, and even then, they were only as strong as bronze. It would take centuries before they surpassed bronze in strength and hardness. As a result, iron metallurgy was unable to prevent Hatti's fall to foreign invaders in the twelfth century BCE.

After the fall of Hatti, the secret of iron making was out, and iron metallurgy spread throughout the Middle East and Europe. It reached Greece by 1000 BCE and western Europe by around 700 BCE. Because iron ore was more common than copper and tin, iron tools and weapons were cheaper than bronze ones. As a result, iron quickly displaced bronze. Reinforcing this displacement was the disruption of established copper and tin trade routes during a period of intense warfare, known as the Bronze Age collapse. Securing iron's position as the new metal of choice was the fact that it would eventually be made twice as strong as bronze, creating harder tools and weapons that kept their edges longer. So while iron metallurgy produced wealth for the Hittites, and shored up their place in history, it did not help to sustain their empire.

Perhaps the most compelling example of iron metallurgy's dominating power can be found in African history. In Africa, iron metallurgy helped spark a migration that caused the Bantu people to spread from their West African origins to eventually encompass all of sub-Saharan Africa.

Iron metallurgy began in West Africa around 1500 BCE after centuries of copper smelting. While East African kingdoms such as Nubia and Axum were in contact with Egypt, and so followed its Copper Age–Bronze Age–Iron Age progression, West African people were not. West Africans did not even have a Bronze Age per se, but they did smelt copper.

Copper smelting emerged in Niger during the latter half of the third millennium BCE. After centuries of copper smelting, the first iron smelting appeared around 1500 BCE in eastern Niger. By 500 BCE, the Nok people of what is now Nigeria had fully mature bloomery furnaces, hotter than those found in the Near East and Europe.

While copper metallurgy produced mainly ornamental objects, iron metallurgy produced tools and weapons. These tools and weapons had a profound impact on the social and economic structure of West Africa. Iron hoes and plows were far more efficient for farming than stone tools ever could be. Iron fishing hooks aided hunting, and iron arrowheads and spears aided both hunting and warfare. All of these and other iron products stimulated the West African economy, generating wealth and military power for early iron-working societies.

By 500 BCE iron metallurgy had stimulated the agricultural and military development of the Bantu. The Bantu originated near the Nigeria-Cameroon border around 3000 BCE; the Nok were members of this group. This development spurred a wave of migration, which began around 1000 BCE. An earlier wave of Bantu expansion had begun around 3000 BCE, not long after their development of food production. Now a second migration was being fueled by iron metallurgy.

The expansion began in eastern Nigeria and spread east and south. When the eastern stream reached the African coast, it too turned south. Then the two streams both headed toward southern Africa along each coast, with smaller streams approaching through the center of the continent. These streams, however, were not the march of an advancing army; rather, they were the continual push for agriculture lands for farming and grazing, activities made more productive by new iron tools.

As the migration progressed, the original land inhabitants, the Khoisan, were displaced or assimilated. These hunter-gatherers posed no threat to the Bantu, who had iron tools and weapons. As the migration continued, it brought agricultural techniques, iron-making technology, and even forms of governance to new areas. In the wake of the expansion, trading empires such as Zimbabwe sprang up. In addition, chieftains such as the Xhosa, Zulu, and Swazi later appeared.

By around 300 CE, the expansion had reached into southern Africa. It reached South Africa by 500 CE. Bantu dominance would last until Europeans arrived in the late eighteenth century.

Africa provides the clearest picture of the power brought to a society by iron metallurgy. The Bantu expansion was largely stimulated by the increased productivity, wealth, and military power that iron metallurgy conveyed. The Bantu were its exclusive owners, and as a result, went unchallenged in their migratory path. Not until another people arrived centuries later were the Bantu ever seriously challenged.

Ancient India provides yet another example of iron metallurgy's power. Iron metallurgy first appeared in India around 1500 BCE. Originally, the process was believed to have been introduced from the Middle East during the Vedic migrations around 700 BCE. However, excavations in recent decades have revealed that Indians practiced iron metallurgy much earlier. With natural deposits of iron ore, iron smelting was evident in several locations by the thirteenth century BCE. By 300 BCE, India was producing a high-grade steel, called wootz steel, whose quality was unsurpassed in the ancient world.

As in other places, iron metallurgy in India was used to create farm tools and weapons. In addition, household items, such as spoons, chisels, tongs, and saucepans, became common between 600 and 200 BCE. By the Roman era, iron tools and weapons had become valuable export items.

Around 600 BCE, sixteen city-states covered northern India. By the end of the fifth century, four had risen to power: Vatsa, Avanti, Kosala, and Magadha. Ultimately, Magadha would defeat its three rivals to become the dominant empire in ancient India.

Much of Magadha's success was rooted in its use of iron metallurgy to create weapons and wealth. Magadha contained India's richest iron deposits. This gave Magadha an advantage in equipping a large army with the most effective weapons, achieving greater agriculture productivity with heavier iron plows, and selling surplus iron on nearby trade routes.

Magadha also had factors besides iron going for it. Magadha was located in a fertile agricultural region, the Gangatic plain, which enabled it to feed a large army. Magadha was located in a prosperous trade zone, and it controlled the trade routes. Magadha's capital was located in a highly defensible position. Magadha had strong leadership and was a military innovator, being the first to use elephants in combat. And being located in eastern India, Magadha avoided some of the political and cultural problems associated with repeated invasions from the northwest. Nonetheless, in many ways, iron metallurgy provided the initial advantage that allowed it to exploit these other factors.

Magadha's power waned as it went through a series of dynastic changes over the next couple of centuries. Meanwhile, the Persians invaded northwest India in the fifth century BCE, and were followed by the Greeks in the fourth century BCE. Then the Maurya dynasty arose in Magadha in 322 BCE. It immediately began to expand westward, and by 320 BCE, had ousted the remnants of Greek authority from northwest India. It then began expanding to the south. At its height, the Maurya empire would stretch from western Afghanistan and southeast Iran in the west, to the Himalayas in the north and east, and down toward the southern end of the subcontinent. It unified much of the subcontinent for the first time in history and contained an estimated 50–60 million people—likely the most populous empire of its day.

Maurya exploited the same advantages of iron, agriculture, and trade that the earlier empire had. Upon this, it built a sophisticated government and a civil service that furthered prosperity and productivity. The standard of living rose in large part due to the increased use of iron in agriculture, trade, and other industries.

Ultimately, the Maurya empire fell in 185 CE, and another dynasty arose. Over the centuries, dynasties would change, but steel making continued to develop. India became an exporter of world-class steel, a trade that did not end until British colonization and European use of the blast furnace emerged in the nineteenth century.

Indian history provides another example of the power potential of iron metallurgy. There, it enabled two empires to rise. While other factors certainly contributed, their success was largely enabled by this innovation and the political conditions that favored its use. However, as we have seen before, this was not the case everywhere.

China provides our last insight into iron metallurgy's potential power. China invented cast iron around 500 BCE. Metalworkers in the southern state of Wu developed a technique that completely melted the ore and poured it into shapes, instead of using a bloomery as was done in the rest of the world. Often, molten iron was poured to form ingots, which were later remelted to form the ultimate object. This form of iron would become known as pig iron centuries later in the West. The process was far less arduous than pounding the impurities out of iron over an anvil, as is done to make wrought iron, and therefore is far more conducive to mass production. However, early cast iron was brittle—too brittle to be used for weapons—so its use was largely confined to farm tools.

By 300 BCE the Chinese had learned how to make cast iron less brittle, and so it began to be used for weapons as well. By this time, the Zhou dynasty had broken into seven fiefdoms that were vying for control of China. This was the Warring States period. Warfare in general changed during this period, with several innovations being introduced such as massed infantry formations, cavalry, new logistics systems, and new organization approaches. Armies grew in size from tens of thousands to hundreds of thousands.

This period also saw the introduction of iron weapons. Swords, halberds, knives, arrowheads, polearms, and armor all made from iron began to appear. However, every state had access to iron metallurgy and iron weapons, so no one gained an advantage. In addition, adoption came slowly, with most states clinging to older bronze weaponry, which was reaching the height of its development. As a result, the introduction of iron weapons did not have an impact on the outcome of the wars.

At the end of the period, the Qin won and unified China again in 221 BCE. After its victory, it instituted many reforms including a centralized bureaucracy and a new legal system. It also began to develop the Chinese iron industry, which it saw as a tax revenue generator and a way to strengthen its rule.

However, the Qin dynasty did not last long: it fell to the Han dynasty in 206 BCE. Under the Han dynasty, the Chinese iron industry fully matured. The Han government nationalized iron production in 117 BCE, making it a state-run business, mainly to counter the growing power of iron industrialists.

Under this new management, government officials began to control iron production. The Han also began a large-scale building program of iron production facilities, building over a dozen blast furnaces in Henan Province, each capable of producing tons of iron a day. Iron production technology also advanced under the Han, with innovations such as a new type of bellows to force more air over the flames, the use of refractory materials, and better control of carbon content, leading to steel making. This was the greatest expansion of China's iron industry in its history to that point.

Also during this time, iron objects became commonplace in Chinese households and in industry. Cooking pots, tweezers, tongs, scissors, and other iron items became common. Plowshares, pickaxes, shovels, hammers, saws, and nails all became common on Chinese farms or in industry.

The Han also fully converted the Chinese military from bronze weapons to iron weapons. At the beginning of the Han dynasty, bronze weapons were still in use. However, as iron metallurgy further developed, the military accelerated its replacement of bronze with iron weapons.

Thus the political situation in China was different from that in Africa or India. During China's Warring States period, everyone had access to iron metallurgy, so no one gained an advantage. Later, a unified kingdom existed that already had a monopoly on power. As such, iron metallurgy could never become the power differential between rivals, so iron metallurgy did not play a major role in altering leadership in China.

So metallurgy was a dominating innovation, but it only had an impact under the right conditions: there had to be a plurality of powers vying for control, and one of those powers had to possess a monopoly on its use. This pattern would be repeated a few more times in our history.[XXVI]

Horse Warfare

Horse warfare is the use of horses to add mobility and striking power to an army. Horse warfare played a role similar to metallurgy in that it had the potential to raise up kingdoms. Whether it did so would depend upon local conditions, both political and geographic. However, the power generation capability was there. Societies with the innovation became members of a select group that had power over those without the innovation. Even when member societies fought against each other, and in some ways cancelled out each other's power, they remained more powerful than those outside the group. This power differential would persist for centuries, until another innovation came along that made the previous innovation obsolete. And all this began with the chariot.

Horses were first domesticated on the Eurasian steppes around the middle of the fifth millennium BCE. The broad grasslands of present-day Russia-Ukraine-Kazakhstan provided ideal conditions for both using horses and developing them. By the third millennium BCE, horse domestication had spread elsewhere though, and by the end of the millennium, Sumerians were beginning to use horses to pull logistics wagons in their wars. While oxen or asses were still the preferred animal for pulling logistics wagons, the early use of horses was the first implementation of horse warfare.

Horse warfare became dominating with the advent of the chariot. Around the time horses started pulling logistics wagon in Sumer, ca. 2000 BCE, the first chariots were being developed back in Kazakhstan, southeast of the Ural Mountains. Chariots were developed from wagons by dropping from two axles to one. This gave them more mobility, which proved useful in hunting—their first application. Their transition to warfare became possible when the spoked wheel was invented. Solid-wheel chariots were slow, heavy, and burdensome for horses to pull with any speed. (Horses were much smaller in ancient times than they are today.) The spoked wheels lightened the vehicle considerably, not only because the wheels were lighter, but also because the vehicle structure could be made lighter, not requiring as much strength to secure the axle. Now it became feasible to use chariots in the attack, rather than just in logistics: now they could outrun infantry.

Chariots became mobile archer platforms. They were too light to charge infantry, and infantry could swarm them, so they had to keep their distance. But if one person drove the chariot while a second person shot arrows or threw javelins, then chariots could be effective. If enemy infantry began to charge, the chariot could nimbly make haste away. This shoot-and-scoot tactic became devastating to infantry in the middle of the second millennium BCE. The chariot had become a formidable weapon.

The chariot was made even more formidable by the invention of the composite bow. Invented by the middle of the second millennium BCE, the composite bow used multiple types of material—wood, bone, and horn—laminated together to create a bow considerably stronger than the traditional one made from a single piece of wood. The composite bow was able to hit targets up to three hundred meters away. With this, companies of charioteers could ride into battle, pull within range of the enemy, shoot two or three volleys, and retreat before the enemy could counterattack. Whittling down enemy infantry, they could change the outcome of battles, while remaining largely impervious to counterattack—moving chariots were difficult to hit with slings or javelins even if infantry came close.

In later centuries, heavy chariots were introduced. Horses had become large enough to pull heavier loads, so they could pull larger, stronger chariots carrying three or four riders who were holding javelins, spears, or axes. These chariots would charge enemy infantry formations, breaking them up and overrunning soldiers. They were also slow enough for light infantry to run beside them, offering some protection. The challenge in using them was that they had limited mobility and could only be used on favorable terrain.

Chariots spread from the central Asian steppe to the south, east, and west—across Eurasia. Kingdoms rose in their wake. Chariots started the world's first strategic arms race.

The Hittites were the first to rise to power due to the chariot. Around the time the Hittites were mining iron ore and making ornamental objects from it, they were also grasping onto this new invention. While they never used iron in their chariots (it was still too soft), they were able to make a chariot with lighter wheels (four spokes instead of eight) and with greater carrying capacity (three soldiers instead of two). This newer chariot helped them build an empire, expanding from present-day Turkey across the Near East starting around 1700 BCE. Chariots helped the Hittites establish and control metals trade routes that ran from the Mediterranean to Mesopotamia, securing a constant supply of ore and access to distant markets.

Other kingdoms also rose because of the chariot. The Hurrians, in the Caucasus; the Mitanni, in northern Syria; the Mycenaeans in Greece; and the Kassites, in Mesopotamia—all gained early access to the chariot and grew as a result. In 1650 BCE, the Hyksos, a Semitic Canaanite people, used superior chariots to invade Egypt and establish themselves as a dynasty that lasted about a hundred years. Chariots reached China before the end of the thirteenth century BCE, during the Shang dynasty. The Shang incorporated them into their army, using them primarily as command and control vehicles for senior officers. Later, the Zhou would use them more effectively to overthrow the Shang in 1046 BCE. During the Battle of Muye, with an army of 45,000 infantry and 300 chariots, the Zhou used chariots as mobile archer platforms and in direct assaults, in close coordination with infantry. Though greatly outnumbered, this combined arms approach helped bring down the six-hundred-year-old Shang dynasty.

By the end of the second millennium BCE, the chariot was an essential component of any aspiring Eurasian society. Kings had built up their support infrastructure with trainers, craftsmen, feed, horse farms, or supply routes to maintain this expensive army component. Chariots even became status symbols for kings and the elite of a society. Noblemen rode in them and made a point of being seen riding in them. Noblemen inscribed chariots on their tombs, or even had chariots buried with them. Everyone wanted to be closely associated with the supreme weapon of the age.

Eventually, however, the supreme weapon became standard. Every kingdom that wanted it had it; and its development had matured, so there was nothing particularly new or innovative coming out. This led to massive clashes of chariots where no one gained decisive victory because of them. By the time of the greatest chariot battle of all time, the Battle of Kadesh in 1274 BCE, the chariot was an essential component in every army. The battle was fought in present-day Syria, between the Hittites and the Egyptians. Both sides had chariots, and used them effectively. While numbers are approximate, the Hittite are said to have had around 37,000 infantrymen and 2,500 chariots. The Egyptians had around 20,000 infantrymen and at least 2,000 chariots. The Egyptians had moved north into Syria to challenge Hittite dominance of the area. After heavy casualties on both sides during the two-day battle, the Hittites stopped the Egyptian advance. In China, by the Spring and Autumn period, 770–476 BCE, the chariot was a standard component of every army; and by the Warring States period, 475–221 BCE, each of the seven warring states fighting for hegemony had a chariot force numbering in the thousands.

By the beginning of the Iron Age, 1000 BCE, the horse had finally reached a size where a man could ride directly on its back. This enabled the advent of cavalry, which was far more mobile than the chariots. By around 500 BCE cavalry began to replace chariots in western Asia.

In China, the crossbow also helped to hasten the end of chariot usage. The crossbow had been invented in China in the sixth century BCE and became standard equipment in most Chinese armies by the third century BCE. Whereas a composite bow required a skilled archer, the crossbow was simple enough for any basic infantryman to use effectively. Now nearly any infantryman could shoot back and hit the target; this effectively put an end to the chariot's shoot-and-scoot tactic. Mass production of crossbows commenced, and in 307 BCE the Zhao replaced their chariot units with cavalry units. The other states quickly followed suit, bringing an end to the age of the chariot in China.

While chariots were the first implementation of horse warfare, they were not the last. The power they generated made them the most sought-after weapon of the second millennium BCE, and this power would continue in another form, cavalry, into modern times.

Cavalry replaced the chariot because it had higher mobility. Cavalry could be deployed in terrain where chariots could not go. While chariots were at their best on the broad grasslands of central Asia, cavalry was less constrained, effective in hill country, deserts, or rocky terrain. In addition, cavalry employment was more flexible than chariot employment. Employment is easier with a force composed of one person–one horse elements than two people–three horse elements:

commanders could more dexterously divide, aggregate, or redirect their horse-borne forces as cavalry than as chariots. In replacing the chariot, cavalry increased the power that horse warfare generated.

The first version of cavalry was as mounted infantry. The simplest way to use larger horses was to put infantrymen on their backs. Mounted infantry would ride to the point of assault, dismount, and engage the enemy on foot. This created a mobile force that could cross the entire battlefield quickly, redeploying from one flank to the other if necessary, to wherever they were needed at the moment. This technique, and the horses that could accomplish it, were developed by the nomadic tribes on the central Asian steppe, the same people who domesticated the horse and invented the chariot centuries earlier.

These Iranian tribesmen, in addition to being excellent horsemen and breeders, also had occasion to raid Assyrians lands to their south. Assyria had twice been a large empire in the region, but by the tenth century BCE, the empire had fallen back to its original homeland. To respond to these raids, the Assyrians copied Iranian mounted infantry techniques—the first city-state to do so. The empire even made cavalry a standard component of its army.

The Assyrians put two riders on each horse. The front rider handled the horse, while the back rider typically carried a bow, a spear, or a sword. Both riders sat farther back on the horse than do today's riders, perhaps to make it easier on the horse. There were no saddles or stirrups, so riding the back of a horse was difficult enough, let alone fighting from it. As such, the best practice was to ride to the point of battle, dismount, and then engage. To shoot arrows, the handler would often dismount and hold the horse steady while the archer used his weapon. Mounted infantry fought in concert with foot infantry and chariots.

In the ninth century BCE, this military capability helped the Iranian tribes push southward from the Caucasus Mountains onto the Iranian plateau, present-day northwestern Iran. They would dominate the region for the next two centuries, even eventually giving it their name.

Also in the ninth century, Assyria reemerged as an empire. It had begun to reemerge around the end of the tenth century BCE: likely about the time mounted infantry techniques were observed in Assyria. By the end of the ninth century, Assyria once again controlled much of the Near East and Middle East. While mounted infantry techniques were not the sole reason for this reemergence, they did contribute military strength.

In the centuries that followed, mounted infantry techniques spread across Eurasia, and the once novel innovation became commonplace. The Iranians tribes[1] and the Assyrians would eventually be challenged by others who also acquired it. Nevertheless, it continued to be a branch of cavalry that would see use even into modern times.

Light cavalry could be considered the first true cavalry. In the ancient world, it took the form of mounted archers, who replaced chariot-borne archers. The Assyrians developed light cavalry in the seventh century BCE, a couple of centuries after acquiring mounted infantry. Saddle technology enabled this new development. Made of cloth and cinched around the barrel of the horse, saddles allowed Assyrians to sit farther forward, into the position riders use today. Moreover, they allowed one person to handle both the horse and a weapon, so each horse had only one rider. The main weapon used was a bow, though a lance might be used for close combat. This tended to be avoided, however, since close combat was usually avoided.

With these changes, cavalry became its own separate branch of the army, distinct from infantry, though still working closely with it. Mounted archers replaced the now antiquated chariots, but adopted their shoot-and-scoot tactics, which were applied at a much faster speed. Cavalry also acquired a new role in forward screening, scouting, and reconnaissance. With the expanded role, cavalry units expanded. The Assyrians would deploy hundreds or even up to a thousand cavalrymen during battle.

Light cavalry undoubtedly helped sustain the Neo-Assyrian empire throughout the eighth century BCE, but as before, Assyria's rivals would eventually acquire it. The Scythians, as the Iranians tribes were now called, developed it roughly when the Assyrians did. And now Media, in present-day northwest Iran, was developing its own cavalry, one whose mounted soldiers would become even better archers than the Assyrians.

By the late seventh century BCE, cavalry had spread across the Near East, and several societies had acquired it. Some of these societies would band

---

[1] The term "tribe" in this context is the historical term used for this group of people, but it is not necessarily representative of their societal level.

together to challenge Assyrian hegemony. As Assyria roiled from infighting and internal division, Scythians and Cimmerians started raiding their northern colonies. Then Media, with its ally Babylon, challenged Assyria from the south in 616 BCE. By 614 BCE they sacked Ashur, the capital of Assyrian. By 612 BCE, Nineveh, its largest city, fell. In 609 BCE the Assyrian empire went out of existence altogether. Throughout the campaign, the Medes and their northern allies employed thousands of cavalrymen. Though less useful in siege warfare, such as during the four-year siege of Nineveh, the allied cavalries played a vital role in weakening Assyria. While Assyria had its own cavalry, it could not match the combined cavalries of its opponents.

Light cavalry continued to spread. By Alexander's time, it had become a standard part of most major armies. Alexander defeated the Scythians in 329 BCE at the Battle of Jaxartes (present-day Uzbekistan-Tajikistan area); this remains a testament to his use of deception, cavalry, and integrated combat arms. Mounted archers reached China in the fourth century BCE, brought in by nomadic tribes from the west. Each warring state quickly made it a component of its army. Soon their cavalries numbered in the tens of thousands.

Mounted archers continued to see use into the Middle Ages until finally replaced by firearms in the sixteenth century.

Heavy cavalry was introduced shortly after the Mede coalition defeated the Assyrians. The Medes had been breeding ever larger horses. By the sixth century BCE, a Mede horse could carry a rider wearing armor, and even wear armor itself. Persia, Media's ally to the south, developed the first heavy cavalry units in the sixth century BCE. These units, called cataphracts, were melee weapons—used to smash into and break up enemy infantry formations.

By the time of Darius the Great (558–486 BCE), the Persians had begun to use heavy cavalry in their campaigns. Mounted archers would first weaken the enemy with repeated volleys of arrow, and then heavy cavalry would charge into the infantry with lances. Once the formation was broken, the infantry would attack and cut down isolated enemy soldiers. These same basic tactics would be used into the Middle Ages.

After seeing that it well worked for the Persians, other societies across Eurasia began adding heavy cavalry to their armies. By the fourth century BCE, both

Persians and Greeks were using heavy cavalry against each other. By the second century BCE the Parthians had integrated heavy and light cavalry tactics with devastating effect. In 53 BCE, they so soundly beat the Romans at the Battle of Carrhae that the Romans overhauled their cavalry structure and tactics to more closely resemble those of the Parthians. By the fourth century CE, the Chinese and other East Asian societies had also adopted heavy cavalry.

Heavy cavalry continued to see use into the Middle Ages. In the early Middle Ages, many armies were still using the old-style cataphracts, where both rider and horse were covered in scale armor (Figure 15). In the tenth century, the Byzantine Empire was using integrated formations of cataphracts and mounted archers with devastating effectiveness in its Syria campaigns. In East Asia, the Xia and Jin became so effective at using cataphracts that the reigning Song dynasty sought to copy their use of them, though they achieved only mixed results.

Figure 15. Horse and rider in ancient Persian cataphract armor.
Source: By John Tremelling (http://www.remountdepot.com/) [GFDL (http://www.gnu.org/copyleft/fdl.html)], via Wikimedia Commons.

By the late Middle Ages, plate armor was replacing scale armor on horses, and was used to cover the chain mail armor worn by infantry and cavalrymen. This created the picture of knights in shining armor so well known today. Charging in a line with lances lowered, smashing infantry formations, and then dismounting to fight on foot; these heavy cavalries still provided incredible striking power for the European armies in their day.

Plate armor had scarcely begun to be used when its demise also began. By the fourteenth century, English longbows could pierce armor from two hundred meters away, if the shot were square to the armor. As such, longbows changed the outcome of battles such as Crecy, Visby, and Laupen. The defensive technique of pike squares—infantry with long, sharp poles (pikes) used to impale horses or riders without breaking their square formation—were developed. This tactic further reigned in the cavalry's effectiveness on the battlefield. By the end of the century, in East Asia, the Yuan dynasty had phased out the use of cataphracts, and in the middle of the fifteenth century, the fall of the Byzantine Empire meant the end of Europe's last cataphracts units.

Heavy lancers in plate armor continued to see use into sixteenth-century Europe, however, even as firearms were introduced. Armor manufacturers began making breastplates and backplates thicker to withstand bullets. Horses lost their plating to provide greater mobility and to compensate for the added weight of the rider. By the latter half of the century, heavy cavalrymen dropped their lances in favor of pistols. And by the end of century, the suit of armor had shrunk to just a breastplate, a backplate, and a helmet. The age of plate-armor cavalry had come to an end.

Unlike earlier versions of cavalry, heavy cavalry did not spawn new empires. It did, however, help preserve the power of horse warfare. It helped armies project power for centuries, until other technologies finally came along to dissipate it. However, those technologies—firearms—did not end heavy cavalry: they transformed it.

Firearms transformed cavalry. Firearms could penetrate iron or steel plates, even if the shots were not square. So maneuverability became primary in importance—not getting hit was the key to survival and success on the battlefield. Cavalry transformed to this new reality. During the seventeenth and eighteenth centuries, each type of cavalry would transform.

European cavalry began their transformation in the middle of the sixteenth century. Though firearms had been around for two centuries by this time, it was not until the wheel lock was invented in the early 1500s that cavalry had a weapon it could use. So now they had to both protect themselves from firearms and learn how to use them as well. Throughout the sixteenth and seventeenth centuries, cavalries experimented with how to adapt to these weapons.

By the end of the eighteenth century, cavalry had standardized into its three basic types again, but they looked different.

- Mounted infantry discarded its swords and crossbows and began to use rifles. They became known as *dragoons*, but their role was largely the same: use horses to ride to a point of dismount, and then fight like infantry.

- Light cavalry dropped the bow, but kept the sword, now in the form of a saber. It also acquired the lance from heavy cavalry, though it was much lighter since no one was wearing armor anymore. They became known as *Hussars*, *Lancers*, or *Uhlans*, depending upon their country of origin. They were effective for attacking scattered infantry, though they retained their reconnaissance and skirmish role as well.

- Heavy cavalry dropped the armor, but kept a breastplate, a backplate, and a helmet to cover critical organs. They became known as *cuirassiers*, for the heavy breastplates, which were called cuirasses. They traded in their lances for pistols, which they shot from horseback, to keep their role as the maximum power, yet mobile assault force. Their tactics reflected this role, and they continued to be used for close-order charges.

Transformed, these branches continued to be used effectively in the firearms age. Their roles became more specialized. They were the first choice for attacking enemy cavalry. They were effectively used to strike enemy flanks or rear areas. In the American Civil War, they strengthened their roles of screening, scouting, and skirmishing.

The success of their transformation translated into employment on a larger scale. In the Battle of Eylar, during the Napoleonic Wars, 11,000 French horsemen assaulted Russian infantry in what would be the largest cavalry charge in history. In the Battle of Waterloo, 9,000 French cavalry assaulted British and German infantry lines, but failed to break their tightly formed squares. A century later, in the opening days of World War I, two full cavalry divisions squared off against each other—one Austria, one Russian—in the Battle of Jaroslavice, the last time thousands of cavalry would engage each other in such a battle.

Despite its success on the Turkish front during World War I, in colonial environs, and later during the Russian Civil War, the western front in World War I had shown nations that horse cavalry, in any form, was no match for barbed wire and machine guns. After the war, armies began to phase out their cavalry. The French tried to integrate horse cavalry with mechanized infantry briefly in the 1930s, but the experiment failed. The British army converted its horse cavalry into the Royal Armored Corps and Royal Tank Regiment in the 1930s. And in 1940, the US Army found its replacement for the horse when it fielded the jeep. Developed in just forty-nine days, over 700,000 were ultimately manufactured for service in World War II. The time of horse warfare had come to an end.

Horse warfare was a dominating innovation for four thousand years. From the twentieth century BCE to the twentieth century CE, horse warfare generated so much power that societies who had it, all else being equal, could defeat those without it. When two societies both had it, then parity was established. However, whenever a new society that did not have horse warfare was encountered, the power difference resumed. Nowhere would this differential become more evident than in the Americas during the Spanish wars of colonization. In the sixteenth century, Spanish conquistadors, using mounted horsemen and other weapons, were able to defeat much larger native forces. Interestingly, after the horse was reintroduced to America by the Spanish (they had died out 10,000 years earlier), native people learned to fight on horseback, reducing this power differential. However, there was still another power differential to overcome: gunpowder.[XXVII]

Chapter 10
Dominating Innovations, Part II

In this chapter, we examine the third dominating innovation: gunpowder. Gunpowder has all the traits of a dominating innovation. It created power for its early adopters; however, it had to mature for a time before its impact was felt. That power could make a society into an empire, but whether that happened depended upon regional geopolitics. Once everyone had it, the power dissipated, though it left a residual power barrier between those with it and those without it.

Moreover, gunpowder provides us with a detailed example of how changes in technology can have a ripple effect to create changes on the world stage. This example shows that part of that ripple effect is a society's ability to put in place the structures needed to use it effectively. Finally, it reveals how cultural attitudes, resource decisions, and local policy can hinder or support putting those structures in place and using the technology once it becomes available.

Gunpowder

Gunpowder is a mixture of chemicals: sulfur, carbon (usually in the form of charcoal), and potassium nitrate (historically known as saltpeter). The sulfur and charcoal are the fuel while saltpeter is the oxidizer, providing the oxygen needed for the mixture to burn quickly. When ignited, the mixture can flare into a flame or create an explosion depending upon the amount of saltpeter used.

Gunpowder was discovered in the middle of the ninth century CE in China. Its components had been discovered in the previous centuries, as Chinese alchemists searched for an "elixir of life." Then around 850 CE, they discovered a mixture that burns with intense fury. A Taoist text records

> Some have heated together sulfur, realgar and saltpeter with honey; smoke and flames result, so that their hands and faces have been burnt, and even the whole house where they were working burned down.[1]

Despite the danger, the alchemists continued experimenting with the new mixture, calling it "fire chemical" and finding new ways to make it more powerful.

The Chinese also found applications for it. They found that when they poured it into a bamboo tube, and threw the tube into a fire, it made a ferocious bang and blew apart the tube: the firecracker was born.

In the tenth century, the alchemists were still experimenting and finding new applications. Predictably, fire chemical would find wartime use. At first, these uses were relatively benign because gunpowder was not that powerful— it did not have the explosiveness it would later gain. However, that did not stop the Chinese from attaching these firecrackers to arrows and shooting them at an enemy. These "fire arrows" were intended to frighten, confuse, and disrupt an enemy more so than kill them.

Another early wartime use was in slow-burning wicks. By the eleventh century, the Chinese had developed flamethrowers. Each flamethrower needed a slow-burning wick to light the fuel as it came out of a tube. These gunpowder wicks were first used during an epic naval battle in 1044 CE, when the fleet of Wuyue burned the fleet of Wu using "fire oil."

By the late eleventh century, the Chinese had made gunpowder explosive by increasing its saltpeter to roughly 75 percent of the overall mixture. This

---

[1] Jack Kelly, *Gunpowder: Alchemy, Bombards, and Pyrotechnics: The History of the Explosive That Changed the World* (New York: Perseus Books Group, 2005), p.4.

opened up an entirely new range of military applications. One such application was the gunpowder bomb, which was hurled against enemy fortresses using catapults. Another application was the "fire lance." A fire lance was a bamboo tube attached to a spear. The tube was sealed on one end, while gunpowder, darts, sand, led pellets, bits of metal, or pottery shards were forced down the other end. When fired in close combat, fire lances wounded, killed, or simply confused an enemy soldier long enough to follow up with the spear. Fire lances had been designed a century earlier, but they became more prolific after the more explosive gunpowder was developed during the Song dynasty. They were used for centuries, well into the Ming period.

By the twelfth century, the Chinese had detached the tube from the spear, made the tube larger, and added more gunpowder. This early "fire cannon" shot a flaming missile at an enemy, though its distance was limited since the tube was still made of bamboo. Fire cannons were first used in combat in 1126. An 1132 account describes a fire cannon that had to be carried by two people, and was fired from a moving platform at a city wall during a siege. By the end of the twelfth century, the Chinese started making tubes out of metal, and the true cannon was born. They also replaced fire arrows with rockets, an application where the tube itself flew through the air toward the enemy.

Over the next few centuries, cannons continued to develop as advances in metallurgy and gunpowder made them ever more powerful. By the fourteenth century, cannons had spread across Eurasia. Cannons continued to grow in size as well. The bombard became a favorite siege weapon during the late Middle Ages. Bombards tended to have a short, but wide barrel and could launch a 400- to 500-pound stone ball 100–200 meters against an enemy fortress (Figure 16). The large bore was needed to inflict damage on castle walls when shooting stone projectiles. During the sixteenth century, armies switched from stone balls to metal balls. Correspondingly, the bore size of the cannon shrank from upward of 20 inches down to 9–12 inches. Small iron balls could do as much damage as large stone ones, but with smaller and more transportable cannons. In the nineteenth century, when explosive shells were invented, bore size began to increase again, until 16-inch and larger guns were found on battleships and some artillery in World War II.

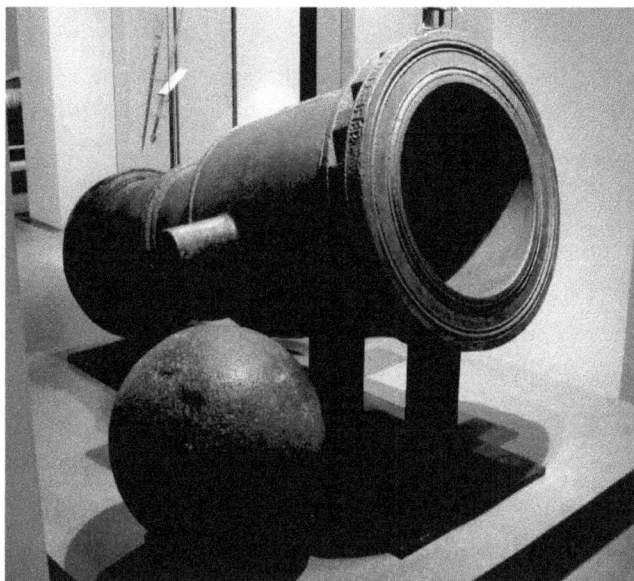

Figure 16. Medieval bombard, ca. 1480-1500
Source: By PHGCOM (self-made, photographed at the Musee de l'Armee) [GFDL (http://www.gnu.org/copyleft/fdl.html) or CC BY-SA 3.0 (http://creativecommons.org/licenses/by-sa/3.0)], via Wikimedia Commons.

The Chinese fire cannon was also the ancestor of the rifle. While Song metallurgists devised ways to make cannons larger, they also found ways to make them smaller, to the point where one person could carry a cannon into combat. These "hand cannons" date to the middle of the thirteenth century: a hand cannon dating to around 1280 CE was found in Manchuria, and they were reportedly even used in a battle between Mongol and Mamluk forces in Egypt as early as 1260. These metal devices were heavy and clumsy to use in combat. Like the fire lance, they were simply a tube, sealed on one end, with objects and gunpowder inserted in the other.

True advancement in rifle technology came with the invention of the matchlock. Developed in the middle of the fifteenth century, this wood-and-metal predecessor to the musket used a trigger device to lower a smoldering fuse into a gunpowder flashpan. The resulting burst set off a second, main charge that propelled a bullet down its barrel. With the matchlock, the shooter could keep both eyes on the target and both hands on the rifle. The resulting leap in accuracy enabled almost any infantryman to attain shooting proficiency quickly. In contrast, it took years for an archer to learn to shoot proficiently. Musketeers began to replace archers on the battlefield once "volley fire" was developed. Volley fire is a tactic where one line of soldiers fires its muskets at the enemy, while another line standing behind the first, loads; and then the two lines switch places. This enabled infantrymen to rain down a continuous volume of fire, a job that had been the role of the archer.

After the matchlock, rifles continued to evolve. The matchlock was replaced by the wheel lock in the sixteenth century and the flintlock in the seventeenth century. These latter rifles replaced the matchlock's slow-burning fuse with a spring-loaded lever that struck a piece of pyrite or flint to create a spark in the flashpan. Like before, the resulting burst would set off the main charge. These rifles were more reliable in rain or damp conditions than the matchlock. The flintlock was replaced in the middle of the nineteenth century when the percussion cap became popular. This device replaced the flashpan with a tiny cylinder containing highly explosive material. One cap was inserted at the rear of the barrel each time the rifle was to be fired. When the gun's hammer struck the cap, the cap exploded, and the main charge exploded. This device eliminated having to pour gunpowder into a flashpan. By the end of the nineteenth century, the percussion cap would be replaced by the metal cartridge. This was a bullet, propellant (gunpowder), and primer (which ignites the propellant) all wrapped together in a brass jacket. These eliminated the need to pour any gunpowder whatsoever. These are still in use today.

With cannons that could knock down castle walls, Europeans started abandoning their castles. With rifles that could shoot through armor, the armor suits of the late Middle Ages became fit only for ceremonial use. With rifle-bearing musketeers, infantry became the dominant force on the battlefield, displacing heavy cavalry. With gunpowder, the age of medieval warfare was over; modern warfare had arrived.

Gunpowder weapons enabled societies across Eurasia to subdue rivals and build empires. Gunpowder technology was spread by the Mongol conquests of the thirteenth century, though it may have reached some central or southern Asian societies a few decades earlier by way of the Silk Road, an ancient trade route.

The Mongol Empire began as a collection of nomadic tribes coalesced into a single entity by Genghis Khan in 1206 CE. Genghis Khan immediately began campaigns of conquest, and defeated the Western Xia of northwest China in 1210. While the Xia had gunpowder, the technology was not mature enough to help them stave off defeat at the hands of the Mongols. Mongol dominance, in contrast, was based on their sophisticated use of horse warfare, which worked great on the open plains but was less useful when laying siege to cities and fortresses. Since gunpowder worked quite well in sieges, it became a complementary enhancement to the Mongol arsenal.

The Mongols began to employ Chinese catapult units, acquired from their former foe, in campaigns to the south and west. As early as 1219, these units were hurling gunpowder bombs in support of the Mongol invasion of Transoxania (present-day Uzbekistan-Tajikistan area). Later campaigns included use of the Chinese cannon (the *huochong*), rockets, and grenades.

The Mongols eventually conquered most of Eurasia, and they spread the use of gunpowder as they went. The Mongols invaded northwest India in the 1220s. In 1241, they invaded eastern Europe and used gunpowder during the Battle of Mohi in Hungary. In 1258 they conquered Bagdad. And in 1274 and 1280, they invaded Japan, though they failed in both attempts.

The Mongols' longest and most arduous campaign was against the Song dynasty of China. After conquering the Western Xia in 1210, and the Jin in 1234, they turned to fight the most powerful kingdom, the Song. The war raged for four decades—by far the longest war of the Mongol conquests.

The war with the Song took so long in part because the Song also had gunpowder technology. In addition to fire lances, rockets, and flamethrowers, the Song had developed increasingly powerful bombs. Ultimately, the Song lost the war, not because of weaponry, but because of treachery. One of the Song's most able generals felt disrespected by the Song court, and so he changed sides and joined the Mongols. This turned the tide of the war. After a series of defeats over the next few years, the Song court finally surrendered in 1276. The Mongols became the Yuan dynasty in China, which would last for a hundred years.

The maturation of gunpowder technology would not come until after the Mongol Empire had dissolved, however. The Mongol Empire went through a series of power struggles after the death of Genghis Khan in 1227. Initially, his third son and chosen successor, Ögedei, assumed power; then Ögedei's nephew (Genghis's grandson) Kublai ruled. By the time of Kublai's death in 1294, the empire had been split into four regions, and various cousins were vying for the title of Great Khan. Civil wars broke out and fracturing resulted. Ultimately, the Mongol Empire dissolved into independent fiefdoms.

In the wake of the Mongol dissolution, four societies in particular, each located on the western edge of the former empire, embraced gunpowder weaponry and used it to make themselves into empires (Figure 17).[XXVIII]

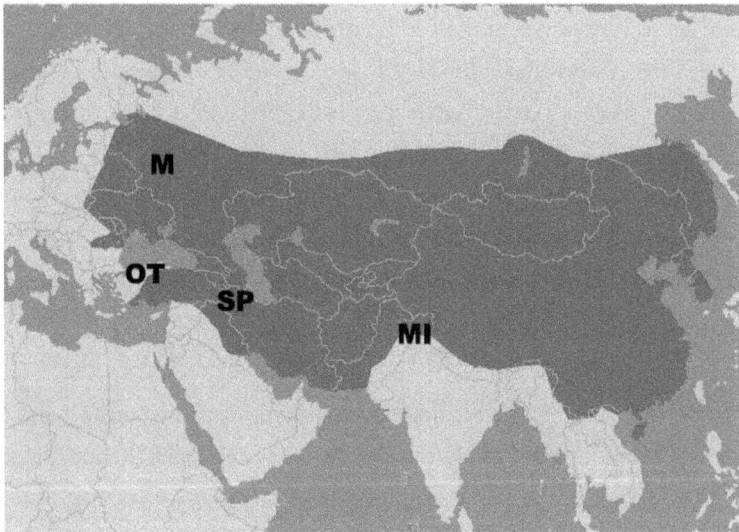

Figure 17. Gunpowder empires along the western Mongol border.

The Ottoman Empire began when Osman I consolidated disparate Turkish states of the Anatolian plateau into a regional power in 1299 CE. He primarily used cavalry forces to do this, but the Ottomans would acquire cannons after an invasion of the Timurids in 1402, and a subsequent civil war that nearly destroyed the budding sultanate.

The Ottomans employed their cannons in the first siege of Constantinople in 1422. The aging Byzantine Empire was able to withstand the siege even though the two sides were technologically matched and both sides had gunpowder weapons.

The Ottomans, however, began a program of aggressive weapons development, even employing a Hungarian expert named Orban to develop long-range artillery. By the early 1450s, Ottoman long-range artillery could hurl 600-pound stone balls up to a mile away. In their second attempt to conquer Constantinople in 1453, the Turks used 68 bombards. This time they succeeded.

The Ottoman program of gunpowder innovation advanced every aspect of weaponry. The Ottomans embraced the rifle as soon as it became available: their elite Janissary Corps shifted from bows to matchlocks in the 1440s. The Ottomans were among the first to mount cannons on ships, which they used to win the first naval cannonade, the Battle of Zonchio, in 1499. The Ottomans were also among the first to use explosives for mines and engineering. Perhaps the Ottoman's greatest strengths, however, were industrial and organizational. The Ottomans had a natural advantage in gunpowder raw materials, which they exploited to the fullest by developing a highly efficient state-run industry for its production and distribution.

Between the fifteenth and seventeenth centuries, the Ottoman Turks became one of the world's largest empires. By the middle of the fifteenth century, the Ottomans had conquered much of eastern Europe, and the Ottoman navy dominated the Mediterranean Sea.

Eventually, however, others caught up with the Ottoman innovations. The empire began to fade in the late seventeenth century when other states overtook the Turks technologically. The remnants of empire were finally dismantled after World War I, after having sided with the Central Powers (Germany and Austro-Hungary) against the victorious Allies.[xxix]

To the north of the Ottomans were the Muscovites, who also used firearms to expand their territory. Muscovite conquests took them across the entire continent of Asia, to the Pacific Ocean during the sixteenth and seventeenth centuries.

Muscovy started out as a trading post in the late 1200s. It eventually grew to become a vassal state of the Mongolian Golden Horde—one of the four kingdoms into which the Mongol Empire had split in the thirteenth century. In 1480, Muscovy became independent from the Horde and began campaigns to subdue and subsume its smaller neighboring states. Muscovy, however, could not defeat its largest rivals: the Kazan khanate to its east (a remnant of the Golden Horde) and the Kingdom of Lithuania to its west. Muscovy fought decades-long on-again, off-again wars against these two enemies well into the sixteenth century.

In the early sixteenth century, Muscovy began acquiring firearms and incorporating them into its army. As the century progressed, Ivan IV ("the Terrible" or "the Formidable"), who was tsar at the time, established close ties with Europe, particularly with England, which he used to secure commerce and arms. By midcentury, firearms had become a mature and effective part of his army. The Muscovites had even developed the Streltsy—an elite standing unit of skilled riflemen that used harquebuses (matchlocks and wheel lock muskets). This unit would often fire from behind mobile walls that were moved to the front, offering protective cover for the shooter. The Streltsy were also early adopters of volley fire tactics, enabling them to pour nearly continuous fire on opposing forces.

With a modern gunpowder army, which included cannons and mines in addition to the Streltsy, Russia (as it was now called) was able to defeat the Kazan khanate in 1552. It was also able to rebuff an Ottoman attack from the south in 1557. The Streltsy, experienced from their battles with the Kazan khanate, armed with harquebuses, and firing from behind their mobile defensive walls, decisively defeated the Ottoman army of 120,000—a force nearly twice its size—thus permanently ending Ottoman expansion plans against Russia.

At the end of the sixteenth century, Russia defeated the Sibir khanate, opening up lands in Siberia to the east. After an initial victory by a Cossack mercenary force was later reversed, Russian forces returned, and with the help of artillery, defeated this second khanate in 1598. With the fall of the khanates, Russia became a regional power and began its expansion across Asia. It reached the Pacific Ocean in 1639.[xxx]

To the south of the Muscovites and Ottomans were the Persians. The Safavid dynasty, founded in the early sixteenth century, rose to rule Persia for two centuries. The Safavid's power came from gunpowder weapons, which helped make them into a regional power.

The dynasty began in 1501 when Ismail I, then fourteen years old, started conquering territory around present-day Azerbaijan. Within ten years, he had conquered all of Persia and even checked the Uzbek advancement on Persia's northeastern border. He did this, however, not with gunpowder, but with the support of the Qizilbash, tribes of skilled warrior horsemen whose slavish devotion to duty was part of their worship of Allah.

Nonetheless, these skilled warrior horsemen were no match for the gunpowder weaponry of the Ottoman Turks. After a humiliating defeat in 1514, the Safavids began to lose territory to the Ottomans. Wars between these powers continued, generally going in favor of the Ottomans and the resurgent Uzbeks in the east.

In 1587, the Safavid's greatest leader, Shah Abbas, grandson of Ismail I, came to power. He had seen how ineffectual his army was compared to the Ottoman Turks, so he launched a program to convert his army to gunpowder. His greatest challenge was the entrenched cultural repugnance against gunpowder weaponry. This notwithstanding, in 1598, he procured the services of two English brothers and their company, who began to convert the Persian army to a gunpowder one based on the European model.

The new army was a success. With it, the Persians regained territory previously lost to the Ottomans and Uzbeks. They went on to expand both to the west and to the east, recapturing Bagdad in 1622 and taking Kandahar in 1649. At its height, Safavid Persia controlled an area that ranged from present-day Syria and Turkey in the west, to the Caucasus and Turkmenistan in the north, to Pakistan in the east. They also developed strong trade relationships with both the English and the Dutch.

The Safavid reigned until the eighteenth century. Eventually others obtained gunpowder and began to raid Safavid territory. Trade relationships with the British and the Dutch eroded. After ineffective leadership and several religious wars, the Safavids fell to an Afghani army that overthrew them and established a new dynasty in Persia.[XXXI]

While the Safavid were growing in power, so was another kingdom to its east—Mughal India. During the sixteenth and seventeenth centuries, Mughal

India became a de facto gunpowder weapons research and development center, and it used the resultant weapons to conquer the Indian subcontinent.

The Mughal Empire was founded in India in 1526 by Babur, a descendant of Timur and Genghis Khan. Born in present-day Uzbekistan, he became ruler of Kabul at the age of twenty-one. While in Kabul, he formed an alliance with the Ottoman Turks, who helped him modernize his army by giving him matchlocks and cannons, and the training to use them. Not strong enough to dislodge the Uzbeks to his north, he launched a campaign to his south in 1519. With a victory at the Battle of Panipat in 1526, he conquer Punjab and founded the Mughal Empire. He died in 1530, but his descendants continued expanding the empire.

Babur's grandson, Akbar, assumed the throne as a child, but when he became an adult, he substantially expanded the development and production of gunpowder weaponry. Mughal India began mass producing matchlocks and became a leader in their development. Mughal engineers created an early machine gun, which used multiple barrels for rapid fire. The Mughals found innovative applications for explosives that included mines, grenades, and antifortress bombs. They developed long-range rockets, which were particularly effective when used in mass bombardment against cavalry and war elephants. They also had the most sophisticated artillery of their day. Eventually, the Mughals would build an industry around gunpowder and gunpowder weaponry, and were exporting firearms and gunpowder raw material to Europe by the seventeenth century.

This expertise in gunpowder and gunpowder weaponry, along with leadership, diplomacy, and alliances, enabled the Mughals to conquer most of the Indian subcontinent by the end of the seventeenth century. The population ultimately under their control is estimated at 110–150 million, about one-quarter of the earth's population at the time.

As with other empires, however, the Mughals eventually felt the effects of a series of poor leaders. In the eighteenth century, revolts broke out and religious feuds erupted. Over time, the Mughals lost power to their rivals, the Marathas, until both were subsumed into the British Commonwealth in the middle of the nineteenth century.[XXXII]

Beyond the western border of the now fallen Mongol Empire lay Europe. Europe acquired gunpowder in at least three ways: in the east, the Mongols introduced Europeans to gunpowder during their invasion of Hungary; in the west, Islamic Moors used gunpowder against Christian kingdoms in present-day Spain; and in the center, the Franks and the papacy learned of gunpowder through liaisons and missionaries to the Mongols. As a result of these three, largely simultaneous introductions, the whole of Europe adopted gunpowder roughly concurrently. As a result, no one society stood out to become a gunpowder empire. While empires were rising in western Asia, where the differential between gunpowder haves and have-nots was greatest, European societies stayed at rough parity as all kingdoms transitioned to gunpowder together.

In eastern Europe, the Mongols attacked Hungary in 1241. The main battle of this campaign was the Battle of Mohi, where the Hungarians squared off against Mongol forces in April. During this battle, Mongols made extensive use of gunpowder weapons such as "flaming arrows" and "napthta bombs." While the campaign devastated the Hungarians, the Hungarians survived and the Mongols retreated, primarily for political reasons. Having seen what gunpowder can do, the Hungarians became early European adopters of these weapons. They would develop large-scale cannons and even provide the Ottomans with experts in their use. They were also one of the first European armies to integrate matchlock-bearing infantry into their ranks.

In western Europe, the Christian kingdoms of Spain were well into the Reconquista, or Reconquering of Spain, from Islamic Moors when the Moors began using gunpowder weapons against them. Cannons had spread along Arab trade routes across North Africa from the Middle East and central Asia. In Spain, cannons were first used during the Siege of Seville in 1248 (a date that suggests the diffusion of gunpowder technology from central Asia likely began prior to the Mongol invasion there in 1219). After Seville, cannons were recurrently used in Reconquista battles. Observers from other parts of Europe came in to watch these new weapons in action. In the end, however, the weaponry was not mature enough to give the Moors a decisive victory, and eventually the Christian kingdoms acquired their own cannons, neutralizing any gunpowder advantage.

In central Europe, gunpowder information was brought in by papal missionaries to the Mongols. The papacy sought an ally in its crusade against Islamic forces in the Near East. The pope sent missionary teams to central Asia to try and convert the Mongols to Christianity, a precondition for any military alliance. In addition, the Franks in particular were interested in forming an alliance with the Mongols against their common enemy, the Islamic caliphate. In 1253, Louis IX sent a Flemish Franciscan named William of Rubruck to convert the Mongols to Christianity in hopes of forging an alliance. While the Mongols refused the conversion, they gave William a demonstration of gunpowder. He was even able to copy down the ingredients for making it, which he later passed to his friend and fellow Franciscan Roger Bacon. Bacon published the account in a book in 1267. During the rest of the century, other books with formulas for gunpowder were published. While the Franco-Mongol alliance never truly came to fruition, routine contact with the Mongols provided the Franks, and the papacy, with multiple opportunities to witness gunpowder weapons. Consequently, Italian city-states would be among the earliest manufacturers of high-quality gunpowder weapons.

By the middle of the fourteenth century, gunpowder weapons were appearing on battlefields across Europe. Gun-making guilds sprouted up in Italy and elsewhere as blacksmiths responded to growing demand for firearms. European states began producing gunpowder, and introduced wet grinding to reduce the risk of explosion. Furthermore, the Hundred Years' War gave France and England ample opportunity to develop, test, and advance gunpowder weapons.

While gunpowder empires were rising in western Asia, no such empire arose in Europe. Because every European society gained access to gunpowder at roughly the same time, no society acquired a monopoly on its use or obtained a lead in weapons development that could be used to dominate other societies. This egalitarian competition between European states, as it turns out, provided ample incentive to develop more and better weapons. This led to a rapid advancement of firearms technology. While Europeans were initially behind other parts of the world in firearms sophistication, they became the leader by the seventeenth century, even surpassing the previous leader, Mughal India.[XXXIII]

In the Far East lay the remnants of the Mongol Empire and other states. The Yuan dynasty (the Mongols) fell in 1368 to the Ming. Because of the Ming dynasty, no other gunpowder empires were able to rise in the Far East, though Japan did try in the late sixteenth century.

The Ming overthrew a decaying Yuan dynasty in 1368, removing the last vestiges of Mongol rule from China. Because of this, the Ming had a virtual monopoly on gunpowder use in the Far East. The Japanese were on the receiving end of gunpowder firepower during the Mongol invasions of 1274 and 1281, but both invasions were cut short when the invasion fleets were destroyed by typhoons. After this, gunpowder weaponry did not take hold in Japan.

Portuguese traders brought firearms to Japan in 1543. These matchlocks were crude, and not considered better than Japanese archers. However, almost immediately, the Japanese began making design improvements. They increased the caliber of the barrel, they put protective coverings over the matches so they would work in the rain, and the Japanese even developed their own volley fire techniques. By the 1560s, the Japanese began converting their armies to rifles, and in 1575, during the feudal Battle of Nagashino, the rifle units proved their effectiveness in combat by stopping both infantry and cavalry charges.

After that, the Japanese were determined to build their own gunpowder empire. By 1592, the Japanese had built up their rifle-bearing forces. They invaded Korea with 158,000 troops, about one-quarter of which were riflemen. The Japanese ground forces had overwhelming success. They landed at Pusan, capturing Seoul in just eighteen days and most of Korea within three months. However, the Korean navy was still able to harass Japanese supply lines, and then Ming China entered the war with a large army and longer-ranged cannons than the Japanese had. This forced the war into a stalemate that lasted for five years. In 1597, the Japanese again invaded Korea, and again were stopped by Korean and Ming Chinese forces. This time Japan withdrew its troops for good. After this, the Japanese largely gave up on gun production and adopted a policy of isolationism.

Other parts of the Far East also acquired firearms from Portuguese traders, but primarily used them in internal conflicts. The Vietnamese acquired firearms through trade during the sixteenth century, and used them in dynastic battles. The Indonesians were likely first exposed to gunpowder weapons by Arab traders in the middle of the fourteenth century, but they would later adopt Portuguese firearms and use them in internal battles as well. Hence, no Far East gunpowder empires, other than the Chinese who originated gunpowder, were able to rise up as they did in other parts of the world.

Gunpowder was the quintessential dominating innovation. The Ottoman Turks, Muscovites, Safavid Persians, and Mughal Indians used it to grow into empires that lasted for centuries. It took a while, however, for gunpowder weaponry to mature. In Mongol conquests, its use was largely confined to sieges, but with the creation of the matchlock—or more specifically, the matchlock trigger mechanism that lowered a lit fuse onto a gunpowder flashpan—gunpowder was ready to move onto the open battlefield.

Gunpowder's greatest impact occurred when one side acquired it and the other did not; or at least when one side had developed it more than the other. Such was the case along the western border of the Mongol Empire. Having been brought in by the Mongols, some societies had used it, while others were less familiar with it. In the case of Muscovy, the khanates simply did not keep up with its development, and so were eventually outgunned by the Muscovites even though they had had exposure to it.

In cases where everyone acquired gunpowder at roughly the same time, such as in Europe, parity was established and no individual society could stand out. Yet the group as a whole elevated in power as a result.

In cases where a new society, such as Japan, tried to use gunpowder against a society that already had it, such as Ming China, the attempts were stalemated or defeated.

Yet for each society that used gunpowder to become an empire, some internal changes had to be made. It may have been reorganizing the army to create elite corps of riflemen, as was done by the Ottoman Empire and the Muscovy. It may have been changing attitudes and culture to embrace what had been looked down upon, as was done in Safavid Persia. It may have been the sustained commitment to invest in becoming an industrial firearms production and development center, as was done in Mughal India. Each society had to respond in its own way to exploit the potential of this new technology.

And then once a society had gunpowder, it still had to develop a policy on how best to use it. Fatigued by generations of foreign campaigns, the Ming turned inward, avoided outside contact, and chose not to exploit gunpowder weapons in the way their predecessor, the Yuan, had (though in later years that decision would have its own repercussions as the Ming would find a need to import advanced weaponry from Europe).

In each case, however, the society that acquired gunpowder obtained a new level of power. Societies that never acquired it, never gained that power. They would fare worse in the years ahead, as would be seen in the colonial wars of the eighteenth and nineteenth centuries.[XXXIV]

Chapter 11
Dominating Innovations, Part III

The final two dominating innovations bring us into the modern age. Petroleum propulsion and nuclear power came along after the world had begun its transition to the nation-state. Even in the modern era, however, each of these innovations had the same characteristics as previous ones: it led to a leadership role for a society, it promoted wealth and/or military strength for the society, its impact dissipated as other societies acquired it, and it left a residual power barrier between those societies with it and those without it. Interestingly, though, the impact of these innovations was for a shorter time than for previous innovations, reflecting how much our world is speeding up.

Petroleum Propulsion

Petroleum propulsion accelerated England's rise to become an empire. This rise began with the English explorers of the late fifteenth century who discovered new lands for the crown; then it took a quantum leap when England transitioned to the nation-state in the late seventeenth century; and then it accelerated forward with the advent of petroleum propulsion in the eighteenth century. In addition, while petroleum propulsion began with the steam engine, this innovation family would continue in other forms, principally in the form of the internal combustion engine, which would be developed a century and a half later.

In the late seventeenth century, British mines were limited in how deep they could go because water collected at their bottom. As a result, most mines ran along the surface in the form of inverted bell-shaped pits that followed a coal seam. The deeper the mine was, the more likely it collected water, so most mining stayed near the surface where water could be removed by hand. An attempt to use steam to suck water out of mines came at the end of the eighteenth century, but this was not very effective and depths were limited to just thirty feet.

Then, in 1712, English inventor Thomas Newcomen introduced a new way to use steam to remove water from mines (Figure 18). His engine created steam in a boiler and injected the steam into a cylinder, and when the steam was cooled, a vacuum was created inside the cylinder that pulled a piston. The piston was connected to a long shaft that extended down into the mine, and the shaft actuated a pump, which removed the water from the mine. The steam was introduced to, first, one side of the piston and then to the other, to create an oscillating motion. This "steam engine" was two stories high, slow, and delivered only five to ten horsepower, yet it was enough to remove water from mines.

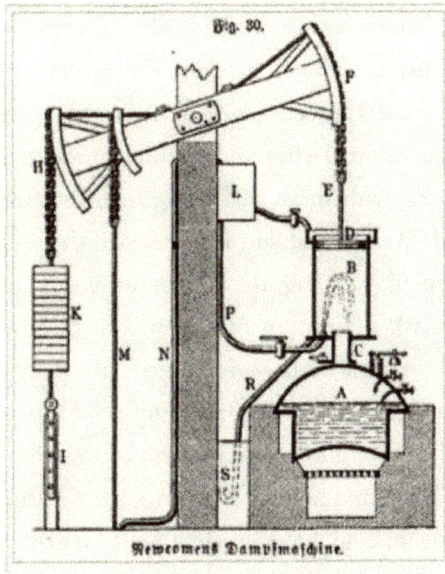

Figure 18. Newcomen steam engine

The Newcomen engine enabled mines to go deeper, which changed coal mining across Europe. Mines could reach deeper into deposits, and new mines opened that had not been feasible before. Newcomen engines were shipped to the Continent, and by the time the patent expired in 1733, 110 had been built, 14 of which were in continental Europe.

The steam engine remained relatively unchanged for decades until the Scottish engineer James Watt discovered ways to make improvements to the design. Watt, who repaired scientific equipment at the University of Glasgow, was asked to fix the university's steam engine model. In doing so he learned that 75–80 percent of the engine's energy was being wasted by heating and cooling the cylinder every cycle. He separated the cooling from the heating by introducing a separate chamber, a condenser, where the steam could be cooled while the cylinder remained hot. He also began using steam pressure to move the piston, instead of just relying on vacuum. He also introduced an air pump to exhaust the cylinder after each stroke. By 1769, he had a working model and had patented the condenser.

More critical than any other factor, the Watt engine was powerful enough and fast enough to drive rotary equipment: this opened the door to a host of new applications across a variety of industries. In mining, the Watt engine enabled deep-shaft mining to begin. In addition to better water removal, the Watt engine could turn fans that pumped air down shafts, clearing out deadly gases and enabling miners to breathe easier. With better water removal and better airflow, mines went deeper and mining productivity surged. Mines became more efficient with more coal being removed from existing mines. New mines opened: Britain had so many reserves that supply could match any increase in demand. In 1700, the annual output of coal was around 2.5 million tons. By 1780, the output of coal was roughly 7 million tons. By 1800, roughly 10 million tons were mined. By 1815, output reached approximately 18 million tons; by 1830, output was over 30 million tons; and by 1861, roughly 57 million tons were mined. Much of this productivity increase was possible because hosts of inventors after Watt continued making improvements on steam engine design after Watt's patents ran out in 1800.

Textile production was the first industry outside of mining to put the steam engine to use. In the early eighteenth century, textiles were made by hand, usually in family-run businesses on home premises. Then in the middle of the eighteenth century, spinning jennies, water frames, and flying shuttles were invented, taking textile manufacturing out of homes and moving it into mills located next to streams where flowing water could turn the equipment. In 1784, the first steam-powered loom was invented, decoupling cotton mills from streams. In subsequent decades, textile-manufacturing centers, such as Lancashire and Manchester, grew up.

From textiles, the steam engine spread to other industries. In iron making, steam engines began to be used for pumping air through blast furnaces, increasing operating temperature and productivity. Steam engines began to turn shafts on assembly lines, giving rise to mass production. Steam engines began driving printing presses, enabling the expansion of both the printing and the publishing industries. Steam engines were put onto watercraft, turning paddles to create the first steamboats. Steam engines replaced horses in rail hauling of coal, freight, and later passengers, giving rise to the modern railroad. In short, during the first half of the nineteenth century, nearly every British industry was experimenting with rotating or reciprocating equipment, driven by the steam engine, in hopes of increasing productivity and cashing in on this new marvel.

These industry changes had secondary and tertiary impacts. Increased textile production required the development of roads, canals, distribution warehouses, cotton exchanges, and other infrastructure to support the rapidly growing production centers. Mass production required better machine tools to build and repair equipment, which in turn required better standards, measures, measurement tools, and the science behind them. More newspapers and books increased calls for literacy and development of the education system. Hence, the impact of industrialization rippled across the entire economy: few areas were unchanged by it.

These industrial changes continued in the second half of the century, and were only accelerated by the advent of the internal combustion engine. Scientists had long known that if the fire that powered an engine were burned inside the cylinder rather than outside of it, the engine would be far more efficient. In 1876, German engineer Nikolaus Otto achieved this goal when he created the first effective internal combustion engine. Earlier versions had lacked the sustained power that Otto's four-stroke engine now provided. Along with the maturing transportation industries of railroads, shipping, and canals, productivity once again began to surge.

The Second Industrial Revolution was characterized by a new wave of innovation. Improvements to the internal combustion engine gave birth to the automotive industry at the end of the century. They also gave birth to the airplane industry at the beginning of the next. Meanwhile, electric generators began to convert petroleum fuels such as coal and oil into electricity to light cities and power factories.

So what began with the steam engine in the eighteenth century was furthered by the internal combustion engine in the nineteenth century. Petroleum propulsion—the conversion of petroleum fuels into mechanical motion—took less than two centuries to transform Britain's economy from agricultural to industrial: even the pace of change had increased.

The crux of the Industrial Revolution was the shift from animal and human labor to machine labor. Now humans were controlling machines that did the work. Humans would feed raw material into the machines, and keep the machines running, but humans were no longer doing the actual manufacturing anymore.

Being the first to have machines do the work had its advantages. Mass production, along with an emerging transportation infrastructure that could send British goods to far-flung parts of the world, made Britain into the world's manufacturing center of the nineteenth century. Britain's share of world manufacturing output rose from 4 percent in 1800, to 10 percent in 1830, to 20 percent by 1860.

This of course put more wealth in British hands. British gross domestic product, which grew at about 1.5 percent annually between 1770 and 1815, grew at 3 percent between 1815 and 1830. British per capital gross national product, which was $346 in 1830, rose to $785 by 1890.[1] Britain's closest rivals, Germany and France, hovered at about two-thirds of this level in 1890.

Mass production also contributed directly to British military might by

---

[1] Both figures are in 1960 US dollars.

creating cheaper, standardized weapons and ammunition. The British were creating warship parts and small arms as early as the Napoleonic Wars in the 1810s, though on a scale still too small to impact the outcome of the wars. The British produced engines, also on a small scale, for warships during the Crimean War in the 1850s. However, the British were mass producing rifles by the 1860s and explosives by the 1870s. Mass production of weaponry helped ensure that British forces could protect British commercial interests abroad. Newfound wealth helped ensure those forces received a continuous flow of arms and ammunition. Together the tandem forces of wealth and military strength elevated British power throughout the nineteenth century.

Of course, none of these gains implies that the Industrial Revolution in Britain did not have its adverse consequences as well. Increases in wealth, healthier diets, and longer life expectancies were accompanied by increased pollution, population blight, easily communicated diseases, and child labor abuse. Though many of these problems were eventually addressed through legislation, historians have debated whether the average British citizen was made better or worse by industrialization. In any event, it is undeniable that industrializing first helped secure Britain's place as a leading power and aided in building the British Empire.

Because industrialization came so soon after Britain's shift to a nation-state, the effects of the two were entangled. However, it is most accurate to say that industrialization accelerated Britain's rise to power, rather than to say that it created the rise outright.

British expansion began in the late fifteenth century as England responded to Portuguese and Spanish explorations. Portugal and Spain were exploring the Americas and opening trade routes to Africa, the Middle East, India, and the Far East. England, France, and the Netherlands, not wanting to be left behind, began their own explorations. The first English exploration was led by John Cabot, who discovered present-day Newfoundland in 1497. He left no settlers behind though.

For most of the sixteenth century, England was preoccupied with waging war against Spain and settling Ireland rather than establishing overseas colonies. The English fought wars with Spain and established the province of

Northern Ireland. The first English settlement in the Americas (The Roanoke Colony) was attempted on the coast of present-day North Carolina in 1584, but this failed for reasons that are still unclear.

English overseas exploration took off in the seventeenth century. England would establish its first permanent settlement (Jamestown) on mainland America in 1607 in present-day Virginia. In the following decades, it would establish several more colonies in America and on Caribbean islands. It would charter commercial companies, such as the English East India Company (later changed to British East India Company), to continue exploration around the globe and to establish trading posts and settlements. England would also fight three wars against the Netherlands, as the two Crowns vied for control of the transatlantic trade routes.

Between 1649 and 1688, England shifted power from its king to its Parliament. While both continued to function, under the new constitutional monarchy, primary responsibility for governance now rested with Parliament. This nation-state structure gave Britain the political and legal foundation needed to effectively manage disparate colonies in far-flung places across the globe.

Instead of a royal sovereign or his representatives making the key decisions, members of Parliament now had primary decision-making authority. Since they were generally easier to access than the king, private entities, such as commercial enterprises, educational interests, financial firms, and other special interest groups, could now share their views with a legislative decision maker more easily. As a result, these entities gained a greater voice in government, leading to more encompassing, more balanced laws. Many of the social reforms that would later occur during the nineteenth century, such as the abolition of the slave trade and social reforms that made the Industrial Revolution palatable to the majority of people, and perhaps even sustainable, may not have occurred without this form of representative governance already being in place.

Also with the new government, policy, procedure, and regulation became a tool not only for capturing decisions made but also for retaining the collective expertise that went into those decisions. New approaches for starting colonies, establishing trading routes, managing tax revenue, establishing oversight bodies, and other ministerial tasks could be replicated across the globe.

These policies could also be tailored to a specific situation. A new territory could become a dominion, a colony, a protectorate, or another form of governed region according to the needs of the local situation. The British government could change the terms of a charter company, authorizing the use of force or giving it authority to collect taxes, if it was deemed necessary in a particular region. Such was the case with the British East India Company in the middle of the eighteenth century. As such, policies provided a flexible way to facilitate acquiring new territory, managing local populations, and defeating foreign rivals.

All of this enabled a more complex level of coordination to exist, with far greater capacity to manage than would have been possible under a fiefdom. Unlike earlier empires, such as the Mongol Empire, which had to be contiguous to maintain order, Britain could manage disparate realms, all coordinated under central policy yet operated largely independently by chartered entities whose operations were aligned to parliamentary intent.

One of the results of this new governance structure was that Britain gained the upper hand in wars against rival empire builders, such as France, during the eighteenth century. British holdings steadily grew through these conflicts, and Britain became the dominant naval power in the world. Only the noteworthy loss of the American colonies blemished this growth.

In the nineteenth century, France would again challenge Britain's hegemony. Led by Napoleon Bonaparte, and buoyed by momentum from the French Revolution, France began wars of conquest on the European mainland. However, these wars were ultimately settled in favor of Britain and her allies, eliminating France as a threat to British sovereignty for the rest of the century.

Into this context, the Industrial Revolution arrived. What began in the mining and textile industries in the eighteenth century spread to other industries in the nineteenth century. Mass production, in its infancy during the Napoleonic Wars, was making Britain into the world's manufacturing center by midcentury as raw materials were brought in from distant lands, converted to finished goods, and then shipped back across the globe to distant markets. The steamship, the railroad, and the telegraph (which had emerged in the 1830s) made it all work:

connecting the enterprise by enabling information, material, goods, and people to flow across its breadth. And this enterprise generated wealth for Britain, fueling its desire for more land with more raw materials.

This land had to be acquired through political and military operations. The British government took direct control of India from the British East India Company in 1858 and began administering it as a dominion. The Scramble for Africa began in the 1880s as the British Empire vied against other European powers for possessions there. Mass production provided cheaper and increasingly sophisticated weaponry for its army. Steamships could move its troops across the seas, under the protection of the world's most powerful navy, and railroads could deliver supplies deep inland to sustain the troops for as long as necessary to subdue local populations. With capital and assets, smaller British forces could often defeat larger non-European armies.

Ultimately, a government would be established, making permanent colonies of these remote regions. These regions could then be administered using laws and policies that integrated commercial, financial, educational, and even religious interests with those of the state. Detachments of colonial troops remained in place to ensure enforcement of the new laws, and local civil services were developed to allow a degree of autonomous rule to emerge over time and to help solidify loyalty to the empire.

By the twentieth century, through wealth and territorial expansion, the British Empire had become the largest empire in world history. While the British Empire had reached its commercial peak in the 1880s,[2] it reached its territorial peak after World War I, when it assumed responsibility for lands formerly belonging to the defeated Central Powers. Ultimately it held dominion over one-fifth of the world's population and almost one-quarter of the world's land.

Of course, the British were not the only ones who industrialized, and in time others caught up—particularly America and Germany. Industrialization began in America back in the middle of the eighteenth century when the

---

[2] Britain had the largest share of world total manufacturing output in 1880, at about 23 percent; the United States was second at less than 15 percent.

owner of a New Jersey copper mine (the Schuyler Copper Mine) brought over an English steam engine to remove water. Mass production began when New England textile mills acquired production techniques from Britain in the late eighteenth and early nineteenth centuries; these techniques spread to many northern states by midcentury. In present-day Germany, Westphalia industrialized the Ruhr Valley by the early nineteenth century. And industrialization spread across the globe to Japan by the 1870s, where the Meiji government was rapidly converting from the feudalism Japan had retained until just a couple of decades before.

By the end of the nineteenth century, with the industrialization of the chemical industry, petroleum industry, electrical industry, and the automotive industry, America and Germany had caught up with Britain. Many American and German conglomerates had emerged as the technological leaders in their industries.

Of course, this industrial competition also meant territorial competition. The Scramble for Africa of the late nineteenth century was followed by an East Asian land grab by Japan after its victories in the First Sino-Japanese War in 1895 and the Russo-Japanese War in 1905. It accelerated after the Allied victory in World War I when Japan acquired Germany's Pacific Island possessions.

World War I was the result of escalating competition between industrial powers. In World War I, mechanized armies fought each other for the first time, but with both sides at industrial parity, the war bogged down into an early stalemate. Ultimately, America's entry on the side of Britain and France delivered the resource superiority needed to end the conflict. After Germany's defeat, Britain reached its largest size, but it was no longer the peerless leader it had been.

In many ways, World War I changed the British people's attitude about their empire. Many were no longer keen on preserving it, let alone on building it further. Political pressure grew from within to disassemble it, as it came to be blamed for the loss of 1.1 million young men. After World War II, Britain gave independence to several colonies that appeared capable of stable governance and were not Communist leaning. The British Empire, for all intents and purposes, came to an end with the transfer of Hong Kong back to China in 1997.

Britain was the beneficiary of a dominating innovation developed soon after a societal-level change. Petroleum propulsion came along only three decades after Britain had transitioned from a fiefdom to a nation-state, and unlike previous dominating innovations, which took centuries to mature, petroleum propulsion was generating leadership power for Britain in only decades. The world was speeding up. With a nation-state foundation and petroleum propulsion power, Britain became history's largest empire within a century. It is likely Britain would have become the leading power simply by its transition to a nation-state, but coupled with petroleum propulsion, it grew faster and attained unprecedented size before others could catch up industrially.

Others did catch up, though. Other societies made the transition to nation-state and acquired petroleum propulsion as well. After the great industrial conflict of World War I, Britain lost its position as the world's only superpower. By the end of the twentieth century, further global changes brought the empire to an end. The British Empire did, however, leave behind a legacy of infrastructure, language, culture, governance, and values around the globe that still influences the world today.[xxxv]

Nuclear Power

The final dominating innovation is nuclear power. Nuclear power reshaped the world community around the United States and the Soviet Union in the latter half of the twentieth century. Based on centuries of scientific discovery, it was a power whose magnitude the world had never before known. It stopped a war, and it began another one: a Cold War, between two competing superpowers. Ultimately, nuclear weapons began to spread, and leadership power began to spread with it. Unlike previous dominating innovations, however, nations intervened to stem nuclear weapons diffusion. After the Cold War, the largest nuclear nations took steps to eliminate their nuclear weapons, while a few other nations sought to develop their own. Today the world exists in a quasi-stable nuclear environment, with most nations agreeing to use nuclear power for peaceful purposes only.

Nuclear power is founded on scientific research conducted between the late seventeenth and early twentieth centuries. Long before then, however, ancient philosophers had conceived of atoms and elements. Philosophers in both ancient Greece and ancient India theorized that all material could be divided, and redivided, over and over again, into ever smaller portions. Then at some point, you would reach a portion so small that it could not be divided any further. In fact, the word *atom* in Greek means "not cut," implying that there is a point at which material cannot be subdivided further. Some Greek philosophers also theorized that matter was composed of four basic elements: earth, air, fire, and water. However, since no experimentation was being done in those days, no consensus was ever reached across societies on this perspective.

Then in the seventeenth century, experimentation led to the discovery of the first true elements. In 1649, Hennig Brand, a German merchant, discovered phosphorus by distilling his urine in alchemy experiments. In 1661, Robert Boyle, an Irish alchemist, coined the term *element* to mean "a substance that cannot be broken down into a simpler substance by a chemical reaction." Later, in 1680, Boyle also discovered phosphorus, inducing Brand to finally publish the results of his experiments conducted three decades earlier.

During the eighteenth century, many more elements were discovered. By 1789, French chemist Antoine-Laurent de Lavoisier published a list that contained twenty-three of them. They included phosphorus, oxygen, nitrogen, hydrogen, mercury, zinc, and sulphur.

During the nineteenth century, scientists discovered molecules and atoms. In 1803, John Dalton, an English chemist and physicist, revived the ancient concept of atoms to describe how they combine to form molecules of the substances we find around us. Later, Italian scientist Amedeo Avogadro would precisely identify the weights of atoms. In 1869, Russian chemist Dmitri Mendeleev put the fifty-six then-known elements in weight order to create the periodic table—a table that predicted four new elements, which were later found.

In the late nineteenth and early twentieth centuries, scientists unveiled the nature of the atom. In 1897, J. J. Thomson discovered electrons, which revealed that atoms were not simple blocks of mass; rather, they were composed of subatomic particles. In 1911, Ernest Rutherford discovered the nucleus of the atom, and that it contains 99 percent of an atom's mass. In 1913, Niels Bohr proposed an orbital model of the atom, where electrons circled the dense nucleus in stable, well-defined orbits. Then in 1917,

Rutherford discovered that the nucleus is composed of positively charged particles, which he later named protons.

As the twentieth century progressed, so did the understanding of the atom. In 1916, Gilbert Lewis found that it was the electrons that bound atoms together to form molecules. By 1926, scientists discarded the simple orbital model of the atom for one with more complex electron orbits. And in 1932, James Chadwick, working in Rutherford's laboratory at Cambridge University in England, discovered neutrons.

By 1938, German scientists discovered nuclear fission. Nuclear fission is the action of breaking a heavy atom into smaller atoms (Figure 19). Otto Hahn used a small laboratory device known as a neutron howitzer to shoot neutrons at a uranium atom and discovered that instead of creating a heavier uranium isotope, a new element appeared—barium. Its presence meant that the uranium nucleus had split into two smaller nuclei, forming two smaller atoms, one of which was barium. Other scientists supporting the research found that in addition to barium, the action produced energy and free neutrons, which could, in theory, break open other nuclei and start a chain reaction.

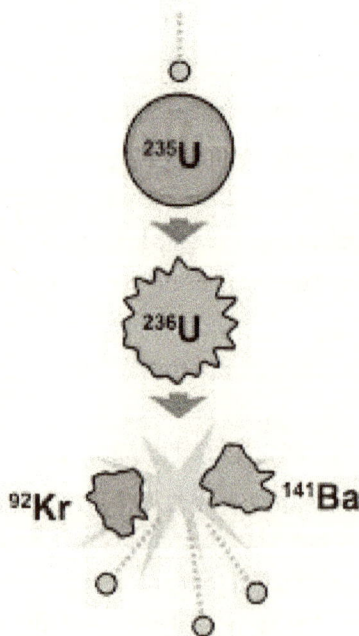

Figure 19. Nuclear fission reaction.

Before this, however, back in 1932, scientists had discovered nuclear fusion. In nuclear fusion, two small atoms are smashed together to form a larger atom (Figure 20). This action also releases energy. The path to fusion's discovery began years earlier as scientists were trying to discover how the sun produces energy. Originally, scientists believed that the sun burned by combustion, the same way a fire burns on earth. However, as geologists were discovering that it took at least several hundred thousand years to form the earth's mountains and oceans, it became clear there was not enough fuel for the sun to burn that long using combustion. A breakthrough came in 1905, when Albert Einstein published his mass-energy equivalence formula, $E = mc^2$, which says that a small amount of matter can be transformed into a vast amount of energy. If hydrogen atoms in the sun were being fused together to form helium atoms, and a bit of the hydrogen's mass is being converted into energy, then the sun would have enough fuel to shine for 100 billion years, as British astrophysicist Sir Arthur Eddington proposed in 1920.

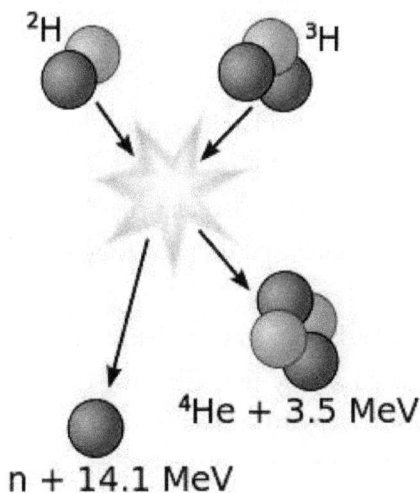

Figure 20. Nuclear fusion reaction.

The first laboratory fusion was accomplished in 1932 by Australian physicist Mark Oliphant, who, along with Chadwick, was working in Rutherford's laboratory at Cambridge University. Oliphant built a particle accelerator, which he used to shoot heavy hydrogen nuclei at various targets.

In one such experiment, he was surprised to find helium present after the collision. Furthermore, the particles that were released by the collision had more energy than the ones he initially shot. He speculated that fusion was occurring—the heavy hydrogen was being converted into helium and releasing energy in the process. In 1939, Hans Bethe, a German scientist working in the United States, would describe this process mathematically, proving Eddington's idea that fusion powered the sun and the other stars.

The discovery of fission by German scientists in 1938 caused quite a stir in the scientific community. Leo Szilard, a Hungarian-born scientist living in the United States, was particularly disturbed. He had formulated back in 1933 that fission could be used to spawn a neutron-driven chain reaction that would release a tremendous amount of energy. He was concerned that Nazi Germany would use this idea to create a bomb.

He sought out his friend and colleague Enrico Fermi to conduct fission experiments with him at Columbia University in New York. Their research confirmed his thesis: a fission chain reaction was possible if the right materials were used. This success gave Szilard even greater concern: German scientists would soon be replicating his work. He decided the US president needed to know about this. With the help of colleagues and friends, Szilard drafted a letter to the president, had Albert Einstein sign it, and had it delivered by Alexander Sachs, an acquaintance who was serving in the Franklin Roosevelt administration.

In October 1939, Sachs brought the letter before President Roosevelt informing him of the possibility that Germany could begin developing an atomic bomb. The letter cited Germany's recent decision to stop selling uranium from its Czechoslovakian mines as evidence of the country's interest. Roosevelt formed the Advisory Committee on Uranium to study the problem. Over the next two and a half years, this advisory committee morphed into the Manhattan Project with the mission to develop a full-scale atomic bomb.

The Manhattan Project became a major covert operation during the war years. It built two nuclear reactors—one in Tennessee and the other in Washington State—to enrich uranium and create plutonium. At its peak, it employed 130,000 at the reactors and various research sites around the country. All told, bomb development cost roughly $2 billion, around $26 billion in 2014 dollars. On July 16, 1945, it detonated the first atomic bomb at the Alamogordo Bombing and Gunnery Range in New Mexico (Figure 21).

Figure 21. First fission bomb test, July 1945.

The idea of developing a fusion bomb was first mentioned by Italian physicist Enrico Fermi in a casual conversation with Hungarian physicist Edward Teller in the fall of 1941. Both scientists were living in the United States and a part of what would become the Manhattan Project. Teller championed the idea of a fusion bomb in the project's early days, but Robert Oppenheimer, the Manhattan Project's scientific leader, decided to focus on the simpler fission bomb. In 1950, however, after the Soviet Union detonated its own fission bomb, US president Harry Truman commissioned a crash program to develop a hydrogen bomb.

Led by Teller, the United States produced and detonated a fusion device in two and a half years. The first device was detonated over the Eniwetok Atoll in the Pacific Ocean, in November 1952. It produced a 10.4-megaton blast—almost five hundred times more powerful than the bomb dropped on

Nagasaki seven years earlier. In 1954, the United States exploded the first genuine hydrogen bomb. Smaller than the first device, it was deployable by aircraft and had a yield of 15 megatons. Nuclear power had not only begun but also was accelerating at a frenetic pace.

The impact of nuclear power on the world was immediate and dramatic. Within two months of the first successful bomb detonation, America used the new weapon to bring an end to World War II. On August 6, 1945, the first atomic bomb dropped on the Japanese city of Hiroshima. It contained 141 pounds of uranium-235 and produced a 16-kiloton blast[3] that killed roughly 75,000 people outright, and perhaps another 75,000 over time due to radiation poisoning. It destroyed 70 percent of the city's buildings: all of the buildings within a mile of the blast center were razed. Fires burned a four-and-a-half-square-mile area.

Three days later a second atomic bomb was dropped; this one on Nagasaki, Japan. It contained 14 pounds of plutonium-238 and produced a 21-kiloton blast. Between 40,000 and 75,000 people were killed outright, but ultimately the number that perished reached around 80,000. Though this blast was more powerful than the first one, a part of the city was shielded by hillsides, reducing the overall impact. Nevertheless, fires raged for days throughout the city.

That night, an Imperial Council was held where the emperor of Japan directed his cabinet ministers to initiate surrender to the Allies. In a speech broadcast over radio on August 15, he informed the Japanese people of his intent to surrender, citing the new weapon as the primary reason for his decision:

> [T]he enemy has begun to employ a new and most cruel bomb, the power of which to do damage is, indeed, incalculable, taking the toll of many innocent lives. Should we continue to fight, not only would it result in an ultimate collapse and obliteration of the Japanese nation, but also it would lead to the total extinction of human civilization.[4]

---

[3] That is, a blast that is the equivalent of 21,000 tons of TNT being detonated.
[4] "Text of Hirohito's Radio Rescript," *New York Times*, August 15, 1945, 3 (accessed August 8, 2015).

A formal ceremony of surrender took place on September 2, 1945, in Tokyo Bay, aboard the battleship USS *Missouri*.

After the war, the United States proposed that the United Nations assume responsibility for atomic weapons. This proposal was rejected, however, by the Soviet Union, which saw that the plan would effectively lock in a nuclear advantage for the United States. Instead they called for universal disarmament, which the United States rejected. Ultimately neither proposal was adopted. America continued testing atomic weapons, conducting blasts in the Pacific's Bikini Atoll in July 1946.

Meanwhile, the Soviet Union leveraged a network of spies to accelerate its own bomb making. Spies within the Manhattan Project had been passing secrets to the Soviet Union since at least 1944. The first Soviet atom bomb was detonated in August 1949. A near replica of the Nagasaki bomb, it came years ahead of when America thought the Soviets should first have such a device.

By 1953 the Soviets also had a hydrogen bomb. In August 1953, only nine months after America detonated its first device, the Soviet Union exploded its first (semi)thermonuclear device. It produced a 400-kiloton blast. Two years later, a second thermonuclear device—its first deployable bomb—was exploded in November 1955. It had a yield of 1.6 megatons.[5] In October 1961, the Soviet Union exploded the largest bomb ever made. It produced a 58-megaton blast over the Arctic Ocean. Soviet premier Nikita Khrushchev boasted, "It could have been bigger, but then it might have broken all the windows in Moscow, 4,000 miles away."

While a thermonuclear bomb could destroy any city or any other target, Americans and Soviets still had to find ways to get them to their targets. Originally, America depended on its fleet of air force bombers for such a task. However, after it was clear that the Soviets were developing missile technology borrowed from the now defunct Nazi program, the United States responded with its own missile development.

Nazi Germany had made the world's first ballistic missile, the V-2 rocket,

---

[5] Debate is still ongoing on how much of a role spies played in the Soviet's rapid development of a hydrogen bomb.

during World War II. The rocket was based largely on research conducted by American professor Robert Goddard during the 1920s. Over three thousand V-2 missiles were launched at London and Antwerp during the last year of the war, killing an estimated nine thousand people. At the end of the war, both the United States and the Soviet Union scrambled to acquire Nazi missile technology. The head of the Nazi missile program came to America, while the Soviets captured many V-2 staff. Throughout the 1950s, both sides would scale up V-2 designs and place thermonuclear warheads on them.

The Soviet Union invested heavily in missile development in the early 1950s. The result was the first intercontinental ballistic missile (ICBM), the R-7, which flew 3,700 miles on its test launch in August 1957. A month later, a missile carried *Sputnik*, the first satellite, into orbit. A year after that, the United States had its own ICBM, launching the Atlas missile in November 1958; and then its own satellite into orbit in October 1959. By the end of the 1950s, both countries had missiles that could strike targets anywhere in the world.

An arms race ensued as each side raced to build more weapons than the other side. By 1964, the United States had over 2,400 missiles, around 6,800 warheads, and a total throw-weight (blast capacity) of around 7,500 megatons. The Soviet Union had around 375 missiles, 500 warheads, and a throw-weight around 1,000 megatons. And this was still early in the Cold War. At that time, the Soviet Union had fewer weapons than the United States (a fact that was not known to the United States at the time), but each side still possessed enough power to destroy the other side and take a good part of the world with it.

The two sides settled into an intense, indefinite stalemate known as Mutual Assured Destruction. This doctrine promoted the idea that it was in neither side's best interest to launch an attack because the other side would still have enough capacity to retaliate and destroy the initial aggressor. This would be the case whether the responder launched after receiving early warning of the aggressor's launch, or it launched after it bore the full brunt of the aggressor's first strike. In either case, neither side could expect to survive the exchange.

While this may have prevented nuclear genocide during the Cold War, it was expensive as both sides built their arsenals to support the second scenario: where it needed a full retaliatory, second-strike capability. Both sides hardened their missile silos, diversified their missile launch capability (ground launched, mobile ground launch, submarine launched, and aircraft launched), and developed rotation and movement strategies to keep the other side from fixing on a stationary target: if the silos in one area were struck, there were always other places that were not hit from where a missile could be launched in short order.

By the 1970s, both sides were ready to discuss slowing the growth and reducing the expense of building nuclear weapons. Early negotiations focused on limiting the size of nuclear arsenals. The 1972 SALT (strategic arms limitation talks) treaty froze the number of missiles each side had at then-current levels. A later treaty, SALT II, actually reduced the size of the nuclear arsenals. Both parties signed the treaty and abided by it for some time, though the United State never actually ratified it to protest the 1980 Soviet invasion of Afghanistan.

In the 1980s, attempts at arms reduction ended and buildup resumed. The Soviet Union was deploying SS-20 medium-range ballistic missiles aimed at targets in western Europe. The United States increased its defense spending by over 40 percent between 1980 and 1987. The buildup included deployment of Tomahawk cruise missiles and Pershing II medium-range ballistic missiles to western Europe. The buildup also included the Strategic Defense Initiative, a research and development program focused on building a capability to shoot Soviet missiles out of the sky, in defiance of the Mutual Assured Destruction doctrine that had been accepted since the early years of the Cold War. In 1986, the United States opted out of the SALT II agreement, claiming the Soviet Union had violated it.

Thus by the mid-1980s, there were an estimated 40,000 nuclear warheads around the world, the vast majority of which were owned by the United States and the Soviet Union. British Intelligence estimated that even a single medium-sized hydrogen bomb could have wiped out London and everything living for a radius of thirty miles. Clearly, there was enough destructive power to wipe out humankind hundreds of times over, in a single day.

Nuclear weapons made the United States and the Soviet Union into the predominant powers in the second half of the twentieth century. However, they did not use their newfound weapons to conquer other nations and confiscate their land, as had been done since the days when bands roamed the earth. Rather, they used their weapons to *influence* other societies, encouraging these societies, directly or indirectly, to join them in embracing their particular ideology.

The world had changed. World War II revealed that nations around the globe would unite to oppose another nation that sought to overrun a third independent sovereign nation. German expansion into Poland and the rest of Europe had been opposed. Japanese expansion into Manchuria and the Far East had been opposed. Of course, national self-interest would govern the speed of the response to such aggressions; however, that a country was free to take land from another country was, for the most part, passing into history.

That land had lost its luster was taken a step further as the world began returning land acquired during the land grabs of the nineteenth century. Indigenous people were receiving their right to self-rule; decolonization was the trend. Britain gave India its independence in 1947. European masters who could not let go of their former colonies were becoming embroiled in long, bitter wars of liberation. France lost its grip on Vietnam in 1954 after an eight-year struggle. It would lose its hold on Algeria in 1962, after another eight-year struggle. And global media, an emerging force during the time, was increasingly portraying the former colonists as the bad guys—the oppressors who sought to deny people their freedom—a freedom the colonial powers themselves enjoyed.

In place of land, *influence* was becoming the primary indicator of a nation's power. Though less tangible than land, it was the true end game as superpowers sought influence over sovereign nations, encouraging these nations to join their side and to embrace their ideology. And the new leader was whoever could wield this kind of influence.

Nowhere was this shift more apparent than during the Suez Crisis in 1956. On July 26, Gamal Abdel Nasser, president of Egypt, announced that he had just nationalized the Suez Canal. Shareholders of the Suez Canal Company, the French and British company that had operated the canal since its construction in 1869, would receive that day's closing market price for their stock. Outraged by the move, Britain, France, and Israel launched a military response to take back the canal, which began on October 29. Within a few days, the military operation had almost complete control of the canal zone.

In response, the Soviet Union threatened to intervene on Egypt's behalf by starting rocket attacks on Britain, France, and Israel by November 5 and by sending troops into the region. Soviet premier Nikita Khrushchev also added that while he did not wish to start a nuclear war, he was more than willing to allow a conventional war to turn nuclear if that was how things played out.

Meanwhile, the United States moved diplomatically and economically against Britain, France, and Israel. The United States did not want to be seen as supporting colonialism, nor did it want to be seen as being duplicitous, given that it was condemning the Soviet invasion of Hungary, which was occurring at the same time. The United States also wanted to avoid World War III, for even though the United States and the Soviet Union were on the same side of this issue, President Dwight Eisenhower knew he would have to back Britain and France if the conflict escalated. Therefore the United States prompted the United Nations to issue a resolution condemning the attack and calling for the withdrawal of British, French, and Israeli troops. The United Nations also blocked the International Monetary Fund from giving assistance to Britain, which was in dire need of cash at the time. It also worked with Saudi Arabia to block oil sales to Britain and France.

Britain accepted a ceasefire on November 6. Britain and France removed their troops by December, and Israeli troops left in March. In their place, a United Nations peacekeeping force was established. The canal reopened, under Egyptian authority, in April.

The influence of the United States and the Soviet Union forced Britain, France, and Israel to withdraw from the Suez Canal zone. This event, perhaps more than any other event of the decade, signified the shift that had taken place in the world. The old world powers of western Europe had given way to the nuclear superpowers of the United States and the Soviet Union. Both of these superpowers had used their influence—diplomatic, economic, or military—to reverse what some nations perceived to be a form of colonial land grab. The United States also recognized that being one of only two nuclear powers gave it the dual responsibility of not only avoiding nuclear war but also protecting its allies from nuclear attack. Hence, the world began to revolve around the two nuclear superpowers.

The world community would shape itself around these nuclear superpowers throughout the middle to late twentieth century. The Soviet Union had annexed some eastern European countries, such as Latvia and Lithuania, at the beginning of World War II. Other countries, such as Poland and East Germany, were brought under the Soviet umbrella at the end of the war. Together, they comprised the Eastern Bloc—a set of countries that embraced communism, an ideology created by philosopher Karl Marx in the 1840s, as their governance structure. They not only embraced communism but also they believed that the entire world should embrace it.

Opposing this view was the Western Bloc, led by the United States. In addition to the United States, countries from western Europe, such as Britain and France, and non-European nations, such as Japan and Australia, worked together to contain communist expansion. The United States and the western European countries formed a military alliance in April 1949, the North Atlantic Treaty Organization (NATO), to support that mission.

In addition to these two groups, there emerged a third set of nations that chose to align to neither superpower. This group, comprised mostly of developing nations, first met in Indonesia in 1955. Later, in 1961, the group formalized the arrangement under the title the Non-Aligned Movement. Led by India, Burma, Indonesia, Egypt, Ghana, and Yugoslavia, the organization pledged a neutral course, resolved to stay out of the Cold War, and committed to focus on peace, disarmament, and later, the economic development of member nations.

So regardless of whether a nation was a member of the Eastern Bloc, the Western Bloc, or the Non-Aligned Movement, its position in the world community was framed by the existence of nuclear weapons and by those who owned them. And having nuclear weapons remained a requirement for leadership within these blocs. In 1958, France complained to the United States and Britain that it was being excluded as an equal partner in NATO leadership (Britain had gone nuclear in 1952). Annoyed that his concerns were not being taken seriously, French president Charles de Gaulle established France's own nuclear program, and later broke ties with NATO in 1966.

The two blocs coexisted in the state of constant tension that became known as the Cold War. This conflict continued for four decades. Rather than risk direct confrontation, however, the two sides fought each other using a series of proxy wars such as in Korea, Vietnam, and Afghanistan, as well as smaller conflicts in Africa, Asia, South America, and Central America. In addition, global propaganda, espionage, assassination, and even the Space Race were used to gain dominance in a region or even psychological advantage, without head-to-head confrontation.

The Cold War finally ended in 1989 following a long period of Soviet economic stagnation. In the 1970s, the Soviet Union had been spending around 25 percent of its gross national product on its military, while neglecting other areas of its economy. When the price of oil (its main export) dropped in the early 1980s, its economy floundered. At the same time, the United States was initiating another arms buildup, and attempts to match it put further strain on the Soviet economy. Perhaps most important, a new generation of leadership began to consider that the Soviet Union's lack of prosperity was the result of internal structural flaws. In the mid-1980s, the Soviet Union desperately sought to reduce military spending so it could focus on internal reforms. The country negotiated an agreement with the United States to reduce nuclear arsenals, and in 1989, at a summit in Malta, both the Soviet Union and the United States declared the Cold War over. The Soviet Union dissolved in 1991.

The story of nuclear weapons did not end with the Soviet Union. As with other dominating innovations, once invented, they began to spread. Britain exploded its first atomic bomb in 1952 and its first hydrogen bomb in 1957. France detonated its first atomic bomb in 1960 and its first hydrogen bomb in 1968. China exploded an atomic bomb in 1964 and a hydrogen bomb in 1967.

Israel is believed to have developed nuclear weapons around 1968, though this has never been publicly confirmed. Rivals India and Pakistan became nuclear nations and have even conducted their own arms race. India detonated its first atomic bomb in 1974, prompting Pakistan to respond with its own nuclear program, which exploded a bomb in 1998. North Korea became the most recent atomic nation, conducting a successful underground atomic test in 2006 and thermonuclear test in 2017.

Of course, to be a credible threat, nations also need to have nuclear delivery vehicles. The original five nuclear nations (United States, Russia, England, France, and China) all have ballistic missiles. Israel's Jericho III ballistic missile went into service in 2008. Pakistan bought short-range DF-11 ballistic missiles from China, and India and North Korea are in the process of developing their own.

As other nations acquired nuclear weapons, American leadership could sense some of its power dissipating. In the early 1970s, American president Richard Nixon and Secretary of State Henry Kissinger sensed the world was shifting from bipolar to multipolar. Kissinger even predicted that China, Japan, and an independent western Europe would eventually join the United States and the Soviet Union in world leadership. Of these regions, all five were emerging economic powers and four were nuclear powers.

In the early twenty-first century, there are nine nuclear weapon nations. There was a common feeling in the 1960s that there would be thirty to thirty-five nuclear nations by this time. The slower-than-expected spread can largely be attributed to the Nuclear Non-proliferation Treaty, whose 189 signatory countries (as of 2014) have decided that a world with fewer nuclear weapons is a better one, even if that means they never get any. In fact, discussions of world leadership power rarely mention nuclear weapons anymore. Forums, books, and articles written over the last ten years tend to focus on whether America is losing economic power relative to other nations. However, despite that nuclear missiles and potential holocaust do not loom large like they did during the Cold War, it only takes one nation (say, North Korea, Iran, or Iraq) to remind us that nuclear weapons are still dominating and they are still spreading. They have not gone away—they have just moved to the background.

Nuclear power was based on centuries of scientific research. When fully developed, it created a destructive power that could raze an entire city in an instant. With missile technology, its destruction power could annihilate an entire nation in a day. Its two principle owners—the United States and the Soviet Union—became world leaders in the latter half of the twentieth century. While their large economies contributed to this leadership, these two superpowers stood out even among industrialized nations. Their leadership power, however, was not manifested in land grabs as leadership power had been until this time. Rather it served to reshape the world community around the two superpowers and their respective ideologies. Eventually nuclear weapons began to spread and with this spread power began to shift. However, nations intervened to stem the diffusion of nuclear weapons, believing that the world would be safer without them. Ultimately, the Soviet Union collapsed, due to internal instability, leaving the United States as the sole superpower. Today, nuclear power exists as part of the world environment, in a quasi-stabile arrangement among nations, though ever present.[XXXVI]

The Dominating Innovation Pattern

Over the last three chapters, we have taken a walk through history to reveal how dominating innovations impact societal leadership. These innovations created leadership power for the societies that acquired them early. This power came in the form of increased military and/or economic power. This power enabled the society to become the leader in its region; though for the last two dominating innovations, that region covered the entire world.

The power derived from these innovations was not permanent. It lasted only as long as the adopting society held a monopoly on it. Over time, the innovation would begin to seep out and the monopoly would be lost. For a time, the monopoly would be replaced by an oligopoly, with a few societies enjoying privileged ownership status. Ultimately, however, the innovation would become widespread and parity would be reestablished across all leading societies. A leading society that did not possess the materials to produce the innovation could acquire it through trade and commerce (e.g., Japanese procurement of steel in the early nineteenth century).

Once the innovation became common, power parity was reestablished (e.g., gunpowder in western Europe). However, this power was still a higher level than that which had existed before the innovation came along. As such, societies that wanted to compete for leadership still had to acquire the innovation before they would be in contention (e.g., acquisition of gunpowder rifles by Native American tribes in the late nineteenth century).

A dominating innovation could be made obsolete by another innovation (e.g., horse cavalry being overrun by petroleum-propelled armies at the beginning of World War II). An originating dominating innovation could even be made obsolete by its own spin-offs (e.g., chariots made obsolete by cavalry).

Moreover, dominating innovations had their impact during the long periods when societies were not changing societal levels. During these times, leading societies existed at the same level, so dominating innovation introduced the power needed to make a society rise above equals. Once societies began to change levels, however, the influence of the dominating innovation waned. The focus shifted to the new way of managing resources, and the dominating innovation became of secondary importance. To be sure, a leading society still needed all of the dominating innovations, but by virtue of being at a higher level, it could invariably acquire it as needed (e.g., again, Japanese procurement of steel in the nineteenth century).

...

So, acquiring a dominating innovation early is the second way a society becomes a leader. The first was jumping to a new societal level first. But what happens when all societies are at the same societal level, and all have the same dominating innovations? There is a final way that societies have used to become a leader, and it applies in these conditions.

Chapter 12
Four Leadership Power Sources

A quick search on the Internet will reveal different ways a person can fix a lopsided table. The easiest way is just to move the table. Perhaps the floor is uneven and rotating or moving the table will fix the problem. Another technique is putting a sliver of cork from a wine bottle or a piece of clear plastic under the short leg; that will usually do the trick. If that does not work, commercial levelers are usually required. These screw into the bottom of the four legs. One can balance the table by screwing them in or out. Usually, they are so thick that one is needed on each leg. Almost no one recommends sawing down three legs to match the shortest one.

We have identified two ways a society can rise into a leadership position: by being the first society to jump to a new societal level, or by being the first society to acquire a new dominating innovation. This answer, however, begs another question: what happens when all societies are at the same level and all have the same dominating innovation? Who becomes the leader then? Truth be told, there is one more way to become the leader. In the absence of the previous two methods, a society can achieve a leadership position by *best managing the four leadership power sources*. Understanding this, however, first requires that we understand what leadership truly is.

Four Sources of Leadership Power

Former US president and army general Dwight Eisenhower once said, "The essence of leadership is to get others to do something because they think you want it done and because they know it is worth while doing." This summation applies as much to societies as it does to individuals: leadership amounts to influence, whether it is acting on a person or a collective group of people. Societal leadership, therefore, is the ability for one society to influence another society to act consistently with the former's intent. However, power is required for this to happen: societies tend not to defer to those without it. So where does this power come from? There are four principle sources of leadership power: military strength, wealth, population, and foreign reach. By growing these four leadership power sources, a society can grow its influence.

Military strength is perhaps the most ancient and obvious source of leadership power. It is the ability to destroy another society's resources—its labor, its assets, its capital—using force. In preceding chapters, we saw how the societies that acquired dominating innovations gained power over rivals. In each case, that power came in the form of increased military strength. Bronze weapons helped to make Sumer into a military power, while iron weapons enabled Bantu people to more easily expand and to assimilate their neighbors. Chariots enabled the Hittites to grow powerful, while mounted archers propelled Assyria's expansion. Firearms made the Ottoman Turks into a force to be reckoned with, while petroleum propulsion enabled mechanized armies to spread the British Empire. In addition, nuclear weapons militarily set apart the United States and the Soviet Union from their peers.

The increased military strength did not always mean that a society had to conduct warfare and conquer rivals, however. Military strength could give a society the ability to threaten another society into submission (a common tactic of the Mongols). Conversely, military strength could be used to make a society into another society's protector, either by defending it in time of conflict or by announcing that it would defend it should the need arise (England's defense of Poland, 1939). Any of these four approaches increased the amount of influence a society had by using increased military strength.

However, military strength alone was generally insufficient for sustained leadership. The Chinese general Sun Tzu once wrote, "[T]here has never been a protracted war from which a country has benefitted." This has been as true in the modern era as it was during the Warring States period. In 1557, both Spain and France declared bankruptcy, with royal treasuries drained and debts run up from multiple decades of continuous warfare. Another kind of power is also necessary for leadership.

Wealth is the second leadership power source. Some of the dominating innovations also provided this source of power. Bronze weapons and tools generated not only military strength for Sumer but also wealth through a thriving trade. Iron metallurgy did the same for the Hittites, creating a metals trade that extended throughout the Near East. Mogul India became a firearms exporter to Europe and the Near East. Petroleum propulsion and the Industrial Revolution would raise the average real wage in Britain by 80 percent during the last half of the nineteenth century.

All of this wealth generated influence for these societies. A rich society is more likely than a poor one to make another society rich. A rich society is more likely to engage in trade or to give foreign aid to another society. Conversely, the impact of a rich society withholding trade or foreign aid is likely to be felt more acutely. As such, rich societies tend to have more influence than poorer ones.

By the mid-1950s, the United States and the Soviet Union had the world's two largest economies, while western Europe's economic output remained relatively low. Western Europe's share of world manufacturing hovered around 25 percent, a level not seen since the early nineteenth century. At this time, the United States and the Soviet Union emerged as the world powers, not only because they possessed nuclear weapons, but also because they had economic might. During the Suez Crisis, the United States applied economic pressure, while the Soviet Union applied military pressure to force two western European powers to withdraw from the canal zone. For the rest of the Cold War, both military and economic pressure would be applied to developing regions of the world in the East-West struggle for hegemony. Economic power had come to rival military power in the game of world influence.

Population is the third leadership power source. All else being equal, a larger population means more power while a smaller population means less power. Of course, this presumes a society has the ability to effectively manage a large population: a large bulging and starving population has never benefitted any society. Population is the power source underlying elevating innovations. When societies adopted a new elevating innovation, they gained the ability to manage resources over a larger population. Tribes manage more people than bands. Chiefdoms manage more people than tribes. Fiefdoms manage more people than chiefdoms. And nation-states manage hundreds of millions while fiefdoms manage only hundreds of thousands (or a few million). Elevating innovations provide the ability to feed and manage larger populations effectively.

Population amplifies the influence of the other power sources. A larger population potentially means a larger army—a larger army that can threaten or conquer, protect or defend another society. A larger population also means a larger economy—an economy that provides a larger market for foreign goods, or one that creates a larger industrial base for producing internal goods. A larger population can also create larger problems when something goes wrong. A neighbor might be able to absorb the refugee problem of a small country experiencing a catastrophe such as civil war, flood, or famine. However, a neighbor is more likely to be harder pressed to deal with the refugee problem of a larger country experiencing those same catastrophes. As such, a larger population raises the stakes, increasing the potential benefits or consequences that one society can impose upon another.

Throughout history, population change has corresponded with influence shifts, though perhaps not right away. Between 2100 and 1700 BCE the population of Sumer declined by three-fifths as a result of rising soil salinity and declining agricultural productivity. With the population loss, Sumer lost its prominence, never to regain it. In contrast, in the nineteenth century, the United States and Russia had the highest growth rates of the world's major powers. Between 1850 and 1900, Russia's population nearly doubled to 136 million, while the United States was next in line with 76 million.[1] These

---

[1] Historical population estimates tend to vary widely based on assumptions made about changing borders. The Russian estimate considers the population within the territory of the Russian Empire at that time.

populations surpassed those of the western European powers: Britain (41 million), France (39 million), and Germany (56 million). However, these population gains did not immediately translate into leadership positions: those would not come for another half century. As such, population helped to give the United States and Russia the *potential* to be leaders; though, other action was required before they could realize leadership.

Foreign reach is the fourth and final leadership power source. Foreign reach is the ability of a society to engage with another society for its benefit. Usually, this takes the form of projecting oneself into the affairs of another society, or by interacting in a way that ensures it obtains what it needs from another society. In either form, it begins with a decision to reach out and *engage* another society. Foreign reach is an independent source of power for it conveys not only intent but also the means to influence.

Foreign reach translates into greater influence as a society internalizes another society. When one society's words are used by children in a foreign country, a part of that society is permanently introduced into the country, even without thinking about it. When a society's inventions, innovations, and even its food become part of another country, it gains influence. Conversely, a society may engage with another society to absorb something, to learn from it, or to gain tools or insights from it. In today's global economy, reciprocal exchanges that benefit both parties in terms of communication and understanding help to build the global village. However, when one society begins to dominate the exchange, it gains power from it, power that can then be used for influence.

The absence of foreign reach is the primary reason America did not become a world leader until after World War II. Before the war, America had decided to isolate itself—the antithesis of foreign reach. In doing so, it forfeited the leadership position it could have had to the European powers of the nineteenth century. Ultimately, America was forced to engage with the rest of the world. Today, foreign reach expresses itself in a variety of ways. In the United States, one can find a Russian-based news channel, broadcasting in Spanish. Technology has enabled foreign reach to extend further, with more precision, than ever before.

So, by growing these four leadership power sources, a society grows in its ability to convey influence. Military strength conveys influence through the use of *force*. Wealth conveys influence through *economics*. Population conveys influence through *mass*. And foreign reach conveys influence through *relationship*. However, it is not enough for a society to target one particular source to the exclusion of the others. Effectively managing the power sources requires that they grow in concert with each other because they are so intertwined. Effectively managing their growth requires that a society understand not only the power sources but also the interaction between sources.[XXXVII]

Power Source Interaction

The four power sources all interact in ways that reinforce and strengthen each other (Figure 22).

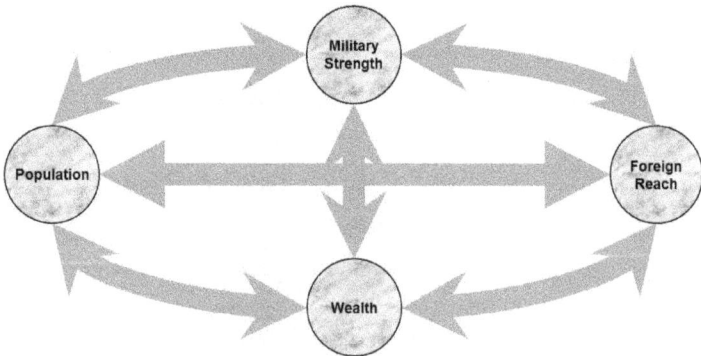

Figure 22. Interaction between leadership power sources.

As mentioned, population builds two other power sources: military strength and wealth. Population supports military strength by providing the labor needed for larger armies and navies. Throughout the Middle Ages, Britain lived in fear of France's larger population and its ability to field a larger army. During the nineteenth century, Russia eclipsed both Britain and France in population and was able to create a larger army than either of its European rivals. By 1900 Russia had a total of 1.1 million army and navy personnel, while Britain and France had 524,000 and 715,000, respectively. Even later in the twentieth century, nations that used human wave tactics (e.g., China during the Korean War and Iran in the Iran-Iraq War) required large populations to establish large infantry divisions that could absorb losses and continue fighting.

However, this link between population and military strength works both ways: military strength enables societies to conquer other societies and annex their populations. This is most obvious in the time-honored military tradition of conquering one's foes and then inducting them into your own army. The Mongols practiced this to a tee. Conquered territories meant a fresh supply of soldiers. No sooner was a society conquered than its young men were impressed into the Mongol army. Centuries later, Russia expanded eastward across an entire continent continued because it had the military capability to conquer and annex disparate Mongol remnants and chiefdoms.

Also mentioned earlier, a large population provides the potential for a large economy, with more people to both produce and consume goods. In 2010, China, with its 1.3 billion people, surpassed Japan as the world's second-largest economy. Both nations ended that year with gross domestic products (GDPs) at around $5 trillion. China began its rise in 1978, when Premier Deng Xiaoping overhauled Chinese economic policies to favor free markets. Since that time, an estimated 300 million people have been lifted out of poverty. However, per capita income in China still lags at around $3,600, roughly on par with Algeria and El Salvador. While population has the potential to generate wealth, it takes time and management ability to realize that wealth.

Of course, wealth supports population. Wealth creates a healthier and more vibrant population. Wealthier nations can spend more on health care and education than can poor countries. A wealthier nation can invest in infrastructure, such as sanitation and water quality, making for a more vibrant and healthy population. Of course, healthier, educated, and more vibrant populations create stronger societies.

The link between military strength and wealth is well documented. Paul Kennedy, in *Rise and Fall of the Great Powers*, summarizes the results of European Wars fought between 1519 and 1659:

All states were placed under severe strain by the constant drain of resources for military and naval campaigns.... The victory of the anti-Habsburg forces was, then, a marginal and relative one. They had managed, but only just, to maintain the balance between their material base and their military power better than their Habsburg opponents. At least some of the victors had seen that the sources of national wealth needed to be exploited carefully, and not recklessly, during a lengthy conflict. They may also have admitted, however reluctantly, that the trader and the manufacturer and the farmer were as important as the cavalry officer and the pikeman.

Hence, wealth becomes the ultimate governor of military strength: its limits define the limits of military strength during sustained, prolonged conflict. However, even in peacetime, wealth governs military strength. Wealth is the means by which superior weapons are developed. In 2014, the United States was able to spend over $67 billion on military research and development alone. And wealth still governs the number of weapons and the size of forces. In the decade before its demise, the Soviet Union routinely spent 20–25 percent of its GDP on its military; such expenditures were no more affordable in the twentieth century than they were in the seventeenth.

The flip side of the military strength–wealth link is just as strong: military strength supports wealth generation. The historical use of military strength has been to protect supply lines and commerce. Such military usage dates back to ancient Mesopotamia and continues today as modern navies patrol the shipping lanes off the coast of Somalia for pirates. Military strength can also generate wealth through conquest. Spanish conquests in the Americas filled coffers with gold in the 1500s. Britain expansion and colonization enabled the import of cheap raw materials to its manufacturing industries in the 1800s. And in 1991, Iraq invaded Kuwait, at least in part to seize its profitable oil fields. Finally, in the short run, military strength can generate wealth by stimulating an economy. Having to establish a wartime infrastructure lifted the United States out of the Great Depression in the early 1940s. Entire industries, such as automobiles, were converted to meet immediate and substantial wartime demand. This created fortunes for some individuals, such as Henry Ford, and full employment for nearly everyone. (Note how these short-term bursts of spending contrasted with the drawn-out European wartime expenditures of the seventeenth century.) So while it happens in different ways, the causal linkage between military strength and wealth remains perhaps the clearest and most conspicuous of all the power source links.

The final and perhaps most obtuse links are those involving *foreign reach*. However, the links become clearer when examined in turn. Military strength can be used to extend foreign reach. Long after a foreign war has ended, aspects of the victor's culture and even its infrastructure become infused in the societies of former foes and allies alike. Roman roads spanned Europe for centuries. American television shows are still seen across Europe. English is commonly taught in Asian as well as European schools. Correspondingly, relationships developed through decades of foreign interaction lead to enhanced military strength through mutual defense treaties, prepositioning of forces and supplies, or even providing soldiers in time of war, as commonwealth states have done for Britain.

Foreign reach enhances wealth because when you have an established presence, business follows more easily. Foreign reach helps to open new markets and makes it more likely profitable trade will occur. Foreign reach means greater access to distribution channels or population segments. It also means copyrights are more likely to be enforced, safety standards are more likely to be followed, and trade agreements are more likely to be equitable. In short, all the arrangements needed to promote wealth generation in another country become easier with greater foreign reach. Conversely, wealthier nations generally have an easier time developing foreign reach than do poorer nations. Wealthier nations can also invest more in relationships, in infrastructure, and in establishing a foreign presence. Poorer countries tend to have to focus internally to address domestic challenges and obligations.

Finally, foreign reach interacts with population. Historically, foreign reach has meant acquiring dominion over remote populations without the use of military force. Vassal states, trade, or diplomacy are typical ways a society has gained access to remote areas. (British presence in India began as a commercial venture.) Conversely, a society with a large population has more people who can emigrate to a foreign land, and in doing so, carry a bit of their home country's culture with them. The immigration waves of the late nineteenth and late twentieth centuries infused and enriched American culture with numerous elements of foreign cultures, from pizza to Cinco de Mayo celebrations.

So the leadership sources interact with each other and can reinforce and strengthen each other. However, this does not happen automatically. History has shown that an imbalance in the sources can have a detrimental effect. Societies that grew one source at the expense of the others often lost influence, and some even grew unstable. In any event, understanding the power sources, and their interactions, enables us to more clearly see how transformative innovations changed the societies that acquired them early.[XXXVIII]

Innovation and the Power Sources

The power sources are the interconnection between the transformative innovations and leadership position. The transformative innovations swelled one or more of the power sources for a society, and that in turn gave that society influence over its rivals. When the society amassed enough influence, it became the leader. Whoever acquired the innovation first gained a head start on amassing power.

As mentioned before, dominating innovations directly impacted military strength and sometimes wealth. Through the interaction between sources, however, they may have impacted the other sources as well but to a lesser extent. Preconditioning innovations acted largely on wealth, but their main contribution was to create an environment for elevating innovations to flourish. Elevating innovations, in contrast, worked on all four leadership power sources directly. This enabled them to create a sustainable platform of power from which a society could build into a new level. Printing provides the best illustration of this.

Printing built population. Printing standardized legal code, making laws more consistent and more credible. This built trust in rule-of-law so that it could ultimately replace remote authority as a governance basis. Rule-of-law can manage more people than can remote authority, so while fiefdoms, through remote authority, governed hundreds of thousands, nation-states, through rule-of-law, could govern hundreds of millions.

Printing built military strength. The period following the advent of printing saw a growth in the bureaucratic machinery needed to sustain larger armies. Improved methods of taxation, which were superior to feudal levies, emerged to sustain larger forces. This period saw a growth in infantry, more complex fortification, and larger fleets of ships. The ability to manage these larger forces improved as operating procedures became more standardized, enabling subordinate units to operate more independently, farther from headquarters, but with greater consistency.

Printing built wealth. Printing spurred on new industries such as publishing, news reporting, and even fiction writing. More broadly, printing helped to create new mechanisms for financing ventures and indemnifying investments. Printing helped to foster these mechanisms by allowing a concept to be put on paper, disseminated widely, adjusted as needed, and updated more quickly than ever before. Printing led to more paper currency, which improved market liquidity. Perhaps most important, printing helped to standardize the rules of commerce and business. Weights and measures could be standardized; accounting could be made more precise, record keeping more sophisticated, and planning more effective. Business knowledge could accumulate.

Printing built foreign reach. The rapid improvement process that printing facilitated also helped to create the bureaucratic tools needed to establish overseas administrations, the commerce tools needed to develop overseas economies, and the navigation tools needed to traverse the high seas. Transatlantic trade increased eightfold between 1510 and 1550, and another threefold between 1550 and 1610.

So, printing directly contributed to all four leadership power sources. It did this by changing the way institutions of these power sources managed their resources. Such changes would have been the case for each of the elevating innovations, since they all shared this common role.

But such power did not come instantly. In ancient times, it often took centuries for an innovation to mature into something useful for generating power (e.g., iron metallurgy). In more recent times, while an innovation may have developed faster, it still took decades for power to well up after it was introduced. Such was the case with printing in the sixteenth century. While the full power of printing would not be realized until the establishment of the nation-state, it helped to drive change long before then. Printing created a swell of technology, which societies then used to gain advantage over each other.

> The fairer aspect of this increasing commercial and colonial rivalry [between European states] was the parallel upward spiral in knowledge in science and technology.... Improved cartography, navigational tables, new instruments like the telescope, barometer, backstaff, and gimbaled compass, and better methods of shipbuilding helped to make maritime travel a less unpredictable form of travel. New crops and plants not only brought better nutrition but also were a stimulus to botany and agricultural science. Metallurgical skills, and indeed the whole iron industry, made rapid progress; deep-mining techniques did the same. Astronomy, medicine, physics, and engineering also benefited from the quickening economic pace and the enhanced value of science. The inquiring, rationalist mind was observing more, and experimenting more; and the printing presses, apart from producing vernacular Bibles and political treatises, were spreading these findings. The cumulative effect of this explosion of knowledge was to buttress Europe's technological—and therefore military—superiority still further.[2]

As printing was applied to different parts of society, change started to occur. Over time, as the innovation was applied to more areas, a web of connections started to form where one application supported, or even reinforced, another. At some point, the web started to fill in, and an inflection point was reached, creating a sudden updraft in power, sending the leading societies in a trajectory toward a new societal level (Figure 23). The more

---

[2] Paul Kennedy, *The Rise and Fall of the Great Powers*, 29.

ambitious societies took steps to embrace the innovation and facilitate this shift, while others resisted the change. The ones who acquired, embraced, and facilitated early gained a head start over rivals in developing their leadership power.

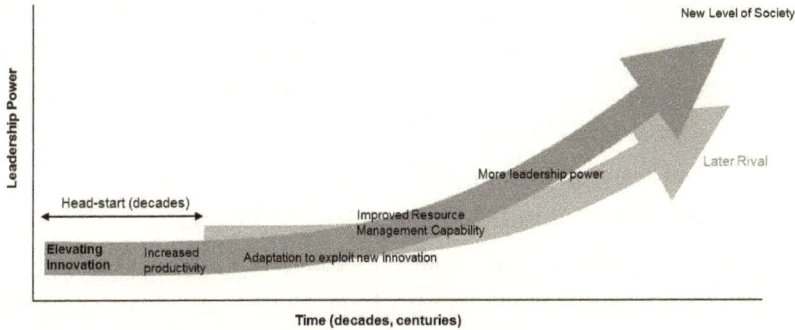

Figure 23. First mover head start.

Because leadership power growth follows an S-curve, a head start of only a few decades could be enough for a society to gain a quasi-permanent advantage. The changes are not always obvious at first, and by the time they become obvious, it is often too late for rivals to catch up. Hence, being the *first mover* has been essential for societal leadership throughout history.[XXXIX]

With this understanding, we can now return to the original question: what happens when no one has exclusive use of a dominating innovation, and everyone is operating at the same societal level? How does a society become the leader?

Power Source Management

Often centuries would pass in between dominating innovations or societal-level changes. Centuries passed between the advents of metallurgy and horse warfare. Even more time passed between the advent of fiefdoms and the nation-state. In the meantime, the leaders continued to change. What governed leadership change during these times?

There was a third way a society could become a leader. A society could become a leader by managing its leadership power sources more effectively than others did. When all countries were at the same societal level, and they all had the same dominating innovations, then the society that best managed these four leadership power sources directly became the leader. Managing the power sources better did not simply mean having more of them; it meant having more of them in the right balance. Having one source rise high above the others could be more detrimental to a society than if they all remained in balance at a lower level. During the nineteenth century, Russia had a large population and a large army compared to its European rivals. However, it did not have the wealth to adequately equip, train, and logistically support it, so its army was less effective. Russia ended up losing the Crimean War and the Russo-Japanese War, and withdrew early from World War I after a disastrous start. So we can see that, in the absence of a dominating or elevating innovation, the society that grows the leadership power sources in balance has the best chance of becoming the leader.

America applied this approach effectively from the middle of the nineteenth to the early twentieth century, rising to challenge European hegemony on the world stage. At the end of the American Civil War, European nations dominated world affairs. In fact, America was viewed by many European states as a rural and relatively unsophisticated nation. However, through immigration and organic growth, America's population rose from 33 million during the Civil War to 133 million by the beginning of World War II. After the Civil War, America shifted from a predominantly agricultural economy to an industrial economy, switching wealth generation from seasonal crops to year-round industrial output. In 1898, America defeated Spain in the Spanish-American War and acquired new holdings in the Caribbean and the Pacific. At the turn of the twentieth century, President Theodore Roosevelt built the US Navy into the third largest in the world, and even sent sixteen ships from the Atlantic Fleet around the world to show its prowess. He commissioned the Panama Canal, which enabled ships to travel from one American coast to the other in thirty days instead of sixty. He also broke up industrial monopolies, realizing that wealth concentrated in the hands of a few was of limited value to the nation. Later, however, after World War I, America retreated into isolationism, self-limiting its involvement in world affairs and its influence on the world stage. Nevertheless, America benefitted from growing its four leadership power sources in balance, giving it potential long before it ever developed nuclear weapons.

Perhaps an even more impressive application of the leadership power approach comes from Meiji Japan. An island with few natural resources, Japan was able to shift from a fiefdom to a leading nation-state in a span of fifty years. Once again, growing the four power sources in balance was the key to its rise.

The Meiji was a reform-minded government that ruled Japan from 1868 to 1912. Its focus was to modernize Japan out of its feudal status. Since the twelfth century, Japan had been ruled by a shogun, or "great general." The shogun loosely oversaw hundreds of semiautonomous local lords, called daimyo. Under the shoguns and daimyo, Japan had remained agricultural, isolated, and outdated—all of which made Japan vulnerable to foreign powers.

Trouble began for the shogunate when it was forced to sign bemeaning treaties that gave foreign powers advantages in trade and other issues. The people, feeling humiliated, rebelled against the Tokugawa shogunate's impotence. A group of reformers wrested authority from the shogun and restored it to the emperor (the emperor had lost authority to rising shogun clans in 1185). The fifteen-year-old emperor adopted the name *Meiji*, which means "enlightened rule." However, while the emperor gained official authority, the reformers made the real decisions on how the country was to be run.

The Meiji pledged to change Japan. This was accomplished symbolically by moving the capital from Kyoto (where it had been since 794 CE) to Edo, now renamed Tokyo, or "eastern capital." The Meiji then issued the Five Charter Oath, which summarized the aims of the new government:

- Establishment of deliberative assemblies;
- Involvement of all classes in carrying out state affairs;

- Revocation of sumptuary laws and class restrictions on employment;
- Replacement of "evil customs" with the "just laws of nature"; and
- An international search for knowledge to strengthen the foundations of imperial rule.

The Meiji undertook reforms to transition from feudalism to a nation-state. In one of their first moves, the reformers replaced *hans* (manors) with prefectures, and daimyo with governors: this placed all the land under the authority of the emperor. (Many of the landowners knew that change was coming one way or another, so by accepting a position as governor, they could preserve some level authority in the new order.)

The Meiji then commissioned a team to study foreign constitutions and identify the one that would best serve as a model for their own. They reviewed several before settling on Germany's. A new constitution was adopted in 1889, establishing Japan as a constitutional monarchy, though much power was retained by the emperor and the constitution contained little provision for personal freedoms.

The Meiji constitution also established a bicameral legislature. Only a small minority of the population could actually vote for their representative in the lower house, though: male land owners, over the age of twenty-five, who paid more than fifteen yen per year in taxes (about 1 percent of the population). The upper house was composed of former nobles and imperial appointees. Furthermore, all new legislation still had to be approved by the emperor.

While the population of Japan grew from 33 million to 51 million during the Meiji period (1868 to 1912), the greater impact came, not from increased population, but from reforms that freed up the population to realize its potential: potential that had been shackled under feudal lords. Political reforms, a new justice system, and a new education system, all based on Western models, gave people more power—to an extent.

Labor reform freed workers from their agricultural land holdings and allowed them to choose their own occupations in the new industries that were forming. Many of the former daimyo and samurai who were able to adapt to the new economy became industrialists.

The Meiji introduced a justice system based on the French model, and an education system based on the American model. The new public school system would ultimately provide at least six years of education for every child, stressing mathematics, reading, and duty to the emperor. The Meiji legal system was patterned after the ones used in France and Germany.

The Meiji increased wealth for Japan by creating a market economy, building infrastructure, and incubating industries. In the early 1870s, the government continued land reform by legalizing private ownership. They established a national currency, developed commerce law, created a tax code, and built financial institutions such as stock exchanges to make it all work.

The Meiji built infrastructure, such as roads, railroads, bridges, and shipyards, and strung telegraph cable throughout Japan. Government incubated industries by building manufacturing plants at government expense, and ultimately selling them to private investors on reasonable terms. In this way mining, textiles, sugar, glass, cement, chemicals, munitions, and dozens more industries grew at amazing rates, accelerating the shift to a market economy. Even experimental agricultural stations were created to improve output on limited land. Later, after the government curbed direct investment in new industries (by the 1880s, there were enough private investors to continue making progress), the government fostered industry through subsidies and other incentives.

Eventually Japan would become "the Britain of Asia," securing raw materials from remote parts of Asia, converting them into manufactured goods, and either consuming them or exporting them to other parts of Asia. By the end of the Meiji period, Japan had become an industrial giant. After World War I, Japan's industrial success only grew as it expanded to fill the Asian markets vacated by war-weary European nations.

Growing strong militarily was as much a part of Japan's rise as was industrialization. The Meiji believed modernizing the military was essential to keep Japan from being colonized—a fait happening to other Asia countries. It began modernizing by disestablishing feudal militias and replacing them with a national army that used conscription to fill its ranks. Because conscription did not recognize the social distinctions of samurai or daimyo, it infuriated the former ruling classes. Even peasants resisted this new obligation. Nevertheless, every able-bodied adult male, noble or peasant, was to serve at least a five-year commitment in the reserves.

In another departure from samurai ways, the Meiji embraced firearms. No longer were they considered crude or uncouth. The Meiji built factories in Tokyo and Osaka that manufactured rifles, gunpowder, ammunition, and eventually machine guns.

The Meiji also sought help from Western advisors to structure the Japanese army. Once again, the Meiji studied several models and selected the French as the best one for its army. The government brought in French advisors to help form the army, and even sent cadets to France and other parts of Europe, and to the United States to see how modern armies functioned. The Meiji had French doctrine translated into Japanese, and had French officers teach it in the newly established military academy in Kyoto.

The Meiji chose the British to help build its navy. The British took to the request with alacrity, helping to build a fleet that could prevent any foreign incursion like the one that led to the downfall of the Tokugawa shogunate. Japan bought British warships to expand its fleet. Meanwhile, Dutch engineers constructed naval bases and army bases to provide the logistics and maintenance infrastructure needed.

The senior ranks of the military resembled that of Germany. The Meiji established the Supreme War Council, which resembled the German General Staff. Its chief of staff had direct access to the emperor and could bypass any war minister. The War Office was replaced by a War Department and a Naval Department.

The new national army was first tested when it had to put down a samurai rebellion. Some members of the former ruling class had resisted change throughout the early years of the Meiji period. They continued to revolt and foment small uprisings. Finally, in February 1877, a 10,000-man samurai army sought to restore the old order. Early in the conflict, the national army attacked it with a force of roughly equal size. After an eight-day battle, both sides had incurred roughly 4,000 casualties. However, the national army was able to replenish its ranks with conscripts while the samurai rebels could not. By the next major battle, the ranks of the national army had swelled to over 25,000, prompting mass surrender by the samurai. The rebellion ended in

September when the last 40 samurai and their leader were killed. The power of a national army over feudal militias had been proven.

During the 1870s, Japan came to believe that it needed to establish a security perimeter beyond the home islands. Russian encroachment from the north finally prompted Japan to push beyond its borders. It began to occupy the Kurile Islands to the north in 1875, and the Ryukyu Islands to the south in 1879. Eventually, Japan would develop policies to justify expanding farther.

Japan's first national confrontation was against China. In 1894, Korea was a vassal state of China's, but Japan believed China was too weak to stave off Russian aggression: it had to control this strategic peninsula itself. The Japanese navy initiated war by destroying a Chinese squadron off the Bay of Asan, on Korea's west coast. Over the coming months, the Japanese navy and army inflicted a series of decisive defeats upon Chinese forces in Korea, Manchuria, and Taiwan. By March 1895, Japan controlled the sea approaches to Beijing; China sued for peace. In the settlement, Japan gained the rights to Korea, Port Arthur and the Liandong Peninsula, and Taiwan, but Western powers forced Japan to return most of the land (it kept Taiwan). This infuriated Japan and encouraged it to continue building its military to prevent such a humiliation from happening again.

By the turn of the twentieth century, Japan's military had attained nearly equal footing with Western powers. In 1900, it would join the Western powers in China, helping to suppress the Boxer Rebellion. Then in 1902, it signed a military mutual defense pact with the world's reigning superpower, Great Britain—a feat unimaginable a couple of decades earlier.

In 1904, the perhaps inevitable war between Japan and Russia began. Once again, Russia appeared intent on moving into the Korean peninsula. Japan sought a treaty with Tsarist Russia on the matter, but was rebuffed. The Japanese responded by attacking the Russian naval fleet at Port Arthur in February. The Japanese army then landed, and a siege of the harbor began. Russia's Baltic Fleet could not arrive in time to save the harbor before it fell in January 1905. Russia's Baltic Fleet pushed forward anyway toward Russia's other anchorage in Vladivostok. However, the Japanese navy caught it in the Tsushima straits between Korea and Japan and summarily destroyed it in May

1905. Russia sued for peace. The Japanese victory over Russia cemented Japan's position as the leading power in Asia, and showed the world that an Asian nation could defeat a Western power. Korea was formally annexed by Japan in 1910.

World War I gave Japan an opportunity to expand its influence even farther. Due to its alliance with Britain, it entered World War I on the side of the allies. Japan seized the German coaling port at Tsingtao, China; and German controlled islands in the Mariana, Palau, Caroline, and Marshall Island chains. After the war, it kept all the properties except Tsingtao, expanding Japan's security perimeter deep into the Pacific Ocean.

The final leadership power source, foreign reach, was codified in the Five Charter Oaths as the primary way by which the Meiji intended to build the empire. Meiji Japan's ability to acquire knowledge, technology, and practices from the West underlay all of its advances.

At the beginning of the Meiji period, Japan had to remain subservient to Western powers, knowing it was at a military and economic disadvantage. As such, the Meiji pledged continued compliance to the humiliating treaties signed by the Tokugawa shogunate. Despite this, the Meiji quickly reached out to the West, bringing in new technology and state-of-the-art military and economic practices. Over three thousand foreigners came to Japan in the 1870s to teach science, engineering, Western languages, military science, and a host of other fields. Japan also sent its students to Europe and America to gain a firsthand perspective on what made these societies successful.

As decades passed, Japan slowly gained stature in the eyes of European powers. Because it had modeled its society so closely on the West, and because it was a rising Asian power, Western powers begrudgingly began to offer Japan better terms in treaties and negotiations. By the 1890s, Western powers were revising the treaties Japan had been forced to accept. However, Japan still struggled to be considered an equal and a peer with Western powers. This was nowhere more apparent than in the terms European powers granted Japan at the end of the First Sino-Japanese War, where it was denied the colonial holdings that European nations enjoyed.

In time, the playing field leveled. The 1902 Anglo-Japanese Alliance brought not only military support to Japan but also further cultural and technological exchange. By the end of the Meiji period in 1912, Japan had become a military and industrial power on the same level as the Western powers. In 1919, Japan was one of the Big Five powers that shaped the Treaty of Versailles, officially ending World War I. It joined the League of Nations, and it received a mandate over all the Pacific islands it acquired during the war. By developing its four leadership power sources, Japan had become a full player on the world stage.

So in those long spans of history in between dominating innovation, or in the even longer spans between societal-level changes, a society could become a leader by effectively managing its four leadership power sources. Doing so may have required changes in policy, practices, or even culture, and it may have even required social restructuring, but it could make an obscure nation into a leading power in a relatively short time. Both the United States and Japan needed only decades to rise into leadership positions.

That the two nations employed the power source management approach in such different ways, however, suggests that the application has to be tailored to each society. The different applications reflected the different conditions each society faced: America had an abundance of natural resources, while Meiji Japan did not; America was trying to exploit opportunity, while the Meiji was trying to avoid colonization; American culture supported a mixture of deliberateness and laissez-faire, while Japanese culture dictated remaining consistently deliberate. Each nation had to consider its own objectives, conditions, and situation in determining how best to apply the approach. What both applications had in common, however, was management skill, unity of purpose, and a couple of basic principles for using the approach.

The first principle is: Grow the leadership power sources in balance. Allowing one power source to get too far ahead of the others eventually becomes counterproductive for a society. Even when a dominating innovation causes one power source to surge, the others usually catch up at some point. When growing the power sources directly, it is best to keep them somewhat level.

A second principle is: Keep a long-term view. Growing the power sources may require policy changes and infrastructure development, both of which take time to accomplish. Patience is needed to make these changes and to wait for results to appear.

A third principle is: Debt reduces wealth. While debt is a useful tool for temporarily boosting a power source to meet an immediate need, long-term debt is counterproductive, for it gives a society the illusion it is wealthier than it really is. In fact, while per capita national income is a useful metric for indicating a nation's wealth, a better metric may be something akin to

$$Wealth = \frac{Annual\ GDP - National\ Debt}{Population}$$

In this metric, national productivity is offset by the amount of debt a society carries, while normalized on the per capita basis to avoid confusing wealth and population.[3]

The fourth and last principle is: Keep innovating. While the *societal-level change* approach and the *dominating innovation* approach were triggered by specific innovations, the *power sources* approach used innovation in a supporting role. Nevertheless, innovation was a feature of both America's and Japan's rise—from naval ship technology, to industrial incubation, to land reform—finding new and improved ways of doing business was an ever-present requirement for sustaining momentum and progress. Some of the innovations were internally developed, while many innovations were imported from abroad and adapted to a new context. Either way, continuous innovation was, and is, a basic principle of this approach.[XL]

. . .

We have identified the third way a society can become a leader: by effectively managing the four leadership power sources. This is the prevailing approach when societal levels are not changing, and all leading societies have the same

---

[3] While one could challenge whether the units of measure are consistent, the basic idea is that debt works against wealth and needs to be considered as a short-term gap filler rather than added to a long-term power source.

dominating innovation. Under these conditions, the more a society grows and balances its four leadership power sources, the more likely it is to gain the influence it will need to assume a leadership role. While it may be difficult for a society to replicate the unity of effort that drove Meiji Japan, a nation can still use this approach to gradually improve its position on the world stage.

So this completes our walk through history to answer the question: how does a society become a leader? Answering that question required us to develop a framework to explain what has driven leadership throughout history. The framework also highlighted the role innovation played. But having this framework begs another question: what's next? While it is nice to know the past, can it tell us anything about our future? The answers to those questions are "it depends" and "yes."

Part II

OUR FUTURE

Chapter 13
Trend Analysis

In the first decade of this century, the county in which I live built too many elementary schools. The population had grown so quickly that county officials were concerned about overcrowding in schools. Seeking to get ahead of the curve, they built several new elementary schools. However, before the decade was out, the economy went flat, the housing market went bust, and the population growth stopped. Suddenly, the county was faced with the prospect of brand-new schools sitting empty. To deal with the issue, the school board established a series of parent rezoning committees charged with deciding how best to balance attendance across schools and whether to shutter one of the older schools. Neither idea was well received: most committees recommended keeping the status quo. Ultimately, the school board performed some limited rezoning (not without resentment), and the old school remained open. In time, with the recession over and the housing market back, growth resumed, and all the schools filled up, which prompted another round of rezoning. For one Virginia county, looking into the future was not an easy task. However, when it perceived (perhaps overzealously) that a decision had to be made, it made the best decision it could with the information it had.

Part I of this book used history to identify three ways by which a society became a leader: by jumping first to a new societal level, by acquiring first a dominating innovation, or by managing better the four leadership power sources. Part I also revealed how transformative innovations, the elevating and preconditioning innovations, triggered societal-level change.

Part II looks into the future. While all the information presented thus far may have been interesting, one might ask: So what? Can it tell us anything about our world today? Can it tell us anything about our world tomorrow? Let us tackle that second question next. But how do we apply what we have learned to look into the future? The answer is: using trend analysis, but it comes with caveats.

Trend Analysis

Trend analysis is the craft of predicting the future. Unlike fortune telling or soothsaying, however, trend analysis uses analytical rigor to evaluate past events and create a picture of what is plausible or even likely to happen in the future. When the government projects the growth of the economy, it is using trend analysis. When a Wall Street firm projects a company's next-quarter earnings, it is using trend analysis. When a market research firm anticipates the next clothing style, or when the National Weather Service predicts the path of an oncoming storm, they are using trend analysis.

Trend analysis works by identifying a relatively stable pattern in past data and then projecting it into the future. It is rooted in the premise that most things in this world do not change instantly: that which happened yesterday is likely to happen again tomorrow unless disrupted by something else. Therefore, a good trend analysis looks for a long series of repeatable past events, a *trendline*, and projects it into a relatively short future: a *horizon*. Company A may use thirteen weeks of recent sales data to project its sales one week out. Company B might use three years of sales data to forecast its holiday sales. The longer the horizon, the longer the trendline has to be. If the trendline is not linear, say, there is seasonality involved, the firm may have to use additional techniques, such as combining last year's holiday sales with the overall change since last year, to make an accurate projection. Such diverse circumstances and needs have led to the development of numerous approaches for making quantitative trend projections.

Trend analysis is also used in future studies. Futures studies are analyses that attempt to reveal what is likely to happen in our world. They are commonly used by commercial firms trying to predict changes in an industry, or by governments attempting to discern changes in the global environment, or by organizations focusing on the future itself. These trend analyses tend to be more qualitative than quantitative, though mathematical models are often used in a supporting role. Besides trend analysis, techniques such as cyclical pattern analysis, environmental scanning, scenarios, or backcasting are also used depending upon the goal of the analysis. Since Part II is a form of futures study, trend analysis supports this study well. [XLI]

Longevity, Stability, and Disruption

Trend analysis requires making a projection into the future. So what are we trying to project? Using the Part I framework to tell us something about the future requires projecting two trends:

- The progression of societal levels, and
- The development of transformative innovations.

Will the progression of societal levels continue, or has it stopped? Will there likely be another transformative innovation, or have these stopped? Before making these assessments, however, we need to verify that extrapolation is even possible, that is, that the two trendlines have the longevity and stability required, and that they are unlikely to be disrupted.

Concerning longevity, these trends are two of the longest-running trends in human existence. These trends start around 10,000 BCE, with the introduction of food production, and continue to the present day: twelve thousand years of history. So how far out can this project?

With twelve thousand years of data, it is not unreasonable to project forward at least a few centuries. If a sales forecast uses thirteen weeks of data to forecast out one week, then a 13:1 trendline:horizon ratio is being used. If a commercial firm is using three years of earnings to project forward one quarter, then a ratio of 12:1 is at work. Applying a 12:1 ratio to our trendlines would imply that we could project forward one thousand years and stay within forecasting norms. A horizon even half this long—five hundred years—would provide immeasurably valuable insight.

Now none of this says that during the next five hundred years a societal-level shift will occur or a new transformative innovation will come along. It only says that it is legitimate to look that far ahead.

Concerning stability, a trendline has to be stable to be forecastable. Erratic behaviors cannot accurately be projected. Clothing styles tend to have erratic sales or earnings because styles are inherently subjective and lots of alternative styles are available. Oil consumption, in contrast, tends to remain relatively stable, and therefore forecastable, because it is a staple product and few substitutes are readily available. So how stable is our trendline?

These trendlines are some of the most stable in existence. By stepping back and looking at human civilization in its entirety, we see a steady progression from bands to the nation-state, with all the associated, increasingly complex innovations that helped the progression along. These are not the small, noisy trends that shrink to invisibility when viewing the expanse of human history. These are not even the megatrends, which may last for a decade or more but also shrink to invisibility when viewing the expanse. These are *archtrends*: trends that only emerge when viewing the expanse. They capture critical elements of the expanse. They do not track a technique used in resource management; rather, they track resource management itself. They do not follow an innovation; they follow innovation itself. That humankind will continue to manage resources and will continue to innovate suggests almost inviolable stability.

Concerning disruption, one has to consider whether anything is likely to come along to disrupt these trendlines. Even a long and stable trendline can be disrupted by changes in the environment, when the underlying playing field has changed. Is there likely to be anything that could alter these archtrends?

Checking for disruptive threats requires looking for related trends with potentially macrolevel impact that are near their inflection points—points of rapid change. For our archtrends, it is worth looking in the three related areas of technology, population, and resources. Within these areas, we look for trends that have recently reached, or are likely to reach, an inflection point—

a point where the rate of change changes: accelerating, decelerating, or leveling off to an end state. Such points tend to create ripple effects in adjacent or related areas that could cause disruption. Within the three areas, seven underlying trends emerge as having had, or are likely to have, an inflection point:

- Technology development,
- Technology diffusion,
- Weapons of war,
- Population growth,
- Global communication,
- Global interdependency, and
- Natural resource consumption.

Examination is required to determine whether these potential threats are likely to have an actual impact. From a practical point, it is most useful to consider such potential threats based on the likelihood that they will have an impact within the forecast horizon: the next few centuries.

Technology development. Technology development is progressing at a faster rate. It took almost seventy thousand years to move from spoken language to food production, while it took only two hundred years to go from petroleum propulsion to nuclear fission. Will this change of pace have any impact on the archtrends? If so, it would only speed them up. The increasing pace of technology development suggests a reduction in the time it would take to complete a societal-level transition, if such a transition were to begin. The spin-off innovations needed to support such a change would come along quicker, so that what once took centuries to spread across a continent could spread worldwide in decades, limited only by humans' reluctance to embrace change. Faster technology development also means an increase in the number of potentially transformative innovations created, and a correspondingly greater chance of societal-level change occurring. If anything, faster technology development means the archtrends will only pick up speed.

Technology diffusion. Technology diffusion is the rate at which an idea spreads across societies, and this rate has been increasing. It took thousands of years for writing to spread across the Eurasian continent, while it only took decades for petroleum propulsion to spread intercontinentally. The increased rate of diffusion may likely be felt within the context of dominating innovations. A dominating innovation generates power for a society as long as the society has a monopoly on its use. If technology diffuses faster, no society may be able to maintain a monopoly on an innovation's use. This may have already taken place. Innovations that may have become dominating, such as electric power generation or even the electric light, spread so rapidly that no society ever monopolized them, and hence no society gathered a military or economic advantage from them. It may be the case that nuclear fission is the last dominating innovation the world will see.

Weapons of war. Weapons of war have continued to increase in lethality since the dawn of humankind. Perhaps beginning with rocks thrown in anger, by the middle of the twentieth century, they reached a point where they could obliterate humankind. Because it is hard to imagine anything more lethal than nuclear weapons, one might say that we have reached an end game concerning lethality, though no doubt weapons will continue to evolve. So what disruption might occur? Obviously, if humankind obliterates itself, the archtrends stop. Short of this, however, the real impact may be indirect. It is possible that the prospect of self-annihilation has forced greater cooperation across societies. The United Nations has survived, while the League of Nations did not. If continued progress requires greater cooperation across societies, the lethality end game may have actually aided the progression. In addition, the lethality end game may suggest that there will be no more dominating innovations that are weapons of war. (Will cyber weapons ever really become dominating?)

Population growth. The population of the world has surged since the eighteenth century when better food production and medical technology reduced child mortality and increased life spans. However, recent models suggest that the earth's population is leveling off. Sometime in the latter half of this century, the world's population is expected to level off at between eleven and twelve billion people. Historically, societal-level change has been associated with population growth. Could this have an impact? It is unlikely. Societal-level change is related to the ability to manage resources across a population. That the population stops growing does not impact the human ability to manage those resources.

Global communication. The speed and frequency of communication has surged in recent decades. Until the twentieth century, mail took weeks or months to reach its destination; even the telegraph and telephone were limited. Today communication is instant, worldwide, and nearly effortless. To know what is happening across the world at any moment, we simply watch television or go online. We contact acquaintances we have not seen in years through social networks. Can this increase in communication speed and frequency have an impact on the archtrends? It would only serve to speed them up. Increased communication and interaction in general increases innovation. This in turn would only speed up the pace at which a society would evolve. Furthermore, increased communication helps us to get to know each other better. A more interactive world is likely to move forward faster than a fragmented or disjointed world.

Global interdependency. In recent decades, societies across the globe have become more connected and more interdependent than ever before. At no time has this become clearer than during the 2009 global economic crisis. The collapse of one New York City financial firm caused a ripple effect that spread throughout the world, creating a worldwide recession. Is this behavior likely to have an impact on the archtrends? Again, a more integrated world would only serve to speed up a societal transition if one ever began. It would also likely produce more innovation with greater sharing of information, resources, and capital. Now it is possible that the world is also becoming less stable in some ways: trouble in one place more easily spreads to other places. However, concerning society and innovation, the pace of change only quickens.

Natural resource consumption. Humankind is consuming the world's natural resources at a faster rate. Natural resource consumption began to surge with the Industrial Revolution and only gained speed in the last century, growing 50 percent in the last thirty years alone. Resource usage efficiency has also started to increase, but only time will tell how effective humankind becomes at managing natural resources. What impact could this have on the archtrends? Of all the potentially disruptive trends, this one is perhaps the murkiest because it depends on how well we adapt. If resources become scarce, will innovation slow down or speed up, as necessity becomes the mother of invention? Perhaps more so than any of the other trends, this one depends upon decisions we make as a collective people in the future.

So, none of these seven trends (with the possible exception of natural resource consumption) appears likely to disrupt the archtrends. Will something new come along to disrupt the archtrends? It is unlikely. A trend with that kind of potential would probably be spotted far in advance: it is doubtful something would surprise us on relatively short notice. (Of course, some sort of cataclysmic catastrophe, e.g., a comet striking the earth, is always a remote possibility, but too remote to consider in this analysis.)

So it seems we can expect the archtrends to continue into the forecastable future because of their longevity, stability, and the low likelihood of being disrupted. But if that is the case, then what will the future look like? What will be the next societal level? What will be the next elevating innovation? What will be the next preconditioning innovation? The remainder of Part II will focus on these questions.[XLII]

Strategic Direction and Forecast Accuracy

One needs to bear in mind that any such projections will be of a general nature. The future simply cannot be known with absolute certainty. One can only project what is more likely to happen than not. In our case, we project that the archtrends are more likely to continue than to stop. If so, then at some point there is likely to be another societal level provided there is another elevating innovation and another preconditioning innovation to initiate it. Anything more granular than this becomes guesswork (although some guesses will be better than others).

Is such information useful? Such is the nature of strategic analysis. Strategic analysis is less concerned with the precision of events than it is with the direction of events. Strategic analysis helps senior officials identify the best path for their organization: whether that organization is a company or a country. Therefore, it only needs to be precise enough to provide accurate direction. And such direction is always based on the available information at the time a decision has to be made. If no decision has to be made, then there is no consequence to allowing the future to unfold further until something forces a decision to be made. If a decision has to be made, however, it is better to make the decision with more insight than less. The final determinant of success is whether the decision maker feels she or he has made the right choice at the time the decision had to be made.

> Many decisions must be made today in the face of great uncertainty about what may happen in the future or even what the effects of today's decision might be in the future. Futures methods help people to deal with this uncertainty by clarifying what is known, what can be known, what the likely range of possibilities is, what the most desirable possibilities are, and how today's decisions may play out in each of a variety of possible futures. [1]

That said, let us see what we can expect in our future.[XLIII]

---

[1] World Futures Society, "Methods and Approaches of Futures Studies."

Chapter 14
The Next Societal Level

Just as the town clock strikes two, the mayor steps up to the podium and begins to read. It's the same story every year. He tells of the history of Panem, the country that rose up out of the ashes of a place that was once called North America. He lists the disasters, the droughts, the storms, the fires, the encroaching seas that swallowed up so much of the land, the brutal war for what little sustenance remained. The result was Panem, a shining Capitol ringed by thirteen districts, which brought peace and prosperity to its citizens. Then came the Dark Days, the uprising of the districts against the Capitol. Twelve were defeated, the thirteenth obliterated. The Treaty of Treason gave us the new laws to guarantee peace and, as our yearly reminder that the Dark Days must never be repeated, it gave us the Hunger Games.[1]

Literature has long toyed with the idea that continent-sized nations will someday emerge. Frequently, these super-nations exist in a postapocalyptic time frame, and are often the remnants, or even a consolidation, of previous, smaller nations that exist today. But will it take near total annihilation for such a thing to come about? Or is it a natural progression that everyone intuitively understands will happen in our future regardless. Can our trend analysis shed any light on this?

---

[1] Suzanne Collins, *The Hunger Games*, Scholastic, New York, 2008, p.18.

The Nation-Union

The next societal level is the nation-union. A nation-union is a group of nations that come together under a single government to share resources and infrastructure. Table 6 provides a summary of why this is likely to be the case.

Table 6. Societal Level Attributes

	Governance	Population	Territory	Center of Authority
Bands	Multiple individuals bound together by relationship and consensus	Half dozen to dozens	None (roaming)	None (roaming)
Tribes	Multiple bands bound together by a tribal council	Dozens to Hundreds	Village	Village
Chiefdoms	Multiple tribes bound together by a chieftain's authority	Hundreds to ten-thousands	Region (e.g., valley, hill country)	Paramount Village
Fiefdoms	Multiple chiefdoms are bound together by royal authority	Ten-thousands to millions	Large geographic feature (e.g., isthmus, mountain range)	City-state
Nation-states	Multiple fiefdoms bound together by a constitution	Millions to hundred-millions	Fractions of a continent	Capital(s)
Nation-unions	*Multiple nations bound by a new form of governance*	*Hundred-millions to billions*	*Continents or large portions thereof*	*Network of capitals, virtual or physical*

From the beginning, societies have joined together under a new form of governance to create the next societal level. Bands joined together under a tribal council to create tribes. Tribes joined together under nonfamilial authority to create chiefdoms. Chiefdoms joined together under remote authority to create fiefdoms. And fiefdoms joined together under constitutional authority to create nation-states. Now this is a very general pattern, and not every society followed it exactly. England was already a single fiefdom when it became a nation-state. Nevertheless, this change gave it the capacity to subsume other fiefdoms and begin forming the British Empire only a few decades later. Other societies, such as Germany, followed the pattern more closely. A continuation of this pattern suggests that someday nation-states, under the right conditions, will join together under the next form of governance to create nation-unions.

So what will the nation-union look like? One feature of nation-unions is that they will likely have more people than nation-states have. Broadly speaking, each societal level contains societies with ten to a hundred times more people than the previous level. Bands ran from a few individuals to a few dozen people. Tribes could have a few hundred people, or a tenfold capacity increase over bands. Chiefdoms could run into the ten thousands, up to a hundredfold increase over tribes. Modern fiefdoms run into the millions—another hundredfold capacity increase. And nation-states easily run into the hundreds of millions,[2] another hundredfold increase. If this trend continues, nation-unions could easily contain societies with populations over a billion, though not every society will necessarily have populations that high. The issue is that the nation-union would have the capacity to manage such numbers effectively to succeed or even come into existence.

Nation-unions will be larger than nation-states. Every societal level has had substantially more territory than the previous level. Bands owned no territory since their existence was nomadic, following animal herds. Tribes settled into villages around lakes, streams, or other sources of water—often with great distances between them. Chiefdoms encompassed groups of tribes, often around some common geographic feature such as a valley or a hilly region. Fiefdoms could extend their territory almost indefinitely, usually until they bumped up against another fiefdom. Fiefdoms often encompassed large geographic regions such as a peninsula, an island, or the plateau between mountain ranges. If they became empires, they could grow even larger. Nation-states can encompass significant portions of a continent, and in the case of Australia, an entire, albeit small, continent. Nation-states are unlimited in their capacity to extend their borders, and are only limited by other nation-states.

If this trend continues, then a nation-union could encompass an even larger portion of a continent, or an entire continent by itself. Clearly, if all the

[2] India and China have populations over 1 billion. These ranges are order-of-magnitude estimates only, so a population of 1.4 billion can also be considered as 14 hundred million.

nations of a particular continent were to form a single union, then the result would be a single continent-sized nation-union. This scenario becomes even more plausible when considering that in all previous societal levels, new societies were formed by amalgamating adjacent societies. It is unlikely that this will be any different for the nation-union—even in the digital age. While advances in communication have made it easier to manage affairs over great distances, many of the potential benefits from such unions, benefits in commerce, transportation, resources, and infrastructure sharing, would only result from joining adjacent territories. Furthermore, discontinuous territories tend to develop their own separate identities, making it harder for such unions to ever form (e.g., Gaza and the West Bank). So it is likely that the size of the nation-union could approach continental levels, limited only by the amount of contiguous land available.

A final feature worth looking at is the center of authority—the seat of power. Nation-unions will likely have a more dispersed center of authority than nation-states have. The center of authority for the band was the individual, the head of the band who facilitated consensus as the band roamed the landscape. Then villages were formed, each one having a tribal council. When chiefdoms emerged, one village—the one where the chieftain resided—became paramount over other local villages. Early fiefdoms were primarily city-states that came to dominate other cities, so the city-state became the capital. Some fiefdoms grew so large that other cities began to have a subordinate role, housing a local authority under the dominion of a ruler who may be hundreds of miles away. This continued into the Middle Ages as castles or other centers of power overlorded local regions. Nation-states developed capitals where their governments resided. There is usually one central capital (i.e., a nation's capital) and several regional capitals (i.e., state, province, territory, or prefecture). The relationship between a nation's capital and regional capitals varies depending upon the government of the society.

If this trend continues, authority in the nation-union could disseminate from a single capital, or from a network of capitals. It may not even be necessary to consolidate the physical governments into a single location: it may be possible for each nation to retain its traditional capital and leverage a centrally coordinating virtual capital. Remember that when a new societal level emerges, the old ones do not disappear. Rather, the new level is formed by adding another layer of coordination and governance on top of the old ones. Likewise, a nation-union will not subsume nation-states, but the people of the nation-states will acknowledge a higher level of authority that crosses former borders. In this structure, the existing capitals may remain intact, but a new capital—whether physical or virtual—comes to represent the ultimate authority in the new union.

These are the primary physical characteristics of the nation-union—the next societal level. They will form when nation-states come together to share resources and infrastructure under a common form of governance. They will have lots of people, with populations often running into the hundreds of millions. They will be huge: reaching continent-sized proportions. And they may coordinate resources from multiple capitals, virtually as well as physically. For many people, this does not sound altogether unfamiliar.

The concept of the nation-union is not far-fetched—even for those who are not science fiction aficionados. At various times over the last century, different regions of the world began to, or attempted to, create such unions. Even today, some regions of the world are closer to it than others, though none have reached the level described above. A look into their attempts, however, can shed some insight on the challenges faced by societies considering such a shift.

Europe

The European Union (EU) is the first region likely to come to anyone's mind when discussing nation-unions. It stands out as the most advanced multinational entity in the world today. The idea to unify Europe originated from the ravages of World War II: some leaders saw it as the only way to make nations stop fighting each other. At first, the goal was only economic partnership. The European Economic Community (informally known as the European Common Market) was founded in 1958 by six European nations. In 1962, it established common prices for agricultural products. A few years later, it removed internal tariffs and created a common external tariff on those products as well as others. In 1967, it added treaties involving coal and steel, and atomic energy, and renamed itself the European Communities (EC).

Over the next two decades, others joined the EC. The Treaty of Maastricht, signed in 1993, officially rolled the EC member into the newly formed EU. The treaty continued the EC political structure, which included a European Parliament and European Court of Justice, and it established a common currency, to be known as the *euro*. In time, the EU would create policies for trade, economic development, criminal justice, education, finance, culture, foreign affairs, energy, health, transportation, and the environment.

By 2012, the EU had twenty-seven member nations,[3] roughly 500 million citizens, and the world's largest economy. The EU's 2012 gross domestic product (GDP) was roughly $16.5 trillion—larger than that of the United States and over 20 percent of the world's total GDP. The EU is the world's largest importer and exporter of goods; it controls about 30 percent of the world's wealth, and it is headquarters to 161 of the world's largest 500 companies (the Global 500). Its Single Market (successor to the Common Market) has added an estimated 2.1 percent to its GDP and created almost 2.8 million jobs since 1992.

While Europe has progressed further toward being a nation-union than any other region of the world, it is still not a union in terms of societal-level change. The EU operates somewhere in between a confederation of independent states and a federation, where governance is shared between independent states and a central body. Some nations have even declared they would need to change their constitutions to be a member of an EU that was a federation. Correspondingly, the EU's budget is small compared to its member nations. The EU's budget runs slightly over 1 percent of GDP, while the member nation budgets may run over 40 percent of GDP.[4] In addition, the EU relies on member nations to enforce its policies (though member nations are expected to consider EU law as equal to their own). And while it has begun infrastructure sharing (e.g., criminal databases and immigration

---

[3] Croatia was added in 2013.

[4] In 2013, the UK's budget:GDP ratio was roughly 43 percent; France's was about 56 percent.

databases), the EU still lacks many of the legal and political enforcement tools it would need to become a full union.

Perhaps the greatest barrier to further integration, however, lies in nationalistic identity. The typical European still identifies with his or her own nation rather than the union, and though one would expect some residual nationalism even in a union (much like pride in one's state), it is currently strong enough to stifle progress. In fact, some leaders even believe that the EU has reached its final state, many Europeans do not see any compelling reason to integrate any further, and Britain has even voted to exit to EU, largely in the name of national pride.[XLIV]

North Asia

The world has already seen one nation-union: the Soviet Union. In 1917, Russia ousted its tsar, moving from a fiefdom to a nation-state. In the civil war that followed, communism was established as the new form of government. In 1922, Russia and three other socialist republics (Transcaucasia, Ukraine, and Belarus) came together to form the Soviet Union. In the late 1930s, the Soviet Union invaded Eastern Europe, occupying several nations including Estonia, Lithuania, and Poland. After World War II, it made these nations into satellite states. By the mid-1950s, the Soviet Union had fifteen socialist republics: all equal in theory, but dominated by Russia.

Whether the former Soviet Union was a nation-union or a nation-state empire depends, to a large degree, upon the level of autonomy each republic really had. If member republics were more or less autonomous—free to make their own decisions while operating under a broader communist constitution—then they were more credibly members of a nation-union. However, if member republics were merely administrative divisions of the Kremlin, the Soviet central authority, then they more closely resembled elements of a nation-state empire. The invasions of Hungary in 1956 and Czechoslovakia in 1968 might suggest more of the latter since they imply the "union" was held together more by arms and intimidation than by mutual benefit. In either case, the Soviet Union resembles a governing body that presages the next societal level.

In the 1980s, the Soviet Union broke up under the weight of a faltering economy. Some nations left the union as early as possible, once they saw Russian military might would not force them to stay. In all, the Soviet Union lasted almost seventy years, making it perhaps not only the world's first nation-union but also its first nation-union fallback.

In May 2014, the leaders of Russia, Belarus, and Kazakhstan signed a treaty that would form the Eurasian Economic Union (EEU). Similar to the EU, it permits free movement of products, services, labor, and capital among member nations to bolster economic productivity. Armenia and Kyrgyzstan have also applied to join. And while member nations insist that the EEU is to remain a purely economic institution, some politicians fear that it portends a political reassembly of the former Soviet Union. In fact, as the EEU was being formed, Russian-backed rebel forces were attacking Ukrainian government positions. Russia's prime minister even began calling Ukraine "New Russia," its former name following Russian conquest in the late eighteenth century. The Soviet Union may not be the last union this part of the world will see.[XLV]

Middle East

The Middle East made a few attempts to build nation-unions during the twentieth century, though none of these lasted very long. The first attempt came in February 1958 when Syria and Egypt merged to form the United Arab Republic (UAR). A group of Syrian political and military leaders proposed the merger to Egypt's president, Gamal Abdel Nasser, who was an Arab hero due to his role in the Suez crisis. Partnership with Egypt would also give Syria a stability it lacked. Not long after the pact went into effect, however, Syrian leadership began to resent Egypt's dominance. In 1961, a Syrian coup deposed the pro-union government and later broke the union. Egypt continued to use the name UAR, however, until 1971, after Nasser died.[5]

In response to the formation of the UAR, and fearing an upset in the

---

[5] North Yemen also joined the UAR in 1958, though later; the loose confederation became known as the United Arab States. It also dissolved in 1961.

Middle East power balance, Iraq and Jordan formed their own union, the Arab Federation. This union was really a confederation of two cousins: King Faisal II of Iraq and King Hussein of Jordan. It lasted only six months, however, ending in August 1958 after King Faisal was deposed in a military coup.

Another union was attempted in March 1972. Libya initiated a union with Syria and Egypt, calling it the Federation of Arab Republics (FAR). While each nation approved the merger in its respective referendums, they could not agree on the specific terms of the merger. As a result, the union never occurred though FAR continued to exist on paper for a little over five years.

By the 1980s, pan-Arabism had largely subsided; nonetheless, in May 1981, six countries along the Persian Gulf's western shore formed the Gulf Cooperation Council (GCC). The GCC established common goals that included promoting industry, establishing a unified military, and creating a single currency. In January 2008, the GCC established a common market to ease the flow of products and labor across member countries. Progress toward the objectives, however, has been slow. Despite this, in December 2013, Saudi Arabia proposed changing the GCC into a Gulf Union. Saudi motives were partly symbolic, hoping to signal greater unity in the region, and partly practical, hoping to establish a stronger defensive shield against Iran. Support for the idea among GCC members has been mixed.

So despite multiple attempts to create a pan-Arab union, none have stuck, though one is still a work in progress. Part of the challenge in creating a union is that so many countries in that part of the world are really fiefdoms. Eight of the twenty-two members of the Arab League are officially monarchies, and many of the rest are fiefdoms culturally. Fiefdoms are inherently relationship based, and introducing new relationships can destabilize the old ones, as Syria found when it united with Egypt.[6] It is inherently easier to introduce new governing relationships to a nation-state, which can alter its process-based governance to accommodate them. As such, the capabilities, mind-set, and

---

[6] Though Syria was officially recognized as a nation-state in the late 1950s, some would argue that it was, in reality, closer to a chiefdom, with different local groups vying for control underneath a thin political and military overlay. Syria technically became a fiefdom when Hafez Assad installed relatives in key ministerial positions and named his son as his successor.

infrastructure needed to sustain a nation-union are formed at the nation-state level: you simply cannot "skip a level."

The Arab Spring of 2011 saw many Arab societies attempt to move either from a fiefdom to a nation-state (e.g., Syria) or from a dictatorship to a democracy (e.g., Egypt). While the results were mixed, continued progress in this direction will be required before Arab countries can legitimately move toward a nation-union.[XLVI]

Africa

The African Union (AU) was established in 2002 with fifty-three member nations, but it faces challenges similar to those in the Middle East. The AU is the successor of previous, more limited, attempts at continental integration. The first attempt was made in 1959 when Ghana and Guinea formed a confederation. Later Mali would join it to form the Union of African States. While its goals included creating a common currency, forming a union bank, and being the genesis of a broader integration movement throughout postcolonial Africa, it faced daunting challenges from the beginning. Because Ghana was not contiguous with the other two nations, it had trouble developing integrating infrastructure. Furthermore, because they had different colonial histories, the three nations had policy differences that were hard to reconcile. Ultimately, the confederation ended in May 1963 when it was superseded by the Organization of African Unity (OAU).

The much larger OAU was created in Addis Ababa, Ethiopia. Its thirty-two founding members had general goals focused on promoting prosperity, fostering long-term integration, and removing the last vestiges of European colonialism from Africa. It made substantial headway in the last goal. It offered bases, weapons, and training to rebel groups fighting colonial and white minority rule in South Africa and Rhodesia. It also closed harbors, denied flyover rights, and even had South Africa expelled from the World Health Organization. It was less successful in the goal of fostering long-term integration, however. Differences within the OAU arose on how best to achieve this, and even though several unifying organizations were created (e.g., Pan-African Telecommunications Union and Organization of African

Trade Union Unity), progress was slow. Even in goals focused on promoting prosperity, the organization came to be seen as having little power. Many member nations were still economically tied to their former colonial masters. There were also splits over whether to side with the West or with the Soviet Union in the Cold War struggle. In addition, the OAU's policy of noninterference in member nations' affairs meant it had little ability to enforce human rights or end civil wars. Ultimately, the OAU came to be derided as a "talking shop," or even a "dictator's club," for its lack of action.

In 1991, OAU member nations created the African Economic Community (AEC), which had a more intense focus on economic development. Its goals included creating a common currency and a common market across Africa. Moreover, it plans called for a graduated path toward economic unity, with the first phase being the creation of eight regional economic communities (some of which had existed already) where economic integration would occur first on a smaller scale. Confusion over how to manage the combined OAS and AEC, however, ultimately led to the creation of the African Union (AU).

In 1999, the president of Libya, Muammar Kaddafi, made another attempt at a nation-union; this time with more success. In a summit in Sirte, Libya, members of the OAS voted to create the AU, an organization that would subsume both the OAS and the AEC. The AU formally stood up in July 2002, with its secretariat, the African Union Commission, headquartered in Addis Ababa. The AU's primary focus has been to foster development, and it has retained the AEC objectives of gradual integration into a common market, with a common currency and a union bank. Toward the end of the decade, it again debated how best to form a single union government, but divisions among members tabled the talks.

In its first decade of existence, the AU faced challenges in having a real impact on the greatest issues facing the continent. It had little influence in the Libyan Revolution of 2011 that deposed its founder. It sent peacekeepers to Sudan, but its troops were ill equipped and its mission underfunded. It had no role in settling the dispute that led to the creation of its fifty-fourth member, South Sudan. It had planned to deploy forces to Mali after an Islamist coup took control, but French forces were used to restore the civilian government. And it was never able to curb the AIDS epidemic that ravaged the continent. Indeed, the AU seems structurally limited. Less than half of its budget comes from its own member nations—the balance is paid by China, the EU, and the United States. Even the AU's headquarters was built and paid for by China. And since its founding, the AU seems almost preoccupied with fixing internal governance rather than fixing external, continent-wide problems.

Perhaps the greatest challenge to the AU, however, lies in the porosity of its institutional rule-of-law. Some member countries are monarchies (i.e., fiefdoms), and though they may be stable, they inherently govern through relationships. Some member countries may have a nominal nation-state government, but huge swaths of land are actually controlled by warlords and militias (i.e., chiefdoms). In some member countries, ethnic ties and tribal loyalty take precedence over national law. Some member countries are so wracked by bribery, corruption, and abuse that they have lost the trust of their people. Other countries change governments by coup d'état rather than by legitimate elections. All of these are symptoms that rule-of-law is not taken seriously, and when rule-of-law is not taken seriously, the nation-state barely functions. As such, the AU's main problem is cultural—making people realize that rule-of-law makes all other aspects of society work and that even the smallest bribe hurts everyone. Until that happens, building a nation-union is like building a skyscraper with mud and straw.[XLVII]

South America

The idea of a nation-union was first presented in the Americas in 1826. Simón Bolivar, president of Gran Colombia (which encompasses all or part of seven present-day Central American and South American countries), convened a summit in Panama City called the Congress of Panama. There he proposed the creation of a league of American republics, with a mutual defense pact, a common military, and even a parliamentary assembly. His motivation was to thwart any attempted recursion into the Americas by the recently ousted Spain. However, of the four countries in attendance (Gran Colombia, Peru, the United Provinces of Central America, and Mexico), only his ratified the proposal. Within a few years, Gran Colombia and the United Provinces both dissolved into smaller independent countries.

Then in 1890, eighteen Western Hemisphere countries met in Washington, DC, to form the International Union of American Republics. Post–Civil War America had begun to seek stronger relationships with other parts of the Americas to open foreign markets and to deter European encroachment. This new body would focus on promoting economic, social, and cultural development, as well as enhancing juridical relationships among nations. In 1948, this organization morphed into the Organization of American States (OAS) with a post–World War II focus on collective security and anticommunism.[7] After the Cold War, the OAS's priorities shifted to facilitating peace among member nations, monitoring human rights and continued economic development.

In 1969, while the OAS was fighting communism and Marxists were calling for the complete unification of South America under a socialist banner, four South American nations established the Andean Community—a trade bloc between Bolivia, Colombia, Ecuador, and Peru. Its early years were focused on setting up a governance structure, and its membership changed a few times. Then in the 1990s it created a free-trade zone among members and approved a common external tariff, creating a customs union.

In 1991, on the other side of the continent, nations formed their own customs union, called Mercosur, or Southern Common Market. Argentina, Brazil, Paraguay, Uruguay, and later Venezuela joined together to eliminate internal customs duties, establish a common external tariff, and coordinate economic policy and legislation. While these objectives were only partially met, Mercursor did promote several deals between members concerning debt reduction, energy cooperation, agricultural exchange, and public health.

Then in 2008, the two trade blocs signed a pact that would create a combined union encompassing all of South America. The Union of South

---

[7] In 1962, Cuba was ousted from the OAS after declaring itself communist and aligning itself with the Soviet Union. In 2009 the OAS offered reinstatement, which Cuba declined.

American Nations (UNASUR)[8] was patterned after the EU. It planned to have a single market, a single currency, a parliament, a secretariat, and several issue-specific councils. A South American Bank was proposed to finance economic, scientific, and technological development, as well as industrial and infrastructure construction. Ultimately, this union would permit the free movement of products, services, labor, and capital. UNASUR has begun hundreds of integrating infrastructure projects, to include an interoceanic highway and common energy-sourcing efforts. Members have taken steps to coordinate their defenses for better regional security. UNASUR has also settled disputes between members that once would have likely resulted in armed conflict. And recently, UNASUR conceptually approved a single citizenship and a single passport.

The target date for complete union had been 2017, but progress has been slower than expected. In 2011, the union's most ambitious objectives—a common currency and a central bank—were tabled after seeing the problems the EU faced during its economic downturn. There is also still much debate on how best to approach economic integration and how much political integration is appropriate. Furthermore, Brazil's dominating economy—a whopping 60 percent of UNASUR's aggregate GDP—is problematic in a union where every country is to have an equal say.

The greatest challenge for a South America union going forward, however, will be to overcome its members' nationalistic priorities. Members still argue with each other as much as they always have, and trade disputes seem to flare up regularly. As a result, UNASUR has been accused of being a discussion forum rather than a working body. Continued progress toward union will require them to clamp down on nationalistic tendencies, believing that union works better for all of them. So far, they are still nations—not members of a union—and it is not clear whether there is a desire to be anything else.[XLVIII]

---

[8] An originally proposed name for the trade bloc was South American Union; however, in Spanish *Union Sudamericana* is abbreviated "USA," so the name was changed to avoid confusion.

North America

North America has not had the same interest in a union that most of the rest of the world has. While other nations struggle with how to better integrate their economies, few North Americans have ever considered such thinking. For those who have, attitudes often range from skepticism to passive resistance. Despite this, some small, integrative steps have taken place.

In 1988, the Canada–United States Free Trade Agreement went into effect. It removed nearly all tariffs between the two counties and opened industries and markets to each other. In 1994, the North American Free Trade Agreement (NAFTA) superseded the Canada–United States Trade Agreement and brought Mexico into the arrangement. It phased out tariffs on products between Mexico and its two northern neighbors gradually, completing the reductions in 2008. It also contained provisions for copyright protection and environmental protection.

Though its impact is difficult to measure, many economists believe NAFTA has had a small, yet positive effect on the economics of all three nations. Trade among the three partners increased from about $290 billion in 1993 to more than $1.1 trillion in 2013. Each nation is among the other two nations' top three trading partners. Canada added 4.7 million jobs to its workforce since NAFTA's ratification (though it may be a stretch to attribute all of this to NAFTA). Some economists say the US economy has been boosted by 0.1 to 0.5 percent due to NAFTA.[9] In Mexico, the impact has perhaps been even greater. NAFTA helped to create new jobs along the border as factories sprang up to become intermediate assembly plants for American supply chains. Mexican consumers could now buy American goods cheaper than they could before. And the Mexican government began to exercise greater fiscal discipline than it had before. Even with these improvements, however, many economists believe NAFTA would have had a greater impact if Mexico had more internal infrastructure, which would help to extend NAFTA's benefits farther away from the border.

In 2001, Vicente Fox talked up the idea of greater integration with the

---

[9] This number may have been higher had not the bilateral United States–Canada Free Trade Agreement already existed.

United States while campaigning for the Mexican presidency. The idea gained little traction, but in 2005, the leaders of the three North American nations did establish a set of advisory working groups, the Security and Prosperity Partnership of North America, to devise better ways of improving collective security and building the economies. Though it made several recommendations, the program was disbanded in 2009 after a change in American administrations.

Despite the seeming indifference, smaller efforts and indicators reveal synergies that are to be realized when the three nations work together and share resources—officially or otherwise. In many regions of the world, labor mobility is considered a key component for growing an integrated economy. In North America, this seems to be the case as well, despite conflicted foreign worker policies. In 2012, only about 12 percent of the 144,000 employment-based requests for legal permanent resident status in the United States came from other North American countries, with 5 percent coming from Mexico and 4 percent coming from Canada.[10] However, in 2012, illegal immigrants, about half of which came from Mexico, comprised about 5 percent of the US workforce. These immigrants worked primarily in the agriculture, construction, and hospitality industries in positions that did not require a high school diploma. This hidden workforce adds an estimated $5–$10 billion per year to the US economy: a slight positive impact.[11]

Additional synergy is revealed by the level of ongoing cross-border cooperation. Canada, Mexico, and the United States have a number of joint initiatives in the areas of public health and safety, security, and energy. Since 1998, the United States and Mexico have partnered in the Border Water Infrastructure Program, spending an average $66 million per year; currently twenty-four projects operate along the US-Mexico border, building water sources and waste treatment facilities. Mexico and the United States have also partnered in the Merida Initiative, where the United States alone has spent

[10] China had the most with 14 percent.
[11] This means they contributed to the labor workforce and helped keep producer costs low. This offset the increased cost to support the population. Most jobs that were filled by illegal immigrant labor would have gone to high school dropouts, which did offset the wages that otherwise could have been earned by this cohort.

over $2.3 billion since 2008 to stem the flow of illegal drugs and violence along the border. This effort has bolstered information sharing, technology sharing, planning, training, and community development, and has even helped refine Mexico's criminal justice system. Since 9/11, Canada has spent over $10 billion on border security and emergency preparedness. Canada and the United States have established Integrated Border Enforcement Teams, where Canadian and US agencies collaborate to ensure security and stop cross-border crime. In energy, the United States and Mexico signed the Transboundary Hydrocarbons Agreement in 2012, which improves the coordination of oil exploration and development in the Gulf of Mexico. In 2015, the US Congress approved the Keystone Pipeline, which moves oil from northern Canada to refineries in the southern United States. The Trump Administration has also supported this initiative.

Some have called out the need to better exploit such potential synergies. In 2014, the Council on Foreign Relations called for a deepening of North American integration using measures such as improving energy infrastructure, strengthening economies through the freer movement of goods and services, establishing a unified security strategy for North America, and building community through freer, but controlled movement of labor across borders. However, North Americans still lack interest in forming any kind of union and the Trump Administration appears to be moving in the opposite direction. Why is there this apparent disconnect from the rest of the world?

One could argue that there is little reason to form a nation-union since things are going so well as nation-states. The 2013 GDPs for the United States, Canada, and Mexico were $16.8 trillion, $1.8 trillion, and $1.3trillion, respectively. This ranks them 1st, 12th, and 16th in the world out of 213 nations. In per capita GDP, the United States, Canada, and Mexico were roughly $53,000, $52,000, and $10,300; placing them in the 95th, 94th, and 66th percentiles among nations. The truth is that most nations aspire to be where North American countries already are, and no nation would consider a union unless it benefitted all members: no society would allow its standard of living to be "averaged out" by creating a union.

Beyond economics, each nation still has issues that would need to be addressed before union would be possible. Overcoming nationalism resistance is a tall order—one of the main arguments against ratifying NAFTA in Canada was that Canadians did not want to see their country become "the 51st state." Mexico would need to complete its industry reforms, and gain control over border security and the drug trade. The United States would likely need to get control over its ballooning debt and entitlement programs, although such problems could actually help further the idea of union, since it would likely take some form of economic calamity—far bigger than the Great Recession—to shake the United States into believing that it needed to look externally for solutions to its problems.

So while even larger trade agreements are in the offing, and some policymakers may call for deeper integration between nations, at present, the idea of a North American union still remains chimerical. As such, this region will likely be one of the last in the world to form a union.[XLIX]

South Asia

A final region worth examining is southern Asia. This region contains the world's two most populous nations: India, with over 1.2 billion people, and China, with 1.4 billion people. These nations are so large that each one has the population and territory of a nation-union already. This makes it less likely they will join any unions: their economies are so large that they would dwarf their surrounding partners, adding little benefit to their own economies while yielding a degree of control to other countries.

Dealing with more people would also increase India's and China's management burden, which is already considerable. In 1991, India changed from a socialist economy to a market economy. In the decade prior to the reform, India's economy grew at 3.4 percent, while in the two decades since, its economy has grown at 6.0 percent and 14.3, percent, respectively. However, along with the economic growth, the ranks of the poor have swollen and income inequality has actually worsened.

China may eventually face its own limitations. While its per capita GDP has grown from around $400 to $7,000 in the twenty-five years since the Tiananmen Square protest, one could question how long this growth can last. In China, "parental connections" are still more important than education as a predictor of a child's future income. From an economic perspective, this will ultimately stifle development since such behavior tends to reduce a political economy's efficiency. Such behavior harkens back to relationship-based governance: "China does not lack laws, but the rule of law," explained one dissident as he described China's proclivity for warrantless seizures and capricious arrests. As such, China's economic future then, as well as India's, probably lies in further internal refinement rather than external union.

There is another part of this region, however, for which movement toward union makes more sense: Southeast Asia. The Association of Southeast Asian Nations (ASEAN, Figure 24) was founded in 1967 mainly to fight communism. It grew out of an earlier organization, the Association of Southeast Asia, founded in 1961; however, in recent decades, it has primarily focused on economic growth and development. In 2012, the ten nations of ASEAN had a combined GDP of $2.3 trillion, which would rank seventh in the world economy if it were a single entity.

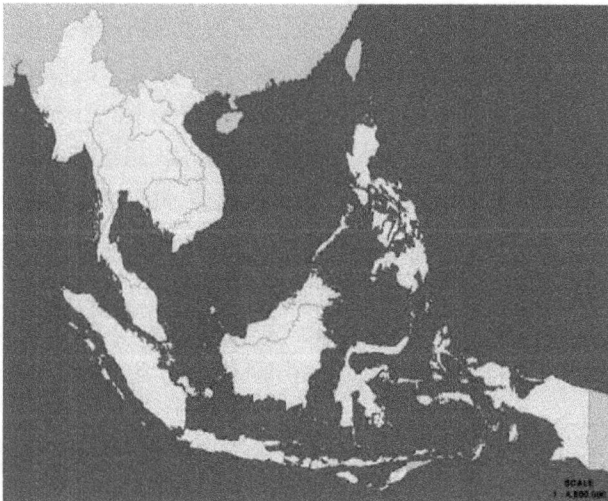

Figure 24. ASEAN member nations.
Source: http://asean.org/asean/asean-member-states/

In 1993, ASEAN began reducing tariffs between members on selected products. In 2007, it set a goal to have an economic community by 2015, which would allow "free movement of goods, services, investment, skilled labor, and freer flow of capital" between member nations, though this has been delayed. It has even discussed a common accounting currency, the Asian Currency Unit (ACU), which would function much like the euro's predecessor, the European Currency Unit (ECU). No date has been set for its adoption.

Over the years, ASEAN has developed strong ties with other nations, particular with the other Southeast Asian nations, namely, China, Japan, and South Korea. These relationships have grown so strong that the three countries have been made adjunct members: the collective group is called ASEAN Plus Three, or APT. They work together most often in matters of regional finance and development.

Like other regions of the world, ASEAN faces challenges in becoming a union. One challenge unique to ASEAN is that so much of its territory is covered by water. Three-quarters of ASEAN's surface area is ocean or sea, making the building of integrating infrastructure all the more difficult. Perhaps a more daunting challenge, however, is the cultural shift that will be required to make full integration come about. The ASEAN Way is a cultural emphasis on politeness, nonconfrontation, and informality over rules, treaties, and hard negotiations. It trades off time for harmony, allowing conflict resolution to take what would be considered an interminably long time to Westerners. Member nations pride themselves on this approach, which they consider to be a unifying element of Southeast Asian culture. Indeed, the ASEAN Way was embodied in the procedural norms of ASEAN at its founding, and ASEAN credits this approach with changing historically warring enemies into mutually supportive allies over the last forty years. Early in the integration process, however, ASEAN found that a more legalistic approach, using formal documents and binding treaties, was needed to begin tariff reduction. Continued progress will require many more changes to domestic laws and regulations to align several disparate economies. Because the ASEAN Way tends to avoid direct confrontation, one can expect the process to be painstakingly slow, as it has been already—some tariffs still have not yet been removed. While ASEAN has been delayed in becoming an Economic Community (with all the typical characteristics), this is not necessarily a problem in a culture that values the process of issue resolution more than the timing of resolution. The challenge remains, however, to retain the ASEAN Way and the cultural cohesion that comes with it, while augmenting it with the formal mechanisms needed to make a union work.[L]

The Path to Union

Altogether, nations have been taking a six-step path to economic integration (Figure 25).[12] The final step, nation-union, goes beyond economic integration by adding political integration.

Figure 25. The path to nation-union

Preferential trade area (PTA) is the first step on the integration path. Prior to this, nations are independent economies, each one having its own import tariffs. When a nation decides to establish a trading relationship with another nation, for economic or political reasons, it creates a bilateral trade agreement. This is an agreement to reduce tariffs on some products imported from each other, making it cheaper for both to buy and sell those products, increasing their trade volume. When nations want to trade with more than one partner, a multilateral agreement can be used to make them all members of the same PTA.

PTAs do not reduce tariffs on all products. PTAs do not eliminate tariffs completely on any products. PTAs do not prevent members from striking deals outside of the PTA. PTAs do, however, create a preference for buying certain products from inside the PTA before going outside of it: a way of "buying local" if the partners are neighbors. And if the partners are neighbors and they begin this process of economic integration, they could be starting down a path toward union.

Free-trade area (FTA) is the next step along the path: it takes the PTA to a higher level. Whereas PTAs reduce tariffs, FTAs completely eliminate them.

---

[12] The names of the steps are quite varied in literature with no clear consensus. These names have been chosen because they seem to be the most common ones and they make the most sense when considering them as a path to nation-union. Also, to some extent, the attributes of each step have been idealized—the real world is a bit messy.

Whereas PTAs apply only to some goods, FTAs apply to all goods. Whereas PTAs apply to goods only, FTAs include services as well. The intent of this broader scope is to expand economic opportunity by creating a community where consumers can buy from other nations as easily as they can from within their own nation. This reduces prices for them and increases demand for producer products and services. Meanwhile, members are still free to create trading relationships outside of the FTA.

Customs unions is the third step. Customs unions impose a common external tariff on nonmembers. Whereas FTAs allow members to trade with nonmembers at their own discretion, customs unions insist that trade with nonmembers be in accordance with terms the union has set. Customs unions also necessitate a single external trade policy that applies to all members (e.g., imported product safety standards and foreign worker occupational safety standards). In this way, no member gains an unfair advantage over other members, and members in effect agree to make internal trade their top priority. Customs unions create a group of nations that have chosen to deal with each other first, and with the rest of the world as a group.

Common market is the fourth step of integration.[13] Common markets enable the free flow of goods, services, labor, and capital within the bloc and across national borders. Whereas FTAs and customs unions eliminated barriers to buying and selling, common markets eliminate barriers to *producing* as well. On goods and services (which includes business-to-business sales as well as consumer sales), both tariff and nontariff barriers are removed (e.g., product safety regulations are harmonized across countries). People have the freedom to live anywhere in the bloc and can move across national borders without a passport. Banks in one country can finance projects in another without added regulations. Companies can merge across borders under common securities law. In the region, production moves to its most advantageous location, resources combine more efficiently, and a single economy begins to emerge.

---

[13] Other names for common market include single market, unified market, and internal market. Some sources use the terms indiscriminately while others make fine distinctions between them. For describing the path of integration, the singular name common market works fine.

Monetary union is the fifth step. It goes beyond common market by introducing a single currency and a common monetary policy (interest rates, quantity of currency in the economy, etc.). National currencies are forced out of existence, and replaced by the bloc currency. In addition, common financial institutions, such as a central bank, may be established. Using a common currency removes the expense and hassle of changing money whenever cross-border transactions are made. Scrapping national currencies provides perhaps the most visible sign of economic integration yet to individuals.

An *economic union* is the ultimate form of economic integration. Economic unions have a common fiscal policy.[14] Common tax rates, deficits, and debt levels are established for all members. By centrally managing these principle tools for controlling economies, the bloc is ultimately able, as close as is possible, to create a single regional economy.

This sequence of steps is not arbitrary: each step responds to a problem that emerged during the previous step. Furthermore, the sequence either facilitates integration or protects member interests.

PTAs begin because countries need to spur economic development in specific industries. The success of the PTA induces nations to broaden their efforts, leading to the creation of an FTA. As goods and services flow more easily, members have to address how nonmembers are handled (or one partner could lower its tariff and get all the imports). Customs unions preserve order by establishing a common tariff.

As the regional economy grows, manufacturers find it more challenging to meet demand. The common market removes barriers to production. As the flow of material throughout the region increases, the financial and administrative costs of changing money become a burden. The monetary union eliminates multiple currencies.

At some point, divergent economies become a problem: either an economic calamity occurs or nations with fragile economies want to join. Because economies are so intertwined, a jolt to one member affects all members. The answer is to manage economic risk as a bloc. The economic union centrally manages the biggest factors impacting an economy—tax rates,

---

[14] Another name for this is fiscal union. Again, there is inconsistency in terms.

deficits, and debt levels. At this point, economic integration has occurred.

Likewise, the sequence of steps protects members. If the PTA is not in place by the time an FTA is started, a nation will lack the experience needed to move forward with more sweeping tariff reductions (the part wisely comes before the whole). If the FTA is not in place when the customs union is started, a nation could not yield control of its external trade to another nation (there is no benefit). If the customs union is not in place when a common market is started, a nation would be unwise to open its borders (the nation with the best external trade relationships will reap the most benefit). If the common market is not in place before a monetary union is started, there is little benefit to having a single currency (without resources flowing across borders, there is no exchange cost). If the monetary union is not in place before the economic union is started, it is too difficult to establish a coherent transnational economic policy.

The net result of all this is that the sequence is set and it does not make sense to skip steps. Each step includes all the attributes of previous steps, so progression means accumulation of attributes. An economic union therefore is the completion of economic integration, and it includes all of the attributes introduced along the way.

Nations have been advancing through these different steps, at varying paces, for several years (Figure 26).[15]

Figure 26. Current state of regional integration

[15] A region was assigned to the lowest category for which it had all the required attributes, provided those attributes are at least halfway effective. Some regions had only token attributes, which received no credit.

As could be expected, there are many preferential trade areas across the globe, both bilateral and multilateral. These begin the integration path. Some of the bilateral PTAs include

- India and Afghanistan (2003)
- ASEAN and the People's Republic of China (2005)
- The United States and Colombia (2012)

Some of the multilateral PTAs include

- South Pacific Regional Trade and Economic Cooperation Agreement (1981)
- Latin American Integration Association (1981)
- Melanesian Spearhead Group (1994)
- South Asian Preferential Trade Arrangement (1999)

Each of these has helped to strengthen the trade relationship of two partners or the region as a whole.

There are four large free-trade areas: North America (NAFTA), South America (UNASUR), Southeast Asia (ASEAN), and Africa (the African Free Trade Zone, AFTZ).

Since signing NAFTA into law, North America has been a free-trade area. However, since then, there has been no forward movement toward establishing a common external tariff or synchronizing foreign trade policy among members. Instead, NAFTA members have chosen to form more bilateral agreements with other parts of the world.

Most of South America, when considered as a whole under UNASUR, is a free-trade area. UNASUR began eliminating tariffs on nonsensitive products in 2014, but will not begin to do so for sensitive products until 2019. UNASUR has shelved long-term projects for creating a common currency and creating a regional development bank.[16]

Southeast Asia, under ASEAN, is a free-trade area. It had eliminated 99% of the tariffs between member nations when it introduced the ASEAN Economic Community at the end of 2015. It has even signed bi-lateral FTAs with Australia, New Zealand, China, Japan, India, and South Korea, showing signs of movement toward a customs union. However, ASEAN has no plans for a common external tariff, and while discussions have begun regarding a common currency, no active plans are in effect.

Africa has a free-trade area. The Tripartite Free Trade Area was formed from three regional FTAs in June 2015. It encompasses twenty-six African nations, with a total GDP of around $625 billion—about half of the continent's total GDP. Also in June 2015, the AU established the goal of creating the Continental Free Trade Area, encompassing all of Africa, by the end of 2017.

Some parts of the world have progressed to the level of customs union: South America (under its older, smaller trading blocs), the Persian Gulf, the Caribbean, and Africa (under an older, smaller trading bloc).

The Andean Community is one of South America's two customs unions. It began in 1969 as a free-trade zone, which became fully operational in 1993. The following year, member nations approved a common external tariff, and in 1998, they developed a framework for joint foreign policy.

Mercosur is the other South American customs union. Mercosur has eliminated internal tariffs on most goods and services and has a common external tariff. The union is fragile, however, in that members can opt out of tariff reduction on select products, and they can even opt out of using the common external tariff, substituting their national tariff instead. Any further forward progress will be led by UNASUR.

The GCC is the Persian Gulf's customs union. The GCC announced the creation of a customs union in 2003, but it only became operational in 2015, and as of this writing still has not yet removed all barriers to the free

---

[16] The Bank of the South was proposed in 2006 by Venezuelan President Hugo Chavez as a way to finance development projects across the continent.

movement of goods and services. It also announced the creation of a common market in 2008, but many barriers remain.

The Caribbean Community (CARICOM) is the Caribbean customs union. The region was a free-trade area before CARICOM was founded in 1973. CARICOM was created, in large part, to establish a common external tariff, which it has been working to develop ever since. Despite a major revision in 1992, by 2004 only three member nations had implemented it. In early 2015, another revision had been proposed, so a more complete common external tariff may finally be close at hand.

Africa has a customs union: the East African Community. It resides within the AFTZ and is composed of five East African nations. It announced its intent to become a customs union in 2004. It became a fully operational free-trade area in 2010 when it eliminated its last internal tariffs. Though it does have a common external tariff, it is still a work in progress since there are a number of exclusions still in effect. It is working to reduce that number and to harmonize its customs procedures as well.

The world has one common market: the EEU. Former Soviet states began discussing forming a customs union and common market in the mid-1990s. A customs union was declared in 2010 when a common external tariff was introduced and members began reducing tariffs and nontariff barriers. Work toward a common market began in 2012. Most of the objectives were achieved in early 2015, when the EEU was formally established.

The world has one monetary union: the EU. Only Europe has gone through all the steps up to and including currency unification. In began as a preferential trade area in 1952 with the creation of the European Coal and Steel Community. It became a fully functioning free-trade area in 1968 after nine years of tariff reductions. It became a customs union also in 1968, when it fixed a common external tariff. It became a common market in 1993, when the EU was formed. It became a monetary union in 2002, when euro coins and currency were introduced.[17]

---

[17] The euro is currently used by nineteen of the twenty-eight members of the EU, but this is considered enough to establish the monetary union.

No region has yet become an economic union; however, Europe is closest to it. In 1997, the EU's Stability and Growth Pact (SGP) outlined what it considered to be proper fiscal management by its members (annual deficits were not to exceed 3 percent of GDP; total debt was not to exceed 60 percent of GDP). In 2005, enforcement teeth were added to the SGP: medium-term objectives were added with the expectation that members would achieve these standards within a reasonable time frame. In 2013, following the worldwide fiscal crisis, the EU adopted a fiscal compact that strengthened enforcement even further by adding penalties for noncompliance. The EU is not a full economic union, however, in that the key macroeconomic policies of spending levels, debt levels, and tax rate are still controlled at a national level.

While many regions began integrating years ago, nearly all have found the journey more difficult than expected. Some have stopped progressing altogether. It will take substantial expected economic benefit for regions to continue making progress. Such economic benefit comes from the underlying presumption that synergy exists between nations. Synergy means combining resources in ways that generate revenue that otherwise would not have happened. Labor, only available from one country, moves to support agriculture in another country. One oil-rich country supplies its oil-starved neighbor. Investors from one country are the only ones interested in funding a start-up in another country. It is presumed that there are enough of these situations out there to justify the hassle and expense of more tightly integrating multiple economies.[18] While results are often difficult to measure, both the EU and NAFTA members have cited their agreements as having boosted their economy (Europe more so than North America). This suggests that, at least to some degree, these potential synergies do exist. Whether there is enough synergy to justify continued integration is a decision each region must make.

Now economic integration does not happen without some level of political integration. Starting with a preferential trade area, national policies have to

---

[18] Economies of scale are often cited as another reason for integration; however, for an entire economy, this impact is small compared to creating new opportunities for generating revenue, though it does help to make economies more efficient.

be aligned to make the bilateral or multilateral agreement work. With each successive stage, greater policy harmonization is needed. In free-trade areas, agreements on common tariffs and quotas for products as well as services are needed. In addition, some rules on industry operation have to be agreed upon to make the arrangement work (e.g., worker safety and pollution controls). Customs unions take this further by requiring external trade policies to be harmonized. All the regulations of internal commerce have to be reviewed and agreed upon at this point.

Common markets require members to agree on border policies to ensure the free flow of goods, services, labor, and capital. Commerce policies must also be harmonized. Members must share common views on industry practices such as monopolistic power, anticompetitive practices, and environmental impacts. These views have to be codified in agreements, often requiring changes in national laws or regulations, and such policy negotiating and crafting is a long, arduous process. When the EU was planning for its common market in the late-1980s, it found that almost 280 pieces of legislation were needed to harmonize industry practices across its (then) twelve members. The process took about six years.[19]

A monetary union requires harmonizing monetary policy: how interest rates are set, who has the authority to make changes to them, who controls the amount of currency in the region, how often is currency printed, whose picture goes on the front it, and so on. In an economic union, the workload balloons as laws concerning the economy are added: how to control spending, who authorizes deficits, what is the process for issuing debt, and so forth. When considering all of this, it becomes understandable why regions have moved rather slowly throughout the integration process.

Of course, managing all of this policy harmonization is full-time work. While the work of an free-trade area may be handled by existing departments within national governments, beginning with customs unions, a supranational structure is needed to coordinate supranational policy. Every trading bloc that is a customs union or higher, and even some free-trade areas,

---

[19] Even with this, there were many residual hurdles that had to be overcome through mutual recognition agreements, which say that one country will accept and acknowledge another country's product, service, or technical standards without having to recertify.

have a governing body whose full-time responsibility is to ensure the relationship works. Most of these are called secretariats, and they become symbols of the trading bloc itself. These institutions often resemble national-level structures with a legislative branch, a judicial branch, and an executive branch. They create laws that ultimately have precedence over national law. Members agree to subordinate themselves to the secretariat, in matters concerning the union.

Without this structure, it is nearly impossible to resolve differences. In Europe, internal tariffs and quotas were abolished in 1968, and plans for a common market were already in play by then, but it took until 1992 to make the common market happen. Much of this delay can be attributed to the absence of a strong supranational and intergovernmental decision-making structure. Only after new powers were given to the European Community in the Single European Act of 1987 did the goal of a common market become achievable.

The other primary reason for supranational governance is to build the infrastructure needed to exploit integration. While potential synergies may exist across borders, it is often too hard for a company to get to it without help. New infrastructure—not only transportation infrastructure, but also energy, communications, finance, and even human resources—is often needed to make integration worthwhile. And the deeper the integration, the more infrastructure needed.

Sometimes infrastructure development takes the form of a specific project such as UNASUR's interoceanic highway. Other times it takes the form of a policy emphasis and associated programs. In 2012, the EU took another step forward in building integrating infrastructure when it issued its Single Market II agreement. Some of the initiatives include

- an action to open the provision of domestic rail passenger services to further intra-EU competition
- the improvement of a single market for maritime transport
- measures to accelerate the Single European Sky
- development of the EURES portal into a fully-fledged cross-border job placement and recruitment tool

- introduction of provisions to mobilize long-term investment funds for private companies and long-term projects
- facilitation of e-commerce in the EU by making payment services easier to use, more trustworthy, and competitive
- measures to make electronic invoicing standard in public procurement procedures
- measures to ensure widespread access to bank accounts, as well as transparent and comparable account fees and easier bank account switching

Such measures could only be enacted by a completely functioning supranational policy-making body, with mechanisms to coordinate investment and a fully functional executive branch to coordinate action.[LI]

The Final Step

So economic integration is occurring—albeit slowly—across the globe. And political integration, to some extent, is occurring just to support economic integration. But what about the final step? What will the move from economic union to nation-union look like, and how will it occur? While there will be many different aspects to this move, the final step from economic union to nation-union will most likely be characterized by two aspects: regions give their supranational institutions the authority to enforce their own policies, and to tax people directly, without going through subordinate nations. While this may sound like a small step from an execution standpoint, it is a huge gulf from an emotional standpoint.

Let us consider the EU, which is the furthest along. Right now the laws and regulations established by the EU's governing bodies (European Parliament, European Commission, and European Court of Justice) are enforced by member nations. Member nations have agreed to treat EU law as equal to, if not superior to, their own. And while this situation works for the present time, it could not support a nation-union. No governing body can exist without the ability to enforce its own laws—otherwise, it remains a coordinating body. So the final step will require not only the authority and capability to create policy at the supranational level but also the ability to enforce it. Nations, of course, will retain their own authority to enforce their own laws, but this will lead to a settling time as regions decide which laws to enforce at the national level and which ones to enforce at the supranational level.

The other requirement for a nation-union is that the supranational governing body has the authority and ability to tax people directly, without going through subordinate nations. Right now, EU member nations fund the EU based primarily on their gross national income. Political integration, however, would require the European Commission to have its own authority to raise taxes, just as local, state, and federal taxes are raised. Taxation has long been used to establish lines of authority: paying taxes directly to the union would make people direct citizens of that union, in addition to their nation, state, and locality. Whether taxes are high or low is not the issue: it is the authority to collect them that counts.

While these legal changes are taking place, however, an emotional change will be needed as well. People today define themselves by their nation. And while nationalism will never go away entirely, political integration requires that a person also define herself as a citizen of the union. As such, loyalties will have to shift somewhat, or there be will inevitable conflict. This is not unlike the confrontations over states' rights in nineteenth-century America (but one could hope the next shift will be handled more civilly). As labor mobility increases, and people spend their youths in multiple countries, some of this shift will naturally occur over time. Yet, for many people, perhaps for ones more stationary, there will need to be some compelling reason to align oneself to this higher-level enterprise. There would have to be such a hope and expectation of imminent prosperity that people would be willing to trust in it. But how could such a thing happen?

...

Well, if history repeats itself for a fifth time, it would suggest that the final step, the step to nation-union, will only occur after the right innovations come along. Specifically, a preconditioning innovation will be needed to create the synergies required for such imminent prosperity; an elevating innovation will be needed to enable resources to be managed in a new way; and a new governance basis will be needed to, in fact, be the next societal level—shifting authority to supranational bodies will only make it work better. But do we have any idea what these innovations might be? Do we know what the next governance basis will look like? Are there any traces of them now? While looking into the future is not an easy task, we can make the best guess with the information we have.

Chapter 15
The Next Governance Basis

NEW YORK—Kelly Clarkson ...was judged America's next pop
star Wednesday by the viewers of "American Idol." After more than
15 million telephone votes were cast by viewers ... more than 100
million votes were cast over the course of the show this
summer....The British [judge Simon] Cowell said he had to
"begrudgingly admit the talent is better here [in America]."[1]

Governance is about making decisions. With a new societal level, a new
way to make decisions about resources will be needed. So how will those
decisions be made in a nation-union? What will be the nation-union's
governance basis? Before going there, however, it would be helpful to know
why we need a new governance basis in the first place.

Nation-State Limitations

Nation-state governments have limitations. These are inherent limitations on
the efficiency and effectiveness of governance. These limitations generally
show up in the form of gridlock and bureaucracy. In the United States, the
amount of gridlock in Congress has soared over the last fifteen years: by one

---

[1] David Bauderap, "Out of 10,000, Texas Cocktail Waitress Kelly Clarkson Wins 'American
Idol'," Associated Press, September 4, 2002.

measure it has more than doubled since 1950. Up to 75 percent of salient issues can be tied up in gridlock with little likelihood of ultimate resolution. Even basic legislation, such as that used to fund government operations, has failed to pass on time, resulting in government furloughs and downgrading of the US debt. Political appointments had been stalled for years until changes in Senate rules finally freed up the logjam. Today discord is the norm: long-gone are the days when President Ronald Reagan and Speaker of the House Tip O'Neill railed against one another during the day, but socialized at the White House in the evenings. The divide appears to have grown so wide that personal relationships cannot bridge it. And of course, all this dysfunction raises frustration and contempt with Congress. Congressional approval ratings have been below 30 percent for the last ten years, even dropping down into the teens much of the time.

However, gridlock and bureaucracy are only the symptoms. This is not just an issue of congressmen behaving badly. The real problem is structural. It lies in the inherent limitations of nation-state governance. These limitations manifest themselves as gridlock, but they are rooted in the very fabric of rule-of-law and the surrogate form of government we use (surrogates can be elected officials or dictators—the people entrusted to run society on behalf of the people). Four dominant limitations exist: delay, distance, deviance, and disconnect. Every form of nation-state government has each of these at least to some degree.

Delay is the length of time it takes to pass and execute legislation under normal operating conditions. Every system of government requires some time to get its work done. Some forms of government are faster than others. Parliamentary systems are generally considered to work relatively fast because the prime minister comes from the legislature, so there is no separation of powers—both branches of government tend to agree with each other more often. In a presidential republic system, there is a strict separation of powers so there is built-in conflict, ideally healthy, but not so much at times. In October 2010, during a period of particular harsh austerity, Britain was able to pass budget cuts that dwarf even Republican proposed budget cuts in America (on a percentage of gross domestic product [GDP] basis). Delay in American government increases when one party controls the White House and the other controls the Congress, but new research has shown that delay soars when one party controls the House and the other party controls the Senate. The bicameral separation causes more delay than legislative-executive branch separation.

Delay is further increased by internal House or Senate rules that slow down the legislative process. These are not rules imposed by the Constitution, or by a republic form of government; these are rules developed over the years by members of the House and the Senate as their preferred way of doing business. While many rules undoubtedly had noble origins, their lingering impact has been to slow down the legislative process—often to a standstill. Take the filibuster, for example. The Senate allows a member to talk ad infinitum about any proposed bill. While this was originally intended to ensure that the minority position was heard, it has long been used to delay a bill from coming to a vote. The senator is allowed to talk as long as he wants, which led to twenty-plus-hour marathon speeches by southern senators during the Civil Rights era. In recent years, it has gotten even easier—the senator does not even have to show up. A senator can stall a vote by introducing procedural issues such as taking role calls or refusing to schedule a time to review amendments to stall the vote. During this time, senators go to dinner, C-span goes to blue screen, and democracy goes to hell. Prior to 1975, it took a vote of 66 out of 100 senators to break a filibuster; wisely, they dropped the requirement to 60 votes, but even that did not fix the problem. When a Senate leader calls for a vote to break the filibuster, the vote does not happen until two days later. In other words, the filibusterer can keep filibustering for another forty-eight hours. And after a vote has been called, taken, and passed, effectively ending the discussion, the Senate can get back to business—after another thirty-hour wait. What's more, a person can filibuster motions to proceed with the bill, amendments to the bill, going to conference on a bill, and so on. In all, up to a half-dozen opportunities exist to introduce a filibuster. While the "nuclear option" reduced the threshold needed to force a vote from 60 to 51 votes, it only applies to certain nominees to the judiciary or executive branch—something that arguably should have been moving along anyway. Efforts to change these rules have often been opposed by the elder leaders, working against younger colleagues who are dismayed at the way things work (or do not work).

While much of this is a self-inflicted wound, representative democracy still has a significant amount of built-in delay. Arguably, dictatorships have the least delay because favored projects proceed rapidly, and unfavored projects are killed off early. However, in either case, a decision is made.[2] So while some forms of government are faster than others, every form of nation-state government has some delay.

Distance is the limitation that occurs when people are physically or emotionally removed from their governmental seat of power. People are often distant from their capitals. Today, some nations span thousands of miles; territories make them even larger. In nations so large, a person on one edge could be days of travel away from the nation's seat of government. This was quite an issue before trains, planes, and automobiles shortened travel times. The logistical problems that once made it difficult to govern large territories have been erased through technological advances in transportation and communication. In that sense, distance is no longer the problem that it once was. This is important in the modern nation-state, where every citizen is supposed to be engaged.

While physical distance is no longer much of an issue, emotional distance remains a big one. This is the degree to which a person lacks connection with the political process. For many people, this takes the form of not caring and not voting. They believe that voting will not do any good, that all politicians are crooks, or that their participation is just not that important. For others, it takes the more active tone of cynicism, agitation, or anger. While such attitudes exist throughout the nation, they are often found in smaller, more isolated communities where such behavior can become reinforcing. In these environs, people can become more susceptible to extremist views, especially when hyped up by an extremist radio, web, or television personality. For

---

[2] Dictatorships are indeed a form of nation-state government. Dictators are often chosen by people before they usurp total power through a coup d'état or other means. They are positioned for power through institutions created by the laws of their country, such as the military, rather than by heredity. Enforcement comes through institutions linked to party rule rather than through a royal family. That said, dictatorships are a form of nation-state government that didn't fully develop. They lack the checks and balances of representative democracies. As such, they act like quasi-fiefdom in a nation-state context.

example, they may hear that mainstream media is the enemy, is inept, or is not to be trusted. Few people are interested or able to sort through the messiness of politics enough to take moderate tones on issues, so most take the easier path of one political extreme or the other. Communities who could benefit from government programs scorn them out of groupthink or blind camaraderie. Distance has gone from disenfranchisement into distrust.

In the early years of this decade, political interest groups were adept at exploiting distance in America. A well-organized group was able to compose a message of frustration and to secure candidates to deliver it. The message preached against compromise and for a take-no-prisoners approach to changing Washington. Local communities that succumbed to their ideology quickly voted out even long-term incumbents who appear to be more moderate. Through political gerrymandering, borders were changed to further isolate and homogenize congressional districts, ensuring that one political party had a lock on it for years to come. And while overall congressional ratings hovered in the teens, their local representative routinely polled well over 50 percent, implying: The problem is not with us—it is with everyone else.

These representatives brought their rancor to Washington, and civil discourse gave way to toxicity. Compromise was collaboration, which of course meant treason, so it was replaced by ardent ideology, bordering on demagoguery. While their numbers were not high enough to pass legislation, they could stall legislation—and they did just that. Rather than offering their own policy ideas, their focus shifted to blocking anyone else's. Ideas about climate change, immigration reform, and gun control never got very far. Even basic legislation—the routine stuff that no one even thought was political—suddenly became a weapon. This led to a shutdown of the federal government in 2013, and to a near default on the federal debt, an action that led to the downgrading of US bonds. Distance went from distrust to disruption to dysfunction.

While it would be easy to blame all of this on one group, in reality, it actually reveals another limitation of nation-state governance. The legislative process in nation-state governments works largely through a culture and a custom of dialogue and compromise. When someone does not want to listen, nor work with the opposition, nation-state governance tends to bog down. In times past, disruptive tactics would not have found a quorum in American politics, except perhaps on extreme social issues. However, with the increased polarization of recent years, such behavior has become a norm. The increased distance between local communities and the nation as a whole has frayed the underlying fabric of cooperation needed to make the system work. Fiefdoms and dictatorships do not expect their people to engage in governance, and neither do they want them to—either directly or indirectly through representatives. For kings and dictators, distance is a good thing. It reduces unwanted meddling. For representative democracy, however, distance, especially when gone to an extreme, is a problem.

Deviance is the limitation created when surrogates work for themselves rather than for the good of society. While institutional deviance began in the era of chiefdoms, its effects are more catastrophic in the era of nation-states. The most obvious examples occur in dictatorships. There, unlimited authority gives dictators an ability to do as they please with the nation's resources. Many of them amass huge fortunes by exploiting these resources: Teodorin Obiang of Equatorial Guinea, $600 million; Saddam Hussein of Iraq, $2 billion; Mobutu Sese Seko of Congo, $1–5 billion; Ibrahim Babangida of Nigeria, $12 billion; Sani Abacha of Nigeria, $3 billion; Daniel Arap Moi of Kenya, $1 billion. For some, their worldwide financial webs of tax havens, bank accounts, private estates, shell companies, and secret trusts appear so complex that running them must have been a full-time occupation.

Clearly these dictators did not feel any obligation to their societies. Their only concern was simply a matter of how much they could get. Since dictatorships lack the checks and balances that democracies have, there was nothing to stop the power grab—only the next coup. If a dictator survived long enough, he accumulated a lot of wealth. When I was in college, on a few occasions, friends from developing countries told me that democracy does not work in the third world (as it was called back then). I bristled at this, refusing to believe that good old American democracy was not a panacea for everyone. Despite that these were different friends, from different parts of the world, telling me this at different times, their stories were similar. Corruption was accepted, bribes were expected, and kickbacks were a business norm. In one case, a friend told me that in his home country of Nigeria, people who went into the government did so with the expressed purpose of pocketing its wealth: they would not go into government if they could not do this because otherwise it would not pay enough.

Democracies are not free from deviance. Stories about a public official being indicted for graft, corruption, bribery, or kickbacks appear in the newspaper from time to time. These can occur at a local, state, or federal level. While reforms over time have reduced the frequency of these crimes, they still occur—examples of someone enriching himself at society's expense. More subtle forms of deviance occur when all the members of a congressional committee are intentionally biased in favor of only one side of an issue: for example, the financial committee that oversees securities regulation stacked with Wall Street executives, or an agricultural committee overseeing farm subsidies composed only of former farmers. (Who represents the urban consumer?) While this may typically happen without much thought going into it, it becomes deviant if it happens intentionally in a way that precludes the committee from coming up with the best solution for overall society.

Deviance in a democracy can take an even milder form still—in the form of partisan politics performed at the expense of overall society. While nearly everyone inside a political party will say: What is good for the party is good for the country; most independent observers will likely say: Not so fast. Take the 2012 US presidential election. In 2012, the US economy was still muddling in the Great Recession. The economic recovery, or the lack of one, was the primary election issue. The Republican Party clearly had a vested interest in the economy *not* recovering: the odds of the party taking the White House were much higher if the economy continued to stumble—or better still, if it tanked altogether. Reporters kept speculating whether the United States was on the verge of a "double dip" recession, which certainly would have led to President Obama being ousted from office. Clearly, having the economy tank was not in the best interest of the American people. This dichotomy of incentives—what was in the best interest of the party versus the best interest of society—set up an unusual environment. Many have argued that Republicans ramped up their obstructionism strategy: any legislation could be perceived as a political victory—jobs bills, stimulus package extensions, and health care legislation were killed or stalled. Indeed, 2011–2012 saw the second-highest gridlock rate on record.[3] (Despite this, the economy recovered enough for the incumbent to win.) So it would appear that representative democracy is not free from deviance—it just shows it in a different form.

So while deviance can be blatant or subtle, all forms of government experience it to some extent: it is part of the political process. Whenever surrogates put self-interest ahead of society's interests, however, the nation-state suffers the consequences.

Disconnect is the fourth limitation. Disconnect results from a fragmented and disjointed legal code. America's legal code is a miscellany of laws and regulations. No one even knows how many federal criminal laws there are—the best estimate is around 4,500. In addition, there are an estimated 300,000 federal regulations that have prosecutorial elements in them: again, no one really knows the exact number. Then there are tens of thousands of criminal state and local laws. And very little structure exists to make sense of any of this. Originally, criminal laws were found under Title XVIII of the *US Code*, but as more laws were added, they spread beyond this boundary. Because Congress finds it easier to pass new laws than to delete old ones, over time the legal code grew like a vine. Today's criminal laws are scattered across all 52 titles in the *US Code*. With context, criminal laws, regulations, and ordinances are difficult to understand; without context, they are nearly impossible to understand.

The problem with all of this is that it weakens governance and wastes money. A convoluted legal code creates rigidity in governance. This rigidity restricts its ability to adapt to a changing environment. Furthermore, a confusing legal code is harder to enforce. Even the president has acknowledged this:

> The Interior Department is in charge of salmon while they're in fresh water, but the Commerce Department handles them when

---

[3] The worst on record according to a Brookings Institute analysis was 1999–2000.

they're in saltwater. I hear it gets even more complicated once they're smoked.[4]

A convoluted legal code also wastes money. Many laws and regulations have programs and expenditures attached to them, so when a law or regulation becomes obsolete, its expenditure continues as a form of waste. Indeed, some Depression-era programs still exist that now pay farm subsidies to millionaires and boost the wages of already overpaid contractors. The 1970s Special Education bill, notwithstanding its noble intent, consumes over 20 percent of the government's K–12 budget despite the tiny percentage of student who receive its benefits. And until recently at least, survivor benefits were still being paid to two descendants of Civil War veterans and ten relatives of Spanish-American War participants.

Some countries aggressively manage their legal code. In Germany, the Federal Ministry of Justice makes sure statutes work together in a coherent way. In South Korea, the Ministry of Government Legislation works continuously to improve existing legal structures. And in the 1980s, New Zealand went as far as to rewrite much of its legal code from scratch—its environmental laws alone went from a 25-inch-thick tome down to 348 pages.

Efforts to eliminate outdated US laws have not gotten very far; in fact, the prospect of streamlining the *US Code* seems so overwhelming that most politicians avoid the subject altogether. Nevertheless, the issue is receiving new focus. In January 2017, President Donald Trump signed an executive order mandating government agencies to eliminate two regulations for every new one introduced, and that any new costs had to be offset by eliminating old costs. Another idea is to attach sunset clauses to new programs so that they do not continue in perpetuity without review. And while few would support rewriting the entire *US Code*, one proposal may help, but with much less pain: moving the 4,500 criminal violations back underneath Title XVIII and cross-referencing them to other parts of the legal code. Indexing and

---

[4] President Barak Obama, "Remarks by the President in State of Union Address," The White House, January 25, 2011, https://www.whitehouse.gov/the-press-office/2011/01/25/remarks-president-state-union-address (accessed August 25, 2015).

cataloging these laws may add a further level of resolution. In addition, making all of this available over the Internet might even give teeth back to the principle of "ignorance of the law is no excuse." (Did you know it was a federal crime to ride a manatee?)

While these limitations create gridlock in a nation-state, they will all but preclude a nation-union from forming. The reality is that, as a nation-state, we can stumble along with these limitations. We may not like all the gridlock and dysfunction, but we can live with it. This is not the case for the nation-union. A nation-union could not form with these limitations, and if one somehow did form, it would eventually fall back to a nation-state. In a nation-union, where more resources are managed at a faster pace, speed bumps become Jersey walls and annoyances become solvents. These limitations will have to be significantly reduced before an aggregate society becomes feasible.

Without a change in governance basis, delay will worsen in a nation-union. Adding another layer of bureaucracy to government will make it even slower than it is now. Elevating issues from a local level to a supranational level, with competing interests at every layer, would take years. And with different ethnic and language groups collected under a single government, there would be more issues. With more issues to address and resolve, a longer deliberation process would be needed. Routine legislation could become so slow that effective governance is unachievable. If internal legislative rules further slowdown the process, nothing would ever get done. Attempts to keep decision making at lower levels would help but ultimately would not suffice— a union that can solve all its problems at a national level is not really a union. Hence, the prospects for a nation-union could be doomed by delay alone. If the nation-union had to operate in the faster world that is expected, delay would mean demise.

Distance will worsen in a nation-union. A larger territory means more people will be, on average, farther away from their government. In addition, some people will now have a national border in between them and their government. With the increased physical distance comes increased emotional distance. The feeling becomes even more acute if language barriers and cultural differences have to be crossed. Even knowing there is another level of governance—one step higher and further away than their national government—could be enough to increase the feeling of distance. With all this, the nation-union will be more susceptible to disenfranchised citizenry than the nation-state. In a larger, more diverse society, with more diverse interests, there will likely be more political opportunists eager to exploit this situation, in which case disenfranchisement turns into distrust. Whether it ultimately reaches to the level of disruption and dysfunction will depend upon the political parties of that day; but whether that happens or not, the nation-union, under the current governance basis, will be more susceptible to disruption than the nation-state.

Deviance will worsen in a nation-union unless there is a change in governance basis. If a nation-union were to form without the proper checks and balances, the results would be disastrous. An unscrupulous leader could pocket the wealth of several nations instead of just one; he would amass a fortune in the tens of billions of dollars instead of just billions. In reality, however, such a union could never form. Nation-unions depend upon rule-of-law to exist, just as nation-states do. If rule-of-law were not robust, nations would not be able to collogue together in the first place—no one would trust each other enough to work together. Even bribes, corruption, and kickbacks would be enough to undermine the fragile workings of a young nation-union. If these problems were overcome somehow, then political jockeying could still do it in. A nation-union will have more political parties than a nation-state. As such, it will be more susceptible to partisan jockeying in the legislative process. This might be avoided through coalition forming, as is done in parliamentary governments, however. In any event, something would have to be different from the nation-state to corral the increased potential for deviance in a nation-union.

Disconnect will also worsen in a nation-union unless there is a change in governance basis. If nation-states create incoherent legal codes, then a nation-union would create a stack of incoherence upon incoherence. When the European Union (EU) was formed, it had to rationalize almost three hundred conflicting national laws. Truth be told, the process was never completed—the EU ended up agreeing to ignore the differences between many of these laws. While this approach has worked for the EU, it would not work in a true nation-union—one that had to operate faster and more efficiently. A convoluted legal code will lead to rigidity in governance, accumulation of outdated laws, proliferation of obsolete (but zealously guarded) programs, and an inability to adapt to a changing environment. This bloated government will have to operate in a world that is faster than today—its incoherent and inconsistent laws will put a drag on society. A continent's worth of outdated programs will consume untold resources. As such, disconnect could be enough to make a forming nation-union into a deformed nation-union.

Because of these four limitations, the nation-state has reached its size limit. Some of the gigasocieties around the world (i.e., India and China) are at maximum capacity for managing resources using the current approach—an approach that has been around since the seventeenth century, mind you. These nations struggle to raise their standard of living, in part due to these limitations. These limitations also provide insight on the only nation-union to have ever existed: the Soviet Union.

The Soviet Union lasted almost seventy years, forming in 1922 and dissolving back into independent nation-states in 1991. While conventional wisdom attributes this to a failure of communism, I would say that this fallback was inevitable—predestined because of these four limitations. Without a true change in governance basis—and communism was not a change in governance basis—a fallback was going to happen regardless of which form of nation-state government was adopted. Early communists likely believed they were changing their governance basis (they obviously did not call it that). The term *soviet* means "council"—almost harkening back to the time when tribal councils made the decisions for the whole of society. While this was a true governance basis during the tribal era, it had long since ceased to be applicable for a modern power.

Most likely the Soviet Union lasted as long as it did by falling back into nation-state status during the 1930s, when the other Soviet republics ceased to be independent and became puppet provinces of Josef Stalin's Kremlin. In this condition, with enough tanks, the nation-union could be sustainable for seventy years. For a nation-union to be sustainable indefinitely, the world will have to see something it has never seen before—a new way of managing resources.[LII]

The Next Step

So if there has to be a new governance basis, what will it be? What new approach to managing resources would remove the nation-state limitations, enabling societies to expand to a new level? Once again, history can be our guide. We can see what trends were at work in past governance bases, and project them forward to make a guess at the next governance basis. Assuming these trends continue (and we have already discussed why they would), we can better understand what it would take to sustain a nation-union.

Each societal level managed resources differently. Bands used consensus; tribes used council consensus; chiefdoms used nonfamilial authority; fiefdoms use remote authority; and nation-states use rule-of-law. In consensus, resource decisions were made by an individual family head or by agreement if the decision involved multiple families. No formal enforcement mechanism was needed because the person who made the decision carried it out.

In council consensus, tribal councils made the decision for families within the tribes. Council members were usually related, and the tribes were large extended families. The only enforcement was based on respect for the elder council member, who was usually a family patriarch.

In nonfamilial authority, a chieftain made the decisions. The chiefdom consisted of multiple tribes, so one person from one of the tribes had final authority. While he received input from other members of the chiefdom, he had the final say. His family enforced those decisions, aided by general loyalty to the chieftain.

In remote authority, a king (baron, duke, pharaoh, sheik, czar, or other titled person) made the decisions. Others may have made smaller decisions, but the king had the ultimate authority. Civil servants enforced those decisions, using royal institutions such as courts and security forces. Members of the royal family were appointed as ministers, overseeing those institutions and civil servants.

In rule-of-law, decisions are made by individuals authorized by law to make them. The law determines which decisions are made and by whom. This could be a president, a prime minister, a representative, or even a dictator. Enforcement comes through institutions established by law to enforce those decisions—a police force, a court, a regulatory agency, and so forth.

Decision making and decision enforcement are the two fundamental dimensions of governance bases: they determine how a society will manage its resources. Interestingly, when you put them on a graph, a pattern emerges (Figure 27).

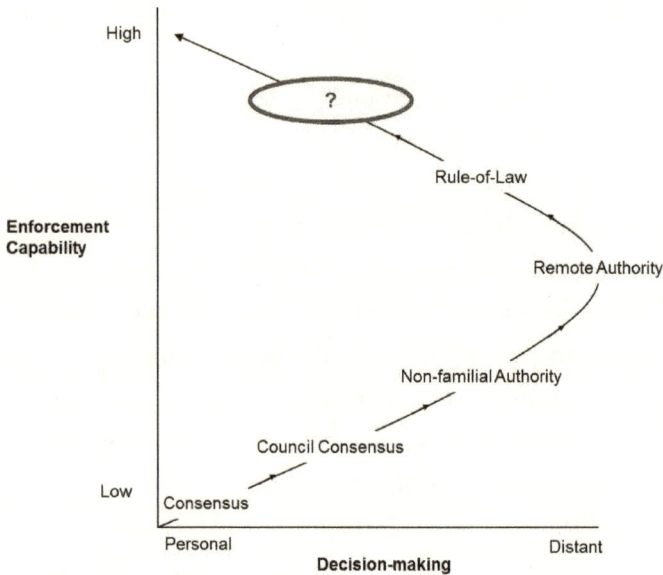

Figure 27. The progression of governance bases.

In consensus, everyone made his or her own decisions. In council consensus, decision making was transferred to a council. In nonfamilial authority, decision making was transferred even further away from the individual, to a chieftain who may not even be a member of the family. Remote authority represented the apex of this transfer—decision making went to someone a person may have never even met. Decision making took a step back closer to the individual with rule-of-law, when it was transferred to authorized individuals (representatives in a democracy).

In consensus, no enforcement was needed because everyone did his own thing. In tribal consensus, enforcement was based on compliance and familial respect for the authority of the tribal council, which was greater than two individuals fighting with each other. In nonfamilial authority, the chief and his family acquired a monopoly on violence. This was used to enforce his decrees when personal respect was not enough. In remote authority, enforcement was delegated to civil servants (scribes, judges, court attendants, and sheriffs) who acted on the king's behalf. Each civil servant had a particular responsibility and enforcement authority commensurate with that area of responsibility. In rule-of-law, institutions (armies, police forces, and regulatory agencies) enforce laws. In total, every change in governance basis increased enforcement capability: it became stronger, broader, or more precise.

Putting these dimensions together reveals the necessities of life over time. Early societies were willing to trade off decision making for enforcement capability. The first three governance basis changes shifted more authority to a more remote figure—from oneself, to a relative, to a chief, to a king. People were willing to give away their authority because it made their lives better—justice became more effective, life became more stable, and at some point prosperity improved, demonstrating the wisdom of the move.

Then it reached a turning point. The Magna Carta was that turning point. In 1215, a group of English barons decided that they had had enough kingly authority and endeavored to take some of it back. Suffering under unbearable taxes, the barons launched a war against King John I. Before the king was killed, and a new one installed in his place (the normal course of action), the Church brokered a peace agreement. By concurring in the peace document, the king agreed to limits on his own authority. This action, though he probably did not realize it at the time,[5] subordinated the king's authority to written law. This was the apogee of decision-making authority.

The rule-of-law used law to move decision making back closer to the individual. It did this through the use of elected officials and representatives (or other surrogates). Eventually, representative bodies emerged. Conceptually, decision making moved back to a point where, though you may not know the decision maker, he was not so far away that you could not

---

[5] King John later claimed he had never agreed to it.

meet him on some occasion—somewhat like a chieftain. Unlike a chieftain, however, people could swap him out if they needed to. In addition, rule-of-law used laws to increase enforcement capability. No longer did these two dimensions have to be traded against each another: society could have both. People could have their cake and eat it too.

So what can we know about the next governance basis? Principally, the next governance basis will continue the trend of more personal decision making *and* increased enforcement capability. Personal decision making is natural. People inherently want to have a say in the things that are important to them. But people will no longer trade off decision making for enforcement. Even twentieth-century examples of this, such as early 1930s Germany, were temporary periods that are not indicative of a new governance basis. The next governance basis will find a way to deliver both or it will never come to light— if people do not embrace a new governance basis, it does not catch on. And the ancient limitations that once necessitated a trade-off no longer exist, so the world of tomorrow will expect more.

But how can a society that may have upward of a billion people make personal decisions? Personal decisions on a grand scale can only be made through more collective decision making. This requires *direct democracy*— giving people an opportunity to vote directly on issues. While this is done sparingly today, it will become the norm in the future. Not every issue will require a public vote, but those issues that are important to people—structural issues, values issues, and big resource issues—will be voted on directly by the people. This will give back to humanity a piece of what it traded away millennia ago—a closer role in the decisions being made for society. It is the first dimension of a new governance basis.

The other dimension is increased enforcement capability. Increased enforcement capability can take different forms. It can mean more than simply hiring more police officers. In the nation-state, it has meant greater specialization—entire government agencies were formed to enforce specific laws. In America they include the Federal Bureau of Investigation; the Department of Alcohol, Tobacco, and Firearms; the Drug Enforcement Agency; Customs & Border Patrol; and the Securities and Exchange Commission, to name a few.

Greater enforcement can also mean better tools, equipment, or weapons to fight crime. DNA testing has been introduced in recent decades to ensure greater accuracy in legal cases. It provides more reliable evidence of wrongdoing or can refute previous blunders that placed innocent people on death row.

Greater enforcement can also mean a more precise application of law enforcement, especially in the use of force. Today's ubiquitous video cameras are changing law enforcement, allowing the public to scrutinize more closely individual police actions involving the use of force and holding senior police officials accountable for the actions of their officers.

Greater enforcement can mean that laws become more precise. Most states now have multiple classifications for murder, each with its own sentencing criteria. This is an attempt to more precisely align punishment with the intent behind a killing. (Nineteenth-century America did not worry about such things.)

Greater enforcement can mean more consistent sentencing. It could mean removing biases in sentencing such as the difference between selling crack cocaine versus powder cocaine despite there being no legitimate reason why there should be a difference.

Moreover, greater enforcement can mean having a more coherent and consistent legal code by which crimes are defined. This is the enforcement change that would most likely come with a new governance basis: the other improvements could, and should, happen anyway.

Each governance basis is an effective and sustainable way that society has used to manage its resources. The dimensions reveal the differences between these ways. The new position indicates that there could be another effective and sustainable way by which society could manage its resources. But this begs the question: Will it work? Could it sustain a nation-union? Conceptually, the indications are positive. Direct democracy could reduce three of the four nation-state limitations, and greater enforcement capability could reduce the last one. If the new position reduced them far enough, then societies embracing it would be free to begin migrating to a new societal level.

Direct democracy could reduce delay by limiting the legislative debate on some issues. While a nation-union would add another layer of bureaucracy, increasing delay, much of this could be reduced by having the public vote directly on more issues. Instead of a bill languishing in a legislature, a time limit would be set for resolution, after which the bill would go to the people for decision. Internal chamber rules would be modified to reduce the time needed to produce legislation, or the public would start making the calls. Even the threat of an issue going to the people would likely be enough to force resolution. Issues that legislators avoid—such as entitlements, gun control, immigration reform, or deficit reduction—would be put on the docket and resolved or at least advanced; in other words, legislators would be forced to legislate. While all of this is still conceptual, and thousands of details would need to be worked out, direct democracy could reduce the limitation of delay by forcing action.

Greater direct democracy could reduce distance by making people feel that they have more personal ownership over what the government does. While a larger society, national borders, and another layer of government could make one feel more distant from the government, giving every adult a vote on issues important to him or her reduces that distance—the person who votes stays engaged. While no one is going to want to vote on every single issue, even voting once in a while would be enough to draw a person into the political process. And because her vote counts, she is less likely to be moved by extremists who prey on feeling of disenfranchisement. The more people brought into the political process by direct voting, the more distance is reduced.

Greater direct democracy could reduce deviance by having more people watch over the governance process, and by placing the public over bureaucrats. Like shareholders who review CEO compensation through a board, or citizens who recall their state governor through a political action committee, direct democracy would establish a more robust oversight structure. With more people observing surrogate behavior, people would become aware sooner if something looked out of order. If a government official were rapidly amassing wealth, a review and possible recall might be warranted. And though partisan deviance could rise with the number of political parties, at some point, every issue has to be decided or it goes to the public. At the end of the day, work has to get done, so there is a time limit placed on infighting and stonewalling. The net effect is that direct democracy could reduce deviance.

Greater direct democracy will not likely decrease disconnect, however. In fact, it could make it worse. A nation-union will not only have to rationalize the disparate laws of multiple nations, but it will have the public creating laws, risking the creation of a legal patchwork that makes governing even more difficult. However while direct democracy may not be the answer, greater enforcement capability could address this. If greater enforcement were to mean instituting and maintaining some kind of coherent legal code, then the limitation of disconnect could in fact be reduced.[6]

So by increasing direct democracy and enforcement capability, a new governance basis could reduce the four nation-state limitations. By managing resources collectively, societies can increase their capacity to manage resources effectively over larger populations and territories. In other words, by embracing *direct governance* societies can move to the next societal level.

But is there any evidence that any of this could work? This may sound good in theory, but can it really happen? The truth is that it is happening already, and has been for a long time.

Referendums

Direct democracy is not new to governance. It has been around for years in the form of referendums. A referendum is an issue-based election: people vote directly on a specific law rather than have legislators vote on the law for them. Referendums have been used recently to settle major issues in Europe. The most glaring example is Brexit, where in June 2016, the United Kingdom voted to leave the EU.[7] However, there are others. In May 2015, Ireland used a referendum to decide whether to legalize same-sex marriage. It passed with over 62 percent of the 1.9 million votes supporting it. In September 2014,

---

[6] How this might work is a lengthy subject treated in an upcoming chapter.
[7] I predict that within a generation, they'll have another referendum to rejoin the EU.

Scotland used a referendum to decide whether to remain a part of the United Kingdom. In the election, 55 percent of the 3.6 million votes cast favored remaining in the union. The UK has had twelve referendums since 1973, many of them relating to their role in the EU. Switzerland has used them even longer, going back to the country's founding as a modern republic in the nineteenth century.

Referendums in America go back even further—to the colonial era when New Englanders used them to develop town ordinances. Since then, referendum usage in America has gone in cycles. They were used quite a bit in the late nineteenth and early twentieth centuries rising with the populist movement. They also faded with the populist movement, hitting an all-time low in the 1960s. Resurgence began in 1978 with California's Proposition 13—an initiative that reduced property taxes from almost 3 percent to only 1 percent of assessed value. (It passed with almost 63 percent of more than 6.8 million votes favoring it.) Within two years, fifteen other states passed similar referendums. California continued using referendums; one was even used to recall its governor in 2003. By the end of 2014, Californians had held their sixth referendum within a decade, their forty-ninth since referendums were legalized in 1912.

Referendums have been used to decide issues across the board—liberal, conservative, libertarian, and populist. Referendums have been used for national issues and local issues. Referendums have been used for issues where elected officials lack legitimacy, such as changes to a voting law.

Despite this long-time usage, direct democracy has been criticized as being susceptible to manipulation. Referendums have been used by politicians who need the people to legitimize a pet project that lacked votes in the legislature. In addition, referendums have been vulnerable to charismatic leaders who used them to build support for their own agendas: Adolf Hitler and Benito Mussolini were particularly effective at using referendums to endorse oppressive policies, claiming it was the will of the people.

Critics also say that they are susceptible to the transient whims of the public. James Madison warned that they undercut the rights of the minority; he called them the "tyranny of the majority." And some legislators have complained that referendums constrain their ability to govern in a logical and cohesive manner—particularly where budgets are concerned. During California's 2009 fiscal downturn, one state senator denounced "ballot box budgeting" and the governor decried, "This is no way to run a state."

Despite these drawbacks, some areas have made it work. Contrary to some fears, people tend not to overreact: voters have shown adeptness at screening out initiatives that seem too extreme. Of the 2,051 US initiatives between 1904 and 2014, only 41 percent were approved; and only about one-quarter of initiatives ever made it to the ballot box.

Nevertheless, referendums have a knack for getting lethargic legislatures unstuck. The direct democracy movement in America grew in the 1890s as a way to bypass legislatures that would block desired reforms such as women's suffrage, direct election of US senators, and voting privacy. Twenty-four states eventually adopted the referendum process, starting with Oregon in 1904; and of course, these reforms became reality. More recently, despite the failure of the 2014 Scottish referendum, the process induced Britain to make concessions to Scotland—giving more power to its parliament. Scotland's first minister declared, "Scotland will expect these to be honored in rapid course—as a reminder, we have been promised a second reading of a Scotland Bill by March 27 next year."

Even the threat of a referendum is enough to induce legislators to act. In Switzerland, they have names for it: "referendumsdrohung" (threat of referendum) and "mit referendum drohen" (threaten to call for a referendum). When referendum usage there increased at the end of the twentieth century, many believed it was because the political parties grew less willing to compromise, so more votes had to go to the people.

Finally, referendums also have the effect of bringing people into the political process who have never participated before. The Scottish first minister also said, "Whatever else we can say about this referendum campaign, we have touched sections of the community who have never before been touched by politics." This has long been one of the main benefits (or evils, depending on your point of view) of the referendum process. In 1890s America, direct democracy was opposed by many in the ruling class. In the South, the gentry feared it would give more power to blacks; in Massachusetts, some power brokers expressed the same concerns about Irish Catholics. Like it or not, direct democracy gets people involved.

Concerning the future, referendums will likely have to become cheaper and easier to run if societies are ever going to use them more frequently. The British House of Lords declared in their 2010 session report, a referendum is "very expensive to do properly and if you are not going to spend the money on it, it is not worth doing it." As such, a new kind of supportive infrastructure—tools, techniques, processes, and technology—will be needed to make them happen more easily.

Part of this infrastructure would involve having a well-planned process for their execution. Such a process would identify when to call a referendum (to eliminate ad hoc political reasons historically used to call them); how to word the referendum and decide the acceptable responses (some referendums are more than yes/no); any constraints on political party and campaign behavior; and how to count the votes (not every issue is decided by simple majority).[8] Such a process, well defined in advance, would remove at least some of the confusion and partisanship that could derail a successful election.

Furthermore, new tools will be needed. The House of Lords identified a consolidated written legal code as a useful tool for helping Britain's referendum execution.[9] A coherent legal code would help societies avoid creating a legal patchwork. Some form of budgetary framework, one that highlights new expenditures or constraints, would be helpful for avoiding spending conflicts.[10]

Even without such infrastructure, referendums have long been a part of democratic governance. In some aspects, they take us back to the era of bands, when every family made its own decisions. While some of its most ardent supporters would have it become the exclusive form of government, and see the use of representatives as a necessary expedient only, most of its supporters see it as a useful augmentation to our current form of representative democracy. Few people want to do away with legislators entirely.[LIII]

---

[8] When modern Switzerland was formed in the nineteenth century, the leading party insisted on a double-majority to approve the new constitution: a majority of the popular vote and a majority of the Swiss cantons (states). The constitution passed by 73 percent of the popular vote and by fifteen of twenty-one cantons.

[9] Unlike in the United States, the legal code in Britain is not contained in a single document.

[10] California's Proposition 98, which mandates funds directly for K–12 education, has been accused of undermining legislative efforts to balance the budget.

Collective Intelligence

While history has shown a sporadic use of referendums, the prospect of expanding direct democracy in the future raises a nagging question: Can we really trust each other to make good decisions? No less than Alexander Hamilton himself, the father of American government,[11] had concerns that during the 1787 Constitutional Convention, state representatives were giving too much power to an uneducated public. While the citizenry of today is much more educated than that of the eighteenth century, the question lingers. Recent research, however, suggests that the future may look different concerning our ability to make group decisions. Researchers are beginning to better understand collective human intelligence.

The idea that a group of people can make wise decisions has gained much attention in the last decade. In *The Wisdom of Crowds*, author James Surowiecki observes that markets—groups of people—are better at making choices than are the individuals who compose them. A 1950s consumer may have thought his Studebaker was the best thing since sliced bread, but the rest of the market determined that Studebaker would not make the cut. The auto industry went from hundreds of companies in the early twentieth century to four by the 1960s, and Studebaker was not one of the four. It seems the market assimilates bits and pieces of information about a subject to make more informed and better long-term decisions than do individuals.

While the idea that groups of people are wiser than individuals has gained recent attention, it is not new. In a famous example, English mathematician Francis Galton, at a 1906 country fair, found that a crowd of about eight hundred people came closer to estimating the actual weight of a slaughtered ox than did local experts. When averaged, the crowd guessed 1,208 pounds—within 1 percent of the actual weight of 1,198 pounds. This phenomenon plays out in other scenarios. Ask a crowd how many jelly beans are in a jar, or ask the crowd of *Who Wants to Be a Millionaire* for an answer, or ask the crowd at a hockey game some obscure trivia question, and they tend to be pretty accurate.

---

[11] In likely the most comprehensive biography written on Alexander Hamilton, author Ron Chernow credits: "If Washington is the father of the country and Madison the father of the Constitution, then Alexander Hamilton was surely the father of the American government."

While it may seem amazing, the phenomenon is actually based on sound mathematical underpinnings. Some people in a crowd will forecast too high; others will forecast too low—these cancel out. What is left is an average that tends to be pretty accurate. And this has been used with impressive accuracy in various applications. From 1988 to 2004, small "wisdom of the crowd" forecasts were about as accurate as the massive Gallup presidential forecasts. Back in 1968, the navy used a similar approach to find a lost submarine, predicting its location to within two hundred yards after it sunk some four hundred miles southwest of the Azores. The idea behind this type of pooled forecasting is that each person offers a small bit of insight, and those "weak signals from diverse experts accumulate quickly."

The wisdom of the crowd does have its limitations, however; after all, a panic-stricken mob can hardly be considered wise. It is based on a few underlying assumptions that have to be met or the crowd will give biased answers. First, people's decisions have to be independent from one another: the more groupthink there is in a crowd, the more potential for bias there is. Second, the crowd has to be diverse: the more alike members of the crowd are, the narrower their range of answers will be and the less likely those answers will fall equally on both sides of the right answer.

The key to whether the wisdom of the crowd, or collective intelligence in general, will be useful for governance depends upon whether researchers can develop the understanding, tools, and techniques needed to apply it wisely and fairly. And researchers are trying to do just that.

Different research groups around the world are trying to find ways to understand and apply collective intelligence. Researchers at the Cajal Institute in Madrid are finding ways to remove bias from crowd decisions, enabling them to settle on wiser answers. Researchers at the University of Missouri are using statistics to define and measure the intelligence of a crowd and to determine when a crowd could be considered smarter than selected individuals. And at MIT's Center for Collective Intelligence, researchers are building a genome of collective intelligence—identifying the underlying building blocks of crowd wisdom. Another project is finding the best ways to integrate the different ideas from within a crowd to solve complex problems. One specific problem being tackled is climate change—the center is already working with thousands of people across the globe to solve this. Another project is developing a software tool (modeled after the swarming behavior of birds, fish, and insects) to network humans together and help them respond with unified collective intelligence.

The underlying premise for all of this research is that humankind is at a point in history when new technology can enable us to exploit collective intelligence like never before: websites such as Google, Wikipedia, YouTube, and Kickstarter are existing examples of this. Research may lead to solutions to problems that would have been unsolvable in any other way—climate change, poverty, terrorism, and healthcare, or crime, for examples—problems too big for any one expert or group. While this research is still in its early stages, it holds promise that many difficult decisions in the future will be made using collective intelligence.[LIV]

...

So with the future looking bright for making good decisions collectively, and with historical experience at administering referendums, the idea of managing resources collectively becomes plausible. It would continue the trend begun in the thirteenth century with the Magna Carta, of giving back more decision making to the individual, while still increasing enforcement capability. Doing so removes nation-state limitations: governments will become more responsive, and less susceptible to gridlock; people will feel connected to their government again; legislators will have more oversight and less room for errant behavior; and ultimately the legal code will be more responsive to the values and needs of the people. With these limitations removed, societies can assume larger proportions, growing in both population and territory. Nation-unions can begin to form.

But how would all this happen? Could current forms of government adapt to the new governance basis, or will there be the same kind of violent revolution that occurred during the last governance basis shift? Fortunately, this time governments should be able to adapt.

Chapter 16
The Next Elevating Innovation, Part I

Fantasy football has become all the rage in recent years. Millions of Americans glue themselves to television sets every fall, not cheering for football teams, but for individual football players—sometimes on opposing teams in the same game—hoping they contribute to the success of an imaginary team, in an imaginary league, of which the fantasizer is the head coach, general manager, and owner. The annual Draft Day has become a ritual, taking the form of a class reunion every August, and ranking somewhere between Halloween and Christmas in revelry. Fantasy football has become a media event. Television networks sponsor their own leagues and update player points in real time during live broadcasts. And temporary leagues now exist, where stout souls join, compete, and collect (or lose) money every week.

And all of this popularity is the result of the Internet. Over the World Wide Web, players can join leagues, draft players, look up statistics, and choose their starting lineups. Mobile apps have made it even easier since footballers can now do all of this from the convenience of a local coffee shop, restaurant, or work cafeteria. No longer is she tied to the home computer.

I was in a fantasy league back in the dark ages. From 1986 to 1997, every Thursday, I would tramp down to the local newsstand to buy the *USA Today* for the AFC stats. The next day I would repeat the trip for the NFC stats. On Saturday, I would go to a different newsstand, one closer to home, to get the injury report. If the newsstand was out of papers, I would drive to the next closest one, which could be blocks or miles away. If it was raining, I would hope I had an umbrella with me. If I was traveling and the hotel did not provide a paper in the morning, then I made finding a newsstand a priority alongside food and a replacement toothbrush. And despite all of this effort, the best I ever finished was second place—once. Today's footballers are so spoiled.

The next societal level will be nation-union and the next governance basis will be direct governance. The next question: What will be the next elevating innovation? To answer this, we have to ask: What innovation can change the way resources are managed? In the last chapter, we identified that direct governance will require some kind of new infrastructure and new tools to support the more frequent use of referendums; so what innovation could create such an infrastructure and tools? If one takes a giant step back, it becomes intuitive to say that the next elevating innovation is computing.

The computer, with all of its spin-off innovations, has created a communication platform for modern humankind. Computers went from behemoth mainframes to personal devices in half a century. Computers started out as isolated machines, but became nodes on an interconnected web by the end of the twentieth century. Computers moved from binary numerical devices to conveyors of human emotion by the early twenty-first century. With this platform in place, it is not a large step until we begin making decisions collectively about our resources over this device. But how did all of this come about? While computing evolved in different ways and enabled many functions, three aspects or dimensions stand out: personalization, connection, and socialization. And progress was made one step at a time.

Mainframes

Computers went from mainframes to minicomputers to microcomputers to personal computers to mobile devices between the 1940s and 2010s (Figure 28).

Figure 28. Computer progression from mainframe to mobile devices.

However, the mainframe did not suddenly appear in the 1940s: elements of it began centuries earlier. The first element, *programming*, was developed in 1206 CE when Al-Jazari, a mechanical engineer working at the local palace at Artuklu (present-day Cizre, Turkey) built the Castle Clock. The face of the clock was a large rectangle, about eleven feet tall and nine feet wide. As the day passed, a crescent moon pointer traveled horizontally across the face, starting at sunrise and ending at sunset. Each hour, one of twelve shutter doors opened, puppet musicians played, and marbles dropped onto a cymbal. A water wheel drove the clock, turning levers, cams, and pulleys to move the displays. Floats precisely controlled the water flow enabling phenomenal accuracy for its day, especially when compared to sundials.

Before sunrise, an operator reset the clock for the day. Because each day is slightly longer or shorter than the day before, the crescent moon pointer had to travel slower or faster than it did the day before. The operator adjusted the water flow regulator, which in turn changed how fast the float would drop, ropes would pull, and pulleys would turn. While earlier clocks and other devices performed a single function the same way each time, this clock performed a function differently depending upon the instructions given to it. These instructions were stored within the device to direct the machine's operation. As such, this was the first programmable device.

The next element, *binary programming*, was introduced nearly six centuries later, when in 1801, French weaver and merchant Joseph Marie Jacquard invented a weaving loom that used punch cards to prescribe a garment's pattern. One punch card corresponded to one row of the pattern. Holes punched in the card (or their absence) determined when to raise or lower the harness (the weft) that held the garment. Thread then passed either above or below the weft, creating a pattern. A stack of cards prescribed a full pattern, and cards were changed to change patterns.

The Jacquard loom used binary programming: whereas the Castle Clock introduced analog programming, binary programming would become the basis for computing a century later. Later, player pianos and tabulating machines would also use binary programming.

The next element of modern computing, *binary data storage*, was created toward the end of the nineteenth century. In the early 1880s, Herman

Hollerith began to develop tabulators (counting machines) based on punch cards. He became fascinated with punch cards when he saw how train conductors stored information about passengers by punching holes in different places on their tickets. In 1882, he went to work at MIT to do research; then a couple of years later, he went to work for the Census Bureau, where he filed a patent.

The 1880 census had taken seven years to complete. During the 1880s, America had grown so fast that the Census Bureau believed it would take thirteen years to complete the next census. To avoid a calamity, in 1888 the Census Bureau held a competition, where three companies vied for the contract to tabulate data for the upcoming census.

Hollerith created a device that resembled a waffle iron. Punch cards would be placed into the device. When closed, metal pins passed through a card in locations where a hole existed, and dipped into tiny wells of mercury. This completed a circuit that incremented a counter. About eighty cards per minute (one family per card) could be tabulated. Cards could also be grouped into aggregates using simple circuitry.

The Hollerith tabulators easily won the competition. They captured the test data in 72.5 hours (vs. 100.5 for the next competitor) and prepared the data in 5.5 hours (vs. 44.5). Later, the Hollerith machines completed the 1890 census in less than a year—"months ahead of schedule and far under budget."

The use of punch cards for data storage was revolutionary: it effectively created modern information processing. Until this time, programmable devices controlled mechanical actions (looms and pianos). Now, punch cards stored binary data while a programmable device read them, performed a function, and output new data. Later machines would print counter totals on paper (instead of requiring an operator to write them down). In 1896, Hollerith created a machine that could add numbers—going beyond counting, and plug boards, which contained different circuitry for different operations. Tabulators became popular for inventory management across industries. Ultimately, Herman Hollerith's company was one of the four that merged in 1911 to found what would become IBM.

The final element, *language*, was added in the late 1930s. Claude Shannon, a graduate student at MIT, noticed a similarity between Boolean algebra and relay circuits. Boolean algebra is a branch of mathematics that focuses on processing ideas that are either false, represented by 0, or true, represented by 1. (Shannon had been introduced to Boolean algebra as an undergraduate at the University of Michigan.) Relays were electromechanical switches commonly found in telephone routing equipment, as well as the early analog computer he was working with at the time. A relay had to be either open (conducting no current, 0) or closed (conducting current, 1). Since Boolean algebra had been developed in the previous century, it was a fairly robust science. Since relay circuitry was still fairly new, designs were plagued by ad hockery. Shannon wrote his 1937 master's thesis on how to apply Boolean algebra to relay circuit design in computers; perhaps most vitally, his thesis included a way to create conditional if-then operations.

The result was the creation of machine code—the language underlying all digital computers, even to this day. It provided the foundation needed for robust circuit design and for systematic programming. The modern computer exists because of it. And it became the final element of modern computer architecture.

With these four elements in place, the modern computer architecture was in place (Figure 29). Thenceforth, computer development would be a matter of refining ideas, improving components, and advancing technology. However, the main conceptual elements were set.

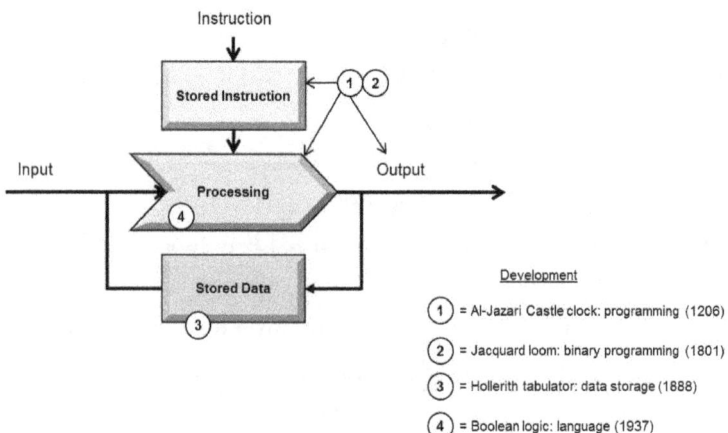

Figure 29. Key elements of a basic computer architecture.

With the architecture established, computers continued to grow in size and power. The first digital computer prototype was the Z-1, built entirely using relays by Germany's Konrad Zuse in 1938. While it was not a complete computer in the modern sense, it was an entirely electric, programmable device.

In 1942, the Atanasoff-Berry computer, or ABC, was built at Iowa State University. It was the first computer to use vacuum tubes instead of relays. Vacuum tubes had been invented at the beginning of the twenty-first century as an outgrowth of the lightbulb, and were extensively used in radios and telephones at the time. Despite this and other innovations, ABC was not a complete computer either.

The first complete computer was ENIAC, completed in February 1946 by the University of Pennsylvania. By then, most computers had switched to vacuum tubes; in fact, ENIAC had over 17,000 of them, as well as some 1,500 relays, 7,200 diodes, 70,000 resistors, 10,000 capacitors, and about 5,000,000 hand-soldered joints. Initially, vacuum tubes burned out several times a day, but a better tube came along in 1948, cutting the failure rate to one every couple of days. ENIAC was 8 feet wide x 3 feet deep x 100 feet long, weighed almost 50 tons, and consumed about 150 kW of electricity. It was the first complete computer because it was programmable, had conditional branching (essential for problem solving), and was Turing complete, meaning it was general purpose rather than specialty focused. As such, ENIAC was the first mainframe computer (Figure 30).

Figure 30. ENIAC ca. 1946.

While large and clunky by today's standards, these early mainframes were successfully built by universities for government projects such as calculating artillery tables, breaking codes, supporting guidance system development, and a host of other military and civilian tasks. Computers ran on machine code in those days—higher-level languages would not appear for a decade. Programming was done by inserting wires into plug boards, changing the way voltage flowed through the machine. Nevertheless, the foundation of the computer and all of its necessary components were established: subsequent developed merely improved on these components.[LV]

Minicomputers

The minicomputer was the first major step toward computer personalization; however, the path to the minicomputer had to be paved with many technical innovations along the way. The first post-ENIAC innovation came in 1948 when computers began storing programs in memory. Before then, computers were programmed using cable patch cords and plug boards. Programming instructions were introduced by moving the patch cords from one location to another to reroute the voltage flow through the machine—it took days to reprogram ENIAC. Meanwhile, data storage was done using punch cards, not unlike data storage in the old Hollerith machines, or punched tape, like in a player piano. In June 1948, the University of Manchester developed the Small-Scale Experimental Machine (SSEM), also known as the Manchester Baby. The Manchester Baby stored not only data on punch cards but also programs. So instead of rerouting patch cords, instructions were entered on punch cards; this cut programming time from days to hours.

Another major innovation of the late-1940s came when mathematician John von Neumann standardized computer architecture.[1] Computer architecture describes the layout—where memory goes, where calculations are made, and how information flows through the machine. Von Neumann created an architecture whose benefits were readily apparent. The von

---

[1] The von Neumann architecture was considerably more complex than the schematic shown in Figure 2.

Neumann architecture reduced the number of instructions required to execute the full command set from dozens to only twenty-one. This was first demonstrated on EDVAC, ENIAC's successor, in August 1949. By 1950, his architecture had become the industry standard.

Innovations continued throughout the 1950s. In November 1953, the University of Manchester created the first transistor computer. Transistors had been invented at Bell Laboratories only a few years earlier in 1947.[2] Transistors replaced vacuum tubes, and prompted designers to find new materials for other components as well. Within a few years, solid-state resistors, diodes, and capacitors began to replace older, clunkier versions, enabling computers to shrink.

Then in September 1958, Jack Kilby of Texas Instruments took the next step and developed a way to manufacture multiple transistors on a single semiconducting wafer, or chip. He then connected the transistors using fine gold wire to create a component (e.g., an oscillator). In September 1960, Robert Noyce of Fairchild Semiconductor obviated the gold wires by forming the chip with linkages in place. The integrated circuit was born.

IBM was the first to exploit this new innovation when it launched the System 360 in April 1964. The System 360 product line had memory ranging from 8K to 64K, was scalable as users' needs changed, and contained a full range of peripheral devices. IBM's $5 billion investment began paying off right away with over one thousand orders received in the first four weeks. Eventually, it would replace all five of IBM's existing products. By 1989, it accounted for half of the world's total inventory of mainframe computers.

Computer language did not stand still during this time either. Assembly language was invented in the late 1940s after computers began storing program instruction. It replaced endless 1s and 0s with words like "jump" and "add." *Assemblers* were written to convert assembly language into machine code to run computers.

Before long, programmers were looking for alternatives to assembly language. In 1949, short code was written with words that sounded more like

---

[2] John Bardeen, Walter Brattain, and William Shockley received the Nobel Prize for their work.

English. It was installed on a computer and tested.[3] While easier to use than assembly language, the programs had to be converted from short code to machine code every time a program ran, making it too slow to be useful.

Then in 1952, the University of Manchester invented the autocode language and a *compiler* to go with it. A compiler is a program that converts other programs, written in a higher-level language, into assembly language or machine code (a step more sophisticated than an assembler). Programs written in autocode were compiled once, then run on the university's Mark I computer as many times as desired. This changed programming forever: now entire languages could be developed to write understandable programs and that were then automatically converted into machine code. It was a game changer.

A number of compilers were written soon after autocode, each one supporting a particular language running on a particular machine. Then in 1953, IBM began looking for its own alternative to assembly language. IBM estimated that half of the cost of a computer center was spent on programming labor, so any reduction in programming time would deliver substantial savings. However, the user community was skeptical that a compiler could create efficient code. When the FORTRAN compiler was delivered in April 1957, it cut programming time twentyfold—any code inefficiencies were quickly forgiven. By 1960, almost all IBM mainframes had FORTRAN compilers. Then competing firms began creating FORTRAN compilers for their own machines—making it the first cross-architecture language. By 1963, more than forty versions of FORTRAN compilers were in operation. The success of FORTRAN spurred development of other languages. Over a dozen were created, COBOL emerging as the second dominant language of the period. "Third-generation languages" (after assembly language and machine code) became the norm for programming.

One other notable language innovation occurred during this time. In the early 1950s, hardware controls were still being handled within application programs. Programmers had to write code that not only solved a problem but

---

[3] An earlier language, Plankakul, was written in 1945 by Konrad Zuse for his Z3 computer, but it was never installed.

also ran the machine—batch processing, input/output interrupts, memory allocation, buffering, spooling, link-loading, run-time libraries, record sorting, to name a few. Programmers had to decide which computer hardware functions were needed by their program and then write it into code. To make things more difficult, these controls differed from machine to machine, so a particular program had to be tied to a particular computer.

As FORTRAN gained popularity, programs written in it had to become portable across platforms as well. This meant separating programs from machine controls. Initially, programmers started keeping ad hoc functions libraries that were architecture specific; they could then link their program to the controls needed for a particular type of machine. Then in 1959, the University of Michigan created a single program that controlled all of the hardware functions for its mainframe computer. The Michigan Algorithmic Decoder (MAD) supplied everything a program needed to run on its mainframe. Soon similar programs began to appear for other computers: these became an intermediary layer between a FORTRAN or COBOL program and the hardware upon which it ran. Later that year, IBM launched its own program, SHARE, for its 704 and later 709 mainframes. In 1964, IBM launched OS/360, an *operating system* that supported its entire System 360 product line. As a separate entity, operating systems bloomed, becoming optimized across architectures and increasing system speed and performance.

By the mid-1960s, Digital Equipment Corporation (DEC) was ready to take advantage of all these hardware and language (now called software) innovations to launch an entirely new type of computer. Since the UNIVAC was launched to satisfy business demand in the mid-1950s, corporate computers had been large mainframes shared by the entire company. In March 1965, DEC introduced the *minicomputer* to target departments within a company. While mainframes cost hundreds of thousands of dollars, the PDP-8 cost $18,000. Instead of taking a floor to house, the PDP-8 was the size of a refrigerator. While it did not have the capability of a mainframe, it had 4K 12-bit memory and used a teleprinter for input-out, which generally sufficed for business or academic departments.

The first PDP-8s were a throwback to assembly language and even used front panel switches instead of an operating system (a throwback to plug wires). They gained power and usefulness when the PS/8 (later OS/8) operating system was introduced in the late 1960s. By the mid-1970s, 16-bit and 32-bit processers were running UNIX and VMS operating systems, giving minicomputers the power formerly possessed by mainframes.

With minicomputers, individual departments within business, academia, or government now had immense computing power available directly to them. No longer did they have to share resources with everyone else. The computer had become more personal.[LVI]

Microcomputers

In 1971, Intel launched the first microprocessor, the 4-bit Intel 4004. It had been developed for a Japanese calculator company, Busicom. Both large-scale integration, which put hundreds of transistors onto a single chip, and random access memory, which greatly expanded memory capacity, had been invented in the late 1960s. Intel combined these onto a single board, consolidating core computer functions, which had been performed by multiple chips on multiple boards in multiple racks inside minicomputers. At $60 per chip, demand grew rapidly for its use in other applications. The following year, Intel released the 8008, an 8-bit version, which exponentially expanded processing power. Soon microprocessors spread from the computer's core to peripherals devices, such as signal processors, network interfaces, disk controllers, and graphics cards. They even began to replace integrated circuits in mainframe computers, causing an overhaul in mainframe architectures. Microprocessors then spread to noncomputer devices, from radar to appliances to devices across every industry.

Inside these microprocessors was microcode: multistep instructions stored in memory. Just as stored programs replaced plug wires in the late 1940s, microcode replaced tasks performed by wired chips. This enabled a further shrinking of the computer's core. This migration also simplified circuitry and created a smaller, more flexible architecture that was easier to debug—an important feature given the growing complexity of computer programs.

In short time, this new technology was being used to make smaller computers. The first attempt was the Kenback-1 in 1971. However, with limited functionality, only forty units were sold. In 1974, MITS launched the Altair 8800. Up to this time, only enthusiasts who built computers from scratch had their own computers; parts had to be ordered separately and assembled. The Altair 8800 was a complete kit that included a motherboard with an Intel 8080 chip on it, assembly instructions, a metal case, and a power supply. The input-output was a switchboard with lights on the front panel. Memory ranged from 1K to 4K depending on which options you bought. Despite its advanced features, programming was done in machine code, and there was no operating system—only operating programs called monitors that performed some low-level functions. Furthermore, it took several days for new owners to solder parts together before it could be used.

The Altair 8800 was featured in the January and February 1975 editions of *Popular Electronics* and listed for $439. By summer, Bill Gates and Paul Allen had written Altair BASIC and sold it to MITS for inclusion in the kit (they would later call their fledgling company Micro-soft.) About ten thousand Altair 8800 units were sold in its first two years of production, effectively beginning the *microcomputer* era. Now more individual hobbyists could enjoy assembling and using their own computers. The computer had taken another step toward personalization.[LVII]

Personal Computers

Despite the commercial success of the Altair 8800, microcomputers remained the province of hobbyists—people who liked tinkering with machines. The average person did not want to spend days soldering wires together. By 1977, three companies decided that there was a market for preassembled computers. Commodore introduced the Commodore PET, which came with a monitor, keyboard, cassette drive for storage, and BASIC software. Tandy introduced the TRS-80, which came with a keyboard and Microsoft BASIC. And Apple introduced the Apple II, which came with a color graphics card (the monitor remained separate), a keyboard, expansion slots, and BASIC. These three computers would eventually become known as the Trinity.

The difference between the microcomputer and the new *personal computer* was night and day. It was not computing power or internal hardware that made the difference: it was the overall experience with the computer that had changed. People were willing to try a computer if they could take it out of the box and use it right away.

Even preassembled machines, however, would likely not have been successful had it not been for third-party software companies that offered programs other than BASIC. Early consumers needed some familiarity with BASIC to even use the machine. Then third-party programs appeared: VisiCalc, a spreadsheet program, was released with the Apple II starting in 1979; and writing programs, such as WordPerfect and later Microsoft Word, enabled PCs (as they came to be known) to displace word processors.[4] Other programs ran databases, offered utilities, or provided games.

Even operating systems became more user-friendly. Early operating systems, such as CP/M and MS-DOS, required users to know something about computers to run them (e.g., c:\run to start a program). Then in 1984, Apple introduced a user-friendly, icon and menu-driven format with its Macintosh operating system. (This became known as a WYSIWYG format: what-you-see-is-what-you-get.) Microsoft Windows copied this format in 1995, and it became the industry standard.

All three of the original computers were big sellers. The Commodore PET sold almost a million units in its lifetime; the Tandy TRS 80 sold about 1.5 million units before the model was discontinued in 1981; and the Apple II sold more than 4 million by the end of its production run in 1993. In addition, in 1981, IBM changed its long-standing position against the personal computer, and entered the PC market. It became the leading brand almost overnight.

By the end of the twentieth century, dozens of PC companies had been started, over 500 million PCs were in use around the world, and over 1 billion had been sold since 1977. About three-quarters of those sold were used in the workplace, while one-quarter went into homes. The third party "packaged software" industry soared throughout the 1980s and 1990s, putting thousands

---

[4] Word processors were descendants of the electric typewriter and were common in the late 1970s and early 1980s. While they resembled electric typewriters, they had some built-in computer editing functionality.

of products on the market, and reaching over $100 billion in sales by 2000. The computer had become not only personalized but also ubiquitous.[LVIII]

Mobile Devices

While early personal computers individualized the computer experience, you could not walk around with them. In the early 1980s, laptop computers were introduced. These were small enough to carry like a briefcase and became especially popular for business travel. By the mid-1980s, personal digital assistants (PDAs) were introduced as a form of electronic day planner. They typically contained a calendar, to-do list, address book, notes page, and calculator. Around the same time, cellular phones were introduced. While they had been invented back in 1973, the first service subscriptions became available in 1983. By the 1990s, many consumers were carrying both PDAs and cell phones at the same time, so in 1994, IBM introduced Simon—the first combination PDA and cell phone, later to be called a *smartphone*. In addition to being a PDA and phone, Simon could send and receive faxes, and provided email service.

Then BlackBerry came along. Initially introduced as a pager, it launched its email-capable RIM 850 in 1999. Then in 2003, it began selling email capability as a service to other devices, such as the Palm Treo. By the end of 2004, it had 2 million email subscribers; by 2007, it had 10 million. Overseas mobile devices were even bigger. In Japan, the NTT DoCoMo smartphone had 40 million email subscribers by 2001. And in 2013, over 1 billion smartphones were sold worldwide.

Though personal computers may appear to have been eclipsed by mobile devices, they made a smashing comeback, albeit in a new form. In April 2010, Apple introduced the iPad—a tablet computer. Roughly the size of a book, iPads were lighter and more mobile than laptop computers, but they had more functionality than a smartphone. A touchscreen display obviated a keyboard, though that remained an option. The iPad was a worldwide sensation, and by October 2013, Apple had sold its 100 millionth tablet.

These mobile devices placed unprecedented computing power at a person's fingertips, anytime, anywhere. Independent email services sprouted up to satisfy the new demand, offering access to email, the Internet, online data storage, and other services. America On-line, Yahoo, and Google all became huge companies during the 1990s. Service became 24/7 and device independent, so no one was locked into any particular smartphone or tablet. A person might access her account from home, work, or while commuting. For the first time, most people in the world could be continuously connected from anywhere. The computer had become personalized. This was quite a change from the days of mainframes built in university basements.[LIX]

Internet Research and Foundation

While computers were shrinking from mainframes to mobile devices, another phenomenon was occurring: computers were becoming more connected. Starting out as isolated mainframes, computers became small devices that were connected to each other in a web that crossed the entire world—an evolution that took decades to accomplish.

In the early 1960s, there were hundreds of mainframe computers scattered throughout the country at universities, government agencies, and commercial enterprises. Each mainframe computer had its own community of users, tied together by time sharing. A few years earlier, mainframes began shifting from batch processing to time sharing, where multiple users could engage the computer at the same time. The social result was that a small community of users grew up around each mainframe. Users within the community could talk to each other using internal programs, but communities could not talk with each other.

During this same time, an ARPA director, J. C. F. Licklider, was proselytizing his message of computer connectivity. The Advanced Research Projects Agency (ARPA) was a Department of Defense activity formed in 1958 to investigate new far-flung technologies. It was created in 1958 by President Dwight D. Eisenhower after the Soviet Union caught America off guard by launching *Sputnik*. The president created ARPA to ensure America was never again surprised technologically.

In 1961, while still vice president at Bolt, Baranek, and Newman, Licklider wrote a series of memos called *The Intergalactic Computer Network*, in which he envisioned that someday computers would talk to each other over an integrated network: a presage of today's Internet. Licklider became the first head of ARPA's Information Processing Technologies Office (IPTO) in October 1962, and began impressing his vision on colleagues.

By the mid-1960s, the problem of nonconnectivity was growing. ARPA director Charles Herzfeld had been frustrated by a lack of computer connectivity since his days of processing ballistic missile test data: using a network of computers would have been much faster and easier than using only the one he had. Now, as director, he remained frustrated that there were only a handful of powerful mainframe research computers and none of them could talk to each other. His new IPTO director, Bob Taylor, had three terminals in his office: one talked to MIT, one talked to UC Berkeley, and one talked to Systems Development Corporation in Santa Monica, California; none of them talked to each other. "There ought to be one terminal that goes anywhere you want to go," he would rant.

In February 1966, ARPA was ready to solve the problem. It funded a project and sought out a project manager. The call went to Larry Roberts, a twenty-eight-year-old postdoctorate doing ARPA-funded research at MIT's Lincoln Laboratory. The year before, Roberts had connected a computer at MIT to another one at Systems Development Corporation in California, using a dial-up phone line; now ARPA wanted to expand his work.[5] Roberts moved to Washington, DC, in late 1966 and wrote a proposal for a test network, which was accepted in 1967.

The test network would be based on packet switching, a change from the circuit switching of the day. Long-distance computer connectivity was hindered by the phone network. When a caller placed a long-distance call, the phone company connected multiple independent segments of a phone line from caller to receiver for the duration of the call—circuit switching. While this was fine for voice calls, it was inefficient for computer traffic. Computers transmit information in bursts, unlike a voice call, which transmits a continuous stream. During a computer call, the line segments sat idle much

---

[5] At first Roberts refused the offer, several times. Eventually, the ARPA director reminded the Lincoln Lab director that ARPA provided half of the lab's research funding. After a few internal discussions, Roberts came around to the idea.

of the time. Hence circuit switching proved inefficient (tying up lines needlessly), expensive (paying for unused time), and unreliable (segments were known to go down routinely—a bigger issue with computers than with voice calls).

Packet switching, in contrast, only used a phone line when the computer transmitted something. Packet switching broke computer transmissions into small packets of information and independently sent them over a variety of paths from sender to receiver. Packets waited in queue at IMPs[6] along the route until a line segment became available (each IMP was connected to several segments) and was then forwarded to the next IMP. Upon reaching their final destination, packets were reassembled into the original message.

This approach meant that a phone line was tied up only when a packet was moving through it. As a result, more line segments remained available, users only paid when data was transmitted, and the connection was more reliable since packets were rerouted whenever a line segment went down. It was easily a better approach.

Two other groups were working independently on packet switching in the mid-1960s. Initially, none of these groups were aware of each other's work, but they each later contributed to the ARPA project. Since 1959, the RAND Corporation had been working on an air force project to make America's communication network more reliable in the event of a nuclear attack. Paul Baran presented a paper on his version of packet switching in 1964. The following year, Donald Davies proposed packet switching to Britain's National Physics Laboratory (NPL) as a way to reduce the cost of remote computer connections. In 1966, Davies started a team to build NPL's network.[7] Back at ARPA, Larry Roberts was building on theoretical work laid out by his former officemate in 1961, when they were both graduate students at MIT. Larry Kleinrock had applied queuing theory (his specialty) to computer networking and published the first paper on packet switching in July 1961. He wrote a book on it in 1964.

In 1968, ARPA hired Bolt, Baranek, and Newman as the primary support

---

[6] IMP stands for interface message processor.
[7] Davies actually coined the term "packet switching."

contractor to build the IMPs. The ARPANET (as it was called) was constructed in 1969. It linked four nodes: UCLA; the Stanford Research Institute (SRI) at Stanford University; the University of California at Santa Barbara; and the University of Utah. Four nodes allowed them to test the IMPs' routing capability, and message traffic was routed over 50-Kbps phone lines—the fastest available at the time.

In September 1969, Bolt, Baranek, and Newman installed the first IMP at UCLA. A month later, the second one was installed at SRI, 350 miles away. By this time, Leonard Kleinrock had left MIT and taken a teaching position at UCLA, where he also led UCLA's portion of the development effort. He was present when the first ever Internet message was sent. UCLA was supposed to send the word "Log" to SRI, and in the spirit of collaboration, SRI would respond, "in." However, the "g" in "log" never made it. So the first message was "Lo," as in "Lo and Behold," Kleinrock says. "We couldn't have asked for a better message."

In December the two other nodes were brought online, and the ARPANET was complete. The Internet was born.[LX]

Internet Expansion and Features

Throughout the 1970s and early 1980s, ARPANET grew rapidly, and the technical foundations of the Internet were laid. In 1970, the approach used to break down, send, check, receive, and reassemble the data packets was formalized and called NCP (network control protocol). Soon afterward, work began on a new protocol—one friendlier to new networks joining (open architecture). By 1978, TCP/IP (transmission control protocol/internet protocol) was in near-final form; it became the standard in 1983.[8]

Email helped people make greater use of the Internet. An early version had been developed for a mainframe time-sharing environment in 1965. In 1971, Ray Tomlinson of Bolt, Baranek, and Newman adapted it for the Internet. He wrote the first email program in March, which included the basic send and read functions. In July, the program enabled users to see a list of email

---

[8] Other standards emerged overseas, such as X.25 in Britain.

messages received, select the ones to be read, respond, forward, and file them. He also invented using the "@" to separate the user and host in the sender name. Email was the primary Internet communication application for almost two decades.

Organizationally, the Department of Defense transitioned ARPANET from ARPA (now DARPA)[9] to the Defense Communications Agency in 1975. DARPA's mission was to focus on cutting-edge research. ARPANET was declared operational and a better fit under the department's standing information systems organization.

Finally, domain names (.com, .gov, .org., .net, etc.) were added to help manage the growing Internet in 1983. Behind every user name (user@host) is an IP address (e.g., 128.8.74.1), which is the user's location on the Internet. SRI maintained a table of user names and IP addresses, but as the Internet grew, keeping the table up to date became problematic. In 1983, Paul Mockapetris of the University of California at Irvine created the domain name system, which grouped host names under domain names (user@host.domain). Now different organizations could maintain different domain tables, spreading the maintenance workload, and a potential bottleneck to Internet growth was eliminated.

Throughout the late 1970s and 1980s, networks proliferated. With ARPANET having demonstrated network feasibility and usefulness, other government agencies and universities began building their own networks. The Department of Energy built MFENET (1976) and HEPNET (1980); NASA built SPAN (1981); the Department of Defense split military traffic from ARPANET to create MILNET (1983); and the National Science Foundation created CSNET (later renamed NSFNET, 1984), to name a few. Many universities had internal networks by the end of the 1970s, but some networks expanded beyond the university, including USENET (University of North Carolina at Chapel Hill, 1980) and BITNET (City University of New York and Yale University, 1981). Overseas networks sprang up as well, including Mark II (Britain, 1973), IPSS (Britain, 1978), JUNET (Japan, 1984), and

---

[9] ARPA's name was changed to DARPA, Defense Advanced Research Projects Agency, in 1972.

TUNET (China, 1991). New networks joined old networks, expanding the network of networks concepts into what would become the Internet.

In addition to network expansion, the 1980s saw the Internet's infrastructure upgraded. T1 lines replaced the old 56-Kbps phone lines. The new lines carried traffic at 1.5 Mbps—twenty-six times faster than the old ones. Also, new organizations formed to manage the Internet. In January 1985, the Internet Engineering Task Force (IETF) was formed to guide Internet development. It consisted primarily of government researchers who used the Internet in their work and desired to ensure its continued interoperability. The Internet Assigned Numbers Authority (IANA) assumed responsibility for coordinating domain name usage.

Commercial interest in the Internet grew during this time. Firms began developing products that incorporated TCP/IP protocols to help businesses connect to the Internet. Then in the late-1980s, the Internet service provider (ISP) industry began. Consumers could buy access to the Internet through PSINet, UUNET, Netcom, or by creating their own access point using portal software. Email providers emerged, offering accounts and even news published over the Internet. This rapid introduction of commerce led to a cultural clash between the newcomers and those who held to the more traditional perspective on the Internet as an open-access information-sharing tool. Ultimately, the academic community accepted the commercial providers since they lowered the cost of accessing the Internet; junior colleges, in particular, benefitted from this change.

In the 1990s, new features made the Internet more useful to the average person. In 1989, Tim Berners-Lee, of the European Organization for Nuclear Research (CERN), invented the World Wide Web. Convincing his bosses it should remain free, he helped ensure it would spread across the globe. In 1993, Marc Andreessen of the University of Illinois invented the web browser Mosaic. He built Navigator the following year and formed Netscape Corporation to sell it. In 1994, the search engine WebCrawler became popular because of its ability to search not only webpage titles but also their content. In 1998, a new search engine, Google, introduced a search approach based on webpage relevancy; this displaced the old directory model for searching the Internet. In 1999, Wi-Fi emerged after IEEE[10] ratified the 802.11b frequency standard in July.

These new features helped make the Internet accessible to the average person. As a result, the Internet experienced unprecedented growth during the 1990s. No longer was the Internet the province of university research and government institutions: it had reached the common man and woman. The 1990s also saw the government phase-out of Internet management. By 1990, there were so many networks that the original ARPANET had become obsolete and was shut down. Residual restrictions on commercial providers were lifted, and commercial networks would soon become the primary access point for engaging the Internet. In 1992, the Internet Society, an international nonprofit organization, replaced IETF as the primary internet oversight body. In 1993, the National Science Foundation (NSF), whose NSFNet had become the primary backbone of the Internet after a 1986 upgrade, began contracting out functions such as directory management, registration, and information services. In 1995, the NSF began contracting out access management. By 1996, more Internet traffic was carried over commercial backbones over than NSFNET (now called ANSNET). By 1998, the NSF passed its Internet management responsibilities over to a nonprofit corporation in California, contracted by the Department of Commerce.

In the 2000s, the Internet underwent another change—this time in how people accessed the Internet. By 2008, more people around the world accessed the Internet from a mobile device than from a personal computer. Personal computers had been the leading way since the ISP industry began in the late-1980s. Now the mobile device was the leading way—and this was especially true in developing countries, where more people had cell phones than personal computers.

With the introduction of mobile device access, by the mid-2000s, it had become easy for people across the world to connect to each other through the Internet (Figure 31).[LXI]

---

[10] IEEE (Institute of Electrical and Electronics Engineers) is the governing electronics industry trade organization; it has over 400,000 members.

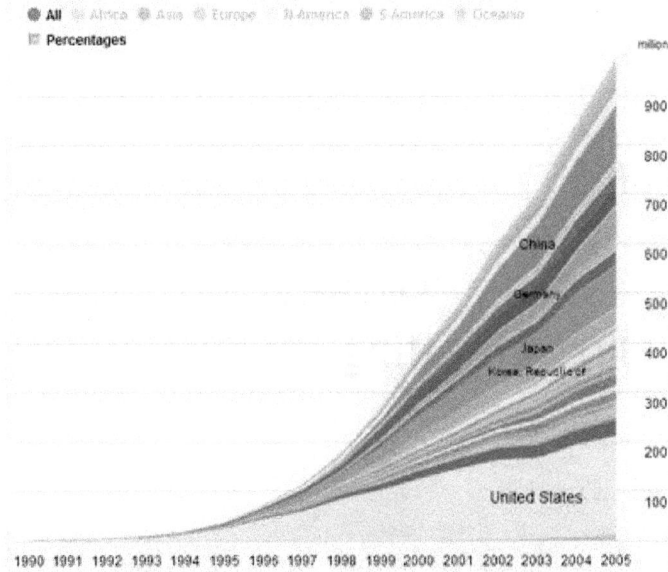

Figure 31. Worldwide Internet user growth, 1990–2005.

Source: UNData, "Who Populated the Internet?"
http://data.un.org/Host.aspx?Content=Tools (accessed October 26, 2015).

Chapter 17
The Next Elevating Innovation, Part II

Computers have shrunk from mainframes to handheld devices. Connectivity has gone from government agencies and universities working in isolation to everyday people connected all over the world. As the dimensions of personalization and connection grew, the span between them created space for a third dimension to appear: socialization. Independent from either the size of the computer or the number of point-to-point connections, this dimension focuses on content—specifically, what we share about ourselves, how we share it, and how we respond to others' sharing. With all of its challenges and growing pains, this is the dimension that leads us to the next governance basis.

Computer Socialization

With computers shrinking to the size of a phone, and with the growing ability to talk to people around the world, it was perhaps inevitable that people would use these devices to deepen their communication with each other. Starting in the 1960s and gradually increasing over time, by the 2010s, people were living portions of their lives on the computer.

Content communication began in the time-sharing environment. In 1965, MIT's Compatible Time-Sharing System introduced a text-only messaging utility, MAIL, so users with accounts on the computer could communicate with each other. Other time-sharing systems quickly developed their own capability. This form of communication, however, was text only, though some systems developed real-time chat capability. Most discussions were focused on technical support issues (e.g., how do I …) or collaborations on research.

By the late 1960s many operating systems had mail utilities. One of these utilities was SNDMSG, written for the TENEX operating system, which ran on DEC PDP-10 computers. In late 1971, Ray Tomlinson, a programmer at Bolt, Baranek, and Newman, began adapting this utility for the ARPANET by combining it with another program used to copy files over a network. The first version copied a document written at a sender's computer, and then sent it over the ARPANET, where it could be opened and read by the recipient. The recipient could then compose a response in a separate email. In that sense, the first Internet email traffic was similar to exchanging postal letters, with each letter going one way.

The next year Larry Roberts added functionality to help manage inboxes. Emails could now be sorted by subject or date, and users could choose to read, save, or delete emails in any order instead of having to go straight down the list. Several releases followed, each making incremental enhancements. Then John Vittal created the Answer command for his program, MSG. Users could now tap a single button and have the return address appear properly formatted for a response. Email now seemed more like a conversation than an exchange of letters.

Over the following six months, email usage over ARPANET exploded. Email would even create its own language. Email users were more tolerant of relaxed standards for grammar, sentence structure, and punctuation. Senders could be less concerned with formality, even when emailing senior-level people with whom formality is normally expected. In this manner, email filled the void between a formal letter and a telephone conversation. Eventually, Internet users embraced email, with its informality, as the primary form of communication.

By the late 1970s, mailing lists and multiparty discussion groups had emerged. Mailing lists were first published at universities. In 1979, The News, a program that sent out email updates over UNIX machines, quickly grew into discussion groups that covered a wide range of topics. In other parts of the Internet, users began forming discussion groups on topics ranging from technical issues to science fiction—of course, the inevitable joke distribution list emerged.

Email remained the primary web application throughout the 1980s. Eventually, companies saw business potential in email, and companies began offering email services over their private networks for a subscription fee. Toward the end of the decade, these networks (MCI Mail, CompuServe mail system, and later America Online) tied into the Internet, linking users to the broader Internet community. So by the end of the 1980s, email had enabled worldwide conversation over the Internet.

During the 1980s, social interaction tools appeared, enhancing online communication. Primarily email derivations, they expanded the number of users who could interact online, or the speed of that interaction to make the online experience more closely resemble a real-world experience.

Chatrooms gained popularity over private networks (e.g., CompuServe CB Simulator). Chatrooms allowed multiple users to converse online at the same time. Real-time discussions were held on politics or social topics. When a person sent a message, everyone in the chatroom saw it at the same time, sometimes a word or even a character at a time. Old messages remained visible, so visitors could catch up on the discussion. Anyone in the room could jump in, so it became the online version of a coffeehouse conversation.

Instant messaging also gained popularity over private networks in the 1980s. Like chat rooms, instant messaging transmitted text; however, the conversion remained one on one, and both users had to be online at the same time. Users were typically acquaintances called from a friendlist. Pop-up messages alerted a user which friends were online at the moment. At the end of the conversation, the message trail was deleted, leaving no record. All of these features made instant messaging feel like an online phone call.

Perhaps the greatest social interaction tool of the pre–World Wide Web era was the bulletin board system. Throughout the 1980s, high-speed, low-cost dial-up modems had entered the marketplace, starting at 300 bits per second (bps) and reaching 9600 bps by the end of the decade. This speed permitted more content to be streamed online, and with that, bulletin boards emerged as sustained platforms for social interaction. Bulletin boards were graphical, similar to today's webpages. Boards were often based on a theme, and the site manager would post related news and information. Nearly all boards provided email, and some had chatrooms. Users could post private or community-oriented information on a public board. Users could upload data or download information someone else had posted. As such, bulletin boards brought all the tools together in one place. Typically a login was required, making it a semiclosed community—visitors could not simply walk onto the board. On these boards, users could interact with like-minded friends and form bonds with people who shared an interest. No longer was geography a barrier to finding someone to chat with about a hobby—boards were full of people eager to hear about it. A board was an open invitation to join a body of like-minded fellows. Immensely popular, there were an estimated 60,000 bulletin boards across America alone, serving 17 million users at their peak in the mid-1990s. There were even three bulletin board magazines serving the industry. However, just as quickly as they had emerged, they began to disappear, the seeds of their demise having already been planted in 1989 by Tim Berners-Lee.

By the mid-1990s, social interaction tools were adapting to the World Wide Web. Internet forums became the web-based version of bulletin boards. Like bulletin boards, they generally focus on a single topic, such as software technical support, sporting events, video games, music, religion, or politics. Users could hold ongoing conversations in the form of posted messages, and messages stayed posted so others could follow them. Sometimes a moderator actively managed the site to ensure the continued relevance and appropriateness of the conversation. And with the World Wide Web underpinning their foundation, they proliferated. A multitude of online microcommunities formed, some focused on even the narrowest of topics.[1]

---

[1] I remember joining one Internet forum around 1997. It was focused on song lyrics, and I was looking for the words to "Buttons and Bows" so I could sing it to my one-year-old daughter (who, being held captive in her crib, could not flee). I marveled at how, in a nation of 300 million people, there were a dozen or so of us who had actually been interested in finding the words to that song over the previous year. A microcommunity, indeed.

Another social interaction tool to pop up was the *blog*. These were web-based postings by a single writer (at least in the early days) on a single topic. A person might write a blog on digging for fossils in Wyoming, or how to find one's ancestors. In many ways, they were like one-person magazine articles or newspaper editorials, commenting on the latest happenings in a particular field. Old posting were left up, so a continuous record, or log, emerged (blog is short for "weblog"); the most recent posts appeared on top. Blogs emerged when web-publishing tools became available in the late 1990s. Before these tools, users had to know HTML or FTP programs to post on the Internet. With these tools, ordinary people found a new way to express themselves before an audience larger than they could have imagined only a few years earlier.

Social interaction was gaining substance. What started with minimalistic email conversations had grown into microcommunity-building websites and tools of expression. Yet this was only the beginning. None of these early sites had yet taken full advantage of the new World Wide Web's potential. But that was about to change.

Also in the mid-1990s, while bulletin boards were at their peak and social interaction tools were being converted to a web-based existence, a new kind of online social experience was emerging. A new kind of website—one not based on email derivatives or ideas conceived before a World Wide Web existed—quietly began to appear. The fresh perspective offered by these websites unfolded from minds that entertained possibilities rather than technical constraints. While lacking maturity at first, their offspring would gain sophistication and change the world.

The first of these websites sprang up to support existing social relationships. PlanetAll supported microcommunities within universities, employers, or other organizations—about one hundred thousand in total. Users signed into a microcommunity to receive a calendar, address book, and to-do list that could be shared with other members of the community. Classmates.com supported high school alumni, helping to rekindle relationships that may have waned in the years since graduation. SixDegrees.com sought to formalize the inherent tiered linkages between people. Based on the idea of "six degrees of separation," it had users form groups with people they knew (1st tier), the people who knew someone they knew (2nd tier), the people who in turn knew those people (3rd tier), and so forth (a practice later popularized by LinkedIn.)

GeoCities was perhaps the first website that acknowledged that a person's online persona did not have to equate to his real-world persona. A user created an address in an online neighborhood—a neighborhood such as RodeoDrive, SunsetStrip, Hollywood, WestHollywood, Colosseum, or WallStreet—and could socialize with like-minded neighbors. Tripod.com gave users a place to exist online by offering space for a webpage, a place to blog and post photos, and even twenty megabytes of storage space.

Each of these web sites sought to tap into relationships, real or desired, by providing online tools; that was just the beginning. By the mid-2000s a wave of new websites appeared. (Many of the old ones perished in the dot-com bust of 2000.) People swarmed onto these new sites as the online experience grew more vivid.

Myspace was the first big social networking site. It was founded in August 2003 by eUniverse, a small company that financed Internet start-ups. Myspace went beyond earlier websites that only allowed users to post photos: it provided each person with a webpage to post photos; update a profile; write a blog; or post music, videos, or other personal items. All of this could be shared with friends, or with anyone on the site, if desired. Myspace allowed each user to create her own online persona. The company actively sought high-profile artists to join Myspace to make it the cool place to hang out online. Myspace grew rapidly: in August 2006, a user from the Netherlands became its 100-millionth account. By 2008, it was the largest social networking site in the world.

The title of world's largest social networking site would eventually pass to a newcomer, Facebook. Facebook was founded in February 2004 by three Harvard undergraduates. The site included a user profile, a wall to post photos and information, the ability to declare someone a friend (or not), a timeline to share latest activities, and the ability to affirm another person's posting with a Like. The site started at Harvard University as a way to help students get to know one another. Soon it was expanded to other Ivy League schools and then universities throughout the country. It was then opened up to everyone.

Overlaying established communities to reinforce relationships (rather than having users build them from scratch) likely benefitted the new website. At the end of 2014, Facebook had almost 1.4 billion users worldwide.

YouTube is a video-sharing site launched in February 2005. Users can watch videos already posted, or upload their own videos for sharing with others. Clips now include personal videos, TV clips, music videos, video blogging, short original videos, and educational videos. By 2012, the site had 800 million unique users each month; streamed 4 billion videos every day; and received sixty hours of uploaded videos every minute. Most of the new videos—about three-quarters—came from sources outside the United States.

Twitter was launched in July 2006. Twitter is a site that harkens back to the days of text-only messaging, but with a twist: users can send and read short 140-character messages called "tweets" from their mobile devices. This allows users to describe what they are doing at that moment of the day, continually throughout a day or as long as desired. By March 2011, 140 million tweets were being posted daily. By May 2015, Twitter had over 300 million active users, and more than 500 million users in total.

By the mid-2010s, social networking sites were fostering new forms of social engagement among large groups of people. Each site emphasized its own particular form of engagement by offering different features. By allowing users to post unlimited photos, videos, and text, Facebook became the tool for "chronicling one's life story before a wide audience, as it is being written." By emphasizing photos over text, and allowing only one photo to be posted at a time, Instagram became the "documenter of life's memorable moments before an audience." By limiting text to short bursts, Twitter became the tool for "bringing people into your moment." It even had the effect of creating temporary communities surrounding an event (e.g., a concert), allowing people to share more richly in the moment, together. And with pictures sent to a small group and deleted ten seconds after receipt, Snapchat became the tool for keeping in touch with close friends.[2] The makers of these sites and

---

[2] These are the experiences my kids have with the networking sites and applications. Others may have different experiences, but each website does enhance a different form of interaction.

applications were not passively providing space online—they were actively enhancing a particular form of social experience, making those relational aspects of life richer in the process.

The social networking sites were a big hit: people love to stay involved in other people's lives, and these sites helped them do it. By 2013, almost three-quarters of all Americans were using at least one social networking site. In addition, many countries have their own sites: Nexopia in Canada, Badoo in Russia, Glocals in Switzerland, Skyrock in Germany, Tuenti in Spain, Hi5 in South America, Mxit in Africa, Cyworld in Asia, to name a few.

So by the mid-2010s, social networking had become part of life for much of the world's population. Besides general interaction, some sites focused on specific social activities: dating sites such as eHarmony or Match.com pledged to help a person find a soul mate; business sites such as LinkedIn were helping people to find jobs and businesses to find opportunities; and crowdsourcing websites such as Kickstarter were helping people raise money for business start-ups, nonprofits, or charities.

This online living has had its downside, however. As people spent more of their lives online, real-world abuses followed them online. The early days of online social interaction were filled with horror stories about sexual predators lurking in every chatroom, waiting to prey upon unsuspecting children. Now some sociologists are concerned that people—particularly young people—are spending too much time online, inhibiting their real-world social skill development. Other researchers have, almost counterintuitively, associated spending too much time online with loneliness and depression, as addicted social networkers find the real world too harsh once they leave their trusted site. Worse still, cases of "cyberbullying" have become all too common. Individuals are targeted for public abuse over social networks: in extreme cases, this bullying has led to suicides.

Even with all of its warts, social networking has become part of our world. One almost has to be intentional about not using networking sites to avoid them. By avoiding them, however, a person risks missing upcoming events or neighborhood news. For many people, being connected 24/7 has become the norm. In our modern society, we now live part of our lives on the computer.

From the 1940s to the 2010s, computing has changed our world. While this change has had many facets, three particular dimensions of change stand out (Figure 32). *Personalization*: Computers started out as huge mainframes and successively shrunk until they became personal handheld devices, without losing the power of those huge mainframes. *Connection*: Point-to-point connectivity of computers users moved from a few universities and government agencies to billions of individuals, worldwide. *Socialization*: The ability to relate to each other over computers grew from sending simple text messages about system functionality to the enhanced sharing of common social experiences. As these dimensions grew, computers became a greater part of people's lives. Now there is a generation that never knew a time when they did not exist. With the computer being such a part of our lives, is it a big deal to start using them to collectively make resource decisions? Emotionally, no; it is really not even a thought. Technically, however, there is still a major hurdle to overcome before taking that final step toward direct democracy.[LXII]

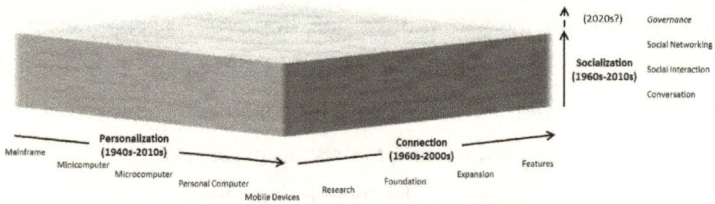

Figure 32. Computer platform for direct democracy.

Computer Governance

In 2008 in Weng'an, China, an estimated thirty thousand people rioted to protest the shabby handling of a local teenage girl's death investigation. In less than twenty-four hours, provincial officials pronounced her death as being the result of suicidal drowning. Protestors suspected rape, murder, and cover-up by two men whose families were well connected to the local security bureau. The protests turned violent, and local government buildings were burned. Fanning the protest were posts on popular online bulletin boards that came out in support of the family, against the government. While many posts were deleted soon after they appeared, ostensibly by government censors, web users began using euphemisms that avoided detection. (Ultimately, local officials quietly reached a settlement with the girl's family.)

In 2011 in Tunisia, about 5 percent of online blogs normally discussed President Ben Ali's leadership. In the month before he resigned, 20 percent of Tunisia's blogs were commenting on his leadership (or lack of it). Blog comments and tweets on liberty, democracy, and revolution preceded nearly every mass protest, including the one-hundred-thousand-person rally that eventually forced him from office. In Egypt, one week before President Hosni Mubarak resigned, the rate of tweets on political change went from 2,300 per day to 230,000 per day. Twenty-three videos showing some form of protest received nearly 5.5 million views. In 2015, ISIS was purportedly able to send tweets from 90,000 accounts around the world to aid its recruiting efforts.

In 2012, one month before the US presidential election, incumbent President Barak Obama had 20.4 million Twitter followers, compared to challenger Mitt Romney's 1.2 million. President Obama's Facebook page had over 29 million likes compared to Romney's 8 million. Obama had 1.4 million Instagram followers, compared to Romney's 38,000. Obama had 233,000 YouTube followers versus Romney's 21,000. Social media experts say that even knowing which songs a candidate downloads tells voters something about the candidate's personality and interests. Today, presidential campaigns leave nothing to chance when it comes to presenting a candidate over social media. And most recently, President Donald Trump has used Twitter to bypass traditional media channels, which he views as hostile to his administration.

All of the above points to the idea that social networking is here to stay and has even grown into a powerful influence on politics and governance around the world. As more people around the world go online, we can only expect this influence to increase. People see no barrier to using online sources and computers to support elections and governance. Furthermore, social networking is training people to make decisions online. Facebook asks users whether to Like someone else's post, what status they are, and who is allowed to see their profile. Twitter asks users to decide whether a post is worthy of being retweeted, or simply favorited. Instagram asks users whether to filter, what caption is needed, and whether to Like or Not Like a post. Snapchat asks users to decide which posts should be captioned or to whom they should be sent. While these choices may seem trivial (especially to the nonuser), they do train people to make social decisions: who they like (or do not like); what information to accept (or reject); what are a person's motives (and their hidden agenda); who is a rising star (and who is fading away). This level of comfort translates easily to a political environment, where the decisions are whom to vote for or which issue to support. It is a modest extension at best, and someday the entire electoral process will probably be conducted online.

But if social networking has brought us this close, what is holding us back? Why have we not begun to hold online elections already? The answer is that some countries have already held such elections. However, for the rest of us, security remains the biggest hurdle. But can this hurdle be overcome?

The US government has been pursuing Internet voting for years, primarily as a means to ensure voting access for the elderly, handicapped, and overseas uniformed personnel. US law requires this access, and Internet voting pilot tests have been proposed. States are also pursuing Internet voting as a means to make voting easier. In 2015, ten states considered some form of Internet voting legislation, with the idea of giving residents easy access to the ballot box from inside their homes, workplaces, or local community centers. Alaska, in particular, has taken a lead on this issue. Alaska's size and mobile population make it difficult for many voters to be at their polling places for an election. Users can sign up for web-based polling when they register, but have to voluntarily waive their right to a secret ballot and accept the risk of a faulty transmission. Users must also sign, scan, and send in a (witnessed) "voter certificate" for identification.

Overseas, a few countries have been moving even faster. In March 2015, New South Wales, Australia, used Internet voting in its state election; voters cast over 280,000 ballots online. In Britain, a parliamentary committee recommended introducing some form of electronic voting in the 2020 national election. According to one survey, one in six people thought that allowing voters to use smartphones or tablets would increase young adult turnout.

By far, however, the most advanced nation concerning Internet voting has been Estonia. This country of 1.3 million people, located in the Balkans, has successfully used Internet voting for more than a decade. In the first election in October 2005, fewer than 2 percent of ballots were filed online. In 2015, more than 30 percent were filed online. Estonia found that Internet voting captures voters who otherwise would find polling difficult—the elderly, the handicapped, overseas voters, and those who live more than thirty minutes from a polling station. One study estimates this boost the vote count by 2–3 percent, while other surveys suggest the figure is higher: perhaps by 5–15 percent.

Despite demand for the convenience of online voting, and its successful (albeit sporadic) application, most experts say that the technology is not ready yet—it is not secure enough. In 2004, the Department of Defense cancelled a pilot test that would have enabled overseas service personnel to vote online in the upcoming presidential election: experts determined the Internet was too unsecure. In 2010, a District of Columbia mock online election was hacked: it only took thirty-six hours for a team from the University of Michigan to break in and gain near-complete control of the election server. In 2014, a team from the University of Michigan analyzed the Internet voting systems used in Australian and Estonian Internet elections and found they were both vulnerable to undetectable attack. And in the summer and fall of 2016, the Russian Federation (or criminals within Russia, according to the Kremlin) hacked into Democratic Party member emails, conducted a cyber-attack against a US voting system manufacturer, gained access to voting systems in 39 states, and tried to take control of the computers of at least 122 local election officials. While it does not appear that the outcomes of the elections were impacted, the vulnerability threatened the democratic process in the 2016 US presidential election.

Making Internet voting systems secure is challenging: elections have even higher security requirements than e-commerce. If someone electronically hacks into a bank account, the bank can simply reimburse the customer for any lost funds, close the account, and open a new one. Elections, in contrast, are not so easy to fix: declaring an election fraudulent has serious societal repercussions.

The Internet, as it currently is configured, is vulnerable to different kinds of attacks. One kind of attack is to change a ballot en route to its tally station. A ballot, once cast and transmitted over the Internet, can take any number of different paths until it reaches the destination where votes are tallied. It would be difficult to ensure that the contents of a ballot are not changed along the path. Verification is difficult because ballots are supposed to remain secret, and verification would require knowing which choices the voter made. This kind of attack is particularly concerning since the populace may never know an election was fraudulent.

A more likely and potentially easier to perform attack is deniability of service. During an election, an enemy or lone wolf protestor could launch viruses that clog the Internet, overloading servers and grinding transmission to a halt. While this kind of attack would be recognized as it happens, the election may have to be repeated in areas hit by the attack, creating numerous legal and technical challenges.

Perhaps the most difficult attack to defend against would be an attack made against the personal computer or mobile device used by the voter. In such an attack, a vote could be changed or deleted without the voter's knowledge, before it ever leaves the device. This attack would be delivered by a virus in advance of an election. Requiring every device to be certified or carry encryption could be an enormous and expensive proposition.

Researchers have begun to address this towering challenge with the logical first step of defining Internet voting system requirements. The three primary requirements for a robust and working system fall into the categories of security, usability, and transparency. *Security* means voters are certain that their personal vote was correctly recorded, transmitted, and tallied; that all votes were correctly tallied (without extraneous ones throw in); and that the election results were accurately reported. This is known as being *end-to-end verifiable*. *Usability* means election officials find the system interface simple, intuitive, and easy to operate: otherwise they will not adopt it. *Transparency* means the entire pathway—from vote to final reporting—is open for public review. All documentation, source code, and system logs need to be available for inspection and certification. And all of this needs to happen inside a network that has the ability to withstand outside attack. Needless to say, this is not the Internet voting system of today.

One idea, long-proposed as an interim step between today's unsecured Internet and tomorrow's perfect system, is the idea of having secure voting kiosks set up in convenient locations such as shopping malls, post offices, or even airports. These would provide greater voting access to people in their more habitual environments. In 2010, the Election Assistance Commission[3] proposed kiosk voting as a way to give greater voting access to overseas service personnel. Using a military-grade secure network to transmit ballots avoids many of the problems of online voting. Scaling up this approach to a general population, however, presents a new set of problems. An unsupervised or semisupervised kiosk might be fine on a military base, but it could be risky in a strip mall. Furthermore, the endeavor might be cost prohibitive—far more expensive than simply having volunteers administering biennial elections.

So the question is not whether the Internet is secure enough to handle an election, but whether it will *ever* be secure enough to handle an election. Security experts have differing views on this. While some challenge the notion, others believe it is not out of reach, especially with the new encryption technology in development. While the historic attitude has been "no way; never," in recent years, it has shifted more toward "What would it take?" One cyber-security expert explained to me that a secure Internet is not just a possibility, but an eventuality. Kevin McTarsney, cofounder of Conscious Security, a cyber-security consulting firm, spoke of a completely secure Internet once everyone receives an encrypted identification card—similar to today's military CAC card or the chip being used on credit cards. An encrypted chip gives holders an unbreakable identification key, which could then be used for authentication. Ultimately, even this will go away once a physiologically unique identifier can be detected. Someday people may be recognized online by their electromagnetic signature, which is different for every person on earth—like fingerprints. He did point out that while the basic Internet can be encrypted, vulnerability still lies in the layers of applications built on top of the Internet. But even these can go away by applying the right expertise—this is not an unsolvable problem.

---

[3] The US Election Assistance Commission is an independent, bipartisan government commission charged with developing guidance and serving as a national clearinghouse of information on election administration.

This sea change in perspective portends to continued research in the area. Britain has allocated about a £100 million to develop online voter registration capability. Estonia is now issuing government identification cards with scannable chips and PINS. US government reports suggest continually monitoring technological progress. Many places have started with the simpler and less risky actions of online registration and issuing blank ballots. Some more aggressive cyber experts say that another small pilot test (most likely for overseas military personnel) could be ready within the next few years. With the lure of easy access over the Internet being too compelling to ignore, governments are already tasking agencies to come up with finding ways to do it; this will likely continue until Internet voting has been achieved or proven impossible.

Perhaps an even more compelling reason to believe in an Internet voting future, however, is *blockchain* technology. A blockchain is a ledger, distributed to a network of people, that records transactions in an openly verifiable and permanent way. Blockchain software appends data to a public ledger every time a transaction occurs so no information can be diverted or changed after the fact. Blockchains were invented to exchange currency and transfer ownership without the need of a central bank, and this is the technology underlying bitcoins.[4]

Governments around the world are pursuing blockchain technology for registry functions: Honduras, Greece, Georgia, and Sweden are considering or piloting blockchain land management and title services, and Estonia is piloting a blockchain notary service. Governments have also expressed interest in its potential to reduce money laundering, improve tax collection, and self-manage passports.

Blockchains even have the potential to make online elections secure. They could make voting completely transparent, and create an unalterable record for verification. Votes would be counted in minutes instead of hours, without the possibility of being double-counted, and problems would be flagged immediately for resolution in days rather than weeks. The Russian Federation

---

[4] Bitcoins are an internet currency, not linked to or indexed to any established government paper currency.

has already begun a pilot project using Blockchain 2.0 as a platform. (Incidentally, blockchain tends to make borders more porous. It incentivizes sharing tax information between countries, and it facilitates transnational shipping—one of its first applications was to track diamond shipments across borders.)

Blockchain is considered a foundational technology—having the potential to disrupt industries and even establish entirely new economic or social systems. A June 2015 World Economic Forum report predicted that by 2025, 10 percent of the world's gross domestic product will be stored on blockchains or blockchain-related technology. Bitcoin transactions surpassed $92 billion in 2016, just seven years after its advent. While widespread Internet voting may still be generations away, it certainly looks more feasible than it did just eight years ago.[LXIII]

Reaching Toward a New Level

In his 1995 landmark book, *The End of the Nation-State*, renowned strategist Kenichi Ohmae predicted the rise of regional states—governing bodies that no longer conform to the nation-state model, rather that whose borders surround natural economic zones, such as the San Diego–Tijuana corridor or the Hong Kong–southern China region. Whether regional states could be the societal level after the nation-union is not clear, but both the regional state and nation-union concepts seem to concur in that borders in the future will be less strict, more porous, and perhaps more flexible (fluid even?).

Driven by economic interest and enabled by the computer, we can see the antecedents of this happening already. In the Arab Spring, in the days following Tunisian president Ben Ali's resignation, there was an average of 2,200 tweets per day from people in neighboring countries discussing Tunisia's political situation, likely with people in Tunisia. Similarly, in the two weeks before Egyptian president Hosni Mubarak resigned, there were 2,400 tweets per day from people in neighboring countries discussing Egypt's revolution. Those revolutions did not stop at the borders. Commercially, we have seen the softening of borders: medicines not available in the United States have been available for purchase from Canada over the Internet since the millennium began. Electrons just do not recognize borders.

Like electrons, some problems do not recognize borders either. Whether a refugee crisis in the Near East that spills into Europe or a drug war in Juarez that spills into El Paso, some problems are inherently regional, cutting across state or national borders. And solving problems across borders is far harder and more time consuming: governments do not readily focus on border issues. In 2000, the Washington, DC, area successfully renumbered the exits on the highway surrounding the city, the DC Beltway. Initially, the Maryland portion of the beltway had its numbers, and the Virginia portion had its own numbers. Virginia, Maryland, and the federal government all had to agree on a common numbering scheme before making any change: a continuous sequence, starting at "1," going all the way around the beltway. It took almost twenty years. Had people in the region been able to vote on this over the Internet, it would have taken twenty days.

Once people start voting from their homes, cross-border problems will be easier to solve. Changes in technology have always changed the electoral process—presidential inaugurations moved from March to January when it became easier to travel in winter. Likewise, governments will have to adapt to accommodate changes wrought by Internet voting technology. If governments develop ways to flexibly allocate resources to support such decisions, regional problems will be addressed faster, across borders, distance, customs, and even language.

Over time, Internet voting across borders will strengthen regional problem solving, and governmental borders will become more porous. Borders that remain will be defined by major geographic boundaries, such as oceans. Hence, a gradual shift to the nation-union will occur, with computers being the elevating innovation.

Now some fear that under an Internet voting scenario, the real division will shift from borders to a digital divide, where Internet savvy people gain the upper hand and people less connected are left out of the electoral process altogether. However, such a perspective presumes that the change occurs overnight: that Internet voting starts tomorrow and people are connected or lose out. This will not happen. The most likely scenario is that in the years it will take to develop secure technology, there will be corresponding research into how to fairly apply it to everyone. Whether this results in training, changing in the education system, providing a terminal to everyone, or doing something novel and creative, steps will be taken to remove the divide. A change as dramatic as Internet voting will have to be approved by the people—over non-Internet systems—and would not be approved if perceived as unfair. Such is our electoral process even today.

Another concern for some people is the move to direct democracy itself. Such was the concern of a 2001 National Science Foundation panel convened to examine the feasibility and implications of Internet voting. Coming at it from the technology-first vantage (instead of a governance-basis vantage), it came to the same conclusion: that Internet voting could eventually lead to directly democracy.

> By reducing the economic and logistical barriers associated with poll site balloting, remote voting might ... allow for elections to be conducted more frequently than at present. Instead of putting a few referenda to vote each year, it could become easy and cheap to do hundreds.[5]

They, however, viewed this as a bad thing. Several members believed it would undermine the deliberative legislative process, leading to bad laws and corrupt ideas becoming enacted into law. And while panelists acknowledged that the current legislative process is slow, they point out that it was meant to be that way—to preclude rash behavior from guiding law making. Without a deliberative process, the reason for having representative governance in the first place would be cast aside with potentially catastrophic consequences. They ultimately recommended further study of the issue.

I agree that the issue should be studied further, though I consider the described end result unlikely. This scenario also presumes that everything happens at once—that Internet voting is introduced tomorrow and direct democracy the day after tomorrow, without the benefit of deliberation or

---

[5] National Science Foundation, Internet Policy Institute, Report of the National Workshop on Internet Voting: Issues and Research Agenda, March 2001, http://www.verifiedvoting.org/wp-content/uploads/downloads/NSFInternetVotingReport.pdf (accessed 2009).

thought in setting up these systems. There will undoubtedly be issues to be worked out, but with study, as the panel recommended, there is still enough time to get a head start on any transition that would occur. One might look to Switzerland as a starting point. In time, a mature process could be conceived, with the appropriate controls in place. The key is not being caught by surprise.

…

The march of societal progression is a strong one. And it is likely that computers will someday make it easy to make resources decision over the Internet. But will that alone lead to the next governance basis? Thus far, we have only addressed half the issue. The next governance basis will require not only direct democracy but also *greater enforcement capability*. How could computing lead to this? What change can it make that we have not already seen? Again, the clues lay in history.[LXIV]

Chapter 18
The Last Transition, Part I

In his 1995 book, *Dreams of My Father*, then-senator-elect Barak Obama described a conversation he once had with his Kenyan step-grandmother.

> Like other boys, your father would be influenced by the early talk of independence, and he would come home from school talking about the meetings he had seen. Your grandfather agreed with many of the demands of the early parties like KANU, but he remained skeptical that the independence movement would lead to anything, because he thought Africans could never win against the white man's army. "How can the African defeat the white man," he would tell [your father] Barack, "when he cannot even make his own bicycle?" and he would say that the African could never win against the white man because the black man only wanted to work with his own family or clan, while all white men worked to increase their power. "The white man alone is like an ant," Onyango would say. "He can be easily crushed. But like an ant, the white man works together. His nation, his business—these things are more important to him than himself. He will follow his leaders and not question orders. Black men are not like this. Even the most foolish black man thinks he knows better than the wise man. That is why the black man will always lose."

Barak Obama's grandfather rightfully discerned the challenges facing a fiefdom about to contest a colonial nation-state for independence. Amazed by the integration and systemization by which his colonial overlords operated, he knew the contest would not be easy: the two societies were worlds apart (a level apart, in our terminology). Kenya did ultimately gain its independence in 1963, after considerable politicking and bloodshed. But a question still remains: How did these societies grow to be so different in the first place?

In an earlier chapter, I introduced the next governance basis: direct governance. I described how the next governance basis will not only make resource decision making more personal but also increase enforcement capability. Then I introduced computing as the next elevating innovation and described how it will lead to more personalized decision making through direct democracy. Now we come to the other half of the issue: greater enforcement capability. How will computing bring this about? To understand this, we need to look at how printing brought about the transition to nation-state.

The next transition will likely be similar to the last transition. Both transitions move in the same direction (Figure 33), suggesting parallels may exist. In fact, one could even surmise that the next governance basis could even be an extension of the current governance basis (just as remote authority could be considered an extension of nonfamilial authority).

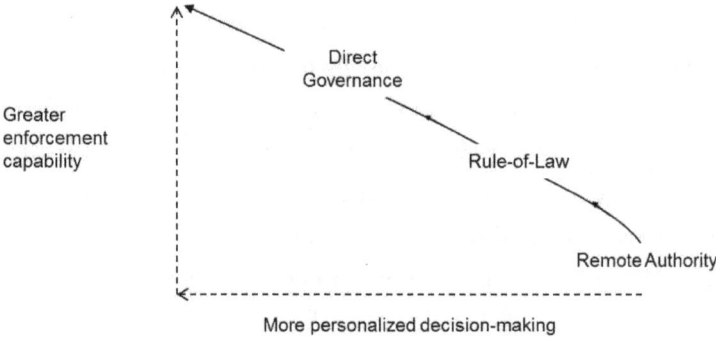

Figure 33. Most recent governance basis transition and the upcoming one.

So by examining how the last transition occurred, we can gain insight into how the next one will likely occur.[LXV]

Transformation of the Magna Carta

England was the first society to transition from a fiefdom to a nation-state. Many people believe this transition occurred instantly when the Magna Carta was signed, but this is wrong. The transition took place over centuries. This gradual shift can be seen in the changing perspective on the Magna Carta. As England transitioned to a nation-state, its perspective on this famous document transitioned from a failed peace treaty to the foundation for English law.

The Magna Carta was originally a truce treaty between King John I of England and his barons. King John's ruthless and capricious ruling style fomented rebellion among his own barons in the early thirteenth century. In August 1212, John received word that some of his barons planned to either murder him or desert him during a planned invasion of Wales. He cancelled the invasion. In February 1214, John invaded France without the military support of many of his barons. He used mercenaries to fill his ranks. The invasion failed; John returned to England in October.

In January 1215, forty barons met with King John in London to discuss terms of reform. John would have none of it. In the months that followed, both sides prepared for war. In May the barons struck first by capturing London; they forced John to come to terms. At this point, John turned to his old vexation, Stephen Langton, the archbishop of Canterbury, to organize mediation. In June, with the barons in London and the king holed up in Windsor Castle, the two sides met in a meadow in the middle named Runnymede. There the barons presented their terms of truce—a peace agreement, crafted by Langton, to which the king agreed and applied his seal. The document went far beyond terms of truce, however; rather, it established a new basis for governance. Among other things, Clause 61 stipulated that a council of twenty-five barons would be selected to oversee the king's compliance to the agreement, and that the barons had the authority to seize the king's property until he complied. As many as forty-one copies of the agreement were produced, one for each county in England.

Within three weeks, King John had the document voided by the pope, claiming that he had been forced to agree to it under duress. Evidently, neither side had believed it would resolve its problems since both sides had prepared to resume the war right after the agreement was signed. In October, John attacked Rochester Castle, which was held by the barons. The barons then invited John's relative, Prince Louis of France (later King Louis VIII) to lead them. The two sides battled up and down England for the next year until John suddenly contracted dysentery and died in October 2016. His successor, his son Henry III, was only nine years old. The boy's well-respected regent, William Marshall, urged the barons not to blame the son for his father's sins. Many barons accepted this, and Henry was crowned by the end of the month. In November, Marshall reissued the Magna Carta in Henry's name (Clause 61 omitted), and Henry gained the support of the barons. Prince Louis, however, was not ready to give up his perceived claim to the throne of England. He continued the war even though most of the barons had switched to Henry's side. At this point, the seventy-year-old Marshall led Henry's forces until they finally defeated Louis about a year later. Louis signed a treaty relinquishing all claims to the throne in September 1217. Later, the barons formed the Great Council, which continued to advise the king.

The Magna Carta was reissued several times during the rest of the thirteenth century. It appeared in some version in 1216, 1217, 1225, 1237, 1253, 1265, and 1297, usually corresponding with the king's need to levy more taxes from the barons, who in turn obtained them from the populace. Despite this manipulative use, each reissue planted more seeds for rule-of-law. Thirteenth-century jurist Henry de Bracton wrote in his treatise *On the Laws and Customs of England*: "The king should not be under man, but under God and the law."

The document continued to have important symbolic meaning throughout the fourteenth century. By this time, the Great Council had evolved into two houses of Parliament, which met periodically. During the reign of Edward III (r. 1327–1377), the relationship between king and barons needed clarification, so Parliament passed six statutes. One statute defined "the law of the land" to mean the judicial procedures that protected a subject's liberties; another coined the term "due process of the law," referring to the Magna Carta's procedural guarantee of individual rights. Parliament continued to extract confirmations of the Magna Carta in exchange for providing the king with new taxes, and Parliament made a practice of publicly reaffirming the document—at least forty-four times until 1423.

While it remained a potent symbolic gesture, the Magna Carta had little practical value. It was rarely cited in legal cases during the thirteenth and fourteenth centuries, and many of its clauses had been superseded by newer laws. Nonetheless, it remained a political contract between king and Parliament, so long as both parties chose to recognize it as such.

In 1476, William Caxton introduced the printing press to Britain. Over the next century, the Magna Carta and other legal documents were printed and widely distributed throughout the country. The first English law book was printed in 1481—an abridged compendium of English statutes by John Lettou and William de Machlina. In it, laws were categorized and the Magna Carta's Clause 29 (1225 version) was summarized under the heading "Peers of the Kingdom." In 1508, Richard Pynson printed the 1225 version in small book format. It was immensely popular and appeared in at least twenty subsequent editions until 1587. The Pynson printing also compelled rival printers to publish their own versions of legal documents and law collections. Even Bracton's treatise enjoyed renewed interest after its reprinting in 1569.

With such distribution and so many eyes laid upon them, legal documents began to spawn a new ideology. Sixteenth-century humanists began to see the Magna Carta no longer as a symbolic gesture, or even as a contract between king and Parliament; rather, it became an affirmation of individual rights and principles that predated the document itself.

By the early seventeenth century, the Magna Carta and its new interpretation was making its way into the courts. It was cited as evidence in many civil cases. Leading legal minds were starting to reference it as the foundation that undergirded all other English law: while other laws could be repealed, the Magna Carta never could because it captured the original liberties that people held against government power. Sir Edward Coke wrote in his treatise *The Second Part of the Institutes* a detailed commentary on how the Magna Carta was the central safeguard of individual liberties against arbitrary actions by the king: and this was not a new right—it was a declaration of the rights that the English people have held since antiquity. (Not happy with the treatise, King Charles I had its publication delayed until 1642, long after Coke's death.)

By 1627, the Magna Carta's new interpretation had worked its way into the halls of governance. In the Case of Five Knights, Parliament and king argued over whether the king has the authority to force knights to loan the Crown money—Charles had imprisoned the knights for refusing to make the loans. The following year, both houses of Parliament passed the Petition of Right, which prohibited the king from raising taxes apart from Parliament, banned capricious imprisonment, and guaranteed habeas corpus—all liberties prescribed by the Magna Carta. Desperate for money to finance the Thirty Years' War, Charles ratified the document.

Challenges to the king's prerogative escalated throughout the 1630s and 1640s, and the new interpretation of the Magna Carta helped fuel antiroyal sentiment. Finally, in August 1642, Civil War finally erupted between king and Parliament. Parliament's forces prevailed. Charles I was captured and executed in January 1649. Parliament assumed control of government and passed laws restraining royal power. The Magna Carta was the unchallenged foundation for English law.

Within in a few years, however, the new Commonwealth of England became a dictatorship. Parliament then decided to bring back the monarchy, considering it the lesser of two evils. King Charles II, son of Charles I, was set on the throne in 1661. Once in power, however, the wrangling between Parliament and king resumed. This went on for another quarter of a century.

During this time, Parliament continued to pass laws guaranteeing the rights of the individual. The Habeas Corpus Act of 1679 expanded and solidified the principle against unlawful and capricious imprisonment. Later, the Bill of Rights of 1689 codified the principle of no taxation without representation—a concept that originated in the Magna Carta. Also in 1689, another civil war took place, this time with less bloodshed. At its end, Parliament and the new king and queen, William and Mary, agreed that Parliament was the right body to make laws. With the king's former powers permanently transferred to Parliament, the first modern nation-state was born.

So English history reveals how the perception of the Magna Carta changed over time: from a symbolic document and contract between Parliament and king to the legal basis for interpreting and creating laws. This change in perspective coincides with the introduction of printing and the widespread distribution of the document. Yet this change is not the total story: it is but one element of a broader transformation in English society—a change that impacted every walk of life.[LXVI]

Transformation of British Society

The change in perspective on the Magna Carta was emblematic of a change in English society in general. Between the late Middle Ages and the early modern era, major transformation occurred in nearly every aspect of English life. The contrast between the two periods is startling—and printing was right in the middle of it.

The late Middle Ages ran from 1300 to 1500 CE.[1] When the period began, Britain was feudal. Feudalism had been firmly reestablished by the Norman Conquests and was characterized by a rigid social hierarchy. At the top was the king; next in line were the land-holding barons, followed by knights who fought for those barons. At the bottom were peasants, most of whom farmed the barons' property. The majority of people living in England during the Middle Ages were peasants: in fact, there were so many peasants they were subdivided into the categories of freemen and serfs, and serfs could be villeins, bordars (also known as cottagers), or slaves. Peasants owned no property. While an outbreak of the bubonic plague (1348–49) began to weaken the feudal system, the social order remained largely intact.[2]

The early modern era ran from 1500 CE to 1800 CE. At its beginning, society started to open up. Schools were founded for the poor, and literacy improved. The monastery system, which had fallen into decay, was abolished by Henry VIII, and the state assumed responsibility for providing for the poor and educating the masses. The country began receiving more imports from abroad, and people began obtaining more goods through foreign exchange. People could now buy potatoes, tomatoes, tea, coffee, and chocolate. Serfdom was abolished altogether by Queen Elizabeth I in 1574.

In the late Middle Ages, five major dialects were spoken across Britain, and each one had a good deal of variation within it. While Old English had been fairly uniform across Britain during the Anglo-Saxon period, the Norman Conquest

---

[1] Some scholars put the late Middle Ages as ending in 1450, while others go as late as 1509.

[2] The Black Death wiped out one-third to one-half of Britain's population, causing labor shortages across the isle. Serfs began working for cash instead of just the opportunity to work their own parcel. They began traveling from one baron to another in search of the highest wage. Attempts to suppress this newfound freedom and wage growth led to the Peasants' Revolt of 1381, which was brutally suppressed. Despite these advances, the social pecking order was still largely fixed by the institutions of the day.

made French the language of the upper classes and relegated English to the commoner. Because peasants were immobile, each region developed its own way of assimilating new French words. Regions approximated French pronunciation and improvised spelling. In time, five separate dialects emerged across Britain: Northern, East Midlands, West Midlands, Southern, and Kentish. Each one of these had a good amount of variation within it as well.

In the early modern era, English standardized on the East Midlands dialect. Most books were published in London, where East Midlands was spoken. The Royal Court and administrative centers were in London. And London was a major educational center. As a result, the East Midlands dialect became Modern English. The first English dictionary was published in 1604, and by 1630 even spelling became standardized.

In the late Middle Ages, life was centered on the local village. Most people lived in small villages of 20–30 families, composed of neighbors who farmed the same baron's estate. Only a knight or a baron lived in a castle, and less than one in ten people lived in a town. And those towns were small: they might have a few shops, a church, perhaps a church-run hospital, but rarely a school. Travel between towns was slow. Roads were dirt or mud. On horseback, a traveler could make perhaps 50–60 kilometers per day, so travel between towns could take a couple of days. Travel by river was often preferred, particularly when carrying wares to a market. Even cities were small by today's standards: York approached 10,000 people and London grew to about 40,000 people at the end of the Middle Ages.

In the early modern era, Britain became more urban and nationalistic. While in 1600, only 8 percent of the population lived in an urban area, by 1800, 28 percent lived in urban areas. The outlook of citizens became more nationalistic. Newspapers and books became tools of social discourse at coffeehouses, which became meeting places for middle-class men to discuss current events. The upper classes began to speak English instead of French, which contributed to a new sense of nationality. People were even speaking the same version of English, further strengthening nationalism.

In the late Middle Ages, agriculture was fragmented and inefficient. While cash farming had replaced the demesne system (the feudal system under which farmers worked land owned by lords), plots remained isolated and independent. Land was held in common, and there was no separation between crops and grazing animals. The crops grown and animals raised varied from region to region, and grain even varied from plot to plot. The farming lifestyle generally was one of subsistence with the excess brought to local markets for sale.

In the early modern era, agricultural productivity soared. While the English agriculture revolution is often associated with the Industrial Revolution, a steady rise began at the beginning of the era (Figure 34). Several innovations contributed to this rise, including crop rotation and the seed drill. Farms consolidated, providing scale economies and reducing the crop and animal variation within a region. Yield management began, and the per acre output of wheat, rye, and barley exponentially increased over time. Selective breeding was introduced, yielding more offspring per animal than ever before. Livestock specialization took hold within the industry, and integrated mixed-farming practices were introduced, where the fertilizer from livestock was used to grow more food, which in turn was used to feed more livestock. By the time of the Industrial Revolution, British agriculture had moved from mere subsistence to being an exporter of surplus food to foreign markets.

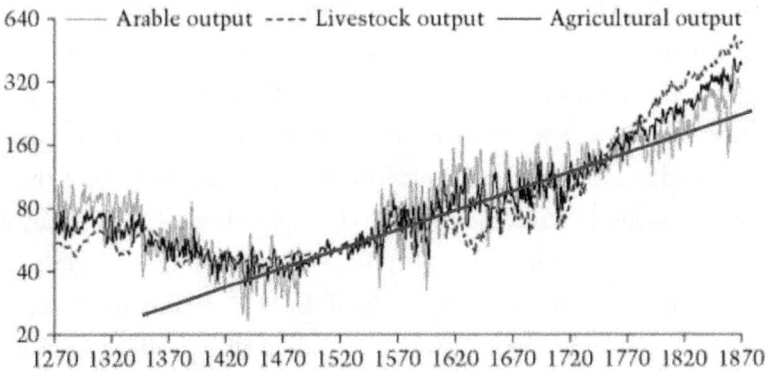

Figure 34. Increased agricultural productivity in England, 1270–1870.

Source: Stephen Broadberry et al., *British Economic Growth, 1270–1870* (Cambridge: Cambridge University Press, 2015), 114. (Line added by author.) Copyright © 2015 Stephen Broadberry, Bruce M. S. Campbell, Alexander Klein, Mark Overton, and Bas van Leeuwen. Reprinted with the permission of Cambridge University Press.

In the late Middle Ages, businesses were run by guilds and moneylenders. Nonagricultural craftsmen worked in villages as blacksmiths, bakers, butchers, bowyers (bow makers), fletchers (arrow makers), fullers (wool workers), potters, and so on. For each trade, there was a guild—a trade organization that had been granted a monopoly by the local baron so that only its members could practice in the area. (The reigning authority received licensing fees in exchange.) The guild oversaw the practices of its members, developed new members through apprenticeships, and promoted business in general. Some of the wealthier guilds even insured their members in the event of fire, theft, disability, or even death. (This encouraged young men to join the guild.) Moneylenders financed the guilds. Moneylenders loaned businesses money and even bought royal debt to finance governments. In time, moneylenders became financial brokers, exchanging debt to spread risk—one lender might exchange a high-risk loan for a lower-risk, lower-return loan. As the practice evolved, moneylenders learned how to buy government debt, divide it, and sell off portions to third-party investors.

In the early modern era, the corporations began running trades, financing ventures, and providing insurance. After the British defeated the Spanish Armada in 1588, it became safe for British companies to undertake long-distance trade. The East India Company was chartered in 1600 by Queen Elizabeth to grab a share of the Indian spice trade, then dominated by Portugal. The company sought investors to help finance voyages and share the risk of a loss at sea. While each voyage was initially separately funded, soon the advantages of using capital from one voyage to finance the next became apparent. In 1612, the East India Company became a temporary joint stock company—which meant that instead of funding a single voyage, investors began to fund the company itself. In 1657, the company became a permanent joint stock company when it removed all expirations on company shares. This enabled it to command a higher price for those shares, and the new capital was used to build a larger fleet. This form of financing caught on in other industries, and the modern corporation was born. Businesses could now raise capital, spread risk, and expand in ways not before possible.

Long-distance trade had two other offshoots: capital markets and modern insurance. When trading companies began issuing shares of stock to investors,

investors in turn began to sell shares to each other rather than back to the company. This led to a financial boom across England with individuals and brokers meeting in coffeehouses around London to buy and sell shares of stock.[3] The first official stock exchange opened in London in 1773.[4]

In addition to finding investors who would share financial risk for a portion of the revenues, ship owners wanted investors who would share financial risk for a fee. Ship owners would meet with prospective investors to review the cargo list for a particular voyage, and if the investor was interested, he would sign the bottom of the ship's manifest. Since the principal meeting place for such arrangements was Edward Lloyd's coffeehouse, "underwriting" began at Lloyd's of London. This practice grew throughout the seventeenth century. In the 1650s, Blaise Pascal and Pierre de Fermat developed probability science, and soon actuary tables were developed to set insurance rates. When a fire broke out in London in 1666, destroying 14,000 buildings, groups of underwriters came together to sell fire insurance. By 1693, mortality tables were developed and companies began selling life insurance.

The change between the late Middle Ages and the early modern era was so dramatic and happened so rapidly that it could not have been the result of the natural evolution of society. Something caused it.

The printing press was brought to England in 1476. William Caxton, a merchant who had traveled extensively in Europe during his tenure as a diplomat, brought it back after living in Cologne, Germany. In short order, a printing boom began. It reduced the cost of printed material, making books affordable to the average person and the publishing business profitable. Within a few years, over twenty thousand books were in print across Britain, and writers gained a new level of status in society.

It is inconceivable that any transformation could have happened in any area of society—language, life, agriculture, or business—without printed documents. Documentation provided a foundation for organization. Documents undergirded each advance by providing a stable, permanent, and

---

[3] Because of a lack of regulation, this first financial boom would go bust as phony companies began selling stock in specious ventures such as reclaiming sunshine from vegetables.
[4] The first debt exchange had opened in Antwerp in 1531.

widely disseminated record of an event, be it a historical occurrence, a planned course of action, or the record of a transaction made. As such, it provided the infrastructure for advancement, for elevation. Thus, in the late 1400s, the last elevating innovation appeared, creating the transformation that ended the Middle Ages and ushered in the modern era. But what does this say about the next transition? To understand this, we still have to look deeper at the last transformation.[LXVII]

Four-Phase Transformation

The English transformation occurred in four phases: conversion of script to print, coherence of printed material, new ideas emerging, and new structures built (Figure 35). This transformation occurred in several areas, but we will focus on a few key areas to see it most clearly: publishing, science, and law.

After the printing press was introduced, the first decades were spent converting hand-scribed documents into printed documents. These early manuscript-to-print conversions were direct—misspellings, poor grammar, and all. The personal libraries of many scholars expanded during this time. With books at a fraction of their former cost, scholars could fill out their libraries with established reference documents—collecting far more volumes than ever before possible.

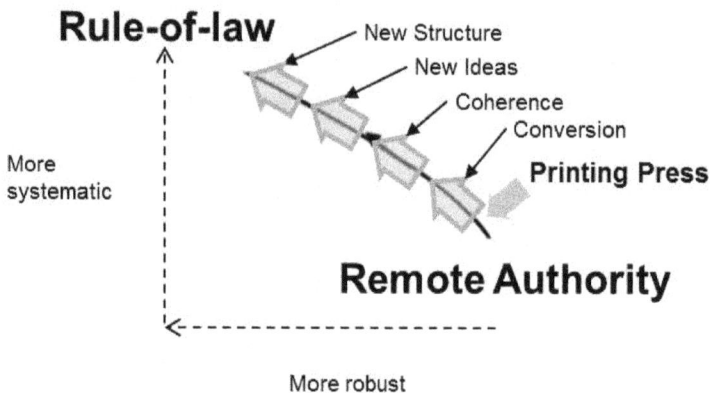

Figure 35. Four-phase transformation.

Also during this time, the printing process itself became more standardized. The process became more precise, systematic, and regularized as it was executed over and over again. In time, the entire field of publishing began to standardize its processes, as printers learned best practices from each other.[5] New techniques emerged to become industry standards, such as publishing errata—a compiled list of errors found within the document being converted. Even lettering standardized on basic groups: Gothic and Roman.

This standardization worked its way into printed content. Publishers began taking the liberty to remove misspellings and other mistakes from authors' works. And why not? Better books sold more. Standard edition books became the norm. Now the same text could be used for the entire country, rather than making dialect-specific versions. This idea of standardization even spread to fields touched by printing. Royal proclamations were no longer tacked to walls and doors in public squares. Rather, they were organized into volumes, with a table of contents added, and issued through distribution channels. In time, society began to appreciate the concept of standardization more: things seemed to be working better than they did before.

This effect spread to other industries as well. Publishers continued the push for greater standardization and process orientation, and it caught on in the rest of society—society became more systematic in general as people began to see its benefits. A new *esprit de systeme* arose, whereby those who performed by using a systematic approach were viewed positively, whereas it had not been such a concern before. Being able to access the right materials in a timely manner added new efficiency to small businesses. In fact, it became a concern of conservative educators and craftsman that an increased reliance on rules and standard procedures actually hindered experiential learning: rules-of-thumb were being replaced by rulebooks; head knowledge was coming at the expense of hand knowledge. Despite these concerns, however, printed textbooks and industry books continued to lay a foundation for future development.

---

[5] Printing and publishing were the same industry at this time. The two diverged in the nineteenth century.

Once most scripted documents had been converted to print, a secondary effect emerged. Inconsistencies and outright contradictions between similar documents became more glaring. By flipping between pages, a scholar could take two books on the same subject, compare them side by side, and see the contradictions between them. Contradictory maps, physicians' texts, and even astronomy tables were exposed for all to see. This must have been embarrassing for the authors and publishers of books that were supposed to be leading references in their field.

Publishers began expecting more consistency in the material they printed. They began using techniques that brought more structure to printed works. While alphabetic order, indexing, cataloguing, and cross-referencing had all been developed in previous centuries, they were applied in innovative ways and with new vigor to printed material in the sixteenth century.

While a publisher's structure helped make sense of a field, it did not remove the inconsistencies; in fact, it exposed them even more. Soon it became apparent to practitioners in various fields that inconsistencies and contradictions could only be removed by taking a holistic look at the entire field of study. This had never been a concern before. Before printing, few law professors had access to the entire *corpus juris*, so no one even conceived that anything should be done with it. Now, what had previously only been a concern in the humanities was a concern in all fields of study, especially the sciences. Leaders in various scientific fields began scrambling for ways to incorporate the observations of the past into some form of holistic framework that made sense of everything and removed contradictions along the way.

After about a century of printing, most fields of study had some kind of holistic framework: geographic maps now saw the world in the same way; historic chronologies had roughly the same dates; astronomical charts projected roughly the same orbits (Copernicus spent much of his career resolving this); bibliographies became comprehensive; and most fields of study shared the same general outline in their textbooks. A new coherency had taken hold in nearly every field of learning.

Once fields of study had a holistic and coherent framework, practitioners entered a new phase: they began to gain new insights into their work. By the seventeenth century, with material amply available—charts, diagrams, maps, dictionaries, grammar books, and tables—a person could look into his field and see things that had not been visible before. In astronomy, Tycho Brahe was able to rationalize two ancient theories of planetary movement. Printing had removed the burden of hand copying and memorization needed to preserve documents—to preserve knowledge itself—freeing researchers to focus on content rather than task.

Knowledge itself would now be preserved through replication. No longer would a scientist have to rely on a single papyrus document that could decay or be destroyed by fire. With dozens of copies widely distributed, the scientist who lost a key document in a fire could simply find another copy from someone else. Knowledge would now accumulate over time rather than dissipate.

Not only did knowledge now begin to accumulate, but it would accumulate faster through expanded data collection. Researchers could leverage the power of a wide audience to advance data collection in ways not possible before. A wider audience, reached through printed material, increased the number of people who could contribute to science. A navigator could respond to an inquiry with his own observations about the shape of a coastline; an amateur horticulturalist could describe the results he obtained from crossing two different types of flowers; the remote stargazer could describe astronomical observations from the Southern Hemisphere. Whereas prior scientific research depended on a single library or chart house, research now could rely on the collaborative efforts of a thousand people.

Knowledge not only accumulated faster but also did so with greater accuracy and precision. Printing gave rise to iterative improvement, which enabled new researchers to build upon the work of predecessors more easily. Published work was widely disseminated and remained available for correction; corrections could then be incorporated into a subsequent edition. Mistakes would be eliminated; generalizations replaced with specificity; and findings peer reviewed by more researchers than ever before. Scientist and philosopher David Hume once wrote to his publisher, "The Power which Printing gives us of continually improving and correcting our works in successive Editions appears to me the chief advantage of that art."

Knowledge even developed greater resilience, as widespread dissemination of printed material became an effective way to get around Church censors. Many publishers, particularly Protestant ones, were willing to ignore papal bans on censored material. Hence, Martin Luther could get his points across despite every attempt to suppress them; a century later, Galileo could share his findings despite forced recantations.

All these advancements—knowledge accumulation, widespread data collection, iterative improvement, and increased resilience—gave printed work a credibility that scripted work never had. Maps came to have new authority as the definitive way the world looked. Astronomical charts were the way the stars actually moved, not merely someone's best guess. The results of hundreds of researchers and thousands of hours of research were now captured for all to see. Hence, printing not only changed the way people thought about a subject but also gave that subject new credibility to go with it.

In the final phase of transformation, practitioners began building new structures to take advantage of the new insights. New structures took the form of new tools, new buildings, or even new organizations that could support research. By the early seventeenth century, most of the advances that could be easily obtained by making sense of ancient observations had already been acquired. Continued advancement would need better tools and a greater support structure to sustain arduous research.

During this period, scientists across Europe developed many new tools that afforded them deeper insights into their fields. In 1595, Zacharias Janssen invented the microscope. In 1608, Hans Lippershey invented the refracting telescope. In 1624, William Oughtred invented the slide rule. In 1636, William Gascoigne invented the micrometer. In 1642, Blaise Pascal created the first adding machine. In 1643, Evangelista Torricelli invented the barometer. In 1645, Otto von Guericke made the first vacuum pump—a necessity for later physics experiments. And many improvements were made to existing tools as well.

Not only were new tools required but also new institutions: without such institutions, advancement might grind slowly to a halt. One of the early and rather novel institutions was Uraniborg, Tycho Brahe's observatory. In 1576, the Danish crown gave the renowned astronomer an island off the coast of Sweden (then under Danish control) and the funds to build a three-story observatory, staff it with more than fifty students and professors, and equip it with the latest tools of the pre-telescope era. The effort cost an estimated 1 percent of the king's annual budget. In this building, and another one built later, researchers and students lived and worked, side by side, to obtain the most accurate and precise measurements of planetary and star movements ever seen. Uraniborg pumped out publications at factory levels, and scientific collaboration reached unprecedented heights during its twenty years of operation. Ultimately, however, the Danish king pulled the plug on funding and the observatory shut down in 1597.

A more common institution than Brahe's observatory was the professional society, where researchers and research sponsors came together to advance science. An early society was formed in 1603, by Italian aristocrat Federico Cesi. This eighteen-year-old son from a wealthy Roman family established the Lyncean Academy to advance experimental scientific research. Its most famous member was Galileo, who joined in 1611. He published his *Letters on Sunspots* from the academy in 1613. At the academy's height, it had thirty-two scientists from across Europe, and published many works in the fields of astronomy, physics, botany, anatomy, and mathematics. The academy disbanded after Cesi's death in 1630.

Perhaps the most famous professional society was the Royal Society of London. The Royal Society was formed at Oxford University in November 1660 after a lecture by Christopher Wren, the renowned architect. Many of its first members had been meeting informally since 1648. In 1663 it received a charter from the king and a charge to advance all fields of science through rigorous experimentation. In 1665, the Royal Society was the first to establish the concepts of scientific priority and peer review, which became permanent practices for managing scientific advancement. Its many works included Isaac Newton's *Principia Mathematica*, the results of Benjamin Franklin's kite experiment (proving lightning was really electricity), and the approval of Charles Babbage's difference engine, a forerunner of the computer. The Royal Society exists to this day and furthers scientific research by contributing almost £42 million annually in grants and donations.

Universities also advanced science in the seventeenth century. Historically, universities were a place where professors were paid to teach classes and tutor students, but not do research. (In 1588, the University of Pisa provided Galileo with a stipend to teach classes, but he had to find funding from the Medici family to do his research.) Then in 1663, the first private endowment for a professorship chair in science was established.[6] Henry Lucas, the member of Parliament from the area surrounding Cambridge University, endowed what has become the most famous academic position in science—the Lucasian Chair at Cambridge University. Isaac Newton became its second holder. Endowments reduced the teaching workload, freeing up professors to do more research. In time, other private endowments followed. Cambridge alone gained several endowments, each focused on a particular discipline in the coming decades: astronomy and experimental philosophy (1704), anatomy (1707), botany (1724), geology (1728), and astronomy and geometry (1749). With these and other endowments, universities were able to go beyond simply teaching science; they began to advance it.

Government was not left out of the scientific revolution. In 1666, France established the Academy of Sciences as a government activity. The French Academy of Science was founded by Jean-Baptiste Colbert as an organization within the government to encourage and protect the spirit of French scientific research. A small group of scholars first met in December 1666 in the king's library; they met every two weeks thereafter. In 1699, King Louis XIV reformed the organization, moved it to the Louvres, and issued operating rules that included publishing a volume a year to summarize the year's research efforts and findings.

With these new tools and institutions (as well as many others), science continued to advance. Many breakthroughs came during this time. In 1604, Johannes Kepler published groundbreaking work in optics. In 1621, Willebrord Snell published the mathematical law of light refraction. In 1628, William Harvey detailed the structure of the heart. In 1661, Robert Boyle separated chemistry from alchemy and described the behavior of gases a year

---

[6] Henry VIII had endowed the first chair in science (physic) at Oxford and Cambridge universities back in 1540 (previous chairs had been in subjects such as divinity or Latin). However, it was not until wealthy private individuals began endowing chairs that universities had enough resources to begin conducting sustained experimental research.

later. In 1687, Sir Isaac Newton published *Principia*, in which he explains the laws of motion, describes gravity, provides mathematical support for Kepler's planetary motion findings, and established the underpinnings for the fundamental theorem of calculus.

The new structures enabled science to advance, but science was not the only field to move ahead. In fact, similar advancements took place across the whole of British society, as is evidenced by British productivity growth (Figure 36). British gross domestic product (GDP) took off right after the printing press was introduced in the 1470s. This growth kept pace with population increase for the next 160 years while transformation was occurring. By the 1630s, the new structures enabled GDP growth to exceed population growth. However, to fully realize the benefits of printing, another structural change was needed—and in the 1630s that change was already getting started.[LXVIII]

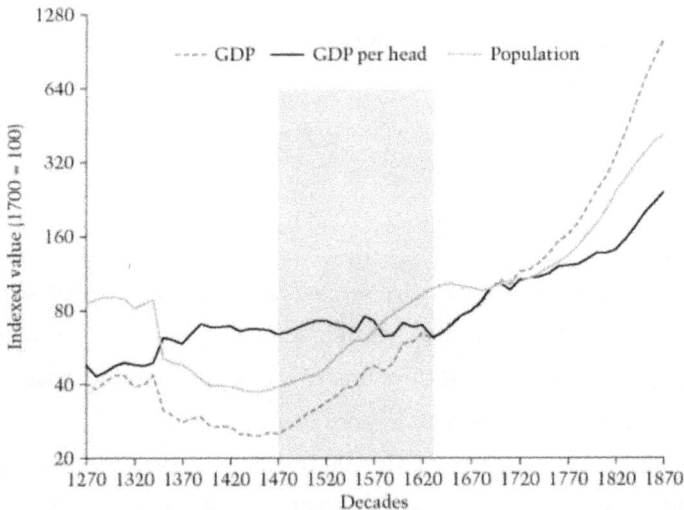

Figure 36. Period of British transformation.
Source: Stephen Broadberry et al., *British Economic Growth, 1270–1870* (Cambridge: Cambridge University Press, 2015), 403. (Shading added by author.) Copyright © 2015 Stephen Broadberry, Bruce M. S. Campbell, Alexander Klein, Mark Overton, and Bas van Leeuwen. Reprinted with the permission of Cambridge University Press.

Chapter 19
The Last Transition, Part II

The transition of England from fiefdom to nation-state was driven by a transformation that was manifested in many areas. Publishing, science, and nearly every walk of life experienced a lot of change in a relatively short time. The area of change with the greatest impact on governance, however, was the legal field. When the legal field transformed, it led to structural changes of the highest magnitude.

Early Parliament

Before printing, Parliament had limited authority relative to the king. Parliament began when the king began holding meetings with his barons and the archbishops in the twelfth century. It was purely an advisory body, providing thoughts on politics and taxes.

The Magna Carta changed this body from an advisory council to an oversight council. Clause 61 of the Magna Carta established a council of twenty-five barons who would oversee compliance to the provisions of the charter. This became known as the Great Council; in time, it would become known as the House of Lords. However, it was not a standing body; rather, it was called to meet periodically by the king, and it had little authority if the king chose to ignore it.

The Great Council became known as Parliament in 1236;[1] it still met only when summoned by the king. In the 1250s, tension between King Henry III and his barons grew because of his expensive plan to rebuild Westminster Abbey and his plan to install one of his younger sons as the king of Sicily, which required a tighter alignment with foreign powers. In 1258, Parliament imposed the Provision of Oxford, which established a permanent baronial council and took control of key appointments. When Henry had the provision overturned by the pope, relations deteriorated and the Second Barons' War broke out.[2] In an effort to boost support for its cause in the war, Parliament began inviting knights of the shire (who represented counties) and burgesses (who represented towns) to meetings. While the war initially favored Parliament's forces, the king's son eventually broke out of prison, rallied the king's forces, and won the war. Kingly authority was firmly restored by agreement and subsequent purge. Regardless, thenceforward, knights and burgesses continued to attend whenever Parliament was called.

In 1341, the two groups began meeting separately, forming an upper house, the House of Lords, which contained the barons and archbishops, and a lower house, the House of Commons, which contained the knights and burgesses. Both houses slowly grew in power over time, particularly in the areas of taxation and law making. In 1362, Parliament passed, and Edward III ratified, a statute that required parliamentary consent over all new taxes. In 1414, Parliament passed, and Henry V ratified, a statute that all new laws required parliamentary approval from both houses. This ruling, in theory, made both houses equal; however, in reality, the House of Lords remained more powerful in influence, and both remained less powerful than the king. After the Wars of the Roses (1455–1487), which decimated the ranks of nobility, both houses lost even more power relative to the king. Then printing was brought to England.

---

[1] Parliament is a derivation of the French word *parlement*, meaning "a speaking" or "a conference."

[2] The First Barons' War occurred after King John (King Henry III's father) reneged on the Magna Carta.

Legal Transformation

Like publishing and science, the legal field transformed in the early modern era. Its transformation followed the same four phases at roughly the same time. Conversion was the focus from the fourth quarter of the fifteenth century through the first quarter of the sixteenth century.[3] Coherence was the focus in the second and third quarters of the sixteenth century. *New ideas* was the focus in the last quarter of the sixteenth century through the first quarter of the seventeenth century. And *new structures* was the focus from the second quarter through the end of the seventeenth century.[4] While these are general in nature, they capture the flow of activity central to transformation. Unlike publishing and science, however, the new structures phase of the legal transformation would have a profound impact on how society was to be governed.

Conversion was the focus of the first phase of transformation. In the decades after printing's arrival in England, old legal manuscripts were converted into print. Yearbooks—a set of volumes containing high court decisions made throughout the year—were converted from script to print. Law reports, treatises, and lectures by law professors were put into print. New yearbooks were now printed instead of scripted. The histories of past legal proceedings came to light as old legal texts were converted to print. Publishers competed to find the best legal material to print. And with all this printed material, law libraries began to expand. In the early sixteenth century, there was a marked increase in the number of professional legal documents that became available (and which can still be found). Even manuscript versions could be found in increasing numbers. Such wide dissemination ensured unprecedented availability of legal material.

Also during this time, standardization caught on in the legal field, just as

---

[3] I purposely choose a large metric to convey the generality of the timing of these phases: they are not meant to be prescriptive.

[4] The phases do not mean that only one type of activity was practice during that time: there was overlap across phases in that regard. The earliest abridgement of English law—summaries of cases under broad topic headings allowing for actual use of the concept of precedent—was published in 1490. However, the phases do identify the preponderance of activity that was most influential at that time.

it did in publishing and science. As legal volumes were pumped out, the content within those volumes became more standardized. Fonts standardized; formats standardized; external volume appearance standardized. The printing process contributed to this: a standard set of books is cheaper and easier to print than a variety of books. Legal professionals even worked with publishers to create outlines for legal texts, making them more consistent and easier to read.

With standardization and widespread distribution, vagueness and errors in legal texts became more apparent. While the initial euphoria of simply having more legal material available may have caused some to overlook errors, in time, legal professionals became less tolerant of them. Legal professionals—attorneys, solicitors, law professors, barristers, or other jurists—began working with publishers to remove these errors and clean up the texts. And their efforts were bearing fruit: by the end of this phase, printed books were becoming more authoritative than the error-prone scripted books.

With standardization of legal volumes, the law itself began to standardize. Lawyers and courts began taking the law more literally, leaving less room for subjectivity. With so many eyes looking at the same legal passage, the only way to move forward in a court case was to agree on a legal interpretation that was close to how it was actually written.[5] As such, the law and the courts that used the law were losing some of their flexibility.

Perhaps the most important aspect of legal transformation in this first phase was the shift from an oral tradition to a written one. In late Middle Age England, oral agreements were the basis for legal agreements, and witnesses were the evidence of an agreement. A written document was merely a reminder that the oral event had taken place. (This in turn had replaced the exchange of dirt clods in ancient Britain.) Wills and land conveyances were the most common oral agreements. However, things began to change with printing. With printing, it became easier to document agreements. Printed agreements were more precise: they were less ambiguous in what property was exchanged, by whom, and when. Multiple copies of an agreement helped ensure the event became part of a permanent record. When the Statute of

---

[5] Sound familiar? This same issue appeared in the 2000 US presidential election.

Wills was enacted in 1540, Parliament and Crown formally recognized the superiority of the written agreement. The Statute of Wills gave landowners the right to pass their property to anyone they chose using a written will, rather than having property passed automatically to the closest relative. This statute made the written document the basis for a legal action despite whatever oral agreements may exist. It forever changed a tradition.

Coherence was the second phase of legal transformation. During this time, England embraced rule-of-law as a concept, as well as the legal concept of *stare decisis*—legal precedence.

With the biggest problems of material availability and glaring vagueness, errors, and omissions solved, those in the legal field turned to the next problem of making sense of what they had. Like the scientific field, the legal field began to strive for greater coherence in legal material and the law itself. Publishers began to index and catalogue legal works like they did the works of other professions. In printed yearbooks, publishers began cross-referencing cases. Cross-references and the ability to compare laws side by side from printed documents helped to expose the lack of coherency in the *corpus juris*, the legal code. Soon books of precedence began to appear, comparing recent cases with older similar one, noting the disconnects and contradictions between decisions. It was not long before the idea that laws ought to be more consistent began to rise. While this had been a rule-of-thumb in common law since antiquity, the exposure of so many contradictory rulings led jurists to believe that something more needed to be done. With judicial decisions now published and widely disseminated, judges were already beginning to be more influenced by prior decisions.

The result was the elevation of *stare decisis* to a principle of law. *Stare decisis* is short for "*Stare decisis et non quieta movere,*" which is Latin for "to stand by decisions and not disturbed the undisturbed." It generally has two dimensions. One dimension establishes that previous court decisions will be taken as correct until proven to be baseless and without merit. As member of Parliament and law professor William Blackstone would put it two centuries later: "Precedents and rules must be followed unless flatly absurd or unjust; for though their reason be not obvious at first view, yet we owe such as deference to former times as not to suppose that they acted wholly without consideration." Court decisions may deviate from precedence, but would need to justify the departure, which may or may not hold up upon appeal. The other dimension of *stare decisis* states that lower court decisions are to be bound by higher court decisions. As such, Supreme Court decisions are binding upon appellate courts, which in turn are binding upon common courts.

Such deference on two dimensions establishes stability in jurisprudence, inhibiting random judgments that would rapidly cause the legal system to deteriorate into confusion. Requiring new laws to be consistent with earlier laws further eliminated some of the capriciousness of the courts. The first recorded use of *stare decisis* in a court decision appeared in 1584. After that time, it became more commonly acknowledged in proceedings.

Another feature of this phase began in the 1530s. There arose a push to make the law more available to the average citizen. It would be printed in English, not Latin or French. It would be affordable to the commoner. The idea was that the law would no longer be kept in the holds of lawyers, jurists, and judges. Now anyone who wanted to find out what he might be accused of could find the law, if he wanted.

With a cleaner, more consistent, more coherent, and more available body of law, another phenomenon arose in the legal field: more credibility. English law was maturing, becoming more robust. With it came the ability to make sounder, wiser judgments. And with better judgments came trust: the trust of the people. And with this trust came rule-of-law.

Back in the fifteenth century, personal relationships were still the basis for governance and society. Common law courts were ineffective and seldom used. No court system existed whereby constitutional disputes could be heard. Among aristocracy, kinship was a more important guide for behavior than any concept of law. Personal honor was a defining concept, and feuds were settled either by neutral arbitration or as often as not by bloodshed.

By the middle of the sixteenth century, that had all changed. Gone were the blood feuds between rival clans as aristocrats resorted to courts to settle disputes. In fact, litigation soared as all people turned to the courts to settle personal grievances rather than resort to violence. It became common to hear rule-of-law touted as the best means of maintaining an orderly and stable society. Peace and prosperity were to be had with rule-of-law. In Elizabethan times, this still meant faithful obedience to the queen's edicts and respect for authority, and the Crown made no small effort to promote this view. So by the end of the second phase, rule-of-law had become so reified that people seemed to laud it with misty eyes. As one jurist put it in 1589,

> I cannot sufficiently, nor amply enough magnifie the majestie and dignitie of the lawe, for it is the devine gifte and invention of god, and the profound determination of wise men, the most strong synewe of a common wealth and the soule w[i]thout w[hi]ch the magistrate cannot stand.[6]

Of course, the legal profession itself had no small stake in promoting this perspective as well. The ranks of the legal profession swelled starting in the 1550s. Part of this growth can be attributed to the ease with which new practitioners could join the profession. With the legal profession now based on writing instead of oral recitation, more practitioners could partake. The mass production of legal books made it possible for more people to engage. Law students could now afford textbooks, whereas before the price of scripted books had precluded many young people from entering the field. Primers could now be obtained for a few pence, and law students could now compile their own canon of legal texts during their studies: a canon that would serve them throughout their career.

Growth in the legal field can also be attributed to the soaring demand for legal services. The amount of litigation boomed between the 1550s and the 1640s. In 1600, the litigation rate was four times higher than it is today. Four law schools (inns, as they were called) flourished during the Elizabethan period, even attaining stature on par with Oxford and Cambridge. By the end of the sixteenth century the number of lawyers reached modern-day proportions.

---

[6] British Library Additional MS 48,109, recorded in "Magna Carta in 16th Century English Legal Thought," by Christopher Brooks, April 10, 2014, Online Library of Liberty, http://oll.libertyfund.org/pages/magna-carta-in-16th-century-english-legal-thought (accessed December 21, 2015).

Despite the number of new lawyers, the Court of Chancery (the lower court system that heard most of the routine cases not heard by the Common Court) saw its caseload swell to the point of dysfunction. A slow pace of adjudication, a large backlog, and rising costs led to cries of ineptness. At one point, Attorney General Francis Bacon calculated that roughly two thousand orders were being issued a year, but the court's backlog was around sixteen thousand.[7]

Even the queen expanded her own legal staff as the attorney general and king's solicitor could no longer handle the workload. The King's Counsel was born, generally acting as assistants to the attorney general.[8] The age of rule-of-law, and legal proceeding, had arrived.

The third phase of legal transformation was one of new ideas. In the late sixteenth century, the *corpus juris* was more complete and coherent. Rule-of-law had become an established principle. Jurists were no longer struggling to make sense of the law; they could now step back and ponder implications and inferences. And as the jurists looked, new ideas began to emerge.

One new idea that emerged during this time was the notion of the equality of man. In feudal systems, notions of equally were not common. Feudal societies were based on a rigid hierarchy of class and wealth. With rule-of-law, however, such divisions did not make much sense. Under rule-of-law, how could any divisions be legitimate? Rule-of-law itself had little meaning if laws could be overridden by class, kinship, or wealth. Either the law applies equally to everyone or it does not apply to anyone. As one seventeenth-century writer put it: "If we would perfectly execute justice wee must make no difference betweene men for their frends[hi]p, parentage, riches, pov[er]tye, or dignity."[9]

Another idea that emerged in the 1590s was the inalienable rights of the individual. Every individual had rights. These rights were neither afforded nor

---

[7] Unfortunately, these cries of dysfunction persisted until the Court of Chancery and the common court system were merged in 1875.

[8] This is not to be confused with the thirteenth-century King's Council that would become the House of Lords.

[9] British Library Additional MS 12,515, recorded in "Magna Carta in 16th Century English Legal Thought," by Christopher Brooks, April 10, 2014, Online Library of Liberty, http://oll.libertyfund.org/pages/magna-carta-in-16th-century-english-legal-thought (accessed December 21, 2015).

could be removed by any court since everyone possessed them innately. Rule-of-law exists to protect these rights from the arbitrary abuse of others. The Magna Carta even came to emblemize this doctrine. It was an early attempt to capture in writing these inalienable rights, which have existed since the dawn of English society. This interpretation of the Magna Carta was cited in two court cases in the 1590s. In the decades to come, more court cases would begin using similar interpretations.

A third important idea that arose during this time involved the role of government itself. If a person had inalienable rights, and no other person could afford or remove those rights, then the law and the courts had to be the protector of those rights against any encroachment—including that of government. Whereas in Elizabethan times, rule-of-law meant obedience to the Crown, now it was being said that, while that remains true, the Crown had to be obedient to the law. The leading proponent of this principle was Edward Coke, who while attorney general in 1604 wrote, "[L]et the King attribute that to the law, which from the law he hath received, to wit, power and dominion; for where will and not law, doth sway, there is no king." (At least some of this new thinking was encouraged by the death of beloved Queen Elizabeth and the succession of her distant cousin James I, who was an absolute monarchist.) By the end of the third phase, lawyers were repeating the virtues of not only the Magna Carta and the inalienable rights of man but also the rights of commoners and laymen. The idea had reached the populace.

This phase also saw the continued growth of the legal field. Enrollment at the Inns of the Court rose by about 40 percent between the 1590s and the 1630s. In 1605, the distinction between solicitors from the Court of Chancery and attorneys of the common court began to ebb as the same new statutes applied to both groups. Throughout the seventeenth century, the legal profession became an avenue where a commoner could rise in society to become a landowner, standing alongside the merchant class, which had arisen a century before. (While legal distinctions between classes were diminishing, social distinctions persisted.)

In the fourth phase, leading jurists and members of Parliament began to push for change. By 1625, some of the new ideas had been around for decades, yet there were barriers to seeing them implemented: the government structure did not lend itself to supporting these ideas. Members of Parliament, mostly lawyers by profession, had long been more effective at creating new laws than the king and his council. Past kings had even acknowledged their role. Yet the true monarchist still held that only the king had such authority, though he might delegate it to Parliament if he so chose. Naturally, this perspective would at some point conflict with the idea that the king was under the law.

By 1625, the simmering tension between king and Parliament began to boil over. That year, James I passed away and his son Charles I acceded to the throne. Like his father, Charles was an absolute monarchist, and the tension between the new king and Parliament was instant. In his first year on the throne, Parliament granted Charles customs duties for one year instead of for life, which had been the precedent. In need of money to prosecute the Thirty Years' War, Charles levied forced loans on knights and barons, without parliamentary approval. More than seventy landowners who refused to pay were imprisoned. This set off a debate between Parliament and the king, and within Parliament, on the rights of the individual versus royal prerogative. In 1628, Parliament produced the Petition of Right. It demanded that the king recognize four principles of the law: there would be no taxation without parliamentary consent; there would be no imprisonment without due cause; there would be no billeting of soldiers or sailors forced upon any citizen; and there would be no martial law declared during peacetime. After much resistance, Charles relented and accepted it as a parliamentary bill, mostly because he needed money for the war, which dragged on.

A year later, after another confrontation with Parliament, Charles just dissolved it. In its absence, Charles sidestepped the Petition of Right to a degree when exchequer judges confirmed he had the right to levy knighthood fees on landowners. Ultimately, this was not enough money, however; so in 1640, he summoned Parliament again—twice, in fact. Parliament took the opportunity to pass a new law barring taxation without parliamentary approval and another one to help ensure its own continuation.

During this time of government frustration, literacy rates rose across England. By 1640, adult male literacy rates in London had reached about 80 percent. Adult male literacy in the countryside reached over 30 percent. This literacy, and the easy access to printed material, gave rise to the political pamphlet. In 1640, 22 pamphlets were published; in 1642, 1966 pamphlets were published. These made their way into alehouses across England. Members of Parliament could enhance their careers by giving rousing street corner speeches, stoking the flames created by these pamphlets, and being seen as a "leaders of the people" and defenders of the inalienable rights of the common man against unjust tyranny.

The power struggle escalated. In November 1641, the Commons passed the Grand Remonstrance (admonitions) against Charles. It was rejected by the king before it even reached the House of Lords. In January 1642, Charles himself entered the Commons chamber to arrest five members of the house (who had already fled). In March, both the Commons and the Lords passed the Militia Ordinance, which established parliamentary control over county militias. (This did not receive Charles's assent.) By August, Charles had had enough. He raised his standard at Nottingham—an ancient symbol for calling for the assembly of an army—the English Civil War had begun.

In the first few months of the war, forces on both sides swelled into the tens of thousands. In the first skirmish of the war, Royalist cavalry defeated Parliamentarian cavalry near Worcester. By June 1643, Royalist forces controlled most of Yorkshire. Then in the fall, things started turning around for the Parliamentarians as they rang up a string of victories over the next year. Then Royalist forces began to dominate once again.

In the wake of these latest setbacks, the Parliamentarians moved to restructure their army. In what is perhaps the clearest depiction of value of process over relationship, the Parliamentarians built an army where rank was based on capability—not peerage or social class. Urged on by Oliver Cromwell, a member of Parliament who had been aggressively leading forces in the field since the beginning of the war, both houses of Parliament passed the Self-Denying Ordinance in April 1645. It required any member of Parliament who had a command in the armed forces (which were many) to relinquish it. The army was to be centrally funded and centrally commanded rather than a collection of regional forces. A professional officer's corps was created and training protocols standardized. A harbinger of things to come, they called it the New Model Army.

In June, the New Model Army routed the king's forces at the Battle of Naseby. In July, the army destroyed Charles's forces at the Battle of Langport. For the next several months, the New Model Army continued to rack up victories. In May 1646, Charles fled to Scotland for protection, effectively surrendering; though by summer 1648, a Royalist uprising and Scottish invasion resumed the war. In August, Cromwell and the army bested Charles's forces at the Battle of Preston, ending the war once again. This time, several members of Parliament were less lenient toward Charles for having resumed the war. He was tried for treason and beheaded in London in January 1649.[10]

With the king gone, the House of Commons abolished the monarchy and established a republic in February 1649. It also abolished the Privy Council (the king's advisory board) and even the House of Lords. With revolts in Ireland and Scotland, Oliver Cromwell returned to the field for another two years. The Council of State was formed to take over executive functions formerly performed by the monarchy, though its power principally came from Cromwell and the army.

In 1653, with the revolts put down, "The Long Parliament" was dissolved and Cromwell was named "Lord Protector of the Commonwealth." The country was divided into military districts with a commander in each one. Cromwell was offered the Crown, but he refused it. However, he did request that upon his death his job as Lord Protectorate would be passed to his son Richard.

In September 1658, Cromwell died, and as requested, his son Richard took over his post. Richard, however, did not have the confidence of the New Model Army and was ousted after only seven months. In May, the army called Parliament back into session to establish direction. In the months that followed, the army and Parliament persisted in an ongoing tug-of-war. Even generals within the army were contending with each other. England, which had become a de facto military dictatorship under Cromwell, was now dealing

---

[10] To his end, Charles did not recognize this charge: "Princes are not bound to give an account of their actions but to God alone."

with rival factions vying for power.

The need for order brought calls for a return of the monarchy. Charles II, son of Charles I, had been living in France during much of this time. He was brought back to England and crowned king at Westminster Abbey in April 1661. Upon his return, he imprisoned or executed many of those he deemed responsible for the death of his father twelve years earlier.

The monarchy would last another thirty years. Charles II himself reigned until 1685. Under Charles II, social mores relaxed from where they had been under the staunch Puritan Cromwell, and society seemed to rest a bit easier. In February 1685, James II succeeded his older brother to the throne after Charles II died from a sudden apoplectic fit.

Like his father, James II believed in the total sovereignty of the king, so royal struggles with Parliament resumed. Ultimately matters came to a head, in part because Parliament wanted a king who would uphold its authority, and in part to remove a king that they considered too pro-Catholic. Key members of Parliament made arrangements to have James's daughter Mary and her husband William of Orange (who was a Dutch ruler and her first cousin) take over the monarchy. In what is called, the Glorious Revolution, William landed his army on the coast of England in November 1688 and received much welcome from the local population. In December, James II fled England. In April 1689, Mary II and William III were crowed co-rulers as queen and king.

This pair of monarchs fully recognized Parliament's right to make the laws of the land. In December, a Bill of Rights was passed that forever gave primacy to legislators over royalty in running the country. It prohibited the monarch from suspending any laws passed by Parliament and from interfering in parliamentary elections. It decreed that only Parliament could levy taxes, and it guaranteed their freedom of speech. It established a constitutional monarchy. England became the first modern nation-state and endures to this day.[11][LXIX]

---

[11] See endnotes for a discussion on what it means to be a nation-state.

A New Infrastructure

England has been a nation-state since 1689: more than three hundred years. It has lasted longer than the Athenian democracy (508–404 BCE), though not as long as the Roman Republic (509–27 BCE). Both of those ultimately turned into fallbacks. What is to say that Britain, or any other modern nation-state, will not become a fallback in time?

Greece and Rome fell back because it was too easy to disregard written law. Rule-of-law requires a robust legal code that serves the public's needs, an almost slavish dedication to process, and precise procedures that can be followed to enforce laws. Greece and Rome never had any of these. The legal code was not robust enough to address people's needs without substantial interpretation; and whoever does the interpreting becomes powerful. There was no *system of process* since that did not exist before publishing introduced standardization. Procedures were not precise enough to enforce the law systematically; as a result, powerful leaders were occasionally required to restore order through their own charisma or militia. As such, ancient Athens and the Roman Republic never had the infrastructure needed to sustain rule-of-law indefinitely.

Early modern era England acquired the infrastructure needed to sustain rule-of-law. The legal code became more robust as Parliament added more laws to it, refining it over time. A group can inherently create a more robust legal code than an individual (Table 7): language has to be more precise and specific for a group to make decisions than for an individual to make them. As such, Parliament created a legal code that was more coherent, precise, and specific than a king ever could have created.

Table 7. Requirements for group and individual decision making.

	An Individual	A Group (Representatives)
Coherence	A perspective or desire about an issue	A common language and context for understanding the issue, otherwise they will continually talk past each other
Precision	Can prescribe a course of action as general intent or even vague terms, and let ministers develop specifics	To prescribe a course of action, need to agree upon more precise details of execution or action is unlikely to lead to a solution.
Specificity	General understanding of the issue, since there really is no one to challenge it	Common agreement on what the specific issue is; otherwise they'll keep going around the issue and never resolve it

England developed a high regard for systematic approaches as standardization spread across industries. With printing, society became more "rules based." In 1620, philosopher Francis Bacon developed an early version of the scientific method, which took a systematic approach to studying and furthering almost any subject. Later that century, Englishman William Penn extolled the virtue of taking a systematic approach to business:

> Method goes far to prevent trouble in business: for it makes the task easy, hinders confusion, saves abundance of time, and instructs those that have business depending, both what to do and what to hope.

In the following century, British economist Adam Smith would publish *The Wealth of Nations*, the first work to lay out a comprehensive view of the entire system of political economy. Clearly, a systematic approach to occupation took hold during the early modern era. This regard for system and rules also meant that laws were more likely to be obeyed by the majority of society.

A final requirement for rule-of-law to be indefinitely sustainable is precise operating procedures. Without these, the civil service cannot enforce the laws with enough rigor. The civil service dates back to the emergence of the fiefdom when writing enabled chieftains to expand their authority by using nonfamily members to begin to perform administrative functions. The ancient Egyptians used different offices for different administrative functions such as justice, food collection, and redistribution. Rome developed separate hierarchies for justice, military affairs, finance and taxation, foreign affairs, and internal affairs. Each of these hierarchies was run by a single principle officer of the state. China's civil service structure lasted from antiquity until 1912. In the Middle Ages, European civil service took the form of secretariats serving the royal household. In the thirteenth century, the administrative state functions were separated from royal household functions. Eventually, three departments would arise across most monarchies: the high court, the treasury, and the royal council.

With printing, the civil service grew into its modern form. The modern civil service differs from its previous implementations in that it is rooted in policy and procedure rather than patronage. It recruits, trains, and promotes (or separates) individuals based on merit rather than a relationship to someone in a high position. A professional corps carries out the functions of the state; this was essential since the civil service had to expand as the legal system expanded: when laws became more comprehensive, the civil service became more comprehensive. By the late eighteenth century, public administration had even developed into its own field of study, with research projects and professorships at various universities across Europe.

Oddly enough, despite being the first nation-state, England did not develop a modern civil service until the middle of the nineteenth century. England was hampered by internal politics that focused more on the relationship between Parliament and the king than on administrative development. As a result, England's royal civil service persisted, staffed by aristocracy, with position based on patronage, with little regard for administrative efficiency. By the end of the eighteenth century, the British Civil Service had become obsolete. In the middle of the nineteenth century, the nation was forced to assess whether its civil service was fit to assume control of East India Company overseas holdings.[12] A stinging report (the Northcote-Trevelyan Report) exposed the poor, antiquated state of the British Civil Service in 1854. In response, Parliament established the Civil Service Commission, and major restructuring began.

The modern civil service actually began in Prussia, in the middle of the seventeenth century, while Prussia was still a fiefdom. The royal government needed more effective control over provinces and cities, so Frederick William, the great elector of Brandenburg, cashiered feudal administrators and replaced them with an efficient administrative organization. The new organization was staffed by civil servants selected on a competitive basis. Courses were developed at universities to train professionals, and research in administration approaches began, resulting in a continuous evolution and refinement of the civil service. By the early eighteenth century, this civil service was fully

---

[12] Until that time, the British Empire had largely been administered by the East India Company, which had developed its own civil service and even founded a college in 1806 to develop a corps of civil service professionals. After an uprising against Britain in India, Parliament decided to assume direct responsibility for Britain's overseas possessions.

developed. Different administrative units handled the different affairs of the Crown, and ordinances prescribed organization structure, recruitment procedures, and performance and promotion requirements. The Prussian model became the model for the rest of Europe.

In France, Napoleon instituted a modern civil service after the French Revolution. He converted the old royal civil service to a nation-state civil service, and in doing so, he changed crown servants into public servants. Rationality, hierarchy, and competency became the expectation. The French civil service expanded rapidly as the public law defined what "public service" meant, how it was to be structured, who performed it, and what the obligations and responsibilities of public servants were. In France, the nation-state first fulfilled its final requirement for sustainment: a modern civil service.

Together, legal code, a commitment to process, and a modern civil service created the infrastructure needed to sustain the rule-of-law as a governance basis. The legal code became more robust and more useful to society. With representatives in Parliament, people at least knew whom to go see when they did not like something—moving a step closer to personal decision making. A culture of process was able to overcome a natural dependency on relationship in governance. The modern civil service enforced the laws, making them credible and effective. And with all this, things seemed to work better. Life got better for people; therefore, the entire governance basis gained credibility and stability. And so the evolution continued. In 1911, the House of Lords would lose much of its power; it lost even more in 1949, making the Commons the sole governing force. Yet rule-of-law endures.[LXX]

Other Transitions

Rule-of-law would become the world's predominant governance basis over the next two centuries. It seems that once one society had proven the concept, others were willing to embrace it—it seemed to work pretty well. Of course, embracing it required ousting the reigning sovereign, which in turn required armed conflict. It is unclear when a society began to think about transitioning to nation-state, but it is generally documented when it took up arms to achieve it, and when it finally attained a stable government. England began its armed struggle in 1642 and attained a stable government when it established a constitutional monarchy in 1689—a period of forty-seven years. Four decades is an average time frame for this period (Table 8).

Table 8. Timing of follow-on nation-state transitions.

	Start of Conflict	Beginning of Nation-state	Conflict Duration (years)
England	1642	1689	*47*
France	1789	1830	*41*
Germany	1806	1871	*65*
Italy	1820	1871	*51*
Russia	1905	1923	*18*
China	1911	1949	*38*

France shifted from a monarchy to a nation-state in forty-one years. The French Revolution started in 1789. From 1789 to 1792, the war was fought and various versions of rule-of-law governance were tried. Napoleon became a dictator in 1792. Over the next few decades, France alternated between a dictatorship and a restored monarchy. Quasi-stability came in 1830 when the "July Monarchy," led by Louis-Philippe, replaced the Bourbon dynasty. The Charter of 1830 contained reforms, one of which stripped the king of his power to enact legislation. France, however, would continue to change forms of governance, vacillating between republic and dictatorship through World War II, when it stabilized on a republican form of governance.

Germany was formed from over three hundred cities and kingdoms into a nation-state in sixty-five years. In 1806, France defeated Prussian in the battle of Jena and Napoleon dissolved the Holy Roman Empire. In 1815, with France defeated, an enlarged Prussia and thirty-eight other German states were placed under Austrian rule. In the 1860s, Prussian minister-president Otto Von Bismarck fought three wars, defeating Austria and unifying the German states. In 1871, Germany adopted a constitution that established a bicameral parliament with the Bundesrat as the upper house, the Reichstag as the lower house, and a chancellor as a type of prime minister. Only the chancellor could initiate new legislation, though both houses had to approve it.

Italy shifted to a nation-state in fifty-one years. At the beginning of the nineteenth century, Italy was composed of independent city-states (e.g., Florence and Rome) ruled by large families, all of whom were under Habsburg dominance and King Ferdinand II of Spain. Italian nationalism took hold after the fall of Napoleon. Uprisings and revolts took place over the next three decades, and many city-states were given their own constitutions by Ferdinand II in appeasement. Finally, three wars of independence and unification were fought (begun in 1848, 1859, and 1866). When Sardinian general and unification leader Victor Emmanuel captured Rome in 1870, the fighting came to an end. A year later, Italy formed a constitutional monarchy with Victor Emmanuel as king. He quickly passed power to the new prime minister and Parliament and retired from active political life.

Russia transitioned from tsardom to communist nation-state in only eighteen years. While dissatisfaction had been brewing for years, active rebellion began after Russia's defeat in the Russo-Japanese War in 1905. With Russia's economy severely weakened, violence erupted. The violence ended months later when the tsar signed the October Manifesto, making Russian into a constitutional monarchy. Violence returned in 1917, as disenfranchised elements of Russian society sought relief from a collapsing economy and poverty brought on in part by World War I. Early defeats in the war further discredited the tsar's regime and the opposition gained strength. In November, Bolshevik and other forces impelled Tsar Nicholas II to abdicate, and a provisional government was established. Civil war broke out a year later when Bolshevik forces under Vladimir Lenin and Leon Trotsky ousted the provisional government and established themselves as the ruling party based on socialistic ideology. Bolshevik forces ultimately won the way in 1923, firmly establishing a communist government.

China transitioned from dynastic rule to nation-state in thirty-eight years. The Qing dynasty, the last monarchy in China, was overthrown in the 1911–1912 Xinhai Revolution. Unrest had been growing for decades as youth began advocating for a republic. China's losses in the Sino-Japanese War and the Boxer Rebellion weakened the dynasty's credibility, and unrest boiled over. This led to the abdication of Emperor Puyi and the establishment of a provisional government. In the coming years, various forms of governance were tried, but China remained politically fragmented and unstable. An attempt to restore a monarchy led to two revolutionary leaders battling for control, and eventually Chinese politics broke into a period ruled by warlords. Much of the country was reunified under nationalist forces led by Chiang Kai-Shek, but war then broke out between nationalist and communist forces in 1927. During World War II, the nationalists and communists continued to fight each other, though they were nominally united to fight the Japanese. After the war, the Nationalist Party was given rule over China by the allied powers, but civil war resumed. In 1949, communist forces, led by Mao Zedong, defeated nationalist forces. Chiang Kai-Shek fled to the island of Taiwan, and China became a communist nation-state.[LXXI]

...

So while countries took different paths, and ultimately took different forms (constitutional monarchy, republic, and communist dictatorship), they all moved away from remote authority to rule-of-law. And now there was an infrastructure that could sustain this new governance basis—an infrastructure enabled by printing. Words captured on paper and widely disseminated changed the way the world worked. It took a few centuries for new structures to develop, but once those structures were in place, people obtained more decision-making authority, since their representatives began making the laws, and the new structures had the power to enforce these laws through a modern civil service.

But what does all of this tell us about our future. Can these past experiences shed light on our future? Once again, though it may not be that precise, we can apply what we have learned.

Chapter 20
The Next Transition

One morning in April 2013, I was going to my barber in McLean, Virginia. I had about an hour to wait, so I decided to kill time in the local wine store. In there, I bumped into Gus, a co-worker from a previous company, LMI, a consulting firm to the federal government. I asked him what project he was working on, and he told me about a client who had just taken over a job as shipping manager on a local army base. His client was new to the job and did not really know what to do. Due to high turnover, there was no one to show him how the office typically ran. He asked for a policy manual describing his duties and was told nothing existed. He was then shown shelves of old manuals, orders, and standard operating procedures for other activities and told he was welcome to go through them to get some ideas. He did this for a while until it became a futile effort.

Somehow the client found Gus, who was working on a new software tool. In the subsequent engagement, they scanned into software these dozens of old manuals, documents, orders, and procedures and posted them online. After they had finished, the tool pulled the right information from these documents to create a virtual manual, where the client could see all of his responsibilities as though someone had written one for his position.

I was stunned. I had expected that something like this would be developed, but I did not expect to see it for another twenty years. Suddenly, the future was a lot closer than I realized. I went back to my car and jotted down notes from this chance meeting. I had learned a valuable lesson: good things happen when you browse through wine stores.

In the last two chapters, I described how the world transitioned from fiefdoms to nation-states. We saw how people began electing representatives to make resource decisions instead of a king. We saw how enforcement improved by expanding the civil service through policy and procedure. We also saw how a four-phase transformation occurred, and how printing triggered that transformation.

Now we look to the future. While we cannot be certain, we can expect that the next transition will be similar to the last one. Both transitions move in the same direction (Figure 37), so decision making will grow even more personal and enforcement capability will grow even stronger. In fact, the next transition could be considered an extension of the last transition, in the same way that remote authority could be considered an extension of nonfamilial authority. This parallelism helps us to grasp what we can expect to see next. So, what will the next transition look like?

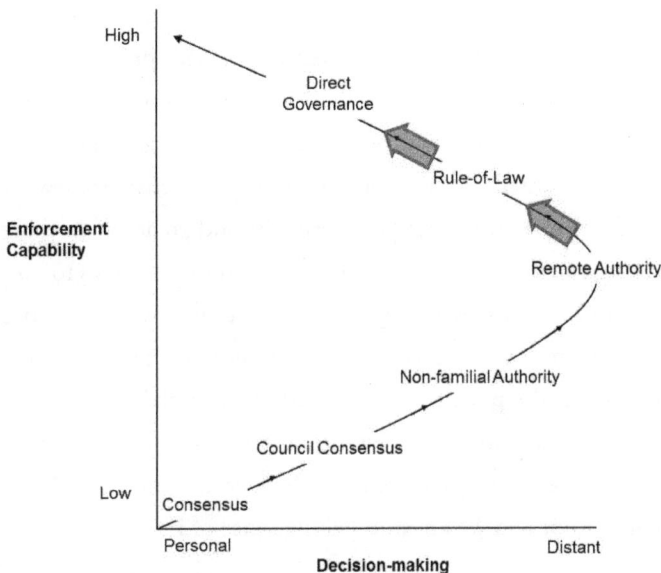

Figure 37. Trends in governance bases.

Similar Transitions

We can expect the next transition to be similar to the last one, though not identical. One way the two transitions will likely be similar is that the next transition is likely to have its own form of four-phase transformation. This is because the four phases are based on how humans make sense of new things, and just as printing revealed new things, the world in the early modern era, computing is revealing new things to the world of today.

Imagine you suddenly take over someone else's job, someone who left quickly so there was no transition time. You walk into your new office and find stacks of papers covering the desk, filing cabinets full of old documents with terms and acronyms you do not recognize, and thumb drives scattered in the desk drawer.

To make sense of what you have, you ask a co-worker what the stacks of material are, or at least what some of the terms and acronyms mean. You make notes on the documents, replacing foreign terms with words familiar to you. You organize the stacks by combining those with like material while throwing out obsolete documents. You clear the file cabinet of outdated material and consolidate folders in a way that makes sense to you. After a while, you start to see things amiss—projects started but left unfinished, projects that duplicate efforts, or opportunities left untapped. You ask your boss and co-workers for their take on these things. You learn that some of these things were more difficult than expected, so you adjust your perspective somewhat. Then, working with your boss, you set your priorities and go about working the top ones, building consensus and teams where needed to get things rolling.

The common experience just described followed the pattern of conversion, coherence, new ideas, and new structure. It is a natural sequence of events whether the pattern is performed by an individual or a society. An innovation opens the door to a new room, but that room was full of clutter and requires someone to make sense of it. Just as printing did, computing opened a new door and we are still making sense of it.

Computing, however, is different from printing, so the impact computing makes will be different from the impact printing made. The easiest way to see what the difference might be is to step back and look at the similarities and differences between computing and printing.

Language, writing, printing, and computing are all innovations within *knowledge management*. At its most basic, knowledge management is about how an organization—or, in this case, humanity—handles the data, information, and knowledge it produces. This involves how it captures knowledge, how it stores knowledge, how it processes or uses that knowledge, and how it conveys or disseminates that knowledge (Figure 38). In principle, the field has been around forever, but it gained special focus when software companies began developing IT tools for specific elements of it in the 1990s.[1]

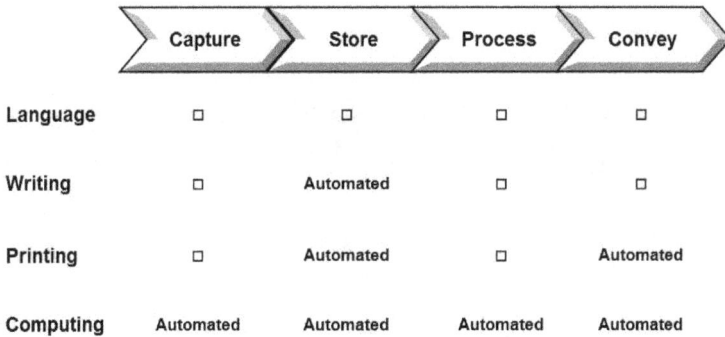

	Capture	Store	Process	Convey
Language	□	□	□	□
Writing	□	Automated	□	□
Printing	□	Automated	□	Automated
Computing	Automated	Automated	Automated	Automated

Figure 38. Knowledge management innovations.

Knowledge management really began with the development of language. Before language, knowledge management did not exist. Protolanguage (hand signals, grunts, and gestures) did not carry specific information, so knowledge management never developed. Knowledge management and language appeared together during the Great Leap Forward starting around 80,000 years ago. At that time, humankind began a rapid advance in development. We see remnants of this in caves in eastern South Africa. The world's first

---

[1] Knowledge management is a loosely defined field that emerged in the 1990s when software companies began developing computer applications for specific elements of it. Knowledge management has dozens of definitions and even more frameworks, but in general, it is the way in which organizations handle their collective brainpower and experience. The model presented here is the simplest and broadest model, which best serves the discussion of how knowledge management has impacted society as a whole.

jewelry, cultural artifacts, and ritual objects such as ornamental shell beads; inscribed ostrich shells; sophisticated bone tools for engraving including awls, needles, and fishhooks; sophisticated stone working; more sophisticated hunting of larger game; bows and arrows; local trade routes; and even land clearing by fire all began during this 20,000-year period.[2]

The Great Leap Forward required passing accumulated knowledge from generation to generation. Passing along accumulated knowledge required some form of knowledge management to learn, store, and teach the next generation. Modern language was needed to convey the specific knowledge needed to build more sophisticated tools and other items. One recent study suggests that language arose because humankind needed a better way to communicate techniques for making more sophisticated stone tools. One could infer that better tools led to new developments (e.g., hunting techniques and fishing techniques), which in turn required better language to explain. Hence a positive feedback loop developed between language and skill development, resulting in The Great Leap Forward.[3] This loop was knowledge management—and so in a sense, human history began with language.

Writing took knowledge management to the next level. Writing removed the requirement to store knowledge in one's head; so in a sense, it "automated" storage. One can see the difference this made by visiting societies that still have an oral tradition. Author Alex Hayley described such an event in his book *Roots*. He traveled to West Africa to find the source of his African heritage. He made his way to the remote village of Juffure, Gambia, one of the shrinking number of places where the oral tradition still exists. There he was met by a village elder, a griot [GREE-oh], or village historian. Griots have been known to spend years learning to recite the history of a family or village.

---

[2] While this sounds like a long time, compared to the inactivity that took place before it, it happened relatively fast.

[3] This development would necessarily have been preceded by another triggering event. There are two prominent theories of what this event was. The first says the human voicebox attained a modern level of development, enabling modern speech. The other says that the brain changed the way it organized information, probably the result of a protein-rich seafood diet in the local coastal area. Both events occurred roughly 100,000 years ago.

They sat down, and the griot began reciting the history of the Kinte clan (Hayley's clan) from its beginning in the empire of Old Mali. From memory, he listed chains of descendants and mentioned odd facts about various clan members. After about two hours of speaking, he reached the year 1750 and mentioned that a young man named Kunte Kinte had been kidnapped and taken away. This was Haley's American ancestor. Hayley would write a best-selling book about his family tree in America, starting with Kunta Kinte. In the book, Hayley lauded the importance of the griot in societies that still practice the oral tradition:

> I acknowledge the immense debt to the griots of Africa—where today it is rightly said that when a griot dies, it is as if a library has burned to the ground.

Today griots and their great memorization skills have almost faded into history. Writing obviated these skills by capturing family or village histories on paper, clay, stone, or animal skins. Information could now last indefinitely and did not require intentional memorization. Capturing that information remained a manual process, however: someone still had to record events by writing them down. Processing remained manual: people still had to decide how to use that information. And conveyance remained manual: people had to determine how to transmit the processed information. Nevertheless, automating the storage function changed history itself by giving rise to *recorded history*.

Printing took knowledge management to a higher level by automating the convey function. No longer was it necessary to create handwritten copies of documents to transmit them—printing presses with movable type could produce thousands of copies in the same time it took to make a dozen by hand. This being the case, printing could help Martin Luther's *95 Theses* spread from a single copy hung on the Wittenberg castle door on October 29, 1521, across Germany within two weeks, and across Europe within two months. In January 1518, when the *95 Theses* was translated from Latin to German, printing was used to repeat this rapid, widespread distribution. Furthermore, with thousands of copies available, the ideas contained in it could not be destroyed in a single accidental fire.

Capturing still remained a manual function, however: someone still had to write down the initial observation or understanding. Processing remained manual: individuals still had to work to translate documents from Latin into German. Despite this, printing still changed history.

Computing automated the remaining two functions of knowledge management: capturing and processing. Capturing could still be done manually by using a keyboard; or it could be done automatically using sensors or scanners, or by receiving it from another computer. Processing was automated when programs were invented. With programs, programmers could set up a job to run overnight and then leave it—they did not even need to be present. In the morning, the data was processed.

Of course, computing improved storage as well. Data was digitized and moved into computer memory, tapes, disks, hard drives, CD-ROMs, thumb drives, and even the Cloud—that nebulous network of online storage facilities. By 2013, Cloud data storage was estimated to have reached over 1 Exabyte—or 1 billion computer hard-drives of 1 gigabyte each. The ability to convey information has clearly improved as well. In 2013, an estimated 640 terabytes of data (640 thousand 1-gigabyte hard drives) passed through the Internet every minute. Furthermore, displaying that information has reached new heights as the computer graphics found in any recent video game will attest.

One of the more interesting aspects of computing emerges when you combine capture and convey, or better stated—convey and capture. When a computer conveys information to another computer where it is then captured, communication is fully automated. When a computer conveys information to itself, where it is then recaptured, *iteration* is fully automated. This opens up new possibilities. Rather than having to get something perfect the first time, iteration creates the possibility of converging on an answer. While printing enabled this to a degree, computers made it a routine occurrence. Iteration has given us an ability to solve complex mathematical equations, test new theories, or even write better books.

So in a way, computing extended what printing began. In fact, all knowledge management innovations are related to each other to some degree. It is no coincidence that four of the six elevating innovations are in the field of knowledge management—how a society learns and uses its learning is one of the most critical attributes it can develop. Computing fully automated each knowledge management function and enabled the feature of iteration to solve complex problems, leading to countless historical breakthroughs.

Yet despite these wonderful achievements, technophiles who grew up in the 1960s and 1970s may be feeling a bit underwhelmed. Depending on what your expectations were, one could say the world really has not changed that much. There are no moon bases, no submarines with windows in them, no hover cars, and no Hal the Computers. Few reasonable people would dispute the economic and political reasons why such things have not come about or that in some ways we have advanced into areas we had no idea even existed. Yet some of us may still feel that something is missing, or maybe we just have not seen it yet. One might still expect that we have not yet seen the full impact that computing is preparing to make on our world.[LXXII]

Conversion

If computing is going to politically transform our world, and that transformation occurs in four phases, then the first phase will focus on converting print media to digital media. So far, the most prominent political digital conversion has come in the form of communications channels. Digital media has replaced, or at least augmented, much of communication formerly done in print. Every US presidential campaign has a social media strategy, making it a fifth channel that has to be actively managed, alongside print, television, radio, and door-to-door. Twitter feeds became an obsession in the 2016 election as candidates used it to keep media attention focused on themselves. In addition, campaign news coverage included online articles that came out almost while the news was being created. And online fund-raising made it easier for new contributors to donate small sums that added up to huge amounts. In the 2012 US presidential campaign, about half of the funds raised came in through digital channels (online, email, and text). This amounted to $504 million for the Obama campaign alone.

As compelling as this may sound, a more substantive conversion (for the long term) is the digitization of the legal code. Back in 1996, the US House of Representatives' Oversight Committee conducted a feasibility study on putting the *US Code* online. By 2004, the House was releasing congressional bill data to the public online. In 2013, the entire *US Code* was made available for download. Now it is available for online browsing. Just as law books and yearbooks were converted from script to print in the sixteenth century, the *US Code* has now been digitized and put online for everyone to see.

The *US Code* contains all of the permanent laws of the United States. It is organized under 54 titles, which range from the President to National Parks (Figure 39).

Title 1 - General Provisions	Title 21 - Food and Drugs	Title 41 - Public Contracts
Title 2 - The Congress	Title 22 - Foreign Relations and Intercourse	Title 42 - The Public Health and Welfare
Title 3 - The President	Title 23 - Highways	Title 43 - Public Lands
Title 4 - Flag and Seal, Seat of Government, and the States	Title 24 - Hospitals and Asylums	Title 44 - Public Printing and Documents
Title 5 - Government Organization and Employees	Title 25 - Indians	Title 45 - Railroads
Title 6 - Domestic Security	Title 26 - Internal Revenue Code	Title 46 - Shipping
Title 7 - Agriculture	Title 27 - Intoxicating Liquors	Title 47 - Telecommunications
Title 8 - Aliens and Nationality	Title 28 - Judiciary and Judicial Procedure	Title 48 - Territories and Insular Possessions
Title 9 - Arbitration	Title 29 - Labor	Title 49 - Transportation
Title 10 - Armed Forces	Title 30 - Mineral Lands and Mining	Title 50 - War and National Defense
Title 11 - Bankruptcy	Title 31 - Money and Finance	Title 51 - National and Commercial Space Programs
Title 12 - Banks and Banking	Title 32 - National Guard	Title 52 - Voting and Elections
Title 13 - Census	Title 33 - Navigation and Navigable Waters	Title 53 [Reserved]
Title 14 - Coast Guard	Title 34 - Navy (Repealed)	Title 54 - National Park Service and Related Programs
Title 15 - Commerce and Trade	Title 35 - Patents	
Title 16 - Conservation	Title 36 - Patriotic and National Observances, Ceremonies, and Organizations	
Title 17 - Copyrights	Title 37 - Pay and Allowances of the Uniformed Services	
Title 18 - Crimes and Criminal Procedure	Title 38 - Veterans' Benefits	
Title 19 - Customs Duties	Title 39 - Postal Service	
Title 20 - Education	Title 40 - Public Buildings, Property, and Works	

Figure 39. Titles of the *US Code*.

The *US Code* receives its content from the *US Statutes at Large*. Whenever a bill has been passed by both houses of Congress, and signed by the president, the new law goes to the National Archives and Records Administration where it is logged into the *US Statutes at Large*, published, and ultimately stored in the national archives. The *Statutes at Large* serves as a logbook and is the final authoritative source for wording of laws in case of disputes. However, the *Statutes at Large* is not very friendly for routine usage. It simply captures the laws as written, in chronological order. The laws are not related to each other. In legal cases, a lawyer would have to look in many places to find the laws pertaining to a single topic. When a law is repealed, the *Statutes at Large* simply notes it.

The *US Code* was invented in 1926 to add structure to America's legal code.[4] The House Office of Law Revision Council maps the permanent laws from the *Statutes at Large* into the *US Code*. The *US Code* contains only permanent federal laws. Laws that are temporary, that is, they only last a year, such as an appropriation bill, or laws affecting a specific area of the country or element of society (private laws) are not pulled in from the *Statutes at Large*. Executive orders and federal regulations, neither of which makes it into the *Statutes at Large*, are recorded by a different process.

The *Code*'s fifty-four titles can be subdivided into as much as fourteen layers using subtitles, parts, subparts, chapters, subchapters, and sections; subsections, paragraphs, subparagraphs, clauses, subclauses, items, and subitems. Not every title uses every level, and there are no standard lengths to any division—a section might be one sentence in one area and run for several pages in another. Furthermore, sections are numbered sequentially across an entire title, regardless of higher-level divisions, and are considered the principle operating level of the *US Code*. Appendices contain related material that is not considered federal law.

Mapping new laws from the *Statutes at Large* to the *US Code* often requires breaking them up and slotting the pieces under different sections. A law providing support to family farms might be divided up and portions put into Title 7 (Agriculture), Title 26 (Tax), and Title 43 (Public Lands). The originating act might be placed in the notes sections of the *Code*. Deletions and expansions require special handling as well. Unlike the *Statutes of Large*, which never deletes anything, the *US Code* will remove sections of law that have been repealed. This ensures that the latest version is completely consistent with current law. To support research, however, the *Code* will leave a note in the spot where the law once was.

---

[4] Private enterprises and even the federal government began offering a more coherent version of the law, complete with categories and cross-referencing in the late 1800s. The federal government created a version in the 1870s, but it was not kept up-to-date and eventually died out. Another effort at the turn-of-the-century came to nothing. Then in the 1920s, the federal government created another version, and this time resolved to keep it up-to-date. This became the *United States Code*, created in 1926. The first version contained all the federal laws of the United States in a single volume. Now it takes multiple volumes to do so.

The digital version of the *US Code* has proven handier in some ways than its printed version. Being online, it is more accessible—people can download entire copies of it within minutes from nearly anywhere.

It is also updated more frequently than printed versions. Printed versions are only updated every six years, with annual supplements issued in the intervening years, after a congressional session has closed. The online version is updated in an ongoing manner, after each bill passed.

In addition, online versions have links to related material. Most law offices use private (nonofficial) versions of the *Code*, which contain substantial amounts of annotations for each section.[5] Annotations include summaries of court decisions, law review articles, uncodified provisions that related to the section, as well as the implied authorities within the section. Online versions contain hyperlinks to other online material relating to the section, such as court opinions referenced. Hyperlinks make searching for new material far easier than was possible before, often reducing hours of legal work to minutes.

Despite these benefits, it still feels that computing would deliver more substantive advances than this. Indeed, the techniques used to structure the *US Code* were developed during the printing revolution, hundreds of years ago. Even hyperlinks are a digital version of cross-referencing, born in the early days of printing.[6] Fundamentally, the legal code is still flat text, and the tools used today are tools developed to support flat text.

This, however, is consistent with the last transition. In the first phase, conversion, only the easy stuff happened. The first few quarter centuries of printing saw the same kind of slow incremental change. Real change began in the second phase, coherence, when people began seeking to make sense of the material they now had to work with. Whether the current phase will last fifty years as it did last time cannot be determined: today's environment is so different from the sixteenth century. However, the progression suggests that there is more still to come.[LXXIII]

---

[5] Private versions of the code, however, are not considered an authoritative source for the law itself and cannot be used in legal documentation.

[6] Technically these methods existed before printing, but printing greatly expanded their use.

Coherence

Today's *corpus juris*, body of law, is full of inconsistencies, limitations, and disconnects. They are not big ones that would undermine the entire legal structure; rather, they are small ones that are too hard to fix so they are tolerated. Take penalties for drug trafficking. The US Food and Drug Administration categorizes controlled substances into five schedules, or levels of danger, with Schedule I being the worst (heroin and methamphetamine) and Schedule V being the least dangerous to society (cough syrup). Under this framework, one might expect the penalties for illegal trafficking of such substances to look something like Figure 40.[7]

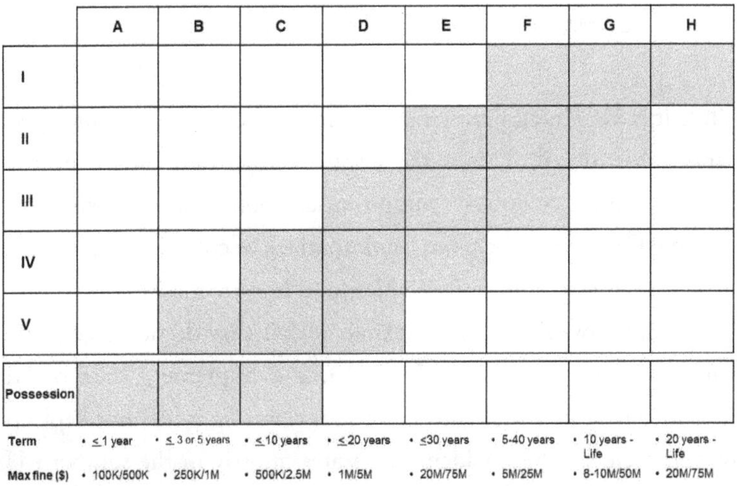

	A	B	C	D	E	F	G	H
I						▓	▓	▓
II					▓	▓		
III				▓	▓			
IV			▓	▓				
V		▓	▓					
Possession	▓	▓	▓					

Term	• ≤ 1 year	• ≤ 3 or 5 years	• ≤ 10 years	• ≤ 20 years	• ≤ 30 years	• 5-40 years	• 10 years - Life	• 20 years - Life
Max fine ($)	• 100K/500K	• 250K/1M	• 500K/2.5M	• 1M/5M	• 20M/75M	• 5M/25M	• 8-10M/50M	• 20M/75M

Figure 40. Coherent penalty structure for drug trafficking in the United States.

In this scenario, each schedule, I–V, has its own corresponding range of penalties. Having a range accommodates factors such as the amount of substance trafficked and repeat offenses. In reality, the actual penalties actually look like Figure 41.

---

[7] The lettering across the top is my own creation to help illustrate the problem: it is not included in federal law though the terms and fines the letters represent are.

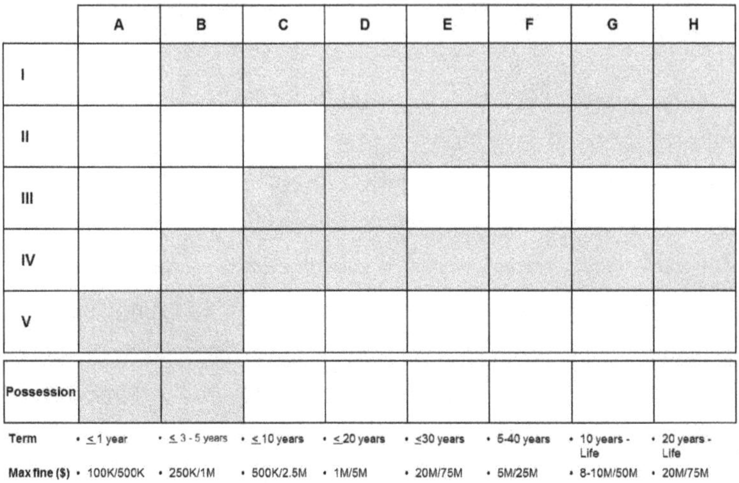

	A	B	C	D	E	F	G	H
I								
II								
III								
IV								
V								
Possession								

Term	• ≤1 year	• ≤ 3 - 5 years	• ≤10 years	• ≤20 years	• ≤30 years	• 5-40 years	• 10 years - Life	• 20 years - Life
Max fine ($)	• 100K/500K	• 250K/1M	• 500K/2.5M	• 1M/5M	• 20M/75M	• 5M/25M	• 8-10M/50M	• 20M/75M

Figure 41. Current penalty structure for drug trafficking in the United States

While it is not a total perversion of common sense, one might expect it to look more intentional. This is the result of legislation by committee (i.e., Congress), which requires compromise, politicking, posturing, and positioning. One cannot help but think this lack of coherence has contributed to states' decisions to contest federal law and legalize marijuana.[8]

Also, today, laws are rather inflexible in that they do not necessarily keep up with changing conditions. In 2013, the Supreme Court overturned portions of the Voting Rights Act of 1965, claiming it had not kept up with changes in society. The act identified states, mostly in the southern United States, where a pattern of discrimination prevented African Americans from voting. In 2013, a divided Supreme Court claimed the Voting Right Acts had not kept up with changes in society—that a better racial climate had developed in the states under scrutiny and that Congress needed to factor this into in any law concerning this issue. Chief Justice Roberts had warned Congress about using "40-year-old facts" to justify the law a few years earlier.

The Court decision invalidated much of the law, but stated Congress

---

[8] According to federal law, marijuana is as bad as heroin and worse that cocaine. While the current US heroin epidemic has claimed many lives, I have not heard of an incident where someone overdosed on marijuana. Even those who do not use marijuana know there is something awkward about this. Arguably, this lack of coherence has led to a gap between federal and some state laws on the issue.

could restore the legislation provided it used a new formula based on recent data to show there was still a need for it. The reality is that there is little or no chance of this happening. "As long as Republicans have a majority in the House and Democrats don't have 60 votes in the Senate, there will be no pre-clearance [update]," said Senator Charles Schumer (D-NY). This issue highlights the sometimes all-or-nothing limitations that daily politics place on long-term legislation: coming up with a new formula is too difficult, or unsupported, so the entire act is gutted.

Unfunded mandates highlight the recurrent disconnect between the law and the resources needed to enforce it. Unfunded mandates occur when the federal government tasks a government agency or a state to do something that will cost it money, but does not provide funds to support it. For small taskings this usually is not a problem—the taskee simply pays for it from operating funds. For big taskings, though, it becomes a problem when operating funds simply cannot cover the expense.

In September 2008, a Metrolink passenger train collided with a Union Pacific freight train near Los Angeles, killing 25 people and injuring 135. In response, Congress passed the Rail Safety Improvement Act, which mandated installation of Positive Train Control (PTC) on all passenger and large freight lines by the end of 2015. PTC is an automated communication network control system designed to prevent collisions, derailments, and other accidents. By the end of 2014, despite the rail industry having spent over $5 billion, only 6% of the planned track miles had PTC installed. The railroads were finding the new technology difficult to develop, the radio frequency spectrum hard to obtain, and the funding hard to acquire.

In May 2015, AMTRAK train 188 jumped the tracks near Philadelphia, killing 8 people and injuring over 200. The train was going 106 mph going into a curve with a 50-mph speed limit. In the congressional hearing held two weeks after the accident, representatives learned the reasons for the slow PTC rollout. In response, Congress has allocated another $224 million to the PTC project and extended the deadline by three years. (The Federal Railroad Administration had requested $825 million.) This disconnect between a law passed and the funding required for its enforcement highlights another inherent limitation of today's governance system.

Finally, how many debates never seem to reach any resolution? While debate is good and healthy in a democracy, one might expect some conclusions to be drawn eventually. The gun rights/gun control debate never ends. The minimum wage debate pops up every few years. The wealthy still pay less tax in proportion to their income than the middle class: is that bad or a necessity? Penal sentencing continues to be racially biased: but how do you fix it? When you think about it, so many of these debates recur so often that you do not even notice them: they are just life as usual.

All of these point to a lack of coherence in our legal code and legal system. This lack of coherence—the inconsistencies, inflexibility, disconnects, and general confusion—creates situations that range from annoyance to injustice. Yet somehow our system of government continues to function—and one might add, function quite well. Incoherence has not been a problem in our society thus far; we simply live with it. We complain about the disconnects, but we can scarcely image a world without them.

But in a larger, faster society, incoherence would be a greater problem. In a faster world, in a world of larger societies, in a world where societies are composed of multiple nations, with different historical backgrounds, and even different languages, incoherence would increase exponentially. People would stand up for their rights, with different understandings of what rights are. Legal speed bumps would turn into legal jersey walls preventing forward progress. Legal proceedings would slowly grind to a halt. Increasing the size of the government to match the increased size and complexity of society would not work: that would only slow things down even more. Today we do not have to worry about such things; however, in the future, we might.[9]

One way to deal with this problem is to create a more coherent legal system. This means improving laws so that there are fewer misalignments that consume time and make laws harder to enforce. This means making laws more adaptive so that they change with the environment, becoming politics independent. This means connecting laws and budgets so passing a law and enforcing the law are more intertwined. This means basing laws on coherent frameworks that obviate having the same recurrent debate every couple of years.

---

[9] Why we would ever concern ourselves with such things will be discussed in a later chapter.

Other fields have already achieved greater coherence, and are starting to reap the benefits from it. Meteorology experienced this a few years ago. Techniques for predicting the weather were developed in the 1920s. However, those calculations took so long that the weather actually occurred by the time the forecast was complete. That all changed in the 1950s when computers were first used to support weather forecasting: hand calculations were converted into computer code. While this improved forecasting, it was not until the 1980s that weather forecasting truly came into its own. At this time, computer models began receiving input from novel sources: ocean wave heights and speed, ocean wind speeds, water temperatures, soil and vegetation types, even gravity. In addition, global models and regional models were linked more tightly, and models were run several times over the same forecast period with statistical methods forecasting the most likely outcome. This was brought together with the use of supercomputers that could process this new input in a timely manner. Subsequently, the 1990s and 2000s were a period of rapid model development. This enabled forecasters to accurately predict both local and global weather patterns further into the future: local 10-day forecasts were introduced, El Nino and La Nina ocean patterns became more measureable, and seasonal weather forecasts, such as hurricane season intensity, became more accurate.

In genetics, something similar happened. In 1944, researchers determined that DNA contained the genetic code for life.[10] In 1953, researchers discovered that DNA looked like two long twisted strands of chemicals—a double helix. Furthermore, each of these strands was composed of only four base chemicals called nucleotides (labeled with the letters A, C, G, and T) repeated in a complex sequence.[11] Efforts then focused on identifying the sequence these four nucleotides took in the DNA of various cells (bacteria, diseases, etc.). Sequencing methods were developed in the 1970s, but they were slow, cumbersome, and used toxic and radioactive substances. In the mid-1980s, however, the processes were automated, greatly reducing the time

---

[10] DNA had been discovered back in 1869, but it was not until experiments conducted in the 1940s determined that DNA, not protein, contained life's code.

[11] The four nucleotides are adenine (A), cytosine (C), guanine (G), and thymine (T). In addition, these nucleotides always come in pairs: A with T, C with G.

and cost of sequencing. This led to newer techniques enabled by supercomputers that could handle sequencing of increased scope. In 1990, the US National Institute of Health and the Department of Energy announced a project to map the entire human genome—the complete set of human DNA, all three billion letters of it. Mapping was completed in 2003. This piece of coherent, holistic information about human DNA has since led to the identification of roughly 1,800 disease-causing genes, reduced the time needed to isolate a disease-causing genes from years to days, led to the creation of 350 new medical products, and spurred the growth of the biomedical industry. Research continues to focus on using this foundation to understand new ways for attacking genetic diseases, finding new cures, and developing specialized treatments for various diseases.

The four-phase progression occurs in fields that have lots of data suddenly made available by a new tool or innovation. Where such a backlog of data does not exist, normal evolutionary development takes place. We can expect the four-phase progression to occur once again in the legal field, where all the legal code generated since the dawn of printing is available. A new kind of insight, made possible by the computer, may now be possible to grasp. In the transition to nation-state, printing created an expectation that laws should be consistent, which led to *stare decisis*. One could expect computing to create its own version of *stare decisis*.

Coherence in the legal field would mean that relationships between laws are explicitly understood and mapped out. Not only are the relationship between laws fully understood but also the relationships between laws and the environment, laws and appropriations, federal laws and state laws—all of the principle areas that a law touches. Lawmakers will know in advance how changing one law changes the body of law, to include rewording other laws. Legislators will not vote on a particular law, rather changes to the body of law relating to a specific area. Changes will ripple across laws, statutes, orders, appropriations, and even state codes. Controls will have to be developed to ensure nothing illegal or unconstitutional occurs, but when a problem is flagged, that is where the debate focuses.

With this fully networked legal code, a new kind of *stare decisis* emerges—

a three-dimensional *stare decisis* that includes other federal laws (horizontally), state laws (vertically),[12] as well as previous laws (longitudinally). This three-dimensional *stare decisis* creates a greater awareness of our legal structure: instead of a flat legal code, our *corpus juris* begins to resemble the holistic network it really is. In this context, contradictions and inconsistencies emerge, and disconnects become more apparent.

Today, fixing every inconsistency or contradiction would bog down the legal system. Hence, there is a need for a digital legal infrastructure. A digital legal infrastructure would allow a broader range of changes to occur more rapidly. It would also allow for legal code to adapt. Laws will evolve, adapt, and converge on a desired end state based on criteria, metrics, and methods of measurement. Condition-based legal code emerges—old laws are automatically deleted, or flagged for deletion upon obsolescence. Changes are phased in, based on predetermined conditions in the environment. Laws change as the environment changes.

This legal system is different from today's legal system. Misalignments decrease. Enforcement becomes more consistent as court sentencing is benchmarked continually. Laws are set up based on objective metrics and measurement tools to track progress and automatically adjust without direct intervention from Congress. Appropriations are linked to bills, ending unrealistic unfunded mandates. Formulas replace politics in resource allocation so "pork" is precluded from budgets. Federal and state laws remain in alignment, yet preserve the freedom that states have to tweak their own laws.

Capriciousness is reduced. Political excellence is reflected by a profound understanding of an issue rather than wheeling and dealing. Positions that exist because of vagaries in law and language are exposed and eliminated. As Parliament reduced the capriciousness of the king in the sixteenth century, people will reduce the capriciousness of legislators in the future.

Moreover, the legal system is more efficient. More laws evolve automatically. Less time is spent passing and repassing the same laws. The

---

[12] States will probably want the ability to block, or at least check, any changes being made to their code before it happens. However, since potential changes will be known in advance, these checks can occur while the bill is still passing through Congress.

legal system becomes more responsive. Coherency has created a more efficient legislative process.[LXXIV]

New Ideas

After the legal code has been made more coherent, new ideas will emerge. It is hard to guess what new thoughts might arise after full coherence has been established, but one could guess that legislators will turn their attention toward addressing some of the principles underlying the laws. These underlying principles will be easier to see once coherence has been established.

One issue that fits this kind of discussion is the age of adulthood. Our current legal code is murky about this. In most jurisdictions, eighteen is the adult age demarkation: eighteen-year-olds receive the right to vote. At eighteen, a person can join the military and be trained to kill; but an eighteen-year-old adult cannot buy a beer. States grant sexual rights to youth between ages fourteen and eighteen, but insist bus drivers be eighteen to twenty-one. The state of Michigan is being sued for sentencing too many youths to adult prison, but federal law allows dependents to remain on their parents' health insurance until age twenty-six. So, at what age do we believe a person becomes responsible for his own behavior? If the answer is that maturity is a sliding scale so adulthood varies with the form of behavior (as some psychologists have said), then defining this scale would be the new thinking required to create a coherent set of laws touched by this issue.

Another incoherent issue is the recurrent gun rights versus gun control arguments. This issue recurs because people continually talk past each other. At some point, new ideas might include creating a common spectrum—with the government taking away everyone's gun at one end and the government issuing everyone a gun upon high school graduation at the other—then society could decide where on this spectrum it wanted to live.

Minimum wage would be defined by how much support society intends to provide to achieve a specific standard of living. Then it would be tied to metrics in the environment and adjusted automatically. Taxes would be governed by an underlying framework that considers both individual and corporate roles and needs, and then leads to a consistent, commonsense progressive tax structure. Farm subsidies would be defined by their original intent to provide support. They are then adjusted or phased out based on how the environment has changed and the continued need for protection. Affirmative action programs would be defined by their original intent and tied to metrics in the environment and set to evolve automatically.

Any of these discussions could be had today, but none of them would go anywhere. It will take a different society, one that cares—one that expects things to make sense—and one ready for the new ideas needed to address these kinds of issues. If these issues were successfully addressed, then the resulting legal code would more closely reflect the values of society and resources would be more precisely allocated to the things society cares most about.[LXXV]

New Structure

In the final stage of transition, societies will implement new structures, that is, governments. These will be needed to take advantage of the new ideas introduced in the previous phase. More likely than not, the new structures will resemble the old ones for a long time. Eventually, however, they will diverge in appearance to adapt to the values of their respective societies. Just as rule-of-law spawned the structures—constitutional monarchy, republic, communism, and even military dictatorships—direct governance will spawn different structures as well.

These structures will expand the use of direct democracy. Perhaps societies will decide that the weighty issues of the previous phase need to be decided by the people rather than their representatives.[13] In any case, the voting process will be done online by this time, making it a far easier thing to do. At some point, it will even feel natural to make major decisions collectively.

Different structures will apply direct democracy in different ways. Some societies will only use referendums for major issues, such as constitutional amendments or altering national borders. Others societies may vote more

---

[13] In reality, there will be overlap between phases so this discussion will likely take place while the third and fourth phases are running concurrently.

often, on less substantive issues. Different structures will develop different ways to count their votes. Some societies may weigh all votes equally, while others may invoke schemes such as double majority (e.g., where the popular vote *and* the majority of states are required for adoption). Some societies may even vary the voting age depending upon the issue being decided; this could ensure that only voters with enough history to make a wise decision are eligible. Societies will develop their own rules based on what they believe fairly represents the interests of their people.

The role of the legislator will shift in the new structures. Legislators will continue to vote on many issues, especially the smaller ones—people will not want to be forced to decide every issue. Legislators will decide which issues are put to vote—not every issue will go before the populace. (Each society will develop its own set of rules on how to approach this.) Legislators will frame issues for public decision; they will decide how to present an issue and even decide what the issue really is (often confusing). After a vote, legislators will fill in the details and craft the legislation needed to enforce the decision. Hence, the role of the legislator remains an important one, whether making the decision or managing the decision-making process. However, emphasis will shift understanding and adding value rather than bartering (and intransigence).[14]

Legislators will also play a key role in precluding populism—an emotional wave running through the people that sometimes induces poor decision making. To be sure, having a coherent legal structure is the best way to prevent society from being led astray by a charismatic leader capable of seducing the people: laws that have to work together constrain capriciousness. Nevertheless, legislators will still play a key role when deciding which issues come to the populace for vote. Also, legislators can help by establishing a stable working tempo to the legislative process—neither gridlocked nor

---

[14] The role of the legislator will change something akin to the way the role of the financial manager changed after online brokerage was introduced. Online brokerage made the complex and mysterious subject of securities understandable to the ordinary person. With the right information, people could make their own decisions. The role of the financial manager then shifted to that of information provider, and executor of decisions made. Full service financial managers filled niches where specific expertise was needed. Likewise, the legislator role will focus on where it can truly add value.

running rampant. Legislators will have a role in ensuring that society is protected from itself.

There will likely be a trial-and-error period when implementing new structures. Just as England had to learn to balance power between king and Parliament to establish rule-of-law, there will likely be some big learning required to establish direct governance—perhaps what controls are needed to guard against populism. Any kind of development is trial-and-error to some extent, so it is likely to be the case here as well. Societies just have to prepare for it.

A slow evolutionary process would be the most secure way to transition. There need not be any revolutions. While lawmakers may resist their initial loss of authority, most will make the adjustment. If there is resistance, a groundswell of public opinion will be able to force the change, yet this can be done without resorting to violence—change mechanisms exist today that were unavailable in the seventeenth century (i.e., more elections). The pace of transition also will be driven by how quickly a society can learn to manage its new structure. Ultimately, however, the pace at which a society expands its use of referendums comes down to, at least in part, a philosophical attitude about who governs whom. Regions where people tend to believe in sovereignty will likely transition faster.[15] Conversely, regions that tend toward traditional structures will transition slower, if at all.[16] [LXXVI]

Transition to Nation-Union

Simply adopting a new structure will not result in a nation-union, however. It will increase a society's capacity to manage resources over a larger population and area, but it will not create a society of greater population and territory. That move will be driven by other factors, and motivated by the self-interest of the times. Once people begin to see the opportunity they have available, they will want to take advantage of it.

---

[15] Of the 24 US states that have legalized the referendum process, 60% of the activity has taken place in the six Western states—Arizona, California, Colorado, North Dakota, Oregon, and Washington—where people are more inclined toward individualism and sovereignty.
[16] In 2012, the British House of Lords wrote: "We recognize that because of the sovereignty of Parliament, referendums cannot be legally binding in the UK, and are therefore advisory. However, it would be difficult for Parliament to ignore a decisive expression of public opinion."

Once the shift does begin, some kind of supranational executive committee oversight will be needed. These already exist, in some form, in most regions of the world. The question will be how much independence and authority to give it. The committee could be fully independent on one extreme, or "slaved" to the referendums of the people, with little interpretative power of its own. It can have lots of authority, with its own resources to manage, or have little authority, relying on member nations for execution. These choices create a two-dimensional spectrum where each region can determine where it wants its own executive committee to operate.

So where are we now in this transition? One could argue that we have completed the conversion phase, and perhaps are at the start of the coherence phase. In the United States, nearly all of the legal code has been digitized and is now available online. Little has been done beyond this, however. A few forward thinkers have introduced the idea that our legal code needs to be streamlined, or at least indexed to make more sense. But so far these have only been individual callings.

Perhaps most interesting, we are seeing the first computer tools with the potential to reveal much of the incoherence at a granular level. These tools involve understanding words and language. Xerox Corporation began developing such tools when it introduced "smart document technologies" back in 2007. It acquired a company called Amici to help it do so. Amici specialized in legal documentation and had tools with the ability to distill facts from thousands of pages of legal documents. These tools used machine learning and linguistics in their search. Another tool intelligently redacted information from legal documents, and added formal structure to unstructured text such as emails or laboratory reports.

Perhaps further along is a tool I described earlier, OpenPolicy™, by LMI. This tool pulls different pieces of information from different documents (most often regulations) to create a coherent picture of a subject. An entire library of manuals can be loaded into a database, and then searched for the right words and interpretations to create a composite picture of the issue. While the structure of the regulations may not cover a specific topic, this tool can create that topic, from existing regulations—and it is legally binding, just as any regulation is. In essence, it creates a third dimension from the regulations, aligned to the topic. If this type of approach were expanded and applied to the entire legal code, then people really would begin to see how coherent or incoherent our code really is.

When all is said and done, and the transition has been completed, society will have a new governance basis and an accompanying new sustaining infrastructure. Together, these enable humankind to manage resources on the scale of a nation-union. They do this by removing the nation-state limitations.

Expanding into a nation-union without changing the governance basis would mean delay worsens because there is a larger territory with more people and more issues to deal with. With direct democracy, however, delay is reduced because government becomes more responsive and less susceptible to gridlock. With a digital legal infrastructure, delay is eliminated because the greater flexibility in the legal code means fewer issues have to be revisited, freeing up legislative time for more new business.

Expanding into a nation-union without changing the governance basis would mean distance will worsen because people are farther and further away from their government. With direct democracy, however, distance is reduced because people will feel more connected to their government again. With a digital legal infrastructure, greater alignment in the legal code means people can be aligned without having to be identical for each and every locale, so it can better adapt to local needs.

Expanding into a nation-union without changing the governance basis would mean deviance will worsen because there are even more political entities to deal with. With direct democracy, however, deviance is reduced because lawmakers have more oversight and less room for errant behavior. With a digital legal infrastructure, capriciousness is further constrained by three-dimensional *stare decisis*.

Expanding into a nation-union without changing the governance basis would mean disconnect will worsen because there are more laws from different nations that will need to be reconciled and rationalized to make sense. With direct democracy, however, disconnect is reduced because the legal code will become more aligned to the values of the people over time.

With a digital legal infrastructure, adaptive legal code enables easier convergence of laws across nations.

So, expanding into a nation-union without changing the governance basis would mean attempts to form a nation-union would fail because the inherent limitations in the nation-state would only get worse. Direct democracy, however, will reduce the nation-state limitations, and augmenting that with a digital legal infrastructure will remove them altogether, enabling humankind to effectively manage the resources of a society on the scale of a nation-union.

This pattern of forming a new sustaining infrastructure every time a new governance basis arises is nothing new: it happens with every new societal level (Figure 42). In bands, the infrastructure was the *self*. The band leader made his own decisions and enforced the rules in his own family. In tribes, the infrastructure was the *family*. A council of relatives made the decisions and extended family relationships ensured their enforcement. In chiefdoms, *organization* became the infrastructure. For the first time, a non–family member, the head of an organization, made the decisions; members of the organization enforced them. In fiefdoms, the infrastructure was *paper*. Paper (or other writing material) conveyed decisions made by the king; it also conveyed procedures (and consequences) resulting in enforcement. In nation-states the infrastructure was *books*—volumes of paper, the documents and manuals needed to capture decisions made by representatives.[17] Paper also conveyed the civil service policies used to enforce those decisions. In nation-unions, computer *networks* will be the infrastructure, capturing the will of the people and conveying the code by which decisions are enforced.

This progression gives us more insight on what the future is likely to hold. This progression supports a pattern of increasingly dispersed authority and enforcement. Authority in society has shifted from an individual, to a council, to a chieftain and his advisors, to the cumulative edicts of kings written over a period of time, to the decisions made by thousands of representatives over the years, captured in extant legal code. The next step will involve decisions

---

[17] Or decisions made by dictators and other surrogates in a dictatorship.

made by the collective citizenry—even greater dispersion. Enforcement has both expanded and become more precise as it shifted from self, to family, to a small group carrying out the chief's directives, to a civil service operating under royal directives, to a civil service following extensive and detailed procedures. While it is not clear how the civil service will change, one can expect it to have broader and more finely tuned enforcement capability. Along both dimensions, the infrastructure granted society the ability to manage, coordinate, and hold together the increased dispersion.

The key for making any new infrastructure work is that it has to be both fair and consistent. Each new infrastructure had to be greeted with a fair amount of mistrust. It took a leap of faith for the head-of-band to hand over authority to a relative. In time, as the relative proved trustworthy, the new arrangement became the norm. It took a leap of faith to trust someone who was not a family member to make decisions for one's family. Over time, when it was found that a non–family member can be fair, this too became the norm. The same leaps of faith had to occur with written edicts from the king and legislation written on paper. A new leap of faith will be needed over whether collective citizenry is capable of making wise, fair, and consistent decisions; and whether those decisions will be fairly and consistently applied using a computer infrastructure. Only time and proof of trustworthiness will enable this to happen. And that will determine how quickly a society progresses to the next level.

How well this new governance basis works will be determined by how well government reflects the values of its people. Even more striking: the character of the people being governed becomes more critical since there will be less "buffer" between the people and the decisions effecting society. No longer will society rely so heavily on the character and talents of a few: to a greater extent, everyone will need character and talent. [LXXVII]

...

Through close examination of the last societal-level transition, we have seen how an innovation can drive changes that ultimately lead to more personal decision making and greater enforcement capability in a new societal level.

We can expect the next societal-level transition to follow a similar pattern, with the computing changes that lead to direct democracy and enforcement made possible by a digital legal infrastructure. We have ascertained that the world has already begun to transition, though it is still early.

Yet something else is needed to complete the transition. In fact, the transition may not go much further without it. It is: the compelling reason to transition. Just because we *can* transition does not mean we *will* transition. Something else must come along and give us the incentive to move forward. That is the role of the next preconditioning innovation. History has shown us that a preconditioning innovation is necessary for every societal level to change, and that each preconditioning innovation does so in a different way—making a different kind of impact. This next one will give us incentive to change. But, as we have asked all along, what will the next one be?

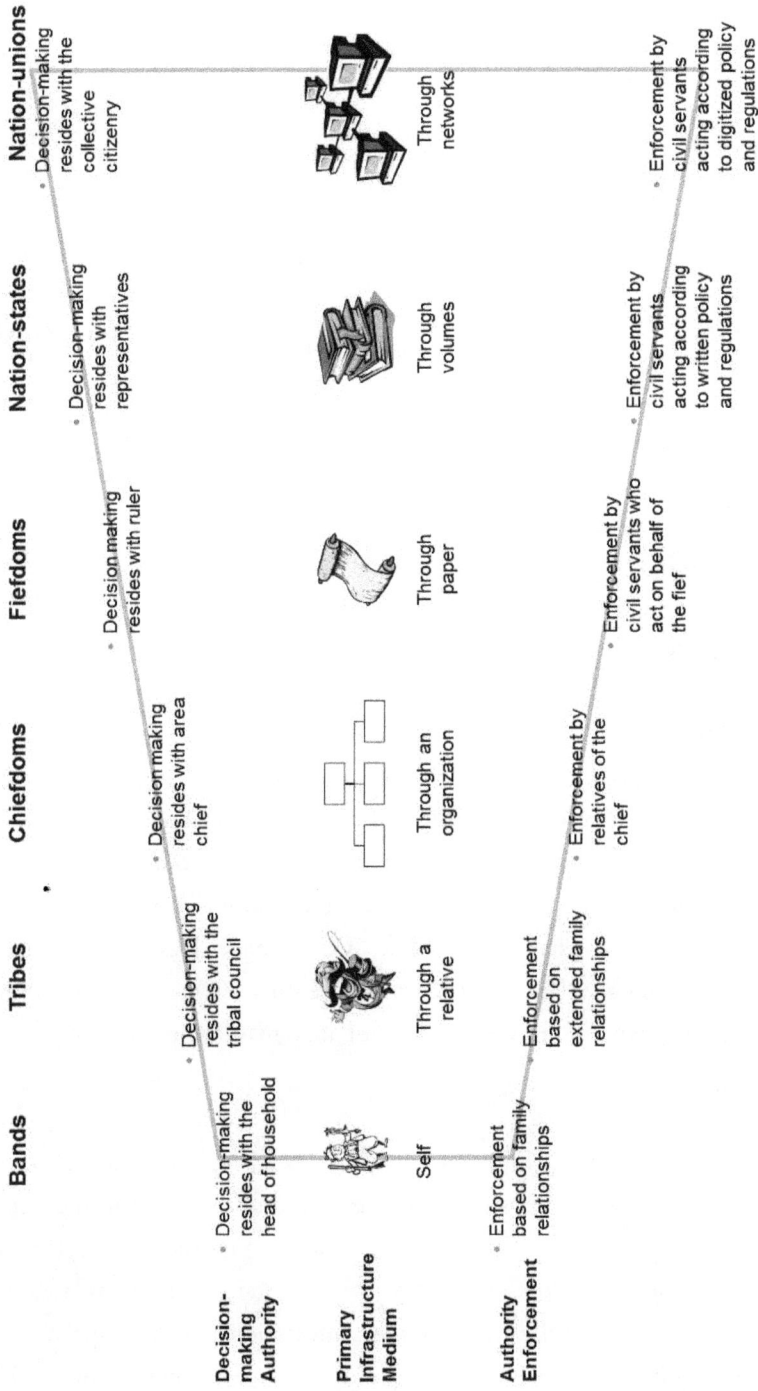

Figure 42. Trends in infrastructure, authority, and enforcement.

Chapter 21
The Next Preconditioning Innovation

In the 1960s, there was a Saturday morning cartoon called *The Jetsons*. In the opening credits, a man in the twenty-first century, George Jetson, left his atmospherically high apartment building, jumped into his flying car, crammed onto a narrow freeway in the sky, and went to work at Spacely's Space Sprockets. His commute only took a few minutes because his car flew at incredible speed. Once at work, he promptly put his feet up on his desk and began to sip coffee, presumptively for the rest of the day. Clearly, the writers at Hanna Barbera had something in mind about what the future would be like. In fact, most of us have some ability to extrapolate into our future and imagine what it may be like. If anything, it does not seem that the future is coming that fast. Our twenty-first-century world does not look much like George Jetson's. However, some of that may begin to change in the coming decades.

The European Union (EU), the most integrated region of the world, is a monetary union with signs of becoming an economic union in the not too distant future. However, it does not show any real indication of becoming a nation-union; neither does any other region of the world for that matter. It seems that no one really wants to take integration that far, especially if it would require changing the constitutions of some member nations. What would it take to make nations want to take that final step to nation-union?

Well, if history were to repeat itself for a fifth time, we can expect to see a familiar process. A preconditioning innovation will come along; it will change the world. This new world will need a new way to manage resources; that is, a new governance basis. Implementing this new governance basis, however, will require employing a new elevating innovation. However, using that new elevating innovation will require a shift in authority. That shift in authority will establish a new societal level. Once a leading region has demonstrated the value of this new societal level, other regions around the world will soon follow suit.[1]

So the process will begin with the creation of the next preconditioning innovation. But what might that innovation be? And has it arrived already? Can its beginnings be found in a laboratory on a desert island in some remote corner of the world? Or is it hidden in plain sight, right beneath our eyes? Identifying the next preconditioning innovation is perhaps the most speculative task we will undertake, but perhaps history can give us clues to guide us.

Preconditioning Innovations

In the past, every societal-level jump began with a preconditioning innovation that changed the environment. We have already established that preconditioning innovations enabled the efficacy of elevating innovations. Food production gave bands the need for property rights. Labor specialization led to the feasibility of a full-time criminal justice system. Mathematics compelled language to carry more precision. Christianity reduced day-to-day violence, enabling printed laws to take hold. However, preconditioning innovations also performed another function: they improved *transactional resource exchange*.

Preconditioning innovations made it easier to transactionally exchange resources: they increased the volume of resource exchange, or they increased the efficiency of resource exchange, or they increased the frequency of

---

[1] At this point, history usually includes a step that involves warfare and conquest; however, this is (optimistically) less likely to be the case in the future for reasons we will discuss toward the end of the book.

resource exchange. Table 9 summarizes the changes. Food production gave bands products to exchange (grain and livestock above consumption level), effectively beginning resource exchange. Labor specialization gave tribes services to exchange, increasing resource-exchange volume. Mathematics enabled chiefdoms to make more precise exchanges, improving resource-exchange efficiency. Christianity enabled fiefdoms to exchange resources more safely, enabling them to occur more frequently.

Table 9. Preconditioning innovation functions.

	Societal Level	Improved Exchange	Supported Elevating Innovation
Food Production	Bands	Started growing food for exchange	Created need for people to own property
Labor Specialization	Tribes	Created services to exchange for food	Made criminal justice possible
Mathematics	Chiefdoms	Made exchange more precise, systematic	Infused content into writing
Christianity	Fiefdoms	Increased freedom of exchange	Leveraged use of printed material

These improvements in resource exchange increased economic activity in a society, and by no small amount. It was not simply an incremental increase, but an order of magnitude leap, as was evidenced by the population that could now be supported within an area. Presuming this pattern continues, the next preconditioning innovation will also create an economic boom. But what could create such a boom?

The Energy Constraint

Right now, energy is the *superordinate constraint* on economic activity. More than anything else, it governs how much an economy can grow. Since the last societal-level change took place, starting in the 1600s, machinery has displaced animal and human power in much of the work performed in society. Automobiles rather than carriages transport people. Diesel tractors rather than horses are used to plow fields. Electric motors rather than oxen turn mills. Machines need energy. Whether gasoline, diesel fuel, or electricity, every machine needs a source of energy to operate. As the world industrialized, energy—particularly petroleum energy—came to hold more sway over every sector of the economy. When energy becomes limited or expensive, economies slow down, as the United States found out during the 1973 Arab Oil Embargo, an event that precipitated a multiyear recession in America.

A new, abundant, and affordable energy source would remove the energy superordinate constraint. It would do this by changing the economics of resource exchange. If energy is cheaper, material can be shipped farther more affordably. If energy is cheaper, products will move faster since there will be less concern about burning the extra fuel to get material to its destination faster. If energy is cheaper, products can be shipped more frequently, in smaller quantities, since the cost of ordering will also decrease.[2]

With the superordinate energy constraint removed, economic activity will soar to a new level. Farther, faster, more frequent resource exchange will create a step-change increase in the world's economies. The pace of life will increase, not unlike the difference between the medieval world and the modern world. While this "step-change" may actually take decades to fully emerge, the change will be so stark that the world will need to find new ways to cope with it. But what source of energy could remove this superordinate constraint?

In 2002, the world consumed energy at a rate of 13.5 terawatts (TW). By 2050, the world is expected to consume roughly 30 TW of energy.[3] In 2012, petroleum supplied roughly 82 percent of the world's energy (oil: 31 percent, coal: 29 percent, natural gas: 21 percent). Nuclear power contributed another 4.8 percent. Renewables contributed 13.5 percent (biofuels: 10 percent, hydro: 2.4 percent; solar, wind, and geothermal: 1.1 percent). To remove the

---

[2] In logistics, the size of an individual shipment is called an economic order quantity. If the cost of shipping decreases, the ideal size of a single order also decreases.

[3] The range for energy consumption in 2050 is 28–35 TW; this presumes that new conservation methods are put in place; otherwise, the world could consume roughly 100 TW.

superordinate energy constraint, a new source of energy would have to be found—either a new supply of an existing form of energy or a new source altogether. It would have to be cheaper than petroleum sources, and it would have to be available at future consumption rates. Is there anything on the horizon that might satisfy these requirements?

Petroleum energy sources will continue to be the dominant source of energy for the foreseeable future. Though there are varied estimates on how long supplies will last, most expect reserves to last well into the next century. Crude oil production peaked around 2008 at roughly 70 million barrels per day and is expected to drop another 3 million barrels per day each year over the next two decades. However, this decline in crude output is being offset by unconventional oil sources (e.g., oil sands). Growth in petroleum demand will be almost exclusively satisfied by natural gas. With an estimated 790 trillion cubic meters of worldwide reserves, supplies are expected to last for another 230 years at today's consumption rates. Coal will also continue to support petroleum demand: US reserves are expected to last another 400 years. As such, petroleum will remain the dominant source of energy, until some new form or source of energy can take its place.

Nuclear power supplied about 15 percent of the world's electricity in 2009. Scattered around the world, 438 nuclear fission plants consume about 70,000 tons of uranium each year. With about 16.5 million tons of reserves that can be affordably mined, there is roughly another 235 years of fissionable material available. For fission plants to become the dominant supplier of electricity, five times the number of plants would be needed, however, and the available supply of uranium would be consumed in a century. So nuclear fission will likely continue to contribute, but will not replace petroleum as the dominant energy source.

Alternative energy sources such as solar power (Figure 43) could partially shift the world off petroleum supplies, but it would require new materials to make it cheaper than oil. By one estimate, solar photovoltaics could satisfy up to two-thirds of the world's 2050 energy demand. Six solar photovoltaic fields of 150 km^2 each, dispersed around the globe in remote sunny areas, could produce 20 TW of energy at a steady rate. However, with today's materials and prices, construction would cost roughly $50 trillion, and photovoltaic manufacturing capacity would have to surge from 14 acres of material per day[4] to 14,000 acres per day. And while new materials are being developed, there is an inherent three-way trade-off between efficiency, availability, and price. The most effective materials are approaching 44 percent energy conversion, but they are very expensive. As such, new developments will be needed to make the economics of solar energy compete with petroleum.

Figure 43. Alternative energy sources.

Other potential sources of energy are on the horizon, but they each have their own challenges. Biofuels (e.g., ethanol) require lots of water to make a comparably small amount of fuel (approximately 1,000 gallons of water is needed to produce 1 gallon of ethanol). This limits the scale of practical production. Solar thermal, thermoelectric, and hydrogen splitting are all new forms of energy still in laboratory development.

So it is unlikely that existing or near-term forms of new energy are going to supplant petroleum as the dominant energy source. This makes it unlikely that the superordinate energy constraint will be removed anytime soon. However, if we are looking into the future for an innovation that would

---

[4] 2010 production levels.

affordably remove, or just lessen, the world's dependency on fossil fuels, there is still one source of energy that might work.[LXXVIII]

Nuclear Power (Revisited)

The atomic research of the 1930s began to see peacetime application in the 1950s and 1960s. Scientists knew that the energy that destroyed cities in Japan and islands in the Pacific could be converted to commercial use if harnessed effectively. In December 1953, US president Dwight Eisenhower made his Atoms for Peace speech to the United Nations, calling for international cooperation in the development of atomic energy for peaceful use.

The first nuclear reactor was built in December 1951. Built by Argonne National Laboratories in Idaho, it passed its first test by powering four lightbulbs. Later it would produce upward of 100 kilowatts. In June 1954, the Soviet Union created the first power plant that contributed power to an electric grid. The 5-megawatt plant was located in Obninsk, about 60 miles southwest of Moscow. In 1956, the world's first commercial plant began operating in Windscale, England, producing around 50 megawatts.

Over the next two decades, nuclear power took off. It grew from less than 1 gigawatt worldwide output in 1960 to 100 gigawatts by the late 1970s. In 1971, the United States alone had 22 commercial reactors in operation, producing 2.4 percent of America's electricity. By 1979, 72 reactors produced 12 percent of its electricity. By 1989, 109 reactors produced 19 percent of the electricity; and by 1991, production peaked with 111 reactors producing 22 percent of America's electricity. By 2005, worldwide power production reached 366 gigawatts.

Despite the continuous increase, nuclear power growth slowed during the 1970s. In the United States alone, 63 nuclear units were canceled between 1975 and 1990. Worldwide, about two-thirds of all plant orders after January 1970 were cancelled, though capacity continued to climb due to improvements to existing plants. In the 1980s, worldwide nuclear power leveled off at around 16–17 percent of all electricity produced. The leveling off was caused primarily by increased construction costs and litigation costs, both of which began to rise after an accident in March 1979 at the Three Mile Island, Pennsylvania, nuclear plant. Even more impactful, oil prices dropped throughout the 1980s, eventually making oil more economically attractive than nuclear power.

In recent years, the industry has had somewhat of a rebound as the need for a secure energy source and the anticipated growth in energy demand in the coming decades have led several nations to take another look at nuclear fission. China, India, and South Korea have led the way, ordering the new and more efficient third-generation reactors. China plans to introduce 100 units by 2020.

While nuclear fission was being successfully moved from the laboratory to commercial use, nuclear fusion stayed behind in the laboratory. Adapting fusion for peacetime proved too difficult to move forward as quickly as fission. Even today, it is still in the experimental stage. Nevertheless, nations continue to pursue its promise of a safe never-ending energy supply.

The fuel used in fusion is readily available and virtually inexhaustible. Deuterium and tritium are isotopes of hydrogen, the most abundant element in the universe. Deuterium occurs naturally in seawater—about 30 grams of it in every cubic meter. Tritium can be bred in nuclear reactors from lithium, which is abundant in the earth's crust at about 30 parts per million. Furthermore, fusion is safer than fission. Deuterium and tritium are far less radioactive than uranium. And though some components of a fusion reactor will become radioactive during power production, the public has nothing to fear from fusion power production. When something goes wrong with fission, radioactive gas is released into the atmosphere; when something goes wrong with fusion, the fire simply goes out and the plant grinds to a halt.

With this kind of appeal, nations have been working together since the late 1950s to make fusion work. They began working together as soon as they learned there was no military value in fusion research. (Peacetime fusion research has so little in common with the military version that advancing the one does nothing to advance the other.) American, British, and Soviet fusion research programs were declassified in 1958.

Despite this cooperation, fusion power production has proved elusive.

Because of differences in pressure and fuel, fusion on earth has to be ten times hotter than it is at the center of the sun—100 million °C instead of 10 million °C. Moreover, at those temperatures, the fuel, which is a gas, liquid, or solid before the reaction, turns into a *plasma*—a state of matter where the electrons are stripped away from the nucleus of the atoms. (Remember the plasma globes of the 1980s—the "cold" plasma?) The challenge became how to hold—how to confine—the plasma. This issue became so dominating that approaches to fusion were named after it: *magnetic confinement fusion* and *inertial confinement fusion.*

Magnetic confinement fusion was the first approach developed—early patents date back to 1946. Magnetic confinement uses a magnetic field to hold the plasma in place (i.e., in midair, though there is no air inside a reactor). Deuterium-tritium (D-T) gas, or pellets, are introduced into the reactor at a high speed, where fusion occurs. Because plasma is electrically charged, magnets can control its movement and keep it away from reactor walls, where direct contact would both slow and cool the plasma, possibly extinguishing the reaction.

The first fusion reactor was a "pinch" device. In it, a current was passed through the D-T gas inside the reactor. This created a magnetic field that made the gas collapse into a high-density, high-pressure, and high-temperature plasma. Because plasma creates a stronger magnetic field, which causes it to compress even further, a chain reaction is created, and under the right conditions, theoretically could lead to fusion. This device proved problematic, however. It could never produce the power needed because the plasma was never stable as it collapsed—too much of it leaked out of the reaction.

Another device, called a stellarator, was built in 1951 at what would become the Princeton Plasma Physics Laboratory. This device was also challenged by plasma instability and leakage. By the mid-1950s, it was clear that more theory had to be developed before any device would work. Slowly the laws of plasma physics were codified and performance improved. By 1958, an experiment at Los Alamos National Laboratory achieved a temperature of 15 million °C—hotter than the core of the sun.

Meanwhile, Soviet researchers were working on a different reactor design.

This research paid off big when they unveiled the *tokamak* in 1968. The tokamak pioneered a new shape and electromagnet configuration that improved plasma flow (Figure 44). It produced the highest temperatures obtained to date as well as the first quasi-sustainable fusion reaction. This reactor design would become the foundation for magnetic confinement fusion in the coming decades.

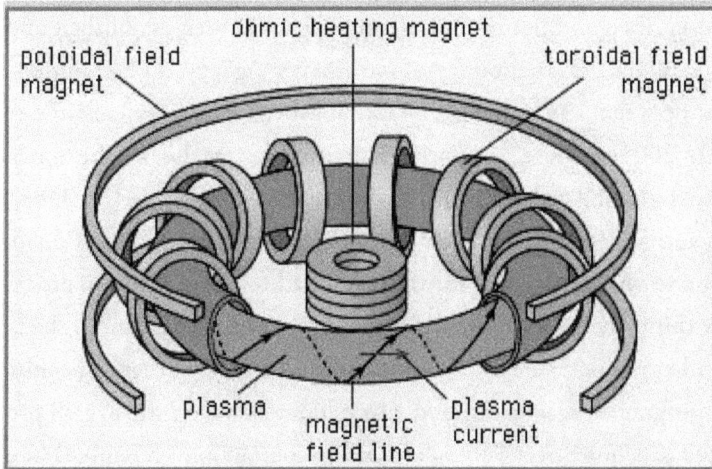

Figure 44. Tokamak reactor.
Reprinted with permission from Encyclopædia Britannica, ©1999 by Encyclopædia Britannica, Inc.

Over time, tokamaks spread across the globe, and performance climbed. In 1997, Europe's JET, located in the United Kingdom, produced 16 megawatts of fusion power—still a record. In 1998, Japan's JT-60 produced a fusion amplification factor, Q, of 1.25—meaning the energy achieved from the reaction was 1.25 times greater than the energy put in to start the reaction—also a record.[5] In 2013, China's EAST tokamak achieved a record plasma confinement time of 30 seconds, an order of magnitude higher than the previous record. Even older designs—stellarators and pinch devices (now reverse field pinch devices)—are seeing new life with technological advances.

---

[5] Q is the most significant metric in fusion energy production. It is believed that commercial fusion requires a Q of 10–20 to be viable.

Now the magnetic confinement community is focused on ITER—the International Thermonuclear Experimental Reactor. It is a seven-nation effort to build a supertokamak in France. When complete, the tokamak reactor will weigh 23,000 tons (about the weight of three Eiffel Towers); it will reside in a building 60 meters high (about 18 stories), on a 103-acre site (roughly the size of 57 soccer fields).

The Soviet Union first suggested building the device soon after the 1985 Reagan-Gorbachev Summit in Iceland. ITER was then established under the auspices of the International Atomic Energy Agency. ITER crafted initial designs between 1988 and 1990, and approved a comprehensive design in 1996. In 2005, it chose Cadarache, France, as its test site. By this time, ITER membership stabilized with Russia, the United States, the EU, China, India, Japan, and South Korea as members. In 2006, member-nations divided the budget and workload going forward, and had to commit to the program for at least thirty-five years. (The EU agreed to put up 45 percent of the budget, while other nations were to contribute around 9 percent each. The initial cost of the program was set at around $13 billion; however, the overall project is expected to require over $40 billion before completion.) Site preparation was performed from 2007 to 2009. Civil construction began in 2010, and the first building foundations were poured in 2013. Hardware installation began in 2015, and testing is set to begin around 2020.

The goal of ITER is to achieve $Q = 10$; that is, it will produce ten times the amount of energy that is needed to start the reaction ($Q = E_{out}/E_{in}$). It also needs to produce 500 megawatts of electricity, about one-sixth the size of a typical fossil fuel plant, for at least 400 seconds. None of this electricity will go to a power grid, however; it will simply fulfill the goal of demonstrating the viability of magnetic confinement fusion as a power source—an aspiring achievement, indeed.

The other approach to fusion power generation is inertial confinement. Inertial confinement fusion (ICF) uses lasers to implode a 2-millimeter pellet of D-T, which then fuses and releases energy. ICF was first proposed only a couple of years after the invention of the laser in 1960. Its name comes from the fact that the plasma, so unstable and difficult to contain in magnetic fusion, is confined within the pellet. The plasma, which ignites at the center of the spherical pellet, expands radially faster than the fuel pellet can explode; so in effect, the fuel holds the plasma in place through its own structural slowness (inertia).

When experiments began in 1965, the lasers were low-power instruments. However, within a few years, lasers became strong enough to achieve the first fusion in 1974. Then researchers began adding mores lasers to blast the pellet. More lasers make the pulse more even across the pellet's surface, creating a more uniform compression. In 1976, Livermore Laboratory began operating a dual-beam laser. A year later, it created a twenty-beam laser that delivered 10.2 kilojoules to the target.[6] By 1984, a ten-beam laser delivered 120 kilojoules to a target. And the escalation continued. During the 1980s, a twenty-four-beam and a ninety-six-beam laser were developed—in the quest for *ignition*; that is, Q = 1.

Progress toward ignition has not been limited to simply adding more and bigger lasers—new implosion techniques offer great promise for achieving ignition and even *gain* (Q > 1). In the original, conventional ICF, laser beams blast the surface of a D-T pellet, causing the surface (the ablator) to explode both outward and inward at the same time. The inward explosion (the implosion) compresses fuel, creating a *hot spot* at the center where the pressure and temperature climb high enough to start a fusion reaction.[7] The trick is that the lasers have to be strong enough to implode the fuel fast enough to create the hot spot, before backpressure and other effects halt the implosion.[8]

A newer technique, called fast ignition, uses lasers to compress the target, and then another laser to deliver a short-burst pulse to trigger ignition. The short burst, only about 1/1000th as long as the long burst (20 picoseconds vs. 20 nanoseconds), uses a smaller laser (10–20 kilojoules vs. 500–1000 kilojoules). This means that less energy is needed to spark ignition. Input energy is further reduced because the initial compression does not have to be as tight, nor as symmetrical, as it does in hot-spot ICF. Because of the lower

---

[6] This is roughly the same amount of energy needed to light a 60-watt bulb for a minute, though laser pulses only last for microseconds.

[7] In a hydrogen bomb, a fission reaction (i.e., an atomic bomb) is needed to create the hot spot.

[8] The implosion has to be faster than 35.4 centimeters per microsecond to create a hot spot.

input energy required, the gain is expected to be 10–20 times higher than hot-spot ICF, although it has not been tested yet.

The newest technique, shock ignition, may provide the same results as fast ignition, but with a simpler and cheaper laser system. Shock ignition also uses a second pulse to spark ignition, but that second pulse comes from the same lasers as the first pulse. The burst pulse ignites fusion at the peak of compression, just as the material starts to rebound. Because the compression pulse is longer and weaker than in hot-spot ignition, it requires less input energy. Because shock ignition uses one laser system, instead of two separate and physically distinct, time-synchronized laser systems, it is simpler and cheaper than fast ignition. This dual benefit has created much optimism in the ICF community.

These techniques will be tested at the United States' National Ignition Facility (NIF) and the recently constructed Laser MegaJoule (LMJ) facility in France. Back in March 2009, the 192-laser NIF opened at Lawrence Livermore National Laboratory in California. The facility cost $4 billion and houses the world's largest laser system, one that can deliver over sixty times more energy to a target than any previous laser system. Experiments began in 2011. In one hot-spot ignition experiment in July 2012, more than 1.8 megajoules—500 trillion watts—was directed at a target. The target compressed to almost a 100,000-fold reduction in volume: a record by far. A year later, NIF announced that an experiment had produced more energy from a fusion reaction than went into the target—another milestone. (This, however, was not ignition, which is defined as the ratio of energy produced over the energy put into *the lasers*, not the target; and since lasers are only a few percent efficient, another order-of-magnitude of gain is still needed for ignition.)

In 2014, a new facility, LMJ, was commissioned in France. LMJ was built between 2003 and 2014 on the site of an earlier, smaller facility. Its 176 laser beams will deliver 1.5 megajoules to a target once the laser system reaches full capability. Experiments began in 2014 using an eight-laser system; more lasers are being added over time. One laser system that has been added is the PETawatt Aquitaine Laser (PETAL). This short-burst laser will help to test fast ignition and shock ignition, working in concert with LMJ's 176 other beams. Construction on PETAL began in 2005, and experiments are expected to begin by the end of 2017.

The goal of both approaches to fusion, magnetic confinement and inertial confinement, is to achieve gains in a sustainable fusion reaction. This will prove that fusion can be used for long-term energy production. Once this is done, however, work is still far from over. Nations will still need to ensure that power plants can be constructed to produce the energy economically. Rather than waiting until ignition to begin thinking about such things, nations are already moving forward on plant development. Two efforts stand out—one in magnetic confinement and one in inertial confinement.

South Korea has taken the lead to construct a magnetic confinement plant in a program it calls K-DEMO (Korea Demonstration). The program will pick up where ITER leaves off and continue the research until full power production. Korea, which has invested roughly $1 billion in the project so far, is a likely choice for this program since it imports 90 percent of its energy from other countries. Korea is supported by the US Department of Energy through the Princeton Plasma Physics Laboratory in New Jersey.

Phase 1 of the program calls for developing plant component technologies. This began in 2012 and will take about ten years. Before it is complete, nearly 2,400 workers will be employed at designing, building, and testing the requisite components. Plant construction is set to begin in 2022, with a prototype plant near Daejon to be completed in 2037. K-DEMO will perform component testing before being converted to long-term energy production in 2050.

HiPER is a European program aimed at demonstrating the viability of inertial confinement fusion power production. A plant site has not been selected yet, but it will most likely be in the United Kingdom. HiPER's three-phase approach begins with ignition at LMJ or NIF, and ends with a prototype plant built and demonstrating economic viability sometime around 2040. Phase 1 of HiPER incorporates the work being done at LMJ and NIF to produce ignition. Energy gain is also required before any further development can begin. Phase 1 is expected to run from 2020 to 2025, starting when the LMJ becomes fully operational.

Phase 2 is technology development. Once ignition has been achieved, HiPER will begin developing the plant components needed to repeatedly introduce D-T pellets into a fusion chamber at high velocity. This includes the mechanisms and controls to introduce targets, track targets, fix lasers onto targets, and engage targets. Components will include target design, the next-generation laser, the fusion chamber, and even community building. Major development is expected to run from 2022 to around 2034–35, though preliminary work has already begun.

Phase 3 is plant prototype development. Once the components have been designed, they will be assembled into a single plant for production start-up. D-T pellets will be fed into the chamber, at a rate of about 16 Hertz, where they will be engaged by the laser beams. The resulting fusion reaction will release high-energy neutrons that will be captured by a lithium blanket covering the chamber walls. The lithium blanket will heat up, and the heat will be transferred into water jackets behind the blanket. The water will turn into steam and be routed to a turbine that produces electricity. The electricity will then be sent to a local grid. The plant is expected to produce only about 1500 megawatts of electricity—the size of a typical oil- or coal-burning plant today—but will test the neutron heat conversion scheme, the long-term sustainability of the process, and the economic viability of the energy production in a commercial environment. This phase is expected to run from 2027–28 to 2040.

In general, researchers are confident of success. When I asked him about the odds of success, John Glowienka, ITER program manager (retired) for the US Department of Energy, said, "Even if we don't get Q = 10—if we only get Q = 7, for example—that's still a success." He also added that the program has learned how to deal with the many curve balls that nature has sent its way over the years and that learning how to do this is part of the program's goals as well.

If successful, nuclear fusion could become a source of energy that is both more abundant and cheaper than oil. There is virtually no limit to the amount of energy available from fusion power. Deuterium comes from seawater, while lithium deposits can be found in the soil all over the world. As such, the world has the opportunity to inherit a fuel source where "a single pickup truck can deliver sufficient deuterium and lithium to equal ... combusting 25,000 railroad cars filled with coal."

Some economic analyses, however, challenge the cost effectiveness of fusion. They say that even though deuterium and tritium are abundant, producing electricity from them will cost more than producing electricity from oil. One study estimated that the cost of most energy sources in the middle of the twenty-first century, the earliest that fusion would become available, will be roughly 30–50 mills per kilowatt-hour (where a mill equals a thousandth of a dollar). Fusion, in contrast, will cost 70–100 mills per kilowatt-hour, with the primary expense being the high cost of constructing a fusion plant. Some use this information to say that other forms of energy are a better investment.

However, many forecasts do not look far enough ahead to consider the long-term, uncertain price of petroleum in a world where reserves are dwindling. Furthermore, many do not account for the further development needed to make the alternative form of energy viable enough to replace petroleum as the dominant energy source. Making "clean coal" for example, by one estimate, would double its current price to around 60–120 mills per kilowatt-hour. (This assumes that reducing its pollutants would be expected for widening its use in the latter twenty-first century.) Also, making wind and solar viable as the primary energy source would require energy storage capability that has not been invented yet. One estimate suggests this development could increase the cost of wind power to 80–300 mills per kilowatt-hour, making it comparable or more expensive than fusion.

That said, if fusion were simply the cheapest among very expensive energy options in the future, it would not have a major impact on the world's economy. However, most economic analyses—even ones that challenge fusion's viability—acknowledge there is a way to reduce fusion energy costs: scale economies. By far the greatest cost of fusion energy is the cost to build the plant. This cost has to be tacked on to every kilowatt produced from the plant over the next thirty years.[9] However, serving more customers from the

---

[9] Most economic analyses amortize plant construction cost over a thirty-year period.

same plant spreads this cost across more customers, reducing the price that each one has to pay. So the larger the plant, the cheaper the energy.

In magnetic confinement fusion, the cost driver is the reactor: the more energy produced from the single reactor, the lower the unit cost. By one early estimate, the unit cost of energy drops 10 mills for every 30 percent increase in reactor size. The same can be said about ICF. In ICF the cost driver is the laser system: the more targets ignited from the same set of lasers, the lower the unit cost of energy produced. Larger ICF plants can drive multiple target chambers from the same lasers—up to ten, by one estimate. When three or four chambers are driven from the same laser system, the cost of fusion energy becomes comparable with that of petroleum energy. While it is not clear how large fusion plants can become, either magnetic confinement or inertial confinement, scale economies favor them both and offer the hope of affordable energy in the future.

Another consideration that has to be acknowledged when examining fusion economics is the technology lifecycle. Comparing petroleum economics to fusion economics right now is a lot like comparing the cost of a horse to the cost of a Ford Quadricycle around the year 1900. At the turn of the twentieth century, the horse was cheaper and faster than the automobile. Furthermore, society was built around the horse, with saddles, plows, carriages, and other associated equipment having been developed to a high degree. Automobiles were slow, expensive, and rather clunky. Roads were gravel if they existed at all, and streetlights were only found in major cities. Over time, this would all change: the automobile would surpass the horse in speed, power, and efficiency; and society would adapt to it. Likewise, fusion is at the beginning of its lifecycle, and is poised to make gigantic strides, whereas more mature forms of energy—petroleum, hydroelectric, even wind—are likely to make smaller, incremental gains.

Thus far, research has been focused on achieving ignition and plant prototyping; however, ultimately the focus will shift to affordability. In fact, ways to take costs out are already being identified: stronger magnetic fields, which reduce the required plasma current and reactor size; better "quality" plasma; more efficient ways to drive current through plasma; better materials; and even better reactor designs. New, nontokamak designs are already being conceptualized. Some of these have garnered interest in the fusion community.[10] Whether any of these designs pan out remains to be seen, but it is safe to say that economic estimates based on early concepts likely do not capture the ultimate potential of the technology. Like most new fields of study, continuous innovation will be required and expected.[LXXIX]

Hence, the world has the potential to create an energy source that is both more abundant and cheaper than petroleum. This energy would remove the world's superordinate constraint and change the economics of the world by making transactions cheaper. The resulting "surge" in economic productivity would not be sudden though: it will likely take generations. However, it would be a change of profound proportions. But how will fusion power help push the world toward nation-unions? Though speculative, we can take a guess.

A Changing World

Once the viability of fusion power plants has been demonstrated by prototype plants, nations will seek to build more plants with regularity. Eventually, fusion power plants will spread across the globe, replacing many coal- or oil-fired plants. The real change, however, will not come until fusion is cheaper than oil—when fusion plants have grown large enough to fully exploit their inherent scale economies. And this will not happen overnight.

Power generation in America started out small and grew over time. The earliest applications (e.g., telegraphs) used batteries. Then crude dynamos (generators) were invented and were connected directly to a point of application, usually a mill or a small manufacturing company. When arc lighting was invented, a few major cities installed direct current (DC) stations and began to replace kerosene street lamps. The lightbulb only increased demand for electricity. Dynamos grew stronger and more efficient, and generating plants became large enough, and standard enough, to service

---

[10] One experimental design by the University of Washington, called the spheromak, when fully scaled up to production size, may produce five times more energy at one-tenth the cost of the typical tokamak.

multiple companies or a local village within a two-mile radius.

Conversion to alternating current (AC) meant power could be transmitted over long distances. Engineers created converters that tied local DC application to intercity AC high-voltage lines. Generating plants grew large enough to service entire cities: Buffalo, New York, was the first city powered by a hydroelectric generator. Then plants grew in scale to service multiple cities and industries within a region, and the price of electricity correspondingly dropped.

Eventually multiple plants were tied together by a common electric grid, and power was sent to distant locations across state borders. Service became more reliable and cheaper. By 1914, fifty-five power systems were operating in the United States at voltages above 70 kilovolts. The rapid industrialization of the early twentieth century, and World War I, spurred on demand for expanded electrification of the United States and all Western nations. We can expect a similar growth with this new source of energy.

Nuclear fission also started out small and grew over time as well. Fission plants grew from 100 kilowatts in the early 1950s to 8.2 gigawatts by the end of the 1990s.[11] Fusion plants are likely to follow a path similar to electricity and fission, taking generations to reach ultimate scale.

Technology-wise, there is no telling how large plants may grow and what challenges may be faced as they do: these will have to be addressed when the time comes. However, a couple of external limitations are known today—and these will have to be eliminated before large-scale fusion plants can become a reality. Fortunately, plans are already under way to do this.

One of these external limitations is the power grid. Today's power grid could not handle the massive amounts of power, coming from a few concentrated sources, and transmitted to consumers thousands of miles away. Transmission losses already limit the distances power can be economically transported: in the United States, an estimated 7 percent of the electricity

---

[11] The largest nuclear fission plant, the Kashiwazaki-Kariwa Nuclear Plant in Japan, was commissioned in 1985. At its peak, around 2000, it produced 8.2 gigawatts. It was shut down after an earthquake in 2011.

generated is lost in transmission before it ever reaches the consumer.[12] However, existing technology can help to fix this problem.

One existing technology that is just starting to see use in power transmission is *high-temperature superconductivity*. Superconductivity is the phenomena where some materials lose their electrical resistance when cooled below a critical temperature. Mercury loses its resistance at –452°F, and lead loses its resistance at –447°F. This means a current induced in a closed-loop wire of those materials at those temperatures would circulate forever with no resistance to slow it down. (Some materials, such as copper, never entirely lose their resistance, no matter how cold they become.) In 1986, some ceramic materials were found to lose their resistance at a balmy –297°F ("high temperature" is relative after all). At this temperature, liquid nitrogen, which is relatively cheap and abundant, can be used as a coolant instead of liquid helium, which is rare and expensive.

This discovery gave new life to the superconductivity field and rise to a host of potential applications, one of them being electric power transmission. The first test of superconductive power transmission began in 2014 when Essen, Germany, installed a 1-kilometer superconducting cable to link two large transformers. The 10-kilovolt cable carries five times the power of its 110-kilovolt predecessor. The city's objective is to use superconductivity to reduce the number of transformers it needs and to move the remaining ones to the outskirts of town, freeing up valuable land. If this technology were applied to long-distance bulk power transmission, losses could be cut in half.[13] In the United States alone, this would save an estimated $10 billion each year, and would make long-distance power transmission from remote sites more attractive.

The power grid could also be upgraded by expanding the use of *high-voltage direct current* (HDVC). HDVC transmits power for thousands of miles with only small loss. HDVC takes the AC current produced at a generating source, converts it to DC at 500–700 kilovolts, sends it thousands of miles away, and converts it back into AC, where it is distributed to a

---

[12] This was the estimate for 1995.

[13] It is estimated that roughly half of the energy saved using superconductivity would be needed to cool the power lines, so the net savings is only half of the total energy saved.

population center. The reduced energy loss offsets the cost of adding converters. The world's longest HDVC intertie connects a hydroelectric plant in northwest Brazil to a population center in southeast Brazil, 1,482 miles away; it is capable of carrying 7.1 gigawatts. There are currently thirty-five HDVC transmission stations in North America alone; more will be needed to remove the current limitations to the electric grid.

A final problem has to be dealt with concerning the electric grid—expanding HDVC by linking grids will result in scaling problems in network complexity and transmission congestion. An overhaul of the electric grid is needed to fix this. Fortunately, there are already plans in place to do this.

In 2007, the US Congress passed the Energy Independence and Security Act, which provided the legal basis for overhauling America's aging electric grid. Overhauling the electric grid means making it into a *smart grid*, where computer technology reads meters and forwards the information to automated controls, which in turn direct the flow of electricity in real time to where it is needed most. This will eliminate the blackouts and brownouts associated with temporary surges in demand or disruptions in energy supply. It will also facilitate adding more diverse kinds of energy to the power grid such as renewables and ultimately fusion.

In 2008, former vice president Al Gore challenged Congress to go a step further and create a *unified smart grid*. The advantages of a smart grid are most fully exploited when it can direct energy from anywhere in the United States to anywhere in the United States. With this in mind, organizations are now pushing for a unified smart grid that not only automates the electric grid but also unifies it into a single entity. Researchers have even begun proposing architectural designs.

Meanwhile, Europe is moving forward on this front as well. The EU aims to build the Supergrid, which will link disparate electric grids across the continent using a network of HDVC interties. Its immediate motivation is to better leverage renewable energy. Energy, such as wind and solar, is inherently intermittent, but a study revealed that if loads could be balanced across Europe, such energy could meet Europe's growing demand for electricity. Offshore wind power alone could meet an estimated 70 percent of demand. This is a big issue for a region that imported half of its energy from foreign sources in 2012. The program would also reduce Europe's carbon footprint, a growing environmental concern.[14]

Such a concept has only recently been enabled by new technologies, such as new converters, breakers, and bipolar transistors that make it possible to connect HVDC links to form a network. However, smart technology is also needed to make it work. That is why the European Commission (EC) is developing the Supergrid. Like America's Smartgrid, the Supergrid will use sensor technology to detect loads and surpluses, and automatically route electricity in real time across its vast network to where it is needed most.

To build the Supergrid, the EC is funding various programs. One program, MEDOW, is researching the operational issues associated with creating an HVDC network. It will investigate not only the interconnections between HVDC links but also its links to wind power generation stations offshore, and links to AC interconnectors in cities. The program costs €3.9 million and runs from 2013 to 2017. Its intent is also to cultivate a generation of workers who will ultimately engineer, build, operate, and manage the Supergrid. Another €63-million project is studying the best way to incorporate renewable energy onto the grid, looking not only at wind but also at tidal, solar, and hydroelectric as well. The EC's Connecting Europe program provides grant money to nations to build connections between their grids. This €5.8-billion program runs from 2014 to 2020. One €40-million grant is helping to link Norwegian hydroelectric power to the United Kingdom and France. Another grant will help link a tidal generation in the Channel Islands to the United Kingdom.

These US and European programs should make their respective power grids robust enough to handle fusion energy long before it ever becomes available. As such, these regions will have a head-start in this area, assuming they complete their programs. However, another external challenge remains: water consumption.

Large-scale fusion plants will use a lot of water, and this limits the number of places where the plants can be located. Fission plants today are usually

---

[14] Many opponents of fusion argue that renewable energy is a better investment than fusion because it is more likely to produce near-term results. Fusion supporters counter that both paths need to be pursued in parallel to best secure Europe's energy future.

located near lakes, rivers, or oceans, where a water source can be used to cool the steam after it has passed through the power turbines. Since plans call for fusion plants to use the same energy-conversion method, a large-scale fusion plant will face the same challenge—and the larger the plant, the greater the challenge.[15] Ideally, large-scale fusion plants would be located away from population centers. However, since people and water tend to go hand-in-hand, the larger the plant, the fewer the number of available sites.

One possible solution to this challenge is to convert heat into electricity without boiling water: that would obviate cooling any steam and thereby reduce water consumption. While this may sound fanciful, some scientists are working to do just that. Magnetohydrodynamics generates electricity directly from plasma. Magnetohydrodynamics is not unlike having a molten wire carrying electricity. When a normal metal wire passes by a magnet, a current is produced in the wire (like a car alternator). Now if that wire were a molten metal instead, it would still conduct a current when it passes a magnet. What is more, that fluid current could be routed to where some of it could be pulled off as electric power. In fusion, plasma behaves the same way as the molten metal (or any other conducting fluid, such as salt brine).

With plasma flowing around a reactor, and superconducting magnets everywhere, it seems like this would be a perfect fit with magnetic confinement fusion: the pieces already seem to be in place. However, reality is far more complicated. For one thing, pulling off current reduces the temperature and flow of the plasma, and it creates other instabilities as well. Scientists are trying to find a way to make this work. Researchers are using complex computer modeling to better understand plasma flow; however, years of research are still ahead.

Another technology that may help is *direct energy conversion*. Direct energy conversion separates plasma into positively and negatively charged particles to create voltage and current. ICF throws off charged particles at a high speed. These particles can be slowed and separated, with positive ions going in one

---

[15] This process is known as the Rankine Cycle, where water is turned to steam by a heat source, used to turn a turbine, condensed back into water, and reused. The process developed in the mid-1800s and was named after William Rankine, a Scottish engineer, who developed much of the early theory of thermodynamics.

direction and negative electrons going in another. This separation creates a voltage, with the resultant flows of ions and electrons becoming current. While this sounds like a perfect fit with ICF, there is a question of how much energy can be generated from this approach versus simply using heat and boiling water. Scientists are seeking ways to increase its effectiveness.

While either of these technologies can be used alongside a steam turbine, it is unclear whether they would entirely replace the turbine. However, if that is indeed the case, then nations will have greater flexibility in where they can locate plants: a plant might be put in the Atacama Desert instead of along the Pacific Ocean. Such flexibility can have great benefit in power distribution and for minimizing impacts to a local population. If the technologies do not prove fruitful, all is not lost—however, there will be a trade-off between the size of the plant and the number of potential sites for them.

So how large could plants grow? They will continue to grow as long as scale economies exist and technology permits. Assuming the external limitations can be removed,[16] then power becomes cheapest when the fewest plants serve the most people. In the extreme, a few plants would supply the energy for an entire continent of people, limited only where natural barriers such as shorelines and oceans restrict the cost-effective distribution of energy (Figure 45). These plants would become *terawatt* plants.[17]

---

[16] This is a big assumption, but one we will make nonetheless.

[17] The EU is installing an undersea power cable from the United Kingdom to Norway to tap into Norway's hydroelectric surplus—someday only "wide oceans" such as the Atlantic may be the restrictive barrier.

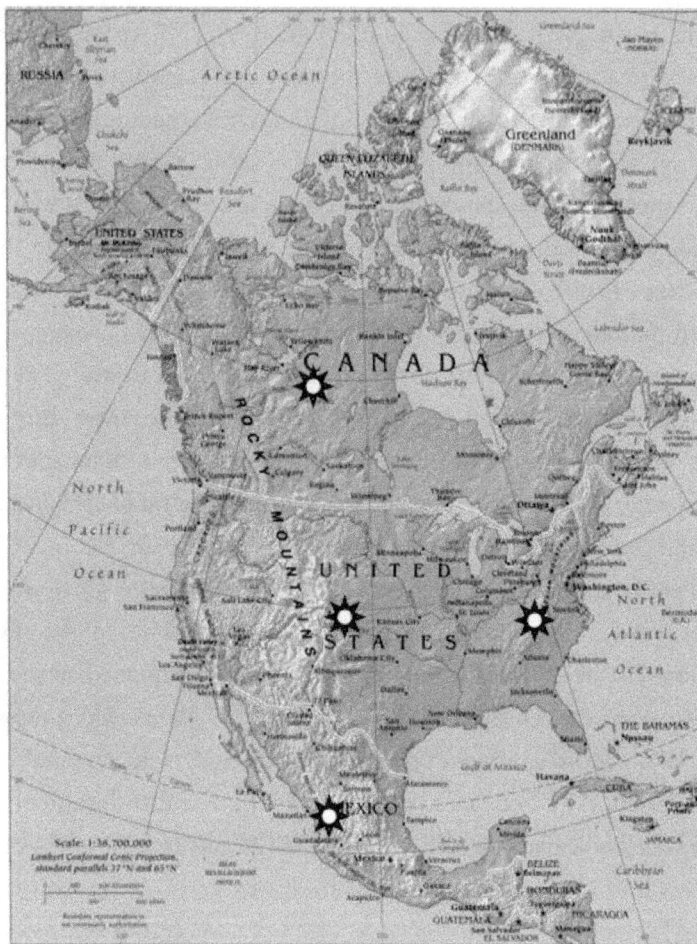

Figure 45. Illustrative location of future fusion power plants in North America.

These plants would be located in remote areas, away from water sources, away from population centers, where land is cheap and urban centers would not be disrupted. Energy would then be distributed to a portion of the continent over a strong electric grid. The plant would be a boon to a local community, industrializing a remote area, creating an industry from scratch.

With terawatt plants, the world will begin to change. The world's energy infrastructure will more fully convert from petroleum to electricity. Electric cars will become the dominant form of vehicle. Filling stations will convert to charging stations. Diesel-electric trains will become electric trains, and may even ride on electromagnetic monorails. Power will become cheaper for consumers.

Of course, petroleum will always have its place. Oils and lubricants will still be needed to run machinery and cars. Petroleum fuel will still to be used wherever energy storage is an issue, such as on a ship or in an aircraft. And of course, oil derivatives, such as plastic, will continue to be a part of our lives. Nevertheless, the world will shift, and will do so in a way reminiscent of its shift from kerosene to electric lighting, but on a larger scale.

Now the creation of a few large central energy sources, and the shift to an electric infrastructure, is likely to have an interesting side effect: it will spur on a move toward supranationalism. Electrons do not naturally stop at borders. As such, a supranational approach is a good fit for energy management. And this will condition people to ask, what else could best be managed at a supranational level?

Electricity generation has nearly always crossed borders. In the early 1900s, power companies extended their distribution capabilities beyond their local areas and eventually out of state. In the 1990s, the United States deregulated the electric power industry, separating power generation from power transmission, and enabling new entrants into both industries. This prompted the formation of nonprofit regional transmission organizations (RTOs) or independent system operators (ISOs) to manage power transmissions across state lines, independent from any particular provider. Today, ten RTOs/ISOs operate in North America, across state and national borders, managing energy in Canada and about two-thirds of the United States' electricity.

Europe has taken this a step further, making energy management almost completely independent from national borders. Europe has been converging its power grids for the last sixty years. In the early 1950s, small groups of power generation and transmission companies would meet to define interoperability standards in their local region. These eventually grew into transmission system operators (TSOs), Europe's version of RSOs, whose focus was to coordinate the exchange of electricity between members. Similar to America, electricity transmission separated from generation (upstream) and local distribution (downstream), and TSOs began to manage transmission networks across borders. Gradually, these TSOs joined together, and in 2009, formed the European Network of Transmission System Operators for Electricity, an association of forty-one TSOs from thirty-four countries that manages the interoperability standards for all members, creating a synchronous network that serves 450 million people.

When fusion comes along, supranational energy management will be not only prudent but also a requirement. Energy will be centrally generated and sent to distant customers, so the sharing of energy cannot be inhibited by borders—local, state, or national. As the world converts to an electricity infrastructure, the demand for more precise routing of electricity will only grow. Policymakers will have to develop a coordinated approach to legally support all forms of power entering the grid[18] and to make the investments required to maintain and continually upgrade the grid. In the future, the region with the smartest power grid, *and the best way of managing* it, will best utilize fusion.

Initiated by fusion, supranationalism will likely migrate into other areas as well. Like energy, transportation, information, and labor do not naturally stop at borders. Material flow industries, such as commerce and logistics, will be the next to pursue supranational management. Cargo bound for Mexico City via high-speed rail will be cleared for uninterrupted travel before leaving a station on Canada's west coast. Passports, if they still exist, will be checked in Santiago so workers can travel uninterrupted to Brasilia. The speed, frequency, and distance of material flow will increase. The need for uninterrupted resource flow will increase. And all of this is best managed supranationally.

And then the world will get faster. Like the difference between medieval fiefdoms and modern nation-states, the pace of life will quicken. Resource transactions will cheapen, and regional economies will expand. Computers will manage the increased flow of resources automatically. And in this environment, borders that were formerly seen as protection will now be seen as a barrier to resource flow, and a limiter of opportunity. Industries will start complaining that governments are not doing enough to work together, to

---

[18] Even with fusion, there will likely be a place where another form of power generation makes sense, such as local hydroelectric.

coordinate their infrastructure, and to jointly create projects that exploit the new form of energy—projects such as new highway construction, high-speed rail, and information standardization. Supranational cooperation will be seen as the only way to remove the lingering barriers to increased prosperity. [LXXX]

...

And so nuclear fusion will create the environment needed for the next societal-level change. If history repeats itself for a fifth time, problems will arise in this faster society. The existing form of governance will begin to show signs of strain. Governments will not be able to keep up with the pace of change. Even economic unions will be inadequate, with too many actions and activities having to be funneled through legislative chokepoints to effectively manage a more dynamic society. And in this faster world, what were formerly speed bumps now flip over the race car. General frustration will increase, and societies will begin to look for new ways to do things. And the rest ... will be history.

So it appears that all of the pieces are coming together, setting the stage for societal-level change in the not too distant future, perhaps as soon as the middle of the next century. And though it will take generations for all of this to play out, many of the critical pieces are already here, and in sociological timing, all of this is just around the corner.

So, all of this begs the question: What do we need to do today?

Part III

OUR PRESENT

Chapter 22
Strategic Positioning

The opening ceremony of the 2014 Winter Olympics in Sochi, Russia, was majestic. It was a presentation of Russian history, which the audience was led through by a young girl. The history was told by dancers, mobile settings that rolled slowly across the arena floor, and aerial settings that floated slowly across the arena sky. The aerial settings were suspended by cables from mobile riggings in the ceiling; they resembled icebergs flowing down a river, each one depicting a different snapshot in time.

Early aerial settings portray Russia's great expanse: a farmhouse in the western woods, a volcano on the Kamchatka Peninsula, a tiny village in the south-central plains, and the cliffs of Lena Island in the arctic north. A family of reindeer herders appears, with round tents, two caribou, and a dog. On the arena floor, singers dressed in beautiful white winter clothing walk through fog. Artificial snow falls. Five huge snowflakes, three or four meters in diameter, hang from the ceiling, as does a crescent moon.

The history lesson breaks for speeches. Then the athletes march in. Afterward, the history lesson resumes with a short film. It shows how Russian was built—an ancient people clear a forest for an enclave of houses. Later, warriors erect an isolated fort deep in the woods. (The film continues into the twentieth century, showing how cities grew up, and ultimately how the arena itself was built.)

The next aerial setting shows three horses pulling the sun across the sky.

This is a Troika, the revered symbol of Russia's first mail and passenger delivery system (something like the stage coaches in the American West). Created in the seventeenth century, it did much to connect the isolated settlements. On the arena floor, a projected sheet of ice breaks into a floe and is carried away by the river. A festive city of onion-top balloons arises, and the dancers suggest a folk carnival is taking place.

This scene gives way to another projection on the floor, this time a raucous ocean. The wind is howling. A lone ship crosses the sea, sailing from right to left, east to west. This scene passes. An army of students, scholarly in appearance, marches in formation across the floor, following the ships. They are going to a grand imperial ball. Ladies in elegant gowns appear. Men are dressed in formal civilian and military attire. The time seems to be around the Patriotic War of 1812, but as the ball goes on, the dancing and music come to increasingly resemble the Romantic Era of the late nineteenth century, the height of imperial Russia.

The final scenes depict the turmoil and later triumph of the twentieth century: war, industrialization, rebuilding, the arrival of the space age, cosmopolitan city life, and the information age. All told, the opening ceremony in Sochi presented in vivid imagery Russia's historic challenge to overcome distance and climate to connect with the rest of the world, and the results of that connection.

Part I of this book looked into the past to understand how leading societies acquired their position. It identified three basic ways: jumping to a new societal level first by acquiring a preconditioning innovation and elevating innovation first; acquiring a dominating innovation first; or managing the four leadership power sources better than anyone else. Part II of the book projected into the future to identify the next preconditioning and elevating innovations, noting that the next elevating innovation has already arrived. This final part of the book applies this understanding to our present. This chapter asks: If a society wanted to become a leader, what would it need to do today?

That the next elevating innovation is already present and the next preconditioning innovation is in development suggests that would-be leaders should seek to be the first society to make the jump. Making the level jump creates the strongest form of leadership. Furthermore, there is no dominating innovation on the horizon. In fact, there may never be another dominating innovation since technology now diffuses so quickly that no society will likely be able to maintain a monopoly on its use—a requirement for dominating innovations. Concerning managing the four leadership power sources, this is something every society should be doing in any case.

So it appears we are at a point in history that we have not seen since the 1500s. The nations that jump first to the next societal level have the potential to be the dominant region for the next five hundred years. But the challenge is that the jump may not happen for decades, even generations. Is there anything a would-be leader should be doing in the meantime? As always, history has a lesson for us.

The Silk Road

The Silk Road was an ancient trade route running from Rome to China. Its western end was located in Rome or Constantinople (it changed over time), and its eastern end was in Chang'an (modern-day Xi'an) China (Figure 46). In between were various paths that merchants used to cross the high desert and connect major cities and trading posts.

The Silk Road began around 200 BCE. The western leg of the Silk Road, running from Europe into central Asia, had begun operating after Alexander the Great's eastern conquests in 330 BCE. The eastern section, running from China into central Asia, began after a Chinese expedition discovered Western empires such as the Parthians around 200 BCE. Thereafter, trade between Europe and China began flowing.

The Silk Road was named for its most precious trade item.[1] Romans became fascinated with the material after learning about it from the Parthians, whom they campaigned against around 50 BCE. Despite being enemies, the Parthians were all too happy to increase the trade flowing through their

---

[1] The name Silk Road was coined by the German scholar Baron Ferdinand von Richthofen, who studied the ancient trade route in the nineteenth century.

territory. By the Tang dynasty (618–907 CE), silk would comprise about 30 percent of the trade along the route.

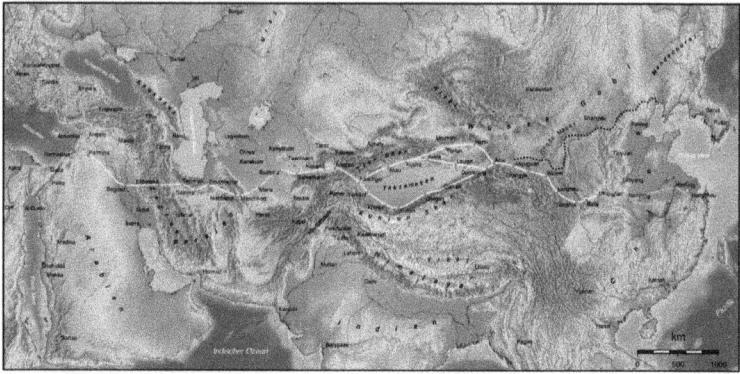

Figure 46. The Silk Road (the main route).
Source: Kelvin Case (File:Seidenstrasse_GMT.jpg revision) [CC BY-SA 3.0 (http://creativecommons.org/licenses/by-sa/3.0)], via Wikimedia Commons.

The Silk Road carried more than just silk, however. Westbound caravans often carried porcelain, bronze, or iron-manufactured objects, jade, furs, or even lacquer. Eastbound caravans carried gold, silver, other precious metals, gems, ivory, or glass. Any item of high value that was transportable and sought after by the elites in Europe and China, who were both willing to pay large sums for these rare items, was worthwhile for merchants to carry across the high deserts and vast empty stretches. Of course, rarely did any single merchant travel the entire length of the Silk Road. The Silk Road was a nexus—a series of connections where exchanges occur. Different merchants handled different segments along the path, and material changed hands several times en route. Exchanges were made at bazaars and oases along the way.

Trade along the Silk Road consisted of not only goods but also ideas. Concepts, technologies, philosophies, and religion were some of the most impactful commodities carried along the Silk Road. Greek language and philosophy was spread early by Alexander. The central Asia region would eventually become a mixing bowl of Greek, Persian, and Indian philosophies. Buddhism began in India in the sixth century BCE and found its way into

China by the first century CE, spread by pilgrims, missionaries, and merchants. China's Northern Wei dynasty (386–535 CE) was particularly encouraging of this new religion, even sending missionaries to India along the eastern route.

Trade along the Silk Road ebbed and flowed, though products and ideas continued to flow even during the lulls. Its first peak came during the Han dynasty (206 BCE to 220 CE) who traded with the Parthians and the Romans. After the Han dynasty, the Silk Road declined, but saw resurgence under the Tang dynasty (618–907 CE). The Tang traded with Iranian and Arab tribes as well as the Byzantine Empire. Islam reached China during this time. After the Tang dynasty, trade ebbed once more. Later, the final peak—with the greatest flow of goods, ideas, and people yet—happened during the Yuan dynasty (1279–1368). This Mongol dynasty provided protection along almost the entire length of the route. The Mongols encouraged the flow of goods, artisans, envoys, missionaries, and merchants, who could now travel its entire length if desired (as Marco Polo did between 1271 and 1295).[2]

The Silk Road remained prosperous throughout the rule of the Yuan. However, merchant ships eventually grew large enough and sturdy enough to make the trip from Europe to China by sea. These ships sailed along the Indian Ocean coastline, which was cheaper, more reliable, and had greater capacity. By the end of the 1400s, the ocean route replaced the overland route. After sixteen centuries, the Silk Road had come to an end.[LXXXI]

A Natural Corridor

It is not happenstance that the Silk Road became such a successful trade route. It had advantages that made it the most effective conduit for the flow of products and ideas in the ancient world.

The Silk Road had no major geographic barriers along its length. While high desert made travel difficult at certain times of the year, it was a continuous landmass, with no major bodies of water to cross. Skirting north

---

[2] The Mongols controlled much of the route even before they officially became the Yuan dynasty.

of the Himalayas meant there were no serious mountains to climb. As such, the route provided a continuum for uninterrupted flow of material along its length. (Probably the biggest problem was bands of robbers and thieves: security was always a challenge.)

In addition, throughout its history, the Silk Road connected some of the largest population centers on earth. In its early era, it connected Rome and Parthia with Han China (Figure 47). Later, it would connect Byzantium and Persia with Tang China. Ultimately, Europe and the expanse of the Mongol Empire were connected. Large population meant large markets for products. Large populations also meant major production centers of food and other items. This holds true for ideas as well. Ideas are more prolific in areas with large populations since there are more issues that require solutions, more competition that provides incentive for them, and more people to conceive them. So the Silk Road was demographically predisposed to the flow of both products and ideas.

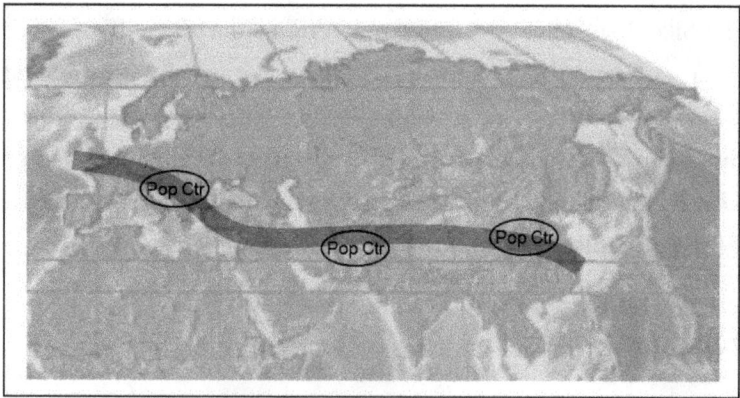

Figure 47. Population centers along the Silk Road.
Source: Tom Patterson (map).

Finally, the Silk Road was aided by its east-west orientation. Products and ideas tend to diffuse faster along an east-west axis than a north-south axis. Farming diffused along an east-west axis from southwest Asia to Europe and into the Indus River Valley at an average rate of about 0.7 miles per year; in the Americas, it diffused along a north-south axis at a speed of 0.2–0.5 miles per year. East-west diffusion is faster because climate is more consistent (no one is crossing from temperate zones to tropic zones), the length of the day is more consistent (which makes travel easier), and seasonality is more predictable (which makes migration easier as people know when the planting season begins). As such, products and ideas could travel faster across Eurasia, the longest east-west landmass on earth, than they could along a north-south pathway. So the Silk Road was a climatically disposed to support the flow of products and ideas.

Thus geographic, demographic, and climatic advantages created a natural corridor for the flow of people, products, and ideas along the Silk Road. This natural corridor is why products and ideas (such as food production) began flowing along its length long before the Silk Road officially "opened."

Because of this natural corridor, societies along the Silk Road were predisposed to acquire an innovation ahead of others. If a Silk Road society did not invent an idea, it could still acquire it early as long as someone else along the Silk Road invented it. In fact, most of the transformative innovations were developed somewhere along the Silk Road, and societies along the Silk Road were the first to acquire them. Food production first appeared in Mesopotamia, where there was enough natural grain diversity and domesticable animals to spawn it. From there, it spread both eastward and westward. Property rights and criminal justice also first appeared in Mesopotamia, where greater population (because of food production) forced the issue. Mathematics and writing appeared first in Sumer, China, and Mesoamerica. They spread across Eurasia, while they remained largely concentrated in Mesoamerica. Metallurgy began in Sumer and spread. Horse warfare began in south-central Asia and spread in both directions, east and west. Gunpowder began in China and diffused westward along the Silk Road.[3] Christianity began in the Near East and spread both to the west and east. Printing began in China and migrated west, all the way to Europe.[4]

---

[3] Many historians attribute gunpowder's spread to the Mongol invasions, although it may have been spread by Islamic traders a few generations earlier. In either case, the pathway followed the Silk Road.

[4] While Gutenberg arguably invented movable type separately, Islamic societies still had exposure to printing along the Silk Road.

Empires on both ends effectively extended the Silk Road. The Roman Empire, and later the Holy Roman Empire, meant goods from the Silk Road would be passed throughout Europe. Trade emerged farther east after the Korean peninsula was unified in the seventh century. Trade flourished under the Song and Yuan dynasties especially, bringing Silk Road goods to Korea and Japan as well.

Conversely, societies not along the Silk Road were at a disadvantage for acquiring innovations early. The geographic, demographic, and climatic features that made the Silk Road a natural corridor also hindered others' access to its products and ideas (Figure 48). Two oceans, the Atlantic and the Pacific, defined the ends of the Silk Road. No ideas made it across the Atlantic Ocean prior to the Spanish invasion in the 1500s. Australia, Polynesia, Micronesian, and other Pacific Islands were largely cut off from large-scale trade.

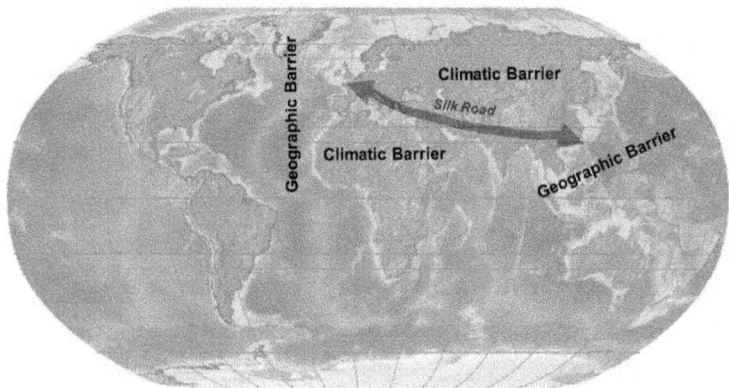

Figure 48. Barriers surrounding the Silk Road.
Source: Tom Patterson (map).

The Sahara Desert provided a climatic barrier south and west of the Silk Road that was not crossable. The desert stretched across North Africa and was a thousand miles deep.[5] While some trade routes worked their way down the

---

[5] From about 9000 BCE to 5500–4000 BCE, the Sahara was actually green and lush due to the onset of monsoon rains that moistened the climate. Population migrated out of the Nile River Valley onto the green savannah. Agricultural and animal husbandry grew as they had along the Nile River. Eventually, however, the desert returned and forced people back toward

east coast of Africa, they rarely ventured into the interior, where larger population centers existed. (When language emigrated from southern Africa 50,000 years ago, there was an exposed land bridge connecting the east coast of Africa to the Arabian Peninsula. In time, the Red Sea would cover this up.)

The Siberian tundra posed a similar problem north of the Silk Road. Thousands of miles of cold weather, along a north-south axis, hindered trade to major population centers north of the Black Sea. The cold also precluded large population centers from developing farther east, in what would become north-central Russia. While ancillary trails eventually made their way into these regions, it was not until the early modern era that Muscovy and other population centers were firmly connected to European trade.[6]

Now societies that were not fortunate enough (at least in this context) to lie along the Silk Road would eventually acquire the innovations anyway. Farming began in the Americas around 3000 BCE. Writing was developed in Mesoamerica by 600 BCE. And metal objects were being fashioned in the Andes by 1000 CE. However, having to rely on separate inventions rather than idea diffusion slowed down acquisition considerably.

Eventually, the geographic and climatic barriers ceased to be trade impediments. The ships that opened up the sea-lanes across the Indian Ocean also brought down most of the barriers. In the 1600s, America received the horse. In the 1700s, Australia received farm animals. In the early 1800s, petroleum propulsion spread from Britain across the world. In the late 1800s, sea routes to southern Africa combined with overland expeditions northward to bypass the Sahara Desert. In the middle of the twentieth century, atomic research traveled across the Atlantic Ocean in the papers and minds of scientists, enabling nuclear power to first be proven in America.

However, while it lasted, the Silk Road (and its natural corridor) gave an advantage to societies along its length, spawning several of the world's empires (Figure 49). Transformative innovations increased a society's leadership

---

the Nile River delta. (Scientists disagree whether this climatic change was abrupt, gradual, or a combination.)

[6] The Mongols swept across this region in the thirteenth century. While this undoubtedly increased the flow of trade to a degree, it was rather short-lived and never comparable to trade along the Silk Road.

power. Whoever acquired them first gained a head start over rivals on building that power. With preconditioning and elevating innovations, a Silk Road society could even transition to higher societal level before other societies, making it the dominant power in the region for centuries.[LXXXII]

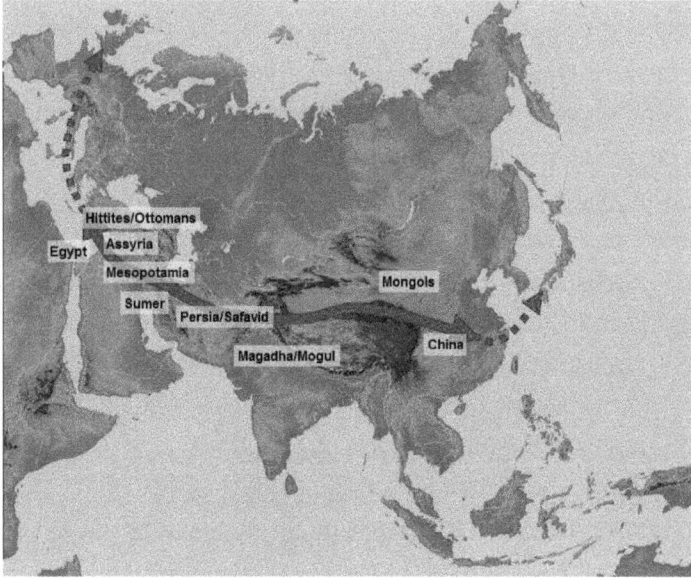

Figure 49. Silk Road empires.

Embracing Innovation

While lying on the Silk Road gave a society early access to innovations, it did not ensure a society would become a leader. Many segments of the Silk Road never spawned an empire. Some of this was due to low population in some areas; however, even densely populated regions such as the Indus River Valley did not see an empire formed in the way other areas did.

Whether a society became a leader was largely driven by whether it embraced the transformative innovation. Embracing an innovation means being transformed by it. If a society ignored an innovation that came along (perhaps because it did not see its value), it was not impacted. Yet if the society allowed itself to be transformed by the innovation, then it could exploit its benefits to the fullest. Sumer was transformed by metal working. It became a part of Sumer's culture and even its religion. The metal-working industry became a primary form of commerce and employment. It even led to the creation of the first banking industry. Hymns were sung to Ea, the god of mining and wisdom, and to his protégé, Gibil, the god of fire and smelting. This level of intensity helped Sumer to fully exploit metallurgy's potential, making it into a regional military and economic power.

A society embraced an innovation in two ways: it had policies that promoted use of the innovation, and an infrastructure conducive to its use. Policies could help a transformative innovation spread throughout society. The rulers of Sumer promoted bronze working. The rulers of Hatti promoted iron working: iron objects became principal trade items and the iron industry became a valuable source of income for the Hittites.

Conversely, policies could stifle an innovation. After initially embracing firearms, the ruling Japanese samurai felt threatened: the sword was a symbol of their prestige. They began restricting firearm development in the 1600s. Ultimately, Japan reached the point where there were few firearms left in the country. In the Middle East, books and even libraries were plentiful in the twelfth century. Many mosques had their own libraries, some of which were larger than any found in Europe. However, they were tightly controlled—lest anyone be led astray by errant teaching. In this atmosphere, the printing press passed through Islamic regions largely untouched, since printing might lead to books that corrupt the correct interpretation of the Koran, challenge the ruling authorities, and may even defile God's name.[7]

Infrastructure also made a difference. A society needed an infrastructure that was conducive to using the innovation to benefit from it. How well a society embraces an innovation is driven largely by how well the new innovation complements the existing tools, systems, and structures in the society. For example, tires will be embraced by a society of automobile drivers more readily than a society composed entirely of pedestrians. When the hunter-gatherer Clo-E Indians of the Amazon were first exposed to twentieth-century products, they found fishing line to be the most useful one since it fit

---

[7] This was not a meritless fear for that is essentially what happened in Europe when Martin Luther posted his *95 Theses* on the door of the Württemberg church.

well with their established routine.

Some societies had infrastructures that were ripe for a transformative innovation. Roman roads and mail helped Christianity spread more easily westward than eastward. Later, European churches, universities, and professional guilds became great producers and consumers of printed material.

Other societies lacked an infrastructure needed to make an innovation useful. Mathematics is not embraced by hunter-gatherer societies because they have no need for it: many indigenous bands use only the numbers *one*, *two*, and *many*. Printing with movable type was never embraced in Asia despite the fact that it was invented in China four hundred years before Gutenberg. Chinese logographic writing did not support its use since it took thousands of characters to tell a story. The syllabic Korean and Japanese writing systems were not very conducive either.[8]

For an innovation to be embraced, a society needed to have both policy and an infrastructure that supported it. If policy was against it, it would be suppressed regardless of its benefit to society. If infrastructure did not support it, then the innovation would likely not be beneficial in the first place. When a society had both, the innovation was effective at changing the society. After Constantine made Christianity the state religion (policy) of the Roman Empire (with all of its infrastructure), Christianity spread quickly throughout the realm. The Moguls not only sought out gunpowder (policy) but also built a research and development center to create weapons that used it (infrastructure). America would pursue an atomic bomb to end World War II (policy), while tapping into vast uranium reserves and building centrifuges to enrich it (infrastructure).

---

[8] In logographic writing systems, such as Chinese Hanzi, each character is a word. When movable type printing was invented in China around 1040 CE, there were an estimated 30,000 Hanzi characters, though only a fraction of these were routinely used. In syllabic writing systems, such as Korean and Japanese, each character is a syllable. This means that fewer characters could represent the language (modern Japanese hiragana has 48 characters). However, Korean and Japanese borrow many Chinese characters and Japanese also uses the syllabic katakana as well. Together, these make printing with movable type less useful. In alphabetic writing systems, such as English, each character is a phoneme, so 26 characters can represent the language.

So history reveals that access to innovation, along with supportive policies and infrastructure, are the keys to societal leadership. For centuries, lying along the Silk Road provided that access, but that ceased being a requirement in the late Middle Ages. Societies could take advantage of this access with the right policies and infrastructure. With these, a society grew leadership power, often becoming an empire.

But how do we apply this today?[LXXXIII]

Strategic Positioning

In modern terminology, societies that lay along the Silk Road were *strategically positioned* for leadership. Their location gave them an advantage over other societies. Strategic positioning is the first step of a competitive strategy that uses a two-step process to achieve results. In the first step, an organization secures a position of advantage. In the second step, the organization strikes from that position to achieve its goal. It is used in warfare, business, athletics, and even academia. A navy fleet maneuvers to a location off the coast of an enemy, from where it can launch air strikes. An up-and-coming football team uses all of its draft picks on offensive linemen, to support a power running game. A retail chain rebrands itself as being healthy, so it can introduce new product lines of vitamins, health food, and cardiovascular services to an aging population. A university acquires a software company so it can launch an online degree program. In general, strategic positioning is needed when victory cannot be achieved in a single stroke—if it could, you would simply strike. Lying along the Silk Road strategically positioned some societies to receive products and innovation early: they innately had the first step. Other societies had to take a first step, such as Russia, when it forged relations with western Europe.

The world's next great leader will come from the first region to reach the next societal level. However, the technology needed to make this jump does not exist yet: there is no preconditioning innovation, and the sustaining infrastructure has not been developed. It may be decades or generations before these things arrive. Is there anything a would-be leader should do in the meantime? Yes, strategically position itself for the jump.

Before a society can strategically position itself, it needs to identify the role it sees itself playing at the next level. There are four basic roles a society can target (Figure 50).

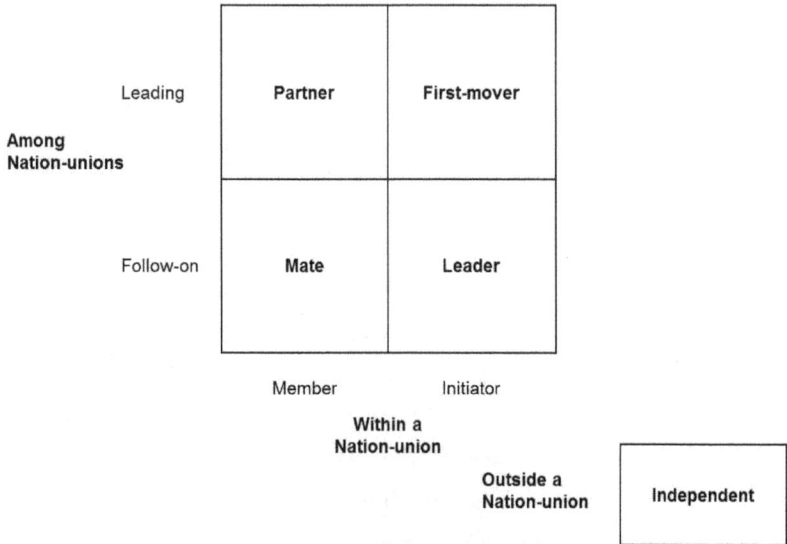

Figure 50. Nation-union roles.

The *first-mover* is the society that wants to be the leader in the next era. The first-mover has decided it is worth whatever time and investment that is needed to secure a place at the head of the table. It requires taking the initiative to form a nation-union; it also requires being the first union. The first-mover cannot wait for this to happen—it has to make it happen. The time between a union's formation and others' formation will be used to accrue leadership power, with the intent of creating a lasting advantage. This role is the most expensive since it requires investments before, during, and after the transition happens.

The *partner* is the society that wants to be a member of the first union, but does not necessarily want to initiate it. This society will let a neighbor take the lead in pulling it together. This allows it to avoid having to make some of the investments that the first-mover will have to make. It also expects that once a true union has been formed, national differences within the union will disappear.

The *leader* initiates a follow-on union. It does not feel the need to be in the first union—a close second may establish near parity with the leading union. It is willing to let another society prove the concept, and work out some of the kinks. It also wants to avoid making some of the investments the first-mover will have to make. Nonetheless, once all signs are pointing in that direction, it will move quickly, working with neighbors to form one.[9] The leader will want to move before the first-mover gets too far ahead in accruing leadership power.

The *mate* is a member in a follow-on union. Most nations in the world will be mates. This requires the least investment, and yet can still take advantage of the anticipated upward spiral of leadership power. It waits until a union is being formed in the region, and then joins. Its goal, therefore, is to simply be an attractive partner to its neighbors.

The *independent* does not join a union. It chooses not to become a member of any union for cultural or other reasons. It will need to forge alliances with nation-unions, however, for security and prosperity. Yet it can retain the autonomy it presently enjoys.

Right now, no region is precluded from becoming the first union: there is enough time for nearly any region to make the right moves to strategically position itself. That means that most of the roles are still open to any society. Realistically, however, some societies will find certain roles more challenging to reach than others, particularly the first-mover. Making a wise role choice entails a dispassionate assessment of one's current position. While there are several investment and affordability factors to considers, perhaps the greatest consideration is where the society is starting from. Some nations simply have further to go than others (Figure 51).

---

[9] This is similar to the role Prussia played in German unification. Once Britain and France had proven the concept, it was ready to move.

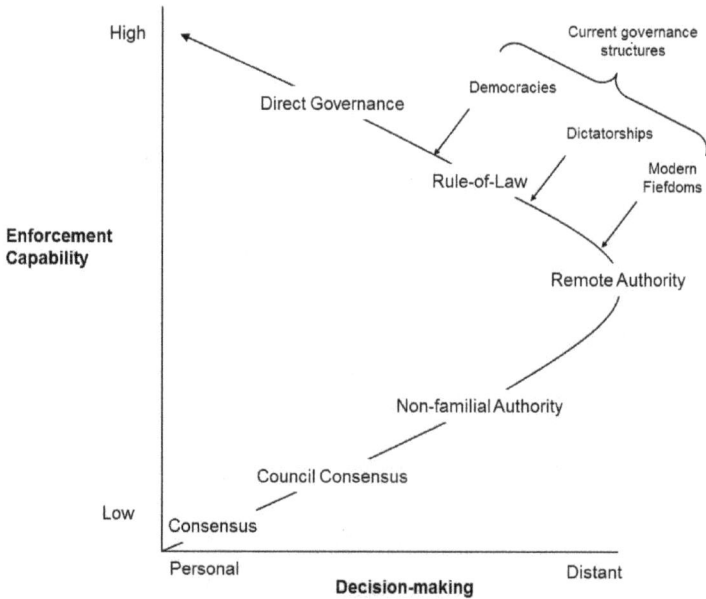

Figure 51. The starting line.

Representative democracies are closest to a nation-union, with its direct governance basis, because they already have regular, meaningful elections. Dictatorships (including those that masquerade as democracies) have further to go since they do not have robust electoral or legislative processes. Moreover, they still have not fully embraced rule-of-law, which is a requirement before any further advance can occur. Fiefdoms, especially those with weak parliaments, are also behind since they do not fully apply rule-of-law either (though some are better than others).

Furthermore, it is not possible to skip a level. No society can jump from being a fiefdom to a nation-union—success at one level requires a cultural mind-set be developed at the preceding level. As such, dictatorship and fiefdoms will necessarily have a longer path than a true democracy. Even democracies that lean toward autocratic rule are disadvantaged compared to truly representative democracies: rule-of-law has to be firmly established to build on.

Now it is not enough to simply change the appearance of one's government: rule-of-law has to be a part of the people and the culture to work. During the Arab Spring, several societies tried to change their governments, but the people were not ready for the change, so they fell back. (No worries: it took European countries four decades to stabilize their nation-state governments.) Creating a government that resembles a democracy but does not operate like one is to no avail. As such, the journey to nation-union is mostly a cultural one; this is even true for democracies.

The good news is that societies can advance faster along the path than their original counterparts. By applying the learnings of the twentieth century, a society can make relatively rapid progress along the path, if it truly desires to change.

All told, the society that has furthest to go needs to begin positioning itself the earliest. Waiting too long means that its role will be defined by others. As other nations migrate into their roles, the roles of everyone become more established; and once established, they are difficult to change. The nation that decides its role early has the best opportunity to secure its position, while the environment is still fluid.

Taking Action

Once a society has decided which role to pursue, it needs to take action. Each role has its own logical course of action. These courses of action are best understood with respect to the first transition to nation-union.

Transition starts when fusion energy has proven to be both technically feasible and economical for widespread power generation. Transitions have historically begun once both preconditioning and elevating innovations are in place, and since computing is already here (even though it is still not in a final form), attention shifts to fusion.

Transition ends when the first region becomes a sustainable nation-union—with a legitimate supranational structure, operating based on direct governance (even though it may only be in an initial form). The focus is on the first transition since that will drive activity across the rest of the globe. Other transitions will continue indefinitely.

This timing defines both the transition and three critical periods: before-transition, during-transition, and after-transition. Each of these periods requires a different set of activities be performed by would-be leaders. Though simplified and idealized, it is fair to say that different roles require action in different periods.

The first-mover needs to initiate transition in his region. To do this, he will make substantial investments before-transition. His focus then is on developing the next transformative innovations. He will invest heavily in fusion research and Internet security, which is a precursor to direct democracy. He will need to engage every area of his political-economy to make it happen (Table 9).

Table 10. Before-transition actions.

	Government	Academia	Industry	Not-for-profit
Nuclear Fusion	• ITER • LMJ • K-demo • LLNL, others	• Magneto-hydrodynamics • Superconductors • Materials • Economics	• Numerous	• Progress • Equity • Environmental
Internet Security	• Encryption • Architecture	• Tools • Techniques	• Numerous • Also larger projects	• Security • Progress • Encryption
Role	• Conduct and fund collaborative and independent research	• Conduct supporting research	• Provide support contractors • Develop niche technologies	• Provide policy, progress, and equity guidance • Coordinate standards and protocols

Government will need to take a leadership role in both conducting and funding research. Both collaborative and independent research programs will be needed. This means maintaining active membership in the International Thermonuclear Experimental Reactor, Laser Mégajoule, and Korea Demonstration. It also means continuing independent research that may take a slightly different approach, such as the inertial confinement fusion work at Lawrence Livermore laboratory. For Internet security, government can fund research in encryption, Internet architecture, and blockchain.

Academia will also need to conduct research. This means not only participating in government programs but also leading supporting development efforts such as in magnetohydrodynamics, superconductivity, materials development, and economics. Government funding will be needed for most of this research. For Internet research, academia may take the largest role in developing new tools and techniques.

Industry can provide contractor support to government programs. Start-ups may develop niche technologies (like they did during the space programs of the 1960s). Industry will probably avoid initiating long-term fusion programs where risk is high and lengthy development times lead to poor rates-of-return. However, since Internet security may be closer than fusion, corporations may take a more active role in larger projects.

Not-for-profits (NFPs) and nongovernmental organizations (NGOs) play a key role in providing policy guidance and coordinating standards and protocols. Key areas include identifying objective measures of success, monitoring progress, ensuring equity in technology and energy sharing, and investigating environmental concerns. NFP/NGOs are needed in areas where an unbiased, nonpolitical perspective is required. They would serve in a watchdog oversight role, and could be advocates for specific areas of development that required attention, but were being overlooked.

Completion of these activities would give a society the reasons to pursue a change in governance, as well as the tools to do it. Without these, it is doubtful that change would ever come. With them, change becomes inevitable.

The partner needs to follow closely behind the first-mover and be ready to move once the transition starts—lagging behind could cost the union its leadership position. As such, his investments are made for the during-transition period and are targeted to facilitate a rapid transition. The partner's focus is to have the policies and infrastructure needed to embrace the transformative innovations once they arrive (Table 11). As such, he will invest heavily in the power grid so it can readily use the energy produced from fusion. It will initiate direct democracy, which has been enabled by improved Internet security. It will push toward a digital legal infrastructure, which will be needed to sustain the union. And it will also begin marching down the path toward union—some variant of the European Union's path, which serves as a prototype. Again, each sector of the political economy plays a role.

Table 11. During-transition actions.

	Government	Academia	Industry	Not-for-profit
Power Grid	• Smart grid • Site locations	• Magneto-hydrodynamics • Superconductors	• Convert retail energy stations • Fuel cells	• Environment
Direct Democracy	• Pilot tests • Structural change	• Political science thought leadership	• Online elections	• Auditing
Digital legal infra-structure	• Legal code development	• Adaptive legal code and controls • Political science	• Identifying and making appropriate legal linkages	• Coordination • Oversight
Union Path	• Make treaties	• Benchmarking	• Advocate specific terms and conditions	• Ensure equity for people
Role	• Conduct small tests • Begin evolutionary change	• Conduct enabling engineering • Provide thought-leadership	• Develop tools and techniques • Build infrastructure	• Provide thought-leadership • Provide oversight • Ensure equity

Government has the role of managing a slow evolutionary change, and conducting pilot tests before adopting anything new. This approach will be required for developing the smart grid, testing direct democracy, making structural changes to support direct democracy, shifting to a digitized legal code, and creating treaties that lead to forming a union. Caution is a watchword in each of these changes, though inactivity will also be costly.

Academia will assist with engineering, thought-leadership, and enabling research. Engineering will be needed to roll out pioneering energy technologies developed before-transition. Political science will be needed to provide thought-leadership on how best to execute a direct democracy. Research will be needed on how best to create an adaptive legal code and on how best to make structural changes to government.

Industry will need to develop the tools, techniques, and infrastructure needed to support energy transition—everything from building the smart grid to converting retail gas stations into retail electric stations. It will develop the tools and techniques for conducting elections online, and for identifying tools that comb the law code for legal relationships. Industry will be its own best advocate for structuring trade agreements as the union progresses.

NFPs play an enhanced role in providing unbiased oversight and thought-leadership to the entire process. Focus areas will include monitoring environmental impacts of fusion introduction, auditing elections performed under direct democracy, and coordinating digital infrastructure development. They also take the leading role in ensuring fairness and equity among people, particularly labor, when forming a union.

Completion of these activities would result in the formation of a nation-union, with direct governance as its basis.

The leader needs to perform the same actions as the partner, but for a different reason. The leader needs to initiate a nation-union, but has conceded that hers will not be the first one. She waited until the technology was proven to avoid making costly and risky investments. Her objective now, however, is to transition as quickly as possible while bringing other members of the region with her.[10] As such, her investments are during-transition. She presumes that she will gain access to all of the technology developed before-transition, preferably sooner rather than later. So her investment priorities are the same as the partner—develop a power grid, plan for direct democracy, shift to a digital legal code, and coordinate movement down the path to union. Successful completion of these activities, in a timely manner, means that her region will also be in contention for world leadership, following closely behind the first-mover to minimize any lasting power differential.

The mate needs to be part of his region's union, but he knows that this union will not be the first one, and he does not have the resources to initiate it. As such, he waits until after-transition to make his investments, most which will be used to make himself more attractive to other union members. Being an attractive prospect requires convincing other members that he will not drag down the upward power spiral of leadership power that is expected once the union has formed. (This spiral parallels the one that occurred after the nation-state was formed.) He will rely on others, even commercial enterprises, to bring him fusion energy and assist with physical and legal infrastructure changes; his investment priorities are focused on generating his four leadership power sources (Table 12).

---

[10] I might editorialize here: without the use of force.

Table 12. After-transition actions.

	Government	Academia	Industry	Not-for-profit
Population	• Education • Disease protection • Disaster protection	• Education • Disease protection • Disaster protection	• Education • Disease protection • Disaster protection	• Health • Environmental protection
Wealth	• Fiscal policy • Commerce policy • Infrastructure • Labor and pollution	• Transnational commerce • Pollution	• International corporations • Common business practices	• Trade practices • Trade organizations • Labor and environment
Military Strength	• Common doctrine • C4ISR • Personnel & training	• ROTC and other personnel systems	• C4ISR • Weaponry	• Capabilities assessments • Family advocacy
Foreign Reach	• Trade agreements • Integration agreements	• Sociological and environmental issues	• Open markets • Production mobility	• Intra-union production and markets
Role	• Policy • Investment	• Research	• Products • Services	• Oversight • Equity

The mate needs his population to be healthy and educated. Health, especially disease protection, is essential. His health care infrastructure will need to be comparable to other members. The 2014 West African ebola outbreak highlights this need. (Not to mention that disease depopulated Europe twice and killed up to 80–90 percent of the Native American population.) He will also need an education system that is comparable to his prospective union partners. They will want this too since they will all be making more decisions jointly. Protection from disasters is another important area. Every region is prone to its own set of natural disasters—typhoons, tornados, or earthquakes. Having building codes in place and emergency preparedness measures that are on par with regional partners gives them confidence that there should not be major population-depleting catastrophes.

The mate needs his area's standard of living to match that of other union partners as closely as possible. This will help convince them that he will not become an endless money-sump, draining their coffers. (Before reunification in 1990, many West Germans had this concern about East Germany.) The mate also needs to eliminate as much debt as possible, since debt makes any mate less attractive (e.g., Greece in the EU). The mate needs fair, but business-friendly policies—ones that are like its regional partners. Abiding by regional labor and pollution standards is required. One society cannot run sweatshops while the other wears fine clothes on-the-cheap. (Otherwise it is a colony, not a partner.)

For military strength, the most important thing is compatibility. The mate needs to implement training and operating doctrine, as well as communication systems,[11] that are common to regional partners. Weaponry will converge over time as new systems replace old systems. (Scale purchases will make this likely to happen quickly.) Logistics doctrine and assets need coordination, with the objective to make the different organizations work together as a single entity.

Most of the mate's foreign reach will focus on moving his region down the union path. He needs to be receptive to trade and monetary policies, while ensuring they are fair and consistent with all regional members. Foreign reach will also need to be proactive and obvious, sharing culture, people, and tourism, so that regional citizens view him as a partner and neighbor rather than a foreigner.

Success for the mate means being accepted into the union as an equal partner, not a junior member. The easiest way to do this is to be ready to contribute the uplift that comes with societal-level change. Once this contribution is acknowledged, long-term social integration is well assured.

The independent needs security and prosperity among giants. It needs to ensure that its borders and sovereignty will be respected by the unions that are forming. It will also want to catch some of the upward spiral. As such, the independent needs to forge alliances with unions who can best provide that protection through mutual defense treaties and aid in that prosperity through commercial relationships. The independent will not have to focus its investments like the others will: it will invest in relationships instead.

The roles provide a strategy for positioning oneself for leadership in the next era. They establish a framework for selecting a desirable, yet achievable objective and provide an investment strategy to go with it. While the

---

[11] Communication in the military is known as C4ISR: Command, Control, Communications, Computers, Intelligence, Surveillance, and Reconnaissance. The more of these that are shared, the more interoperability there will be.

investment strategies have been presented as before-transition, during-transition, and after-transition, they can all begin right now. By beginning these investments before transition begins, a society is strategically positioning itself for a leadership role in the future—a role that will be obtained once transition has been completed.

Starting these investments now makes them more affordable. In reality, the first-mover will have to invest in all three phases. Likewise, partners and leaders have to invest in the last two. As such, the investment grows exponentially with ambition. This kind of sustained commitment can be expensive for a society, yet it becomes easier if spread over time.

However, there is risk involved. The would-be first-mover could begin all the investment phases now and find out that fusion does not work (it is still in development after all). A society needs to assess whether the risk is worth taking, or whether it would pursue any of these actions regardless. (They are all good things to do). However, knowing what is coming in advance—decades in advance—allows ample time to make course corrections if needed—mitigating risk.

...

So the period between now and the birth of nuclear fusion is not an idle one. There is much to do for the society that would position itself to become the leader of the next era. But besides preparing for something that is decades away, can this study help us make decisions about the world we live in today? I think it can.

Chapter 23
Application in the Middle East, Part I

Back in the summer of 2006, I went to Iraq to support a Department of Defense project that was to assess how capable the Iraqi army was at logistically supporting itself once coalition forces left. I had been out of the Marine Corps for thirteen years by then, so my biggest concern was actually whether I would be able to adjust to camp life again. Fortunately, I found that old routines come back in a day or two. I was also concerned about the heat—just the thought of 115° F days was draining and a little scary. Fortunately, I found July in Iraq was a lot like summer in Bakersfield, California, near where I grew up, so that was not too bad either.

After a couple of days in Camp Victory (Figure 52), I was walking along a dirt road when a heard a *BOOM* in the distance. It had a low pitch, so I knew it was miles away. I assumed the army was doing artillery training. Then it occurred to me:

> We're on the outskirts of Bagdad—a city of 8 million people—there are no artillery ranges around here. [My mind blanked.] *I may as well be on Mars.................. This is not my world.* That was an IED. It just blew up somewhere in downtown Bagdad. People were killed.

> This is chaos. And it's not because it's a foreign country either. I've been to third-world countries, where poverty is everywhere: where

people live in square mile after square mile of tin shacks, where boys scrounge and beg and girls hawk wares or prostitute themselves; where traffic signs don't exist and rules of the road are only suggestions. No: this is different. This is medieval. A world like this hasn't existed for five hundred years. [My mind continued to reel.]

But why is this place so different? Why hasn't it progressed like the rest of the world? Rule-of-law. [The phrase popped into my head.] That makes sense. That is why this place is so different from any other place I've been. Rule-of-law has not overlaid this world yet.

Figure 52. Camp Victory, Iraq, July 2006.
Source: Photo by author.

The last chapter focused on preparation: what a society would do today to become a leader tomorrow. This chapter focuses on applications of the frameworks to today's problems. We will focus on the Middle East because that region has seen the most attempts at nation-building in recent years. This provides the greatest opportunity to see how, in particular, the governance basis framework can be used to understand our world today. It also has been the region with the most volatility, so understanding that region better might have the most immediate impact for our world.

Iraq

One of the most important insights to come from this analysis is the trade-off between *relationship* and *process* in governance. Every organization is run by both: relationships between people are needed to do the work, and processes determine how the works gets done. This is the same for governance: both relationships and processes are needed. However, in governance, the relative emphasis has changed over time (Figure 53).

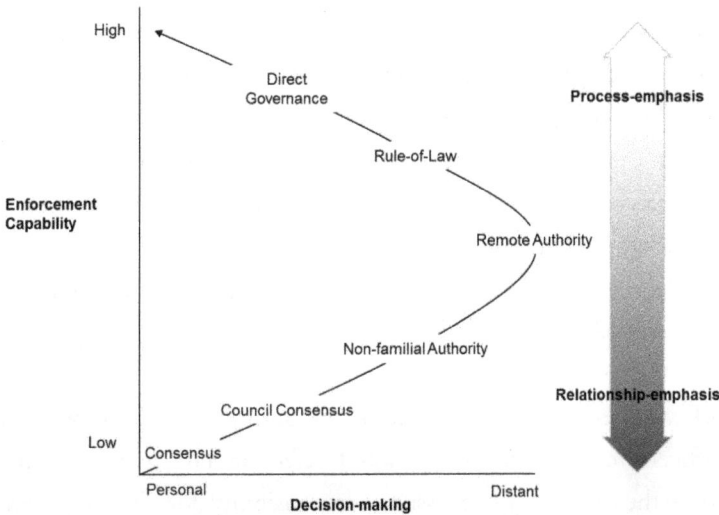

Figure 53. Governance basis emphasis.

In bands, every family made its own decisions, so the relationship was with oneself. Process mainly focused on activities such as tool making and hunting rather than on governance. Rudimentary process was introduced in governance when consensus meetings were held between heads of families. However, even there, relationship dominated.

In tribes, the patriarch took on a greater role. Relationships between patriarchs on the tribal council determined what decisions were made. Enforcement came through the relationship between the patriarch and his extended family members. So relationship was still predominant with tribes.

In chiefdoms, the relationship shifted from the patriarch to someone else who was known and trusted. The chieftain's family members became royalty. The chieftain's friends could also assume high positions, such as priests. Everyone else became commoners. As such, the relation was still the emphasis in governance for chiefdoms.

In fiefdoms, nothing changed—it only expanded. Society stratified further. The sovereign's family members were still royalty. The extended family held positions of power and oversight. Friends or acquaintances became local barons (or their equivalent). Below this were several levels of commoners. As such, relationship was still the emphasis in governance for fiefdoms.

In nation-states, process took over: it displaced much of the emphasis formerly placed on relationship. Societies made this shift to acquire the consistency and systematic approach offered by everyone agreeing to follow what is written on paper. Process became the vehicle for enforcement as well, though it meant that rules could not be overridden by one's relationship to another person. Relationship was still important, however, especially when deciding what gets written on paper. As such, process (due process, rule-of-law, and legal rulings) became the predominant emphasis in governance in the nation-state.[LXXXIV]

When I was preparing to go to Iraq in late Spring 2006, I met with various staff officers in the Pentagon. I was briefed on how the US Army was preparing the Iraqi army to assume responsibility for their logistics after coalition forces left. These meetings had a recurrent theme to them: do not expect the Iraqis to do things the way we do them here in the United States. For one thing, the army was having difficulty making Iraqi contractors comply with their maintenance contracts. The problem was not that the Iraqis did not know how to fix equipment (the army had trained them how to do it); rather, it was that they did not always feel compelled to do it. A piece of equipment (a fork lift, a truck, or an armored personnel carrier) would sit deadlined for weeks without being touched. When the army challenged the contractor, a typical response might be as follows:

"My cousin told me not to fix it."

"Who's your cousin, and what does he have to do with anything?"

"He's an important person in the Interior Ministry. He told me not to fix it."

"But you signed a contract saying you would fix it."

"I know, but I cannot go against my cousin."

Without a Federal Trade Commission or a Federal Commerce Commission to enforce contracts, nor even an understanding of their usefulness, they simply could not be relied upon to transact business the way we do in the United States.

Later, I had a conference call with an army colonel stationed in Iraq. He described how standard operating procedures were a new concept to the Iraqis, and despite training, they were not being followed very well. As a result, efficiency in the distribution depots was abysmal. Supplies simply were not moving very fast.

After that, I met with a former US ambassador to Jordan, who had spent years in the Middle East. His message was the same, only at a government level. He warned me not to expect things to happen in Iraq as they do in the United States. Our challenge in rebuilding Iraq was actually greater than our challenge in rebuilding Japan after World War II—Iraq is not a nation the way Japan was. Furthermore, Saddam Hussein was not a president—he was the head of the Tikrit clan, and he ran the country like he ran the clan.

When I arrived in Camp Victory in July, it was not long before I began to see that some things were different from what I had seen on television in the United States. At the DFAC (dining facility), I would strike up conversations with people who had been in Iraq for a while and hear things I had not heard on the news. For one thing, there did not seem to be three large blocs vying for control of the government—the Sunni, the Shia, and the Kurd. Rather, it seemed that there were a couple of dozen or so rival clans—most were Shia, some were Sunni, and a few were Kurd—all competing against each other. Yes, they did fight together as blocs, but it seemed that if they were not fighting together, they would be fighting each other. There did not seem to be a lot of unity across clans.[1]

Another impression confirmed what the ambassador had told me: that Saddam Hussein was not a president in the way we think of them in the United States. While he was the reigning authority in Iraq, he did not consider every Iraqi to be his fellow countryman. Some were his enemies. Now it made sense how he could "gas his own people" in 1988—*they were not his people.* They were from a different clan in a different region with a different religion. They were no more the same people than the Russians and Germans in World War II. They just happened to live within the same border.

It was not long before I began to feel uneasy about the direction things were taking. Logistically, Multinational Forces Iraq (MNFI) was building a logistics system that resembled the US Army's, but on a smaller scale. This was natural enough—ours works pretty well, so why should the Iraqis not have it too? However, I was not sure it would work for people who were not used to following contracts or standard operating procedures.

I was more concerned, however, that we were building the wrong government for the Iraqi people. I had no role in this part of the nation-building effort—it was "far above my pay grade." But I had seen organization charts of the government we were trying to build. It was a typical parliamentary structure, with various ministries and a prime minister position—just as one would see in Britain. Again, this seemed natural enough, but my gut feeling was telling me: "We're building a House of Commons when we should be building a House of Lords."[2] It did not seem that the Iraqis were of a mind-set that would run a Western form of government properly. They were certainly smart enough, but they just did not do things there the way we do them here in the United States. The project only lasted a couple of weeks, but the impressions I received were enduring.

Two years later, in the summer of 2008, I was waiting for a meeting at Headquarters Marine Corps when I met a lieutenant colonel who had just

---

[1] I've never found out how accurate this was; but it was the perception I was getting.
[2] At this time, my thinking was only beginning to form around these issues.

returned from Iraq. By that time, things were going much better for coalition forces in Iraq. I asked him how we turned around Al-Anbar province so quickly. He replied, "We got the sheiks on board." Sheiks are the local village bosses who are common throughout the Middle East. When they switched from Al Qaeda to the Iraqi government, their towns switched with them. When enough towns switched, the province switched. After the meeting, while driving home, I felt a little vindicated. The principle underlying my House-of-Lords-versus-House-of-Commons notion was that we needed to leverage the existing lines of authority. We needed to use the leaders the people already view as their authority. (In my notion, the lords were the recognized clan leaders.) By getting the sheiks on board, the marines did that—they convinced each locally known and respected sheik to join us, and this had a cascading effect that the central government in Baghdad could not manufacture.

A government has to fit the people being governed. The United States has tried to make Iraq into a nation-state—a democracy no less—and it has been quite a stretch (Figure 54).

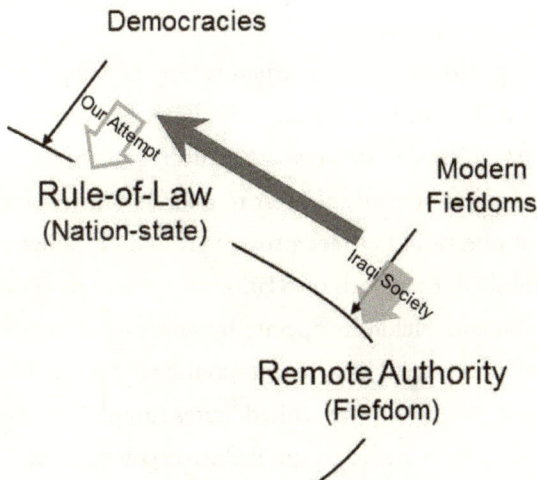

Figure 54. The Iraqi stretch.

The move was a natural enough; given that a war had just taken place, we needed to rebuild a country, and it had worked in Japan after World War II.

And even if it was a stretch, as every MBA student learns that "structure follows strategy"—whenever you want to move a company in a particular direction (strategy), you build the organization in a way that pulls it forward (structure). This must apply to governments, so building a democratic government in Iraq must be the best way to make it into a democracy. While indeed it could apply to governments, when Alfred Chandler coined that phrase in 1962, he based it on corporations that had evolved naturally as technology changed (General Motors, DuPont, Standard Oil, and Sears). In Chandler's research, the fit between the structure and the inherent nature of the products and services being delivered could be presumed—however, that is not always the case. When Lucent Technologies reorganized in the 1990s, it chose a decentralized structure that worked against the integrated nature of its products and the way they had to be sold and serviced. After near disaster, the company went back to its old structure. Hence, a more comprehensive model considers this last factor as well. In essence, structure is the meat in the sandwich—it fills the gap between strategy (the top slice of bread) and the nature of product and service delivery (the bottom slice of bread). So while structure can pull an organization forward, it can also fracture the organization when stretched too far.

In Iraq, the imposed democratic structure was not aligned to the way services had to be delivered. Iraq is really a fiefdom. Never mind that Iraqis have cell phones and microwave towers—the culture is that of a fiefdom. And after the US military left, it tried to revert to one. As prime minister, Nouri al-Maliki did what one would expect a sovereign to do if he were running a fiefdom. He established a network of relationships through which he could manage his government. Fiefdoms operate by relationships, so he filled his cabinet with sectarian cronies. His network was full of Shiites. He even placed relatives in some top positions. The United States complained about his lack of inclusiveness, but in a fiefdom, an inclusive government is a weaker government. He found himself stuck in the middle between his natural inclinations and his powerful overlord, and we did not appear to be much help.

The next prime minister had similar challenges. When ISIS appeared in 2014, it immediately took Iraqi territory, including Ramadi and Fallujah, sites of some of the heaviest fighting during the Iraq War. The cities fell almost uncontested, despite numerical superiority. The primary culprit was sectarianism—Sunni clans would not fight for a Shia central government. In May 2015, the US secretary of defense declared that the Iraqi army does not have the will to fight ISIS.[3] Some Sunni soldiers clearly had no intention of fighting for a rival fiefdom—the government. Nevertheless, Shia militias seemed to fight quite well, despite that some of the fighters came in from Iran. As a Shia authority, the prime minister could gain the loyalty of Shia militia, and in Iraq, national borders are less important than sectarian boundaries. This would naturally be the case when nation-state borders falsely overlay a fiefdom culture.

The United States is betting that the Iraqis can adapt—that they can get used to the idea of being a nation-state and a democracy. And this may still happen, though it will take another generation. The world has to be willing to wait that long for change to occur.

Was there a better way? Perhaps. Hindsight is always 20/20. However, understanding that there is a societal progression may help shape policy in the future. Understanding the concept of *government fit* may allow more flexibility if it should become necessary to help construct future governments. Meanwhile the Middle East offers other insights on nation-building. The Arab Spring in particular offers a wealth of insight into such situations. It is worth examining further.[LXXXV]

Arab Spring

A primary lesson from the Iraqi nation-building experience is that the appropriate end goal is largely determined by the starting point. Stretching too far can have adverse consequences, so knowing where a country starts from helps to decide the appropriate-size steps to take. Nowhere was this more apparent than during the Arab Spring. When it began, six countries sought democracy; one achieved it. Understanding why sheds light on how much change a society can expect to embrace at one time.

---

[3] Does this not sound vaguely similar to something we heard around 1970?

On December 17, 2010, a local police official in Sidi Bouzid, Tunisia, confiscated the cart and produce of a twenty-six-year-old vegetable seller named Mohamed Bouazizi for selling produce without a license. When the vendor tried to pay the fine, he was insulted, slapped, and then beaten. He went to provincial headquarters to protest, but was refused an audience. As the sole breadwinner for an extended family of eight, he could not afford to lose his livelihood. At the zenith of frustration and humiliation, he went back to the headquarters and immolated himself.

News of the event quickly spread through social media. Peaceful protests began immediately; marchers wanted to call attention to the corruption, poverty, and lack of opportunity that particularly young people faced. Security forces responded with violence. The protests spread. The message was heard in other countries, and protests began there as well. Democracy became the goal of the protesters. Within weeks, the entrenched regimes of six Arab countries were fighting for their existence—Tunisia, Egypt, Libya, Yemen, Bahrain, and Syria. In the end, though, only one—the original protest country of Tunisia—became a democracy.

In each case, victory was decided by the country's military. The regimes were not going to go peacefully. In each case, the dictator ordered the military to suppress the revolt, by firing on the people if needed. Forced to make a decision, each country's military had to choose a side. In two cases, Tunisia and Egypt, the military sided with the protesters. In two cases, Libya and Yemen, the military fractured, with some units siding with protesters while other units sided with the regime. And in two cases, Bahrain and Syria, the military sided with the regime.

With military support, Tunisia moved forward to become a democracy. In Egypt, the country was headed for democracy but stumbled along the way and ended up where it started, as a dictatorship. In both Libya and Yemen, civil war ensued, with one part of the military fighting another part of the military. In Bahrain, with military support, the regime soundly won. And in Syria, with military support, the regime likely would have won, but foreign intervention extended the conflict into civil war.

What is most interesting, however, is understanding why each country's military made the decision it did. It turns out that in countries closest to a nation-state, the military sided with the people. In countries closest to a fiefdom, the military sided with the regime. And in countries right in the middle, the military fractured.

Figure 55 describes the situation. Egypt and Tunisia were dictatorships but with nation-state institutions. Yemen and Libya were dictatorships run like fiefdoms, but with some nation-state aspects to them. Syria and Bahrain were dictatorships that were really fiefdoms. In each case, the Arab Spring revolt clarified an individual nation's position along the governance basis progression.

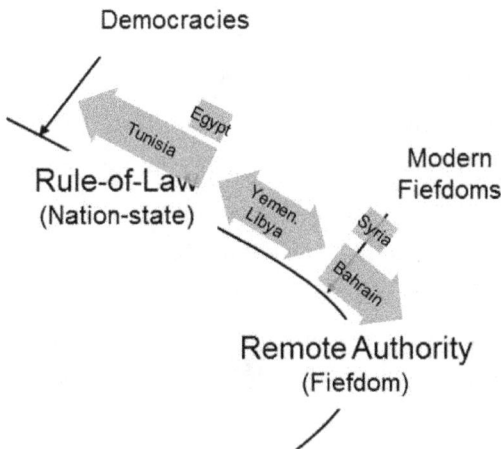

Figure 55. Arab Spring results.

Tunisia became a democracy because Tunisia's military sided with the people, and not the regime. Equally important, after the revolt, Tunisia's military did not try to take over. Rather, it allowed civilian authorities to handle the transition to a democratic government. But why did Tunisia's military behave this way?

Tunisia gained independence from France in 1956. Its first president, Habib Bourguiba, had been active in the independence movement from France, was well liked by the people, and was committed to improving their lives. Nevertheless, he fashioned a one-party system that tolerated no dissent.

Despite this, he was pro-Western, having been educated in France. He passed many Western-style reforms for an Islamic country, including granting women equal status with men and promoting education for every member of society. He also maintained strong relationships with France and the United States. Nevertheless, when his economic programs failed to deliver, calls for a multiparty system began. He responded by having himself declared "president for life" in 1975. In later years, he became even more authoritarian, cracking down on protests and Islamic extremists.

In 1987, after a court ruled Bourguiba no longer medically competent to rule, the prime minister, Zine al-Abidine Ben Ali, deposed the eighty-four-year-old Bourguiba in a bloodless coup. Ben Ali had also grown up with Western exposure, having received military training in France and having studied engineering in the United States. After assuming the presidency, he implemented reforms that boosted the economy and cut Tunisia's poverty rate in half. He also showed signs of progressivism by loosening restrictions on the press. In time, however, he became more authoritarian. He banned Islamic political parties, staged sham elections that guaranteed his victory, and was increasingly criticized for human rights abuses. During his reign, he also created a palace economy, where his family became enriched by rigging the regulations of the country to ensure family businesses prospered at the expense of competition. After two decades of rule, the country's prosperity had still not reached certain segments of society, including the country's young people, who suffered from high unemployment and lack of opportunity.

During both regimes, the Tunisian military had remained largely out of regime politics. The military was kept small and focused mostly on border security. Internal security forces were primarily used to handle uprisings, and military officers could not even join the ruling party. This cleavage developed a rather independent spirit in the military. On the two occasions (1978 and 1984) where the generals were called upon to help put down uprisings, they resented the misuse of force.

This cleavage also left the military to develop itself into a professional institution. Officers trained in France and the United States, learning security techniques, organizational development, and the proper role of the military in a democracy. Troops were conscripted from economically disadvantaged areas where military life was seen as an improvement to them. They could be deployed anywhere in the country, giving them a broader perspective than simply as a member of their local tribe. The Tunisian military ultimately became one of the most respected in the Arab world.

When the revolt began in December 2010, the military watched from the sidelines. Such matters had never been their purview; rather, the large and amply funded internal security forces, run by the Interior Ministry, were in charge. Several senior military officers had even become troubled by the regime's corruption by this time, so no one was anxious to get involved.

The regime called on the Presidential Guard and unleashed gangs of thugs to suppress the revolt; however, these proved insufficient. In January, Ben Ali ordered the army chief of staff, General Rachid Ammar, to deploy troops in support of internal security detachments. While he deployed the troops, he forbade them from firing on demonstrators (unlike the security forces, which had killed many by then). Where troops were deployed, they began fraternizing with protesters. On some occasions, the general even placed troops, tanks, and armored vehicles in between security forces and demonstrators to shield them. Infuriated at this insubordination, Ben Ali tried to sack Ammar, but found himself powerless to do so. On January 14, General Ammar told Ben Ali "he was finished," and Ben Ali fled the country for Saudi Arabia.

Tunisia succeeded in becoming a democracy because by 2011, the country had been an independent nation-state for fifty-five years, even though it had been ruled by a single-party regime and its second ruler had developed a quasi-redistributive economy with himself as the benefactor. Moreover, the army, left to its own devises, became a first-rate nation-state institution. The officer corps could view the dictatorship more objectively, with no particular stake in the regime. Two generations of national conscript meant that soldiers identified more with the people than with the regime. (There is doubt they would have fired on the people even if ordered.) In the minds of both the people and the military, nationalism had taken root, overriding regime allegiance.

In a further expression of nationalism, after the revolution, neither General Ammar nor anyone else in the military tried to take over. Rather, the military subordinated itself to civilian rule and allowed the prime minister, and later a transitional government, to set up elections without interference. When elections were held in October, Tunisia became a democracy—and a stable one at that.

Egypt had a beginning similar to Tunisia. It became a nation-state in 1952, when a group of army officers, led by General Gamal Abdel Nasser, ousted Egyptian king Farouk, and established an authoritarian dictatorship. Egypt has had five "presidents," each of whom has maintained an authoritarian regime. Under Hosni Mubarak, a former air force commander who was elected president following the assassination of Anwar Sadat in 1981, Egypt continued its shift away from socialist leanings, preferring a more capitalist orientation and a Western bent. Mubarak initiated several modernization and economic development programs.

Unlike Tunisia, however, every regime maintained a tight relationship with the military. Every president came from the military, and the military is still viewed as a kingmaker. Under Mubarak, the military was even allowed to establish state-run commercial ventures: such as in construction, consumer goods, tourism, and arms production. These boosted both organizational and personal revenues.

Despite these enticements, by the 2000s the military had concerns about the Mubarak regime. Top on the list was the fear that at the end of his term, Mubarak would pass the presidency to his son, Gamal. Gamal had never served in the military, instead he had come up through finance. Many top officers were concerned about young people, who were increasingly frustrated with unemployment, low wages, government corruption, and a bleak outlook—all of which fomented interest in Islamist groups. Senior officers also grew weary of the growing internal security forces. The regime seemed to be relying upon them more heavily and giving them more privileges—even to the point of rivaling the traditional military establishment. Furthermore, the enlisted ranks, which for two generations had been filled with conscripts from across Egypt and could be deployed anywhere in Egypt, had no particular allegiance to the regime.

When the Arab Spring revolt broke out in late January 2011, the military was in a quandary. It had sympathy for the protesters, but decided to support the regime, in hopes of stabilizing the situation as a compromise was worked out. Mubarak made concessions, hoping that would quell the crowd, but it was not long before the crowds' goals shifted from reform and ending unemployment to regime change. Mubarak called out the military to help suppress the demonstrations. Army units were deployed across the country. The army acknowledged the legitimacy of protesters' demands, but hoped things would return to normal if it maintained an obvious visible presence.

That all changed on February 2, when Mubarak loyalists and security forces fired upon protesters and unleashed massive violence to squash the demonstrations. At that point, the military, which had been quietly supporting the regime, openly ended its support and demanded that Mubarak leave. On February 10, Mubarak fled and the Supreme Council of the Armed Forces took control of the country. It dissolved the nonfunctioning parliament and constitution. A new constitution was crafted in March 2011.

In June 2012, Egypt elected Mohamed Morsi of the Muslim Brotherhood as president. Tension immediately began between Morsi and the military. Exploiting a flaw in the constitution, Morsi then declared himself to be "immune from challenge." After public uproar, the military removed Morsi from power in July 2013. The military then installed an interim president and cracked down on the Muslim Brotherhood. In January 2014 it created a new constitution. In May it held an election where the former head of the Egyptian military became president. Today, the regime of Abdel Fatah al-Sissi is considered one of the most repressive Egypt has seen in recent history.

Egypt failed to become a democracy despite having been a nation-state since the 1950s and having an institutional military from its earliest day. And while historically the Egyptian military has been close to regimes, it was nationalistic enough to know when it was time to side with protesters over the regime. However, Egypt stumbled on its way to democracy. It came down to a few key opportunities where adhering to rule-of-law would have propelled the country forward; rather, by applying brute force progress was stifled.

The first missed opportunity came when the Egyptian people demanded that Mubarak leave office before the end of his term. Had Mubarak been allowed to finish his prescribed term, then the nation would have practiced a respect for rule-of-law. By then precluding Mubarak's son from being installed as president, Egypt would have again push away from fiefdom behavior, and toward democracy. However, the people did not trust Mubarak to leave office, so the military had to act. By doing so, though, progress toward democracy was reset to the starting line.

The next opportunity came after Mohamed Morsi voted himself more power. Clearly this was a flaw in the constitution: balance of powers should not have allowed this to happen. However, such events are common in new constitutions. It took four decades for most European powers to work out the bugs in their constitutions. If Morsi had to be removed while the constitution was "fixed," afterward he needed to be returned to power, being the duly elected president by the people of Egypt. If it was determined that he had to go, having lost legitimacy for his indiscretion, then the next in line, according to the constitution, needed to finish out his term—the vice president, perhaps. Once again, by having the military intervene, progress was reset to the starting line (at best).[4]

Finally, it did not help when the former head of the Egyptian armed forces was elected president in May 2014 (with less than 50 percent voter turnout even). This essentially sealed the deal, continuing the series of dictatorships that has existed since Egypt became independent in 1952.

While Egypt's Arab Spring may seem like an opportunity lost, it also shows that the people were probably not ready for democracy. The missed opportunities reveal a lack of appreciation for rule-of-law—the basis for any democracy. In each case, short-term expediency took precedence over long-term progress. Perhaps all of this was unavoidable—the immediate circumstances precluded any other path. But perhaps a military dictatorship is the best fit for Egypt after all (at least for right now).

In contrast to Tunisia and Egypt, which had been nation-states for decades, and whose militaries had functioned as nation-state institutions, other

---

[4] In reality, every time the military intervened in civilian affairs, progress went backward as the people became less accustomed to rule-of-law and more accustomed to military solutions to every problem.

countries involved in the Arab Spring were run like fiefdoms. Their dictators ran the countries as emirs rather than as officials chosen through the processes of the state. In two of these countries, Libya and Yemen, however, there were enough elements of a nation-state to create tension within the military and society. In those cases, the military fractured and civil war ensued.

Libya was established as a monarchy under King Idris in 1951. King Idris was the emir of Cyrenaica, one of the traditional regions in that area of the Sahara. He was also made the emir of Tripolitania early in 1922, recognized by both Italy and later Britain. He lobbied for Libyan independence from Italy after World War II and was installed as its king upon independence in 1951. He set up a modern monarchy with three provinces, but he later divided Libya into ten provinces to shift more power to the central government. Nevertheless, provincial ties remained more important than national ones throughout his reign. After oil was discovered in Libya in 1959, the country's wealth began to grow, but it was concentrated in relatively few hands. Along with growth, government bureaucracy grew: it eventually became stifling. In 1969, frustrated by poor governance and fueled by Arab nationalism, a group of military officers deposed King Idris in a coup.

The leader of the coup, an air force colonel named Muammar Qaddafi, took power. After attempting some initial national-level reforms, he decentralized government in the country so no one could challenge his authority. He created a government based on local councils; in these councils, tribal allegiances could emerge unencumbered. He was able to make all central government decisions. He used patronage to keep various constituents happy, and played one constituent against another to balance power. He also pocketed much of the country's oil wealth, while his people remained in a general state of poverty.

Libya had no formal constitution. In fact, technically, it did not even have a head of state—Qaddafi considered himself to be the "supreme guide." Tribal affiliations remained of supreme importance in Libya. The Libyan parliament was purely ceremonial. Rather than invest in institutions, Qaddafi ruled through relationships. Most of the key military and security positions were held by Qaddafi's relatives or by his tribesman. His sons and nephews ran various government agencies. His youngest son, Khamis, ran Libya's most elite security force. Nevertheless, to meet military personnel requirements, Libya did resort to conscription, which helped to build a sense of nationalism in the ranks.

In February 2011, when the Arab Spring started, Qaddafi tried to ensure military loyalty by giving cash bonuses to friendly commanders and sacking disloyal ones (this included his brother-in-law, who was the head of the Secret Service). He arrested others, including the top army general, and even held the families of some unit commanders hostage in exchange for loyalty.

The result was a split military. Elite army units, headed by Qaddafi's relatives, remained loyal to the regime. However, army and air force units in Tobruk, Benghazi, and other cities defected en masse. Many of these units became leaders in the rebellion. Those in Benghazi drove other army units out of the city. Qaddafi brought in foreign mercenaries to bolster his dwindling army ranks, but in the end, with support from a NATO bombing campaign, the rebels won. In August, the rebels captured Qaddafi.

Despite the victory, it was not clear that the victors were ready for rule-of-law. An ominous sign appeared when Qaddafi, who was clearly a prisoner of war, was killed on the way to imprisonment. Evidently, the rebels could not wait for a trial.

With Qaddafi's death, Libya fell into turmoil and instability. Civil war ensued. Oil production slumped. Commerce dwindled. Human trafficking networks sprung up. In the end, two rival factions vied for control in Libya, each claiming to be the true government. Much of Libya remained beyond the control of either—held by Islamist groups, rebel groups, or tribal militias. Finally, in December 2015, an agreement between the two leading rival factions was signed to form a unified interim government.

In Libya, the country was run by a dictator who for years ruled more like a prince than a president. Family and personal relationships were used to hold onto power. Yet elements of nationalism took hold in the conscripted army. As a result, regime elements and nationalistic elements would contend during the revolt, with an inconclusive outcome.

Yemen was in a position similar to Libya: a fiefdom with nascent nationalistic attitudes as well as strong tribal affiliations. Yemen had been subject to dynastic rule since the twelfth century BCE. The Ottoman Empire invaded in 1539 but found it difficult to rule with continuous uprisings and rebellions. In 1839, the British, in need of a coaling station for ships traveling to India, invaded Aden on the southern coast and established a protectorate with nine local tribes. The Ottomans left Yemen in 1918, after their defeat in World War I.

In the 1920s, Imam Yahya formed an independent Yemen by consolidating power across the region, with the exception of the Aden protectorate. Arab nationalism swept through the region in the 1960s, fanned by Egypt's Nasser. This eventually led to a civil war and a partitioning of the country in 1967–68. In the north, army officers led a civil war that overthrew the monarchy; they formed the Yemen Arab Republic. In the south, the British pulled out early, allowing leaders to form the socialist People's Democratic Republic of Yemen. The two states remained at odds with each other for three decades.

In 1990, the two countries reunified and Ali Abdullah Saleh, from the north, became president of the Republic of Yemen. Unable to form a cooperative working government, the former rival states fought a brief civil war in 1994, in which northern forces triumphed. Saleh was formally elected president with 96 percent of the popular vote in 1999, and reelected with 77 percent of the popular vote in 2006.

Despite the recent nationalistic history, Yemen operated as a fiefdom. Yemen had few public institutions. It had a royal military—senior positions were held by members of President Saleh's family, and the Republic Guard was led by Saleh's son, Ahmed. Other security forces were led by his nephews. His half-brother ran the air force.

Nevertheless, some of the old nationalistic ideals lingered in senior members of Yemen's military. Furthermore, Yemen had a conscripted army, which tends to promote nationalism among draftees. Almost paradoxically, Yemen's security apparatus also made use of several tribal militias, which also meant those soldiers would maintain strong allegiance to their local tribes (instead of a regime).

When the Arab Spring arrived and protests began, President Saleh initially made nationalistic-sounding concessions to the people. He increased the minimum wage, increased food subsidies, raised civil service pay, and vowed to step down when his term ended in 2013. He even declared that his son would not assume the post after he left. These, however, did not satisfy the crowds, which demanded he step down immediately.

In March 2011, internal security forces cracked down, killing fifty-two protesters. As in other countries, the military was forced to make a choice. Regular army units with strong tribal ties, as well as senior officers with lingering nationalistic leanings, defected to the uprising. Even the head of the Yemeni army in the Northwest (reportedly the president's half-brother) defected to the rebels. A dozen other generals followed him. (Some had been cashiered for failing to use force against the peaceful protesters.) One defecting general even positioned an armored division between protesters and security forces.

Internal security forces and elite army units sided with the regime, resulting in civil war. The Gulf Cooperation Council tried to broker a peace deal, but when Saleh refused the terms (which included that he step down), fighting escalated. Ultimately, however, rebel forces prevailed and President Saleh had to step down. He transitioned power to his vice president.

An interim government was established in February to prepare for elections, but no sooner had the transition begun when a Shia tribe from the north—the Houthis—took advantage of the fractured military and launched attacks. By September, the Houthis had toppled the interim government. Negotiations between the Houthis and the vice president (in absentia) followed, but eventually the Houthis took complete control of the country. This prompted Saudi Arabia to launch a responding invasion to support its Sunni neighbor. Airstrikes began in March 2016.

In the four Arab Spring countries discussed thus far, the militaries had varying degrees of nationalism. This gave them a sense of obligation and loyalty to the people of the country. However, this was not the case in the two other Arab Spring countries. Both Bahrain and Syria are fiefdoms with royal militaries whose loyalty is solidly behind the regime, and not the people.

Bahrain has been a fiefdom since antiquity, having been part of the Persian Empire between the sixth and third centuries BCE. The current ruling family, the Al Khalifa, has been on the throne since 1783. Though dominated by British influence for most of the nineteenth and twentieth centuries, the family remained in power. In 1971, Bahrain declared its independence from Britain and joined the United Nations. The current emir, Hamad ibn Isa Al Khalifa, came to power in 1999. He introduced some progressive policies such as parliamentary elections and women's suffrage. In 2002, however, Bahrain reaffirmed its status as a monarchy when it changed its official name to the *Kingdom of Bahrain.*

The military is a royal military whose sole purpose is to protect the regime. The emir is its supreme commander, and his son is the deputy supreme commander. All important positions in the military are held by family members. The military is small—about 13,000 in a country of 1.2 million. The soldiers enjoy good pay, modern weapons, and top-notch training. Moreover, the military is composed almost entirely of Sunni Muslims in a country whose Muslim population is three-quarters Shia. When the ranks are low, the regime hires foreign Sunnis to fill them rather than conscript from the general population, which would put more Shia into uniform. As it is, the Sunni military has little loyalty or affection for the majority Shia population.

During the Arab Spring, which began in February 2011, most of Bahrain's protesters were Shia. They were seeking democratic reforms and an end to anti-Shia prejudice. However, the Bahraini military squarely opposed the reform movement. When the protests started, the regime used its military, as well as 1,500 soldiers and police from Sunni neighbors Saudi Arabia and the United Arab Emirates to suppress the revolt. What began on February 14 was over by March 14. Altogether 80 people died in the clash and subsequent crackdown, while over 2,900 were arrested.

The final Arab Spring country, Syria, also had a solidly royal military. It too was able to counter the initial uprising, though with defections and foreign support, the Syrian revolt turned into an extended civil war.

Syria had been a part of the Ottoman Empire since 1516. After World War I, it became a French mandate. Syria tried democracy when the French left after World War II, but this turned into a long series of coups and countercoups. Finally, in 1970, the Syrian minister of defense, Hafez al-Assad, took control of the country, in yet another coup.

Assad assumed the post of prime minister and then president. He then effectively shifted the country from one-party rule to one-man rule—himself. He took over much of the decision making that had belonged to his former party, the Ba'ath Party. He suppressed all forms of opposition, through arrest, torture, and execution. He put family members in key positions in the military, security, and intelligence organizations. He accelerated Alawite control of the military. The Alawites are a minority Shia tribe, comprising about 12–15 percent of the population in an otherwise Sunni nation. Assad gave key positions in the military only to Alawites.[5] Sunnis were allowed to hold nonmilitary positions only. Together, these moves effectively ended coup d'états in Syria by making Syria into a fiefdom once again.

Hafez al-Assad died in 2000, after almost thirty years as president. His designated heir, his second son, Bashar, took over the presidency. Bashar continued his father's policies, particularly when it came to control of the military. By 2010, about 70 percent of Syria's career soldiers were Alawite; the officer corps was 80–90 percent Alawite; and nearly all senior positions were held by tribal members. The elite units were exclusively Alawite and led by Assad family members. The regime kept its military modern and well trained. Unlike other Arab nations, it never held secondary status to internal security forces. Senior officers enjoyed status in Syrian society. Advancement came through personal relationships and loyalty to the regime. And as was the case in Egypt, the military was allowed to undertake limited commercial ventures.

Nevertheless, some members of the rank-and-file military had come to identify more with the people than with the regime. Unlike Bahrain, Syria used conscription to fill its ranks, and conscripts could come from any tribe in the country. Also, Syria did not use foreign fighters the way Bahrain did, instead drafting solely from the Syrian people. Furthermore, perhaps through shared struggles with Israel and fighting in Lebanon, Syrian soldiers had developed a greater degree of nationalism than Bahraini soldiers—national borders meant something to them.

---

[5] Alawites had had a strong presence in the Syrian officer corps since the 1950s when they gained control of the military wing of the Ba'ath Party.

When the Arab Spring arrived in Syria in March 2011, the military stood firmly behind the regime. Both internal security forces and the military responded to protests with violence and brutality, even firing on children. However, some soldiers chose to desert rather than shoot protesters.

In Syrian revolt expanded into a civil war. Unlike in Bahrain, military response alone could not put down the protests. Three factors help to explain the different outcomes. First, in Syria there were enough defectors to form a guerrilla insurgency against the regime. Unlike in Libya or Yemen, where whole units switched sides, these defections were by individuals or small groups of individuals disillusioned with their role in the uprising. In July 2011, seven midlevel military officers formed the Free Syrian Army (FSA), citing that it was their duty to protect the people; this required them to bring down the Assad regime. Other senior-level officers joined later. By fall, the FSA and other rebel groups were conducting guerrilla operations across Syria, their ranks swelling into the tens of thousands with new defectors.

Second, critical to the rebels' initial survival was the support they received from foreign governments. Most critical was the safe-haven rebel organizers received from Turkey. In October 2011, Turkey allowed the rebels to meet on Turkish soil where they founded the Syrian National Council, the political wing of the rebellion. This group would coordinate the initial policy for the rebellion. (In November, the council agreed not to attack Syria troops while they were still in their barracks.) Eventually, other foreign powers engaged in supporting the rebellion with arms and materiel. The United States led a coalition against the regime and both the United States and the European Union imposed bilateral sanctions on Syria, straining the Syrian economy. (A United Nations resolution had been defeated.)

Third, and perhaps most critical to the long-term sustainability of the rebellion, foreign fighters became involved. Islamist groups entered the fray as early as December 2011. Others sectarian groups joined later. Eventually, the al-Nusra Front would become the largest and most effective of the rebel forces. The FSA even lost much of its effectiveness as many of its fighters joined Islamist or other sectarian organizations that were highly motivated and better equipped. Some even joined the Islamic State, which captured much of eastern Syria in the summer 2014.

In its death throes, the Assad regime began receiving air support from its old ally Russia in October 2015. This helped restore the regime's military and reestablish parity with rebel forces, prolonging the war.

Six countries were involved in the Arab Spring. Two countries had significant nationalistic elements, which included institutional militaries. One of them became a democracy. Two countries had nascent nationalistic elements in society and in their military. Both ended up embroiled in civil war. Two countries were solid fiefdoms with royal militaries. One, with foreign involvement, put down its rebellion forthrightly. The other, with different foreign involvement, became embroiled in civil war. The likelihood that a country could move forward depended in large part on where it started. The more nationalist the people, and the more institutional the government (in particular, the military), the more likely the society would be able to throw off the old regime and move toward democracy.

A nationalistic mind-set takes time to develop: a generation or more. It has to occur within society as a whole, rather than in the minds of a few leaders. As it develops, loyalty to one's borders and the people within those borders strengthens, while loyalty to a particular regime running the country fades. It is a natural progression. However, not every society is ready for democracy: endless coups and countercoups result when a society jumps the gun to become something it is not. Democracy requires a high regard for rule-of-law, throughout all levels of society.

In a way, through revolt, these societies clarified the form of government that works best for them. Changing one's governance basis is a painful process. Only when the people and key government institutions embrace the right mind-set does it occur. However, transformation has its benefits: so it remains a juicy goal to pursue.[LXXXVI]

...

The frameworks helped us to understand how some situations in the Middle East and the Arab world developed. One can see the progress that societies make and how it takes a readiness on the part of the people to change how their society operates. But in addition to helping us understand the past and the present, can they help us make decisions going forward?

Chapter 24
Application in the Middle East, Part II

In this book, I have spent over twenty chapters developing a framework to help us better understand our world. And over twenty years of consulting experience has shown me that only analysts and engineers really care about frameworks. The rest of the world just wants answers. So with that in mind, I offer the present chapter to show how the frameworks can be used to find answers.

In general, the frameworks in this book provide a long-term strategic perspective on a variety of issues. They do not solve any specific issue entirely. While this may be frustrating to some, it is important not to overstep their intent. Every policy issue has multiple concerns that have to be considered. The long-term strategic perspective is just one of them, but it is often overlooked.

The long-term perspective provides a context for problem solving: it provides a backdrop for all other issues to be weighed against. In the maximum, it provides a default position. A default position will move an organization toward a long-term goal until it is overridden by more immediate concerns (which are often unavoidable). This is useful for policymakers, who now do not have to fly by the seat of their pants, making things up as they go along. They have a starting point for the discussion. This reduces the uncertainty and the chance of making egregious mistakes by starting somewhere out in left field.

In this chapter, we will go beyond understanding recent events to examining courses of action. We will stay in the Middle East for the same reasons stated in the last chapter—there is ample opportunity to demonstrate the frameworks as well as to do some good. We will revisit Iraq and Syria, and pay a visit to Afghanistan. Each of these countries faces different conditions, which drive different approaches to democratization (assuming that is still the goal). We will finish up with a few general thoughts on Middle East politics.

More Thoughts on Iraq

It has been more than ten years since I went to Iraq. In that time, it is safe to say that Iraq has made some progress in its quest to become a nation-state. Iraq has held three parliamentary elections: in 2005, 2010, and 2014. In the 2014 election, 62 percent of the eligible twenty-two million voters cast ballots for 328 parliamentary members. This was roughly the same level as in 2010 (though it had been almost 80 percent in 2005). In 2014 the Independent High Electoral Commission had to annul 300 polling stations for violations and dismiss more than a thousand electoral workers; however, there was still less election fraud than in 2010. In fact, after the 2014 election, it only took four months to work through fraud issues and form a new government, whereas in 2010, it took almost ten months.

Furthermore, many see the new prime minister, Haider al-Abadi, appointed in August 2014, as an improvement over his predecessor, Nouri al-Maliki. Many now blame Maliki for fostering sectarianism and corruption. It seems that the relationships Maliki needed to run the central government are now viewed with derision. This perspective is actually a good sign—a nation-state mind-set is taking root so this is no longer considered normal.

The current prime minister has pledged to reduce sectarianism in government, which has become increasingly seen as a primary cause of bureaucracy and dysfunction, particularly when dealing with economic and governance problems (another sign of a nation-state mind-set taking hold). Abadi began his assault on sectarianism by appointing a nonsectarian cabinet. His appointees are qualified technocrats not affiliated with any party or sectarian group. (In Iraq, political structure requires awarding ministry, undersecretary, and manager positions to Shia, Sunni, Kurd, Christian, and other groups roughly based on their proportion in parliament. Abadi's nominees clearly did not fit that model.) Abadi has received much opposition to this plan. Tribal and religious affiliations are still strong in Iraq. His strongest opponents are even coming from within his own party. Clearly there is a way to go.

Al-Abadi has vowed to fight "corruption" as well (remnants from Iraq's fiefdom years). However, even he had to rein in expectations on what could be expected in the near term. He has focused on the Interior Ministry first.

Meanwhile, the Sunni-Shia rift is alive and well, and many Iraqis still live outside the political process. While sectarian attacks have decreased, Sunnis still have faced murder and abduction from government-aligned Shia militia. One-third of Al-Anbar province, which is predominantly Sunni, did not participate in the last election. Yet the new prime minister believes things are slowly getting better. He says that when he took office, 40 percent of his country was occupied by ISIS, and ISIS still had popular allegiance in some parts of the country; now that allegiance has largely dissolved and ISIS's territory is all but gone.

So over the last decade, the fingerprints of a nation-state have started to take hold. Practices long viewed as normal are now being viewed with disdain. However, there is a long way to go. On average, European countries took about four decades to achieve stable nation-state governments, so one might expect Iraq to take a while longer.[LXXXVII]

More Thoughts on Syria

In December 2015, the United Nations Security Council passed Resolution 2254, which outlined a transition plan for Syria. It specified an eighteen-month time frame for removing the Assad regime and transitioning to a democratically elected government. The Obama administration further developed the outline by specifying that a cease-fire be in place, a transition government established, and work begun on a new constitution by May 2016. There were to be parliamentary and presidential elections by August. The new constitution was to be completed by November, and voted on in January

2017. Bashar al-Assad and his inner circle were to step down in March 2017. The plan initially had the agreement of both the United States and Russia, though no details were worked out on how to enforce it. Eventually, it was ignored.

Currently, the Trump administration has no strategy for dealing with Syria. The administration was initially receptive to keeping Assad in place until he attacked civilians in rebel-held territory with chemical weapons in April 2017. Then, as a punitive measure, the US launched an air strike against the Syrian airfield used in the attack. Since that time, the Trump administration has been equivocal about whether Assad should stay or go, and what involvement the US would have in the process, citing that its first priority was to defeat ISIS. This absence of a strategy does not bode well for civilians in the region or for Europe which continues to endure a refugee problem, and the conflict appears to be no closer to resolution than it was a few years ago.

The frameworks described in this book may be useful for adding clarity to this situation. In any event, it is hoped their usage will stimulate constructive thinking about the situation, starting with the original strategy.

United Nation's Resolution 2254 essentially introduced to Syria the same approach the United States and United Nations used in Iraq. This approach attempted to shift Syria from a fiefdom to a democracy quickly, in a single step, by ousting the current leaders, establishing a transition government, then holding elections for a new government. The problem with this strategy, however, lies with the rebel groups that have joined together in a quasi-coalition with the common goal of toppling the regime. The Free Syrian Army, the al-Nusra Front[1], and others have hundreds or even thousands of fighters who have rallied around the cause of removing a tyrant. However, these rebel groups are actually militias—chiefdom armies—formed around a particular person (a chieftain) with nonfamilial authority as a governance basis. The most likely scenario is that once Assad falls they would start fighting

---

[1] The al-Nusra Front now goes by the name JTF, which stands for the Front for the Conquest of the Levant.

each other. Why? Because that is what chiefdoms do. (Remember the Celts?) Without the common goal of defeating Assad, personal power and ambition become the primary goals of each group. Mostly likely, a second Syrian civil war would begin as each group vies for control. An immature democratic government—where people do not really know how to work together—is unlikely to stop any of this. In the end, one chiefdom would rise above the others and establish itself as the new fiefdom—this is the normal pattern. (Remember Clovis of the Franks?)[2]

Of course, the United States would likely feel obligated to prevent this from happening so it and other Western powers would have to intervene. To maintain order, the United States and coalition forces would become engaged in a multiyear (multi-decade?) peacekeeping mission.

An alternative to the one-step strategy (or having no strategy at all) is to pursue an evolutionary strategy: a gradual transition from fiefdom to democracy—one that gives people and institutions time to adapt to rule-of-law while leaving established lines of authority in place for stability.

Syria has been a fiefdom run by the Assad regime for the last four decades. Fiefdoms are run on relationships more so than on process. As such, Syria will need time to go through a systemization transformation similar to that which Britain went through in the Early Modern era and something similar to what Iraq is going through now (Figure 56). For governance, a graduated path to democracy might also resemble the one Britain took. Over a four-hundred-year period, Britain migrated from king to lords to commons. Syria might be able to do something similar (Figure 57).

---

[2] It is important that Americans not confuse these rebel groups with the thirteen American colonies (as we are sometimes prone to do). While both were fighting to remove a king perceived as being unjust, the colonies had been part of a nation-state for almost ninety years before the American Revolution. America was born a nation-state, inherited from Britain—we have never known it any other way. The rebel groups are chiefdoms and are starting with a different mind-set and a different level of organization. The two are not comparable.

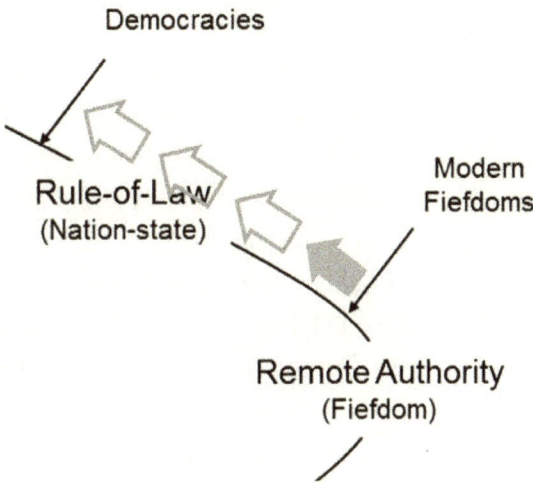

Figure 56. Graduated approach in Syria.

One would expect the transition to begin by assembling something equivalent to a House of Lords, with a power-sharing agreement in place (using a Syrian name for it, of course). This House of Lords would be composed of representatives from tribes, religious bodies, or other established groups. Each representative would have to have some authority in his own sphere of influence. While this house does not need to be a large body, it needs to be large enough and diverse enough to discourage an oligarchy from arising. Above all, the new construct would need the right separation and balance of powers to prevent a dictator from reemerging. The current Syrian house of parliament more closely resembles a House of Commons (and is somewhat of a sham in any case), so it would be disestablished.

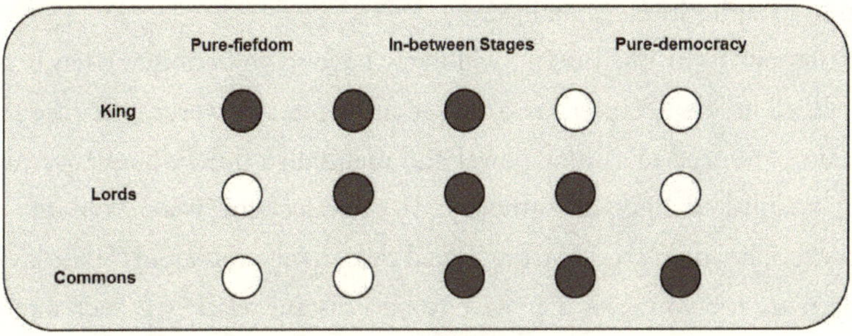

Figure 57. Migration from fiefdom to democracy.

Key institutions would be used to begin the systemization/nationalization process. Education would be required for every man, woman, and child, since this is a driver of progress and nationalism. Civil servants would be required to move around the country when they change positions to get to know other parts of it and other people. Economic development would be transitioned from the regime to House of Lords oversight to ensure fair resource investment. The countryside would be demilitarized: militias eliminated, the armed forces downsized, and a republican security apparatus constructed. A new constitution would codify the values of the new country and its approach to democracy.

With international support, benchmarks could be used to monitor progress, and condition-based milestones could determine when the government is ready to transition to the next stage. Upon successfully reaching the right milestone, some version of a House of Commons would be reestablished. When it does, authority will shift and ministries may change hands.

Of course, this approach means the Assad regime stays in power, at least for a time. This will enable the government to continue operating while it transitions. Tapping into the existing lines of authority, rather than trying to create new ones from scratch based on rules written on paper, is critical for maintaining stability. Perhaps America's greatest mistake in Iraq (besides going in) was not leveraging the established lines of authority (disestablishing the Iraqi army and not recognizing the role of sheiks until 2007). Every society has people to whom other people look for authority. It takes generations to build up these lines of authority. When one person leaves a position or dies, another person has to assume his position so authority is maintained.

Bashar al-Assad, the person, will likely have to go because he has become too sullied to be accepted as a leader anymore. However, his recognized successor will need to assume power and maintain a functioning government using established lines of authority. If the successor were from the next generation, it would send a strong signal that change was afoot. Since his own children are too young, it may have to be a distant relative. If such a relative were not available, then it would have to be someone else most Syrians could recognize as an authority.

Of course, the decision to embark upon such a path would have to be made by the Syrians themselves as part of the war settlement: it would not be legitimate if foisted upon them by the international community. It would, however, be a managed transition. Also, it would not take four centuries or perhaps even four decades to affect—proper milestones and monitoring could accelerate progress. Of course, the approach would need to be adaptive, changing as new developments occur, but remaining focused on the end goal of a more democratic society, which, it is hoped, would help to preclude future civil wars.[LXXXVIII]

Some Thoughts on Afghanistan

Afghanistan is the next place we will take a look at. It is worth examining because it is in a different situation than either Iraq or Syria. It appears to be in a different starting place than either of those countries, so the frameworks reveal a third type of approach may be needed.

Afghanistan appears to be operating primarily at a chiefdom level. That idea first came to me in 2008 when co-workers and clients of mine who had been to both Iraq and Afghanistan performing logistics work told me that Iraqi supply chains were more sophisticated than Afghani supply chains. In Afghanistan, there were no formal supply chains, hardly even rudimentary ones. There was no banking system—people were paid in cash; army disbursers drove around in pickup trucks with trash bags full of cash and soldiers carrying M16s for protection. Basic services in Afghanistan did not exist. Supply chains in general are an indicator of a country's infrastructure, so I gathered that if Iraq was a fiefdom, then Afghanistan was either a simpler fiefdom or a chiefdom.

Later, US military efforts in Afghanistan seemed to confirm this. Part of the campaign strategy in Afghanistan called for US Army and Marine platoons to train Afghani villages to defend themselves, and ultimately aggregate into a cohesive national-level force. The US Army found it almost impossible to do this. While some individual villages learned how to fight, it was impossible to aggregate them above the village level. Similar to Iraq, the required lines of authority did not exist for that to happen. In 2009, a Foreign

Service officer in Afghanistan coined the term "valleyism" to describe how the typical Afghani will fight for his family, his village, and even his valley—but no higher. The illusory central government and its activities have no place in local village life or thought. No one from these remote villages wants the central, national government in their lives, and they will even fight against it, seeing it as an intruder.

Finally, Western concepts of organization and rule-of-law do not appear to have taken hold in Afghanistan. Criminals may be released from prison after pulling strings or paying bribes. Tribal feuds are common and hard to contain. And central government administration is almost viewed as comical.

> [Local tribal leader Amir] Jan has little faith in the government, which he calls corrupt and ineffective. Within the past few months, the district police chief, district governor and top prosecutor have all been dismissed in separate cases of malfeasance.[3]

Elections do not even mean that much in Afghanistan. Local elections carry some weight, but often become vehicles for local chieftains to legitimize the power they already have informally. Prior to the 2014 national elections, experts warned the international community not to expect perfect elections since the Afghans are not even bothered by procedural irregularities or small-scale fraud. Only if a gross aberration of justice propelled an unpopular candidate into office would the Afghans be upset.

The 2014 election revealed the challenge of attempting to overlay a rule-of-law government onto a chiefdom society. Warlords put forth their own presidential candidates, backed up by their own private militias. Rival campaign workers got into fistfights. Some warlords even debated whether they should scrap the entire election and start their own government. Even after the election, warlords kept their militias intact just in case the new government did not work out. At the last minute, the entire democratic process was upended when the losing candidate refused to concede. Rather than asking for a vote recount, he insisted that there be no recount for that

---

[3] Kevin Sieff, "As Marines depart province, Afghans worry," Washington Post, September 30, 2012, p.A16.

would show he had lost. He even forbade releasing the vote count. To prevent a civil war, the winning candidate opted for power sharing: he would become president and the losing candidate would become the "chief executive officer," a made-up position akin to a prime minister. They agreed to modify the constitution in two years to make it a permanent position. Clearly this is not how democratic elections are normally run.

The results of the power-sharing deal are what one might expect: dysfunction. Bickering and an inability to work together have rendered the "unity government" ineffective. The two Afghan leaders have not agreed on many basic issues, and by and large have remained adversaries, competing against each other for power and influence. Requirements of the original power-sharing agreement were not fulfilled: parliamentary elections were not held, economic development programs were stifled, and the 2004 constitution was never updated. In 2016, the CEO declared the president "unfit to govern."

Perhaps worst of all, security within Afghanistan deteriorated. The positions of Minister of Defense and Minister of the Interior went unfilled for over a year. Partisanship undermined the command structure within the Afghan army and the ranks have been thinned by attrition, desertions, and defections. In September 2015, Taliban forces retook Kunduz and made substantial gains in Helmand province. Nearly six thousand members of the Afghan security forces were killed in 2015. By the end of 2016, the Taliban held more territory than at any time since 2001. In April 2017, the Taliban attacked an army base, killing upward of 200 soldiers, forcing the Minister of Defense and Army Chief of Staff to resign.

With unemployment on the rise, violence on the rise, and the economy flatlining, Afghani confidence in the country's future is at the lowest point in a decade, and hundreds of thousands fled the country in 2015 alone. There have been calls to end the unity government, and many Afghans resent the United States for having foisted it upon them in the first place.

On the surface, one might think the problem is that the president and de facto prime minister cannot seem to get along; however, that is not the real problem. The real problem is overlaying a nation-state government onto a chiefdom-fiefdom society. In Afghanistan, every village, or at least every valley, is its own chiefdom. And every chiefdom is independent from every other chiefdom: many of them have their own militias. Every village makes its own decision about whether, or how much, to support the central government, or the Taliban. This makes it incredibly hard to organize anything on a national level in Afghanistan.

Even the federal government seems to work at a fiefdom-level at best. The president is reluctant to acknowledge the power-sharing arrangement, often making unilateral decisions while surrounding himself with small politicians and yes-men. This has alienated many of the powerful politicians within the country. Both men have fallen back to their own ethnic groups as a base of support (the president is Pashtun; the CEO is Tajik), increasing ethnic tensions across Afghanistan. Both men have filled appointments in government agencies and the military with their own people, raising perceptions of discrimination. Both men have failed to consult people outside of their own ethnic group when making program decisions, disenfranchising groups such as the Uzbeks and Hazaras. And in a bit of modern day court intrigue, both men work around each other, trying to strengthen their own base of support at the expense of the other's. These are all elements of fiefdom behavior and it appears that both men favor them over policy, procedure, and rule-of-law.

So what would work better? Given the existing climate and culture, it seems a more natural course for Afghanistan might be to first restore the monarchy and then migrate to a constitutional monarchy over time. This was in fact Afghanistan's original path until a coup in 1973 disrupted it. Understanding why this would work now requires an understanding of Afghan history.

Fiefdom rule began in Afghanistan when the Persians invaded in the sixth century BCE. The Persians, under Darius I, conquered much of central and southern Asia at that time. From then on, empires such as Greece, Parthia, and Mughal India were constantly present in the region.

Afghanistan became an independent monarchy in 1709 when a local tribal leader, Mirwais Hotak, threw off the Safavid Persia overlords. Then Britain entered the region. While it never conquered Afghanistan outright, it did hold considerable influence over it throughout the nineteenth century. Then in

1919, King Amanullah Khan signed a treaty with Britain giving Afghanistan full independence.

King Amanullah then embarked on a path of modernization. He had traveled extensively and saw how the postwar world was being reshaped; he wanted Afghanistan to have a role in it. He crafted Afghanistan's first constitution in 1923, which created a modern monarchy.

The Afghani constitution created a prime minister position, which separated the monarch from the day-to-day government. A government would be formed each year so a state council could approve the budget. A separate judiciary was established; religious and tribal justice was forbidden, shifting all judiciary matters to a national court system. Local assemblies were formed to replace tribalism with nationalism.

The constitution also made a number of social reforms. Torture, slavery, and forced labor were abolished. It introduced freedom of the press and recognized private enterprise and private property. It expanded women's rights and called for universal education. It introduced government employment. It curtailed the aristocracy as well as unorthodox tribal practices. It also reduced the role that Islam played in government.

While the new constitution was reformist, it did much to reaffirm the authority of the monarchy. It centralized power in the government at the expense of tribal and religious leaders. There was no legislative body, so all law making was controlled by the monarch.

The new constitution faced immediate opposition from tribal leaders and Islamic clerics. Opposition was so fierce that in 1923, when the king tried to have it approved by the Loya Jirga (Afghanistan's grand council of elders) it was rejected.[4] In 1925, the king amended the constitution to soften its thornier points, trying to avoid a revolt. Principally, he added back in a role for Islam. Nevertheless, the king was toppled in 1929, so the constitution never really took effect.

A 1931 constitution was much less ambitious and much more amenable to tribal leaders and Islamic clerics. Issued by a new king, it reintegrated Islam into government and even subordinated national law to Sharia law. It made

---

[4] He later had it rubber-stamped by a smaller loya jurga.

no mention of women's rights or their education. Also, the judiciary had to decide cases in accordance with the Holy Hanafite creed.

It did have one considerable reform, though—it created a legislature. The bicameral legislature contained an upper house, whose members were chosen by the king, and a lower house, whose members were elected by their districts. It turned out, however, that in reality the king could, by various means, select members of the lower house as well, so it became a rather perfunctory body. Moreover, the parliament could only advise the king regarding new laws—it had no power to make them independently. This constitution remained in effect for over thirty years.

In 1953, an authoritarian prime minister was appointed to jump-start progress. Mohammad Daoud Khan, who was the king's cousin and his brother-in-law, was appointed prime minister and quickly became the primary force in government. He initiated a nationalization program by codifying the country's laws. He began Afghanistan's civil law system. He opened public education to women and pushed through other reforms that had been rejected a quarter century earlier. He also suppressed all opposition to the regime: throughout the 1950s, his rule was one of authoritarian control. The king, who had deferred much of his power to his uncles since the 1930s, now deferred it to his cousin.

However, events in other countries were causing concern in the royal family. In Middle East countries such as Egypt, Libya, and Iraq, kings had been replaced by revolutionary regimes. In Iraq, the king and his prime minister were killed. The royal Afghan family decided change was needed. They intended that the country gradually shift to a democratic structure under a constitutional monarchy. However, the prime minister would have none of it. He was then pressured to resign, which he did in 1963.

King Mohammed Zahir Shah commissioned the crafting of a new constitution. It was a collaborative affair, with a seven-member committee seeking input from across Afghanistan's multitude of constituencies. After debates, reviews, and revisions, it was sent to a loya jirga for more debate and textual editing. It was then ratified and, after public review, went into effect in October 1964.

The 1964 constitution was intended to modernize Afghanistan as a nation and prepare it for democracy. It established three coequal branches of government, putting the judiciary and legislature on equal footing with the executive branch (still run by the king). In the upper house (the Meshrano Jirga), now the king could only appoint one-third of its members—the rest were selected by provincial councils and jirgas. Members of the lower house (Wolesi Jirga) were elected directly by the people for four-year terms.

Moreover, the legislature now had law-making authority. Both houses had to pass a bill to make it a law. The legislature gained oversight of the budget and treaties. It also had the power to reject, or even dismiss, cabinet appointments. Parliament had to meet regularly—and did not need the king's approval to form. Members could speak with legal immunity. They also had the right to form political parties, though legislation from the king was needed to approve them. Perhaps most intriguing, the new constitution blocked royal family members from entering political life.

Reforms included a bill of rights that guaranteed freedom of thought and expression, protection of private property, the equality of men and women, and the equality of tribes before the law. It subordinated Sharia law to national law—Sharia law could only be applied when no national law existed to cover a specific situation. Islam did remain the official religion of the country, though.

However, the king did retain monarchical power. He exerted power through his cabinet, which controlled government policy and could invoke emergency decrees. The cabinet could slow, halt, or even reverse legislation passed by the legislature. Legislators could not hold any position within the executive branch, and even by appointing one-third of the upper house, the king still had de facto control over it.

Despite all of its good intentions, the government struggled under the new constitution. The judiciary struggled under a lack of qualified judges and entrenched local practices. It was also overshadowed by the king and his prime minister.

The new legislature struggled as well. Its members were not experienced enough for things to run properly. Moreover, the legislature kept getting bogged down in divisions between conservatives, nationalists, clerics, and communists. Furthermore, the laws needed to form legitimate political parties were never forthcoming, so clandestine parties began to spring up in the shadows. Soon a shadow legislature began operating with parties on the extreme left and extreme right meeting in secret. Without the ability to form parties (let alone coalitions), the legislature could never muster a majority to pass anything. It became disparaged as a joke.

Further undermining the legislature's power was the adversarial relationship between the cabinet and the legislature. The cabinet could effectively block any legislation it wanted. This stagnated the government and even led to riots on college campuses. When legislators complained, the cabinet responded by further holding up legislation. Some of these stagnant laws were needed to put the constitution fully into effect. The result was circular gridlock.

The constitution also caused the executive branch to grind to a halt. By prohibiting royal family members from participating in politics, it created a dearth of new leadership, since the only people with experience were royal family members. Inexperienced newcomers stumbled in executive positions, and no vibrant young leadership appeared to be anywhere on the horizon.

On top of the gridlock, many of the reforms did not play well with society. Too much power was left in the hands of too few people. This frustrated perhaps no one more than young people, who had become enthused by the idea of increased freedoms and liberal access to education, but frustrated by a nonfunctioning government, a sluggish economy, and few employment opportunities.

Oddly enough, however, the general public remained largely indifferent to all of these events. Most of the activity and frustration was felt in cities like Kabul; however, the new constitution seemed irrelevant to the lives of people in rural areas. In the 1965 and 1969 elections, voter turnouts were 15–20 percent of eligible voters. Without working political parties to generate enthusiasm and develop support for a slate of candidates, every candidate became a party of one.

Finally, in 1973, the former prime minister, Daoud Khan, reappeared. Cast out by the no-royals clause, he watched as the country suffered years of government dysfunction, a stagnated economy, and a rise in extremist political parties. He led a bloodless coup against his cousin when the latter was in Europe for medical treatments. Khan dissolved the government and proclaimed himself president of a new republic.

Afghanistan's problems did not end with a new government, though. The new republic quickly became a dictatorship. President Khan formed a central committee to advise him, ruled by executive decree, and held absolute power. In 1977, he crafted a new constitution to replace the old one. The document reflected his leftist leanings and was consistent with the socialist ideology of his day. It nationalized resources and introduced land redistribution. It also expanded rights for women (including the right to vote) and eliminated any lingering role for religion in governance. Another loya jirga was convened to ratify this constitution, which it did in February 1977.

Khan's 1977 constitution never went into effect, however; he was deposed in a communist coup, called the Saur Revolution, in April 1978. The People's Democratic Republic of Afghanistan was formed and the Revolutionary Council became its government.

This prompted an immediate response from rural tribes. Mujahedeen— Islamic fighters—began attacking government installations across the country. Then an internal coup replaced one group of communists with another. The new group began ruling with a Soviet-style politburo that issued decrees from a central planning committee. However, the Mujahedeen attacks continued, and were so fierce they threatened to topple this government. In December 1979, the Soviet Union intervened, sending divisions into Afghanistan to save its puppet government. Meanwhile, the Mujahedeen continued to fight.

After ten years, almost 15,000 killed, and over 50,000 casualties, the Soviet Union, now led by reform-minded Mikhail Gorbachev, pulled out of Afghanistan. Between 850,000 and 1.5 million Afghans were killed. Afghanistan's communist government then tried to appeal to the people with economic and military aid, but remained in a state of war. When the Soviet Union dissolved in December 1991, Afghanistan's communist government lost vital foreign aid. The government collapsed in April 1992.

After this, the militia wars began. Saudi Arabia and Iran backed rival militias in a proxy war; chaos reigned. By 1994, the Pakistan-backed militia, the Taliban, was rising to power. By the end of 1994, the Taliban forced the surrender of dozens of local Pashtun leaders and took control of southern Afghanistan. By September 1996, with aid from Pakistan and now Saudi Arabia, Taliban forces took Kabul. Later that month, they declared the Islamic Emirate of Afghanistan.

The 9/11 attacks brought the United States to the region. The Islamic extremists who perpetrated the attacks were headquartered in Afghanistan. The United States coordinated with rebel groups against the Taliban, and by December 2001, the Taliban was out. With US coordination, another republic was formed in 2004. Hamid Karzai, head of the Polpalzai tribe and a leader in the anti-Taliban movement, was selected to be its first president by a loya jurga.

Expectations were high, but Karzai soon found it difficult to govern the new republic. The new president found it difficult to govern unless he leveraged the personal relationships to an almost monarchical level. This appeared as cronyism in the West. He was reelected in 2009 and served until his second term expired in 2014.

Since 1973, Afghanistan has been through a string of governments. It has also experienced unprecedented levels of bloodshed. And in all, it has to be said that however bad the 1964 constitution was for the Afghan people, it was still better than what happened later. The instability brought on by fluctuating governments did incalculable damage to the country, and the country is still reeling from its effects.

On the surface, it may appear that the 1964 constitution failed because people refused to work together: members of parliament, parliament and the cabinet, ministries officials, and a judiciary and local officials. Add to this inflexibility and an unwillingness to adapt, and you have the makings of a disaster. A deeper look, however, reveals a more pervasion issue afoot.

Historically, Afghans are a rural people with little regard or trust in central government. The people of Afghanistan have generally had little concern, or even acknowledgment, of central government affairs. Only when local or religious sovereignty was infringed upon did rural tribes even take notice. It was local tribal leaders and clerics who protested the 1923 constitution, which promoted nationalism at the expense of tribal and religious authority. The

1964 constitution and its resultant parliament were largely ignored by the vast, rural, uneducated countryside, which did not understand it and did not care about it enough to try.

This rural-palace divide even played out in the 1960s legislature, where 90 percent of the legislators in the lower house were commoners from rural Afghanistan, few of whom had any modern education or foreign exposure. The opposite was true of the cabinet members, who had lots of both. Hence, the two groups spoke different languages and had different perspectives on what was important—all this was on top of whatever adversarial relationship the new constitution created. The judiciary had similar problems with the local court system, where tribal customs and practices, though they may have violated the law, were more entrenched. Even provincial governments—which in theory are closer to the people than a central government—have historically been viewed as centers of corruption and ineffectiveness.

Moreover, the 1964 constitution just did not seem to carry enough weight with people. In fact, none of the constitutions have ever meant that much to people in Afghanistan— either rural people or the central government. It is commonly held that the primary reason for creating the original 1923 constitution was to show foreigners how enlightened Afghanistan was— constitutions were in vogue at the time. Even today, a common refrain in Afghanistan is that the first people to disobey the constitution are the people who wrote it (as the 2014 elections might confirm). And without public pressure to make government officials conform to a written constitution, officials feel they have license to go around it.

All of this speaks to an even deeper issue, a foundational issue: that rule-of-law never truly developed in the hearts of the Afghan people. Not only that, it would suggest that remote authority never truly developed in the hearts of the Afghan people—people just do not see the benefit of having a central government. Despite centuries of being a fiefdom, its effects never reached into the rural areas.

Because of this absence of remote authority, Afghanistan still operates at a chiefdom level. When the communists took over, it was chiefdom-level militias that rallied to attack the new communist government, after the perceived legitimate government had been removed. It was the militia that sustained ground offensives until the communist regime fell in 1992. It was militias that battled for control of Afghanistan until the Taliban arose in 1996. It was the Taliban, another chiefdom, that ran the country until overthrown in 2001. It seems the tribal people never embraced the idea that any form of central government, even a fiefdom, had real merit. And this disregard seems to go both ways. While planning the new constitution in 2002, one of the chief complaints heard from tribal representatives was that the central government treated the rural population as an undifferentiated mass of peasants rather than respecting and understanding the differences between tribes.

Without remote authority as a foundation, efforts to build a higher-order government are flawed at best. Each governance basis becomes the foundation for the next one, so if remote authority is missing, then rule-of-law cannot take root.

So instead of starting over with a new government in 1973, Afghanistan would likely have been better off continuing along its original path from absolute monarchy to constitutional monarchy. With a monarchy intact, Afghanistan would have been more likely to develop to remote authority. In fact, one could argue the Afghan monarchy tried to move too far, too fast. The 1950s was the most productive time in Afghanistan's history. Most historians believe this was because of the energetic and forceful prime minister, Daoud Khan. However, it may have been because a strong monarchy was the best fit for the Afghan people at the time.

In the 1960s, out of fear for personal safety, the monarchy embarked on an ambition modernization plan, yet it knew it needed to keep some level of control. So it strengthened the lower house only to build in conflict with its own cabinet. However, the king was fearful of creating a multitude of political parties for fear this would challenge established political powers. It is likely a strong cabinet may have worked better with an upper house of tribal leaders (and not political cronies) to gain their concerns, their inputs, and their cooperation on key issues. Giving too much decision making to the people, when they do not know what to do with it, is not always the right thing to do.

In the 1970s, Daoud Khan perceived that Afghanistan needed to go back to a more centralized structure, but the only way he could do that was through a coup and by declaring a republic. Doing this led to both his and Afghanistan's downfall. Afghanistan tried to skip a step (Figure 58).

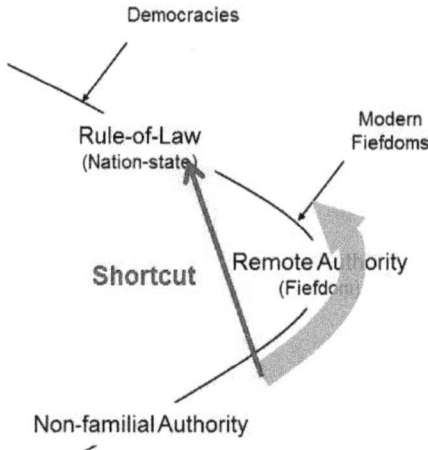

Figure 58. Skipping a step in Afghanistan.

For Afghanistan to progress, it needs to strengthen remote authority as a governance basis. Whether Afghanistan once had it and lost it during the militia wars or never developed it at all, strengthening it is the first priority.

Remote authority is founded upon redistribution, which is essential for governance. At a chiefdom level, societies learned that redistribution of resources can benefit everyone in the chiefdom. At the fiefdom level, writing enabled it to expand. It works the same way today—by collecting taxes and redistributing the money where it is needed most. Every nation-state has this foundation—it is second nature. Through taxation and investing in programs in education, social welfare, defense, and infrastructure development, nation-states function. The only debate is how much tax and where to invest.

Afghanistan needs to strengthen remote authority to solidify the country. Rural Afghans have to see that it works to their benefit. While paying taxes is never pleasant, the people have to see that it makes their lives better, through services such as electricity, clean water, health care, education, and economic development. The government has to give the local Afghans a reason to look beyond the valley. Rural Afghans have to see that the central government can deliver goods that a warlord cannot. Unless this happens, society will remain fragmented with isolated chiefdoms scattered in the hills and valleys across the country. Local chieftains will not want to cede authority to the central government, so it will take time, but it is still needed.[5]

Restoring a monarchy in Afghanistan would allow time for this to occur while preserving stability. A monarchy does not have the distractions and confusion that a nation-state government has—it is simpler. Representation in government is a lower priority at this point. If rural Afghans rarely pay attention to central government, they will not miss representation in government. However, a proper functioning government is required. A monarchy will provide the most stability as the Afghan people evolve.

A good model for this would be Morocco: Morocco is an effective modern monarchy today. While democracy advocates give it low marks, the country is well run and its people are generally happy. It has the fifth-largest economy in Africa and ranks first in quality of life in Africa. Education is free and is compulsory through primary school. Literacy runs around 72 percent. It also has more than four dozen universities and institutions of higher learning. It has a thriving tourist industry, with more than ten million visitors a year. It is a favorite of Europeans who love the Mediterranean and Atlantic coastlines. Its people genuinely like visitors and are generally happy to chat with them. And the arts are alive and well. Moreover, people live relatively simple, but joyful lives. Family, food, and friends are priorities in Morocco.

Since liberation in 1956, Morocco has slowly liberalized its government. The Spanish had ruled Morocco for centuries until it became a French protectorate in 1912. After a protracted war for independence, Morocco became a monarchy and Sultan Mohammed V became king in 1956.

---

[5] In 2011, I was at the Pentagon when I met a marine lieutenant colonel who had just come back from Afghanistan. His assignment involved working with villages on security and development. He told me that in one village, he was talking with the local chieftain about a development plan. When he mentioned setting up a school, the chieftain became uneasy—he was very reluctant to have one. The chieftain then explained that as long as the people were illiterate, they would come to him for understanding and direction. Once they learned to read and write, they would not need him as much. He said this with all sincerity and saw nothing wrong with that viewpoint. When the lieutenant colonel left Afghanistan, construction had begun on several buildings, including a medical center, but a school was not in the plan.

The king's son, Hassan II, assumed the throne in 1961. He created a bicameral legislature in 1962, though he retained much personal authority. Furthermore, he ruthlessly suppressed any dissention against his rule. There were a reported ten thousand human rights violations, including death, detention, and exile during his reign.

His son, Mohammed VI, came to the throne in 1999. He is well liked and is viewed as having great compassion and concern for the Moroccan people. He has commissioned several hospitals, universities, and other public service offerings.[6] To the world, he is viewed as a "cautious modernizer." In 2011, he revised the constitution, granting more power to the parliament and prime minister after the Arab Spring uprising; however, ultimate authority remains in his hands. In September 2015, Morocco held its first ever direct elections for regional councils.

Morocco has succeeded in keeping a stable government by gradually introducing personalized decision making over time (arguably, as the people were ready for it). Morocco's elections are considered free and fair. Yet the government works. After a terrorist bombing in Casablanca in 2003, the government has ruthlessly cracked down on Islamic militants. Morocco is even considered a non-NATO ally by the United States, and has received praise from the latter for its efforts on the global war on terror.

Of course, Afghanistan's unity government has to be allowed to work. Every chance has to be given to it. If it works, and the people are generally happy with it, then keep it. However, if at the end of its tenure, the Afghan people decide that another direction is needed, then they would be wise to consider restoring the monarchy. Both Britain and France restored their monarchies while they worked out issues in search of a stable form of government. Afghanistan had a chance to restore its monarchy back in 2001, but opted for a republic instead; this would be another opportunity. Of course, the people of Afghanistan would still have to recognize the royal family and give them the deference needed to make it work. It also depends upon whether anyone in the monarchy wants the job, and is qualified to do it.

---

[6] My Moroccan barber thinks he is great.

After restoration, however, the monarch would have to be allowed to introduce the controls needed to effectively govern. That could mean allowing royal family members to hold ministerial positions as needed to oversee effectiveness. (Personal loyalty can be a guarantee of performance more than written law.) This could mean disestablishing the lower house, and making the upper house an advisory board. It would almost necessarily mean either standing-down local militia or deputizing them. It would also mean redistribution through fair and appropriate taxation, as well as focused investments that benefit people (education and infrastructure development). With this, the rural parts of Afghan are more likely to gradually coalesce into a single nation.

Afghanistan could then resume its journey to constitutional monarchy. By steadily introducing greater personal decision making over time (like Morocco), the constitutional monarchy may eventually take modern form (like Britain's). Throughout the process, however, the royal family remains a stabilizing force for society as the details of government are worked out. The royal family just needs to remember that theirs is a temporary job—for them and their descendants—and that the better they do their job, the sooner it will end. So it is best to find a royal who is sacrificially committed to the welfare of her people.[LXXXIX]

Some Thoughts on ISIS

The final Middle East situation to be examined concerns ISIS. ISIS emerged out of nowhere in June 2014, establishing itself on the world-stage, declaring itself to be a new caliphate, espousing a version of fundamental Islam, and employing unprecedented levels of violence to achieve its aims. ISIS recruited from across the Middle East, Europe, and even the United States, using social media to attract frustrated and disenfranchised Muslim youth to its cause. Thousands journeyed to Syria to fight for the dream of creating a powerful Islamic country. And while recently ISIS has lost much of its territory, it still promotes its agenda through lone-wolf terrorist attacks upon civilians. Those who would join ISIS, however, particularly young people, would be wise to know more about the challenges it faces in achieving its goals, and even with its basic construction—things our frameworks can illuminate. But first, some background.

ISIS began as JTJ (the Party of Monotheism and Jihad) in 2003, founded by a jihadist Abu Musab al-Zarqawi. The organization changed its name to Al Qaeda in Iraq (AQI) after it united with al Qaeda in 2004. Its primary mission was to foment sectarian violence, which would then require the Sunni population to seek its protection from Shia retaliation. In June 2006, a US bomb killed al-Zarqawi, and the organization went dormant.

Eventually another jihadist, Abu Bakr al-Baghdadi, took over AQI. Charismatic, Sunni, and Iraqi born, he was able to swell ISIS's ranks with former military officers and personnel from Saddam Hussein's army. Their presence gave the organization a more militaristic flair and capability than it previously had. Al-Baghdadi changed the organization's name to ISI, then ISIL, then ISIS (the Islamic State of Iraq and Syria). In 2014, this version of the organization was able to conquer territory in western Iraq and eastern Syria—predominantly Sunni locations that were not opposed to having a Sunni organization protect them against the Shia governments of Nouri al-Maliki in Iraq and Bashar al-Assad in Syria. Al-Baghdadi declared himself to be the new caliph, the spiritual leader of Muslims. With US-led coalition airstrikes, however, Iraq and Syria were able to retake ground lost earlier. Since then, ISIS has turned its attention to promoting independent "home-grown" terrorists to strike at targets in the United States and Europe.

While ISIS has certainly made itself known to the world, it has never had a sustainable construction. ISIS is a chiefdom. It was formed by a charismatic leader who passed the organization to another charismatic leader; hence, its governance basis is nonfamilial authority. While it is not clear whether al-Baghdadi is still alive, his perceived presence (or that of a successor) holds the organization together.

ISIS is not a fiefdom. It is too young to have developed a hierarchical structure based on heredity. It has not been around long enough to develop the relationships through which fiefdoms are ruled. Nor does it have a robust civil service structure or policies and coordination that would indicate it is a fiefdom. In reality, its leader is a warlord with dominion over militias that fight for him.

ISIS was not sustainable because it has a fiefdom on each side of it—Iraq on the east and Syria on the west; and fiefdoms beat chiefdoms in existential warfare. ISIS exists because both Iraq and Syria have been weakened by war in recent years. Furthermore, Iraq is still learning how to become a nation-state and Syria's ruler is trying to hold onto the fiefdom he has. However, there is nothing to suggest that these conditions will last forever. Once these two countries have been restored, whether as fiefdoms or as nation-states, they would be able to crush ISIS in between them. Of course, both societies will have to better address the concerns of their Sunni populations, which is no small task to be sure; but ISIS as a country with territory was at an end from the beginning—coalition airstrikes sped up the process.

A second challenge for ISIS lies in achieving its goal of establishing a multi-continent caliphate. A caliphate is a territory or group of people who have pledged loyalty to a caliph. A caliph is a spiritual leader, whom many Muslims consider to be God's representative on Earth. The last caliph was Abdulmecid Efendi. He was born in Ottoman Turkey in 1868 and became caliph in 1922. He was a scholar, a gifted painter, and an avid butterfly collector. He held the position until 1924 when the new Turkish Republic ousted the remnants of the old Ottoman Empire, including the caliphate. Efendi spent his last twenty years in France. Since that time, there has been no caliph or caliphate.

Most Muslims interpret the position of caliph as a spiritual leader, akin to the Roman Catholic pope. However, ISIS has determined that the caliph is not only a spiritual leader but also a government leader—with territory and a country to run. When this country conquers other countries, God's rule on earth expands.

The problem with this interpretation is that as soon as the caliph becomes a government leader, the caliphate becomes a fiefdom (or a chiefdom). Fiefdoms have a single ruler, which inherently limits their size: the largest fiefdoms have only a few million people. In a fiefdom, decision making is funneled through the leader, and this becomes a bottleneck for governance. (Nation-states have a more "open architecture" type of government so they have less of a bottleneck.) As such, a caliphate would never become large enough to encompass even a portion of the world. More basically, however, is that fiefdoms are less powerful than nation-states, so it is unlikely ISIS would ever defeat the nation-states it needs to accomplish its goal. Creating a worldwide caliphate is simply unrealistic.

But say the caliph's role is modified so that he becomes the head of state while a prime minister runs the government. In principle, the caliphate could then be run like a constitutional monarchy—a nation-state. The problem it would face is that nation-states require a relatively peaceful and stable environment where the majority of people follow the rules. Creating such an environment requires that violence drop below a critical level, to the point where people trust in printed laws instead of their own guns and knives. The violence that ISIS has institutionalized runs counter to this. Their acts of violence, even if only committed against foreigners, breed a culture of instability that would have shielded their society from embracing rule-of-law so their caliphate could not be run as a nation-state.[7] Hence, their violence has worked against them in the long-run.

So for ISIS, its construction is unstainable and its goal is unattainable. While it may grab headlines, and may even be around for years to come, it is not going to be a long-term solution to anyone's problems. So what option then is there for a young man in the Middle East frustrated by his current situation? While I could not begin to address every issue in the Middle East, the frameworks do introduce a path forward, toward democracy.

The allure of democracy is not new to the Middle East. A post-World War II generation espoused the hope of national liberation and democratic freedom. In most cases these hopes were dashed as dictatorial regimes took the place of colonial overlords. While this must have been heartbreaking to that generation, no less heartbreaking were the dreams dashed when the Arab Spring turned into the Arab Winter. However, there is still cause for hope.

We now know more about what it takes to become a democracy. It takes

---

[7] Bear in mind the difference between state-sponsored violence in the form of wars and revolutions and the communal violence in people's daily lives. The revolutions used to form nation-states in Europe were state-sponsored and came to an end, while the communal violence decline steadily. It is ISIS's introduction of violence into communal life would most likely prevent a nation-state from taking hold.

more than simply handing out ballots; it takes a mindset. Developing that mindset is an evolutionary process, and governance cannot evolve until the right mindset develops within the society. Setting the process in motion requires a commitment to rule-of-law. It begins by recognizing that bribery, lying, graft, and corruption are not victimless crimes—they hurt society as a whole, especially the children who will grow up in a country with less opportunity because of it. While the process is neither quick nor easy, it is realistic and hopeful.

For those concerned that this process only applies to Western countries or that is a Christian idea that conflicts with Islam: neither is true. The nation-state does not belong to Europe. Europe gave birth to the nation-state in the 1500s, shifting power westward from the Middle East, which had seen most of the ancient world's early growth and development. But this shift was primarily the result of a change in mentality—there was nothing physiological about it.

The nation-state is secular. It is neither religious nor antireligious, neither sacred nor sacrilegious. Christianity was needed for the first nation-state to emerge, but once the concept was proven, non-Christian nations were able to follow suit, as Japan and China can attest.

Neither do nation-states depend upon relationships based on religion or tribe as fiefdoms do. Nation-states are multiethnic and multitongued. Ethnic and religious differences need not matter. In fact, a nation-state's best interest is served by promoting work and cooperation between everyone rather than by division. In nations-states, the historical barriers between sectarian groups can slowly fade if people are willing. The key is getting everyone to see it.[XC]

As a younger generation looks to make its world a better place, this knowledge should provide a palpable alternative to the violence-filled world of an Islamic state with unattainable goals.

...

The research used in this book was originally intended to understand how some societies become world leaders while others do not. Somewhere along the way, it became apparent that this insight could be more useful and perhaps more meaningful by helping people's lives today. I hope that has been the case. While this book does not have all of the answers, I hope it adds light in a few problem areas. Consider it as you make decisions for yourself and your country.

Chapter 25
A Long Look Forward

In my early twenties, I lived in Cincinnati. While downtown was normally quiet on a Saturday morning, one place that was guaranteed to be bustling was the local farmers' market in the Over-the-Rhine neighborhood, about a mile from where I lived. Occasionally, I would go over and pick up some fresh produce—a handy convenience since the nearest supermarket was across the river in Kentucky. The market was exciting at that time of the week as hordes of shoppers descended downtown to look over the region's poultry, pork, fruits, and vegetables.

One day I decided to drop by in the afternoon, just before the market closed. I found a totally different environment. The crowd was thin, and the vendors had begun packing up. A few were still trying to clear stock, and with fewer people clamoring for attention, I could calmly walk around and get some good deals. While the best items had already been picked over, the residual produce was still decent enough for a bachelor. I once got an entire shopping bag of grapes for a couple of dollars. I liked the price, but I would regret buying an entire bag later that week.

In Part I of this book, we looked through history to understand how some societies rise above others to become leaders. In Part II, we applied those principles to understand what it would take to become a leader in the future. In Part III, we began to address a pressing question: What should we do today? We began by describing how best to prepare for future leadership. Then we looked at an example of our world today to show how it can benefit from this understanding. Now, we ask the final question: How will we human beings need to change to inherit our future world?

No Wars

Perhaps the greatest value in knowing that a societal-level shift is coming is to avoid the greatest mistake of past shifts—war. The last level shift saw bloodshed in a great many countries, including Britain, France, Germany, Italy, Russia, and China. It seemed that it was a requirement to bring about the nation-state. We can avoid this. The nation-state has change mechanisms that fiefdoms generally do not have (i.e., elections). These work reliably well as long as those in power accept the idea that they work for the people, and they need to be ready to relinquish power, slowly, as people begin reaching the point where they can make more decisions for themselves. Perhaps by knowing in advance that such a change is under way, those in power will begin to adapt and make the transition a smooth one rather than a chaotic and forced one.

In addition to civil war, past societal-level shifts have seen a leading society conquer its neighbors in the name of unification. Prussia led the German Wars of Unification. The English Revolution was followed by campaigns against Scotland and Ireland. Russia bullied neighbors into joining its socialist republic. This next transition cannot be a forced marriage—it must be an engagement of partners with a desire for mutual benefit; otherwise, it will not last. To sustain the new governance basis, the political systems can only come together through cooperation. Even more critical, the people will have to see themselves as belonging to one entity. While no nation need lose its history or heritage to join a union (did Scotland lose its heritage when it joined the United Kingdom?), the people ultimately have to see themselves as belonging to the same enterprise—the same union.

Finally, every societal-level shift has been accompanied by bloodshed as the first-mover uses its newly acquired power to dominate other societies. Such empire creation has been the primary motivation for societies throughout history. This needs to change. The future world cannot afford such behavior. In 1942, England, Russia, Canada, and America cobbled together the alliance that would eventually defeat the Axis powers. Early arguments, bickering, and power struggles eventually gave way to cooperative resource coordination. Now imagine a system where similar resource levels were coordinated by an entity whose military and political systems were fully unified on a permanent basis. Even NATO does not have this. The first union needs to use any acquired power for everyone's benefit. Any attempt to exploit an advantage will eventually result in a retaliatory response anyway, so it is better to step off on the right foot in the first place. Those in power need to accept the idea that they need to serve others as well as themselves.

Reduced Competition

It is not enough to simply avoid going to war; societies in the future have to reduce their competitiveness against each other. The desire to beat a rival has been the primary motivation for progress for societies going back to the band era. In fact, the underlying premise of history (and of this book) has been societal competition: every time a society has gained an advantage, it has used that advantage against another society.

However, with nation-unions this becomes problematic. Nation-unions will have so much resource management capacity that even minor actions could have major consequences. Before this happens, the world needs to learn more restraint. Arguably, this has already begun, with the advent of the United Nations after World War II. While this was a good start, it cannot stop there. Ultimately, societies will have to concern themselves less about being on top.

A world of nation-unions may innately have less competition than today's world. There is a good possibility that several regions of the world will arrive at the next societal level at roughly the same time, since, unlike the transition to nation-state, everyone will know this one is happening and will make their move sooner rather than later. Arriving at roughly the same time means that no region will be able to amass a leadership power differential before others arrive. The result is a level of parity the world has not seen before. This could stave off competition as no society feels behind and obligated to catch up. No arms race results, and there is less struggle for power.

Furthermore, there will be fewer independent voices trying to be heard on the world stage. Right now, nations have to be competitive to get their views heard above the cacophony of issues and positions that exist. With the creation of South Sudan in July 2011, the United Nations grew to 193 member nations. In this setting, every nation is like a child in a large family, struggling to be heard. With a few large powers instead of a multitude, however, it is more likely that every region will receive adequate attention and representation. Scientists have determined that the human brain is hardwired to work in groups of about twelve people. When larger groups deal with complex issues, subgroups form to make the large group behave like a group of twelve again. This suggests that humankind may be predisposed toward ultimately having about twelve unions, though geography and values differences will drive the actual number to be higher than this. A marketplace with twelve or so vendors is substantially less competitive than a marketplace with 193 vendors. Hence, the chance to reduce competition among world societies does exist.[XCI]

Problem-Solving World Leadership

With greater parity in the world, a new style of leadership will be needed, one that focuses more on problem solving than on conquering one's neighbors or flexing one's muscles. The leadership motivations of the past will need to give way since they can be far more destructive in the future.

In a world of rough parity, leadership will no longer be based on the amount of leadership power a society has. Rather, it will be based on the stability and value a leader brings to the world stage. The leader that shows it can be a stabilizing force in world affairs will gain influence. The leader that shows it can help others will gain influence. The leader that acts selflessly will gain influence.

New leadership has to focus on problem solving. Problem-solving leaders create stability by ensuring everyone is so intertwined that no one has incentive to attack anyone else. Problem solvers create wealth by getting societies to work together to find new synergies. Problem solvers encourage sharing new ideas, without applying force. Problem solvers create stability by listening to others and addressing their needs.

While the world has slowly been moving in this direction since the creation of the United Nations, we still have a long way to go to achieve it fully. No world leader can afford to do this today—the world is not ready for it yet. However, with nation-unions, it becomes easier. With fewer entities to contend with, a leader can take a broader perspective on world affairs and be less focused on remaining competitive.

There will always be a leader: it is functional and it is human nature to have one. People naturally look to the leader for its opinion—people and nations alike want to see how well their positions align with those of the leader. However, with problem-solving leadership, the world can really focus on issues such as how best to manage our world's limited resources, how to provide a minimum standard of living for all the citizens of the world, and how to protect our world environment—things that take a backseat today.

Character Development

Finally, it is worth coming back to the impact that direct democracy will have on a society. In a society with direct democracy, elected officials will be less of a buffer between people's desires and the laws of society. The good news is that the laws will be more closely mapped to the values of the people. The scary news is that they will also more closely reflect the character of the people. While protections such as three-dimensional *stare decisis* can filter out rash actions due to fleeting passions and whims, the long-term legal code will eventually adapt. So a society composed of self-absorbed people will eventually create a legal code that supports self-absorption.

Because of this, the future of any society will depend more heavily upon the collective character of its people. It is often easy to admire the brash celebrity, the temper tantrum, or the loudmouth who seems to get his way, but ultimately this will have long-term consequences. People with good character will be needed to have a good society. There is no alternative.

As such, character development needs to be a priority. A society needs to value character development to ensure it will continue running properly. Therefore, a society's greatest priority is to develop its character, especially in its children—all of its children. Since the changes described in this book are generations away, there is still time to shape our children to become what society will need in the future. Let us make it our highest priority—otherwise, the consequences could be devastating. Either way, the future belongs to them.

...

The future is now known, more or less. While many of the details will change, it is hoped that the general direction has been accurately forecasted. These are simple trends extrapolated from the past into the future. Of course, the timing of events is subject to great variation; as history unfolds, it can be updated accordingly. In any case, it is hoped that this information will prove useful for many. It is not meant to prescribe policy or behavior as much as to provide a context for it—a framework for decision making. And while it will not be perfect, it provides information that might otherwise be unavailable.

The world is coming to its next inflection point in history; the society that wants to be a leader on the other side of it would be wise to begin planning for it early. Since these events are relatively far in the future, there is no need for a knee-jerk reaction. Rather, conscious deliberation on the type of leader a society wants to be, and on what it has to offer the world, would be an appropriate place to begin a discussion.

Epilogue

So how accurate are the predictions in this book? Only time will tell. My sense is that while the particulars may turn out differently, the overall direction is correct. Much of this sense comes from the events of recent years. I completed the original analysis in September 2010. Since that time, several events have occurred that tell me we are moving forward in the direction described. I will highlight some of the key ones.

Social media is perhaps the biggest change to happen to the world in the last seven years. While it was invented a few years before, it has really become popular within the last decade. I see it as evidence that the world is becoming more personalized and connected using computers. When I formed this idea almost ten years ago, I based it on what I called microcommunities that seemed to be springing up on the World Wide Web. This was based on my own experience looking for song lyrics over the Internet and noting that out of the hundreds of millions of people in America, a few of us had been looking for words to the same song in recent months. It was as though we shared a common bond centered on an old show tune. Now, this example is so passé it did not even rate a mention in the text. Facebook, Twitter, and other websites and apps have accelerated us toward collective decision making sooner than I ever imagined. I thought it would have taken at least another generation.

Also in the original analysis I spent a lot of time examining Barak Obama's use of social media in the 2008 US presidential campaign. I suggested that this was a harbinger of Internet usage in politics. Again, time has sprung forward so that now every presidential campaign has a social media and Internet strategy, and the current US president routinely uses Twitter to bypass the media altogether.

In the original analysis, I based my idea about the rise of a digital legal infrastructure on database taxonomies—essentially the way databases categorize information. Then in 2013 I bumped into a former coworker, whom I had not seen in four years. His new tool OpenPolicy™ blew me away. Twenty years vanished in an instant in that wine store.

I was similarly thunderstruck when I discovered the US Code had been put online in 2013. I had no inkling of it when I completed the digital infrastructure chapter in 2010. Back then, I was struggling to understand when we could expect such a thing to begin. A few years later, Congress answered that question.

In addition, now blockchain technology has made it more likely that secure online elections will be a part of our future. (This is something I added as I was trying to get this book ready for publishing—time is moving so quickly!)

Another momentous change that occurred during the last six years was the Arab Spring of 2011. During 2011 and early 2012, young people in over a dozen Middle East and North African countries revolted against their rulers, seeking reforms and democracy. While I was supportive of their cause, I was also skeptical. My time in Iraq during the summer of 2006 told me that most Arab countries were not quite ready for democracy because they had not embraced rule-of-law firmly enough. Without this underpinning, it was unlikely that democracy was going to succeed. Nevertheless, I hoped for the best.

When it looked like several revolutions were going to succeed, I considered rethinking my model: perhaps I had been too hard on what it took to transition from a fiefdom to a nation-state, or even from a dictatorship to a democracy; perhaps there was enough foundation after all. However, I put away my doubts when the revolutions turned south. Egypt deposed a dictator and replaced it with a military junta—one step forward, one step back. Libya regressed to multiple chiefdoms (militias) fighting for control. Syria degenerated into a prolonged civil war. It did work in Tunisia, however, where its people replaced a repressive dictator with a parliamentary government. So despite the less than ideal results, it did validate the governance basis progression model in that people innately want more control over their future and are looking for opportunities to get it; they just need the underlying foundation of rule-of-law to make it possible.

In a different way, I have gained confidence from another region's lack of progress. In June 2016, Britain held a referendum and decided to leave the European Union (EU)—Brexit they call it. This raises two points.

The first point is that this colloquy is consistent with the idea that the EU has gone as far as it can go without a change in governance. That Britain would leave the EU suggests the entity has remained fragile despite existing for more than twenty years. A preconditioning innovation is needed to create an environment where the nations insist that they strengthen their mutual ties, and an elevating innovation needs to make it possible. My expectation is that Britain will eventually have another vote and rejoin the EU.

The second point raised by Brexit is that it used a referendum to make a collective decision. The 2014 Scottish referendum on whether it should remain part of the United Kingdom was a watershed moment in European governance—as was Ireland's 2015 referendum on the definition of marriage. With Brexit, it has become an accepted tool for making even the highest legislative decisions—even if things did not go as planned. And with each use, the world learns more about how to use referendums, gaining experience as we go along.[1]

---

[1] Quite honestly, Brexit could be considered a lesson in what not to do. That such an important structural decision would be left to a simple majority demonstrates a lack of understanding in how to use this process. A supermajority of, say, at least five points (5%) would have been appropriate, as is common when making big decisions. The US Senate requires 60% to approve some key political appointments, and the US Constitution requires that 75% of state legislatures approve amendments. Alternatively, for Brexit, a double-major may have been the wisest approach. That would have required a simple majority of the overall popular vote, and a simple majority in three of the four member states (England, Wales, Scotland, and Northern

On a different note, in 2014, Russia created the Eurasian Economic Union. After this, it seized Crimea and began supporting separatist rebels in Ukraine. It seems that Russia is already moving toward union using a different approach and has already made it a priority to get there first. Having already been a nation-union may facilitate Russia's progress a second time around. However, the Eurasian Economic Union will reach the same limitation that the European Union encountered: a new governance basis is still required.

The preconditioning innovation is closer than I once thought. In 2007, when I deduced that nuclear fusion would most likely be the next preconditioning innovation, I felt I was going out on a limb—not that the answer was wrong, but that few would believe it; no one talked about fusion back then and even the international energy project, ITER, was struggling with political wrangling that stalled progress. All that has now changed. ITER got past its political bickering to create an enormous campus with buildings and installed equipment. While the National Ignition Facility's grand breakthrough did not occur, shock ignition and other approaches still provide cause for optimism, and the new Laser Mégajoule (LMJ) facility in Europe is going to make another run at breakeven next year. Meanwhile Korea has launched its K-DEMO program to scale prototype designs into operating power plants. (Both LMJ and K-DEMO were launched after my original analysis was completed in 2010.) And more players are getting involved. MIT has started redesigning its reactor to exploit new superconducting material that could shrink reactor size. Lockheed Martin claims it is building a reactor that will fit on the back of a pickup truck. Perhaps most interesting, commercial startups have begun to explore technologies bypassed by government mega-efforts—and they are attracting the capital to do it. As Time magazine put it in 2015,

> There is now a stealth scene of virtually unknown companies working on [fusion], doing the kind of highly practical rapid-

Ireland). Because of the way the referendum was conducted, however, Scotland is now preparing to revisit its 2014 referendum on whether to stay in the United Kingdom. A steep learning curve, indeed.

iteration development you can do only in the private sector. They're not funded by cumbersome grants; the money comes from heavy-hitting investors with an appetite for risk.

So lots of people are betting on fusion—governments, corporations, and even startup investors. Fusion is not the pipe dream it once was.

Speaking of superconductors, when I deduced their role in the future power grid, I was largely basing it on what I remembered as a mechanical engineering undergraduate in the 1980s, with some updated information. Again, it seemed like one of my more precarious positions. Then Germany installed the first superconducting power line in 2014, and it seemed the world leapt forward once again. It was not so precarious after all.

And while we are talking about power transmission, when I did the original analysis, the smart grid was just an idea. My position was based on the realization that the power grid was too old to support fusion and needed to be upgraded. Low and behold, the US government and the EU have already begun making their grids intelligent so they can route power more efficiently to where it is needed on a moment-by-moment basis. This means that even if fusion did not produce all of the power predicted, it may have the same impact because the power was being used more wisely. That I did not anticipate. [XCII]

So does this mean that everything will come to pass as described? Based on events that have occurred since 2010 (when I completed the original analysis), it appears that things are tracking pretty well. However, while I believe nearly all of the high-level direction will come true, I will concede that the particulars may be different. In any event, time is marching forward. And rather than simply waiting to see what happens, we can use an early look to plan, if we choose to do so. We may be able to shape our future by considering long-term implications when making today's decisions. In any event, it is worth starting the discussion.

Appendix
The Five Cons of Online Data Sourcing

Online data sources were indispensable to this analysis; it could not have been done without them. Information that would have taken days or weeks to find was found in minutes. Information that would have remained undiscovered was quickly located with web searches. Information that would have been cost prohibitive was freely available. Information that may have been shallow was treated in depth by crowdsources. Document text that would have required reading books to find was found in minutes with word searches. Indeed, this analysis could not have begun much earlier than it did in 2005.

However, online sources can also be dangerous. Needless to say there is a lot of noncredible information out there. While using online sources, I learned to separate credible information from noncredible information. I summarize those learnings in this appendix, calling it *The Five Cons of Online Data Sourcing*. In this case, *con* does not mean "against"; rather, it is a mnemonic for the criteria I used to discern a source's credibility. The first con is ...

Congruent. Believe it or not, your brain already knows a lot about subjects you never really thought much about. You have some idea of what sounds right or wrong about lots of subjects just from casual awareness. When something does not fit, it draws your attention quickly.

When scanning a lot of information about a new subject, you can generally rely on your intuition to tell you what makes sense and what does not. Your brain does a pretty good job of discerning whether it fits with what you already know (or believe). When it does not, you have to dig a little deeper. This means your brain automatically checks for congruence—how well new information ties in with prior knowledge.

If a source reaffirms what you already more-or-less know to be true, you can generally accept it as accurate. If something does not fit at all, it is a good candidate to be skipped altogether. What is more common, however, is that you will find you were partially right and partially wrong. In that case, you will need to spend time sorting it out. This approach allows you to economize your time. You do not have to drill down into every piece of data equally to ensure it is credible. You can focus your attention where it is needed most.

On the off chance you accepted something as true that was really false, in a large analysis, it will likely be exposed later, when it becomes incongruent with other material. There are lots of checks and balances in a large analysis. However, on occasion, you will know absolutely nothing about a subject, and you are totally dependent upon your sources to tell you. In that case you look for data that is …

Consistent. Sometimes, you will stumble across an idea you have never heard of; or perhaps it contradicts what you already believe. In these cases, you will want to look at multiple sources and check whether they are saying the same thing or presenting different positions. If the bulk of the sources say the same thing, you can generally believe you have discovered the general consensus on a subject. In this analysis, I typically went with the general consensus of the experts working in a field. However, if I found something incongruent between their position and my other research, then had I to dig deeper.

It was often the case, however, that there would be a majority position and a minority position on a subject. Sometimes, I found myself supporting a minority position that was more congruent with my other findings. I do not recall ever having to create a new position in a field that had been researched for a long time.

Again, this approach economizes your time. There is little point in reconfirming what everyone already accepts as truth. It is better to spend your time focusing on other areas. However, sometimes there is no consensus on a subject and the few research papers that do exist contradict each other. All else being equal, you look for the one that is more ...

Convergent. Convergent is how well a source uses data to support its position—that is, how well the facts converge around the point being made. Technical documents and scientific reports are the best for this. Blogs are the worst. Most of the time, the difference is readily apparent. Some authors give a subject a comprehensive treatment, packing lots of precise data around the conclusion they draw. Depending upon what you are using the source for, you will not even use the detail—you will only need the Abstract.

As a rule of thumb, I did not use blogs. Blogs contain lots of general statements and often reflect opinions more than facts. On a couple of occasions I used them when they were written by an insider (such as a Washington staffer writing about the dysfunction in Congress) or by a known expert in the field. Blogs can be useful for ideas or finding new data sources, however, but this means corroborating any information with other sources. The main problem with blogs, and why they were often not trustworthy, is that they were not ...

Consequential. Consequential means there is a consequence to an author being wrong. When it matters that an author is right or wrong, the author will generally put more effort into his work and become more credible. Blogs are often ideas put out for discussion—they are not meant to be authoritative. If the author is challenged, he can simply say he changed his mind and that ends it for him. However, if you mistake a discussion source for an authoritative source, it is a big problem. In general, blog statements are treated as ideas, not data, and cannot be used until corroborated with other sources.

The opposite of blogs are academic sources. By their nature, college and university research had to be scrupulously checked by many people. No university wants to lose its reputation by publishing bogus or weak material. Even when a university posts research from a professor who is considered an outlier in his field (which is how knowledge is often stretched), it is still vouching for the conduct of the research: it is putting its brand behind the professor's work. Disclaimers that these are not the opinions of the university will not work either (though I never encountered this): from a branding standpoint, the university is responsible for what appears on its website, regardless of legalities. Other organizations are in similar positions, including think tanks, certain specialty nonprofit organizations, or anyone with a reputation to lose. (This should not frighten universities from posting material; in general, I found works posted on university websites were some of the best, most comfortable sources to use.)

Regardless of which organization is posting data, however, the would-be user of data needs to ensure the source is ...

Uncontaminated. Uncontaminated means there is no overt bias or agenda present in the data. These are not hard to discern: when people have an agenda, it is usually obvious, and it casts suspicion on everything they write. While we all know that words can paint a backdrop that contains bias (e.g., a newscast), these are generally not the problem. Of greater concern are political articles or articles written by people with an agenda to rewrite history in a certain way. While the source may not be worthless, at best it has to be treated as a blog. If it was grossly biased, I skipped it entirely.

These are the Five Cons. Their value lies in helping the researcher discern trustworthy online data from less-than-trustworthy data. They also help the researcher economize effort, by guiding her through the myriad of material on the web. With these principles, I felt comfortable working with online sources. While my criteria may not have been foolproof, the benefit of using online sources far outweighs the risk. Overtime, online sourcing will continue to improve, becoming even more robust: I saw it improve in the eleven years I took to do this analysis.

ENDNOTES

The endnotes for this book are grouped by section within each chapter. The nature of the analysis used to create the book precluded line citations (too dynamic). However, sources used to help create each section are accurately captured.

¹ Prologue

Central Intelligence Agency, *World Factbook, 2015*, 2015, https://www.cia.gov/library/publications/the-world-factbook/rankorder/2244rank.html (accessed February, 17, 2016).

Am J Hum Genet, *The Use of Racial, Ethnic, and Ancestral Categories in Human Genetics Research*, National Human Genome Research Institute, Bethesda, August 29, 2005, doi:10.1086/491747.

Natalie Angier, "Do Races Differ? Not Really, DNA Shows," *Science*, 22 Aug 2000, http://www.nytimes.com/library/national/science/082200sci-genetics-race.html (accessed May 5, 2017).

"Race in a Genetic World," *John Harvard's Journal*, May-June 2008, http://harvardmagazine.com/2008/05 (accessed May 5, 2017).

Lynne B Jorde and Stephen P Wooding, "Genetic variation, classification and 'race'," *Nature Genetics* 36, no. S28-S33 (2004); doi:10.1038/ng1435.

Mark Schoofs, "What DNA Says About Human Ancestry—and Bigotry," Village Voice, MIT, http://web.mit.edu/racescience/in_media (accessed May 5, 2017).

Maurice White, "Why Your Race Isn't Genetic," Pacific Standard, 30 May 2014, https://psmag.com/environment/why-your-race-isnt-genetic-82475 (accessed May 5, 2017).

II *Chapter 2*

Wikipedia, s.v. "Sociocultural Evolution," last modified February 12, 2009, http://en.wikipedia.org/wiki/Sociocultural_evolution (accessed February 17, 2009).

III This was the main treatise of Jared Diamond's Pulitzer Prize–winning book *Guns, Germs, and Steel* (New York: Norton, 1999).

IV *Chapter 3*

Sesana and Others v. Attorney General, 52/2002 (Botswana HC. Dec. 13, 2006), South African Legal Information Institute, http://www.saflii.org/bw/cases/BWHC/2006/1.html (accessed September 18, 2013).

United Nations Department of Economic and Social Affairs, "State of the World's Indigenous Peoples," December 2009, http://www.un.org/esa/socdev/unpfii/documents/SOWIP_web.pdf (accessed September 18, 2013).

"Botswana: Culture under Threat—Special Report on the San Bushmen," IRIN, March 5, 2004, http://www.irinnews.org/report/48908 (accessed September 18, 2013).

"G/wi React to Desert Life," Peaceful Societies, March 22, 2012, http://www.peacefulsocieties.org/NAR12/120322gwi.html (accessed September 18, 2013).

V Jared Diamond, *Guns, Germs, and Steel* (New York: Norton, 1999), 267–292.

VI *Wikipedia*, s.v. "Prehistoric Britain," last modified September 27, 2006, http://en.wikipedia.org/wiki/Ancient_Britain (accessed September 30, 2006).

Wikipedia, s.v. "Cro-Magnon," last modified September 19, 2013, http://en.wikipedia.org/wiki/Cro-Magnon (accessed September 24, 2013).

Wikipedia, s.v. "Prehistoric Settlement of the British Isles," last modified August 1, 2013, http://en.wikipeida.org/wiki/Prehistoric_settlement_of_the_British_Isles (accessed September 24, 2013)

There is some dispute over the earliest modern man in Britain. Another source places it at only 41,500 years ago, depending upon whether an older finding was Neanderthal or modern man. There is also dispute on when the land bridge disappeared, 8500 BCE or 6500 BCE.

Wikipedia, "Prehistoric Britain" September 27, 2006.

"Celtic Britain (The Iron Age)," Britain Express, accessed September 12, 2006, http://www.britainexpress.com/History/Celtic_Britain.htm

Wikipedia, "Prehistoric Britain," September 27, 2006.

Wikipedia, "Neolithic British Isles," July 18, 2013.

Wikipedia, "Bronze Age Britain," August 18, 2013.

Wikipedia, "Hillforts in Britain," May 27, 2013.

There is another timing dispute over whether the invasions took place between 900 and 500 or 500 an 100 BCE. Different sources say different things.

Wikipedia, "Anglo-Saxon England" September 25, 2013.

Wikipedia, "Cro-Magnon," September 19, 2013.

Wikipedia, "History of Anglo-Saxon England," September 1, 2009.

Wikipedia, "Roman Conquest of Britain," September 7, 2013.

Wikipedia, "Iron Age Tribes in Britain," July 4, 2013.

Wikipedia, "Hadrian's Wall," September 25, 2013.

Wikipedia, "Augustus," September 9, 2013.

Wikipedia, "Roman Republic," September 24, 2013.

"Magna Carta History," St. Edmundsbury Borough Council, accessed September 12, 2006, http://www.steedmundsbury.gov.uk.

"Parliament: The Political Institution," United Kingdom Parliament, January 27, 2007, http://www.parliament.uk/about/history/institution.cfm (accessed February 1, 2007).

Mike Ibeji, "An Overview of Roman Britain," BBC, June 1, 2001, http://bbc.co.uk/history/ancient/romans/questions_02.shtml (accessed September 9, 2008).

VII Diamond, *Guns, Germs, and Steel,* 109.

Geoffrey Orloff, *The Clo-e People,* National Geographic Channel, television documentary, 2008.

Guy Gugliotta, "The Great Human Migration," *Smithsonian,* July 2008, http://smithsonianmag.com/history/the-great-human-migration-13561 (accessed January 9, 2016).

Wikipedia, "Origins of Speech," January 2016.

Wikipedia, "Fertile Crescent," January 29, 2016.

Ancient History Encyclopedia, s.v. "Fertile Crescent," by Joshua Mark, September 2, 2009, http://www.ancient.eu/Fertile_Crescent (accessed February 26, 2016).

Ancient History Encyclopedia, s.v. "Mesopotamia," by Joshua Mark, September 2, 2009, http://www.ancient.eu/Mesopotamia (accessed March 3, 2016).

Wikipedia, "Samarra culture" July 1, 2015.

Wikipedia, "Ubaid period," February 25, 2016.

About.com, s.v. "Uruk Period Mesopotamia: The Rise of Sumer," by Kris Hirst, 2016, http://archaeology.about.com/od/mesopotamiaarchaeology/fl/Uruk-Period-Mesopotamia-The-Rise-of-Sumer.htm (accessed March 2, 2016).

Wikipedia, "Uruk period," February 28, 2016.

Wikipedia, "History of Sumer," February 26, 2016.

VIII Paul Kennedy, *The Rise and Fall of the Great Powers* (New York: Random House, 1987), 347.

Diamond, *Guns, Germs, and Steel*, 289.

Chapter 4

IX Jared Diamond, *Guns, Germs, and Steel* (New York: Norton, 1999), 267–292.

Candice Millard, *The River of Doubt* (New York: Broadway Books, 2005), 223.

Millard, *The River of Doubt*, 228.

"Art and Life in Africa," University of Iowa Museum of Art, November 3, 1998, http://www.uiowa.edu/~africart/toc/people/Frafra.html (accessed October 1, 2013).

Antonio Giustozzi, "Don't Call That Warlord a Warlord," Foreign Policy, February 25, 2010, http://foreignpolicy.com/2010/02/25/dont-call-that-warlord-a-warlord-2/

Wikipedia, *Saudi Arabia,* September 28, 2013, http://en.wikipedia.org/wiki/Saudi_Arabia (accessed October 2, 2013), furnished under Creative Commons License, reference https://creativecommons.org/licenses/by-sa/3.0/

X I use a narrower definition of *nation-state* than typical. My definition of nation-state requires it to operate according to a constitution:

A sovereign state that is inhabited by a group of people who share a feeling of common nationality and that operates according to a mutually shared and accepted constitution.

The typical definition leaves out that requirement:

A sovereign state inhabited by a relatively homogeneous group of people who share a feeling of common nationality (*Random House*).

The typical definition is missing the key attribute that distinguishes modern governments from earlier ones—operating by constitution. The added clause captures this, and with it the change in societies ushered in at the beginning of the Modern Era. The clause even clarifies which societies today are true nation-states and which ones are really monarchies (even if their leader is called president instead of king).

^{XI} *Chapter 5*

innovation. Dictionary.com. Dictionary.com Unabridged. Random House, Inc. http://www.dictionary.com/browse/innovation (accessed February 21, 2017).

Dictionary.com, "Technology," 2013.

^{XII} Jared Diamond, *Guns, Germs, and Steel* (New York: Norton, 1999), 103, 224.

^{XIII} Dan Vergano, "Arrow Origins Traced to Africa," *USA Today*, June 20, 2011, http://usatoday30.usatoday.com/tech/science/columnist/vergano/2011-06-19-bow-arrows-origin (accessed October 8, 2013).

Chapter 6

^{XIV} Jared Diamond. *Guns, Germs, and Steel* (New York: Norton, 1999), 260.

Wikipedia, "Origin of Speech," January 2016.

Ray Jackendoff, "How Did Language Begin?" *Linguistic Society of America*, August 2006, http://www.linguisticsociety.org (accessed January 11, 2016).

Wikipedia, "Linguistic Relativity," January 7, 2016.

Michael Balter, "Human Language May Have Evolved to Help Our Ancestors Make Tools," *Science*, January 13, 2015, http://news.science.org/archaeology/2015/01/human-language-may-have-evolved-help (accessed January 9, 2016).

Greg Downey, "Life Without Language," *Neoroanthropology*, July 21, 2010, http://neuroanthropology.net/2010/07/21/life-without-language (accessed January 9, 2016).

Wikipedia, "Bow and Arrow," January 10, 2016.

Susan Schaller, *A Man Without Words* (Berkeley: University of California Press, 2012).

Guy Gugliotta, "The Great Human Migration," *Smithsonian*, July 2008, http://www.smithsonianmag.com/history/the-great-human-migration-13561 (accessed January 9, 2016).

^{XV} Diamond, *Guns, Germs, and Steel*, 271–277.

James E. Krier, "Evolutionary Theory and the Origin of Property Rights," *Cornell Law Review* 95 (2009): 139–160, edited by University of Michigan Law School.

Robert C. Ellickson, "Stone-Age Property in Domestic Animals," *Yale Law & Economics Research*, paper no. 468 (May 13, 2013), http://ssrn.com/abstract=2241675 (accessed March 12, 2016).

^{XVI} Timothy Wall, "Amazonian Tribal Warfare Sheds Light on Modern

Violence, Says MU Anthropologist," *University of Missouri, News Bureau,* October 2, 2012, http://munews.missouri.edu/news-releases/2012/1002-amazonian-tribal-warfare-sheds-light-on-modern-violence-says-mu-anthropologist.

XVII Diamond, *Guns, Germs, and Steel,* 280–281.

Christopher Dewdney, "The History of Language and Writing," in *Light Onwords/Light Onwards* (Conference proceedings, York University, November, 14–16, 2002).

Wikipedia, "Proto-writing," October 1, 2013.

Wikipedia, "Cuneiform," October 10, 2013.

Wikipedia, "Uruk," September 24, 2013.

Wikipedia, "Uruk Period," October 7, 2013.

Wikipedia, "History of Egypt," October 7, 2013.

Wikipedia, "Egyptian Hieroglyphics," October 2013.

Wikipedia, "History of Ancient Egypt," October 2013.

Wikipedia, "Early Dynastic Period of Egypt," October 9, 2013.

Wikipedia, "Olmec," October 17, 2013.

Wikipedia, "Zapotec Civilization," October 12, 2013.

Wikipedia, "Maya Civilization," September 19, 2013.

Wikipedia, "Maya Codices," October 13, 2013.

Wikipedia, "Shang Dynasty," October 16, 2013.

Wikipedia, "Chinese Character," October 11, 2013.

Wikipedia, "Yellow Emporer," October 16, 2013.

Wikipedia, "Xia Dynasty," October 7, 2013.

About.com, s.v. "Monte Alban," by Kris K. Hirst, http://archaeology.about.com/od/ancientcivilizations/a/zapotec.htm (accessed October 18, 2013).

Ask.com, s.v. "Mesoamerican Writing Systems," September 20, 2013, http://www.ask.com/wiki/Mesoamerican_writing_systems (accessed October 17, 2013).

"Mesoamerican Writing Systems," Ancient Scripts, 2012, http://www.ancientscripts.com/ma_ws.html (accessed October 17, 2013).

XVIII Elizabeth Eisenstein, *The Printing Revolution in Early Modern Europe* (Cambridge: Cambridge University Press, 2007), 42–303.

Kristina Ross, "Mass Culture," University of Minnesota Media History Project, 1995, http://www.mediahistory.umn.edu/masscult.html (accessed March 9, 2007).

Paul Kennedy, *The Rise and Fall of the Great Powers* (New York: Random House, 1987), 73–86.

Wikipedia, "Peloponnesian War," October 18, 2013.

Wikipedia, "Classical Athens," October 15, 2013.

Fred D. Miller, "The Rule of Law in Ancient Greek Thought," Springer Link, 2010, http://link.springer.com/chapter 10/10.1007/978-90-481-3749-7_2 (accessed October 22, 2013).

Thomas R. Martin, "An Overview of Classical Greek History from Mycenae to Alexander," Tufts University, September 25, 1996, http://www.perseus.tufts.edu/hopper (accessed October 23, 2013).

Wikipedia, "Roman Republic," September 24, 2013.

John Baker, The Oxford History of the Laws of England (London: Oxford University Press, 2003).

Wikipedia, "Woodblock Printing," November 1, 2013.

Wikipedia, "Printing Press," November 2, 2013.

"Gutenberg's Print Shop," Harry Ransom Center, University of Texas, http://www.hrc.utexas.edu/educator/modules/gutenberg/invention/printshop (accessed November 5, 2013).

Wikipedia, "Johannes Gutenberg," October 4, 2013.

Wikipedia, "Movable Type," October 21, 2013.

"An Introduction to Printing," Britain in Print, 2003, http://www.britaininprint.net/introtoprint/england.htm (accessed July 24, 2009).

Steven Kreis, "The Printing Press," The History Guide, May 13, 2004, http://www.historyguide.org/intellect/press.html (accessed July 27, 2009).

XIX *Chapter 7*
Damian Carrington, "Da Vinci's Parachute Flies," BBC, June 27, 2000, http://news.bbc.co.uk/2/hi/science/nature/808246.stm (accessed November 18, 2013).

Jan Meyer, "An Introduction of Deployable Recovery Systems," *Historical Review*, excerpt from Sandia Report SAND85-1180, August 1985, http://www.parachutehistory.com/eng/drs.html (accessed November 18, 2013).

Wikipedia, "Parachutes," November 17, 2013.

Levi Buchanan, "The Sega Channel: This Genesis Download Service Was Way, Way Ahead of Its Time," IGN, June 11, 2008, http://www.ign.com/articles/2008/06/11/ (accessed November 19, 2013).

"Sega Channel: The First Real Downloadable Content," Sega-16, 2013, http://www.sega-16.com/2004/12/sega-channel-the-first-real-dowloadable-content/ (accessed November 19, 2013).

"Sega Channel," Sega Retro, October 17, 2013, http://segaretro.org/Sega_Channel (accessed November 19, 2013).

"Technology Before Its Time," Techspot, 2013, http://www.techspot.com (accessed November 15, 2013).

^{XX} Jared Diamond, *Guns, Germs, and Steel* (New York: Norton, 1999), 92, 99, 205, 271.

Gregory K. Dow, Nancy Olewiler, and Clyde Reed, "The Transition to Agriculture: Climate Reversals, Population Density, and Technical Change," January 2005, available at SSRN: https://ssrn.com/abstract=698342 or http://dx.doi.org/10.2139/ssrn.698342.

Robert C. Ellickson, "Stone-Age Property in Domestic Animals," *Yale Law & Economics Research Paper No. 468* (March 29, 2013), Social Science Research Network, http://papers.ssrn.com/sol3/papers.cfm (accessed March 12, 2016).

Ainit Snir et al., "The Origin of Cultivation and Proto-weeds, Long Before Neolithic Farming," edited by Sergei Volis, July 22, 2015, *PLOS One*, http://journals.plos.org/plosone/article?id=10.1371/journal.pone.0131422 (accessed March 16, 2016).

Ancient History Encyclopedia, s.v. "Animal Husbandry," by Joshua Mark, July 27, 2010, http://www.ancient.eu/Animal_Husbandry (accessed March 15, 2016).

Andrew B. Smith, "Animal Husbandry, Nomadic Breeding, and Domestication of Animals," UNESCO-EOLSS, http://www.eolss.net/sample-chapters/c10 (accessed March 15, 2016).

^{XXI} At this point it is worth confirming that Specialized Labor is truly an innovation. Our definition of innovation is "an idea or insight applied to solve a problem or exploit an opportunity." Labor specialization was an idea—it was not practiced before the end of the tribal era; and when it was, it was a scant activity. The innovation was not simply weaving a basket or firing a clay pot—people had known how to do those for centuries. The innovation was whether such tasks could be performed on a full-time basis in exchange for food—something that had never been done before. Furthermore, this idea solved a problem—there were not enough baskets to store food or jars to store liquids; and it exploited an opportunity—it took advantage of new surplus food stores. As such, labor specialization meets our criteria for being an innovation. However, there is another consideration.

Risk made labor specialization an innovation rather than an inevitable next step. As obvious as labor specialization might sound to us today, it involved real risk back when it was conceived. The entrepreneur had to test whether he could make a full-time living at it, instead of producing his own food. Customers had to part with their surplus food, even though they may be one bad crop away from starvation. At some point, people simply had to take a chance and try it. With any innovation, there has to be the risk of failure; otherwise, the idea is simply the inevitable next step in a long course of action. With labor specialization, both suppliers and customers were trying something that had never been done before, and there was risk that it would not work.

It did work, however. Once the concept was proven, it became a foundation that was applied in multiple areas. Basketry was the first area, quickly followed by pottery, then by brickmaking, spinning, weaving, milling, and a host of other specialized inventions created before the first chiefdom ever arose in 5500 BCE. Yes, specialized labor was an innovation that made a permanent impact on our world in the seventh millennium BCE.

[XXII] Diamond, *Guns, Germs, and Steel*, 63, 271–277.

Roy Davies and Glyn Davies, "A Comparative Chronology of Money," Chronology of Money—History 9000-1 B.C., 1999, http:projects.exeter.ac.uk/RDavies/arian/amser/chrono1.html (accessed November 22, 2013).

"The History of Money," NOVA, October 26, 1996, http://www.pbs.org.wgbh/novaancient/history-money.html (accessed November 22, 2013).

Wikipedia, "Barter," November 12, 2013.

Wikipedia, "Gift economy," November 23, 2013.

AP Worldipedia, "The Neolithic Revolution and Early Agricultural Societies," May 17, 2015, http://apworldipedia.com/ (accessed March 17, 2016).

Wikipedia, "Redistribution (cultural anthropology)," October 12, 2015.

Wikipedia, "History of bread," March 8, 2016.

Pat Strauss, "Baskets: These Woven Wonders Are the World's Oldest Multipurpose Utensils," *Morning Call*, April 6, 1986, http://articles.mcall.com/1986-04-06/features/2531312_1_basketmaking-reeds-grasses (accessed March 20, 2016).

Bamber Gascoigne, "History of Pottery and Procelain," HistoryWorld, 2016, http://www.historyworld.net/wrldhis/PlainTextHistories.asp?historyid=ab98 (accessed March 17, 2016).

Gascoigne, "History of Technology," 2016.

Gascoigne, "Inventions and Discoveries," 2016.

Philip E. L. Smith, "Ganj Dareh Tepe," *Paleorient* (1974): 207–209.

"Mesopotamia: Mesopotamian Art (Mesopotamia, 7000–2400 B.C.)," Antiquities Experts, 2016, http://www.antiquitiesexperts.com/near-east_early.html (accessed March 20, 2016).

Wikipedia, "Pottery," March 5, 2016.

"The History of Bricks," Brick Directory, 2014, http://www.brickdirectory.co.uk/html/brick_history.html (accessed March 20, 2016).

"Milling: A Brief History," Cottage Grove Farmhouse, 2016, http://cgfarmhouse.com/home/cgf/page_58/milling_a_brief_history.html (accessed March 17, 2016).

Steven Pinker, "Violence Vanquished," *Wall Street Journal*, September 24, 2011.

XXIII *Wikipedia*, "Ubaid Period," October 27, 2013.

American Heritage Science Dictionary, s.v. "Mathematics," edited by Houghton Mifflin Company, http://dictionary.reference.com/browse/mathematics (accessed December 2, 2013).

Wikipedia, "Proto-writing," October 1, 2013.

Wikipedia, "History of Mathematics," November 27, 2013.

Wikipedia, "Tally stick," Novemeber 12, 2013.

Wikipedia, "Prehistoric Numerals," August 30, 2013.

CDLI:Wiki, s.v. "Uruk (Modern Warka)," edited by University of Oxford, December 13, 2011, http://cdli.ox.ac.uk/wiki/doku.php?id=uruk_mod._warka (accessed December 2, 2013).

Christopher Dewdney, "The History of Language and Writing," in *Light Onwords/Light Onwards* (Conference proceedings, York University, November, 14–16, 2002).

Jack Kilmon, "The History of Writing," http://www.historian.net/bywrite.htm (accessed October 21, 2005).

Wikipedia, "Writing," October 21, 2005.

Wikipedia, "Cuneiform," October 10, 2013.

William N. Goetzmann, "Financing Civilization," Yale University, http://viking.som.yale.edu/will/finciv/chapter1.htm (accessed December 2, 2013).

"Mesoamerican Writing Systems," Ancient Scripts, 2012, http://www.ancientscripts.com/ma_ws.html (accessed October 17, 2013).

Kevin Callahan, "Mesoamerican Writing Systems," 1997, http://www.angelfire.com/ca/humanorigins/writing.html (accessed October 17, 2013).

Wikipedia, "Maya Civilization," September 19, 2013.

Wikipedia, "Zapotec Civilization," October 12, 2013.

About.com, s.v. "Monte Alban: Capital City of the Zapotec Civilization," by K Kris Hirst, http://archaeology.about.com/od/ancientcivilizations/a/zapotec.htm (accessed October 18, 2013).

Wikipedia, "Olmecs," October 17, 2013.

Wikipedia, "Maya Codices," October 13, 2013.

Chen Shimin, "Rise and Fall of Debit-Credit Bookkeeping in China," *Accounting Historians Journal* 25, no. 1 (June 1998): 73–92, http://www.chinaaccounting.cn/resources/2011/0529/61489.shtml (accessed December 9, 2013).

Lawrence Lo, "Chinese," Ancient Scripts, 2012, http://ancientscripts.com/chinese.html (accessed December 3, 2013).

Wikipedia, "Oracle Bone Script," November 20, 2013.

Wikipedia, "Chinese Mathematics," October 3, 2013.

Encyclopedia Britannica, "Shang dynasty," 2013.

"Chinese Calendar," Beijing Xindong International Travel Service, 2012, http://www.beijingservice.com/beijinghighlights/chinesecalendar.htm (accessed December 9, 2013).

Wikipedia, "Burning of Books and Burying of Scholars," December 5, 2013.

Wikipedia, "Chinese Astronomy," November 19, 2013.

Wikipedia, "Chinese Calendar," December 6, 2013.

Wikipedia, "Neolithic Signs in China," October 25, 2013.

Lucy C. Lee, "A Manuscript of China's History of Accounting," Accounting Information, 2013, http://www.accountingin.com/accounting=historians-journal/volume-14-2 (accessed December 3, 2013).

Maxwell Aiken and Lu Wei, "Historical Instances of Innovative Accounting Practices in the Chinese Dynasties and Beyond," *Accounting Historians Journal* 20, no. 2 (December 1993): 163–186, http://www.jstor.org/discover/10.2307/ (accessed December 3, 2013).

Wikipedia, "Chinese Numerals," November 20, 2013.

Wikipedia, "Xia dynasty," October 7, 2013.

Wikipedia, "Shang dynasty," October 16, 2013.

J. J. O'Connor and E. F. Robertson, "An Overview of Egyptian Mathematics," December 2000, MacTutor History of Mathematics Achives, University of St. Andrews, http://www-history.mcs.st-andrews.ac.uk/HistTopics/Egyptian_mathematics.html (accessed December 9, 2013).

Wikipedia, "Egyptian Mathematics," November 20, 2013.

Wikipedia, "Egyptian Hieroglyphs," October 2013.

Wikipedia, "History of Egypt," October 7, 2013.

Wikipedia, "History of Ancient Egypt," October 2013.

Wikipedia, "Early Dynastic Period of Egypt," October 9, 2013.

Wikipedia, "Sequoyah," December 16, 2013.

"Ancient China," British Museum, October 22, 2007, http://www.ancientchina.co.uk/staff/resources/background (accessed April 20, 2016).

"Prehistory," China Connection Tours, 2016, http://www.chinatour.cn/Chinese-History/Prehistory.htm (accessed April 20, 2016).

Ulrich Theobald, "Prehistoric Cultures of China," China Knowledge, 2000, http://www.chinaknowledge.de/History/Myth/prehistory-event.html (accessed April 20, 2016).

Ren Shinan, "Several Major Achievements in Early Neolithic China, ca 5000 BC," *Kaogu Archaeology* (1996): 37–49, translated by Wing Kam Cheung, edited by B. Gordon, Ancient Chinese Rice Archeological Project, http://http-server.carleton.ca/bgordon/Rice/papers/REN94.htm (accessed April 20, 2016).

"Neolithic Period in China," Metropolitan Museum of Art, October 2004, http://www.metmuseum.org/toah/hd/cneo/hd_cneo.htm (accessed April 20, 2016).

Art Encyclopedia, s.v. "Neolithic Art in China," July 20, 2015, http://www.visual-arts-cork.com/east-asian-art/chinese-neolithic.htm (accessed April 20, 2016).

He Nu, "Exploring the Earliest State of China: New Archaeological Evidence from Taosi," Institute of Archaeology, Chinese Academy of Social Sciences, October 20, 2014, http://www.kaogu.cn/en/Research_work/Exploration_on_the_origin_of_Ch/2014/1020/47911.html (accessed April 27, 2016).

He Nu, "Taosi Site Marks the Origin of 'Central Point,'" Chinese Social Sciences Today, December 5, 2014, http://www.csstoday.com/Item/1477.aspx (accessed April 21, 2016).

Wikipedia, "Taosi," August 29, 2015.

He Nu, "The Longshan Period Site of Taosi in Southern Shanxi Province," in *A Companion to Chinese Archaeology*, edited by Anne P. Underhill (Chichester: Wiley, 2013), Blackwell Reference Online, doi: 10.1002/9781118325698.ch13

Ancient History Encylopedia, s.v. "Xia Dynasty," by Emily Mark, January 10, 2016, http://www.ancient.eu/Xia_Dynasty (accessed April 4, 2016).

Wikipedia, "Xia Dynasty," April 20, 2016.

"Xia Dynasty," ChinatownConnection.com, 2005, http://www.chinatownconnection.com/xia-dynasty.htm (accessed April 21, 2016).

"Xia Dynasty," ChinaCulture.org, September 2003, http://www.chinaculture.org/gb/en_aboutchina/2003-09/24/content_22684.htm (accessed April 21, 2016).

Encyclopedia Britannica, "China," December 28, 2015.

World Heritage Encyclopedia, "Burning of Books and Burying of Scholars," World Public Library, http://www.worldlibrary.org/articles/burning_of_books_and_burying_of_scholars#cite_note-12 (accessed April 21, 2016).

Wikpedia, "Cascajal Block," March 19, 2016.

"Late Preclassic (300 B.C.–A.D. 300)," National Institute of Culture and History (Belize), http://www.nichbelize.org/ia-archaeology/late-presclassic/ (accessed April 17, 2016).

Wikipedia, "Preclassic Maya," March 25, 2016.

"The Mayan Pre-Classic Era," History on the Net, August 14, 2014. http://www.historyonthenet.com/mayans/the-mayan-pre-classic-era (accessed April 17, 2016).

"Preclassic Period," University of California Santa Barbara, Mesoamerican Research Center, 2010, http://www.ucsb.edu/research/maya/ancient-maya-civilization/preclassic-period (accessed April 17, 2016).

Ancient History Encylopedia, "Maya Government," by Maria Gomez, May 1, 2015, http://www.ancient.eu/Maya_Government (accessed April 17, 2016).

Ryan Johnson and Cristen Conger, "How the Mayan Calendar Works," How Stuff Works, December 27, 2007, http://people.howstuffworks.com/mayan-calendar.htm (accessed April 16, 2016).

"History," Mixtec.org, Latin American Studies Department, San Diego State University, 2012, http://www-rohan.sdsu.edu/mixtec/history.html (accessed March 29, 2016).

About.com, s.v. "The Mixtec," 2016, http://archaeology.about.com/od/mterms/a/mixtec_culture.htm (accessed March 29, 2016).

"Aztec," Ancient Scripts, http://www.ancientscripts.com/aztec.html (accessed March 30, 2016).

"Mixtec," Ancient Scripts, http://www.ancientscripts.com/mixtec.html (accessed March 29, 2016).

"Mixtec Religion," StasoSphere.com, 2016, http://www.meta-religion.com/World_Religions/Ancient_religions/Central_america/mixte_religion (accessed March 29, 2016).

Encyclopedia Britannica, "Teotihuacan," 2016.

James W. Dow, "Astonomical Observations at Teotihuacan," *American Antiquity* 32, no. 3 (1967): 326–334.

"Aztecs," History.com, 2009, http://www.history.com/topics/aztecs (accessed March 30, 2016).

Ancient History Encyclopedia, "Aztec Civilization," by Mark Cartwright, February 26, 2014, http://www.ancient.eu/Aztec_Civilization (accessed March 30, 2016).

Wikipedia, "Aztec," March 21, 2016.

"Aztec Commercial and Tax Law," Tarlton Law Library, University of Texas, 2014, https://tarlton.law.utexas.edu/exhibits/aztec_commecial.html (accessed

March 30, 2016).

Brian Handwerk, "Aztec Math Decoded Reveals Woes of Ancient Tax Time," *National Geographic*, April 3, 2008, http://news.nationalgeographic.com/news/2008/04/080403-aztec-math.html (accessed March 30, 2016).

Constance Holden, "How Aztecs Did the Math," *Science,* April 3, 2008, http://www.sciencemag.org/news/2008/04/how-aztecs-did-math (accessed March 30, 2016).

Gascoigne, "History of the Aztecs," March 30, 2016.

Wikipedia, "Moctezuma I," February 2, 2016.

Wikipedia, "Moctezuma II," April 8, 2016.

Wikipedia, "Nahuatl," March 20, 2016.

Kenneth G. Hirth and Joanna Pillsbury, *Merchants, Markets, and Exchange in the Pre-Columbian World* (Washington, DC: Dumbarton Oaks, 2014).

Gary J. Previts, Peter Walton, and Peter Wolnizer, *A Global History of Accounting, Financial Reporting and Public Policy: Americas* (Bingley: Emerald Publishing Group, 2011).

"Mayan Religion," ReligionFacts, November 10, 2015, http://www.religionfacts.com/mayan-religion (accessed March 24, 2016).

Andie Byrnes, "Neolithic Cairo," September 17, 2005, http://faiyum.com/html/neolithic_cairo.html (accessed April 22, 2016).

Andie Byrnes, "Neolithic Faiyum," September 17, 2005.

Wikipedia, "Badari culture," February 23, 2016.

About.com, s.v. "Nabta Playa (Egypt)," by Kris Hirst, 2016, http://archaeology.about.com/od/nterms/g/nabta_playa.htm (accessed April 22, 2016).

Fred Wendorf and Romuald Schild. "Nabta Playa and Its Role in Northeastern African Prehistory," *Journal of Anthropological Archaeology* 17 (January 1998): 97–119.

"Egypt and Egyptian Antiquities, Pre and Early Dynastic Period (3100–2686 B.C.)," Antiquities Experts, 2016, http://www/antiquitiesexperts.com/egypt3100.html (accessed April 25, 2016).

"Pre-Dynastic & Early Dynastic Period (5,500–2,700 BC)," CEMML, Colorado State University, https://www.cemml.colostate.edu/cultural/09476/egypt02-02enl.html (accessed April 25, 2016).

Wikipedia, "Gerzeh culture," January 25, 2016.

Diane Leeman, "Abydos Tomb U-j of Predynastic Egypt," Yudu, May 2007, http://content.yudu.com/Library/A1ij30/AbydosTombUj/resources/8.htm

(accessed April 25, 2016).

Wikipedia, "Egyptian hieroglyphs," April 22, 2016.

Jacques Kinnear, "Narmer Macehead," Ancient Egyptian Site, June 10, 2014, http://www.ancient-egypt.org/history/early-dynastic-period/1st-dynasty/horus-narmer/narmer-artefacts/narmer-macehead.html (accessed April 22, 2016).

Wikipedia, "Narmer Palette," March 2, 2016.

Wikipedia, "Early Dynastic Period (Egypt)," April 16, 2016.

Ancient History Encyclopedia, "Early Dynastic Period in Egypt," by Joshua Mark, January 22, 2016, http://www.ancient.eu/Early_Dynastic_Period_In_Egypt (accessed April 25, 2016).

"Early Dynastic Period (3100 B.C.–2700 B.C.)," Theban Mapping Project, August 23, 2002, http://www.thebanmappingproject.com/resources/timeline_1.html (accessed April 25, 2016).

"Pyramids of Giza," Discovering Egypt, 2016, http://discoveringegypt.com/pyramids-temples-of-egypt/pyramids-of-giza (accessed April 26, 2016).

Chapter 8

[XXIV] Identifying *when* European violence started to decline is helpful for determining *why* it started to decline. While data is available for several European countries, the focus here will be England. The available data runs from 1200 to 2000 CE.

Throughout this period, violence was in steep decline. To obtain a rough estimate for when this decline began, I drew a line through the data, which was my best estimate for a regression, Figure A. (I consider this a preliminary analysis since I did not have the source data available.)

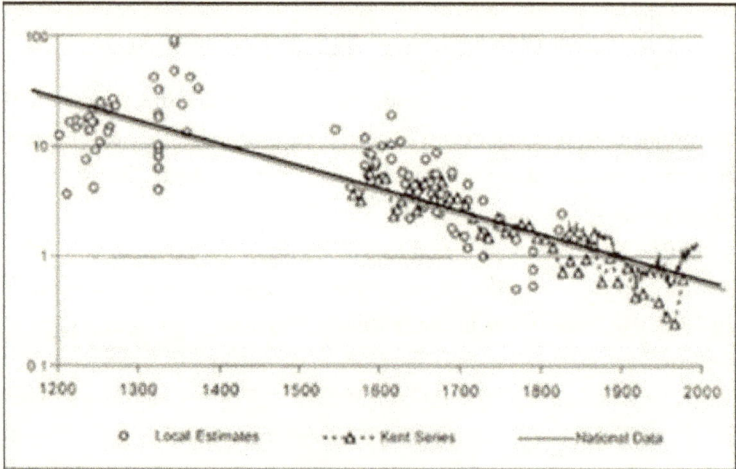

Figure A. English Homicides per 100,000 Population, 1200–2000. Reprinted with permission from Manuel Eisner, "Modernization, Self-Control, and Lethal Violence: The Long-Term Dynamics of European Homicide Rates in Theoretical Perspective," *British Journal of Criminology* 41, no. 4 (2001): 622 (line added by author).

Presenting this curve, along with key data points, on arithmetic axes (instead of semi-log) shows the actual steepness of the decline (Figure B).

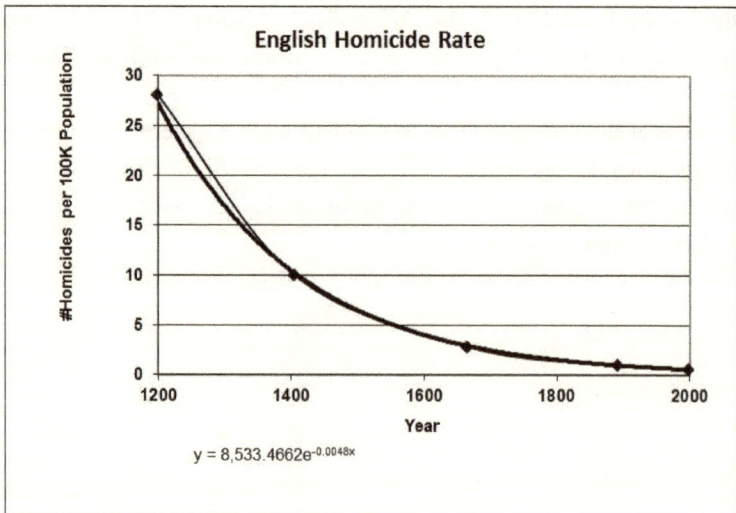

Figure B. Decline in English Violence, 1200–2000.

Because violence was already in steep decline at the start of the data, we can be almost certain that the trend started before the data begins. As such, we need to estimate a realistic starting point for the decline, and this requires making an assumption on how high the violence initially was.

A worst-case estimate (highest violence, earliest start of the decline) would use the maximum sustainable violence rate for a society, which the United Nations estimates is 50–150 homicides per 100,000 in population. (Today's worst nations average in the middle teens.) This extreme figure would suggest that the decline began between 840 and 1070 CE.

Another estimate worth considering is the average birthrate across Europe throughout the Middle Ages. This was generally 40–45 births per 100,000 population per year. If we assume that as many people were killed by homicide as were born, then the decline began between 1093 and 1117 CE, about a century before the data begins.

However, the best estimate will almost assuredly come by changing the shape of the curve. While the data is presented in logarithmic form, reality is likely closer to an S-curve where violence started at one steady-state level then moved to a lower steady-state level. S-curves are used to model many "natural systems" that exhibit patterns of either decay or exponential, but limited, potential growth.

To apply the S-curve, we use the generalized logistics equation, commonly used to model natural systems that exhibit S-curve behavior such as population growth, certain chemical reactions, the spread of disease, changes in language, or even innovation diffusion. Notably, applying this curve reveals that we only have data for the second half of the decline—data for the entire first half is missing. Because we see no evidence of an inflexion in the data we have, we select 1200 CE as the midpoint to make a conservative assumption (lowest violence, latest start). This yields a new curve, Figure C.

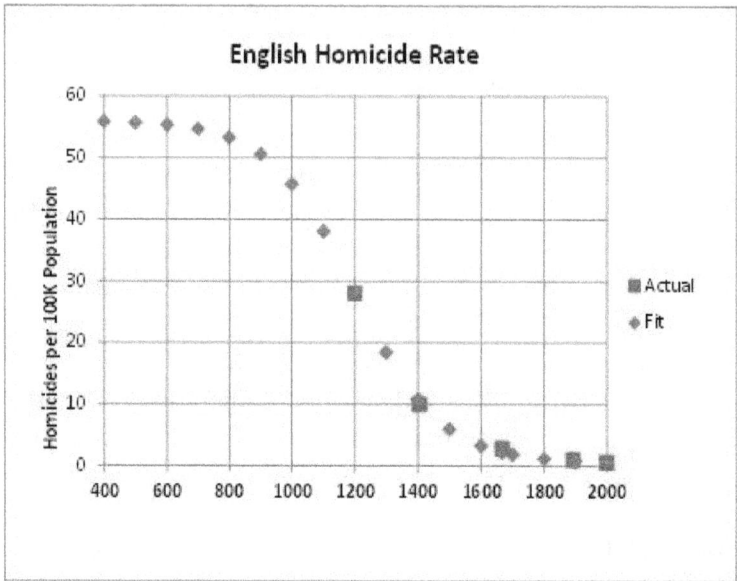

Figure C. Preliminary Model of the Decline of Violence in England, 400–2000 CE.

This curve fits the equation

$$Year = -\frac{\ln\left(\frac{Homicides\ per\ 100K}{8533}\right)}{.0048}$$

From this, we see that the English homicide rate was around 55 homicides per hundred thousand until around the seventh century, when it began to decline.

All together, these three estimates create a bounded timeframe for the start of the decline in English violence—ranging from roughly 600 to 1120 CE, with the earlier timing being more likely. In any event, it is safe to say that violence in England began to decline in the early Middle Ages.

[xxv] I have some personal experience with how the perceived value of life can change over time. I grew up in a small town in central California where stray dogs were abundant and easily acquired. And in my household, there was an unwritten rule that if we had to spend more than $50–$75 to keep a dog healthy, its days were at an end. So a generation later, I am in semidisbelief as I spend $400 to buy my daughter her dream dog, a tiny white bichon frise, from a breeder. This did not stop me from ribbing my neighbor, however, for spending $1600 on a lifesaving operation for his dog. (It was for the kids, he claimed.) Years later I would have to eat my

words when I spent $2200 on diagnosis and attempts to extend the life of our little bichon frise, who had cancer. As a child, I never would have imagined spending that kind of money on a dog. However, even one's perception of life's value can change over time.

Wikipedia, "Early Middle Ages," August 2010.

Encyclopedia Britannica, "England, A Narrative History; Part 4: The Anglo Saxon Period," by Peter N. Williams, 2000.

Brenda Lewis, "Why the Dark Ages?" March 8, 2010, http://suite101.com/article/why-the-dark-ages-a210582 (accessed November, 22, 2012).

Jennifer Tumanda, "The Decline of the Viking," July 15, 2008, http://www.family-ancestry.co.uk/history/vikings/decline (accessed August 12, 2009).

Wikipedia, "History of Anglo-Saxon England," September 1, 2009.

Steven Pinker, "A History of Violence," *New Republic*, March 19, 2007, https://newrepublic.com/magazine.

Wikipedia, "Gladiator," August 31, 2009.

Wikipedia, "Slavery in Medieval Europe," June 2010.

Wikipedia, "Monogamy in Christianity," August 1, 2010.

Kevin MacDonald, "The Establishment and Maintenance of Socially Imposed Monogamy in Western Europe," *Journal of Politics and Life Sciences* (1995): 3–23.

Wikipedia, "Human Sacrifice," August 2010.

Melissa Snell, "The Medieval Child, Part III: Surviving Infancy," ThoughtCo, May 2009, http://historymedren.about.com/od/medievalchildren/a/child_survival_3.htm (accessed Aug 21, 2010).

Wikipedia, "Viking," August 8, 2009.

Wikipedia, "Charlegmagne," September 26, 2009.

Wikipedia, "Roman Catholic Church," September 16, 2009.

"Timeline," History Bookshop, http://www.historybookshop.com/timeline.

Richard Landes, "Peace and Truce of God," in *Encyclopedia of the Middle Ages, Pt. 114, Vol 1*, edited by Andre Vauchez (Cambridge: James Clarke & Co, 2002), 1103–1105

Richard Landes, "Peace of God: Pax Dei," Center for Millennial Studies, Boston University, http://www.mille.org/people/rlpages/paxdei.html (accessed September 25, 2009).

Wikipedia, "Feudalism," January 14, 2014.

Peter N. Stearns, "The Spread of Christianity," in *Cultures in Motion* (New Haven, CT: Yale University Press, 2001), 36–43.

Wikipedia, "Early Centers of Christianity," April 3, 2016.

Jeffrey Hayes, "Early Christianity in Europe," Facts and Details, March 2011, http://factsanddetails.com/world/cat55/sub352/item1415.html (accessed April 7, 2016).

Augustus L. D'Souza, "The Spread of Christianity in Europe," http://avemaria.bravepages.com/articles/jan/spread.html (accessed April 7, 2016).

Gascoigne, "History of Christianity" (accessed April 7, 2016).

Wikipedia, "Edict of Milan," April 3, 2016.

Wikipedia, "Theodosius I," April 2016.

Wikipedia, "History of Christianity in Britain," March 29, 2016.

Wikipedia, "Augstine of Canterbury," April 4, 2016.

Encyclopedia Britannica, "Saint Augustine of Canterbury," 2016.

Tim Lambert, "A Brief History of Christianity in England," World History Encyclopedia, 2014, http://www.localhistories.org/christian.html (accessed April 7, 2016).

Wikipedia, "Christianization of Scandinavia," March 16, 2016.

Bruce Elleman, review of *Persistent Piracy: Maritime Violence and State-Formation in Global Historical Perspective*, edited by Stefan Eklof Amirell and Leos Muller (New York: Palgrave Macmillan, 2014), Criminal Law and Criminal Justice Books, Rutgers University, September 2015, http://clcjbooks.rutgers.edu/books/persistent-piracy.html (accessed April 6, 2016).

Wikipedia, "United Kingdom general election 1945," April 1, 2016.

XXVI *Chapter 9*

Chris Butler, "The Birth of Metallurgy and Its Impact," The Flow of History, 2007, http://flowofhistory.com/units/pre/1/FC8 (accessed July 30, 2007).

Alan Cramb, "A Short History of Metals," accessed January 24, 2014, http://neon.mems.cum.edu/cramb/Processing/history.html.

Wikipedia, "Mesopotamia," August 25, 2010.

Wikipedia, "Sargon of Akkad," September 2010.

Wikipedia, "Bronze Age," June 16, 2007.

Wikipedia, "Sumer," August 21, 2010.

Bert Lott, "Bronze & Iron Age Movements," Vassar College, 2001, http://faculty.vassar.edu/jolott/old_courses/crosscurrents2001/Lefkandi/bronze.htm (accessed February 13, 2014).

Joseph S.Spoerl, "A Brief History of Iron and Steel Production," St. Anselm College, http://www.anselm.edu/homepage/dbanach/h-carnegie-steel.htm (accessed February 17, 2014).

Rit Nosotro, "A History of Metals," Hyperhistory, July 30, 2007, http://www.hyperhistory.net/apwh/essays/cot/t0w03metaluses.htm (accessed July 30, 2007).

Wikipedia, "History of the Hittites," 2010.

Wikipedia, "Steel," October 12, 2005.

Wikipedia, "Ironwork," January 19, 2014.

Wikipedia, "Hittites," August 26, 2010.

Wikipedia, "Iron Age Sword," January 20, 2014.

Jeff Tyson, "How Sword Making Works," How Stuff Works http://science.howstuffworkds.com/sword0-making2.htm (accessed February 13, 2014),

Wikipedia, "Bantu Expansion," February 9, 2014.

"The Story of Africa: Early History," BBC, http;//www.bbc.co.uklworldservice/africa/features/storyofafrica/2chapter5.shtml (accessed February 19, 2014)..

Richard Hooker, "Civilizations in Africa: The Iron Age South of the Sahara," November 15, 1996, http://www.sahistory.org.za/iron-age-kingdoms-southern-africa (accessed February 19, 2014).

Wikipedia, "Ferrous Metallurgy," January 18, 2014.

Wikipedia, "Iron Age," October 9, 2005.

Jared Diamond, *Guns, Germs, and Steel* (New York: Norton, 1999), 393–401.

David K. Jordan, "The Bantu Expansion," University of California San Diego, January 31, 2014, http://weber.ucsd.edu/-dkjordan/resources/clarifications/BantuExpansion.html (accessed February 19, 2014).

"Iron Age Kingdoms of Southern Africa," South African History Online, http://www.sahistory.org.za/iron-age-kingdoms-southern-africa (accessed February 19, 2014).

Malcolm Guthrie, "Bantu Peoples & Migration," TSIME Online, University of Zimbabwe, accessed February 19, 2014, http://tsime.uz.ac.zw.

Encyclopedia Brittanica, "Central Africa: The Iron Age," accessed February 19, 2014.

Wikipedia, "Iron Metallurgy in Africa," February 17, 2014.

Wikipedia, "Iron Age," February 7, 2014.

Wikipedia, "History of Metallurgy in the Indian Subcontinent," October 24, 2013.

Pradip Dutta, "The Rise and Fall of Ancient India's Iron and Steel Metallurgy," Ghadar Jari Hai, October 20, 2009, http://www.ghadar.in/gjh_html/?q=content/rise-and-fall-ancient-india%E2%80%99s-iron-... (accessed February 19, 2014).

"The Mauryan Empire," Library of Congress Country Study, accessed February 25, 2014, http://historymedren.about.com/library/text/bltxtindia5.htm.

"The Mauryan Empire in World History," TimeMaps Ltd., 2014, http://www.timemaps.com/civilization/The-Mauryan-empire (accessed February 25, 2014).

Wikipedia, "History of India," February 17, 2014.

Rakesh Tewari, "The Origins of Iron-Working in India," Archaeology Online, May 6, 2003, http://antiquity.ac.uk/projgall/tewari/tewari.prd (accessed February 19, 2014).

"Iron Age India," IndiaNetZone, April 9, 2013, http://www.indianetzone.com/55/iron_age_india.htm (accessed February 19, 2014).

Puja Mondal, "The Causes of the Success of the Magadhan Imperialism up to the Reign of Ashoka the Great," YourArticleLibrary, accessed February 25, 2014, http://www.yourarticlelibrary.com/history/the-causes-of-the-success-of-the-rnagadhan-imp...

Vinay Pandey, "The Rise of the Magadha Empire," ImportantIndia, August 1, 2013, http://www.importantindia.com/879/rise-of-magadha-empire-geographical-economic (accessed February 25, 2014).

Raghudev, "What Are the Four Causes That Led to the Rise of Magadha?" Preserve Articles, 2012. http://www.preservearticles.com/2011082311533/what-are-the-four-causes-that-led-to-the (accessed February 25, 2014).

Wikipedia, "Maurya Empire," February 16, 2014.

Wikipedia, "History of Metallurgy in China," October 18, 2012.

Cao Hangang, "China from Bronze to Iron," ARS Cives Creativity, http://www.arscives.com/historysteel.cn.article.htm (accessed February 19, 2014).

"Steel," EDInformatics, 1999, http://www.edinformatics.conm/inventions_inventors/steel.htm (accessed October 14, 2005).

"Iron Making History in China," ChinaCulture, 2008, http://www.chinaculture.org/library/2008-02/01/content_26524.htrn (accessed September 14, 2010).

Wikipedia, "Economy of the Han Dynasty," September 2010.

Wikipedia, "Qin Dynasty," February 18, 2014.

Wikipedia, "Science and technology of the Han Dynasty," January 12, 2014.

Wikipedia, "Warring States Period," February 8, 2014.

Wikipedia, "Shang dynasty," October 16, 2013.

XXVII *Wikipedia*, "Domestication of the horse," June 17, 2007.

Wikipedia, "Chariot," August 29, 2010.

Ancient History Encyclopedia, "Chariot," by Rodrrigo Quijada Plubins, March 13, 2013, http://www.ancient.eu.com/chariot/ (accessed February 17, 2014).

Wikipedia, "Composite Bow," February 9, 2014.

Arthur Cotterell, *Chariot: From Chariot to Tank, the Astounding Rise and Fall of the World's First War Machine* (Woodstock, NY: Overlook Press, 2005).

Wikipedia, "Chariot tactics," August 25, 2010.

Wikipedia, "Hyksos," March 22, 2014.

"Hyksos," Jewish Virtual Library, 2012, http://www.jewishvirtuallibrary.org/jsource/judaica/ejud_0002_0009_0_09361.ht ml (accessed March 25, 2014).

Wikipedia, "Shang dynasty," October 16, 2013.

Stephen Roberts, "The Chinese War Chariot," Karwansaray Publishers, September 15, 2013, http://www.karwansaraypublishers.com/cms/karwansaray/ancient-warfare/about/readmore-aw/16-ancient-warfare/ancient-warfare-articles/248-the-chines-war-chariot.html (accessed March 25, 2014).

Wikipedia, "Battle of Kadesh," March 23, 2014.

Rob Wanner, "Kadesh," Military History Online, 2005, http://www.militaryhistoryonline.com/ancient/articles/kadesh.aspx (accessed February 17, 2014).

Cao Hangang, "China from Bronze to Iron," ARS Cives Creativity, http://www.arscives.com/historysteel.cn.article.htm (accessed February 19, 2014).

Wikipedia, "History of crossbows," March 17, 2014.

Wikipedia, "Crossbow," March 15, 2014.

Wikipedia, "Qin Dynasty," February 18, 2014

"Battle of Muye," Asia's Place, September 21, 2009, http://asia.worldgoo.com/t148-battle-of-muye (accessed March 26, 2014).

Wikipedia, "Cavalry," September 8, 2010.

Wikipedia, "Cataphract," February 20, 2014.

Wikipedia, "Military history of the Neo-Assyrian empire," February 24, 2014.

Wikipedia, "Cavalry Tactics," February 27, 2014.

Wikipedia, "Horses in Warfare," June 5, 2007.

"History of Iran: Median Empire," Iran Chamber Society, 2014, http://www.iranchamber.com/history/median/median/php. (accessed March 20, 2014).

Wikipedia, "Assyria," March 16, 2014.

Gascoigne, "History of Warfare—Land," 2014.

Wikipedia, "Battle of Jaxartes," March 7, 2014.

Chapter 10

XXVIII *Wikipedia*, "Gunpowder," April 4, 2014.

Jack Kelly, *Gunpowder: Alchemy, Bombards, and Pyrotechnics: The History of the Explosive That Changed the World* (New York: Perseus Books Group, 2005).

Wikipedia, "History of gunpowder," March 14, 2014

"History of Fireworks & Gunpowder," Pyro Universe, www.pyrouniverse.com (accessed October 11, 2005).

Wikipedia, "Pen Huo Qi," August 30, 2013.

Wikipedia, "Fire lance," March 24, 2014.

"Gun and Gunpowder," Silkroad Foundation, 2000, http://www.silkroad.com/artl/gun.shtml (accessed October 11, 2005).

Wikipedia, "Gunpowder artillery in the Song dynasty," March 24, 2014.

Wikipedia, "List of the largest cannon by caliber," April 26, 2014.

Wikipedia, "Bombard (weapon)," April 2, 2014.

Wikipedia, "Matchlock," March 27, 2014.

Wikipedia, "Wheelock," May 3, 2014.

Wikipedia, "Flintlock," May 3, 2014.

Wikipedia, "Percussion cap," April 30, 2014.

Wikipedia, "Cartridge (firearms)," April 4, 2014.

Wikipedia, "Mongol invasion of China," March 25, 2014.

XXIX *Wikipedia*, "Ottoman Empire," April 10, 2014.

Wikipedia, "Military of the Ottoman Empire," April 3, 2014.

Wikipedia, "Siege of Constantinople (1422)," November 20, 2013.

Wikipedia, "Fall of Constantinople," April 18, 2014.

Wikipedia, "Cannon," April 9, 2014.

Wikipedia, "Janissary," April 16, 2014.

Cameron Rubaloff Nelson, "The Manufacture and Transportation of Gunpowder in the Ottoman Empire: 1400–1800," August 2010, USpace Institutional Repository, University of Utah, http://content.lib.utah.edu/cdm/ref/collection/etd2/id/1276 (accessed April 18, 2014).

ˣˣˣ *Wikipedia*, "Grand duchy of Moscow," April 4, 2014.

Wikipedia, "Russo-Kazan Wars," October 13, 2013.

Wikipedia, "Arquebus," April 16, 2014.

Wikipedia, "Ivan the Terrible," April 16, 2014.

Wikipedia, "Streltsy," April 15, 2014.

Wikipedia, "Yermak Timofeyevich," April 5, 2014.

Wikipedia, "Russian conquest of Siberia," February 26, 2014.

ˣˣˣᴵ *Wikipedia*, "Safavid dynasty," April 4, 2014.

Wikipedia, "Military history of Iran," March 24, 2014.

Wikipedia, "Ismail I," May 3, 2014.

Wikipedia, "Qizilbash," May 2, 2014.

"Qizilbash," Advameg, Inc., 2014, http://www.everyculture.com/Africa-Middle-East/Qizilbash.html (accessed May 6, 2014).

ˣˣˣᴵᴵ *Wikipedia*, "Mughal Empire," April 9, 2014.

Wikipedia, "Babur," May 5, 2014.

Wikipedia, "Battle of Mohi," March 25, 2014.

ˣˣˣᴵᴵᴵ *Wikipedia*, "Siege of Seville," September 14, 2013.

"Early Medieval Cannon," Medieval Combat Society, 2013, http://www.themcs.org/weaponry/cannon/cannon.htm (accessed April 21, 2014).

Wikipedia, "Franco-Mongol alliance," March 25, 2014

Wikipedia, "William of Rubruck," March 18, 2014.

Wikipedia, "Roger Bacon," April 21, 2014.

Wikipedia, "Hundred Years' War," April 17, 2014.

ˣˣˣᴵⱽ *Wikipedia*, "Mongol Invasion of Japan," March 28, 2014.

Wikipedia, "Yuan Dynasty," April 22, 2014.

Wikipedia, "Ming Dynasty," April 19, 2014.

Wikipedia, "Japanese invasions of Korea (1592-98)," April 23, 2014.

Wikipedia, "Firearms of Japan," January 24, 2014.

Chapter 11

ˣˣˣⱽ *Wikipedia*, "Industrial Revolution," August 1, 2007.

Wikipedia, "Thomas Savery," May 17, 2014.

John Lienhard, "The First American Steam Engine," Engines of Our Ingenuity, University of Houston, 1997, http://www.uh.edu/engines/epi1085.htm (accessed June 15, 2010).

Wikipedia, "James Watt," May 5, 2014.

"Industrial Revolution," Citizendium, July 10, 2007,

http://en.citizendium.org/wiki/Industrial_Revolution (accessed August 2, 2007).

Wikipedia, "History of coal mining," May 6, 2014.

Wikipedia, "Textile manufacturing during the Industrial Revolution," May 27, 2014.

"Mechanization of Textiles and New Iron Making Techniques," Red Apple Education, 2014, http://www.skwirk.com (accessed May 29, 2014).

Wikipedia, "Blowing engine," April 13, 2014.

Wikipedia, "History of rail transport in Great Britain," May 17, 2014.

Wikipedia, "History of rail transport in Great Britain to 1830," April 8, 2014.

Stephen Luscombe, The British Empire, May 13, 2014, http://www.britishempire.co.uk (accessed May 13, 2014).

Paul Kennedy, *The Rise and Fall of the Great Powers* (New York: Random House, 1987), 143–158.

Wikipedia, "Mass production," May 5, 2014.

Wikipedia, "British Empire," May 6, 2014.

E. A. Brayley Hodgetts, *The Rise and Progress of the British Explosives Industry* (Essex, UK: Royal Gunpowder Mills, 2013).

"Explosives and Gunpowder," Faversham, 2014, http://www.faversham.org/history/explosives.apx (accessed June 5, 2014).

Wikipedia, "Gun quarter," March 2, 2014, http://en.wikipedia.org/wiki/Gun_quarter (accessed June 5, 2014).

Wikipedia, "Royal Small Arms Factory," December 12, 2013.

William Manchester, *The Last Lion: Winston Spencer Churchill, Visions of Glory, 1874–1932* (London: Little, Brown and Company, 1983), 661–673, 833–841.

XXXVI *Wikipedia*, "Atom," June 11, 2014.

Wikipedia, "History of the periodic table," June 13, 2014.

Wikipedia, "Robert Boyle," June 26, 2014.

Wikipedia, "Timeline of chemical element discoveries," May 24, 2014.

Wikipedia, "Atomic theory," June 17, 2014.

Wikipedia, "Dmitri Mendeleev," June 5, 2014.

Wikipedia, "Ernest Rutherford," June 8, 2014.

Carl R. Nave, "Nuclear Fission," Hyperphysics, Georgia State University, 2012, http://hyperphysics.phy-astr.gsu.edu/hbase/hframe.html (accessed June 17, 2014).

Wikipedia, "Nuclear Fission," June 23, 2014.

Wikipedia, Nuclear fusion, June 11, 2014.

"A Brief History of Fusion Research," European Commission on Energy Research, http://ec.europa.eu/research/energy/fu/fu_int/article_1247_en.htm (accessed July 2, 2009).

Wikipedia, "Einstein-Szilard letter," June 6, 2014.

Wikipedia, "History of the Teller-Ulam design," March 3, 2014.

Wikipedia, "Edward Teller," June 19, 2014.

Wikipedia, "Atomic bombings of Hiroshima and Nagasaki," June 20, 2014.

"Text of Hirohito's Radio Rescript," *New York Times*, August 15, 1945, 3 (accessed August 8, 2015).

"The United States Presents the Baruch Plan," History Channel, 2014, http://www.history.com/this-day-in-history/the-united-states-presents-the-baruch-plan (accessed July 15, 2014).

"Operation Crossroads," Atomicarchive, 2008, http://www.atomicarchive.com/History/coldwar/page02.shtml (accessed July 3, 2009).

"The Beginnings of the Cold War," Atomicarchive, 2008, http://www.atomicarchive.com/History/coldwar/page02.shtml (accessed July 3, 2009).

"The Soviet Atomic Bomb," Atomicarchive, 2008, http://www.atomicarchive.com/History/coldwar/page03.shtml (accessed July 3, 2009).

"The Soviet Response," Atomicarchive, 2008, http://www.atomicarchive.com/History/coldwar/page07.shtml (accessed June 24, 2014).

Marian Smith Holmes, "Spies Who Spilled Atomic Bomb Secrets," Smithsonian, April 19, 2009, http://www.smithsonianmag.com/history/spies-who-spilled-atomic-bomb-secrets (accessed June 24, 2014).

Wikipedia, "V-2 Rocket," June 12, 2014, http://en.wikipedia.org/wiki/V-2_rocket (accessed June 24, 2014).

Wikipedia, "Intercontinental Ballistic Missiles," June 23, 2014, http://en.wikipedia.org/wiki/Intercontinental_ballistic_missiles (accessed June 24, 2014).

Wikipedia, "Mutual assured destruction," May 27, 2014, http://en.wikipedia.org/wiki/Mutual_assured_destruction (accessed June 24, 2014).

Wikipedia, "Nuclear arms race," June 15, 2014, http://en.wikipedia.org/wiki/Nuclear_arms_race (accessed June 24, 2014).

"Reagan's Defense Buildup Bridged Military Eras," *Washington Post*, June 9, 2004, E1.

"The Nuclear Arms Race," History Learning Site, 2014, http://www.historylearningsite.co.uk/nuclear_arms_race.htm (accessed June 26, 2014).

Wikipedia, "British Empire," May 6, 2014.

"The Suez Crisis, 1956," US Department of State, November 1, 2013, https://history.state.gov/milestones/1953-1960/suez (accessed July 1, 2014).

Wikipedia, "Suez Crisis," June 30, 2014.

Wikipedia, "The Cold War," July 5, 2014.

Wikipedia, "Non-Aligned Movement," July 5, 2014.

"Britain Goes Nuclear," Atomicarchive, 2013, http://www.atomicarchive.com/History/coldwar/page11.shtml (accessed June 24, 2014).

"France Joins the Club," Atomicarchive, 2013, http://www.atomicarchive.com/History/coldwar/page11.shtml (accessed June 24, 2014).

"Chinese Nuclear Weapons," Atomicarchive, 2013, http://www.atomicarchive.com/History/colwar/page12.shtml (accessed June 24, 2014).

Wikipedia, "Nuclear weapons and Israel," July 2, 2014.

Wikipedia, "North Korea and weapons of mass destruction," April 16, 2014.

"Safeguards to Prevent Nuclear Proliferation," World Nuclear Association, 2014, http://www.world-nuclear.org/info/Safety-and-Security/Non-Proliferation/Safeguards-to-Prevent-Nuclear-Proliferation (accessed July 7, 2014).

Chapter 12

XXXVII "Quotes," Dwight Eisenhower Presidential Library, Museum and Boyhood Home, http://www.eisenhower.archives.gov/all_about_ike/quotes.html (accessed September 16, 2014).

Paul Kennedy, *The Rise and Fall of the Great Powers* (New York: Random House, 1987), xv–xxi.

Kristina Ross, "Mass Culture," University of Minnesota Media History Project, 1995, http://www.mediahistory.umn.edu/masscult.html (accessed March 9, 2007).

Ang, Peng Hwa, and James Dewar, "Back to the Future of the Internet: The Printing Press," Learning Initiatives on Reforms for Network Economies, http://lirne.net/resources/netknowledge/ang.pdf (accessed May 11, 2007).

Shannon Duffy, review of *The Printing Press as an Agent of Change*, by Elizabeth L. Eisenstein, H-Ideas, H-Net Reviews, June 2000, http://www.h-net.msu.edu/reviews/showrev.cgi?path=24899962821867.

Jared Diamond, *Guns, Germs, and Steel* (New York: Norton, 1999), 258–260.

Sun Tzu, *The Art of War*, translated by Samuel B. Griffith (London: Oxford University Press, 1963).

Wikipedia, "Sumer," August 21, 2010,

"Transformation of Russia in the Nineteenth Century," Library of Congress, 2013, http://countrystudies.us/russia/6.htm (accessed September 24, 2014).

Wikipedia, "United States Census," September 24, 2014.

"World History at KMLA," KMLA, accessed September 24, 2014, http://www.zum.de/whkmla/region/russia/eurrusdemhist17961917.html.

XXXVIII Kennedy, *The Rise and Fall of the Great Powers*, 72.

US Department of Defense, *The Budget for Fiscal Year 2014*, The Whitehouse, 2013, http://www.whitehouse.gov/sites/default/files/omb/budget/fy2014/assets/defense.pdf (accessed October 1, 2014).

"China Overtakes Japan as World's Second-Biggest Economy," Bloomberg, August 16, 2010, http://www.bloomberg.com/news/print/2010-08-16/china-economy-passes-japan-s-in-second-quarter-capping-three-decade-rise.html (accessed October 1, 2014).

"China Passes Japan as Second-Largest Economy," *New York Times*, August 16, 2010, http://www.nytimes.com/2010/08/16/business/global/16yuan.html?pagewanted=all&_r=0 (accessed October 1, 2014).

XXXIX Kennedy, *The Rise and Fall of the Great Powers*, 29.

XL *Wikipedia*, "Meiji period," August 15, 2014.

Wikipedia, "History of Japan," September 28, 2014.

"The Meiji Restoration and Modernization," Asia for Educators, Columbia University, 2009, http://afe.easia.columbia.edu/special/japan_1750_meiji.htm (accessed October 8, 2014).

Tim Lanzendorfer, "A Short History of Japan: From 1850 to the Beginning of World War II," http://www.microworks.net/pacific/road_to_war/japan_1853-1941.htm (accessed October 8, 2014).

Wikipedia, "Russo-Japanese War," October 12, 2014.

Jan Lahmeyer, "Population Statistics," 2006, http://www.populstat.info/ (accessed October 1, 2014).

Wikipedia, "First Sino-Japanese War," October 13, 2014.

XLI *Chapter 13*

David S.Walonick, PhD, "An Overview of Forecasting Methodology," StatPac, 1993, http://www.statpac.com/research-papers/forecasting.htm (accessed January 23, 2009).

"Methods and Approaches of Futures Studies," World Futures Society, Rutgers

University, http//crab.rutgers.edu/goertzel/futuristmethods.htm (accessed January 26, 2009).

Spyros Makridakis, Steven C. Wheelwright, and Victor E. McGee, *Forecasting: Methods and Applications* (New York: Wiley, 1983), 3–13, 547–550, 637–639.

XLII Brenda Lewis, "Why the Dark Ages?" Suite101, March 8, 2010, http://suite101.com/article/why-the-dark-ages-a210582 (accessed 2010).

Clarence Lehman, "We Have Passed Our Sustainability," Univeristy of Minnesota, http://www.umn.edu (accessed January 21, 2009).

"Overconsumption? Our Use of the World's Natural Resources," Friends of the Earth Europe, September 2009, http://www.foe.co.uk/sites/default/files/downloads/overconsumption.pdf (accessed January 29, 2015).

XLIII World Futures Society, "Methods and Approaches of Futures Studies."

Chapter 14

XLIV *Wikipedia*, "European Union," August 5, 2008.

Wikipedia, "European Union," February 7, 2015.

Infoplease, "European Economic Community," 2005, http://www.infoplease.com/ce6/history/A0817889.html (accessed February 23, 2009).

Wikipedia, "Maastricht Treaty," January 30, 2015.

"Europa-How the EU works," European Union, 2015, http://europa.eu/about-eu/index_en.htm (accessed February 5, 2015).

Wikipedia, "European Economic Community," January 20, 2015.

Wikipedia, "Member state of the European Union," February 1, 2015.

"The Single Market Act," European Commission, December 1, 2014, http://ec.europa.eu/internal_market/smact/index_en.htm (accessed February 10, 2015).

"Single Market Act II," European Commission, October 3, 2012, http://ec.europa.eu/internal_market/smact/index_en.htm (accessed February 10, 2015).

"The EU Budget 2012 in Figures," European Union, February 5, 2015.

"Budget 2013," House of Commons, United Kingdom, March 20, 2013, https://www.gov.uk/government/news/budget-2013-documents (accessed February 10, 2015).

"United Kingdom—Data," The World Bank, 2015, http://data.worldbank.org/country/united-kingdom (accessed February 10, 2015).

"France Government Budget," Trading Economics, 2015, http://www.tradingeconomics.com/france/government-budget (accessed February 10, 2015).

"The French Budget: One cheer," Economist, September 28, 2012, http://www.economist/com/blogs/charlemagne/2012/09/french-budget (accessed February 10, 2015).

XLV *Wikipedia*, "Soviet Union," February 9, 2015.

Wikipedia, "Eurasian Economic Union," February 12, 2015.

"Putin Asserts Right to Use Force in Eastern Ukraine," *New York Times*, April 17, 2014, http://nytimes.com/2014/04/18/world/europe/russia-ukraine.html (accessed April 17, 2014).

XLVI *Wikipedia*, "United Arab Emirates," August 5, 2008.

Wikipedia, "United Arab Republic," August 5, 2008.

Wikipedia, "United Arab States," 2008.

Wikipedia, "Arab Federation," June 15, 2008.

Wikipedia, "Federation of Arab Republics," August 4, 2008.

Wikipedia, Pan-Arabism, August 3, 2008.

Wikipedia, "Gamal Abdel Nasser," August 5, 2008.

Wikipedia, "Syria," February 6, 2015.

"Syria," Library of Congress, April 1987, http://countrystudies.us.syria (accessed February 13, 2015).

Wikipedia, "Libya," February 10, 2015, http://en.wikipedia.org/wiki/Libya (accessed February 13, 2015).

Wikipedia, "Cooperation Council for the Arab States of the Gulf," February 10, 2015, http://en.wikipedia.org/wiki/Cooperation_Council_for_the_Arab_States_of_the_G ulf (accessed February 12, 2015).

"Why Is Oman Against a Gulf nation?" Al Arabiya News, December 10, 2013, http://english.alarabiya.net/en/perspective/analysis/2013/12/10/Why-did-Oman-refuse-a-Gulf-nation (accessed February 12, 2015).

Bruce Riedel, "Saudi Arabia Moving Ahead with Gulf union," Al-Monitor: The Pulse of the Middle East, December 22, 2013, http://www.al-monitor.com/pulse/original/2013/12/saudi-arabia-gcc-unity-oman-opposition (accessed February 12, 2015).

Wikipedia, "Arab world," March 3, 2015, http://en.wikipedia.org/wiki/Arab_world (accessed March 4, 2015).

XLVII *Wikipedia*, "African Economic Community," December 11, 2014.

Wikipedia, "African Union," February 6, 2015.

Wikipedia, "African Union," August 4, 2008.

"AU in a Nutshell," African Union, accessed February 16, 2015, http://www.au.int/en/about/nutshell.

"History & Background of Africa's Regional Integration Efforts," United Nations Economic Commission for Africa, February 2015, http://www.uneca.org/oria/pages/history.

Wikipedia, "History of African Union," November 17, 2014.

Wikipedia, "Union of African States," January 8, 2015.

Wikipedia, "Organization of African Unity," February 4, 2015.

"Mali profile," BBC News, January 28, 2015, http://www.bbc.com/news/world-africa-13881978 (accessed February 18, 2015).

"Profile: African Union," BBC News, February 5, 2015, http://www.bbc.com/news/world-africa-16910745 (accessed February 16, 2015).

"Mali's Stability Still at Stake a Year after Coup," France 24, March 21, 2013, http://www.france24.com/en/20130321-mali-military-coup-anniversary-stability-stake (accessed February 18, 2015).

"Will There Be an African Economic Community?" Brookings Institution, January 9, 2014, http://www.brookings.edu/blogs/africa-in-focus/posts/2014/01/19-african-economic-community (accessed February 17, 2015).

"Boko Haram in Nigeria Targeted with African Union troops," Associated Press, January 15, 2015, http://www.cbc.ca/news/world/boko-haram-in-nigeria-targeted-with-african-union-troops (accessed February 16, 2015).

"For Mugabe, Term as African Union Chief Could Salvage a Tarnished Legacy," Christian Science Monitor, February 9, 2015, http://www.csmonitor.com/world/Africa/2015/0209/For-Mugabe-term-as-African-Union (accessed February 16, 2015).

Sarah Chayes, "Boko Haram Isn't Just About Western Education," *Washington Post*, May 18, 2014, B5.

Sudarsan Raghavan, "Trapped in Violence and Forgotten," *Washington Post*, September 28, 2014, A1.

XLVIII *Wikipedia*, "Congress of Panama," April 8, 2014.

Wikipedia, "Gran Colombia," February 10, 2015.

Wikipedia, "First International Conference of America," January 7, 2015.

Columbia Encyclopedia, 6th ed., "Pan-American League," 2014, http://www.encyclopedia.com/topic/Pan-American_Union.aspx (accessed February 20, 2015).

Wikipedia, "Organziation of American States," February 8, 2015.

"Who We Are," Organization of American States, 2015, http://www.oas.org/en/about/who_we_are.asp (accessed February 18, 2015).

"History," United States Permanent Mission to the Organization of American States," http:www.usoas.usmission.gov/history.html (accessed February 19, 2015).

Wikipedia, "Andean Community," February 18, 2015.

Encyclopedia Brittanica, "Andean Community," 2015.

Wikipedia, "Mercosur," February 20, 2015.

Joanna Klonsky, "Mercosur: South America's Fractious Trade Bloc," Council on Foreign Relations, July 31, 2012, http://www.cfr.org/trade/mercosur-south-americas-fractious-trade-bloc/p12762 (accessed February 20, 2015).

"Mercosur: History," Global Edge, Michigan State Univerisity, July 31, 2012, http://globaledge.msu.edu/trade-blocs/mercosur/history (accessed February 20, 2015).

"Profile: Mercosur—Common Market of the South," BBC News, 2015, http://news.bbc.co.uk/2/hi/americas/5195834.stm (accessed February 19, 2015).

Wikipedia, "Union of South American Nations," January 31, 2015.

Nathaniel Parish Flannery, "Explainer: What Is UNASUR?" AS/COA, November 30, 2012, http://www.as-coa.org/articles/explainer-what-unasur (accessed February 20, 2015).

Simon Romero, "Settling of Crisis Make Winners of Andes Nations, While Rebels Lose Ground," *New York Times,* March 9, 2008, http://www.nytimes.com/2008/03/09/world/americas/09colombia.html (accessed February 23, 2015).

"Unasur, Looking at the EU, Freezes Project for Common Currency and Central Bank," MercoPress, June 13, 2011, http://en.mercopress.com/2011/06/13/UNASUR-looking-at-the-eu-freezes-project (accessed February 23, 2015).

XLIX *Wikipedia,* "Canada–United States Free Trade Agreement," January 19, 2015.

Wikipedia, "North American Free Trade Agreement," February 6, 2015.

"20 Years On, NAFTA's Effects Difficult to Measure, Report Says," Sandler, Travis & Rosenberg, P.A., March 11, 2013, http://www.strtrade.com/news-news-197.html (accessed February 26, 2015).

Mohammed Aly Sergie, "NAFTA's Economic Impact," Council on Foreign Relations, February 14, 2014, http://www.cfr.org/trade/naftas-economic-impact/p15790 (accessed February 26, 2015).

M. Angelese Villarreal and Ian F. Fergusson, "NAFTA at 20: Overview and Trade Effects," Congressional Research Service, April 28, 2014, http://fas.org/sgp/crs/row/R42965.pdf (accessed February 26, 2015).

Department of Homeland Security, "2012 Yearbook of Immigration Statistics," July 2013, http://www.dhs.gov/yearbook-immigration-statistics (accessed February

27, 2015).

Jens Manuel Krogstad, "5 Facts about Illegal Immigration in the U.S," Pew Research Center, November 18, 2014, http://www.pewresearch.org/fact-tank/2014/11/18/5-facts-about-illegal-immigration-in-the-us (accessed February 27, 2015).

George J.Borjas, "Does Immigration Grease theWheels of the Labor Market?" *Brookings Papers on Economic Activity* (2001): 69–133.

George J. Borjas, "The Economic Benefits from Immigration," *Journal of Economic Perspectives* (1995): 3–22.

Wikipedia, "Economic impact of illegal immigrants in the United States," February 4, 2015.

"*Q&A: Illegal Immigrants and the U.S. Economy*," National Public Radio, March 30, 2006, http://www.npr.org/templates/story/story.php?storyId=5312900 (accessed February 27, 2015).

Department of Homeland Security, Office of Immigration Statistics, *U.S. Legal Permanent Residents: 2012*, March 2013, https://www.dhs.gov/sites/default/files/publications/ois_lpr_fr_2012_2.pdf.

US Environmental Protection Agency, *Annual Report 2012: U.S.-Mexico Border Water Infrastructure Program*, March 2013, https://www.epa.gov/sites/production/files/2016-02/documents/us_mexico_border-annual_report_2012.pdf

"Merida Initiative," US Department of State, http://www.state.gov/j/inl/merida (accessed March 2, 2015).

"Canada-US Border Cooperation Government of Canada," Canada's Economic Action Plan, Government of Canadahttp://actionplan.gc.ca/en/page/bbg-tpf/canada-us-border-cooperation (accessed March 2, 2105).

US Department of State, *U.S.-Mexico Transboundary Hydrocarbons Agreement*, May 2013, http://www.state.gov/r/pa/prs/2013/05/208650.htm (accessed March 2, 2015).

Wikipedia, "Security and Prosperity Partnership of North America," July 27, 2014.

M. Angeles Villarreal and Jennifer E. Lake, "Security and Prosperity Partnership of North America: An Overview and Selected Issues," Congressional Research Service, May 27, 2009, http://fas.org/sgp/crs/row/RS22701.pdf (accessed March 2, 2015).

Council on Foreign Relations, *North America: Time for a New Focus*, Independent Task Force Report No. 71, David H. Petraus and Rober B. Zoellick co-chair, October 2014, www.cfr.org/north-america/norht-america/p33536?co=C007301 (accessed March 2, 2015).

Wikipedia, "North American Union," January 25, 2015.

"GDP (Current US$)," data from World Bank Group, 2015, http://data.worldbank.org/indicator/NY.GDP.MKTP.CD (accessed February 25, 2015).

"GDP Per Capita (Current US$)," data from World Bank Group, 2015, http://data.worldbank.org/indicator/NY.GDP.PCAP.CD (accessed February 25, 2015).

Marie Arana, "Covering Mexico, on Both Sides of a Bloody Border," *Washington Post*, June 2, 2013, B1.

Lally Weymouth, "Mexico's President: 'We Had to Change,'" *Washington Post*, September 28, 2014, B1.

ᴸ *Wikipedia*, "India," March 9, 2015.

Shivani Gupta, "A Comparative Study of Indian Economy in Pre and Post Reform period: An Econometrics Analysis," *Global Journal for Research Analysis* 3, no. 2 (February 2014): 51–56.

"GDP (Current US$)," data from World Bank Group, 2015, http://data.worldbank.org/indicator/NY.GDP.MKTP.CD (accessed February 25, 2015).

Thor Halvorssen, "A Chinese Dissident's Plea for Freedom and Love," *Atlantic*, 2015, http://www.theatlantic.com/international/print/2014/12/liu-xiaobo-china-i-have-no-enemies (accessed March 10, 2015).

Chen Guangcheng, "Chen Guangchecng: Still Waiting on China to Honor Its Pledges," *Washington Post*, June 24, 2014, http://www.washingtonpost.com/opinions/chen-guangcheng-still-waiting-on-china-to-honor-its-pledges (accessed March 10, 2015).

Chen Guangcheng, "How China Flouts Its Laws," *New York Times*, May 29, 2012, http://www.nytimes.com/2012/05/30/opinion/how-china-flouts-its-laws.html (accessed March 10, 2015).

"Population of China," Worldometers, 2015, http://www.worldometers.info/world-population/china-population (accessed March 10, 2015).

"Population of India," Worldometers, 2015, http://www.worldometers.info/worl-population/india-population (accessed March 10, 2015).

Wikipedia, "Association of Southeast Asian Nations," February 2015.

"ASEAN," Association of Southeast Asian Nations, ASEAN, 2014, http://www.asean.org/asean (accessed March 6, 2015).

Wikipedia, "Asian Monetary Unit," February 28, 2015.

Wikipedia, "European Currency Unit," December 14, 2014.

"Association of Southeast Asian Nations (ASEAN)," US Department of State, http://www.state.gov/p/eap/regional/asean (accessed March 6, 2015).

"ASEAN Economic Community Blueprint," Association of Southeast Asian Nations, 2007, http://www.asean.org/archive/5187-10.pdf (accessed March 10, 2015).

Logan Masilamani and Jimmy Peterson, "The ASEAN Way: The Structural Underpinnings of Constructive Engagement" *Foreign Policy Journal*, October 15, 2014, http://www.foreignpolicyjournal.com/(accessed March 11, 2015).

Gillian Goh, "The "ASEAN Way" Non-intervention and ASEAN's Role in Conflict Management," *Stanford Journal of East Asian Affairs* 3, no. 1 (Spring 2003): 113–118.

Rodolfo C. Severino, "The ASEAN Way and the Rule of Law," ASEAN, September 3, 2001, http://www.asean.org/resources/2012-02-10-08-47-56/speeches-statements-of-the-former-secretary-general-of-ASEAN (accessed March 11, 2015).

Ade M. Wirasenjaya and Ratih Hemingtyas, "ASEAN Way—at the Crossroads," The Jakarta Post, July 17, 2013, http://www.thejakartapost.com/news/2013/07/17/asean-way-crossroads.html (accessed March 11, 2015).

John Pomfret, "The People's Republic of Ambition," *Washington Post*, May 18, 2014: B1.

LI "Economic Integration," Economics On-line, 2015, http://www.economicsonline.co.uk/Global_economics/Economic_integration.html (accessed March 16, 2015).

"Trading Blocs, Common Markets, and Economic Unions," Finance Train, 2015, http://financetrain.com/trading-blocs-common-markets-and-economic-unions (accessed March 16, 2015).

M. Angeles Villarreal and Jennifer E. Lake, "Security and Prosperity Partnership of North America: An Overview and Selected Issues," Congressional Research Service, May 27, 2009, http://fas.org/sgp/crs/row/RS22701.pdf (accessed March 2, 2015).

"What Is a Single Market?" European Commission, March 8, 2015, http://ec.europa.eu/internal_market/20years/singlemarket20/facts-figures/what-is-the-single-market? (accessed March 16, 2015).

Encyclopedia Britannica, "Economic Integration," March 28, 2013.

Wikipedia, "Preferential trading area," February 8, 2015.

Wikipedia, "Caribbean Community," March 18, 2015.

Wikipedia, "Central banks and currencies of the Caribbean," October 4, 2014.

Wikipedia, "African Free Trade Zone," January 6, 2015.

Wikipedia, "East African Community," March 15, 2015.

Wikipedia, "Southern African Development Community," March 19, 2015.

Encyclopedia Britannica, "European Community," March 21, 2015.

Wikipedia, "Stability and Growth Pact," February 3, 2015.

Wikipedia, "European Fiscal Compact," February 26, 2015.

Wikipedia, "Single market," February 22, 2015.

"The EU Single Market: Historical Overview," European Commision, http://eu.europa.eu/internal_market/top_layer/historical_overview/index_en.htm (accessed March 16, 20150.

"European Single Market," Politics, 2015, http://www.politics.co.uk/reference/european-single-market (accessed March 16, 2015).

"Single Market Act II: Twelve Priority Actions for New Growth," European Commision, October 3, 2012, http://ec.europa.eu/growth/single-market/smact/index_en.htm (accessed March 20, 2015).

Wikipedia, "Euro," March 25, 2015.

Wikipedia, "United States—Colombia Free Trade Agreement," January 18, 2015.

LII *Chapter 15*

Aaron Blake, "Gridlock in Congress? It's Probably Worse Than You Think," *Washington Post*, May 29, 2014, http://washingtonpost/com/blogs/the-fix/ (accessed July 21, 2015).

Mark Kesselmen, "Why Gridlock in Washington?" Al Jazeera English, January 17, 2013, http://www.aljazeera.com/indepth/opinion/2013/01 (accessed July 21, 2015).

Shannon McGovern, "Who Is to Blame for Washington Gridlock?" *U.S. News & World Report*, August 23, 2012, http://www.usnews.com/opinion/articles (accessed July 21, 2015).

M.S., "Intransigence Is Good Strategy," *Economist*, May 20, 2014, http://www.economist.com/blogs/democracyinamerica/2014/03/political-gridlock (accessed July 21, 2015).

"10 Richest Dictators of All Time," Futurescopes, 2014, http://www.futurescopes.com (accessed July 21, 2015).

Paul Rosenzweig, "Ignorance of the Law Is No Excuse, But It Is Reality," The Heritage Foundation, 2013.

Philip K. Howard, "Obsolete Laws—The Solutions," *Atlantic*, March 30, 2012, http://www.theatlantic.com/national/archive/2012/03/obsolete-law-the-solutions (accessed August 13, 2015).

Liz Peek, "Outdated Laws Drive Stupid Government Spending," *Fiscal Times*, March 26, 2013, http://www/thefiscaltimes.com/Columsn/2013/03/26/Outdated-Laws-Drive-Stupid-Government-Spending (accessed August 13, 2015).

Erin Kelly, "Some Want Earmarks Back to Help Congress Pass Bills," USAToday, October 29, 2013, http://www.usatoday.com/story/news/politics/2013/10/29/congress-earmarks-legislation-spending (accessed August 16, 2015).

Sarah Binder, "Polarized We Govern?" Brookings Institute, 2014.

Ezra Klein, "Let's Talk," *New Yorker*, January 28, 2013, http://www.newyorker.com/magazine/2013/01/28/lets-talk (accessed August 17, 2015).

Manu Raju and Ginger Gibson, "Reid, McConnell Reach Senate Filibuster Deal," Politico, January 24, 2013. http://dyn.politico/com/printstory.cfm?uuid=BB866D39 (accessed August 17, 2015).

Paul Kane, "Reid, Democrats Trigger 'Nuclear' Option; Eliminate Most Filibusters on Nominees," *Washington Post*, November 21, 2013, http://www.washingtonpost.com/politics/senate-poised-to-limit-filibusters-in-party-line-vote (accessed August 18, 2015).

Wikipedia, "Filibuster in the United States Senate," July 1, 2015.

"Congress and the Public," Gallup, June 2015, http://www.gallup.com/poll/1600/congress-public.aspx? (accessed July 21, 2015).

Cassandra Willyard, "Ballooning Budgets: Why Federal Budgets Grow, but Rarely Shrink," Kellogg Insight, April 6, 2011, http://insight.kellogg.northwestern.edu/article/balooning_budgets (accessed July 15, 2015).

Steven Mufson, "Trump wants to scrapt two rgulations for each new one adopted," *Washington Post*, January 30, 2017, https://www.washingtonpost.com/news/energy-environment/wp/2017/01/30/ (accessed August, 2, 2017).

LIII *Wikipedia*, "Referendum," July 9, 2015.

Jim Miller, "Referendums Are a Big Part of California Ballot History," *Sacramento Bee*, November 22, 2013.

"A Brief History of the Initiative and Referendum Process in the United States," Initiative & Referendum Institute, University of Southern California, 2014, http://iandiinstitute.org (accessed July 21, 2015).

"Switzerlands' Referendums," Direct Democracy, 2005, http://directdemocracygeschichte-schweiz.ch/switzerlands-system-referendums.html (accessed July 21, 2015).

"Referendums Held in the UK," UK Parliament, 2015, http://www.parliament.uk/get-involvedlelections/referendums-held-in-the-uk/ (accessed July 21, 2015).

"Scottish Referendum: Scotland Votes 'No' to Independence," BBC, September 19, 2014, http://www.bbc.com/news/uk-scotland-29270441 (accessed July 21, 2015).

Henry McDonald, "Irish Voters Make History in Gay Marriage Referendum," *Guardian*, May 22, 2015, http://www.theguardian.corn/world/2015/may/22/irish-voters (accessed July 2015).

Matt Qvortrup, "The History of Ethno-National Referendums, 1791–2011," in *Nationalism and Ethnic Politics* (Tarlor & Francis Group, LLC) 18, no. 1 (2012).

Helena Catt, quoted in British House of Lords, *Referendums in the United Kingdom, 12th Report of Session 2009–10*, Parliament of the United Kingdom (London: Parliament, 2010).

"History of Initiative and Referendum in California," Ballotpedia, February 24, 2015, http://ballotpedia.org/History_of_Initiative_and_Referendum_in_California (accessed July 21, 2015).

"Huge Republic of Ireland Vote for Gay Marriage," BBC, May 23, 2015, http://www.bbc.com/news/world-europe-32858501 (accessed August 22, 2015).

Wikipedia, "California Proposition 13 (1978)," July 10, 2015.

LIV Todd Leopold, "The Crowd Is Smarter Than You Think," CNN, July 14, 2004, http://cnn.entertainment (accessed July 21, 2015).

P. J. Lamberson, "Big Data and the Wisdom of Crowds Are Not the Same," March 16, 2014, http://social-dynamics.org/big-data-widom-crowds (accessed April 15, 2014).

"Forget the Wisdom of Crowds; Neurobiologists Reveal the Wisdom of the Confident," Technology Review, MIT, July 14, 2014, http://www.technologyreview.com/view/528941 (accessed July 21, 2015).

Scott McLemee, "The Wisdom of Crowds: Problem Solving Is a Team Sport," *New York Times*, May 22, 2004.

Phillip Tetlock quoted in Benedict Carey, "U.S. Navy Strategists Have a Long History of Finding the Lost," *New York Times*, March 14, 2014.

Wikipedia, "The Wisdom of Crowds," July 16, 2015.

Phillip Ball, "Wisdom of the Crowd: The Myths and Realities," BBC, July 8, 2014, http:www.bbc.com/future/story/20140708-when-crowd-wisdom-goes-wrong (accessed July 21, 2014).

Liz Karagianis, "Collective Brainpower," MIT Spectrum, Summer 2010, http://spectrum.mit.edu/issue/2010-summer/collective-brainpower (accessed June 8, 2010).

Center for Collective Intelligence, MIT, 2014, http://cci.mit.edu (accessed July 21, 2015).

Rob Asghar, "The Dean of Leadership Gurus Passes at 89," August 1, 2014, http://www.forbes.com (accessed August 4, 2014).

Cassandra Willyard, "Ballooning Budgets," April 6, 2011.

Jessica Love, "Is Economic Growth a Question of Culture?" Kellogg Insight, September 2, 2014, http://insight.kellogg.northwestern.edu/article/economic-growth-a-question-of-culture (accessed September 22, 2014).

Ron Chernow, *Alexander Hamilton* (New York: Penguin Books, 2004).

Gallup, "Congress and the Public," June 2015.

LV *Chapter 16*

Wikipedia, "History of Computer Hardware," June 2010.

Salim Al-Hassani, "Al-Jazari's Castle Water Clock: Analysis of Its Components and Functioning," Muslim Heritage, http://www.muslimheritage.org/article/al-jazaris-castle-water-clock-analysis (accessed September 2, 2015).

Wikipedia, "al-Jazari," August 2015.

Wikipedia, "Artuqids," August 2015.

Wikipedia, "Jacquard loom," September 2, 2015.

Wikipedia, "Joseph Marie Jacquard," July 14, 2015.

Wikipedia, "Herman Hollerith," May 6, 2015.

Wikipedia, "Tabulating machine," September 1, 2015.

"The Hollerith Machine," US Census Bureau, August 14, 2015, https://www.census.gov/history/www/innovations/technology/the_hollerith_tabulator.html (accessed September 1, 2015).

M. Mitchell Waldrop, "Claude Shannon: Reluctant Father of the Digital Age," *MIT Technology Review,* July 1, 2001, http://www.technologyreview.com/featuredstory/401112/claude-shannon-reluctant-father-of-the-digital-age (accessed September 1, 2015).

Wikipedia, "Claude Shannon," June 2010.

Wikipedia, "History of Computer Science," August 2015.

About.com, "History of the Software Program" by Mary Bellis, 2015, http://inventors.about.com/od/sstartinventions/a/software.htm (accessed September 9, 2015).

Graeme Philipson, "A Short History of Software," Core Memory, 2004, http://www.thecorememory.com (accessed September 9, 2015).

Wikipedia, "Machine Code," August 19, 2015.

Wikipedia, "Vacuum tube," September 4, 2015.

Wikipedia, "Computer," June 2010.

"When was the First Computer Invented?" Computerhope, http://www.computehope.com/issues/ch000984.htm (accessed June 18, 2010).

"The History of the Calculator,"Calculator Site, March 24, 2014, http://www.thecalculatorsite.com/articles/units/history-of-the-calculator.php (accessed September 2, 2015).

Wikipedia, "Bombe," August 29, 2015.

Wikipedia, "Z3 (computer)," September 1, 2015.

Wikipedia, "Atanasoff-Berry computer," August 2015.

Wikipedia, "Harvard Mark I," August 2015.

Wikipedia, "Colossus computer," August 25, 2015.

Wikipedia, "ENIAC," August 30, 2015.

Walter Isaacson, "Walter Isaacson on the Women of ENIAC," *Fortune*, September 18, 2014, http://fortune.com/2014/09/8/waltter-isaacson-the-women-of-eniac (accessed September 2, 2015).

LVI *Wikipedia*, "Manchester Small-scale Experimental Machine," August 11, 2015.

"1953—Transistorized Computers Emerge," Computer History Museum, 2014, http://www.computerhistory.org/semiconductor/timeline/1953-transistorized-computers-emerge (accessed September 3, 2015).

"Transistor," Computer Hope, 2015, http://www.computerhope.com/jargon/t/transistor.htm (accessed September 3, 2015).

Wikipedia, "EDVAC," July 28, 2015.

Wikipedia, "Solid-state electronics," August 26, 2015.

"History of Transformers and Inductors," CET Technology, 2015, http://www.cettechnology.com/history-of-transformers-and-inductors (accessed September 4, 2015).

"1931—"The Theory of Electronic Semi-Conductors" is Published," Computer History Museum, 2014, http://www.computerhistory.org/semiconductor/timeline/1931-The-Theory.html (accessed September 4, 2015).

Wikipedia, "Capacitor," September 2015.

Wikipedia, "Electronic component," August 20, 2015.

"Invention of Resistor," Radiomuseum, 2011, http://www.radiomuseum.org/forum/invention_of_resistor.html (accessed

September 4, 2015).

Wikipedia, "Invention of the integrated circuit," September 1, 2015.

"System 360," IBM, 2011, http://www-03.ibm.com/ibm/history/ibm100/us/en/icons/system360 (accessed September 4, 2015).

Wikipedia, "History of programming," September 2, 2015.

Wikipedia, "Assembly language," August 24, 2015.

Wikipedia, "Programming languages," September 3, 2015.

Wikipedia, "Compiler," August 26, 2015.

Wikipedia, "Fortran," September 3, 2015.

Wikipedia, "Operating System," September 10, 2015.

Wikipedia, "Minicomputer," August 24, 2015.

Wikipedia, "Digital Equipment Corporation," August 13, 2015.

Douglas W. Jones, "The Digital Equipment Corporation PDP-8," Notes on the History of the DEC PDP-8, edited by University of Iowa, March 23, 1996, http://homepage.cs.uiowa.edu/jones/pdp8/history.html (accessed December 15, 2015).

Wikipedia, "PDP-8," July 6, 2015.

Wikipedia, "OS/8," May 26, 2014.

[LVII] *Wikipedia*, "History of computing hardware (1960s-present)," September 4, 2015.

Wikipedia, "Microprocessor," August 27, 2015.

Wikipedia, "Microcode," August 16, 2015.

"What Was the First PC?" Computer History Museum, 2015, http://www.computerhistory.org/revolution/personal-computers/17/297 (accessed September 9, 2015).

"Altair 8800 Computer," Obsolete Technologies, July 23, 2014. http://www.oldcomputers.net/altair-8800.html (accessed September 3, 2015).

"Altair 8800 Microcomputer (1974)," Computermuseum, 2000, http://www.computermuseum.li/Testpage/Altair-8800-1974.htm (accessed September 17, 2015).

"MITS Altair 8800," PC History, 2015, http://www.pc-history.org/altair.htm (accessed September 17, 2015).

[LVIII] *Wikipedia*, "Personal Computer," June 2010.

Wikipedia, "History of the Personal Computer," September 3, 2015.

"Personal Computers,"Computer History Museum, 2015, http://www.computerhistory.org/revolution/personal-computers/17 (accessed September 9, 2015).

Wikipedia, "VisiCalc," September 4, 2015.

Wikipedia, "Word processor,". September 9, 2015.

"Software and IT Services Industry Data," by Tim Miles, International Trade Administration, US Department of Commerce, March 2010, http://web.ita.doc.gov/ITI/itiHome.nsf/ (accessed September 15, 2015).

LIX *Wikipedia*, "Personal digital assistant," September 14, 2015.

Wikipedia, "Mobile phone," September 12, 2015.

Wikipedia, "Smartphone," September 16, 2015.

"RIM History," BlackBerry, 2015, http://us.blackberry.com/enterprise.html (accessed September 21, 2015).

"BlackBerry Timeline: A Look Back at the Tech Company's History," Global News, September 24, 2013, http://globalnews.ca/news/860689/blackberry-timeline-a-look-back-at-the-tech-company's-history (accessed September 21, 2015).

Wikipedia, "BlackBerry," September 18, 2015.

Wikipedia, "Tablet computer," September 10, 2015.

LX "Brief History of the Internet," Internet Society, 2015, http:www.internetsociety.org/internet/what-internet/brief-history-internet (accessed September 17, 2015).

Wikipedia, "ARPANET," October 18, 2015.

Wikipedia, "DARPA," October 11, 2015.

Wikipedia, "Packet switching," September 15, 2015.

Cade Metz, "Leonard Kleinrock, the TX-2 and the Seeds of the Internet," *Wired*, October 1, 2012, http://www.wired.com/2012/10/leonard_kleinrock/ (accessed October 21, 2015).

Wikipedia, J.C.R. Licklider, September 11, 2015.

Wikipedia, "Charles M. Herzfeld," April 27, 2015.

"How Pacific Island Missile Tests Helped Launch the Internet," Internet Society, August 27, 2012, http://internethalloffame.org/blog/2012/08/27/how-pacific-island-missle-tests-helped-launch-the-internet (accessed October 21, 2015).

"Larry Roberts Calls Himself the Founder of the Internet. Who Are You to Argue?" Internet Society, September 24, 2012, http://internethalloffame.org/blog/2012/09/24/larry-roberts-calls-himself-founder-internet (accessed October 21, 2015).

Wikipedia, "Charles M. Herzfeld," April 27, 2015.

Wikipedia, "Robert Taylor (computer scientist)," May 3, 2015.

Wikipedia, "Lawrence Roberts (scientist)," September 22, 2015.

Encyclopedia Britannica, "Lawrence Roberts," by Erik Gregersen, 2015.

Wikipedia, "Leonard Kleinrock," September 29, 2015.

Wikipedia, "Paul Baran," October 14, 2015.

Wikipedia, "Donald Davies," September 22, 2015.

Wikipedia, "NPL Network," August 28, 2015.

LXI Dave Kristula, "The History of the Internet," 2001, http://www.davesite.com/webstation/net-history.shtml (accessed February 24, 2009).

"Brief History of the Internet," Internet Society.

Dave Kristula, "Internet History Timeline," January 2012, http://www.davesite.com/webstation/net-history5.shtml (accessed September 17, 2015).

Wikipedia, "DARPA," October 11, 2015.

Wikipedia, "J.C.R. Licklider," September 11, 2015.

Wikipedia, "Charles M. Herzfeld," April 27, 2015.

"Pacific Island Missile Tests," Internet Society.

Wikipedia, "Robert Taylor (computer scientist)," May 3, 2015.

About.com, "Charles Herzfeld on ARPAnet and Computers," by Charles Herzfeld, http://inventors.about.com/library/inventors/bl_Charles_Herzfeld.htm (accessed October 21, 2015).

Wikipedia, "Lawrence Roberts (scientist)," September 22, 2015.

Wikipedia, "Packet switching," September 15, 2015.

Wikipedia, "ARPANET," October 18, 2015.

Wikipedia, "Paul Baran," October 14, 2015.

Wikipedia, "Leonard Kleinrock, September 29, 2015.

Metz, "Leonard Kleinrock," *Wired.*

Wikipedia, "Donald Davies," September 22, 2015.

Wikipedia, "NPL network," August 28, 2015.

"Larry Roberts," Internet Society.

Encyclopedia Brittanica, "Lawrence Roberts," by Erik Gregersen, April 22, 2015.

Wikipedia, "Domain Name System," October 19, 2015.

Internet Encyclopedia, "Historical Development of IP Addressing," edited by Brent Baccala, April 1997, http://www.freesoft.org/CIE (accessed October 25, 2015).

Wikipedia, "History of the World Wide Web," September 14, 2015.

Ian Peter, "History of the World Wide Web," Net History, 2004, http://www.nethistory.info/HistoryoftheInternet/web.html (accessed September 17, 2015).

"History of the Web," World Wide Web Foundation, 2015, http://webfoundation.org/about/vision/history-of-the-web (accessed September 17, 2015).

"Web Browser History," Living Internet," http://www.livinginternet.com/w/wi_browse.htm (accessed September 17, 2015).

Wikipedia, "History of the web browser," September 2015.

Aaron Wall, "History of Search Engines: From 1945 to Google Today," History, 2015, http://www.searchenginehistory.com (accessed September 18, 2015).

Ian Poole, "IEEE 802.11b," Radio-Electronics, http://www.radio-electronics.com/info/wireless/wi-fi/ieee-802/11b.php (accessed October 26, 2105).

ᴸˣᴵᴵ *Chapter 17*

"Brief History of the Internet," Internet Society.

"Email History," Living Internet, 2015, http://www.livinginternet.com/e/ei.htm (accessed September 17, 2015).

Wikipedia, "History of the Internet," February 24, 2009.

Wikipedia, "Chat room," July 21, 2015.

Wikipedia, "Instant messaging," September 15, 2015.

Wikipedia, "Bulletin Board System," September 20, 2015.

Wikipedia, "Internet forum," September 3, 2015.

Wikipedia, "Blog," September 20, 2015.

Wikipedia, "Social networking service," September 23, 2015.

Wikipedia, "theGlobe.com," May 31, 2015.

Wikipedia, "PlanetAll," February 14, 2015.

Wikipedia, "Classmates.com," September 23, 2015.

Wikipedia, "SixDegrees.com," May 4, 2015.

Wikipedia, "Yahoo!GeoCities," September 20, 2015.

Wikipedia, "Tripod.com," May 31, 2015.

Wikipedia, "Myspace," September 24, 2015.

Felix Gillette, "The Rise and Inglorious Fall of Myspace," *Businessweek*, June 22, 2011, http://www.bloomberg.com/bw/magazine/content/11_27 (accessed September 24, 2015).

Wikipedia, "History of Facebook," September 23, 2015.

Wikipedia, "YouTube," September 27, 2015.

Wikipedia, "History of YouTube," September 24, 2015.

Wikipedia, "Twitter," September 23, 2015.

Wikipedia, "Email," October 19, 2015.

Wikipedia, "TOPS-20," August 11, 2015.

Ian Peter, "The History of Email," Net History, 2004, http://www.nethistory.info/History-of-the-Internet/email.html (accessed October 27, 2015).

Wikipedia, "Hayes Microcomputer Products," June 25, 2015.

Wikipedia, "SNDMSG," July 5, 2015.

Brianna Hamblin and Brandon Hamblin, interview by Neil Hamblin concerning social networking sites, October 2015.

LXIII Jill Drew, "Before Games, China Puts Conflict on Hold," *Washington Post*, July 8, 2008, A10.

Catherine O'Donnell, "New Study Quantifies Use of Social Media in Arab Spring," *UW Today*, September 12, 2011, http://www.washington.edu/news/2011/09/12/new-study-quantifies-use-of-social-media-in-Arab-Spring (accessed October 29, 2015).

"Why It's So Difficult to Counter ISIS on Social Media," CBS News, June 23, 2015, http://www.cbsnews.com/news/why-so-difficult-counter-isis-social-media (accessed October 29, 2015).

Jenna Wortham, "The Presidential Campaign on Social Media," *New York Times*, October 8, 2012, http://www.nytimes.com/interactive/2012/10/08/technology/campaign-social-media.html (accessed October 29, 2015).

Brianna Hamblin and Brandon Hamblin, interview.

"The Future of Voting," US Vote Foundation, July 2015, https://www.usvotefoundation.org/E2E-VIV (accessed October 6, 2015).

Grant Gross, "Internet Voting Isn't Ready Yet, but It Can Be Made More Secure," *Computerworld*, July 10, 2015. (accessed October 5, 2015).

Hans A. von Spakovsky, "The Dangers of Internet Voting," Heritage Foundation, July 14, 2015, http://www.heritage.org/research/reports/2015/07/the-dangers-of-internet-voting (accessed October 5, 2015).

Tom de Castella, "Election 2015: How Feasible Would It Be to Introduce Online Voting?" BBC, April 27, 2015, http://www.bbc.com/news/magazine-32421086 (accessed October 5, 2015).

National Institute of Standards and Technology, *Security Considerations for Remote Electronic UOCAVA Voting*, February 2011, http://www.nist.gov (accessed October 6, 2015).

Doug Gross, "Why Can't Americans Vote Online? CNN, November 8, 2011, http://www.cnn.com/2011/11/08/tech/web/online-voting (accessed October 5, 2015).

National Conference of State Legislators, *Electronic Transmission of Ballots*, July 27, 2015, http://www.ncsl.org/research/elections-and-campaigns/internet-voting.aspx (accessed October 5, 2015).

Kevin McTarsney (co-founder Conscious Security, an internet security firm) interview by author, Richmond, Virginia, May 19, 2014.

Elizabeth Weise, "Internet Voting 'Not Ready for Prime Time,'" *USA Today*, November 3, 2014, http://www.usatoday.com/tech/2014/11/02/internet-voting-not-secure (accessed October 5, 2015).

Ben Goldsmith and Holly Ruthrauft, *Implementing and Overseeing Electronic Voting and Counting Technologies* (Washington, DC: National Democractic Institute, 2013).

Aviel Rubin, "Security Considerations for Remote Electronic Voting over the Internet," in *29th Research Conference on Communication, Information and Internet Policy* (Florham Park, NJ: AT&T Labs, 2001).

David Jefferson, Aviel Rubin, Barbara Simons, and David Wagner, *A Security Analysis of the Secure Electronic Registration and Voting Experiment (SERVE), Program Review* (Washington DC: Department of Defense, 2004).

John Schwartz, ""Report Says Internet Voting System Is Too Insecure to Use," *New York Times*, January 21, 2004, http://www.nytimes.com/2004/01/21/technology/23CND-INTE.html?pagewanted=print (accessed November 1, 2015).

Investopedia, "Blockchain," 2017, http://www.investopedia.com/terms/blockchain.asp (accessed March 13, 2017).

"Blockchains: The Great Chain of Being Sure about Things," *Economist*, 2015, http://www.economist.com/news/briefing/21677228-technology-behind-bitcoin-lets-people-who-do-not-know-or-trust-each-other-build-dependable (accessed October, 31, 2015).

Wikipedia, "Blockchain," March 2017.

Marco Iansiti and Karin R. Lakhani, "The Truth about Blockchain," *Harvard Business Review*, Jan–Feb 2017.

Laura Shin, "Bitcoin Blockchain Technology in Financial Services: How the Disruption Will Play Out," *Forbes*, September 14, 2015, https://www.forbes.com/sites/laurashin/2015/09/14/bitcoin-blockchain-technology-in-financial-services-how-the-disruption-will-play-out/#6e6412925edf

Ernst and Young, *Blockchain Reaction*, 2016, http://www.ey.com/gl/en/industries/technology/ey-blockchain-reaction-tech-plans-for-critical-mass

Bernard Marr, "How Blockchain Technology Could Change the World," *Forbes*, May 27, 2016, https://www.forbes.com/sites/bernardmarr/2016/05/27/how-blockchain-technology-could-change-the-world/#b075b38725b2

Michael Riley and Jordan Robertson, "Russian Cyber Hacks on U.S. Electoral System Far Wider Than Previously Known," *Bloomberg*, June 13, 2017, https://www.bloomberg.com/news/articles/2017-06-13/russian-breach-of-39-states-threatens-future-u-s-elections (accessed August, 7, 2017).

LXIV Kenichi Ohmae, *The End of the Nation-state: The Rise of Regional Economies* (New York: Simon & Schuster, 1995), 1–5.

O'Donnell, "Arab Spring."

Chapter 18

LXV Barak Obama, *Dreams from My Father* (New York: Three Rivers Press, 1995), 417.

"Dec. 12, 1963: Kenya Gains Independence," *New York Times*, December 12, 2011, http://learning.blogs.nytimes.com/2011/12/12/dec-12-1963-kenya-gains-independence (accessed December 9, 2015).

LXVI "Magna Carta: Muse and Mentor," Library of Congress, Exhibit (Washington DC, 2014).

Wikipedia, "British House of Commons," January 26, 2007.

Wikipedia, "Edward Coke," November 6, 2015.

Wikipedia, "Institutes of the Lawes of England," January 5, 2015.

Encyclopedia Britannica, "John, King of England," by Sir James Holt, 2015.

Wikipedia, "John, King of England," November 17, 2015.

Wikipedia, "Llywelyn the Great," October 7, 2015.

Wikipedia, "First Baron's War," October 18, 2015.

Wikipedia, "Magna Carta," November 9, 2015.

"The U.K. Parliament," UK Parliament, May 6, 2006, http://www.parliament.uk/works/parliament.cfm (accessed September 8, 2006).

Steven Kreis, "The English Civil War," History Guide, February 28, 2006, http://www.historyguide.org/earlymod/lecture7c.html (accessed July 30, 2009).

Wikipedia, "English Civil War," July 22, 2009, http://en.wikipedia.org/wiki/English_Civil_War (accessed July 30, 2009).

"Charles I and the Petition of Right," UK Parliament, http://www.parliament.uk/about/living-heritage/evolutionofparliament/parliamentaryauthority/civilwar (accessed November 17, 2015).

Robert Crowley and Geoffrey Parker, "Oliver Cromwell," History, 1996, http://www.history.com/topics/british-history/oliver-cromwell (accessed November 17, 2015).

Wikipedia, "Charles II of England," July 24, 2009.

Wikipedia, "James II of England," July 24, 2009.

Wikipedia, "Glorious Revolution," July 29, 2009.

LXVII *Wikipedia*, "Social History of England," November 2015.

Wikipedia, "Economy of England in the Middle Ages," November 2015.

Tim Lambert, "Everyday Life in the Middle Ages," World History Encyclopedia, 2014, http://www.localhistories.org/middle.html (accessed November 18, 2015).

Wikipedia, "History of Serfdom," October 29, 2015.

Oxford English Dictionary, s.v. "Middle English—An Overview," by Philip Durkin, 2013, http://public.oed.com/aspects-of-english-in-time/middle-english-an-overview (accessed November 23, 2015).

David Crystal, "The Ages of English," BBC, February 17, 2011, http://www.bbc.co.uk/history/british/lang_gallery_05.shtml (accessed September 27, 2013).

About.com, "Middle English (Language)," by Richard Nordquist, 2015, http://grammar.about.com/od/mo/g/midenglterm.htm (accessed November 23, 2015).

Oxford English Dictionary, "Early Modern English Pronunciation and Spelling," by Edmund Weiner, 2013, http://public.oed.com/aspects-of-english/english-in-time/early-modern-english-pronunciation (accessed November 23, 2015).

"History of the English Language," English Club, https://englishclub.com/english-language-history.htm (accessed November 23, 2015).

Elizabeth Eisenstein, *The Printing Revolution in Early Modern Europe*, 2nd ed. (Cambridge: Cambridge University Press, 2005), 56–101.

"UK Countryside History—1750 AD," UK Agriculture, http://www.ukagriculture.com/countryside_history_1750ad.cfm (accessed November 18, 2015).

Alexander Apostolides, Stephen Broadberry, Bruce Campbell, Mark Overton, and Bas van Leeuwen, "English Agricultural Output and Labour Productivity, 1250–1850: Some Preliminary Estimates" (working paper, Academic Reseach Project, University of Warwick, Coventry, UK, 2008).

Bas van Leeuwen, "Land Use in Britain—The Agricultural Revolution," *Medieval,* May 11, 2014, http://mittelzeit.blogspot.com/2014/05/land-use-in-britain-agricultural.html (accessed November 18, 2015).

Mark Overton, "Agricultural Revolution in England, 1500–1850," BBC, February 17, 2011, http://www.bbc.co.uk/history/british/empire_seapower/agricultural_revolution_01.shtml (accessed November 18, 2015).

Investopedia, s.v. "The Birth of Stock Exchanges," by Andrew Beattie, 2007, http://www.investopedia.com/articles/07/stock-exchanges-history.asp (accessed

November 24, 2015).

Risk Encyclopedia, s.v. "History of Corporations," 2015, http://www.riskencyclopedia.com/articles/corporation (accessed November 23, 2015).

Investopedia, s.v. "The History of Insurance," by Andrew Beattie, 2008, http://www.investopedia.com/articles/08/history-of-insurance.asp (accessed November 24, 2015).

"The History of the Corporation," History of Business," 2015, http://www.historyofbusiness.net/history_of_coporations.html (accessed November 23, 2015).

Encyclopedia Britannica, "East India Company," June 11, 2015, http://www.britannica.com/topic/East-India-Company (accessed November 30, 2015).

George P. Landow, "The British East India Company—The Company That Owned a Nation (or Two)," Victorian Web, September 20, 2013. http://www.victorianweb.org/history/empire/india/eic.html

"An Introduction to Printing," Britain in Print, 2003, http://www.britaininprint.net/introtoprint/england.htm (accessed July 24, 2009).

LXVIII Eisenstein, *The Printing Revolution*, 86, 123–163, 209–311.

Encyclopedia Britannica, "History of Publishing," 2015.

About.com, "17th Century Timelines and Inventions," by Mary Bellis, December 15, 2014.

"Who Invented the Microscope?" History of the Microscope, 2010, http://www.history-of-the-microscope.org/history-of-the-microscope-who-invented-the-microscope (accessed December 18, 2015).

Wikipedia, "Evangelista Torricelli," December 12, 2015.

Wikipedia, "Uraniborg," December 4, 2015.

Encyclopedia Britannica, "Uraniborg," 2015.

Al Von Helden, "Federico Cesi and the Accademia dei Lincei," the Galileo Project, 1995, http://galileo.rice.edu/gal/lincei.html (accessed December 17, 2015).

Wikipedia, "Accademia dei Lincei," December 11, 2015.

Ann E. Egger and Anthony Carpi, "Scientific Institutions and Societies," VisionLearning, 2009, http://www.visionlearning.com/en/library/Process-of-Science/49/Scientific-Institutions-and-Societies (accessed December 17, 2015).

"History," Royal Society, https://royalsociety.org/about-us/history (accessed December 17, 2015).

Wikipedia, "French Academy of Sciences," December 15, 2015.

Wikipedia, "Financial endowment," November 10, 2015.

Wikipedia, "List of professorships at the University of Cambridge," July 19, 2015.

Wikipedia, "*Philosophiae Naturalis Principia Mathematica,*" December 14, 2015.

Wikipedia, "Scientific revolution," December 17, 2015.

Chapter 19

LXIX Conventional wisdom says that the nation-state began when the Treaty of Westphalia was signed in 1848. While that was a necessary precursor for nation-states to emerge on the European continent, it did not create any. The difference lies in the definition of nation-state. The typical definition for nation-state is general in nature.

A sovereign state inhabited by a relatively homogeneous group of people who share a feeling of common nationality (Random House)

This definition misses the key attribute that underlies the success of the modern form of government: operating by a constitution. A more precise definition would include this:

A sovereign state that is inhabited by a group of people who share a feeling of common nationality and that operates according to a mutually shared and accepted constitution

This captures the driving distinction between modern forms of government and those of previous ages. So while the Treaty of Westphalia made the distinction between civil authority and the monarchy, it also allowed that civil authority to run by a monarch, parliament, or other state officials; hence, the lines remained blurred. It would take another forty years for the first nation-state to emerge.

"Charles I and the Petition of Right," UK Parliament (accessed November 17, 2015).

Wikipedia, "Self-denying Ordinance," June 17, 2015.

Robert Crowley and Geoffrey Parker, "Oliver Cromwell," History, 1996, http://www.history.com/topics/british-history/oliver-cromwell (accessed November 17, 2015).

"The English Republic (1649–1660)," Open Door Web Site, 2009, http://www.saburchill.com/history/chapters/chap4008f.html (accessed July 31, 2009).

Wikipedia, "Charles II of England," July 24, 2009.

Wikipedia, "James II of England," July 24, 2009.

Wikipedia, "Glorious Revolution," July 29, 2009.

Wikipedia, "Mary II of England," November 15, 2012.

John F. Rohe, "The Arrows in Our Quiver," review of *Legal Language,* by Peter M. Tiersma, *Michigan Bar Journal* (July 2000): 842–844, http://www.michbar.org/journal/article.cfm?articleID=104&volumeID=9 (accessed July 20, 2009).

John Baker, R. H. Helmholz, and J. Stewart Anderson, *The Oxford History of the Laws of England* (London: Oxford University Press, 2003).

Bradley Steward Chilton, "Star Trek and Stare Decisis: Legal Reasoning and Information Technology," *Journal of Criminal Justice and Popular Culture*, 2001, http://www.albany.edu/scj/jcjpc/vol18is1/chilton.html (accessed July 20, 2009).

Richard J. Ross, "Communications Revolutions and Legal Culture: An Elusive Relationship," *Law and Social Inquiry* 27, no. 3 (2002): 637–684.

"Legal History: The Year Books," Boston University School of Law, http://www.bu.edu/law/seipp (accessed December 2, 2015).

Wikipedia, "Law Report," October 25, 2015.

Amanda Griscom, "Print Media and 17th Century Society," Trends of Anarchy and Hierarchy, http://www.cyberartsweb.org/cspace/infotech/asg/ag14.html (accessed July 27, 2009).

F. J. C. Hearnshaw, "Legal Literature," in *Cambridge History of English and American Literature in 18 Volumes*, edited by A. W. and A. R. Waller Ward (New York: Bartleby.com, 2000).

Steven Kreis, "The Printing Press," History Guide, May 13, 2004, http://www.historyguide.org/intellect/press.html (accessed July 27, 2009).

Steven Kreis, "The English Civil War," February 28, 2006.

Wikipedia, "English Civil War," July 22, 2009.

Encyclopedia.com, s.v., "Statute of Wills," 2005, http://www.encyclopedia.com/doc/1G2-3437704162.html (accessed December 21, 2015).

Thomas Burns, "The Doctrine of Stare Decisis," Scholarship@Cornell Law: A Digital Repository, 1893, http://scholarship.law.cornell.edu (accessed December 21, 2015).

Wikipedia, "Precedent," December 14, 2015.

Wikipedia, "Court of Chancery," November 19, 2015.

Roscoe Pound, "The Legal Profession in England from the End of the Middle Ages to the Nineteenth Century," *Notre Dame Law Review* 19, no. 4 (June 1944): 315–333.

"Lawyers in England and Wales," Family Search, February 2, 2015, https://familysearch.org/learn/wiki/en/Lawyers_in_England_and_Wales (accessed December 21, 2015).

Christopher W. Brooks, *Law, Politics and Society in Early Modern England* (Cambridge: Cambridge University Press, 2008).

Christopher W. Brooks, "Magna Carta in 16th Century English Legal

Thought," Online Library of Liberty, 2008, http://oll.libertyfund.org/pages/magna-carta-in-16th-century-english-legal-thought (accessed December 21, 2015).

Encyclopedia Britannica, "Petition of Right," 2015.

Wikipedia, "Petition of Right," October 22, 2015.

Michael Chiorazzi and Gordon Russell, *Law Library Collection Development in the Digital Age* (London: Psychology Press, 2002).

Le Quart Part des Reportes de Edward Coke, L'attorney general le Roigne (London, 1604), recorded in "Magna Carta in 16th Century English Legal Thought," by Christopher Brooks, April 10, 2014, Online Library of Liberty, http://oll.libertyfund.org/pages/magna-carta-in-16th-century-english-legal-thought (accessed December 21, 2015).

LXX Elizabeth Eisenstein, *The Printing Revolution,* 102–120.

"William Penn Quotes," Quoteland, accessed November 9, 2015, http://www.quoteland.com/author/William-Penn-Quotes/1944.

Wikipedia, "Baconian Method," October 29, 2015.

"Adam Smith Biography," Biography, http://www.biography.com/people/adam-smith-9486480 (accessed November 13, 2015).

Encyclopedia Britannica, "Public Administration," 2015.

Rong Tan and Lifang Hao, "An Analysis on Development of Public Administration Study in Western Countries," *Canadian Social Science* 9, no. 21 (March 2013): 21–27.

Internation Encyclopedia of the Social Sciences, s.v. "Civil Service," 1968, http://www.encyclopedia.com/topic/civil_service.aspx (accessed December 5, 2015).

"Civil Service History," Civil Service Commission, 2012, http://www.civilservicecommission.org.uk/civil-service-history.html (accessed December 5, 2015).

LXXI *Wikipedia,* "French State-General," January 31, 2009.

Wikipedia, "French Revolution," February 3, 2009.

Wikipedia, "Bourbon Restoration," January 21, 2009.

Wikipedia, "July Monarchy," January 30, 2009.

Wikipedia, "Charter of 1830," August 24, 2008.

Wikipedia, "French Second Republic," 2009.

Wikipedia, "French Constitution of 1852," November 22, 2008.

Wikipedia, "French Constitutional Laws of 1875," August 26, 2008.

Wikipedia, "French Third Republic," February 5, 2009.

Wikipedia, "Constitution of France," February 5, 2009.

Wikipedia, "Italian Unification," January 28, 2009.

Wikipedia, "Victor Emmanuel II of Italy," February 11, 2009.

Wikipedia, "Umberto I of Italy," January 23, 2009.

Wikipedia, "History of Italy as a Monarchy and in the World Wars," November 9, 2008.

Wikipedia, "Birth of the Italian Republic," February 15, 2009.

Wikipedia, "Unification of Germany," February 3, 2009.

HW Poon and TK Chung, "The Russian Revolution of 1905," 1979, http://www.thecorner.org/hist/russia/revo1905.htm (accessed February 11, 2009).

Wikipedia, "Russian Revolution (1905)," February 11, 2009.

Wikipedia, "Russian Revolution (1917)," February 5, 2009.

Wikipedia, "Russian Civil War," February 10, 2009.

David Barnsdale, "Russian Revolution in Dates," Febuary 14, 2005, http://www.barnsdel.demon.co.uk/russ/datesr.html (accessed February 11, 2009).

Wikipedia, "Xinhai Revolution," February 3, 2009.

John Bowblis, "China in the 20th Century," King's College, April 12, 2000, http://departments.kings.edu/history/20c/china.html (accessed February 11, 2009).

Wikipedia, "History of China," February 2009.

LXXII *Chapter 20*

Greg Downey, "Life Without Language," *Neuroanthropology*, July 21, 2010, http://neuroanthropology.net/2010/07/21/life-without-language (accessed January 9, 2016).

Wikipedia, "Linguistic Relativity," January 7, 2016.

Michael Balter, "Human Language May Have Evolved to Help Our Ancestors Make Tools," *Science*, January 13, 2015, http://news.sciencemag.org/archaeology/2015/01/human-language-may-evolved-help-ancestors-make-tools (accessed January 9, 2016).

Ray Jackendoff, "How Did Language Begin," Linguistics Society of America, August 2006, http://www.linguisticsociety.org (accessed January 11, 2016).

Alex Haley, *Roots* (New York: Dell Publishing Company, 1976), 10.

Wikipedia, "The Ninety-five Theses," December 28, 2015.

John Callaham, "Research Firm: Over 1 Exabyte of Data Is Now Stored in the Cloud," February 20, 2013, Neowin, http://www.neowin.net/news/research-firm-over-1-exabyte-of-data-is-now-stored-in-the-cloud (accessed January 13, 2016).

Rick Burgess, "One Minute on the Internet: 640TB Data Transferred, 100k tTweets, 204 Million Emails Sent," Techspot, March 20, 2013, http://www.techspot.com/news/52011-one-minute-on-the-internet-640tb-data-transferred (accessed January 13, 2016).

LXXIII Byron Tau, "Obama Camp Fundraising Total: $1.1B," Politico, January 19, 2013, http://www.politico.com/story/2013/01/obama-campaign-final-fundraising-total-1-billion (accessed January 15, 2016).

Aaron Smith, "Presidential Campaign Donations in the Digital Age," Pew Research Center, October 25, 2012, http://www.pewinternet.org/2012/10/25/presidential-campaign-donations-in-the-digital-age (accessed January 15, 2016).

Wikipedia, "United States Code," November 26, 2015.

U.S. House of Representatives, United States Code, 2015, http://uscode.house.gov (accessed December 31, 2015).

U.S. House of Representatives, United States Legislative Markup, October 2013, http://uscode.house.gov (accessed December 31, 2015).

LXXIV US Drug Enforcement Agency, "Federal Trafficking Penalties," www.dea.gov/druginfo/ftp3:shtml (accessed November 18, 2015).

Brian Yeh, "Drug Offenses: Maximum Fines and Terms of Imprisonment for Violation of the Federal Controlled Substancs Act and Related Laws," Congressional Research Service, January 20, 2015, www.crs.gov (accessed November 2015).

Robert Barnes, "Supreme Court Stops Use of Key Oart of Voting Rights Act," Washington Post, June 25, 2013, https://www.washingtonpost.com/politics/supreme-court-stops-use-of-key-part-of-voting-rights-act/2013/06/25 (accessed November 9, 2015).

Wikipedia, "Positive train control," December 31, 2015.

Nora Kelly, "The Life-Saving Train Technology Yhat Congress Isn't Fully Funding," Atlantic, December 18, 2015, http://www.theatlantic.com/politics/archive/2015/12/congress-positive-train-control-amtrak (accessed January 15, 2016).

"Positive Train Control," Association of American Railroads, 2015, https://www.aar.org/policy/positive-train-control (accessed January 15, 2016).

Halimah Abdullah, "Lawmakers on Hill Grill Amtrak Officials on Train Crash," NBC, June 2, 2015, http://www.nbcnews.com/ (accessed January 15, 2016).

Greg Botelho and Dana Ford, "Amtrak Crash: Video Shows Train Speeding Up," CNN, May 14, 2015, http://www.cnn.com/2015/05/14/us/philadelphia-amtrak-train-derailment (accessed January 16, 2016).

"Postive Train Control (PTC) Overview (Railroad Safety)," Federal Railroad Administration, accessed January 15, 2016, https://www.fra.dot.gov (accessed January 15, 2016).

Wikipedia, "Numerical weather prediction," January 7, 2016.

Wikipedia, "History of numerical weather prediction," January 4, 2016.

"Fact Sheet: Human Genome Project," National Institute of Health, October 2010, http://www.genome/gov (accessed January 17, 2016).

"Human Genome Project Completion: Frequently Asked Questions," National Human Genome Research Institute," April 14, 2003, https://www.genome.gov/11006943 (accessed January 17, 2016).

Wikipedia, "DNA sequencing," January 9, 2016.

LXXV Jim Lynch, "Juvenile prisoners in Michigan Allege Rape, Abuse," *Detroit News*, April 1, 2015, http://www.detroitnews.com/story/news/politics/2015/04/01/juvenile-prisoners-michigan-allege-rape-abuse (accessed January 20, 2016).

"Parental Consent and Notification," Planned Parenthood, 2014, https://www.plannedparenthood.org/learn/abortion/parental-consent-notification-laws (accessed January 20, 2016).

Wikipedia, "Age of consent," January 19, 2016.

Wray Herbert, "We're Only Human—The Teenage Brain: How Do We Measure Maturity?" Association for Psychological Science, March 29, 2013, http://www.psychologicalscience.org/index.php/news/were-only-human/the-teenage-brain (accessed January 16, 2016).

Wikipedia, "Maturity (psychological)," January 14, 2016.

LXXVI *Wikipedia*, "Referendum," July 9, 2015.

"A Brief History of the Initiative and Referendum Process in the United States," Initiative & Referendum Institute, University of Southern California, 2014, http://iandiinstitute.org (accessed July 21, 2015).

British House of Lords, *Referendums in the United Kingdom, 12th Report of Session 2009–10* (London: Parliament, 2010).

LXXVII Geoff Colvin, "Ursula Burns Launches Xerox into the Future," CNN Money, April 22, 2010, http://money.cnn.com/2010/04/22/news/companies/xerox_ursula_burns.fortune/index.htm (accessed 2010).

Geoff Colvin, "Xerox's Inventory-in-Chief," CNN Money, June 27, 2007, http://money.cnn.com/magazines/fortune/fortune_archive/2007/07/09/100121735/index.htm (accessed 2010).

Pedro Hernandez, "Xerox Thinks Vertical for Automated Document Management," eWeek, April 28, 2015, http://www.eweek.com/print/pc-hardware/xerox-thinks-vertical-for-automated-document-management (accessed January 18, 2016).

Gus Creedon, director at LMI, discussion with author, April 18, 2013.

Chapter 21

[LXXVIII] International Energy Agency, *2014 Key World Energy Statistics*, 2014, http://www.iea.org/publications/freepublications/publication (accessed April 27, 2015).

"MIT Panel of Experts," MIT Energy Initiative (panel at MIT, Cambridge, MA, June 4, 2010).

Wikipedia, "Energy Development," June 2010.

Wikipedia, "Energy development," March 26, 2015.

International Energy Agency, *World Energy Outlook 2012*, 2012, http://www.iea.org/publication/freepublications/publication/world-energy-outlook-2012.html (accessed April 27, 2015).

[LXXIX] World Nuclear Association, *Outline History of Nuclear Energy*, March 2014, http://www.world-nuclear.org/info/current-and-future-generation-outline-hisotry-of-nuclear-energy (accessed April 28, 2015).

Wikipedia, "Nuclear power," April 9, 2015.

"History of Nuclear Energy," Department of Energy, http://www.energy.gov/sites/prod/files/The%20History%20of%20Nuclear%20Energy_0.pdf (accessed April 28, 2015).

"Outline History of Nuclear Energy,"World Nuclear Association, March 2014, http://www.world-nuclear.org/info/current-and-future-generation-outline-hisotry-of-nuclear-energy (accessed April 28, 2015).

"Brief History of Fusion Power," LPPFusion, 2014, http://lawrencevilleplasmaphysics.com/fusion-power/brief-history-of-fusion-power (accessed April 28, 2015).

Encyclopedia Britannica, "Nuclear Fusion" (accessed April 29, 2015).

"What Is Fusion?ITER," 2015, http://www.iter.org/sci/Whatisfusion (accessed April 29, 2015).

Wikipedia, "Fusion power," May 23, 2007.

Wikipedia, "Timeline of nuclear fusion," April 4, 2015.

Wikipedia, "Fusion power," April 28, 2015.

John Glowienka, "Star-Building on Earth" (presentation at MIT Club of Washington, DC, December 10, 2014).

"Ignition Experiments," Lawrence Livermore National Laboratory, https://lasers.llnl.gov/science/ignition/ignition-experiments (accessed May 5, 2015).

Perkins et al., "Shock Ignition: A New Approach to High Gain Inertial Confinement Fusion on the National Ignition Facility," Berkeley Laboratory, http://www.lbl.gov/public (accessed May 4, 2015).

Wikipedia, "National Ignition Facility," May 1, 2015.

"LMJ/PETAL Laser Facility: Overview and Opportunities for Laboratory

Astrophysics," ScienceDirect, 2014,
http://www.sciencedirect.com/science/articfle/pii/S1574181814000871 (accessed
May 1, 2015).

French Alternative Energies and Atomic Energy Commission, *LMJ-PETAL User
Guide*, September 2014, http://www-
lmj.cea.fr/docs/2014/LMJ_PETAL_Users_guide_v1.0.pdf (accessed April 18,
2015).

Pravesh Patel, "Fast Ignition Program Overview," Princeton Plasma Physics
Laboratory, December 2, 2010, http://fire.pppl.gov (accessed May 21, 2015).

J. C. Fernandez et al., "Fast Ignition with Laser-Driven Proton and Ion Beams,"
IOPScience, 2014, http://iopscience.iop.org (accessed May 21, 2015).

"Facts & Figures," ITER, 2015, https://www.iter.org.factsfigures (accessed May
21, 2015).

Bernard S. Brown, "What Does the Kilojoule Look Like," *Biochemical
Education* (October 1979): 88–89.

Soo Bin Park, "South Korea Make Billion-Dollar Bet on Fusion Power,"
Nature, January 21, 2013, http://www.nature.com/news/south-korea-makes-billion-
dollar-bet-on-fusion-power-1.12251 (accessed May 5, 2015).

"Korea Aims at Completing DEMO by 2037," ITER, January 30, 2013,
https://www.iter.org/newsline/255/1481 (accessed May 5, 2015).

HiPER Project Team, *HiPER Preparatory Phase Final Report*, December 1,
2013, http://www.hiper-
laser.org/Resources/HiPER_Preparatory_Phase_Completion_Report.pdf (accessed
May 1, 2015).

"Laser riven Fusion to Develop the Path to Carbon-Free Energy on a Global
Scale," HiPER, October 6, 2008, http://www.hiper-laser.org/News (accessed May
4, 2015).

Lynn Savage, "HiPER to Expand Europe's Role in Laser-driven Nuclear Fusion
Technology," EuroPhotonics, June 2012,
http://www.photonics.com/Article.aspx?AID=51006 (accessed May 1, 2015).

John Glowienka (ITER program manager for US Department of Energy),
discussion with author at MIT Club of Washington, DC, meeting, December 10,
2014.

Gary J. Linford, "An Overlooked Solution to the Global Energy Crisis," *Infinite
Connectio*n, August 2008.

J. G. Delene, J. Sheffield, K. A. Williams, R. L. Reid, and S. Hadley, *An
Assessment of the Economics of Future Electric Power Generation Options and the
Implications for Fusion*, Oak Ridge National Laboratory, September 1999,
http://www.ornl.gov (accessed 6 May, 2015).

Per F. Peterson, "Inertial Fusion Energy: A Tutorial on the Technology and Economics," UCB Inertial Fusion Energy Tutorial, September 23, 1998, http://www.nuc.berkeley.edu/thyd/icf/IFE.html (accessed May 23, 2007).

D. J. Ward, I. Cook, and P. J. Knight, "The Impact of Physics Assumptions on Fusion Economics," International Atomic Energy Association, accessed May 6, 2015, http://www-pub.iaea.org/mtcd/publications.

"Economic, Safety and Environmental Prospects of Fusion Reactors," *IOPScience*, 1990, http://iopscience.iop.org/0029-5515/30/9/015 (accessed May 6, 2015).

Michelle Ma, "UW Fusion Reactor Concept Could Be Cheaper Than Coal," University of Washington, October 4, 2014, http://www.washington.edu/news/2014/10/08/uw-fusion-reactor (accessed May 6, 2015).

Eric Sofge, "MIT Fights for Clean Power with Holy Grail of Fusion in Reach," *Popular Mechanics,* October 1, 2009, http://www.popularmechanics.com/science/4251982 (accessed June 1, 2010).

Wikipedia, "Ford Quadricycle," April 2, 2015.

LXXX "Niagara Falls History of Power Development," Niagara Falls Info http://www.niagarafallsinfo.com (accessed May 25, 2015).

"Powering a Generation: Power History #1," National Museum of American History, http://americanhistory.si.edu (accessed May 25, 2015).

Wikipedia, "Electric power transmission," February 8, 2008.

Wikipedia, "List of largest power stations in the world," May 17, 2015.

Wikipedia, "Kashiwaszaki-Kariwa Nuclear Power Plant," May 14, 2015.

Wikipedia, "Superconductivity," May 16, 2015.

Graham Templeton, "World's First Superconducting Power Line Paves the Way for Billions of Dollars in Savings, More Nuclear Power Stations," ExtremeTech, May 14, 2014.

"World Premiere in Essen: PWE Integrates Superconductor Cable for the First Time into Existing Power Grid," Nexans, May 5, 2014, http://www.nexans.com/eservice/Corporate-en/navigatepub_142482_-33667/World_premiere_in_Essen_RWE_integrates_superconduc.html# (accessed May 21, 2015).

"How HVDC Works," Clean Line Energy Partners, 2015, http://www.cleanlineenergy.com/technology/hvdc (accessed May 21, 2015).

"The World's Longest Power Transmission Lines," Power Technology, February 18, 2014, http://www.power-technology.com/features/ (accessed May 21, 2015).

PESWiki, s.v. "PowerPedia: Electric Power Transmission," February 17, 2007, http://peswiki.com/index.php/OPwoerPedia:Electric_power_transmission (accessed February 11, 2008).

"Smart Grid," US Department of Energy, http://energy.gov/oe/services/technology-development/smart-grid (accessed May 26, 2015).

"What Is the Smart Grid?" Smartgrid, https://www.smartgird.gov/the_snmart_grid/smart_grid (accessed May 26, 2015).

Wikipedia, "Smart grid," May 24, 2015, http://en.wikipedia.org/wiki/Smart_grid (accessed May 26, 2015).

Wikipedia, "Unified Smart Grid," December 14, 2014.

Matt Smith, "Unified Smart Grid Can Prepare Utilities for Next Superstorm," Electric Lighting & Power, February 17, 2014, http://www.elp.com/articles/powergrid_international/print/volume-19/issue-2/features (accessed May 26, 2015).

Faycal Bouhafs, Michael MacKay, and Madjid Merabti, *Communication Challenges and Solutions in the Smart Grid* (New York: Springer, 2014), 83–95.

Wikipedia, "MHD Generator," January 17, 2008.

Flavio Dobran, "Fusion Energy Conversion in Magnetically Confined Plasma Reactors," *Progress in Nuclear Energy* 60 (September 2012): 89–116.

C. P. C. Wong et al, "Progress on DCLL Blanket Concept," *Fusion Science and Technology* 64, no. 3 (September 2013): 623–630.

MacMillan Encyclopedia of Energy, s.v. "Magnetohydrodynamics," 2006, http://www.bookrags.com/research/magnetohydrodynamics-mee-02 (accessed February 14, 2008).

P. Massee, L. H. T. Rietjens, and A. J. D. Lambert, "Assessment of the Potential of Magnetohydrodynamic Energy Conversion for Tokamak Reactors," *Fusion Science and Technology* 17, no. 3 (May 1990): 439–451.

Ralph W. Moir, "Direct Energy Conversion in Fusion Reactors," *Energy Technology Handbook* (New York: McGraw Hill, 1977): 5-150–5-154.

Ben Harack, "How Do We Turn Nuclear Fusion Energy into Electricity?" Vision of Earth, November 2, 2010, http://www.visionofearth.org/industry/fusion/how-do-we-turn-nuclear-fusion-energy-into-electricity? (accessed May 21, 2015).

Mohamed Abdou, "Introduction to MHD and Applications to Thermofluids of Fusion Blankets," *Fusion Science and Technology* 51, no. 1 (January 2007), http://www.fusion.ucla.edu/abdou (accessed May 21, 2015).

Y. Yasaka, K. Goto, A. Taniguchi, A. Tsuji, and H. Takeno, "Studies on Plasma Direct Energy Converters for Thermal and Fusion-Produced Ions Using Slanted Cusp Magnetic and Distributed Electric Fields," *Nuclear Fusion* 49, no. 7 (2009).

Charles Stein, *Critical Materials Problems in Energy Production* (New York: Academic Press, 1976).

Wikipedia, "Regional transmission organization," Mar 18, 2015.

"Union for the Coordination of the Transmission of Electricity," ENTSO-E, 2014, https://www.entsoe.eu/news-events/former-associations (accessed May 27, 2015).

"Member Companies," ENTSO-E, 2014, https://www.entsoe.eu/about-entso-e/inside-entso-e/member-companies (accessed May 27, 2015).

"UCTE," Centrel, 2015, http://www.centrel.org/ucte.html (accessed May 27, 2015).

Wikipedia, "Super grid," January 3, 2015.

"Developing a Reliable Wind Supergrid," European Commission, December 16, 2014, http://cordis.europa.eu/news/rcn/122208_en.html (accessed May 26, 2015).

Paul Brown, "EU Plans Power Supergrid to Boost Renewables," *Climate News Network*, November 5, 2014, http://www.climatenewsnetwork.net/eu-plans-power-supergrid-to-boost-renewables (accessed May 26, 2015).

"How Close Are We to Realising a European Supergrid?" Power Engineering International, June 20, 2013, http://www.powerengineeeringint.com/articles/print/volumen-21/issue-6 (accessed May 26, 2015).

Chapter 22

LXXXI *Wikipedia*, "Silk Road," October 7, 2005.

"Silk Road History," TravelChinaGuide, 2008, http://www.travelchinaguide.com/silk-road/history (accessed May 23, 2008).

Oliver Wild, "The Silk Road," University of California, Irvine, 1992, http://www.ess.uci.edu/oliver/silk.html (accessed October 7, 2005).

LXXXII Jared Diamond, *Guns, Germs, and Steel* (New York: Norton, 1999), 93–103.

Mark Sincell, "New Clue to Sahara's Origins," *Science*, July 9, 1999, http://www.sciencemag.org/news/1999/07/new-clue-saharas-origins (accessed January 27, 2016).

Bjorn Carey, "Sahara Desert Was Once Lush and Populated," *LiveScience*, July 20, 2006, http://www.livescience.com (accessed January 27, 2016).

"A Slow Birth for the Sahara," *Science*, May 8, 2008, http://www.sciencemag.org/news/2008/05/slow-birth-sahara (accessed January 27, 2016).

Anuradha K. Herath, "How Earth's Orbital Shift Shaped the Sahara," *Astrobiology*, December 20, 2010, http://www.astrobio.net/news-exclusive/how-earths-orbital-shaped-the-sahara (accessed January 27, 2016).

Becky Oskin, "Sahara Went from Green to Desert in a Flashm," *LiveScience*, April 5, 2013, http://www.livescience.com/28493-when-sahara-desert-formed.html (accessed January 27, 2016).

Encyclopedia Britannica, "Sahara," 2016.

Wikipedia, "Sahara," December 30, 2015.

Wikispaces, s.v. "Nation Building—Holy Roman Empire," 2016, https://themedievalera.wikispaces.com/Nation+Building+-+Holy+Roman+Empire (accessed February 2, 2016).

"Song Dynasty in China," Asia for Educators, Columbia University, 2008, http://afe.easia.columbia.edu/song/out/trade.htm (accessed February 2, 2016).

"The Trading World of China, Japan, and the Phillipines," World Economy, http://www.theworldeconomy.org/org/impact/The_trading_world_of_china_japan_and_the_phillipines (accessed February 2, 2016).

Wikipedia, "History of Sino-Japanese relations," December 28, 2015.

[LXXXIII] Ray Smith, "Ray Smith's Notebook of Metalworking Origins," Anvilfire, 2002, http://anvilfire.com/21centbs/stories/rsmith/RSindex.htm (accessed November 10, 2012).

Diamond, *Guns, Germs, and Steel*, 224–233.

Bill Woodley, *The Impact of Transformative Technologies on Governance: Some Lessons from History*, NGO Report (Ottawa, CA: Institute on Governance, 2001).

Film about the Clo-e, an indigenous people in South America, by National Geographic Channel, 2008.

"Iron Making History in China," ChinaCulture, 2008, http://www.chinaculture.org/library/2008-02/01/content_26524.htrn (accessed September 14, 2010).

Wikipedia, "Hiragana," January 17, 2016.

Wikipedia, "Movable type," January 12, 2016.

Wikipedia, "Chinese characters," January 25, 2016.

Chapter 23

[LXXXIV] The principle of *process* overlaid upon *relationship* exists not just in nation-state governance but in nation-state life as well. Every organization is run by both the relationships between people and the processes that deliver the product or service. Corporations develop business policies, which when followed help to grow the business. Street signs are an example of process: everyone's experience on the road goes better when everyone follows the road signs. Corporations also function based on relationship. It is common to hear the cynic make this observation with the adage: "It is not what you know, it is who you know." In corporate downsizings, it is common for people to cling to a director as a form of job protection.

Even in the modern world, however, there are places that still use relationship as the basis for getting things done. The city boss was a prominent fixture in American history well into the twentieth century. In twentieth-century America, many towns, small and large, were influenced by a local boss. Harry Truman got his political start with support from the Kansas City boss. In parts of the world, a town might be controlled by a local "boss," who is a type of local sovereign. He either controls the town or has great influence over it. If you want something done, he has to approve it. If you live there, your opportunities in life are directly correlated with your relationship to him. A few years ago, near Timbuktu, Mali, National Geographic reported how one of its journalists identified such a boss. He was an Al Qaeda operative who had been responsible for kidnapping foreigners between 2008 and 2011. The journalist was warned by one old resident, "The One-eye has eyes everywhere.... I'm sure he knows you are here."

In these regions, process is less important and it shows. Traffic is worse because people do not take road signs seriously. Business is less efficient because bribery and graft are normal practices that override established policies. Justice is even more capricious because courts issue arbitrary rulings rather than follow due process. Governments become corrupt because officials sidestep written law for their own personal gain.

Even in normal situations in a nation-state, when process breaks down, such as after a disaster (Hurricane Katrina or an aircraft goes down), personal contact and relationships are needed to make things happen (rescue, establish order, and comfort the loss). This is innate in our humanity.

LXXXV Clayton M. Christensen and Michael E Raynor, "Why Hard-Nosed Executives Should Care About Management Theory," *Harvard Business Review* (September 2003): 67–74.

Wikipedia, "Alfred C. Chandler Jr.," June 2, 2016.

LXXXVI Derek Lutterbeck, *The Role of Armed Forces in the Arab Uprisings*, University of Malta, April 5, 2015, http://www.um.edu.mt (accessed May 13, 2016).

Zoltan Barany, "Comparing the Arab Revolts," *Journal of Democracy* 22, no. 4 (October 2011): 28–39.

Wikipedia, "Tunisia," May 13, 2016.

Wikipedia, "Tunisian Revolution," May 2016.

Wikipedia, "Egypt," May 13, 2016.

Wikipedia, "History of the Republic of Egypt," April 16, 2016.

"Amid Crackdown, Egypt Sentences 152 People to Prison for Protesting," NPR, May 15, 2016, www.npr.org (accessed May 15, 2016).

Wikipedia, "Libya," May 12, 2016.

Wikipedia, "Yemen," May 15, 2016.

Wikipedia, "Bahrain," May 26, 2016.

Wikipedia, "Bahraini uprising of 2011," May 25, 2016.

Encyclopedia Britannica, "Habib Bourguiba," 2016.

Ali Ben Mabrouk, "Reflecting on Bourguiba, 13 Years After His Death," Tunisialive, April 9, 2013, http://www.tunisia-live.net/2013/04/09/reflecting-on-bourguibab-13-years-after-his-death (accessed June 6, 2016).

Eric Pace, "Habib Bourguiba, Independence Champion and President of Tunisia, Dies at 96," *New York Times*, April 7, 2000. http://www.nytimes.com/2000/04/07/world/habib-bourguiba-independence-champion-and-president (accessed June 6, 2016).

"Habib Bourguiba: Father of Tunisia," BBC, April 6, 2000, http://news.bbc.co.uk/2/hi/obituaries/703907.stm (accessed June 6, 2016).

Wikipedia, "Zine El Abidine Ben Ali," June 2, 2016.

Encyclopedia Britannica, "Zine al-Abidine Ben Ali," 2016.

Tristan Dreisbach, "Revealing Tunisia's Corruption Under Ben Ali," Al Jazeera, March 27, 2014, http://www.aljazeera.com/indepth/features/2014/03/revealing-tunisia-corruption-under-ben-ali-201432785825560542.html (accessed June 6, 2016).

Wikipedia, "History of Yemen," May 31, 2016.

Wikipedia, "Hafez al-Assad," May 30, 2016.

Encyclopedia Britannica, "Hafiz al-Assad," 2016.

Wikipedia, "Syrian Civil War," June 8, 2016.

Wikipedia, "Free Syrian Army," June 4, 2016.

Aleksandar Mishkov, *Syrian Civil War—Quick Timeline Explaining the Story of the Conflict*, DocumentaryTube, November 2015, http://www.documentarytube.com/articles/syrian-civil-war-quick-timeline-explaining-story-of-the-conflict (accessed June 8, 2016).

LXXXVII *Chapter 24*

Wikipedia, "Iraqi parliamentary election, 2010," June 2, 2016.

Wikipedia, "Iraqi parliamentary election, 2014," December 29, 2015.

Wikipedia, "Iraqi parliamentary election, December 2005," June 12, 2016.

Liz Sly, "Maliki's Bloc Leads in Iraq Election," *Washington Post*, May 19, 2014, https://www.washingtonpost.com/world/middle_east/malikis-bloc-leads-in-iraq-election/2014/05/19/f7e695cb-414b-4a63-879e-bd13df8ad8d7_story.html (accessed June 13, 2016).

"Iraq Elections: Maliki's State of Law 'Wins Most Seats,'" BBC, May 19, 2014, http://www.bbc.com/news/world-middle-east-27474518 (accessed June 13, 2016).

Wikipedia, "Prime Minister of Iraq," April 24, 2016.

Anne-Sophie Brandlin, "Haider al-Abadi: 'I Cannot Turn the Country Upside Down in One Day,'" Deutsche Welle, February 11, 2016, http://www.dw.com/en/haider-al-abadi-i-cannot-turn-the-country-upside-down-in-one-day (accessed June 13, 2016).

"Iraqi PM Ready to Resign as Part of Cabinet Reshuffle," Al Jazeera, February 16, 2016, http://www.aljazeera.com/news/2016/02/iraqi-pm-ready-resign-part-cabinet-shuffle (accessed June 13, 2016).

Zalmay Khalilzad, "Haider al-Abadi's Dangerous Gamble," *New York Times*, April 12, 2016, http://www.nytimes.com/2016/04/13/opinion/haider-al-abadis-dangerous-gamble.html (accessed June 13, 2016).

Mustafa Saadoun, "Will Abadi Resign from His Party?" Al Monitor, April 27, 2016, http://www.al-monitor.com/pulse/originals/2016/04/iraq-abdai-resignation-government-technocrat (accessed June 13, 2016).

LXXXVIII Jonathan Tirone, "Syrian Transition Plan Reached by U.S., Russia in Vienna," Bloomberg, November 14, 2015, http://www.bloomberg.com/news/articles/2015-11-14/syrian-transition-plan-achieved-by-u-s-allies (accessed June 10, 2016).

United Nations Security Council, Resolution 2254, December 18, 2015.

"US Timeline Sees Assad as Syria Leader until at Least March," Associated Press, January 6, 2016, http://foxnews.com/politics/2016/01/06/us-timeline-sees-assad-as-syria-leader-until-at-least-march (accessed June 10, 2016).

"US Asks Syria to Stick to Political Transition Timeline," Firstpost, May 4, 2016, http://www.firstpost.com (accessed June 10, 2016).

Ann Barnard, "Syrian Parliamentary Elections Highlight Divisions and Uncertainty," *New York Times*, April 13, 2016: A10.

Wikipedia, "People's Council of Syria," June 8, 2016.

Lizzie Dearden, "Russia open to US plan for Syria 'safe zones' but only with Bashar al-Assad's approval," The Independent, February 23, 2017, http://www.independent.co.uk/news/world/middle-east/russia-us-plan-syria-safe-zones-bashar-al-assad-approval-civil-war-donald-trump-vladimir-putin-a7595011.html (accessed September 5, 2017).

Evan Halper and W.J. Hennigan, "Syria crisis tests Trump's plan for a new world order," LA Times, April 7, 2017, http://www.latimes.com/politics/la-fg-pol-syria-analysis-20170407-story.html (accessed September 5, 2017).

Spencer Ackerman, "What's Trump's plan for Syria? Five different policies in two weeks," The Guardian, April 11, 2017, https://www.theguardian.com/us-news/2017/apr/11/donald-trump-syria-bashar-al-assad-isis (accessed September 5, 2017).

Byrony Jones, Clarissa Ward, and Salma Abdelaziz, "Al-Nusra rebranding: New name, same aim? What you need to know," CNN, August 2, 2016, http://www.cnn.com/2016/08/01/middleeast/al-nusra-rebranding-what-you-need-to-know/index.html (accessed September 5, 2017).

LXXXIX Bing West, "A War, a Love Story, and Dozens of Broken Rules," *Washington Post*, March 30, 2014: B1.

Matthew Hoh, "A Sudden Exit Driven by an 'Irrational' War," *All Things Considered*, National Public Radio, WAMU, Washington, DC, October 29, 2009.

Kevin Sieff, "As Marines Depart Province, Afghans Worry," *Washington Post*, September 30, 2012: A16.

Noah Coburn and Ronald Neumann, "Afghnistan after Karzai," *Washington Post*, March 30, 2014: A15.

Wikipedia, "Afghanistan," May 17, 2016, https://en.wikipedia.org/wiki/Afghanistan (accessed May 17, 2016).

Rod Norland, "After Rancor, Afghans Agree to Share Power," *New York Times*, September 2014: A1.

J.K., "Afghanistan's Dispute Election: Divide and ule," *Economist*, September 14, 2014, http://www.economist.com/node/21619585 (accessed May 17, 2016).

Jawad Sukhanyar and Mujib Mashal, "In Afghanistan, John Kerry Seeks End to Bickering in Unity Government," *New York Times*, April 9, 2016, http://www.nytimes.com/2016/04/10/world/asia/john-kerry-arrives-in-afghanistan-with-message-of-suport (accessed May 18, 2016).

Masood Saifullah and Imam Shamil, "Is the Afghan Unity Government Falling Apart?" Deutsche Welle, April 12, 2016, http://www.dw.com/en/is-the-afghan-unity-government-falling-apart/a-19180730 (accessed May 17, 2016).

Catherine Putz, "19 Months Later, Afghan Government Lacks Core Ministerial Leadership," Diplomat, May 6, 2016, http://thediplomat.com/2016/05/19-months-later-afghan-government-lacks-core-ministerial-leadership (accessed May 17, 2016).

Ali M. Latifi, "Kerry's Comments in Afghanistan on Unity Government Spur Anger, Charges of U.S. Interference," *Los Angeles Time*s, April 11, 2016, http://www.latimes.com/world/middleeast/la-fg-afghanistan-kerry-20160411-

story.html (accessed May 17, 2016).

International Crisis Group, *Afghanistan's Flawed Constitutional Process*, NGO Report (Brussels: International Crisis Group, 2003).

Fausto Biloslavo, "The Afghan Constitution between Hope and Fear," *CeMiSS Quarterly* 2, no. 1 (Spring 2004): 61–75.

An Introduction to the Constitutional Law of Afghanistan, edited by Aghanistan Legal Education Project, Stanford Law School (Palo Alto, CA: Stanford University, 2013).

Wikipedia, "1964 Constitution of Afghanistan," January 6, 2015.

Wikipedia, "Mohammed Daoud Khan," May 13, 2016.

Wikipedia, "Mohammed Zahir Shah," May 27, 2016.

Wikipedia, "Hamid Karzai," May 31, 2016.

Wikipedia, "Loya jirga," March 5, 2016.

Wikipedia, "Soviet_Afghan War," June 23, 2016.

Central Intelligence Agency, "Morocco," *World Factbook*, May 9, 2016, https://www.cia.gov/library/publications/the-world-factbook/geos/mo.html (accessed June 2, 2016).

"Morocco Profile-Overview," BBC, November 11, 2015, http://www.bbc.com/news/world-africa-14121439 (accessed June 2, 2016).

Wikipedia, "Morocco," May 31, 2016.

Lisa Jane Fallon, "Why I Left England and I settled in Morocco," *Morocco World News*, June 1, 2016, http://www.moroccoworldnews.com/2016/06/187917/whi-i-left-england-and-i-settled-in-morocco (accessed June 2, 2016).

Wikipedia, "Parliament of Morocco," January 6, 2016.

Fred Bezhan, "Crisis Looms as Clock Winds Down on Afghan 'Unity Government' Deal," Radio Free Europe, September 4, 2016, https://www.rferl.org/a/afghanistan-crisis-looms-expiring-unity-government-deal/27966465.html (accessed September 7, 2017).

Pamela Constable, "Afghanistan's Shaky National Unity Government Approaches its Second Anniversary," Washington Post, September 28, 2016, https://www.washingtonpost.com/world/asia_pacific/afghanistans-shaky-unity-national-government-approaches-its-second-anniversary/2016/09/28/37495ad4-84e3-11e6-b57d-dd49277af02f_story.html?utm_term=.8d0bbbf9c5d3 (accessed September 7, 2017).

Hamid M. Saboory, "What is Going Wrong with Afghanistan's National Unity Government?" The Diplomat, September 29, 2016, http://thediplomat.com/2016/09/what-is-going-wrong-with-afghanistans-national-unity-government/ (accessed September 7, 2017).

Mujib Mashal and Helene Cooper, "2 Top Afghanistan Military Officials Resign After Taliban Attack," New York Times, April 24, 2017, https://www.nytimes.com/2017/04/24/world/asia/afghanistan-taliban-defense-minister-resigns.html?mcubz=1 (accessed September 7, 2017).

Afghanistan: The Future of the National Unity Government, Crisis Group, Report No. 285, April 10, 2017, https://www.crisisgroup.org/asia/south-asia/afghanistan/285-afghanistan-future-national-unity-government (accessed September 7, 2017).

Thomas Gibbons-Neff and Sayed Salahuddin, "U.S. Defense Chief Arrives in Kabul as Afghan Defense Minister Resigns in Disgrace," Chicago Tribune, April 24, 2017, http://www.chicagotribune.com/news/nationworld/politics/ct-defense-secretary-afghanistan-20170424-story.html

[XC] Martin Smith, "The Rise of ISIS," *Frontline*, television program produced for Public Broadcasting Service, 2014.

Bobby Ghosh, "ISIS: A Short History," *Atlantic*, August 14, 2014, http://www.theatlantic.com/international/archive/2014/08/isis-a-short-history/376030 (accessed June 26, 2016).

Wikipedia, "Caliphate," June 19, 2016.

Karl Vick, "What Is the Caliphate?" *Time*, July 1, 2014, http://time.com/2942239/what-is-the-caliphate (accessed June 23, 2016).

Tim Lister, "What Does ISIS Really Want?" CNN, December 11, 2015, https://www.cnn.com/2015/12/11/middleeast/isis-syria-iraq-caliphate (accessed June 26, 2016).

Wikipedia, "Abdulmecid II," May 28, 2016, https://en.wikipedia.org/wiki/Abdulmecid_II (accessed June 26, 2016).

Anne Aly, "Is It Fair to Blame the West for Trouble in the Middle East?" Conversation, October 5, 2014, http://theconversation.com/is-it-fair-to-blame-the-west-for-trouble-in-the-middle-east-32487 (accessed June 24, 2016).

Zainab Salbi, "What People in the Middle East Say in Private about the West," *New York Times*, May 26, 2015, http://nytlive.nytimes.com/womenintheworld/2015/05/26/what-people-in-the-middle-east-are-saying-in-private-about-the-west (accessed June 22, 2016).

Emily Badger, "Why Are the World's Muslims So Mad at America?" *Pacific Standard*, May 19, 2011, https://psmag.com/why-are-the-world-s-muslims-so-mad-at-america-46d9cea2d759 (accessed June 24, 2016).

Steven Kull, "Why Muslims Are Still Mad at America," CNN, September 5, 2011, http://globalpublicsquare.blogs.cnn.com/2011/09/05/why-muslims-are-still-mad-at-america (accessed June 24, 2016).

Bernard Lewis, "Fundamentalist Muslim Rage," Awesome Library, 2015, http://www.awesomelibrary.org/Muslims-Rage.html (accessed June 24, 2016).

Ramzy Baroud, "Understanding the Roots of the 'Angry Muslim,'" Middle East Eye, June 23, 2014, http://www.middleeasteye.net/columns/understanding-roots-angry-muslim-1195255220 (accessed June 24, 2016).

Chapter 25

[XCI] Mark Sisson, "Dunbar Number: Maximum Human Group Size," Mark's Daily Apple, March 9, 2010, http://www.marksdailyapply.com/dunbars-number-group-size (accessed June 17, 2010).

Edward T. Hall, *Beyond Culture* (New York: Anchor Books, 1976), 203.

"General Assembly of the United Nations," United Nations, 2016, http://www.un.org/en/ga (accessed February 11, 2016).

Central Intelligence Agency, *The World Factbook*, January 27, 2016.

Epilogue

[XCII] Lev Grossman, "A Star Is Born," *Time* 186, no. 18 (November 2, 2015).

BIBLIOGRAPHY

Altenergy.org. *Alternative Energy.* n.d. http://www.altenergy.org (accessed June 2010).

American Heritage Dictionary. *Nexus.* 2004. http://dictionary.reference.com/browse/nexus (accessed June 6, 2008).

American Heritage Dictionary of the English Language. *fiefdom.* n.d. http://dictionary.com.reference/browse/fiefdom (accessed August 15, 2009).

American Heritage Dictionary of the English Language, 4th ed. *Due process.* n.d. http://dictionary.reference.com/browse/due process (accessed August 15, 2009).

Ang, Peng Hwa and James Dewar. "Back to the Future of the Internet: The Printing Press." *Learning Initiatives on Reforms for Network Economies.* n.d. http://lirne.net/resources/netknowledge/ang.pdf (accessed May 11, 2007).

Angier, Natalie. "Do Races Differ? Not Really, DNA shows." *Science,* August 22, 2000.

Baker, John. *The Oxford History of the Laws of England.* London: Oxford University Press, 2003.

Barnsdale, David. *Russian Revolution in Dates.* Febuary 14, 2005. http://www.barnsdel.demon.co.uk/russ/datesr.html (accessed February 11, 2009).

Baronial Order of Magna Charta. *Stephen Langton—Archbishop of Canterbury.* n.d. http://www.magnacharta.com/articles/articles/article01E.htm (accessed August 5, 2010).

Biographybase. *Stephen Langton Biography.* n.d. http://www.biographybase.com/biography/Langton_Stephen.html (accessed August 5, 2010).

Bowblis, John. *China in the 20th Century.* April 12, 2000. http://departments.kings.edu/history/20c/china.html (accessed February 11, 2009).

Bradley, Colin. "History of Fireworks." *History of Fireworks and Gunpowder.* 2005. http://www.pyrouniverse.com/history.htm (accessed October 11, 2005).

Britain Express. *Celtic Britain (The Iron Age).* n.d.
   http://www.britainexpress.com/History/Celtic_Britain.htm (accessed
   September 12, 2006).

Britain in Print. *An Introduction to Printing.* 2003.
   http://www.britaininprint.net/introtoprint/england.htm (accessed July 24,
   2009).

Brookings Institution. "Internet Development in China: Its Impact on Politics and
   Society." *Internet Development in China: Its Impact on Politics and Society.*
   Washington D.C.: Anderson Court Reporting, 2007. 13-15.

Bungale, Prashanth and Swaroop Sridhar. "Eletronic Voting—A Survey." *Citeseer.*
   2003. citeseerx.ist.psu.edu/viewdoc/download?doi=10.1.1.87...rep... (accessed
   February 24, 2009).

Butler, Chris. *The Birth of Metallurgy and its Impact—The Flow of History.* 2007.
   http://flowofhistory.com/units/pre/1/FC8 (accessed July 30, 2007).

Chilton, Bradley Steward. "Star Trek and Stare Decisis: Legal Reasoning and
   Information Technology." *Journal of Criminal Justice and Popular Culture.*
   2001. http://www.albany.edu/scj/jcjpc/vol18is1/chilton.html (accessed July
   20, 2009).

Chiorazzi, Michael and Gordon Russell. *Law Library Collection Development in the
   Digital Age.* London: Psychology Press, 2002.

Citizendium.org. *Industrial Revolution.* July 10, 2007.
   http://en.citizendium.org/wiki/Industrial_Revolution (accessed August 2,
   2007).

CNN. *North American Union?* Atlanta, July 2008.

Collins English Dictionary; 10th Edition. "Innovation." *Dictionary.com.* n.d.
   http://dictionary.reference.com/browse/innovation (accessed November 01,
   2012).

Columbia Electronic Encyclopedia, 6th ed. *European Economic Community.* 2007.
   http://www.infoplease.com/ce6/history/A0817889.html (accessed February
   23, 2009).

Colvin, Geoff. "Ursula Burns Launches Xerox into the Future." *CNN Money.* April
   22, 2010.
   http://money.cnn.com/2010/04/22/news/companies/xerox_ursula_burns.fort
   une/index.htm (accessed 2010).

—. "Xerox's Inventory-in-Chief." *CNN Money.* June 27, 2007.
   http://money.cnn.com/magazines/fortune/fortune_archive/2007/07/09/1001
   21735/index.htm (accessed 2010).

Computerhope. *When was the first computer invented?* n.d.
   http://www.computehope.com/issues/ch000984.htm (accessed June 18,
   2010).

Corbett, John, interview by Neil Hamblin. *Working in East Africa* (July 27, 2009).

Cosmic Log, NBC News. *How Far Away is Fusion.* June 6, 2007.
   http://cosmiclog.nbcnews.com/_news/2007/06/28/4351572-how-far-away-is-
   fusion?

Dewdney, Christopher. "The History of Language and Writing." *Living Literacies Text.* York University, 2002.

Diamond, Jared. *Guns, Germs, and Steel.* New York: W.W. Norton & Company, 1999.

Dictionary.com. *Taxonomy.* n.d. http://dictionary.reference.com/browse/taxonomy (accessed October 22, 2009).

Dictionary.com Unabridged. Random House, Inc. *Forecasting.* n.d. http://dictionary.reference.com/browse/forecasting (accessed January 26, 2009).

Duffy, Shannon E. *H-Net Reviews in Humanities and Social Sciences.* June 2000. http://www.h-net.msu.edu/reviews/showrev.cgi?path=24899962821867 (accessed May 11, 2007).

Duffy, Shannon. "Review of Elizabeth L. Eisenstein, The Printing Press as an Agent of Change." *H-Ideas, H-Net Reviews.* June 2000. http://www.h-net.msu.edu/reviews/showrev.cgi?path=24899962821867.

EdInformatics.com. *EDinformatics.* 1999. http://www.edinformatics.com/inventions_inventors/steel.htm (accessed October 14, 2005).

Eisner, Michael. "Modernization, Self-Control, and Lethal Violence: The Long-term Dynamics of European Homicide Rates in Theoretical Perspective." *British Journal of Criminology,* 2001: 618-638.

Ernst & Young. "Blockchain reaction." 2016.

European Commission on Energy Research. *A Brief History of Fusion Research.* n.d. http://ec.europa.eu/research/energy/fu/fu_int/article_1247_en.htm (accessed July 2, 2009).

European Union. "European Future Internet Portal." *Bled Declaration: Future Internet.* March 17, 2008. http://www.future-internet.eu/publicatinos/bled-declaration.html (accessed February 24, 2009).

Genet, Am J Hum. *The Use of Racial, Ethnic, and Ancestral Categories in Human Genetics Research.* Working Group paper, Bethesda, MD: National Human Genome Research Institute, 2005.

Griscom, Amanda. "Trends of Anarchy and Hierarchy." *Print: Media and 17th Century Society.* n.d. http://www.cyberartsweb.org/cspace/infotech/asg/ag14.html (accessed July 27, 2009).

Hall, Edward. *Edward: Hall: The Perfect Group Size is 8-12.* June 28, 2006. http://37signals.com/svn/archives2/edward_hall_the_perfect_group_size_812.php (accessed June 17, 2010).

Hearnshaw, F.J.C. "Legal Literature." In *Cambridge History of English and American Literature in 18 Volumes,* by A.W. and A.R. Waller Ward. New York: Bartleby.com, 2000.

History Bookshop. *Timeline.* n.d. http://www.historybookshop.com/timeline.

Hoovers. *Internet Service Providers Industry Overview.* 2010. http://www.hoovers.com/industry-facts.internet-service-providers.1584.html (accessed June 25, 2010).

Iansiti, Marco, and Karin R Lakhani. "The Truth about Blockchain." *Harvard Business Review.* Jan-Feb 2017.

Ibeji, Mike. *An Overview of Roman Britain.* June 1, 2001. http://bbc.co.uk/history/ancient/romans/questions_02.shtml (accessed September 9, 2008).

Internet Policy Institute. *Report of the National Workshop on Internet Voting: Issues and Research Agenda.* National Workshop on Internet Voting, Washington D.C.: Internet Policy Institute, 2001.

Investopedia. "Blockchain." *Investopedia.* n.d. http://www.investopedia.com/terms/blockchain.asp (accessed March 17, 2017).

ITER. *ITER History.* 2010. http://www.iter.org/proj/iterhistory (accessed June 2010).

Jefferson, David, Aviel Rubin, Barbara Simons, and David Wagner. "A Security Analysis of the Secure Electronic Registration and Voting Experiment." *Analysis of Intenet Voting Security in the SERVE.* January 20, 2004. http://servsecurityreport.org (accessed February 24, 2009).

Jorde, Lynne B., and Stephen P. Wooding. "Genetic variation, classification, and 'race'." *Nature Genetics* 36, no. S28-S33 (2004).

Karagianis, Liz. "MIT Spectrum." *Collective Brainpower.* Summer 2010. http://spectrum.mit.edu/issue/2010-summer/collective-brainpower (accessed June 8, 2010).

Kennedy, Paul. *The Rise and Fall of the Great Powers.* New York: Random House, 1987.

Kreis, Steven. *The English Civil War.* February 28, 2006. http://www.historyguide.org/earlymod/lecture7c.html (accessed July 30, 2009).

—. *The Printing Press.* May 13, 2004. http://www.historyguide.org/intellect/press.html (accessed July 27, 2009).

Kristula, Dave. *The History of the Internet.* 2001. http://www.davesite.com/webstation/net-history.shtml (accessed February 24, 2009).

Lai, Selena and Waka Takahashi Brown. *The Shang Dynasty, 1600 to 1050 BCE.* November 2006. http://spice.stanford.edu/docs/117 (accessed September 7, 2010).

Landes, Richard. "Peace and Truce of God." In *Encyclopedia of the Middle Ages, Pt 114, Vol 1*, by Andre Vauchez, 1103-1105. Cambridge, UK: James Clarke & Co, 2002.

—. *Peace of God: Pax Dei.* n.d. http://www.mille.org/people/rlpages/paxdei.html (accessed September 25, 2009).

Lehman, Clarence. "Univeristy of Minnesota." *We Have Passed Our Sustainability.* n.d. http://www.umn.edu (accessed January 21, 2009).

Levine, Marsha. "Levine—Domestication, Breed Diversification, and Early History of the Horse." *Domestication, Breed Diversification, and Early History of the Horse.* n.d.

http://www3.vet.upenn.edu/labs/equinebehavior//hvnwkshp/hv02/levine.htm (accessed June 18, 2007).

Lewis, Brenda Lewis. *Why the Dark Ages?* March 8, 2010. http://suite101.com/article/why-the-dark-ages-a210582 (accessed 2010).

Lewis, Paul. "Curb on Population Growth Needed Urgently, U.N. Says." *New York Times.* April 30, 1992. http://query.nytimes.com/gst/fullpage.html (accessed January 21, 2009).

MacDonald, Keving. "The Establishment and Maintenance of Socially Imposed Monogamy in Western Europe." *Journal of Politics and Life Sciences*, 1995: 3-23.

MacMillan Encyclopedia of Energy. *Magnetohydrodynamics.* 2006. http://www.bookrags.com/research/magnetohydrodynamics-mee-02 (accessed February 14, 2008).

Marr, Bernard. "How Blockchain Technology Could Change the World." *Forbes.* May 27, 2016. https://www.forbes.com/sites/bernardmarr/2016/05/27/how-blockchain-technology-could-change-the-world/#b075b38725b2 (accessed March 2017).

Merriam-Wesbters's Dictionary of Law. *Rule-of-law.* n.d. http://dictionary.reference.com/browse/rule of law (accessed August 15, 2009).

Microsoft Encarta. *Silk Road.* 2008. http://encarta.msn.com/encyclopedia_761579956_2/Silk_Road.html (accessed May 23, 2008).

Microsoft. *Gates Shares Microsoft's Vision for a More Secure Future.* February 14, 2006. http://www.microsoft.com/presspass/press/2006/feb06/02-14rsa06keynotepr.mspx (accessed February 24, 2009).

MIT, interview by MIT Alumni Weekend. *MIT Energy Initiatives* (June 3, 2010).

MSNBC News Service. *$13 Billion Nuclear Fusion Site Gets Green Light.* June 28, 2005. http://www.msnbc.msn.com/id/8385911 (accessed August 17, 2007).

National Archives Learning Curve. *Feudal System.* n.d. http://www.spartacus.schoolnet.co.uk/NORfeudal.htm (accessed September 12, 2006).

The Clo-e People. Performed by National Geographic Channel. 2008.

Orloff, Geoffrey. *Alternative Energy Sources.* n.d. http://www.about.com (accessed June 2010).

PESWiki. *PowerPedia: Electric Power Transmission.* February 17, 2007. http://peswiki.com/index.php/OPwoerPedia:Electric_power_transmission (accessed February 11, 2008).

Peterson, Per F. "Inertial Fusion Energy: A Tutorial on the Technology and Economics." *UCB Inertial Fusion Energy Tutorial.* September 23, 1998. http://www.nuc.berkeley.edu/thyd/icf/IFE.html (accessed May 23, 2007).

Pinker, Steven. "A History of Violence." *The New Republic.* March 19, 2007. https://newrepublic.com/magazine.

Poon, HW and TK Chung. *The Russian Revolution of 1905.* 1979. http://www.thecorner.org/hist/russia/revo1905.htm (accessed February 11, 2009).

"Race in a Genetic World." *John Harvard's Journal,* May-June 2008.

Rohe, John F. *The Arrows in Our Quiver.* n.d. http://www.michbar.org/journal/article.cfm?articleID=104&volumeID=9 (accessed July 20, 2009).

Ross, Kristina. "Mass Culture." *University of Minnesota Media History Project.* 1995. http://www.mediahistory.umn.edu/masscult.html (accessed March 9, 2007).

Ross, Richard J. "Communications Revolutions and Legal Culture: An Elusive Relationship." *Law and Social Inquiry, Vol. 27, No. 3,* 2002: 637-684.

Schoofs, Mark. "What DNA Says About Human Ancestry—and Bigotry." *Village Voice,* n.d.

Shin, Laura. "Bitcoin Blockchain Technology in Financial Services: How the Disruption will Play Out." *Forbes.* September 14, 2015.

Silkroad Foundation. "Gun and Gunpower." *Gun and Gunpower.* 2000. http://www.silkroad.com/artl/gun.shtml (accessed October 11, 2005).

Sisson, Mark. *Dunbar Number: Maximum Human Group Size.* March 9, 2010. http://www.marksdailyapply.com/dunbars-number-group-size (accessed June 17, 2010).

Smith, Ray. *Mesopotamia—Part I.* 2002. http://www.anvilfire.com/21centbs/stories/rsmith/RSindex.htm (accessed September 14, 2010).

—. "Ray Smith's Notebook of Metalworking Origins." *Mesopotamia—Part I.* 2002. http://anvilfire.com/21centbs/stories/rsmith/RSindex.htm (accessed November 10, 2012).

Snell, Melissa. *The Medieval Child, Part III: Surviving Infancy.* May 2009. http://historymedren.about.com/od/medievalchildren/a/child_survival_3.htm (accessed Aug 21, 2010).

St. Edmundsbury Borough Council. *Magna Carta History.* n.d. http://www.steedmundsbury.gov.uk (accessed September 12, 2006).

Tech Connection. "Will the Ignitor Make Fusion Power Possible?" *Tech Connection,* May 2010.

The Economist. "Blockchains: the Great Chain of being sure about things." *The Economist.* 2015. http://www.economist.com/news/briefing/21677228-technology-behind-bitcoin-lets-people-who-do-not-know-or-trust-each-other-build-dependable (accessed October 31, 2015).

The National Archives Learning Curve. *Feudal System.* n.d. http://www.spartacus.schoolnet.co.uk/NORfeudal.htm (accessed September 12, 2006).

The Open Door Web Site. *The English Republic (1649-1660).* 2009. http://www.saburchill.com/history/chapters/chap4008f.html (accessed July 31, 2009).

TravelChinaGuide.com. *Silk Road History.* 2008. http://www.travelchinaguide.com/silk-road/history (accessed May 23, 2008).

Tumanda, Jennifer. *The Decline of the Viking.* July 15, 2008. http://www.family-ancestry.co.uk/history/vikings/decline (accessed August 12, 2009).

—. *The Decline of the Vikings.* July 15, 2008. http://www.family-ancestry.co.uk/history/vikings/decline (accessed August 12, 2009).

U.S. Department of Energy. *Nuclear Energy.* n.d. http://www.ne.doe.gov (accessed October 30, 2009).

UK Parliament. *Birth of the English Parliament.* June 30, 2009. http://www.parliament.uk/about/livingheritage/evolutionofparliament (accessed July 28, 2009).

United Kingdom Parliament. *Parliament: The Political Institution.* January 27, 2007. http://www.parliament.uk/about/history/institution.cfm (accessed February 1, 2007).

Walonick, Ph.D., David S. "StatPac." *An Overview of Forecasting Methodology.* 1993. http://www.statpac.com/research-papers/forecasting.htm (accessed January 23, 2009).

White, Maurice. "Why Your Race Isn't Genetic." *Pacific Standard,* May 30, 2014.

Wikipedia. *African Union.* August 4, 2008. http://en.wikipedia.org/wiki/African_Union (accessed August 6, 2008).

—. *Ancient Warfare.* August 21, 2010. http://en.wikipedia.org/wiki/Ancient_warfare (accessed September 8, 2010).

—. *Arab Federation.* June 15, 2008. http://en.wikipedia.org/wiki/Arab_Federation (accessed August 6, 2008).

—. *Birth of the Italian Republic.* February 15, 2009. http://en.wikipedia.org/wiki/Birth_of_the_Italian_Republic (accessed February 16, 2009).

—. *Blockchain.* March 2017. https://en.wikipedia.org/wiki/Blockchain (accessed March 13, 2017).

—. *Bourbon Restoration.* January 21, 2009. http://en.wikipedia.org/wiki/Bourbon_Restoration (accessed February 6, 2009).

—. *British House of Commons.* January 26, 2007. http://en.wikipedia.org/wiki/British_House_of_Commons (accessed February 1, 2007).

—. *Bronze Age.* June 16, 2007. http://en.wikipedia.org/wiki/Bronze_Age (accessed June 18, 2007).

—. *Chariot.* August 29, 2010. http://en.wikipedia.org/wiki/Chariot (accessed September 8, 2010).

—. *Charlegmagne.* September 26, 2009. http://en.wikipedia.org/wiki/Charlegmagne (accessed September 26, 2009).

—. *Charles II of England.* July 24, 2009. http://en.wikipedia.org/wiki/Charles_II_of_England (accessed August 3, 2009).

—. *Charter of 1830.* August 24, 2008. http://en.wikipedia.org/wiki/Charter_of_1830 (accessed February 6, 2009).

—. *Claude Shannon.* June 2010. http://en.wikipedia.org/wiki/Claude_Shannon (accessed June 22, 2010).

—. *Clovis I.* September 22, 2009. http://en.wikipedia.org/wiki/Clovis_I (accessed September 26, 2009).

—. *Commonwealth of England.* July 21, 2009. http://en.wikipedia.org/wiki/Commonwealth_of_England (accessed July 31, 2009).

—. *Computer.* June 2010. http://en.wikipedia.org/wiki/Computer (accessed June 18, 2010).

—. *Constitution of France.* February 5, 2009. http://en.wikipedia.org/wiki/Constitution_of_France (accessed February 6, 2009).

—. *Contingent Valuation.* October 2, 2009. http://en.wikipedia.org/wiki/Contingent_valuation (accessed February 16, 2010).

—. *Early Middle Ages.* August 2010. http://en.wikipedia.org/wiki/Earky_Middle_Ages (accessed August 16, 2010).

—. *Energy Development.* June 2010. http://en.wikipedia.org/wiki/energy_development (accessed June 2010).

—. *English Civil War.* July 22, 2009. http://en.wikipedia.org/wiki/English_Civil_War (accessed July 30, 2009).

—. *European Union.* August 5, 2008. http://en.wikipedia.org/wiki/European_Union (accessed August 6, 2008).

—. *Federation of Arab Republics.* August 4, 2008. http://en.wikipedia.org/wiki/Federation_of_Arab_Republics (accessed August 6, 2008).

—. *French Constitution of 1852.* November 22, 2008. http://en.wikipedia.org/wiki/French_Constitution_of_1852 (accessed February 6, 2009).

—. *French Constitutional Laws of 1875.* August 26, 2008. http://en.wikipedia.org/wiki/French_Constitutional_Laws_of_1875 (accessed February 6, 2009).

—. *French Revolution.* February 3, 2009. http://en.wikipedia.org/wiki/French_Revolution (accessed February 5, 2009).

—. *French Second Republic.* 2009. http://en.wikipedia.org/wiki/French_Second_Republic (accessed February 6, 2009).

—. *French State-General.* January 31, 2009. http://en.wikipedia.org/wiki/French_States-General (accessed February 7, 2009).

—. *French Third Republic.* February 5, 2009. http://en.wikipedia.org/wiki/French_Third_Republic (accessed February 6, 2009).

—. *Fusion power.* May 23, 2007. http://en.wikipeida.org/wiki/Fusion_power (accessed May 23, 2007).

—. *Fusion Power.* June 1, 2010. http://en.wikipedia.org/wiki/fusion_power (accessed June 2010).

—. *Gladiator.* August 31, 2009. http://en.wikipedia.org/wiki/Gladiator (accessed August 31, 2009).

—. *Glorious Revolution.* July 29, 2009. http://en.wikipedia.org/wiki/Glorious_Revolution (accessed July 31, 2009).

—. *History of Anglo-Saxon England.* September 1, 2009. http://en.wikipedia.org/wiki/History_of_Anglo-Saxon_England (accessed September 1, 2009).

—. *History of China.* February 2009. http://en.wikipedia.org/wiki/History_of_China (accessed February 11, 2009).

—. *History of Computer Hardware.* June 2010. http://en.wikipedia.org/wiki/History_of_computing_hardware (accessed June 22, 2010).

—. *History of Italy as a Monarchy and in the World Wars.* November 9, 2008. http://en.wikipedia.org/wiki/History_of_Italy_as_a_monarchy_and_in_the_World_Wars (accessed February 9, 2009).

—. *History of Metallurgy in China.* October 18, 2012. http://en.wikipedia.org/wiki/History_of_metallurgy_in_China (accessed November 12, 2012).

—. *History of the Internet.* February 24, 2009. http://en.wikipedia.org/wiki/History_of_the_Internet (accessed February 24, 2009).

—. *Hittites.* August 26, 2010. http://en.wikipedia.org/wiki/Hittites (accessed August 27, 2010).

—. *Horses in Warfare.* June 5, 2007. http://en.wikipedia.org/wiki/Horses_in_warfare (accessed June 18, 2007).

—. *Human Sacrifice.* August 2010. http://en.wikipedia.org/wiki/Human_sacrifice (accessed August 2010, 2010).

—. *Iron Age.* October 9, 2005. http://en.wikipedia.org/wiki/Iron_Age (accessed October 14, 2005).

—. *Italian Unification.* January 28, 2009. http://en.wikipedia.org/wiki/Italian_unification (accessed February 5, 2009).

—. *ITER.* January 2, 2009. http://en.wikipedia.com/wiki/iter (accessed January 2009).

—. *James II of England.* July 24, 2009. http://en.wikipedia.org/wiki/James_II_of_England (accessed July 31, 2009).

—. *July Monarchy.* January 30, 2009. http://en.wikipedia.org/wiki/July_Monarchy (accessed February 6, 2009).

—. *Manhattan Project.* August 31, 2010. http://www.en.wikipedia.org/wiki/manhattan_project (accessed September 2010).

—. *Mary II of England.* November 15, 2012. http://en.wikipedia.org/wiki/Mary_II_of_England (accessed November 21, 2012).

—. *MHD Generator.* January 17, 2008.
    http://en.wikipedia.org/wiki/MHD_generator (accessed February 15, 2008).
—. *Monogamy in Christianity.* August 1, 2010.
    http://en.wikipedia.org/wiki/Monogamy_in_Christianity (accessed August
    2010).
—. *Nuclear Weapon.* May 31, 2010. http://en.wikipedia.org/wiki/Nuclear_weapon
    (accessed June 2010).
—. *Online Service Provider.* June 2010.
    http://en.wikipedia.com/wiki/Online_service_provider (accessed June 12,
    2010).
—. *Personal Computer.* June 2010. http://en.wikipedia.org/wiki/Personal_computer
    (accessed June 25, 2010).
—. *Prehistoric Britain.* September 27, 2006.
    http://en.wikipedia.org/wiki/Ancient_Britain (accessed September 30, 2006).
—. *Roman Catholic Church.* September 16, 2009.
    http://en.wikipedia.org/wiki/User:Ottava_Rima/Roman_Catholic_Church
    (accessed September 24, 2009).
—. *Russian Civil War.* February 10, 2009.
    http://en.wikipedia.org/wiki/Russian_Civil_War (accessed February 11,
    2009).
—. *Russian Revolution (1905).* February 11, 2009.
    http://en.wikipedia.org/wiki/Russian_Revolution_of_1905 (accessed February
    11, 2009).
—. *Russian Revolution (1917).* February 5, 2009.
    http://en.wikipedia.org/wiki/Russian_Revolution_of_1917 (accessed February
    5, 2009).
—. *Sargon of Akkad.* 2010. http:en.wikipedia.org/wiki/Sargon_of_Akkad (accessed
    September 27, 2010).
—. *Shang Dynasty.* September 7, 2010.
    http://en.wikipedia.org/wiki/Shang_Dynasty (accessed September 7, 2010).
—. *Silk Road.* October 7, 2005. http://en.wikipedia.org/wiki/Silk_Road (accessed
    October 7, 2005).
—. *Slavery in Medieval Europe.* June 2010.
    http://en.wikipedia.org/wiki/Slavery_in_Medieval_Europe (accessed June 16,
    2010).
—. *Sociocultural Evolution.* February 12, 2009.
    http:en//en.wikipedia.org/wiki/Sociocultural_evolution (accessed February 17,
    2009).
—. *Sumer.* August 21, 2010. http://en.wikipedia.org/wiki/Sumer (accessed August
    27, 2010).
—. *Teller-Ulam Design.* May 28, 2010.
    http://en.wikipedia.org/wiki/teller_ulam_design (accessed Jun 2010).
—. *Umberto I of Italy.* January 23, 2009. http://en.wikipedia.org/wiki/Umberto_I
    (accessed February 16, 2009).

—. *Unification of Germany.* February 3, 2009.
   http://en.wikipedia.org/wiki/Unification_of_Germany (accessed February 5, 2009).

—. *United Arab Republic.* August 5, 2008.
   http://en.wikipedia.org/wiki/United_Arab_Republic (accessed August 6, 2008).

—. *United Arab States.* 2008. http://en.wikipedia.org/wiki/United_Arab_States (accessed August 8, 2008).

—. *Victor Emmanuel II of Italy.* February 11, 2009.
   http://en.wikipedia.org/wiki/Victor_Emmanuel_II_of_Italy (accessed February 16, 2009).

—. *Viking.* August 8, 2009. http://en.wikipedia.org/wiki/Viking (accessed August 12, 2009).

—. *Xinhai Revolution.* February 3, 2009.
   http://en.wikipedia.org/wiki/Xinhai_Revolution (accessed February 11, 2009).

Wild, Oliver. *The Silk Road.* 1992. http://www.ess.uci.edu/oliver/silk.html (accessed October 7, 2005).

Williams, Peter N. *England, A Narrative History; Part 4: The Anglo Saxon Period.* 2000. http://www.britannia.com/history (accessed September 12, 2006).

Woodley, Bill. *The Impact of Transformative Technologies on Governance: Some Lessons from History.* NGO Report, Ottawa, CA: Institute on Governance, 2001.

Wooldridge, Dan. *The Internet and Politics.* November 7, 2006.
   http://insidework.net/resources/articles/entry-0000022000/print (accessed October 8, 2009).

World Futures Society. *Methods and Approaches of Futures Studies.* n.d.
   http//crab.rutgers.edu/goertzel/futuristmethods.htm (accessed January 26, 2009).

Index

www.ingramcontent.com/pod-product-compliance
Lightning Source LLC
Chambersburg PA
CBHW021849090426
42811CB00033B/2196/J

9 780999 238820